MOYASIMON
TALES OF AGRICULTURE

2

Masayuki Ishikawa

Translated and adapted by
Stephen Paul

Lettered by
North Market Street Graphics

Ballantine Books * New York

Moyasimon: Tales of Agriculture volume 2 is a work of fiction. Names, characters, places, and incidents are the products of the author's imagination or are used fictitiously. Any resemblance to actual events, locales, or persons, living or dead, is entirely coincidental.

A Del Rey Manga/Kodansha Trade Paperback Original

Published in the United States by Del Rey, an imprint of The Random House Publishing Group, a division of Random House, Inc., New York.

Publication rights arranged through Kodansha Ltd.

First published in Japan in 2005 by Kodansha Ltd., Tokyo

ISBN 978-0-345-51473-8

Printed in the United States of America

www.delreymanga.com

9 8 7 6 5 4 3 2 1

Translator/Adapter: Stephen Paul
Lettering: North Market Street Graphics
Cover design: Yoichi Yamakami (ARTEN)

Contents

HONORIFICS EXPLAINED

Throughout the Del Rey Manga books, you will find Japanese honorifics left intact in the translations. For those not familiar with how the Japanese use honorifics and, more important, how they differ from American honorifics, we present this brief overview.

Politeness has always been a critical facet of Japanese culture. Ever since the feudal era, when Japan was a highly stratified society, use of honorifics—which can be defined as polite speech that indicates relationship or status—has played an essential role in the Japanese language. When addressing someone in Japanese, an honorific usually takes the form of a suffix attached to one's name (example: "Asuna-san"), is used as a title at the end of one's name, or appears in place of the name itself (example: "Negi-sensei," or simply "Sensei!").

Honorifics can be expressions of respect or endearment. In the context of manga and anime, honorifics give insight into the nature of the relationship between characters. Many English translations leave out these important honorifics and therefore distort the feel of the original Japanese. Because Japanese honorifics contain nuances that English honorifics lack, it is our policy at Del Rey not to translate them. Here, instead, is a guide to some of the honorifics you may encounter in Del Rey Manga.

-san: This is the most common honorific and is equivalent to Mr., Miss, Ms., or Mrs. It is the all-purpose honorific and can be used in any situation where politeness is required.

-sama: This is one level higher than "-san" and is used to confer great respect.

-dono: This comes from the word "tono," which means "lord." It is an even higher level than "-sama" and confers utmost respect.

-kun: This suffix is used at the end of boys' names to express familiarity or endearment. It is also sometimes used by men among friends, or when addressing someone younger or of a lower station.

-chan: This is used to express endearment, mostly toward girls. It is also used for little boys, pets, and even among lovers. It gives a sense of childish cuteness.

Bozu: This is an informal way to refer to a boy, similar to the English terms "kid" and "squirt."

Sempai/
Senpai: This title suggests that the addressee is one's senior in a group or organization. It is most often used in a school setting, where underclassmen refer to their upperclassmen as "sempai." It can also be used in the workplace, such as when a newer employee addresses an employee who has seniority in the company.

Kohai: This is the opposite of "sempai" and is used toward underclassmen in school or newcomers in the workplace. It connotes that the addressee is of a lower station.

Sensei: Literally meaning "one who has come before," this title is used for teachers, doctors, or masters of any profession or art.

-[blank]: This is usually forgotten in these lists, but it is perhaps the most significant difference between Japanese and English. The lack of honorific means that the speaker has permission to address the person in a very intimate way. Usually, only family, spouses, or very close friends have this kind of permission. Known as *yo-bisute*, it can be gratifying when someone who has earned the intimacy starts to call one by one's name without an honorific. But when that intimacy hasn't been earned, it can be very insulting.

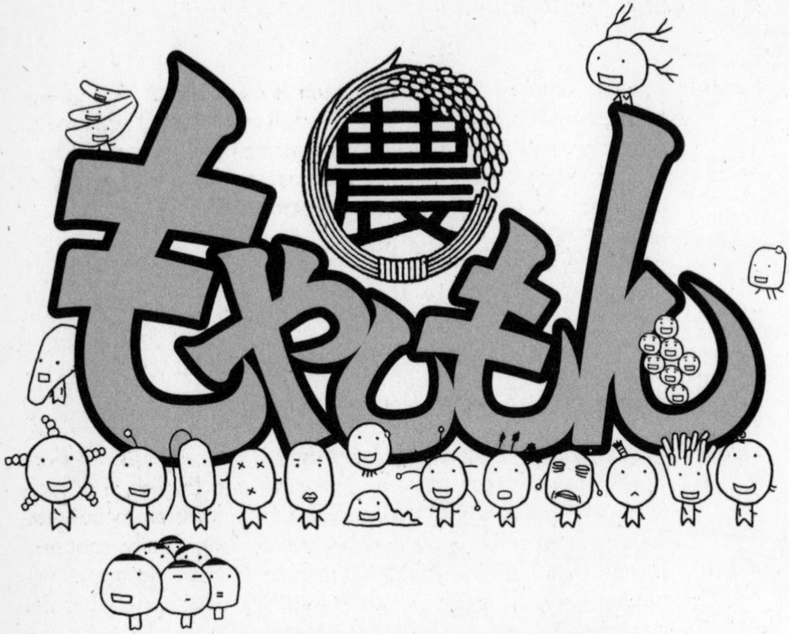
農
もやしもん

TALES OF AGRICULTURE

2

Masayuki Ishikawa

Contents

THIS MANGA IS COMPLETE AND UTTER FICTION. JUST IN CASE.

S. Cerevisiae
A yeast. Taught humanity about fermentation.

L.Lactis
Lactic acid bacteria. Beats up other germs.

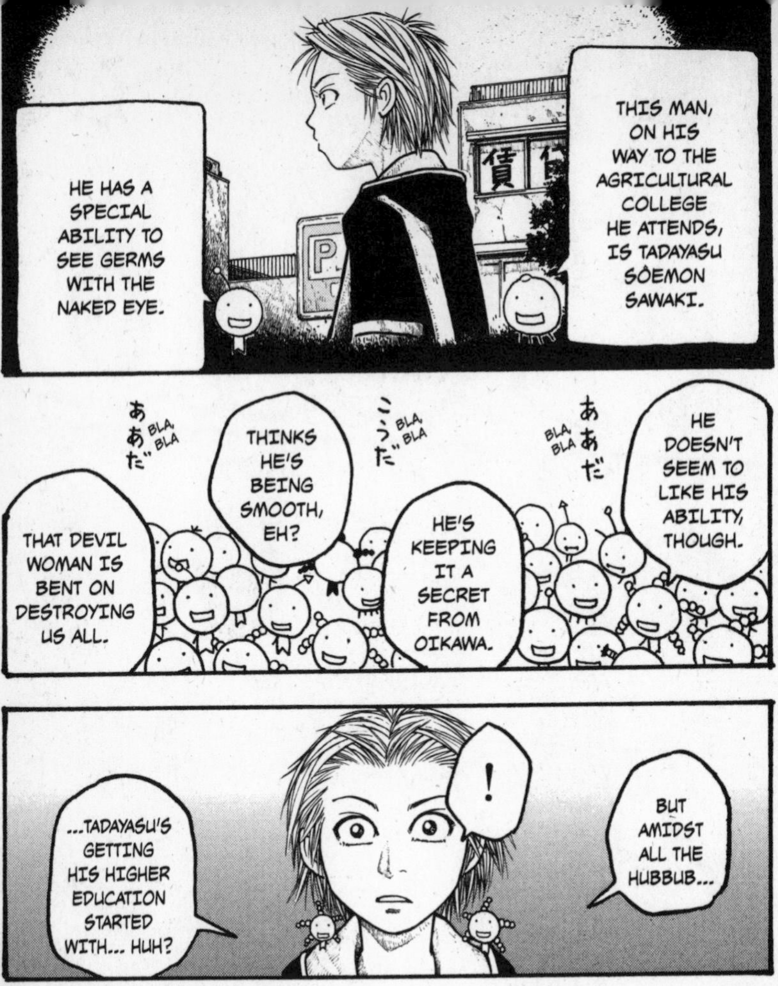
THIS MAN, ON HIS WAY TO THE AGRICULTURAL COLLEGE HE ATTENDS, IS TADAYASU SÔEMON SAWAKI.
HE HAS A SPECIAL ABILITY TO SEE GERMS WITH THE NAKED EYE.
HE DOESN'T SEEM TO LIKE HIS ABILITY, THOUGH.
ああだ
BLA, BLA
HE'S KEEPING IT A SECRET FROM OIKAWA.
こうだ
BLA, BLA
THINKS HE'S BEING SMOOTH, EH?
ああだ
BLA, BLA
THAT DEVIL WOMAN IS BENT ON DESTROYING US ALL.
BUT AMIDST ALL THE HUBBUB...
!
...TADAYASU'S GETTING HIS HIGHER EDUCATION STARTED WITH... HUH?

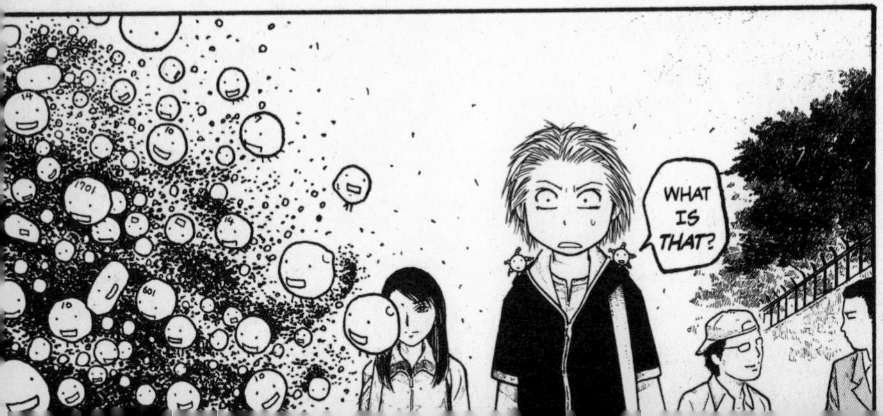
WHAT IS *THAT*?

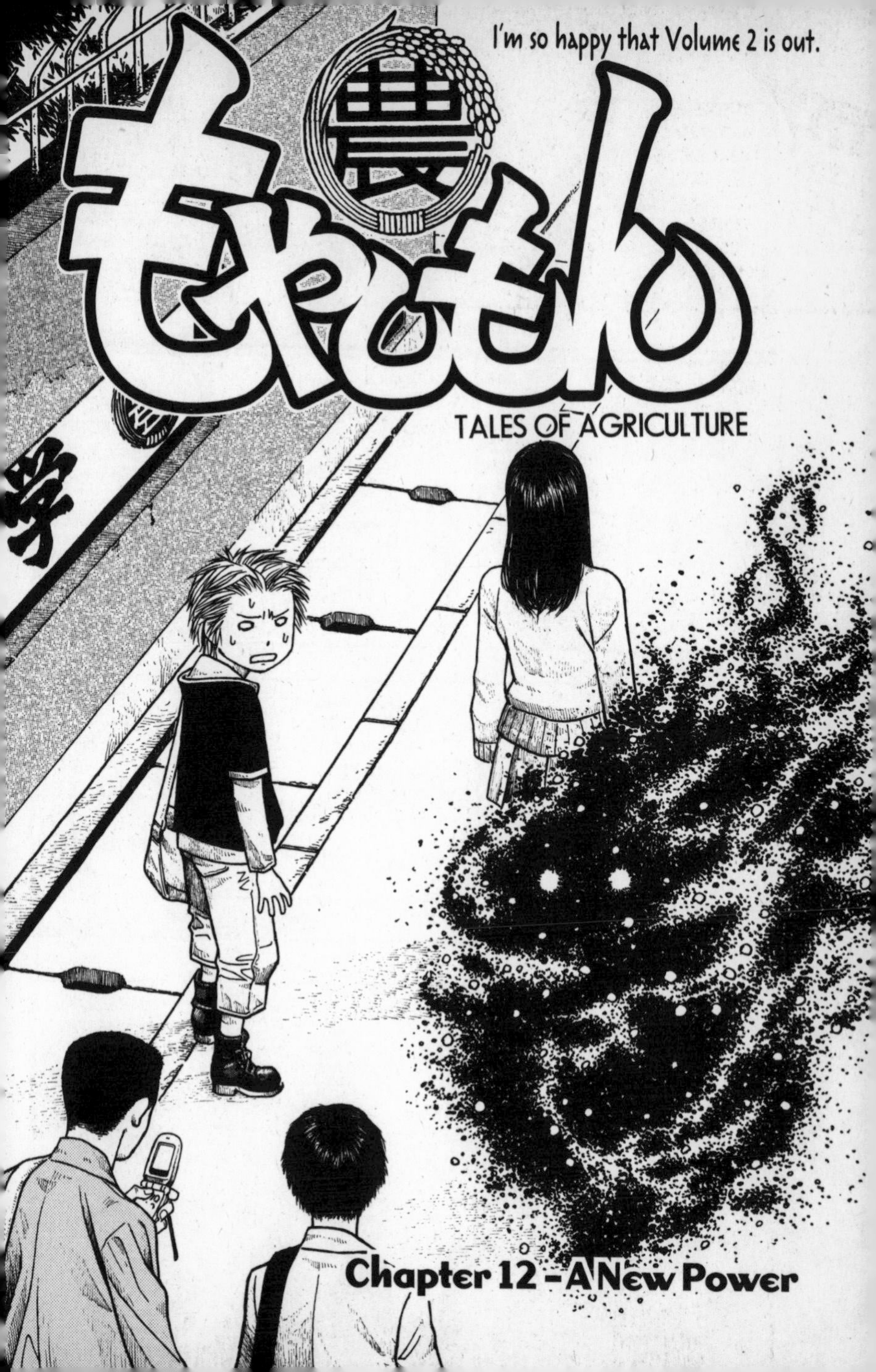
I'm so happy that Volume 2 is out.
農
もやしもん
TALES OF AGRICULTURE
学
Chapter 12 - A New Power

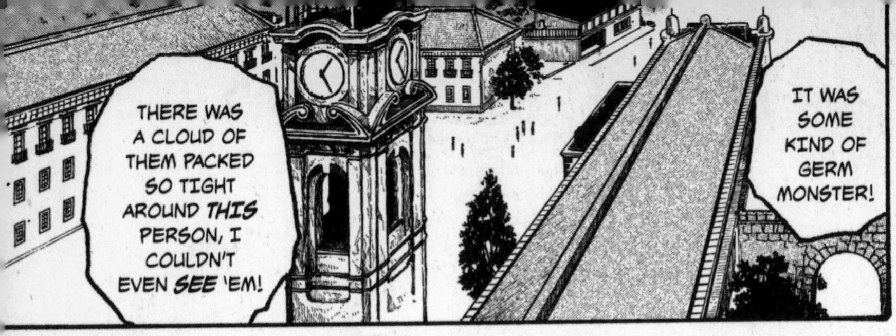
IT WAS SOME KIND OF GERM MONSTER!
THERE WAS A CLOUD OF THEM PACKED SO TIGHT AROUND *THIS* PERSON, I COULDN'T EVEN *SEE* 'EM!

This Is the Story... ...of Tadayasu Sawaki, an agricultural university student who can see microbes with the naked eye, for some reason. This ability gets him involved in all sorts of trouble. He had a hell of time in Volume 1.

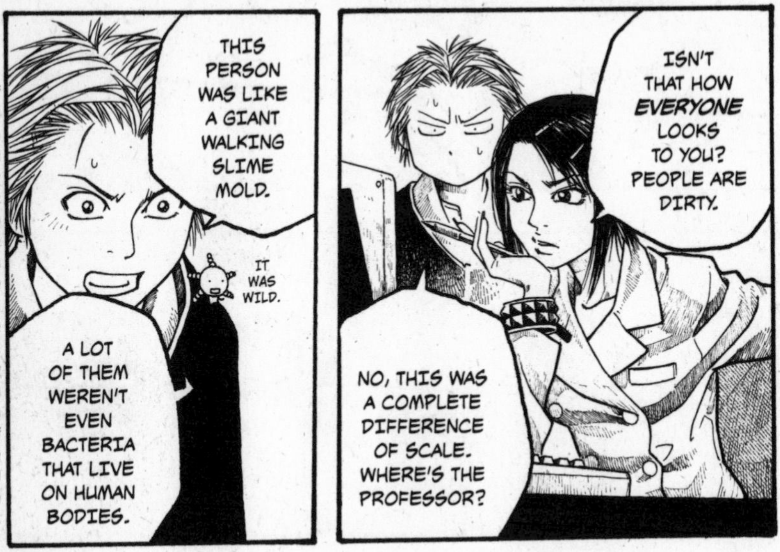
ISN'T THAT HOW *EVERYONE* LOOKS TO YOU? PEOPLE ARE DIRTY.
NO, THIS WAS A COMPLETE DIFFERENCE OF SCALE. WHERE'S THE PROFESSOR?
THIS PERSON WAS LIKE A GIANT WALKING SLIME MOLD.
IT WAS WILD.
A LOT OF THEM WEREN'T EVEN BACTERIA THAT LIVE ON HUMAN BODIES.

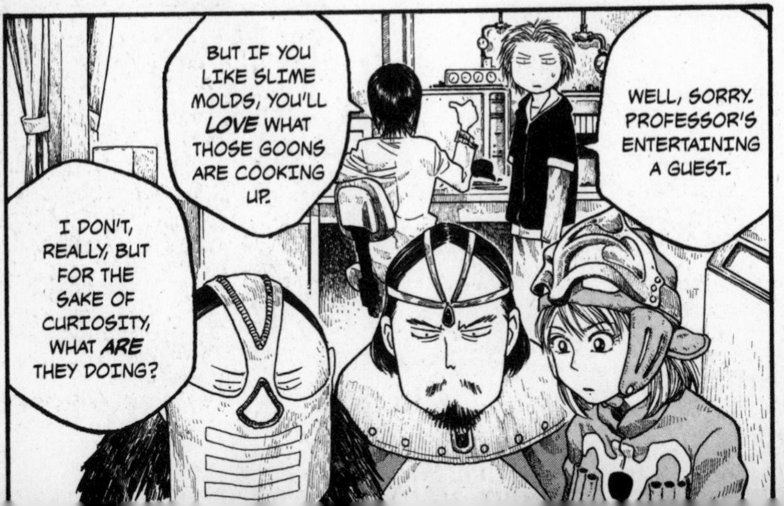
WELL, SORRY. PROFESSOR'S ENTERTAINING A GUEST.
BUT IF YOU LIKE SLIME MOLDS, YOU'LL *LOVE* WHAT THOSE GOONS ARE COOKING UP.
I DON'T, REALLY, BUT FOR THE SAKE OF CURIOSITY, WHAT *ARE* THEY DOING?

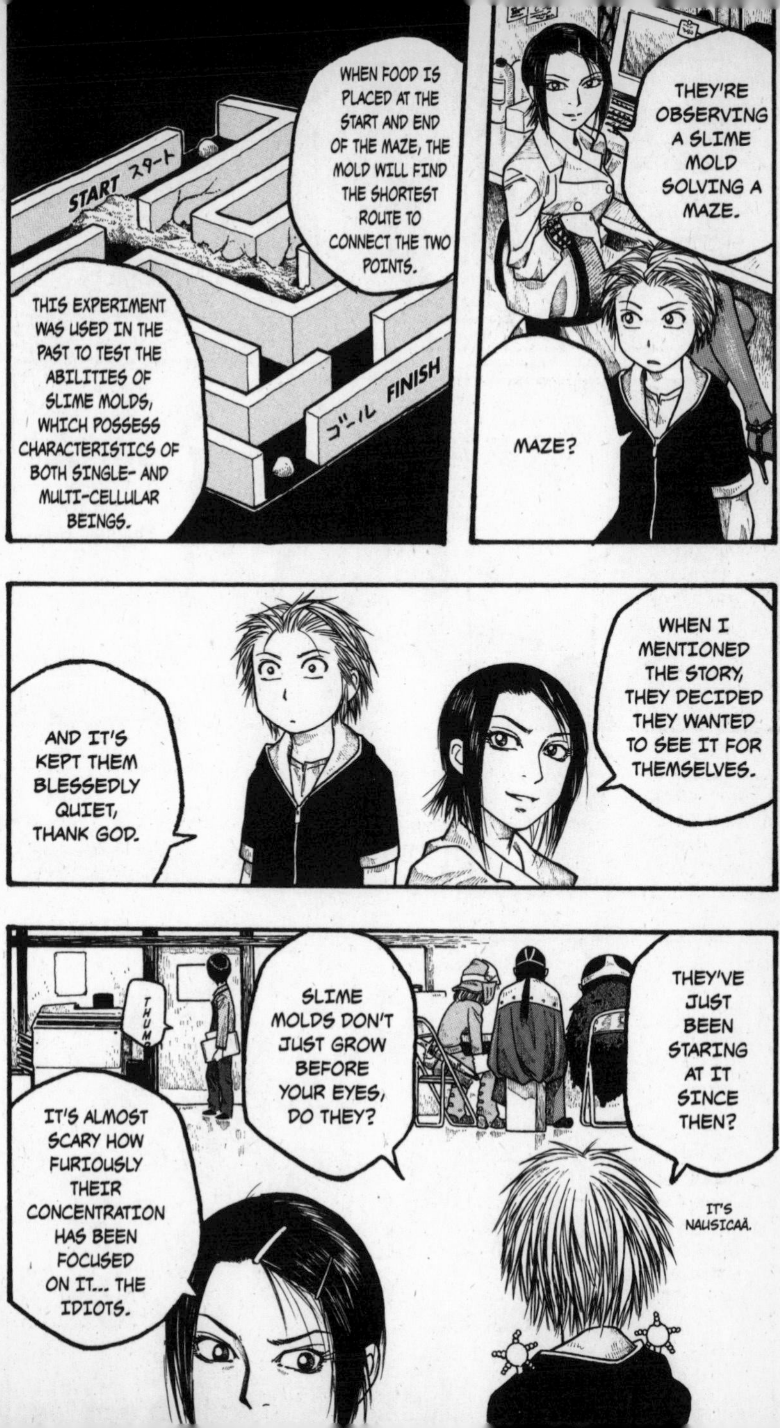
THEY'RE OBSERVING A SLIME MOLD SOLVING A MAZE.
MAZE?
WHEN FOOD IS PLACED AT THE START AND END OF THE MAZE, THE MOLD WILL FIND THE SHORTEST ROUTE TO CONNECT THE TWO POINTS.
START スタート
FINISH ゴール
THIS EXPERIMENT WAS USED IN THE PAST TO TEST THE ABILITIES OF SLIME MOLDS, WHICH POSSESS CHARACTERISTICS OF BOTH SINGLE- AND MULTI-CELLULAR BEINGS.
WHEN I MENTIONED THE STORY, THEY DECIDED THEY WANTED TO SEE IT FOR THEMSELVES.
AND IT'S KEPT THEM BLESSEDLY QUIET, THANK GOD.
THEY'VE JUST BEEN STARING AT IT SINCE THEN?
SLIME MOLDS DON'T JUST GROW BEFORE YOUR EYES, DO THEY?
THUMP
IT'S ALMOST SCARY HOW FURIOUSLY THEIR CONCENTRATION HAS BEEN FOCUSED ON IT... THE IDIOTS.
IT'S NAUSICAÄ.

Physarum polycepharum
A slime mold. Its body is made up of many nuclei and a moving plasma. It acts solely using DNA information. Some say it even has all five senses.

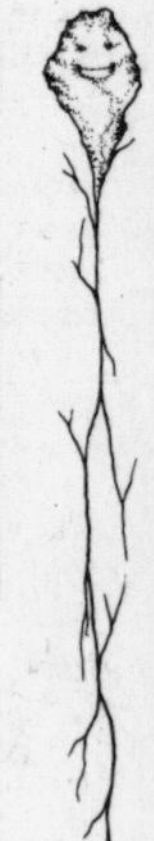

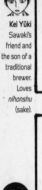

Tadayasu Sawaki
Protagonist. Can see microbes for some reason. That's *A. oryzae* sitting on his shoulder.

Kei Yûki
Sawaki's friend and the son of a traditional brewer. Loves *nihonshu* (sake).

Haruka Hasegawa
Ag school grad student. Professor Itsuki's chief assistant. Secretly treating athlete's foot.

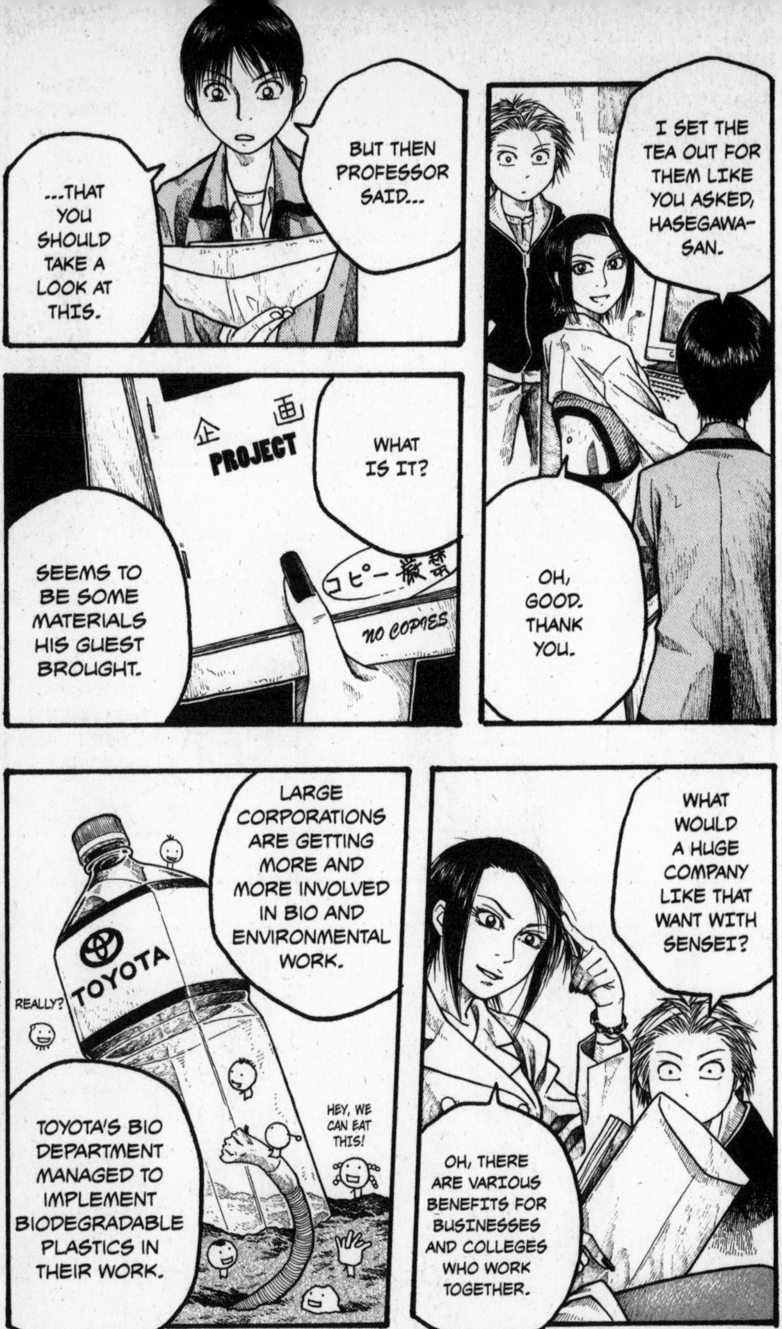
I SET THE TEA OUT FOR THEM LIKE YOU ASKED, HASEGAWA-SAN.
OH, GOOD. THANK YOU.
BUT THEN PROFESSOR SAID...
...THAT YOU SHOULD TAKE A LOOK AT THIS.
WHAT IS IT?
企画
PROJECT
コピー厳禁
NO COPIES
SEEMS TO BE SOME MATERIALS HIS GUEST BROUGHT.
WHAT WOULD A HUGE COMPANY LIKE THAT WANT WITH SENSEI?
OH, THERE ARE VARIOUS BENEFITS FOR BUSINESSES AND COLLEGES WHO WORK TOGETHER.
LARGE CORPORATIONS ARE GETTING MORE AND MORE INVOLVED IN BIO AND ENVIRONMENTAL WORK.
TOYOTA
REALLY?
HEY, WE CAN EAT THIS!
TOYOTA'S BIO DEPARTMENT MANAGED TO IMPLEMENT BIODEGRADABLE PLASTICS IN THEIR WORK.

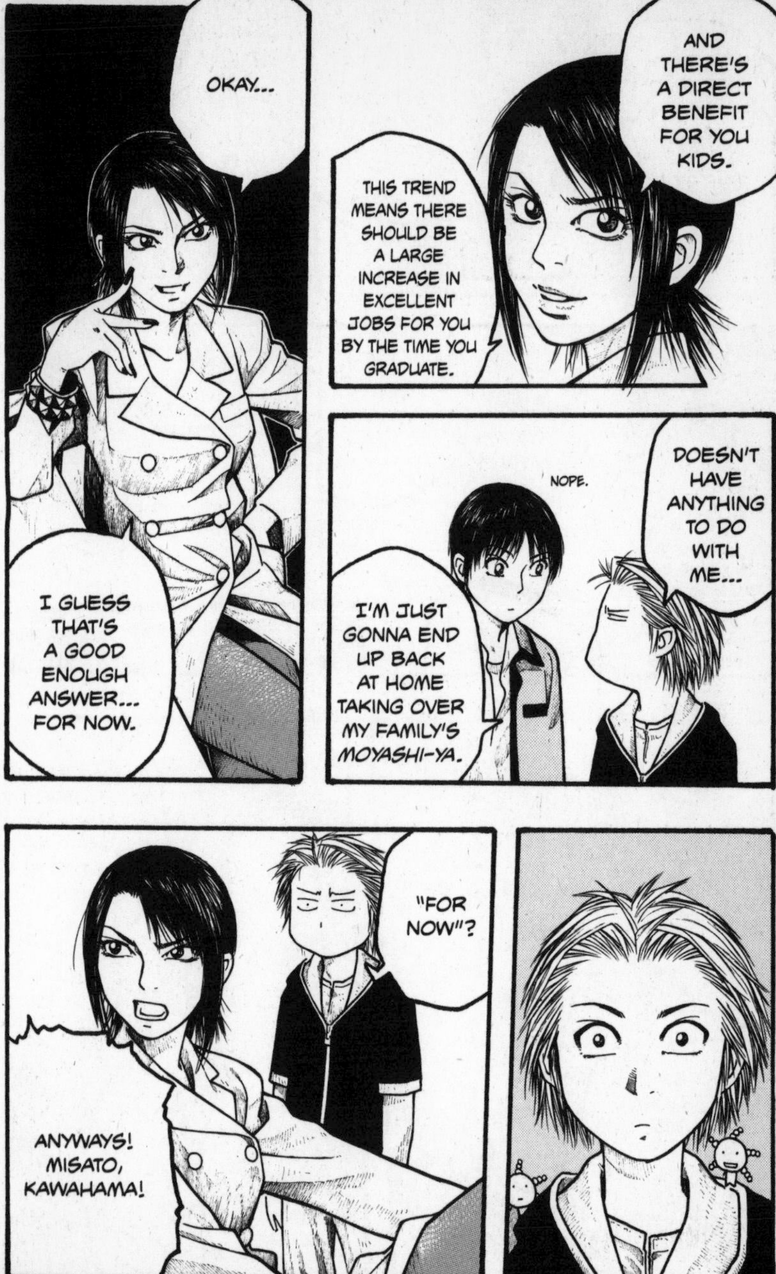
AND THERE'S A DIRECT BENEFIT FOR YOU KIDS.
THIS TREND MEANS THERE SHOULD BE A LARGE INCREASE IN EXCELLENT JOBS FOR YOU BY THE TIME YOU GRADUATE.
DOESN'T HAVE ANYTHING TO DO WITH ME...
NOPE.
I'M JUST GONNA END UP BACK AT HOME TAKING OVER MY FAMILY'S *MOYASHI-YA*.
OKAY...
I GUESS THAT'S A GOOD ENOUGH ANSWER... FOR NOW.
"FOR NOW"?
ANYWAYS! MISATO, KAWAHAMA!

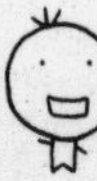

A "**moyashi-ya**" is another word for a place that sells **tane-kôji** molds for brewing *sake*.

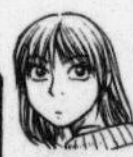

Hazuki Oikawa
A freshman like Sawaki and Yûki. She wasn't born yet when *Nausicaä of the Valley of the Wind* (1984) was released.

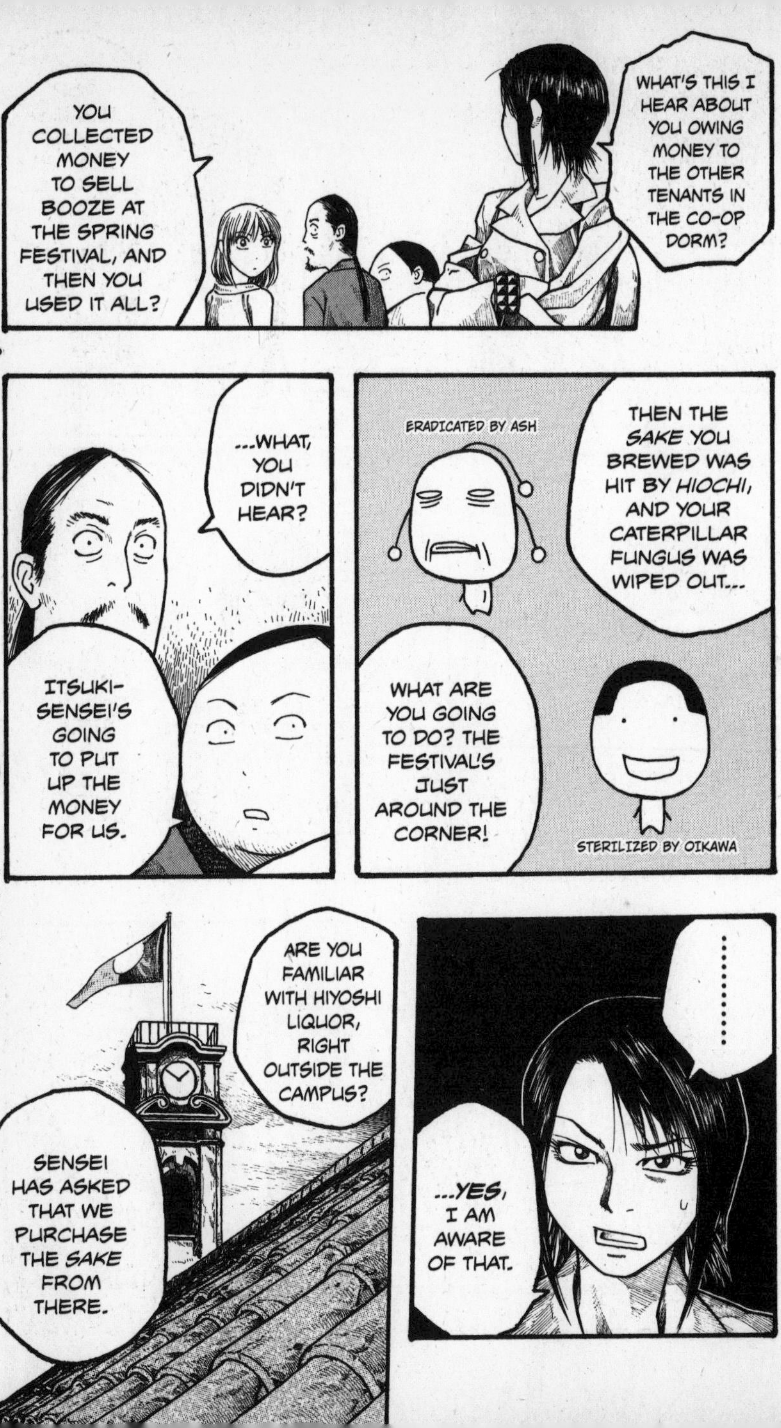
WHAT'S THIS I HEAR ABOUT YOU OWING MONEY TO THE OTHER TENANTS IN THE CO-OP DORM?
YOU COLLECTED MONEY TO SELL BOOZE AT THE SPRING FESTIVAL, AND THEN YOU USED IT ALL?
THEN THE *SAKE* YOU BREWED WAS HIT BY *HIOCHI*, AND YOUR CATERPILLAR FUNGUS WAS WIPED OUT...
ERADICATED BY ASH
WHAT ARE YOU GOING TO DO? THE FESTIVAL'S JUST AROUND THE CORNER!
STERILIZED BY OIKAWA
...WHAT, YOU DIDN'T HEAR?
ITSUKI-SENSEI'S GOING TO PUT UP THE MONEY FOR US.
......
...*YES*, I AM AWARE OF THAT.
ARE YOU FAMILIAR WITH HIYOSHI LIQUOR, RIGHT OUTSIDE THE CAMPUS?
SENSEI HAS ASKED THAT WE PURCHASE THE *SAKE* FROM THERE.

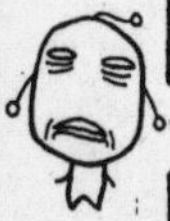

The **hiochi** bacteria caused havoc in chapters 2–3 (Volume 1).

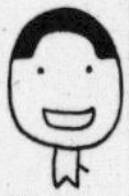

This fungus is the cause of "caterpillar fungus." They were wiped out by Oikawa in Chapter 8 (Volume 1).

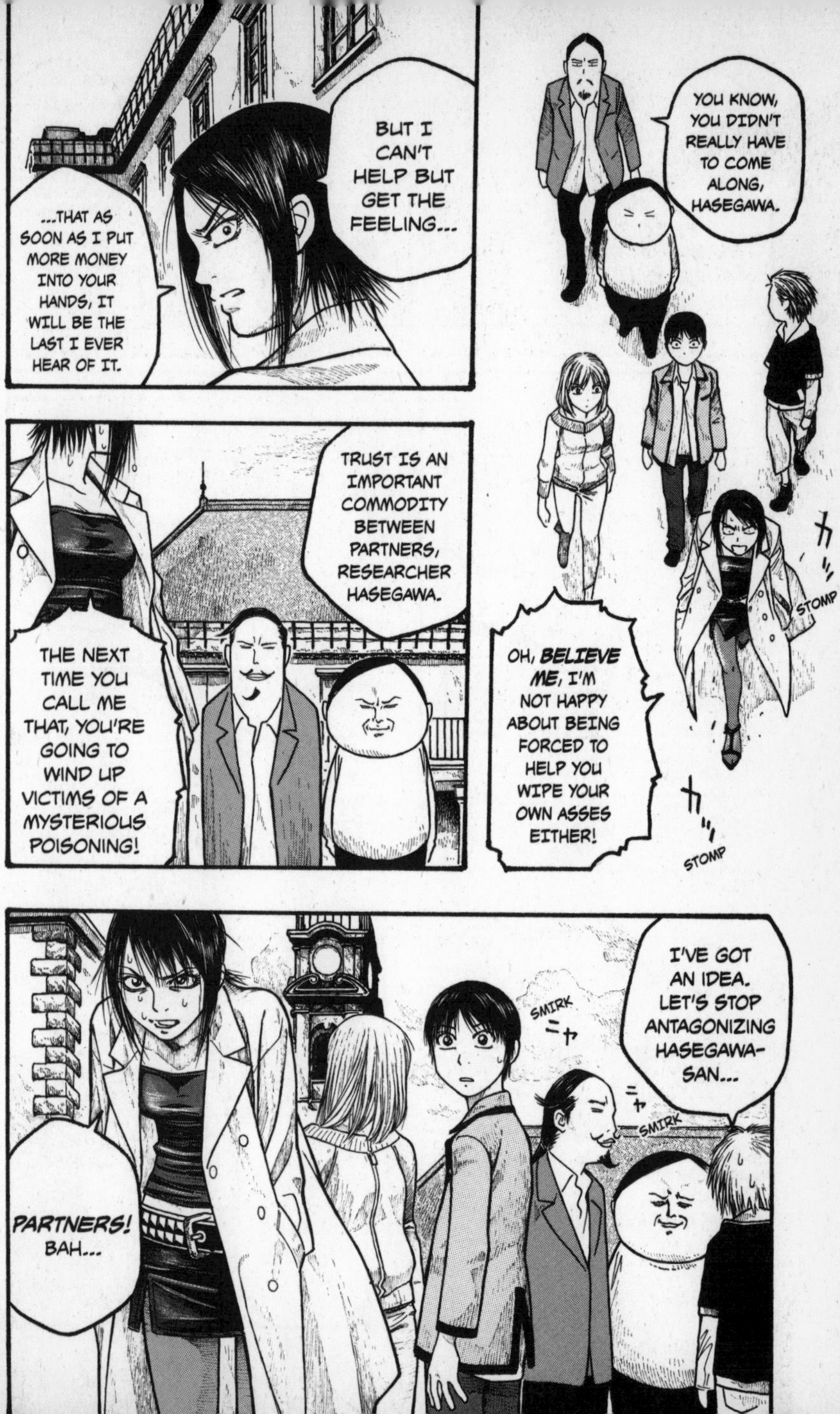
YOU KNOW, YOU DIDN'T REALLY HAVE TO COME ALONG, HASEGAWA.
OH, BELIEVE ME, I'M NOT HAPPY ABOUT BEING FORCED TO HELP YOU WIPE YOUR OWN ASSES EITHER!
カッ STOMP
カッ STOMP
BUT I CAN'T HELP BUT GET THE FEELING...
...THAT AS SOON AS I PUT MORE MONEY INTO YOUR HANDS, IT WILL BE THE LAST I EVER HEAR OF IT.
TRUST IS AN IMPORTANT COMMODITY BETWEEN PARTNERS, RESEARCHER HASEGAWA.
THE NEXT TIME YOU CALL ME THAT, YOU'RE GOING TO WIND UP VICTIMS OF A MYSTERIOUS POISONING!
I'VE GOT AN IDEA. LET'S STOP ANTAGONIZING HASEGAWA-SAN...
ニャ SMIRK
SMIRK ニャ
PARTNERS! BAH...

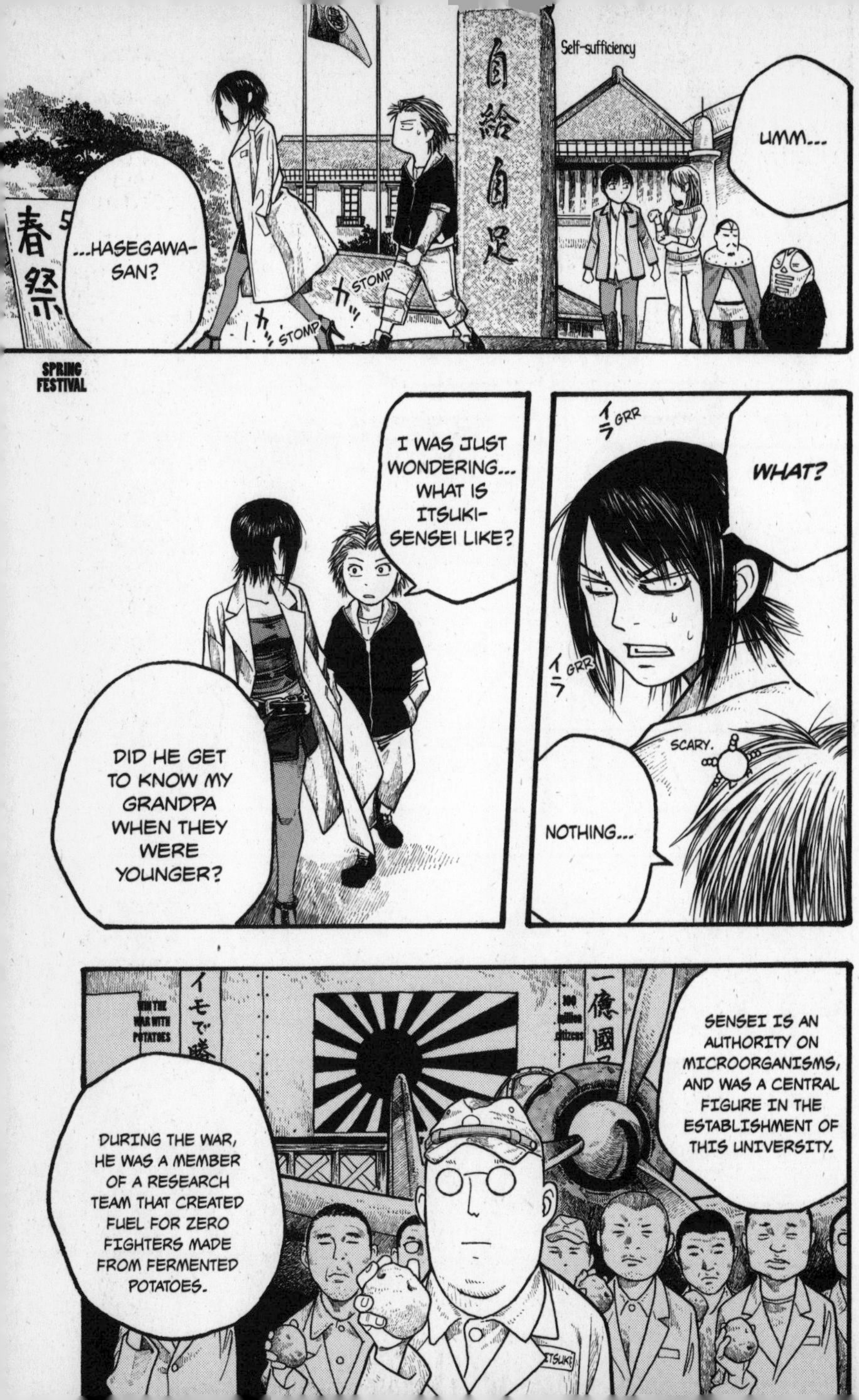

自給自足
Self-sufficiency
UMM...
春祭
...HASEGAWA-SAN?
STOMP
STOMP
SPRING FESTIVAL
WHAT?
GRR
GRR
SCARY.
NOTHING...
I WAS JUST WONDERING... WHAT IS ITSUKI-SENSEI LIKE?
DID HE GET TO KNOW MY GRANDPA WHEN THEY WERE YOUNGER?
SENSEI IS AN AUTHORITY ON MICROORGANISMS, AND WAS A CENTRAL FIGURE IN THE ESTABLISHMENT OF THIS UNIVERSITY.
100 million citizens
WIN THE WAR WITH POTATOES
DURING THE WAR, HE WAS A MEMBER OF A RESEARCH TEAM THAT CREATED FUEL FOR ZERO FIGHTERS MADE FROM FERMENTED POTATOES.
ITSUKI

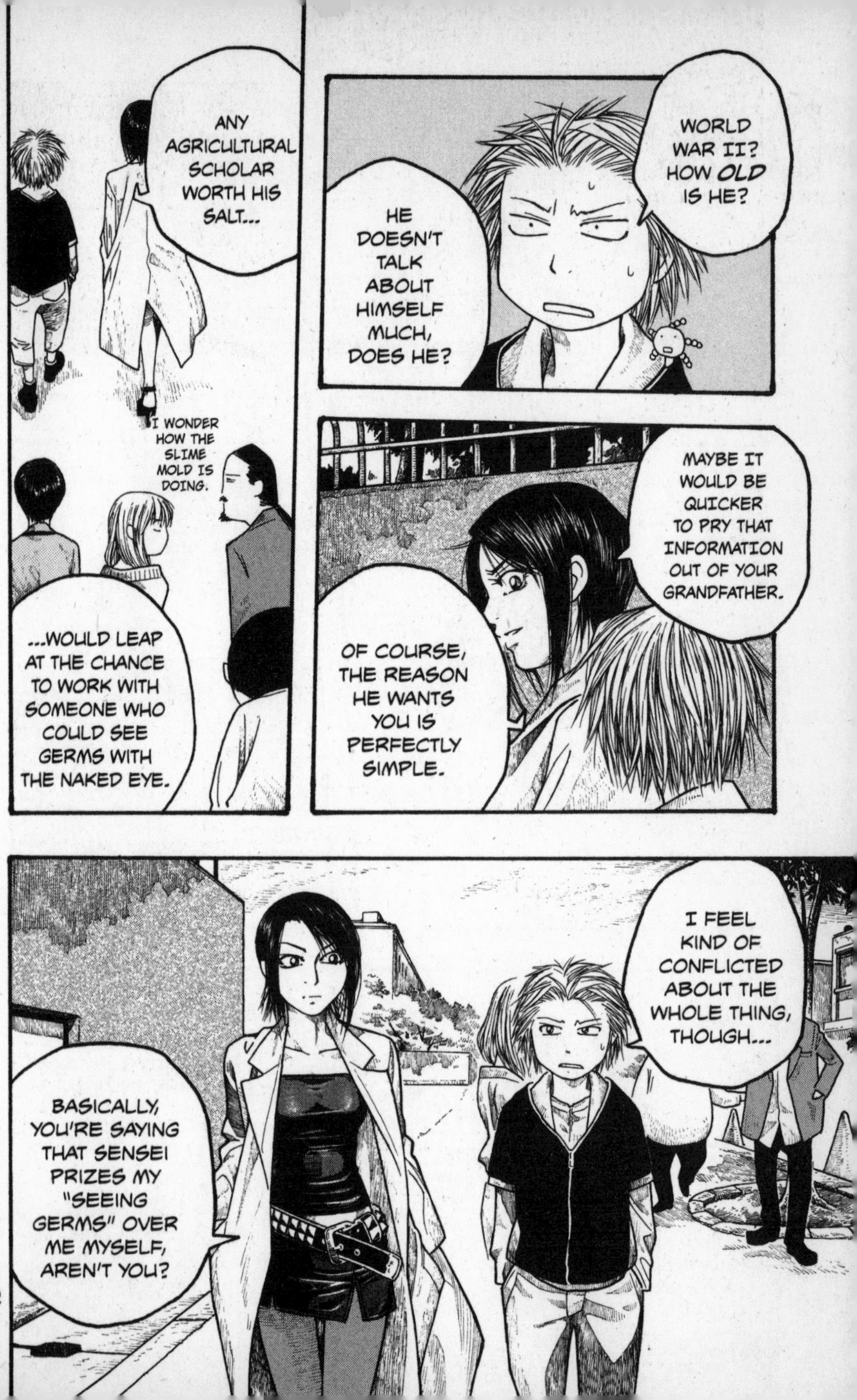
WORLD WAR II? HOW OLD IS HE?
HE DOESN'T TALK ABOUT HIMSELF MUCH, DOES HE?
MAYBE IT WOULD BE QUICKER TO PRY THAT INFORMATION OUT OF YOUR GRANDFATHER.
OF COURSE, THE REASON HE WANTS YOU IS PERFECTLY SIMPLE.
ANY AGRICULTURAL SCHOLAR WORTH HIS SALT...
I WONDER HOW THE SLIME MOLD IS DOING.
...WOULD LEAP AT THE CHANCE TO WORK WITH SOMEONE WHO COULD SEE GERMS WITH THE NAKED EYE.
I FEEL KIND OF CONFLICTED ABOUT THE WHOLE THING, THOUGH...
BASICALLY, YOU'RE SAYING THAT SENSEI PRIZES MY "SEEING GERMS" OVER ME MYSELF, AREN'T YOU?

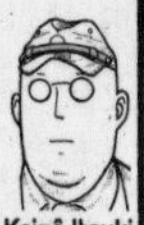

Keizô Itsuki
Ag school professor, age unknown.

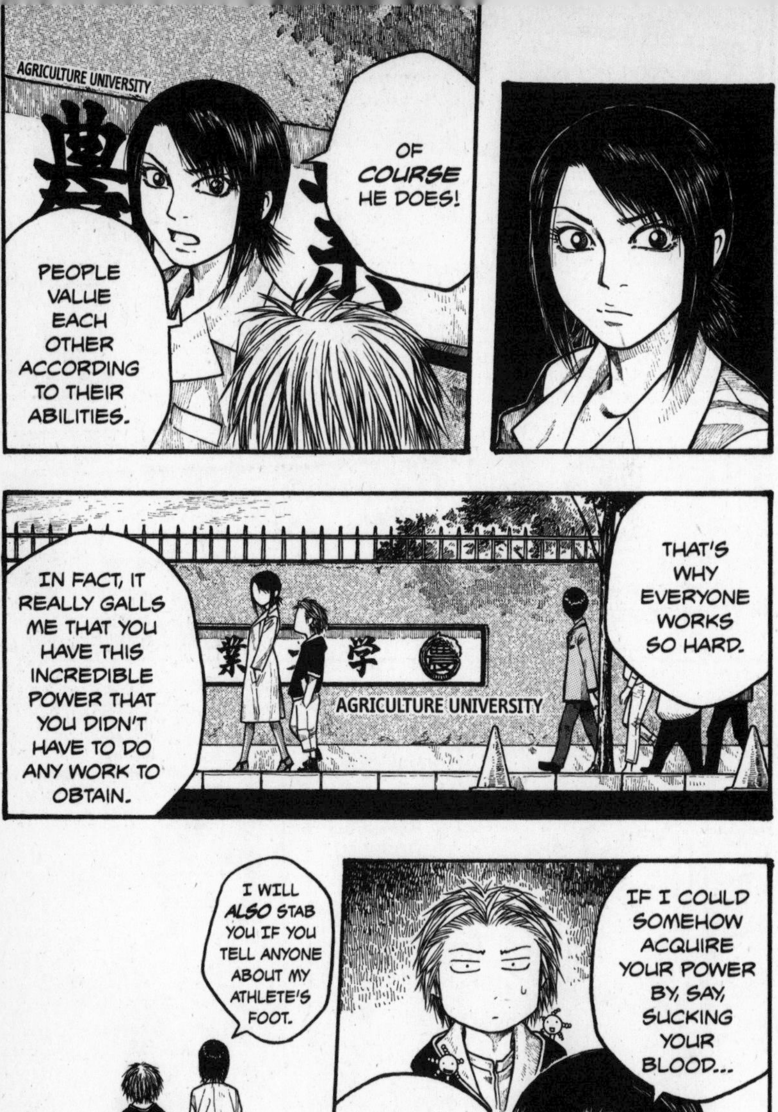
AGRICULTURE UNIVERSITY
OF COURSE HE DOES!
PEOPLE VALUE EACH OTHER ACCORDING TO THEIR ABILITIES.
THAT'S WHY EVERYONE WORKS SO HARD.
AGRICULTURE UNIVERSITY
IN FACT, IT REALLY GALLS ME THAT YOU HAVE THIS INCREDIBLE POWER THAT YOU DIDN'T HAVE TO DO ANY WORK TO OBTAIN.
IF I COULD SOMEHOW ACQUIRE YOUR POWER BY, SAY, SUCKING YOUR BLOOD...
...YOU'D BE RECOVERING FROM A STAB WOUND IN YOUR NECK RIGHT ABOUT NOW.
I WILL *ALSO* STAB YOU IF YOU TELL ANYONE ABOUT MY ATHLETE'S FOOT.
WHY WOULD I TALK ABOUT THAT?

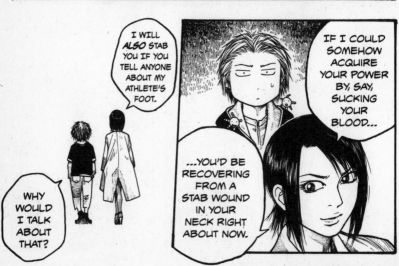

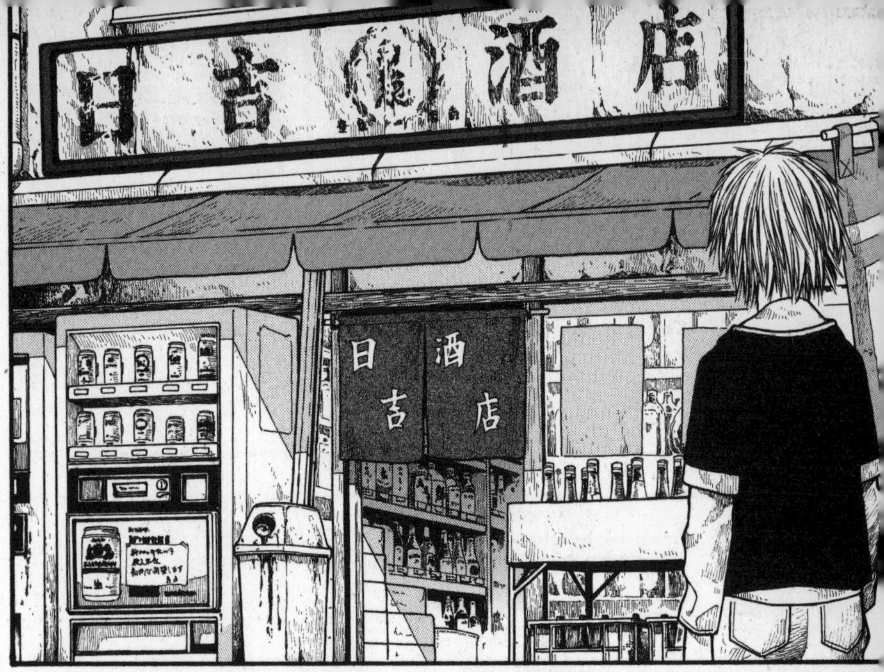
日吉酒店

Hiyoshi Liquor

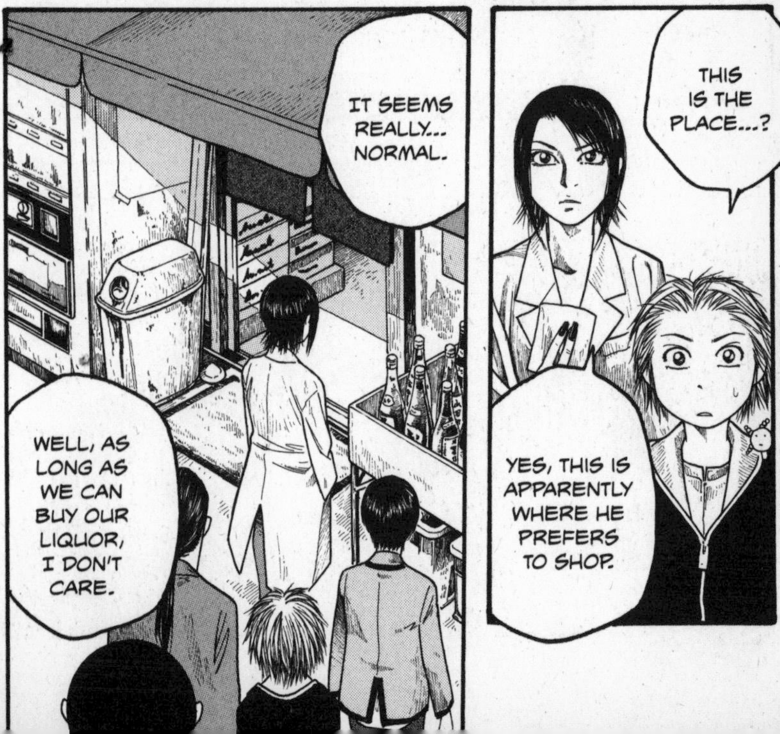
THIS IS THE PLACE...?
YES, THIS IS APPARENTLY WHERE HE PREFERS TO SHOP.
IT SEEMS REALLY... NORMAL.
WELL, AS LONG AS WE CAN BUY OUR LIQUOR, I DON'T CARE.

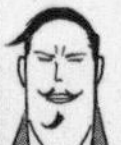

Kaoru Misato
Sophomore. His cosplay in this chapter was of the aide to Kushana, Princess of Torumekia.

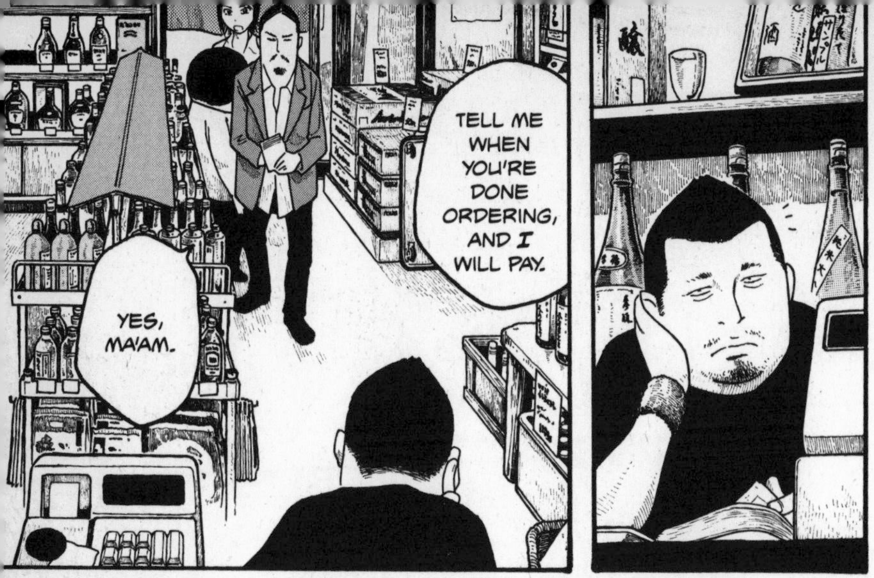
TELL ME WHEN YOU'RE DONE ORDERING, AND *I* WILL PAY.
YES, MA'AM.

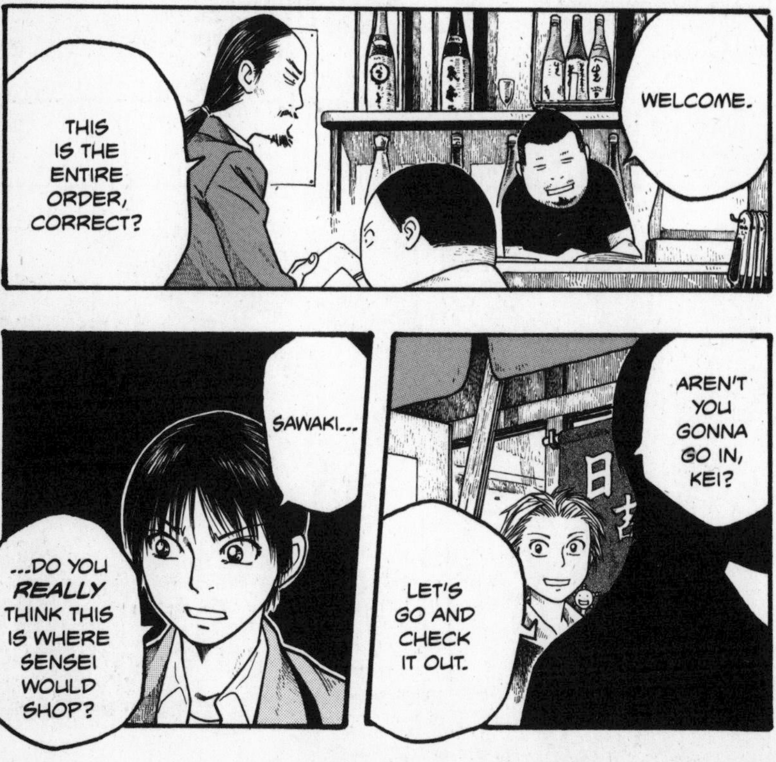
WELCOME.
THIS IS THE ENTIRE ORDER, CORRECT?
AREN'T YOU GONNA GO IN, KEI?
LET'S GO AND CHECK IT OUT.
SAWAKI...
...DO YOU *REALLY* THINK THIS IS WHERE SENSEI WOULD SHOP?

Takuma Kawahama
Sophomore. His cosplay in this chapter was of the Mani elder of the Dorok Principalities. Even after dying, he was a big part of the story.

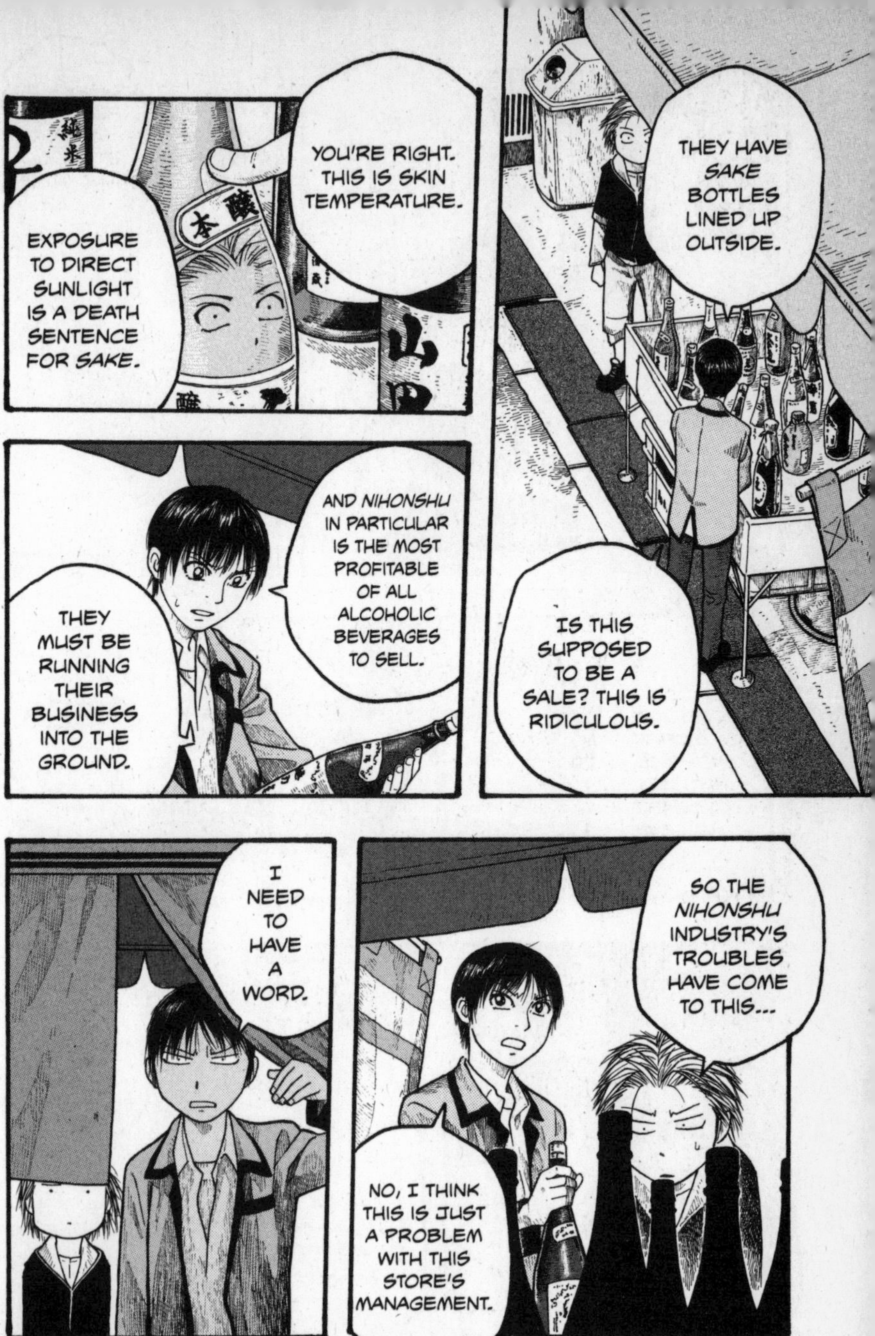
THEY HAVE SAKE BOTTLES LINED UP OUTSIDE.
IS THIS SUPPOSED TO BE A SALE? THIS IS RIDICULOUS.
YOU'RE RIGHT. THIS IS SKIN TEMPERATURE.
EXPOSURE TO DIRECT SUNLIGHT IS A DEATH SENTENCE FOR SAKE.
AND NIHONSHU IN PARTICULAR IS THE MOST PROFITABLE OF ALL ALCOHOLIC BEVERAGES TO SELL.
THEY MUST BE RUNNING THEIR BUSINESS INTO THE GROUND.
SO THE NIHONSHU INDUSTRY'S TROUBLES HAVE COME TO THIS...
NO, I THINK THIS IS JUST A PROBLEM WITH THIS STORE'S MANAGEMENT.
I NEED TO HAVE A WORD.

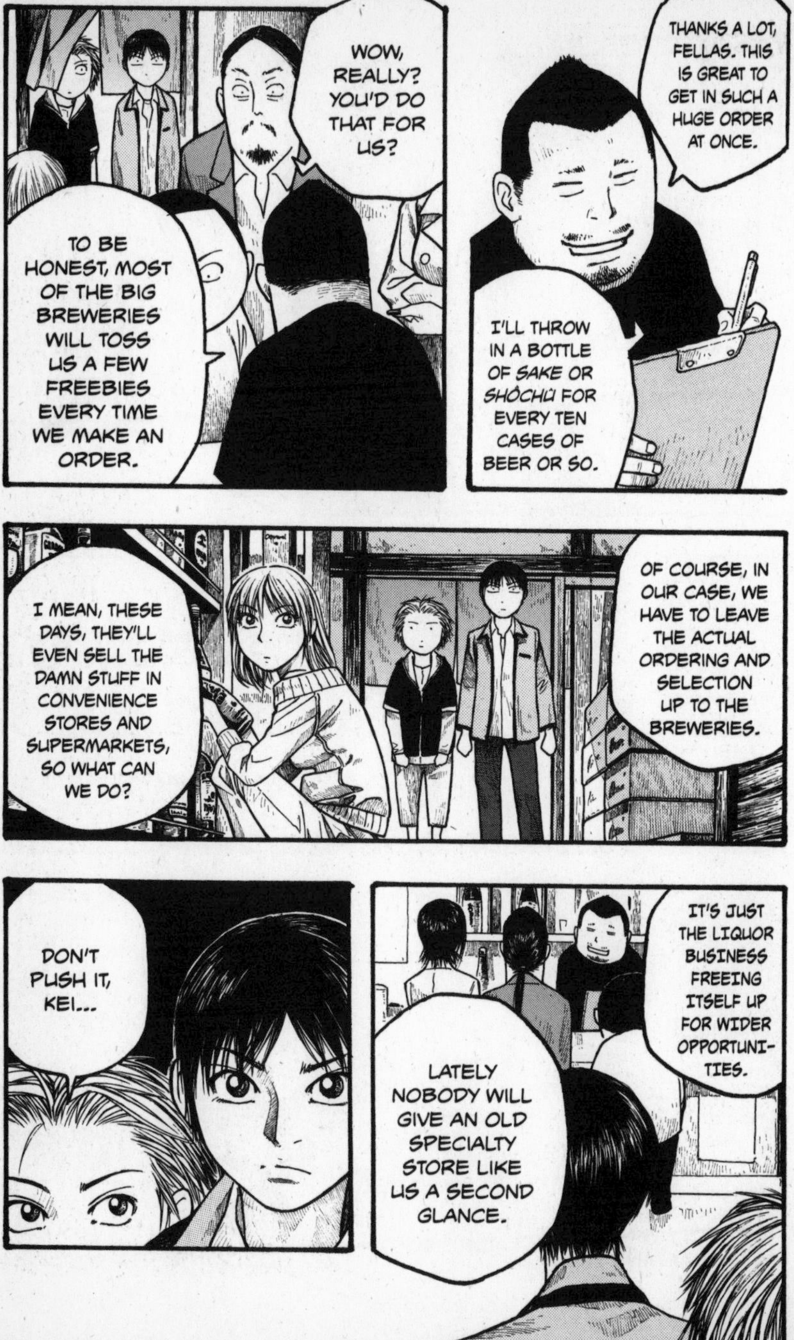
THANKS A LOT, FELLAS. THIS IS GREAT TO GET IN SUCH A HUGE ORDER AT ONCE.
I'LL THROW IN A BOTTLE OF *SAKE* OR *SHŌCHŪ* FOR EVERY TEN CASES OF BEER OR SO.
WOW, REALLY? YOU'D DO THAT FOR US?
TO BE HONEST, MOST OF THE BIG BREWERIES WILL TOSS US A FEW FREEBIES EVERY TIME WE MAKE AN ORDER.
OF COURSE, IN OUR CASE, WE HAVE TO LEAVE THE ACTUAL ORDERING AND SELECTION UP TO THE BREWERIES.
I MEAN, THESE DAYS, THEY'LL EVEN SELL THE DAMN STUFF IN CONVENIENCE STORES AND SUPERMARKETS, SO WHAT CAN WE DO?
IT'S JUST THE LIQUOR BUSINESS FREEING ITSELF UP FOR WIDER OPPORTUNITIES.
LATELY NOBODY WILL GIVE AN OLD SPECIALTY STORE LIKE US A SECOND GLANCE.
DON'T PUSH IT, KEI...

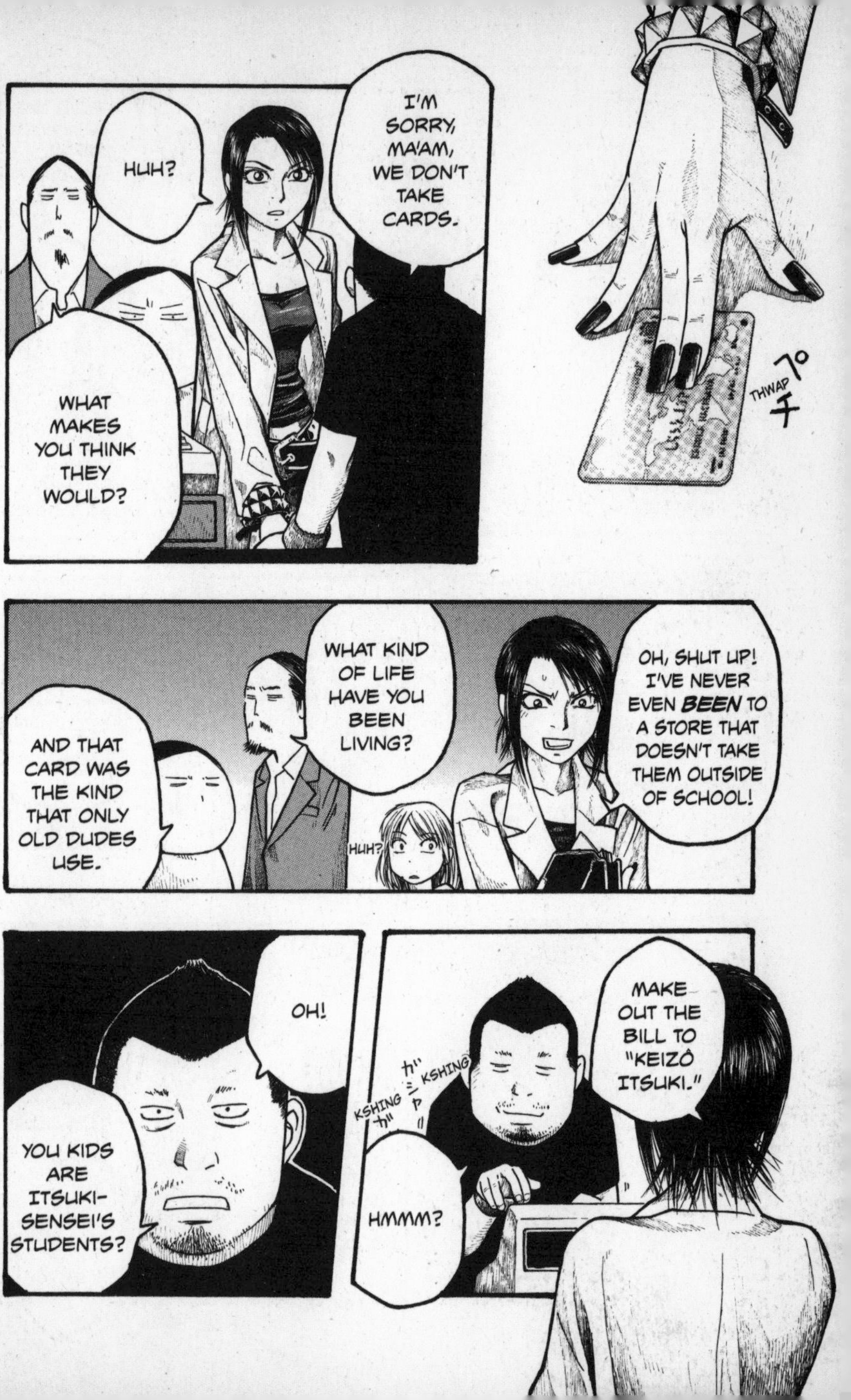
THWAP
I'M SORRY, MA'AM, WE DON'T TAKE CARDS.
HUH?
WHAT MAKES YOU THINK THEY WOULD?
OH, SHUT UP! I'VE NEVER EVEN **BEEN** TO A STORE THAT DOESN'T TAKE THEM OUTSIDE OF SCHOOL!
WHAT KIND OF LIFE HAVE YOU BEEN LIVING?
HUH?
AND THAT CARD WAS THE KIND THAT ONLY OLD DUDES USE.
MAKE OUT THE BILL TO "KEIZÔ ITSUKI."
KSHING
KSHING
HMMM?
OH!
YOU KIDS ARE ITSUKI-SENSEI'S STUDENTS?

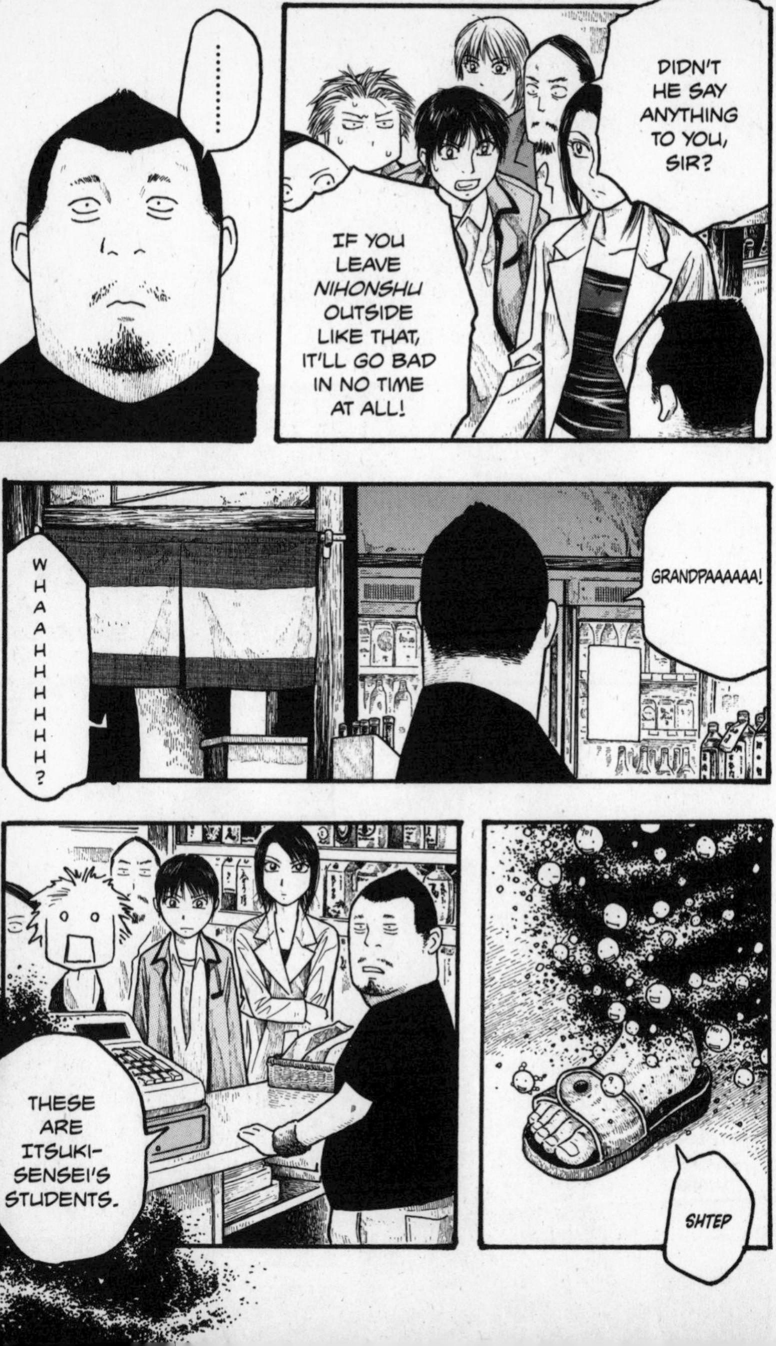
DIDN'T HE SAY ANYTHING TO YOU, SIR?
IF YOU LEAVE NIHONSHU OUTSIDE LIKE THAT, IT'LL GO BAD IN NO TIME AT ALL!
......
GRANDPAAAAAAA!
WHAAAHHHHHHH?
SHTEP
THESE ARE ITSUKI-SENSEI'S STUDENTS.

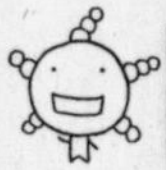

A. oryzae Kôji mold. Always found on Sawaki's shoulder.

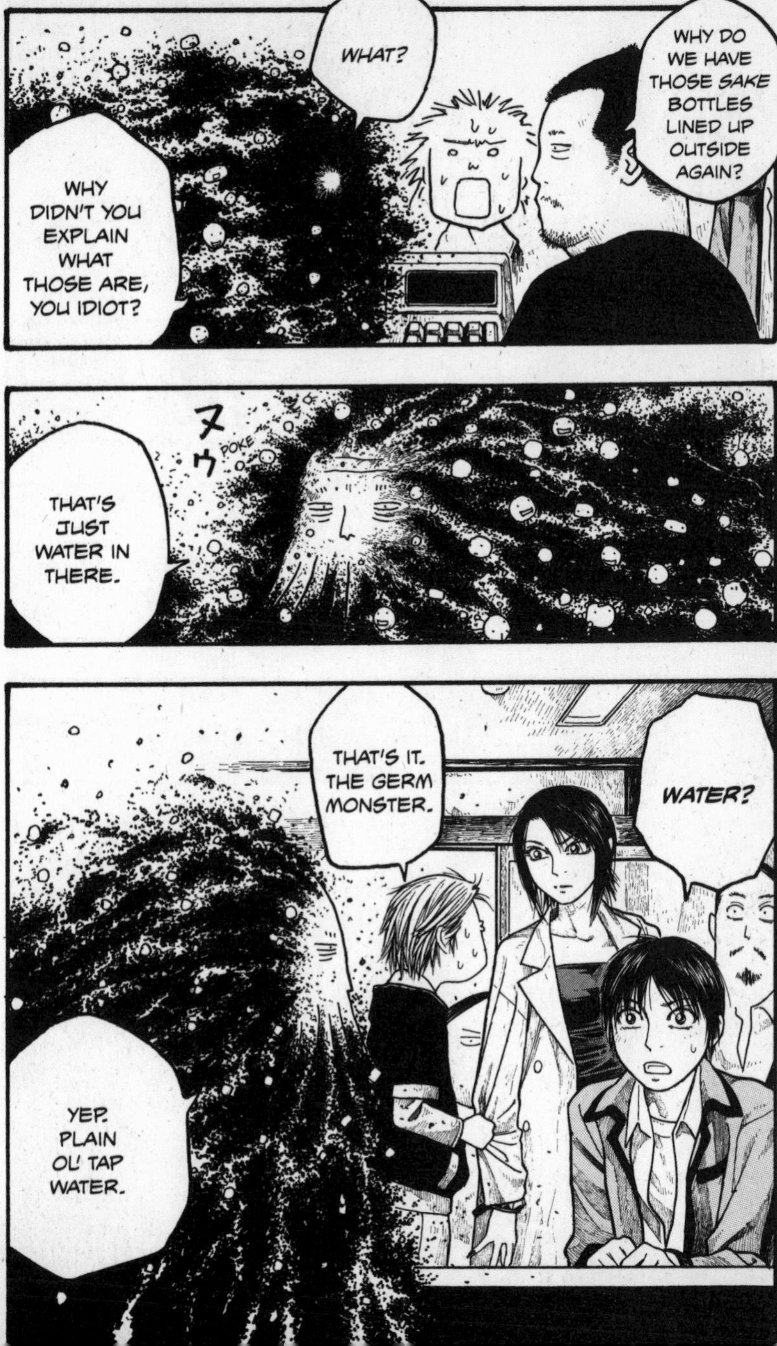
WHY DO WE HAVE THOSE SAKE BOTTLES LINED UP OUTSIDE AGAIN?
WHAT?
WHY DIDN'T YOU EXPLAIN WHAT THOSE ARE, YOU IDIOT?
ヌウ POKE
THAT'S JUST WATER IN THERE.
WATER?
THAT'S IT. THE GERM MONSTER.
YEP. PLAIN OL' TAP WATER.

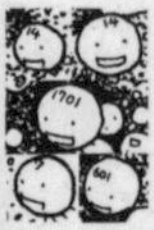

Society Yeast Yeast that is developed and distributed by the Brewing Society of Japan. One must have a distilling license to purchase these. High quality.

12 END

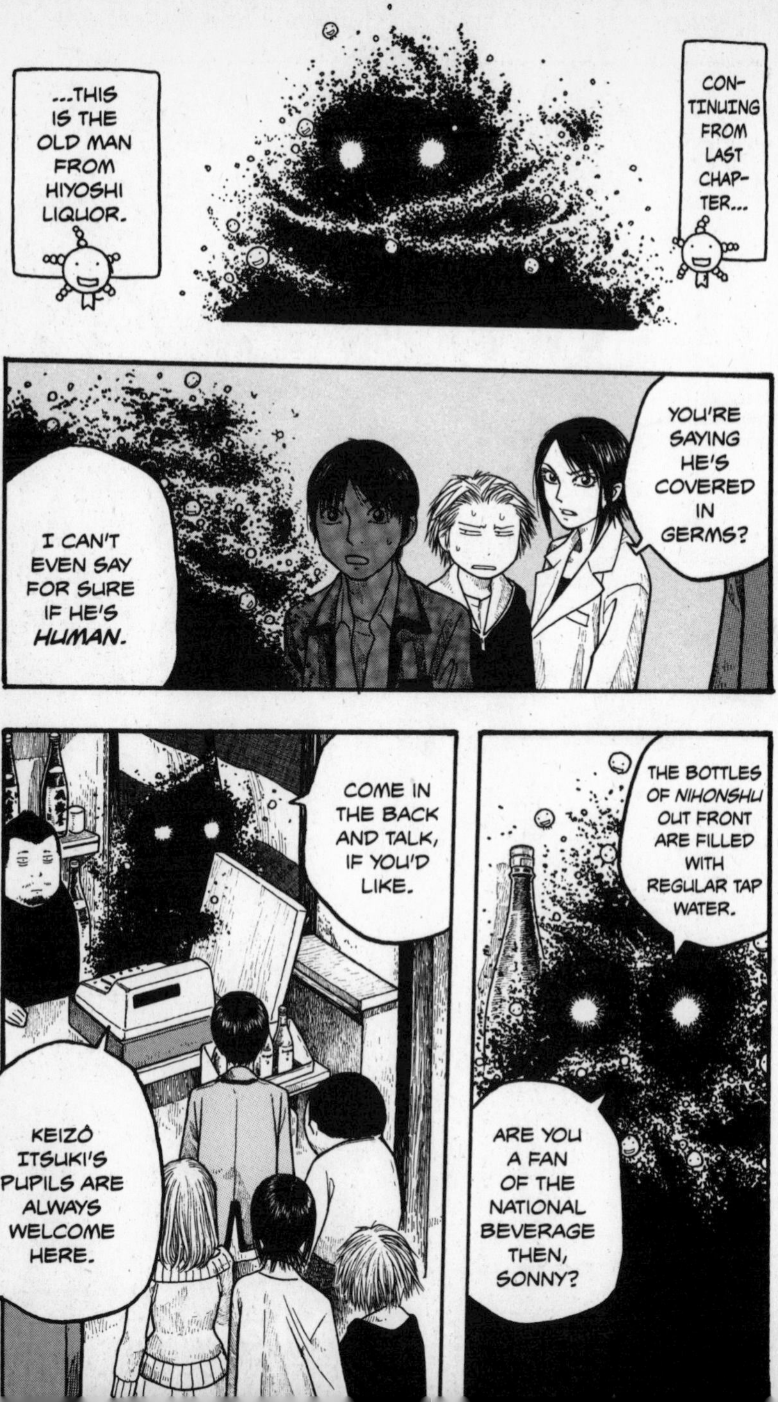
CONTINUING FROM LAST CHAPTER...
...THIS IS THE OLD MAN FROM HIYOSHI LIQUOR.
YOU'RE SAYING HE'S COVERED IN GERMS?
I CAN'T EVEN SAY FOR SURE IF HE'S *HUMAN*.
THE BOTTLES OF *NIHONSHU* OUT FRONT ARE FILLED WITH REGULAR TAP WATER.
ARE YOU A FAN OF THE NATIONAL BEVERAGE THEN, SONNY?
COME IN THE BACK AND TALK, IF YOU'D LIKE.
KEIZÔ ITSUKI'S PUPILS ARE ALWAYS WELCOME HERE.

A. oryzae
When *sake* is finished and ready to be consumed, the kôji molds are completely gone.

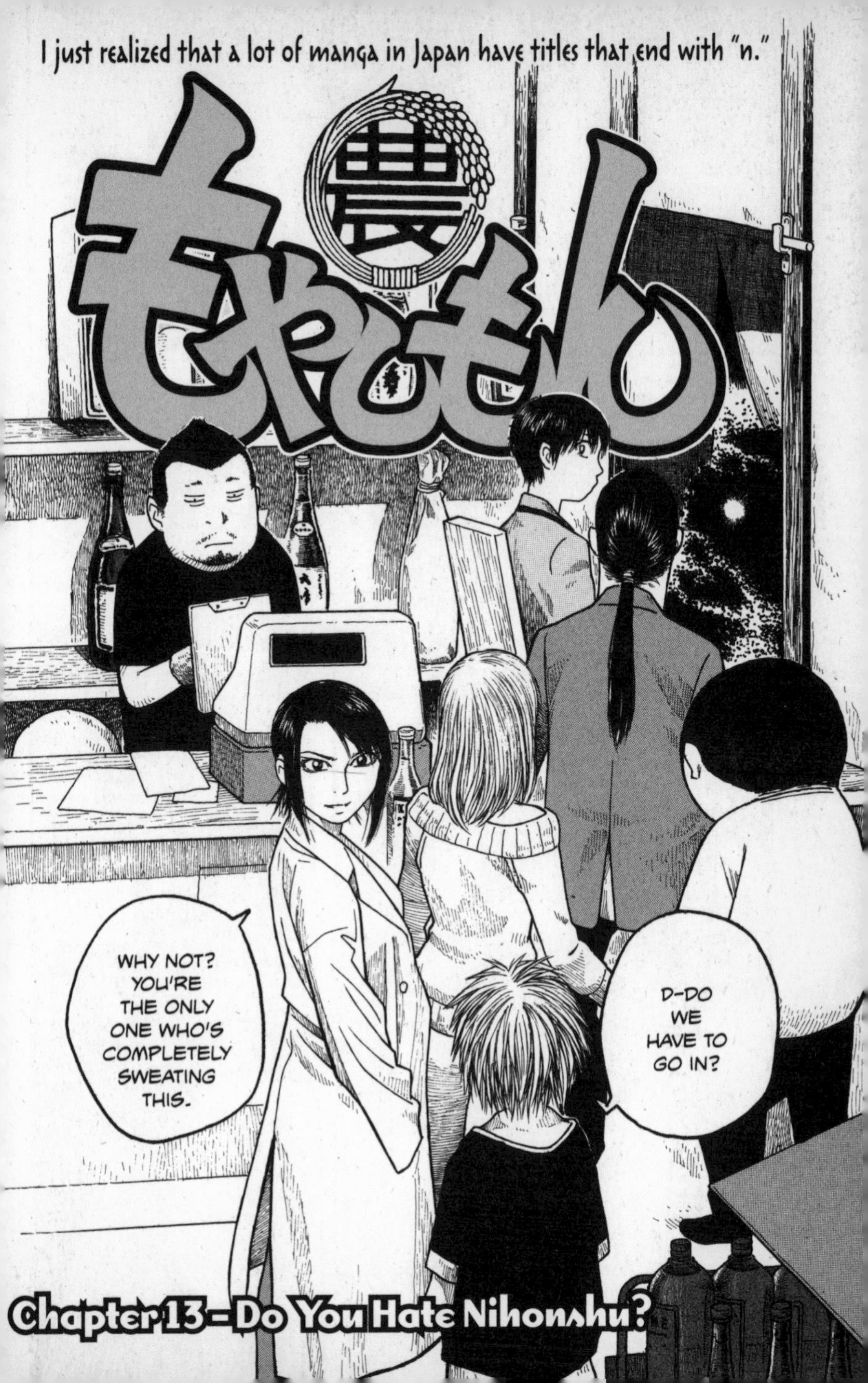

I just realized that a lot of manga in Japan have titles that end with "n."
もやしもん
D-DO WE HAVE TO GO IN?
WHY NOT? YOU'RE THE ONLY ONE WHO'S COMPLETELY SWEATING THIS.
Chapter 13 - Do You Hate Nihonshu?

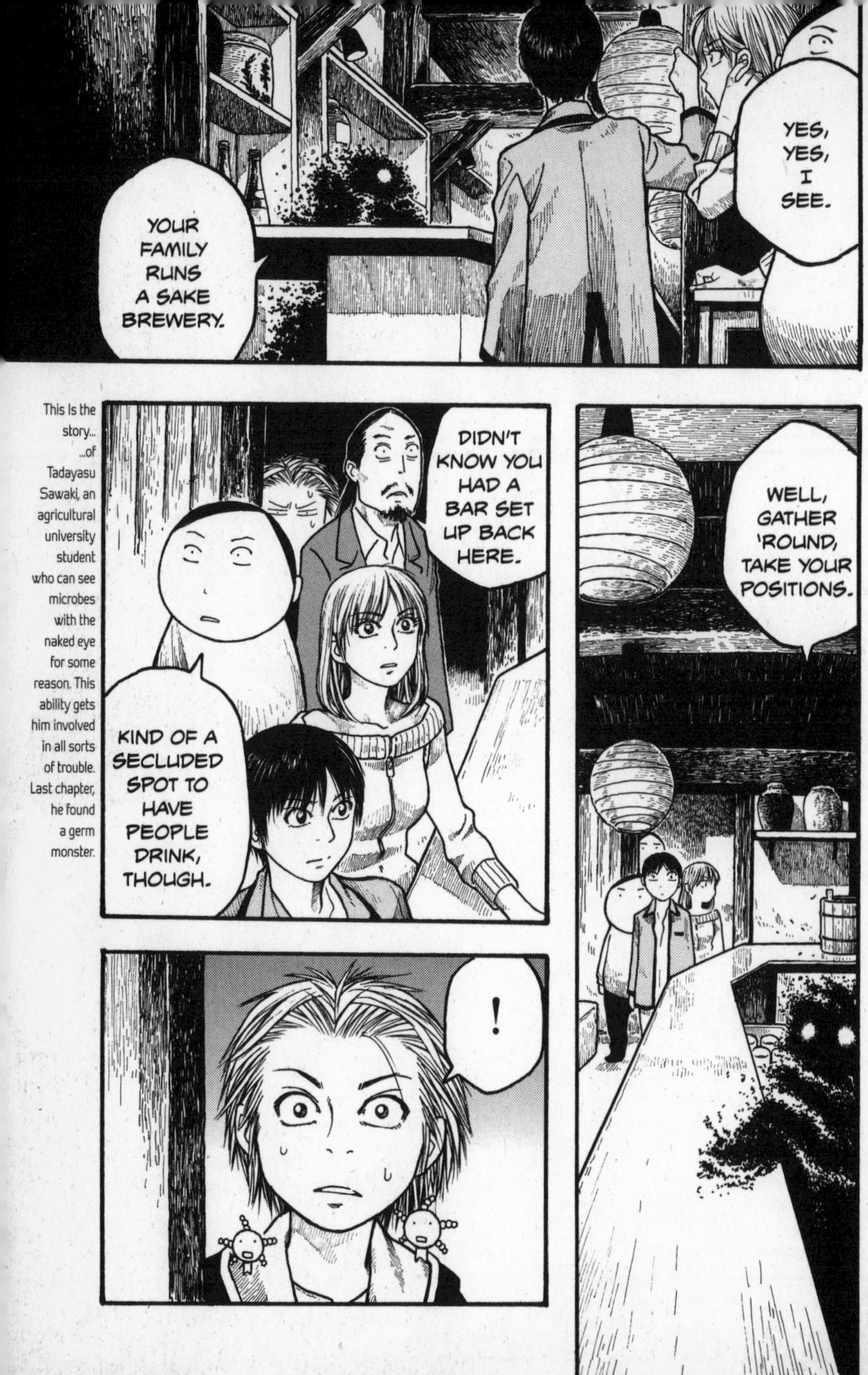
YES, YES, I SEE.
YOUR FAMILY RUNS A SAKE BREWERY.
WELL, GATHER 'ROUND, TAKE YOUR POSITIONS.
DIDN'T KNOW YOU HAD A BAR SET UP BACK HERE.
KIND OF A SECLUDED SPOT TO HAVE PEOPLE DRINK, THOUGH.
!

This Is the story... ...of Tadayasu Sawaki, an agricultural university student who can see microbes with the naked eye for some reason. This ability gets him involved in all sorts of trouble. Last chapter, he found a germ monster.

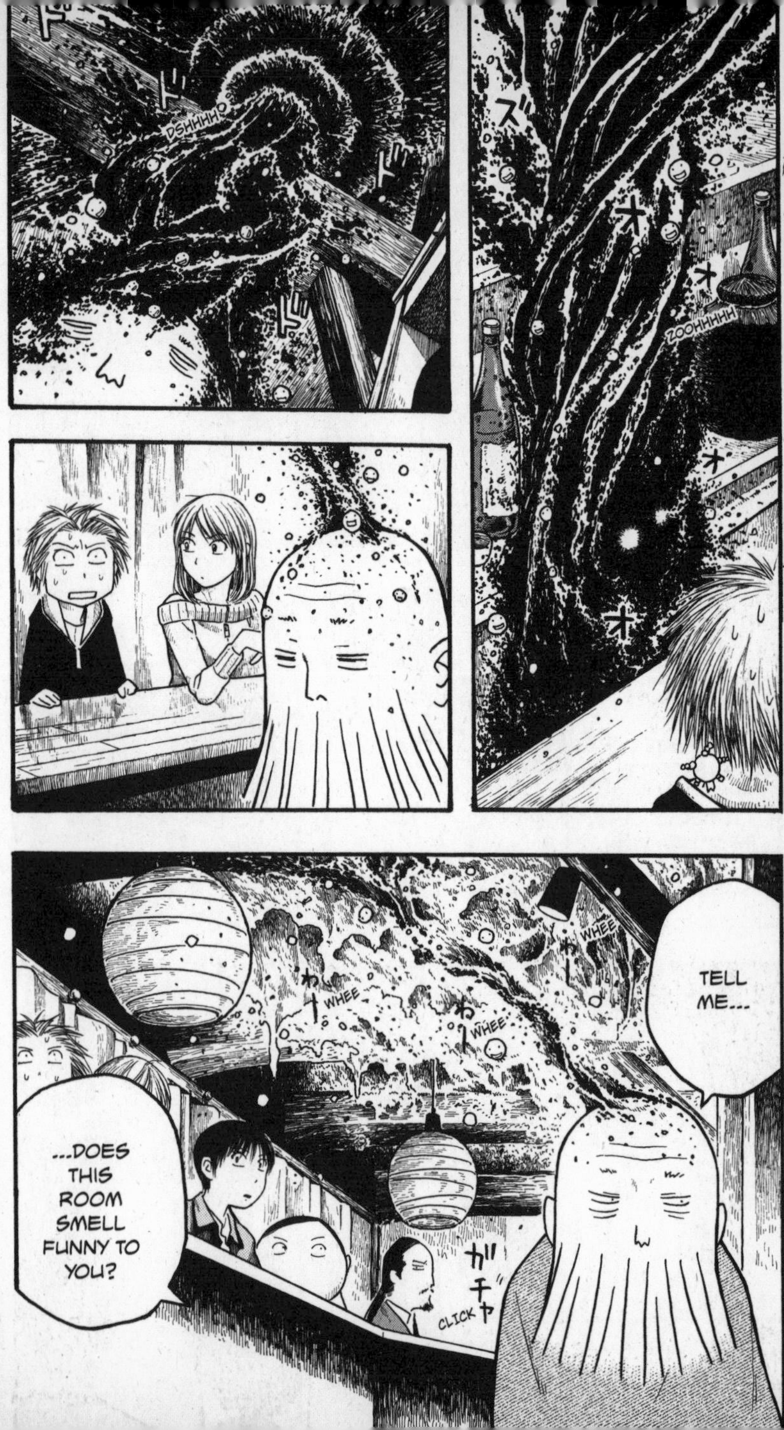
ズ
オ
オ
ZOOHHHHH
オ
オ
ド
ド
DSHHHH
ド
ド
TELL ME...
...DOES THIS ROOM SMELL FUNNY TO YOU?
WHEE
わー
WHEE
わー
WHEE
ガチャ
CLICK

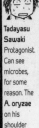

Tadayasu Sawaki
Protagonist. Can see microbes, for some reason. The **A. oryzae** on his shoulder came from home.

Kei Yûki
Sawaki's friend and the son of a traditional brewer, which is the reason for his indignation in this chapter.

Hazuki Oikawa
A freshman like Sawaki and Yûki. Does very little in this chapter.

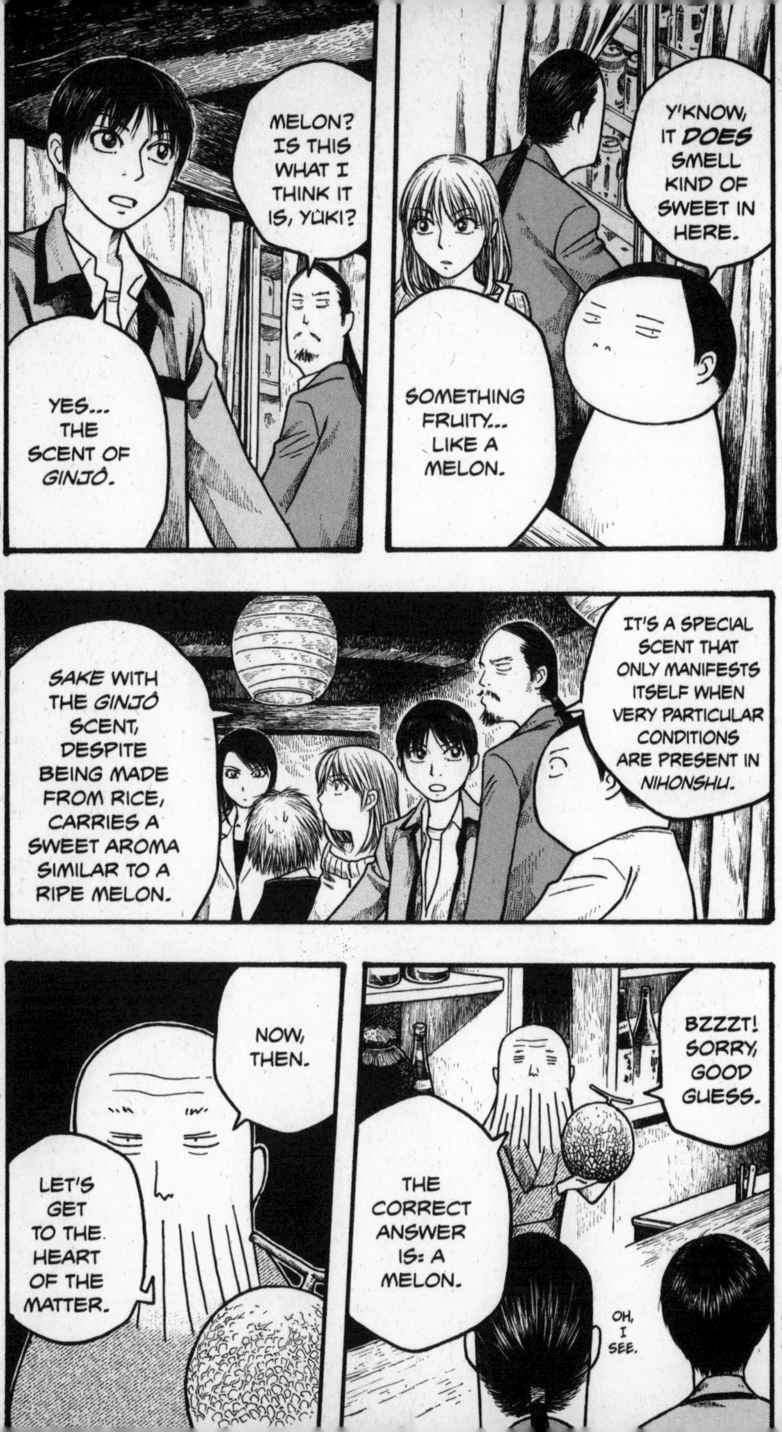
Y'KNOW, IT *DOES* SMELL KIND OF SWEET IN HERE.
SOMETHING FRUITY... LIKE A MELON.
MELON? IS THIS WHAT I THINK IT IS, YŪKI?
YES... THE SCENT OF *GINJŌ*.
IT'S A SPECIAL SCENT THAT ONLY MANIFESTS ITSELF WHEN VERY PARTICULAR CONDITIONS ARE PRESENT IN *NIHONSHU*.
SAKE WITH THE *GINJŌ* SCENT, DESPITE BEING MADE FROM RICE, CARRIES A SWEET AROMA SIMILAR TO A RIPE MELON.
BZZZT! SORRY, GOOD GUESS.
THE CORRECT ANSWER IS: A MELON.
OH, I SEE.
NOW, THEN.
LET'S GET TO THE HEART OF THE MATTER.

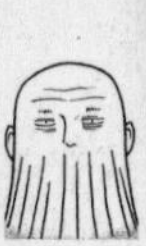

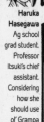

Kikuji Hiyoshi
The retired owner of Hiyoshi Liquor. An old acquaintance of Keizô Itsuki's... but in what way?

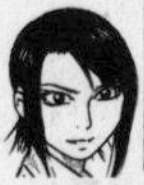

Haruka Hasegawa
Ag school grad student. Professor Itsuki's chief assistant. Considering how she should use ol' Grampa Hiyoshi.

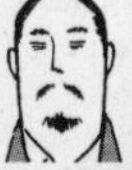

Kaoru Misato
Sophomore. Loves *sake* enough to brew his own. He will speak in this chapter.

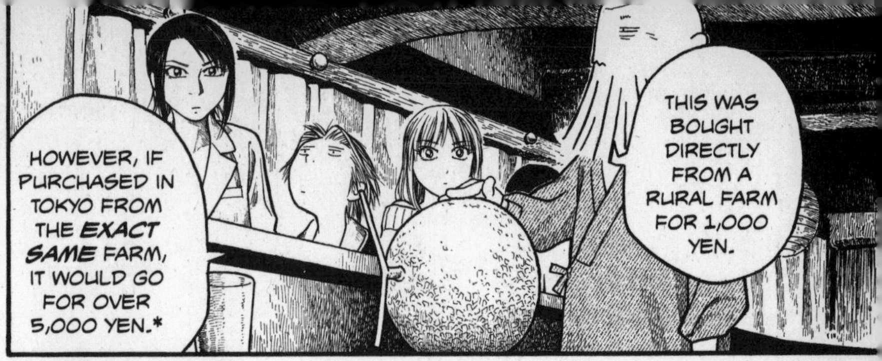
THIS WAS BOUGHT DIRECTLY FROM A RURAL FARM FOR 1,000 YEN.
HOWEVER, IF PURCHASED IN TOKYO FROM THE ***EXACT SAME*** FARM, IT WOULD GO FOR OVER 5,000 YEN.*

*$50

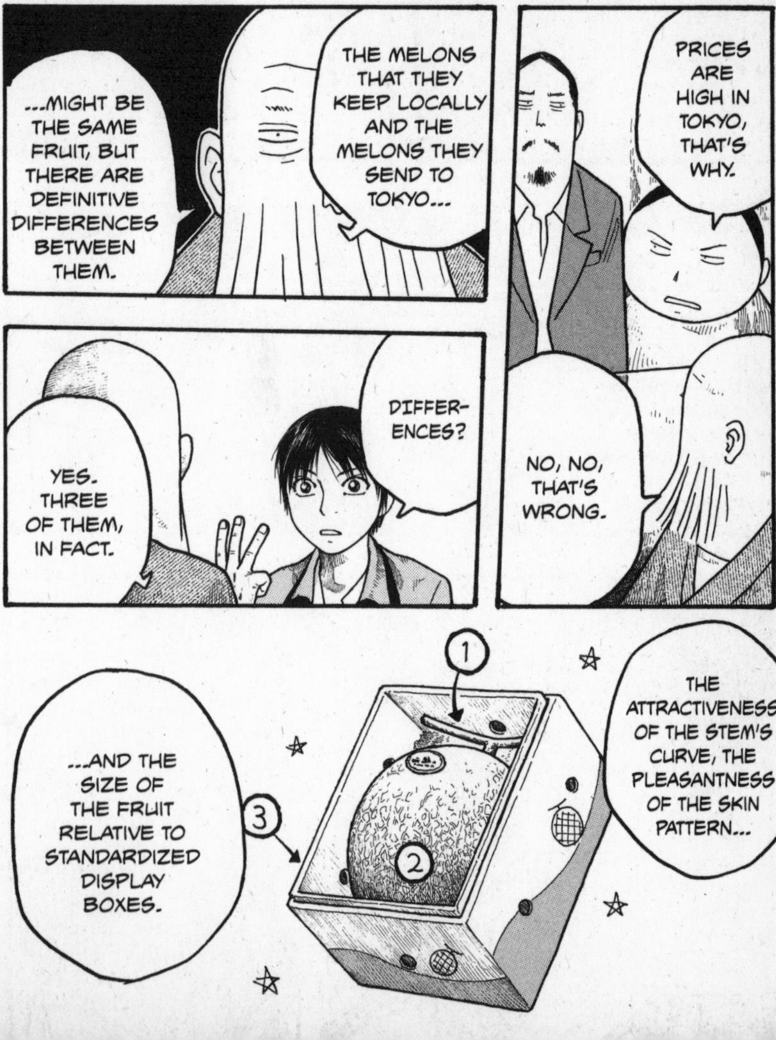
PRICES ARE HIGH IN TOKYO, THAT'S WHY.
NO, NO, THAT'S WRONG.
THE MELONS THAT THEY KEEP LOCALLY AND THE MELONS THEY SEND TO TOKYO...
...MIGHT BE THE SAME FRUIT, BUT THERE ARE DEFINITIVE DIFFERENCES BETWEEN THEM.
DIFFER-ENCES?
YES. THREE OF THEM, IN FACT.
1
2
3
THE ATTRACTIVENESS OF THE STEM'S CURVE, THE PLEASANTNESS OF THE SKIN PATTERN...
...AND THE SIZE OF THE FRUIT RELATIVE TO STANDARDIZED DISPLAY BOXES.

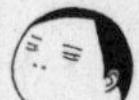

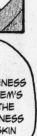

Takuma Kawahama
Sophomore. His face gets bigger and bigger as the story continues.

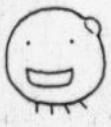

S. cerevisiae
Yeast. Kind of a ditz.

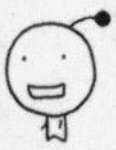

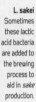

L. sakei
Sometimes these lactic acid bacteria are added to the brewing process to aid in *sake* production.

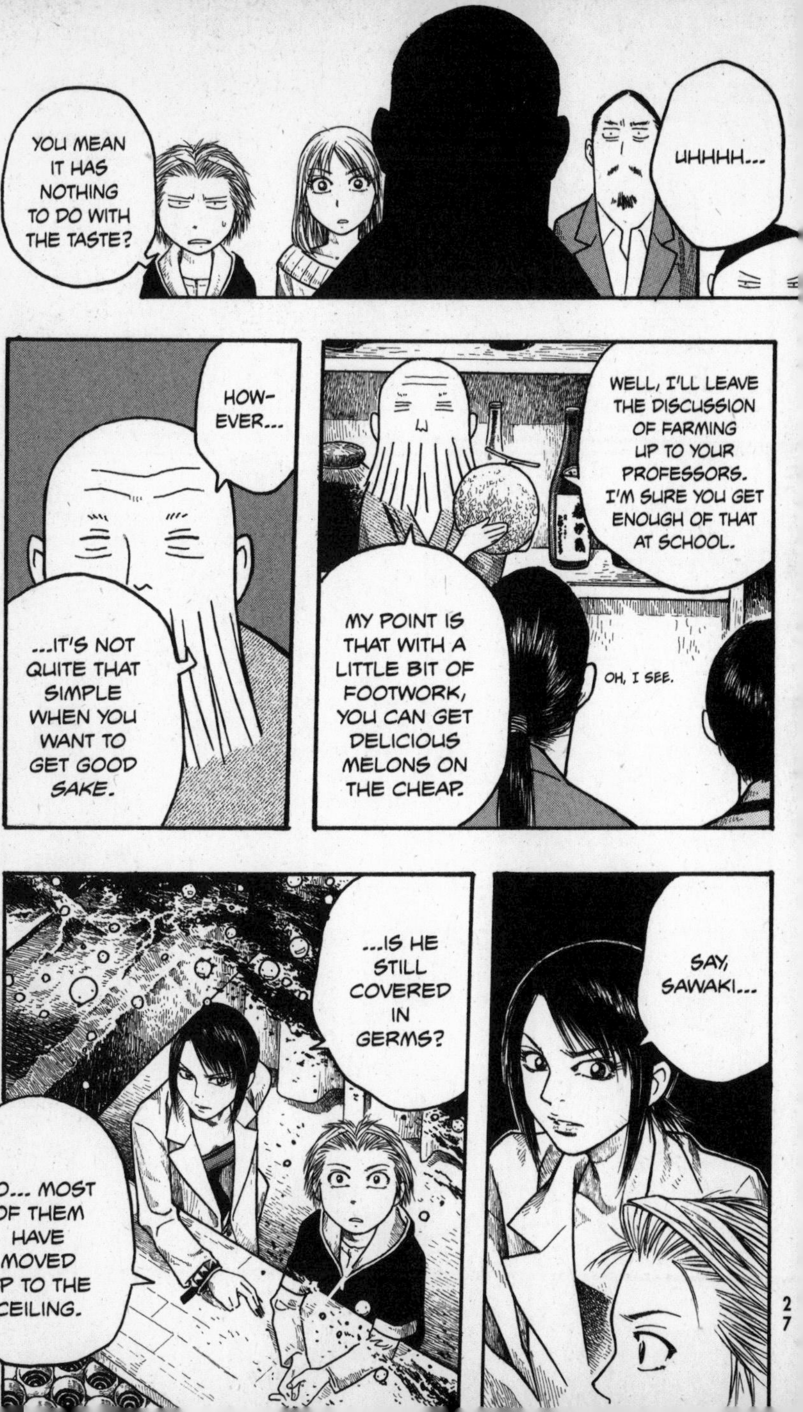
UHHHH...
YOU MEAN IT HAS NOTHING TO DO WITH THE TASTE?
WELL, I'LL LEAVE THE DISCUSSION OF FARMING UP TO YOUR PROFESSORS. I'M SURE YOU GET ENOUGH OF THAT AT SCHOOL.
MY POINT IS THAT WITH A LITTLE BIT OF FOOTWORK, YOU CAN GET DELICIOUS MELONS ON THE CHEAP.
OH, I SEE.
HOW-EVER...
...IT'S NOT QUITE THAT SIMPLE WHEN YOU WANT TO GET GOOD SAKE.
SAY, SAWAKI...
...IS HE STILL COVERED IN GERMS?
NO... MOST OF THEM HAVE MOVED UP TO THE CEILING.

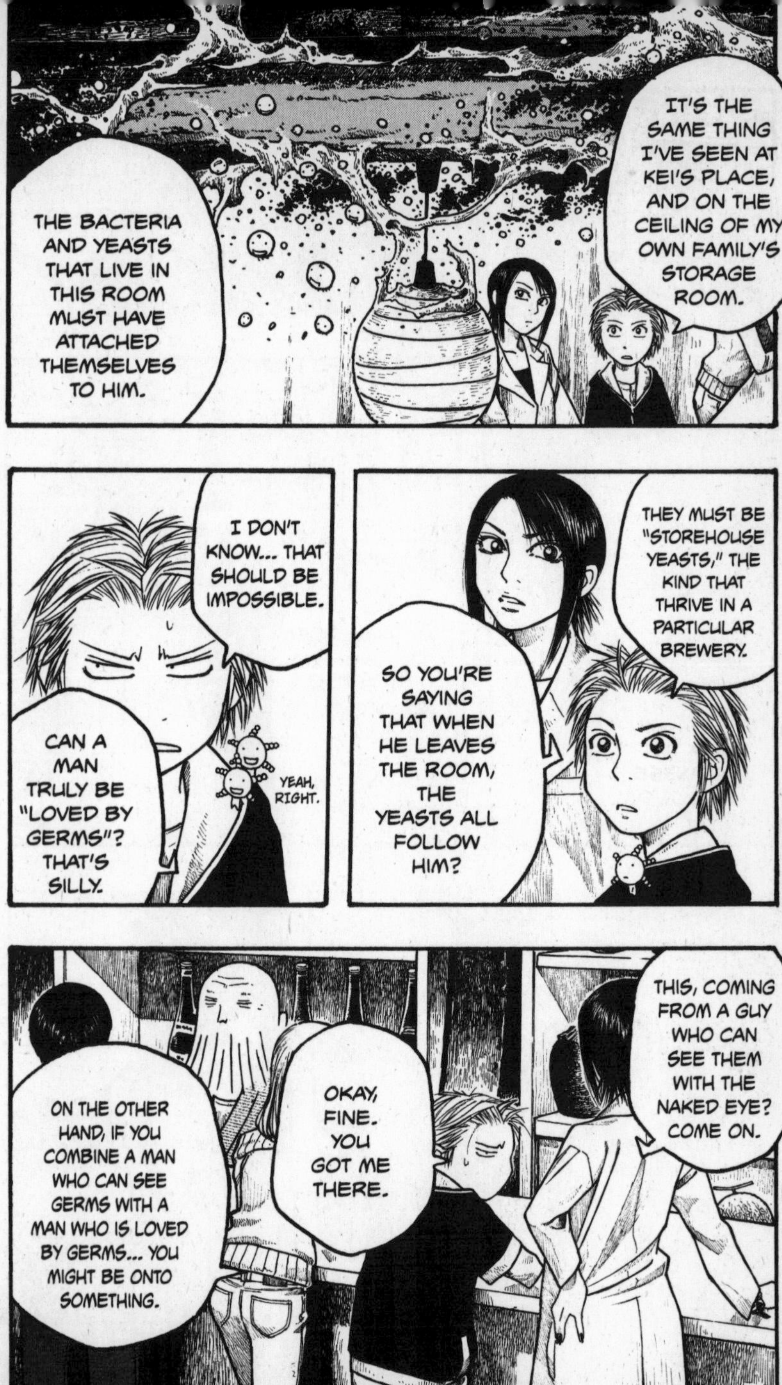
IT'S THE SAME THING I'VE SEEN AT KEI'S PLACE, AND ON THE CEILING OF MY OWN FAMILY'S STORAGE ROOM.
THE BACTERIA AND YEASTS THAT LIVE IN THIS ROOM MUST HAVE ATTACHED THEMSELVES TO HIM.
THEY MUST BE "STOREHOUSE YEASTS," THE KIND THAT THRIVE IN A PARTICULAR BREWERY.
SO YOU'RE SAYING THAT WHEN HE LEAVES THE ROOM, THE YEASTS ALL FOLLOW HIM?
I DON'T KNOW... THAT SHOULD BE IMPOSSIBLE.
YEAH, RIGHT.
CAN A MAN TRULY BE "LOVED BY GERMS"? THAT'S SILLY.
THIS, COMING FROM A GUY WHO CAN SEE THEM WITH THE NAKED EYE? COME ON.
OKAY, FINE. YOU GOT ME THERE.
ON THE OTHER HAND, IF YOU COMBINE A MAN WHO CAN SEE GERMS WITH A MAN WHO IS LOVED BY GERMS... YOU MIGHT BE ONTO SOMETHING.

S. sake
Sake yeast. An expert in brewing nihonshu.

Yeast #7
Its ancestor was the yeast that made "Masumi," from Nagano's Miyasaka Brewery.

Yeast #11
A variant of #7. Has a naughty personality.

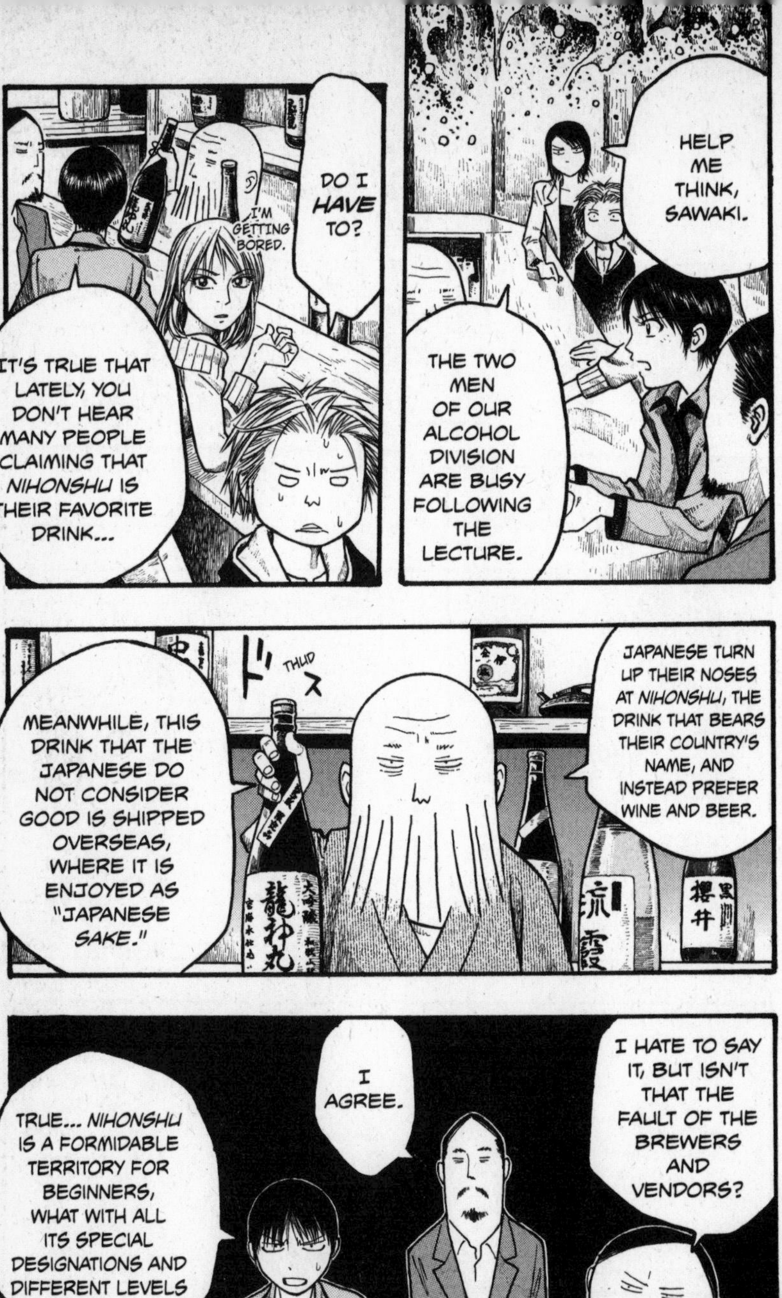
HELP ME THINK, SAWAKI.
THE TWO MEN OF OUR ALCOHOL DIVISION ARE BUSY FOLLOWING THE LECTURE.
DO I *HAVE* TO?
I'M GETTING BORED.
IT'S TRUE THAT LATELY, YOU DON'T HEAR MANY PEOPLE CLAIMING THAT *NIHONSHU* IS THEIR FAVORITE DRINK...
JAPANESE TURN UP THEIR NOSES AT *NIHONSHU*, THE DRINK THAT BEARS THEIR COUNTRY'S NAME, AND INSTEAD PREFER WINE AND BEER.
ドス
THUD
MEANWHILE, THIS DRINK THAT THE JAPANESE DO NOT CONSIDER GOOD IS SHIPPED OVERSEAS, WHERE IT IS ENJOYED AS "JAPANESE *SAKE*."
I HATE TO SAY IT, BUT ISN'T THAT THE FAULT OF THE BREWERS AND VENDORS?
I AGREE.
TRUE... *NIHONSHU* IS A FORMIDABLE TERRITORY FOR BEGINNERS, WHAT WITH ALL ITS SPECIAL DESIGNATIONS AND DIFFERENT LEVELS OF QUALITY...

Yeast #6
Its character is carefree and cheery. Based on the yeast in "Aramasa," from Akita.

Red Sake Yeast
An active part of the creation of pink nigori (cloudy) *sake*.

There are plenty more of these, so I'll try to introduce them bit by bit.

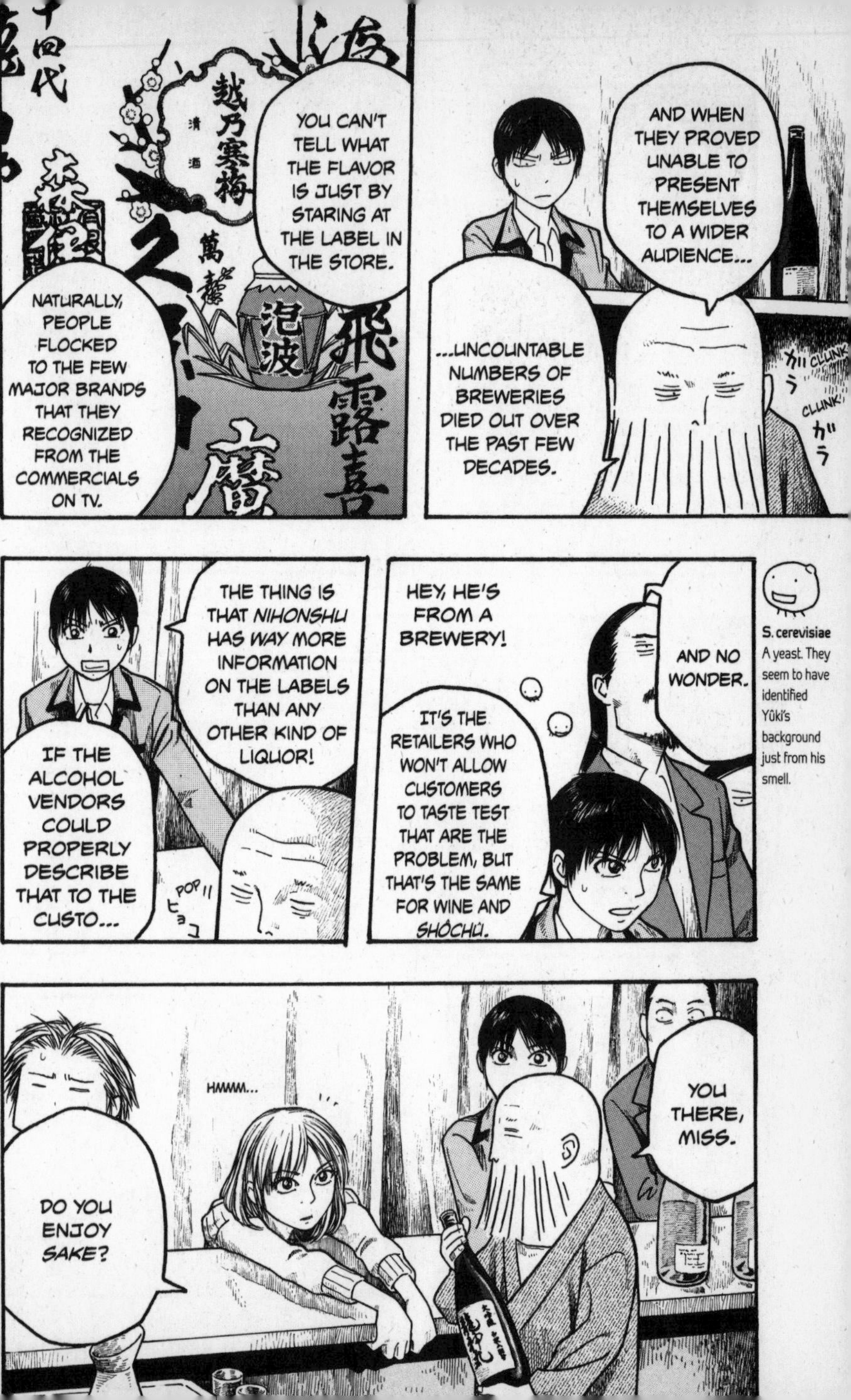
AND WHEN THEY PROVED UNABLE TO PRESENT THEMSELVES TO A WIDER AUDIENCE...
...UNCOUNTABLE NUMBERS OF BREWERIES DIED OUT OVER THE PAST FEW DECADES.
ガラ CLUNK
ガラ CLUNK
十四代
越乃寒梅
清酒
泡波
飛露喜
YOU CAN'T TELL WHAT THE FLAVOR IS JUST BY STARING AT THE LABEL IN THE STORE.
NATURALLY, PEOPLE FLOCKED TO THE FEW MAJOR BRANDS THAT THEY RECOGNIZED FROM THE COMMERCIALS ON TV.
HEY, HE'S FROM A BREWERY!
AND NO WONDER.
IT'S THE RETAILERS WHO WON'T ALLOW CUSTOMERS TO TASTE TEST THAT ARE THE PROBLEM, BUT THAT'S THE SAME FOR WINE AND *SHÔCHÛ*.
THE THING IS THAT *NIHONSHU* HAS *WAY* MORE INFORMATION ON THE LABELS THAN ANY OTHER KIND OF LIQUOR!
IF THE ALCOHOL VENDORS COULD PROPERLY DESCRIBE THAT TO THE CUSTO...
ヒョコ POP
YOU THERE, MISS.
HMMM...
DO YOU ENJOY SAKE?

S. cerevisiae
A yeast. They seem to have identified Yûki's background just from his smell.

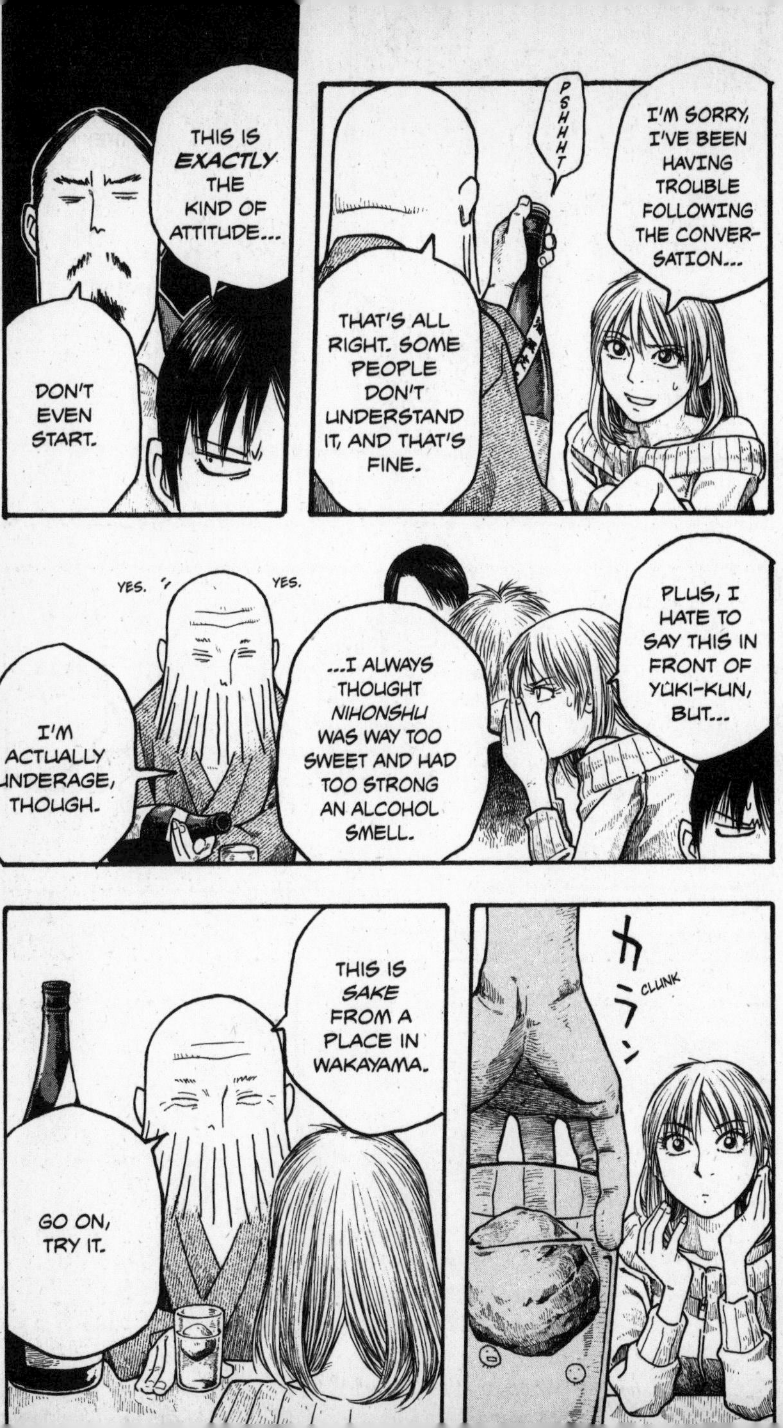
I'M SORRY, I'VE BEEN HAVING TROUBLE FOLLOWING THE CONVER-SATION...
PSHHHT
THAT'S ALL RIGHT. SOME PEOPLE DON'T UNDERSTAND IT, AND THAT'S FINE.
THIS IS *EXACTLY* THE KIND OF ATTITUDE...
DON'T EVEN START.
PLUS, I HATE TO SAY THIS IN FRONT OF YŪKI-KUN, BUT...
...I ALWAYS THOUGHT *NIHONSHU* WAS WAY TOO SWEET AND HAD TOO STRONG AN ALCOHOL SMELL.
YES.
YES.
I'M ACTUALLY UNDERAGE, THOUGH.
カラン
CLUNK
THIS IS *SAKE* FROM A PLACE IN WAKAYAMA.
GO ON, TRY IT.

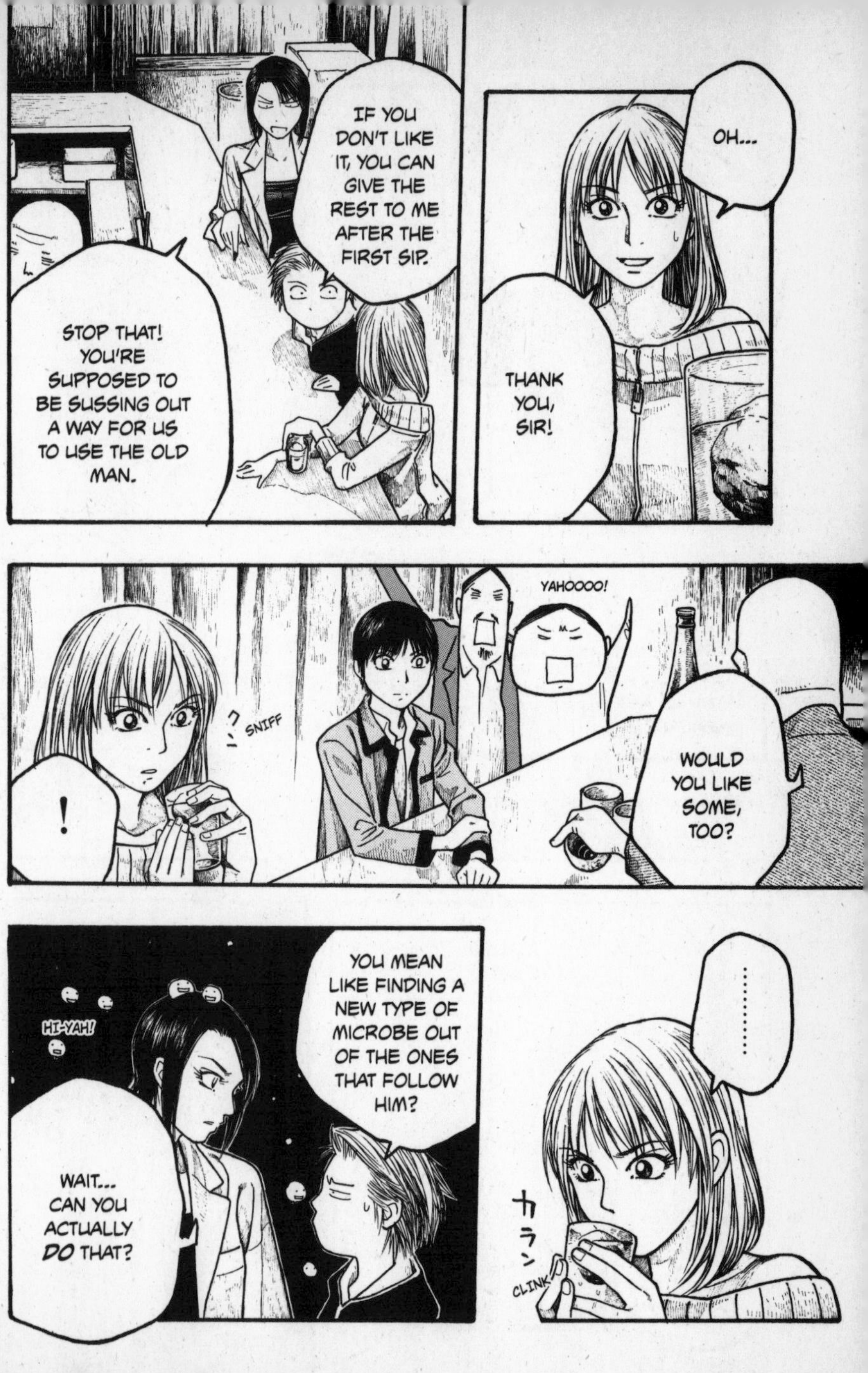
OH...
THANK YOU, SIR!
IF YOU DON'T LIKE IT, YOU CAN GIVE THE REST TO ME AFTER THE FIRST SIP.
STOP THAT! YOU'RE SUPPOSED TO BE SUSSING OUT A WAY FOR US TO USE THE OLD MAN.
WOULD YOU LIKE SOME, TOO?
YAHOOOO!
SNIFF
!
......
カラン
CLINK
YOU MEAN LIKE FINDING A NEW TYPE OF MICROBE OUT OF THE ONES THAT FOLLOW HIM?
WAIT... CAN YOU ACTUALLY *DO* THAT?
HI-YAH!

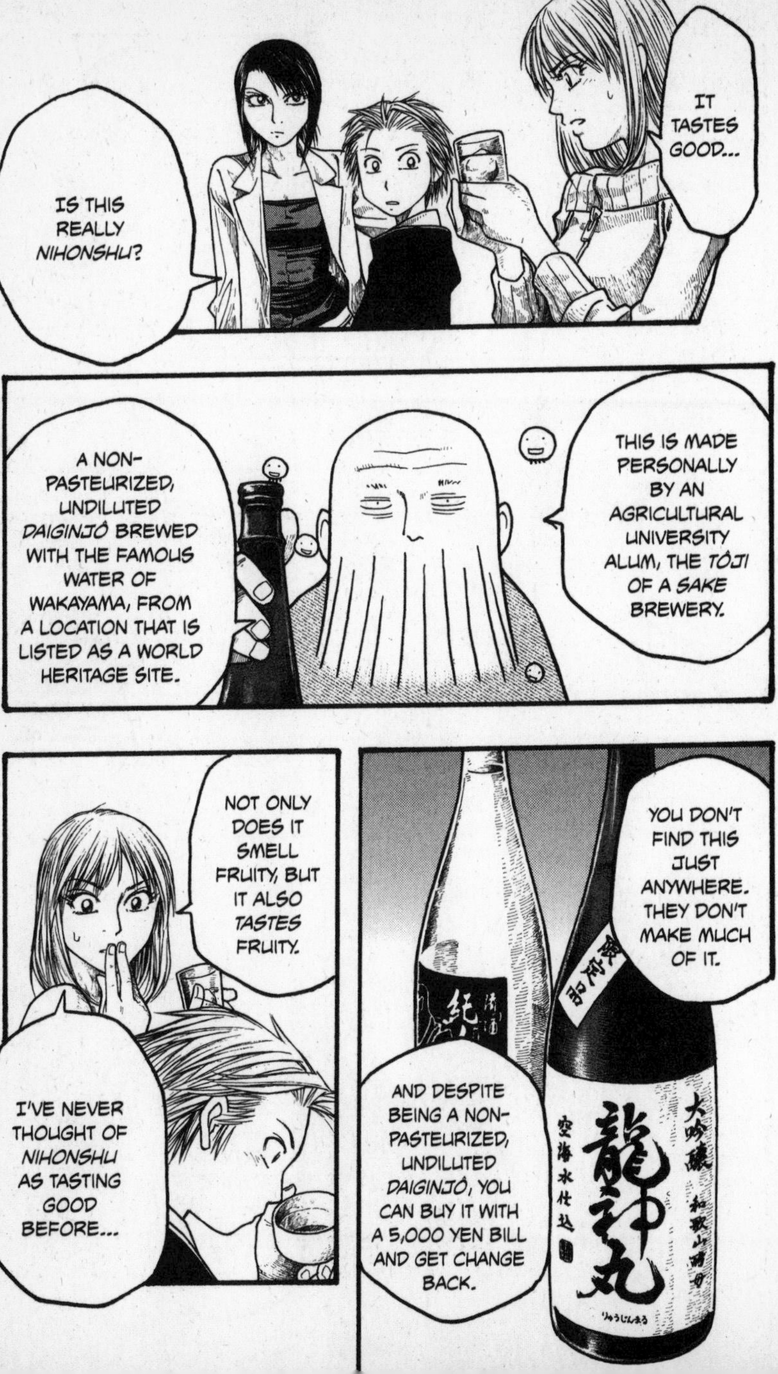
IT TASTES GOOD...
IS THIS REALLY *NIHONSHU*?
THIS IS MADE PERSONALLY BY AN AGRICULTURAL UNIVERSITY ALUM, THE *TÔJI* OF A *SAKE* BREWERY.
A NON-PASTEURIZED, UNDILUTED *DAIGINJÔ* BREWED WITH THE FAMOUS WATER OF WAKAYAMA, FROM A LOCATION THAT IS LISTED AS A WORLD HERITAGE SITE.
YOU DON'T FIND THIS JUST ANYWHERE. THEY DON'T MAKE MUCH OF IT.
AND DESPITE BEING A NON-PASTEURIZED, UNDILUTED *DAIGINJÔ*, YOU CAN BUY IT WITH A 5,000 YEN BILL AND GET CHANGE BACK.
限定品
大吟醸
龍神丸
和歌山酵母
空海水仕込
りゅうじんまる
NOT ONLY DOES IT SMELL FRUITY, BUT IT ALSO *TASTES* FRUITY.
I'VE NEVER THOUGHT OF *NIHONSHU* AS TASTING GOOD BEFORE...

Ryûjinmaru
A brand of *ginjô sake* made using pure trickling water and Wakayama yeast in the dead of winter. And it's non-pasteurized. And it's undiluted.

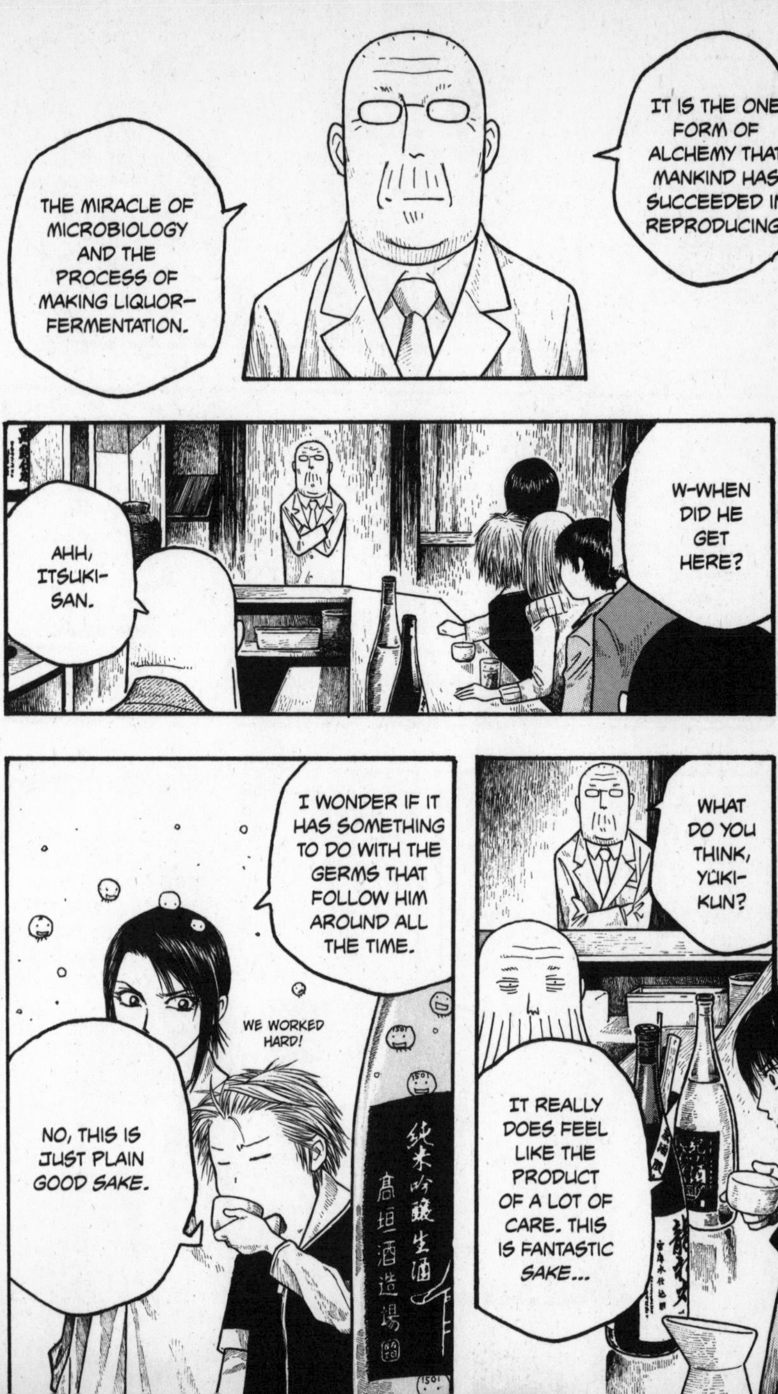
IT IS THE ONE FORM OF ALCHEMY THAT MANKIND HAS SUCCEEDED IN REPRODUCING.
THE MIRACLE OF MICROBIOLOGY AND THE PROCESS OF MAKING LIQUOR—FERMENTATION.
W-WHEN DID HE GET HERE?
AHH, ITSUKI-SAN.
WHAT DO YOU THINK, YŪKI-KUN?
IT REALLY DOES FEEL LIKE THE PRODUCT OF A LOT OF CARE. THIS IS FANTASTIC SAKE...
I WONDER IF IT HAS SOMETHING TO DO WITH THE GERMS THAT FOLLOW HIM AROUND ALL THE TIME.
WE WORKED HARD!
NO, THIS IS JUST PLAIN GOOD SAKE.
純米吟醸生酒
髙垣酒造場

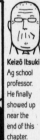

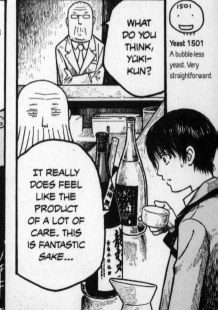

Keizô Itsuki
Ag school professor. He finally showed up near the end of this chapter.

Yeast 1501
A bubble-less yeast. Very straightforward.

I'm happily accepting thoughts and opinions on the first volume now. Hopefully, they will reach me in Japan.

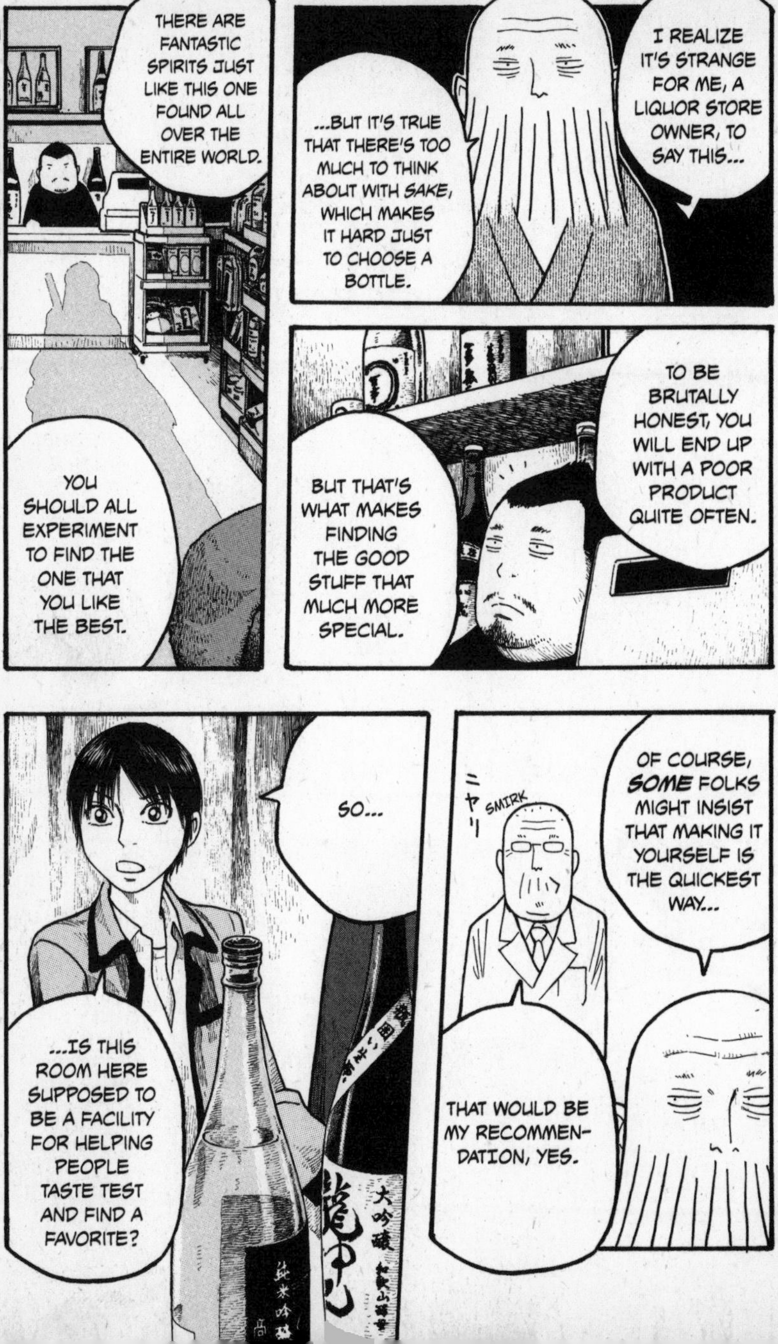
I REALIZE IT'S STRANGE FOR ME, A LIQUOR STORE OWNER, TO SAY THIS...
...BUT IT'S TRUE THAT THERE'S TOO MUCH TO THINK ABOUT WITH *SAKE*, WHICH MAKES IT HARD JUST TO CHOOSE A BOTTLE.
TO BE BRUTALLY HONEST, YOU WILL END UP WITH A POOR PRODUCT QUITE OFTEN.
BUT THAT'S WHAT MAKES FINDING THE GOOD STUFF THAT MUCH MORE SPECIAL.
THERE ARE FANTASTIC SPIRITS JUST LIKE THIS ONE FOUND ALL OVER THE ENTIRE WORLD.
YOU SHOULD ALL EXPERIMENT TO FIND THE ONE THAT YOU LIKE THE BEST.
OF COURSE, ***SOME*** FOLKS MIGHT INSIST THAT MAKING IT YOURSELF IS THE QUICKEST WAY...
ニヤリ
SMIRK
THAT WOULD BE MY RECOMMEN-DATION, YES.
SO...
...IS THIS ROOM HERE SUPPOSED TO BE A FACILITY FOR HELPING PEOPLE TASTE TEST AND FIND A FAVORITE?

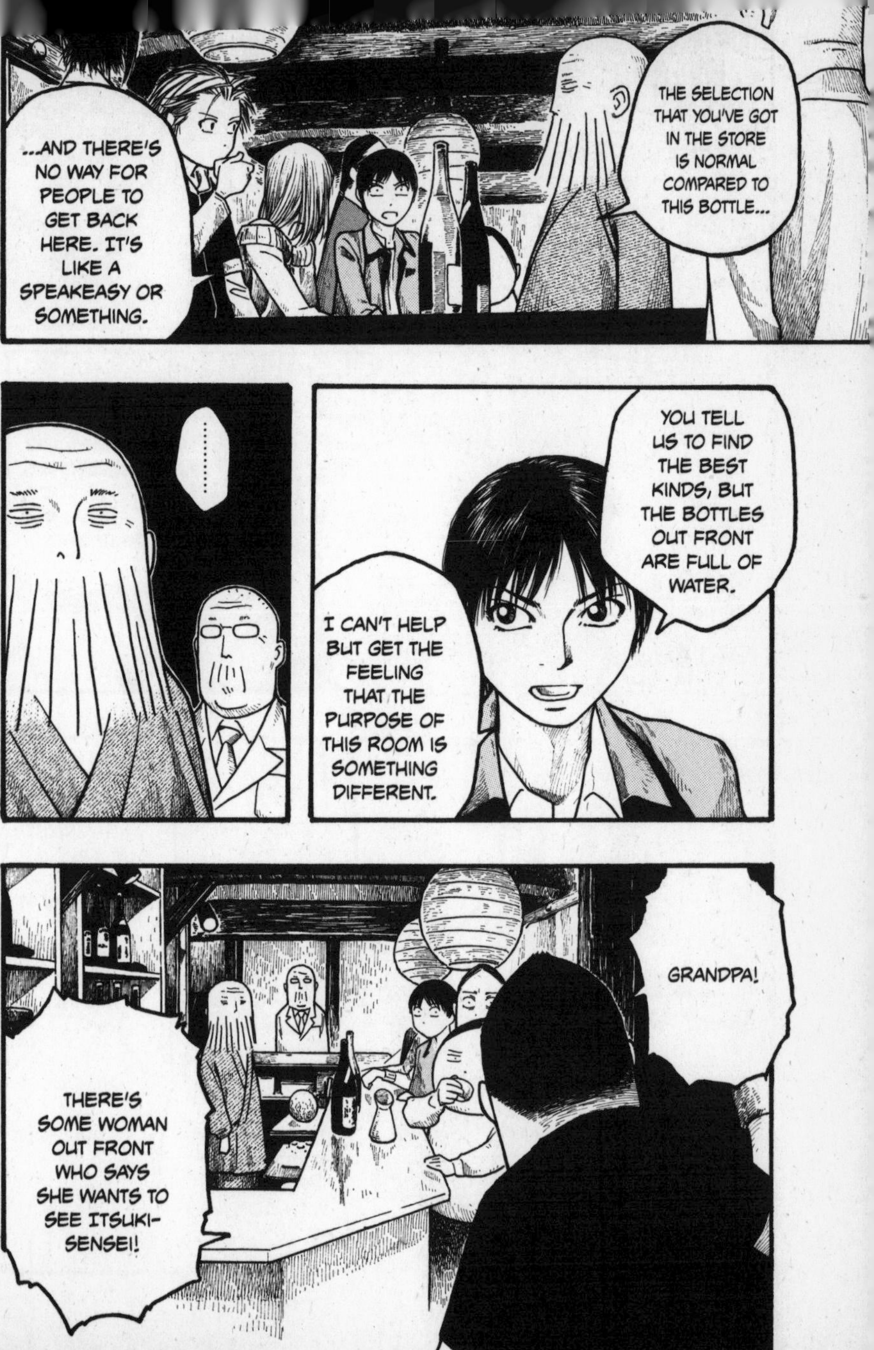
THE SELECTION THAT YOU'VE GOT IN THE STORE IS NORMAL COMPARED TO THIS BOTTLE...
...AND THERE'S NO WAY FOR PEOPLE TO GET BACK HERE. IT'S LIKE A SPEAKEASY OR SOMETHING.
YOU TELL US TO FIND THE BEST KINDS, BUT THE BOTTLES OUT FRONT ARE FULL OF WATER.
I CAN'T HELP BUT GET THE FEELING THAT THE PURPOSE OF THIS ROOM IS SOMETHING DIFFERENT.
......
GRANDPA!
THERE'S SOME WOMAN OUT FRONT WHO SAYS SHE WANTS TO SEE ITSUKI-SENSEI!

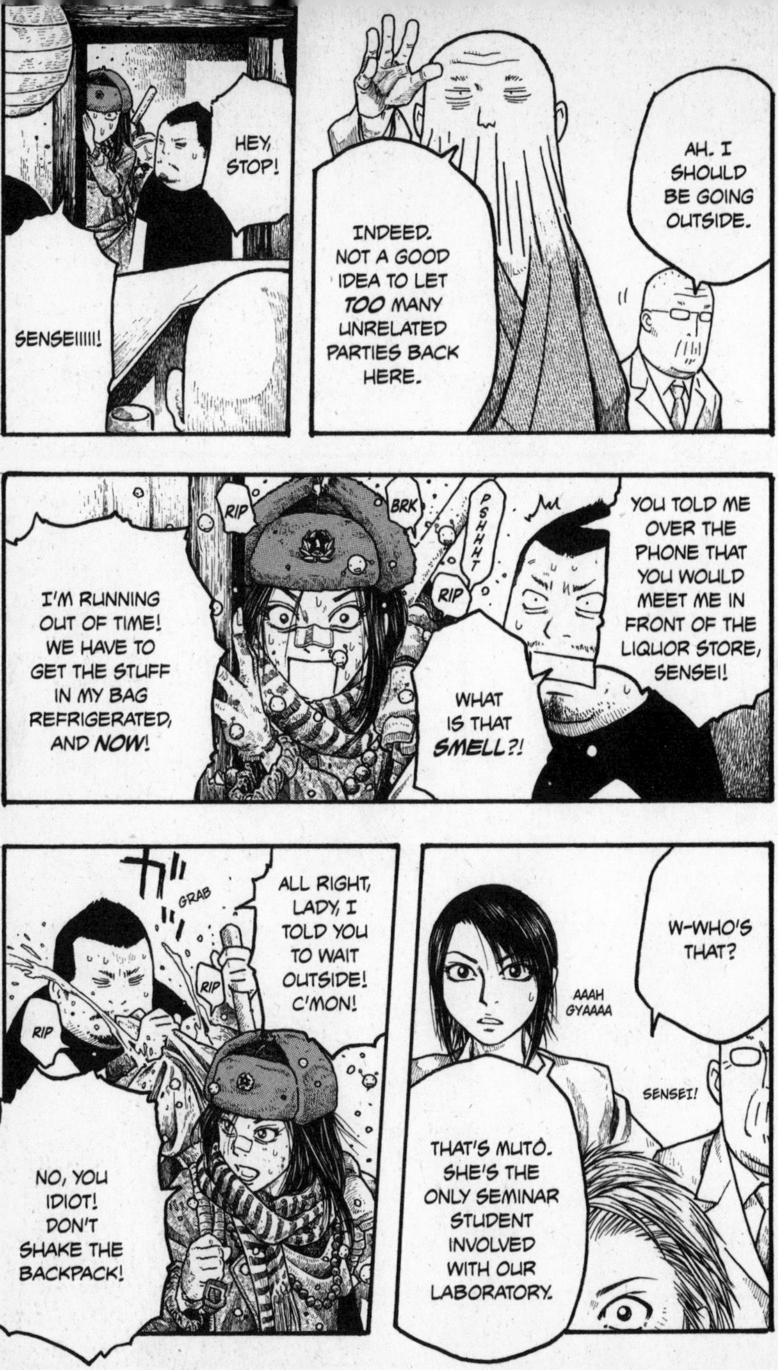
AH. I SHOULD BE GOING OUTSIDE.
INDEED. NOT A GOOD IDEA TO LET *TOO* MANY UNRELATED PARTIES BACK HERE.
HEY, STOP!
SENSEIIIIII!
YOU TOLD ME OVER THE PHONE THAT YOU WOULD MEET ME IN FRONT OF THE LIQUOR STORE, SENSEI!
WHAT IS THAT *SMELL*?!
PSHHHT
RIP
BRK
RIP
I'M RUNNING OUT OF TIME! WE HAVE TO GET THE STUFF IN MY BAG REFRIGERATED, AND *NOW*!
W-WHO'S THAT?
SENSEI!
AAAH GYAAAA
THAT'S MUTÔ. SHE'S THE ONLY SEMINAR STUDENT INVOLVED WITH OUR LABORATORY.
ALL RIGHT, LADY, I TOLD YOU TO WAIT OUTSIDE! C'MON!
GRAB
RIP
RIP
NO, YOU IDIOT! DON'T SHAKE THE BACKPACK!

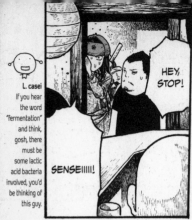

L. casei
If you hear the word "fermentation" and think, gosh, there must be some lactic acid bacteria involved, you'd be thinking of this guy.

B. brevis
This one came from Germany. It has seen the brevises of many places.

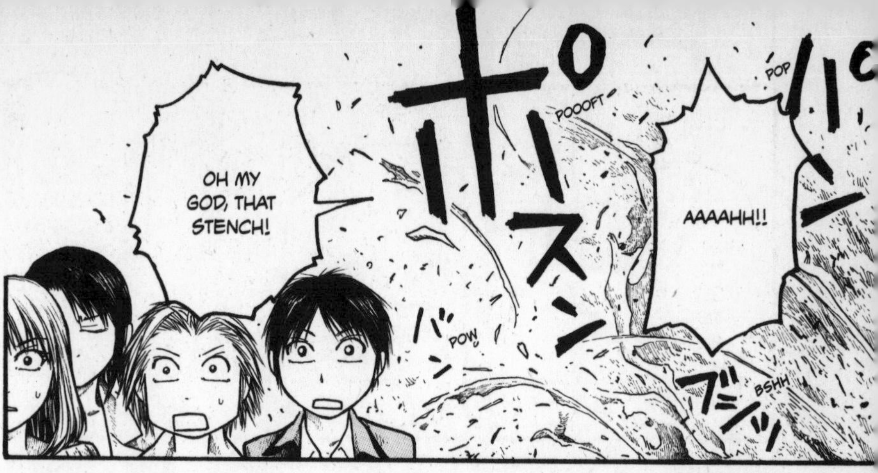
POP
AAAAHH!!
POOOFT
ポスン
POW
BSHH
OH MY GOD, THAT STENCH!

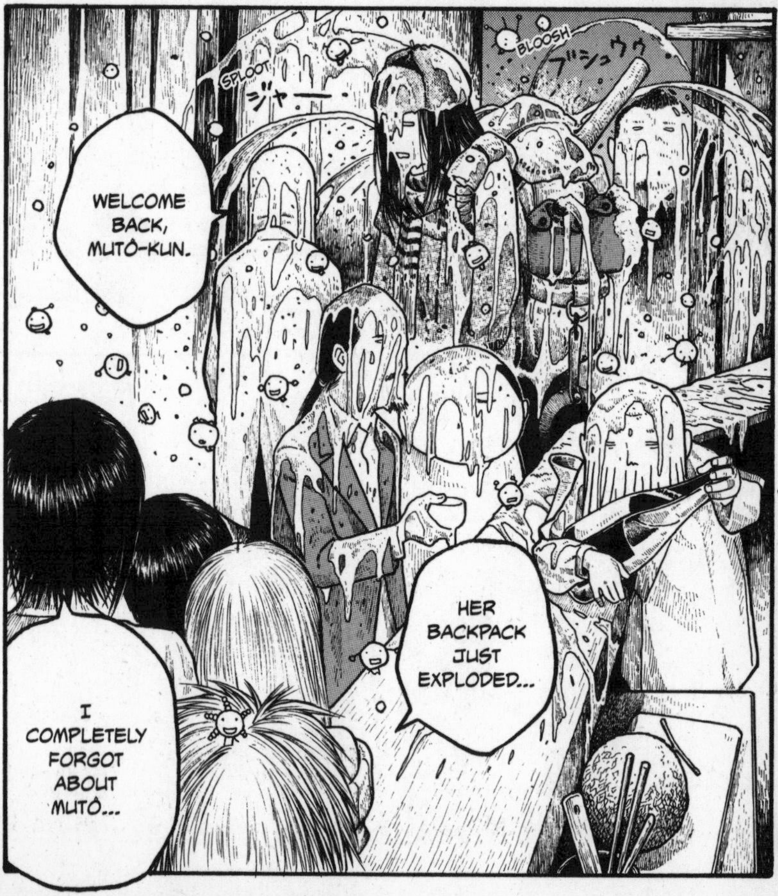
BLOOSH
ブシュウ
SPLOOT
ジャー
WELCOME BACK, MUTÔ-KUN.
HER BACKPACK JUST EXPLODED...
I COMPLETELY FORGOT ABOUT MUTÔ...

B. cinerea
Came from France. Helps rot the grapes that make "noble rot" wine.

R. oligosporus
Also known as "tempeh fungus." As it was traveling, it thought, "Asia is truly under our control."

13 END

This Is the Story... ...of Tadayasu Sawaki, an agricultural university student who can see microbes with the naked eye, for some reason. This ability gets him involved in all sorts of trouble. I saw this was labeled as an "Agricultural School Germ Manga" on some homepage so I guess that must be its genre.

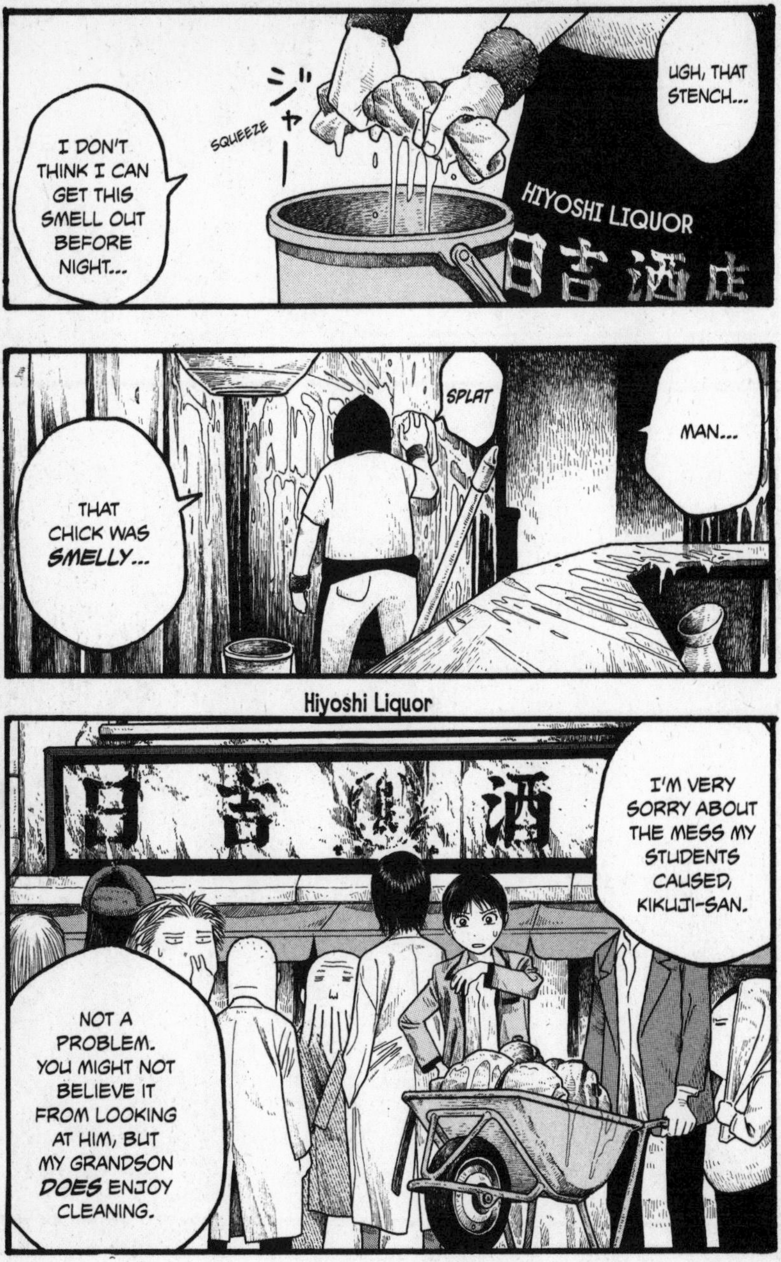
UGH, THAT STENCH...
HIYOSHI LIQUOR
ジャー
SQUEEZE
I DON'T THINK I CAN GET THIS SMELL OUT BEFORE NIGHT...
MAN...
SPLAT
THAT CHICK WAS *SMELLY*...
Hiyoshi Liquor
I'M VERY SORRY ABOUT THE MESS MY STUDENTS CAUSED, KIKUJI-SAN.
NOT A PROBLEM. YOU MIGHT NOT BELIEVE IT FROM LOOKING AT HIM, BUT MY GRANDSON *DOES* ENJOY CLEANING.

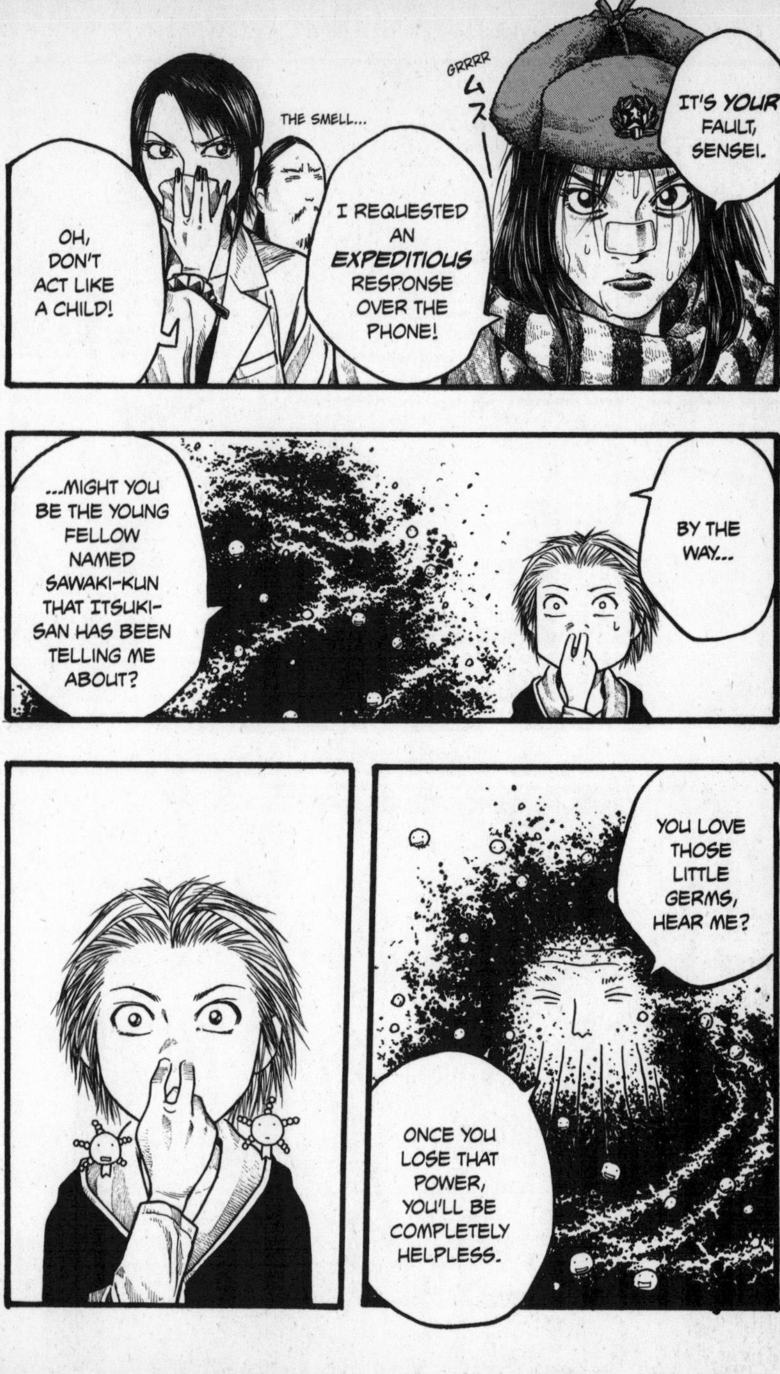
IT'S YOUR FAULT, SENSEI.
GRRRR
ムス
I REQUESTED AN EXPEDITIOUS RESPONSE OVER THE PHONE!
THE SMELL...
OH, DON'T ACT LIKE A CHILD!
BY THE WAY...
...MIGHT YOU BE THE YOUNG FELLOW NAMED SAWAKI-KUN THAT ITSUKI-SAN HAS BEEN TELLING ME ABOUT?
YOU LOVE THOSE LITTLE GERMS, HEAR ME?
ONCE YOU LOSE THAT POWER, YOU'LL BE COMPLETELY HELPLESS.

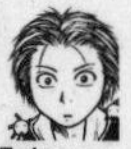

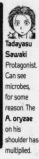

Tadayasu Sawaki
Protagonist. Can see microbes, for some reason. The **A. oryzae** on his shoulder has multiplied.

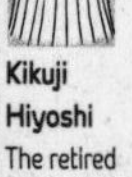

Kikuji Hiyoshi
The retired owner of Hiyoshi Liquor, and the inside of the "germ monster."

Whenever I Google "Moyasimon" (in English), it only spits out results for the anime version. I wish I could find a review of the Manga to read.

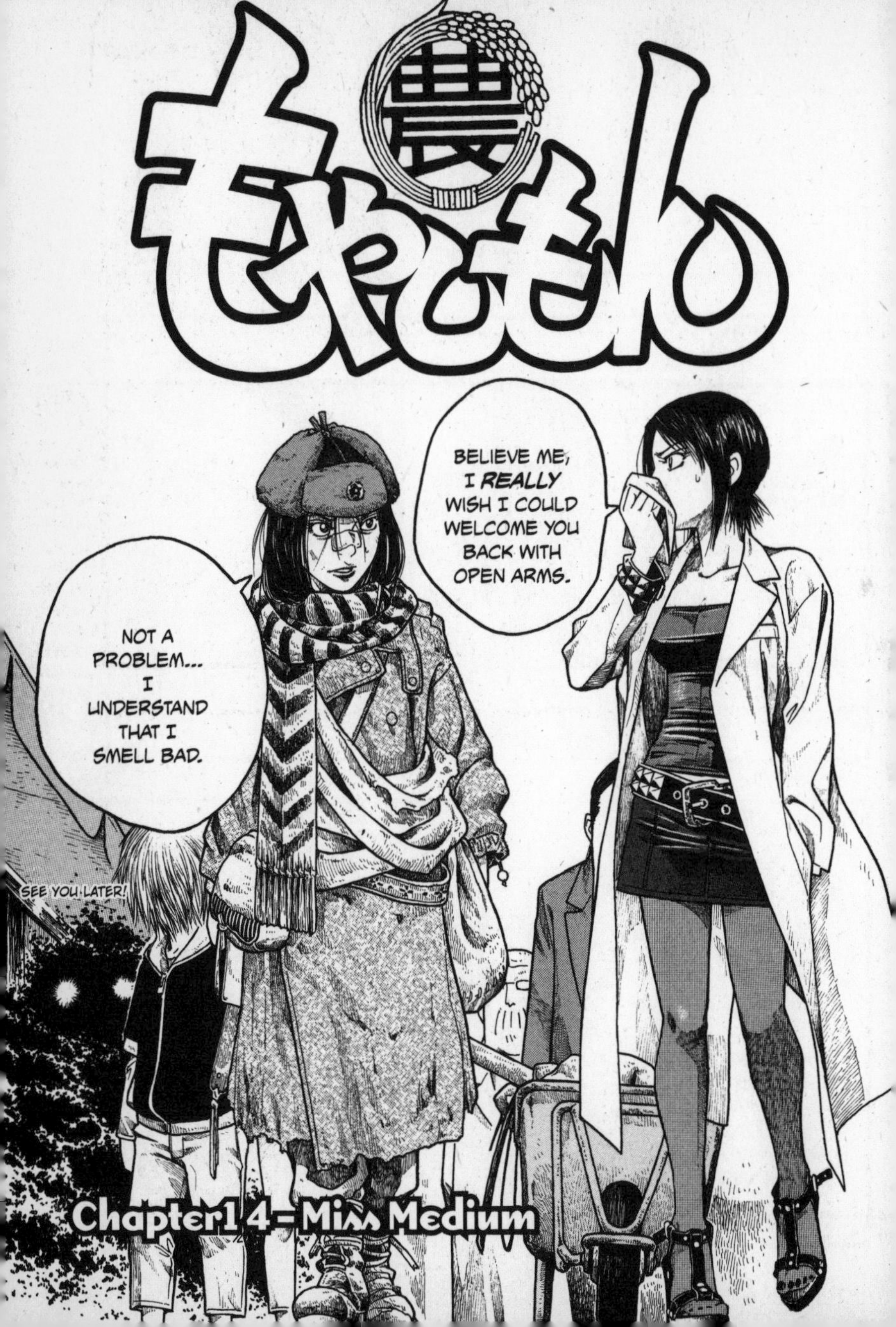
もやしもん
BELIEVE ME, I *REALLY* WISH I COULD WELCOME YOU BACK WITH OPEN ARMS.
NOT A PROBLEM... I UNDERSTAND THAT I SMELL BAD.
SEE YOU LATER!
Chapter1 4 - Miss Medium

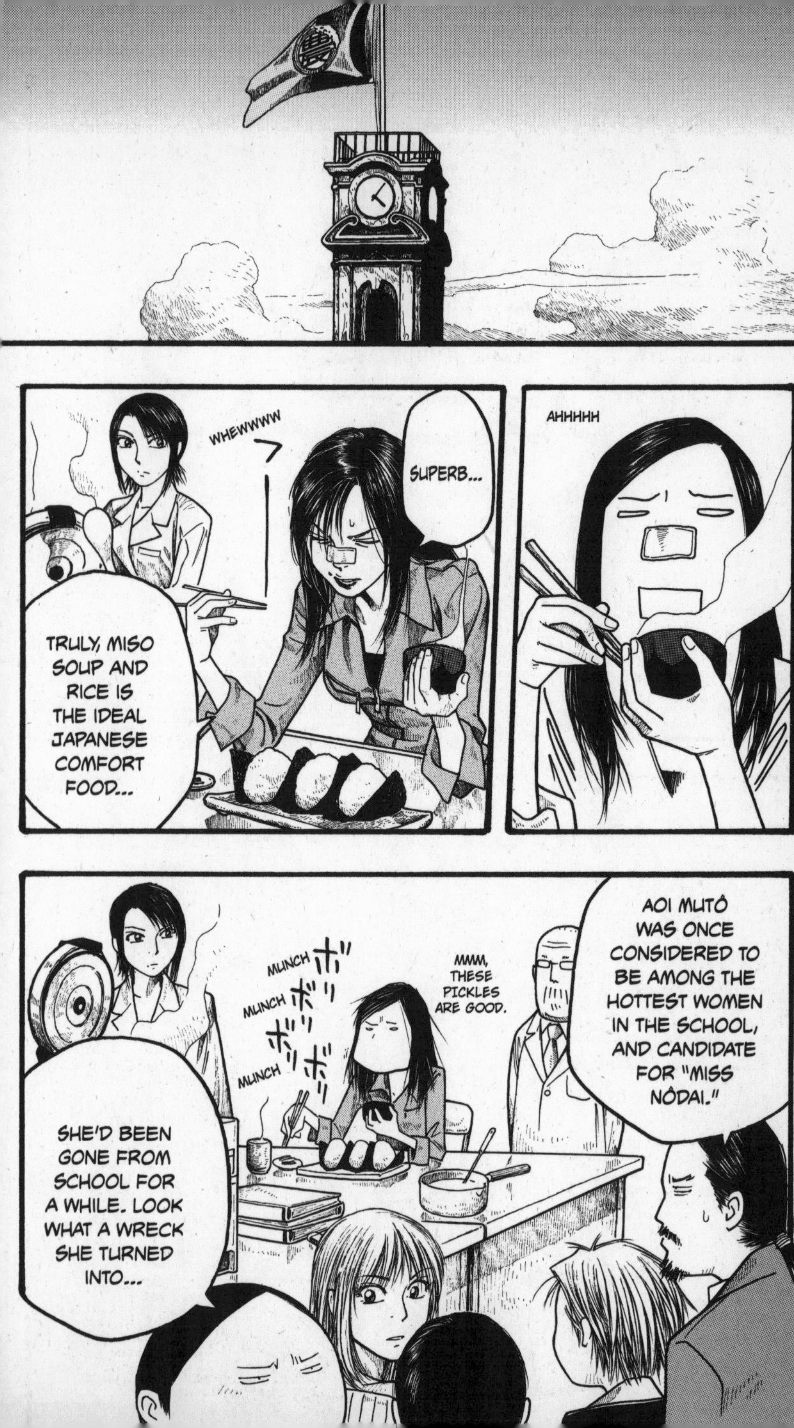
AHHHHH
SUPERB...
WHEWWWW
TRULY, MISO SOUP AND RICE IS THE IDEAL JAPANESE COMFORT FOOD...
AOI MUTÔ WAS ONCE CONSIDERED TO BE AMONG THE HOTTEST WOMEN IN THE SCHOOL, AND CANDIDATE FOR "MISS NÔDAI."
MMM, THESE PICKLES ARE GOOD.
MUNCH ボリ
MUNCH ボリ
ボリボリ
MUNCH
SHE'D BEEN GONE FROM SCHOOL FOR A WHILE. LOOK WHAT A WRECK SHE TURNED INTO...

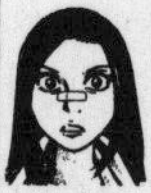

Aoi Mutô (1)
The only seminar student of Itsuki's lab. She just came back from a worldwide quest for fermented foods.

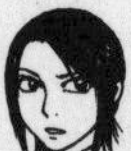

Haruka Hasegawa
Ag school grad student. Professor Itsuki's chief assistant. She has tricophyton living in between her toes.

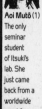

Scarborough Fair
An English folk song tracing back to the Middle Ages. It was made famous by Simon & Garfunkel's 1966 rendition. It is a song of love utilizing lyrics about the herbs parsley (good for digestion, masks bitter flavors), sage (a symbol of eternal strength), rosemary (symbol of faithfulness, love and remembrance) and thyme (symbol of courage). Incidentally, Scarborough is the name of a town that was known for frequent criminal trials ending with a hanging. Actually, everything in this explanation is kind of incidental.

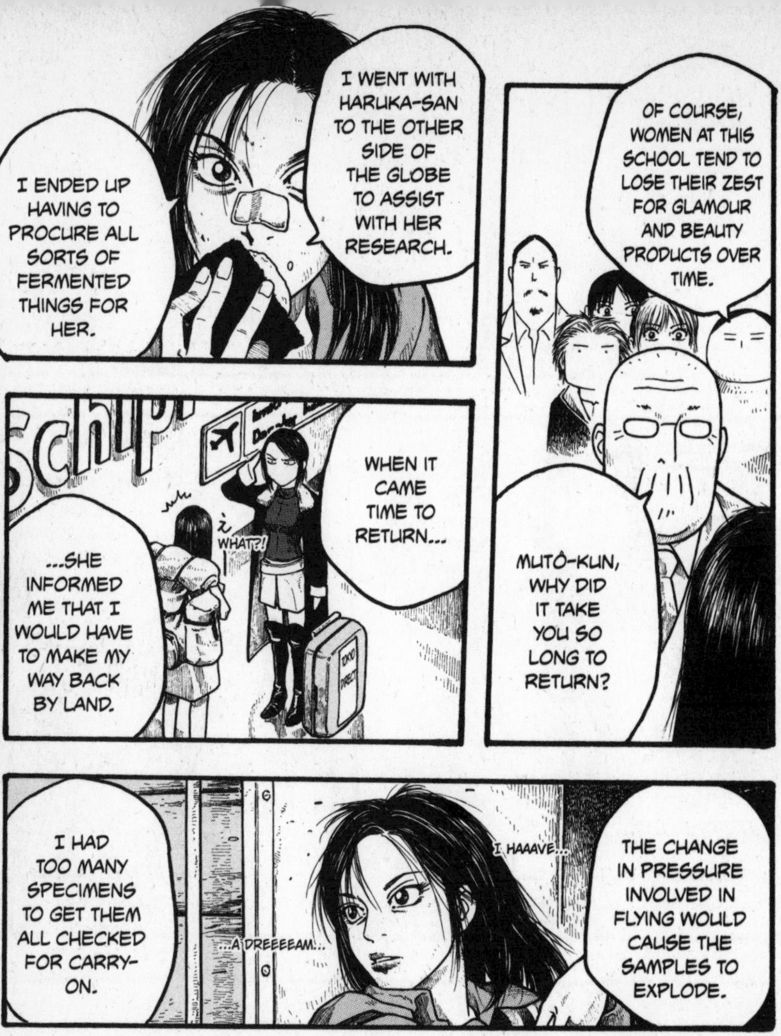
OF COURSE, WOMEN AT THIS SCHOOL TEND TO LOSE THEIR ZEST FOR GLAMOUR AND BEAUTY PRODUCTS OVER TIME.
MUTÔ-KUN, WHY DID IT TAKE YOU SO LONG TO RETURN?
I WENT WITH HARUKA-SAN TO THE OTHER SIDE OF THE GLOBE TO ASSIST WITH HER RESEARCH.
I ENDED UP HAVING TO PROCURE ALL SORTS OF FERMENTED THINGS FOR HER.
WHEN IT CAME TIME TO RETURN...
WHAT?!
...SHE INFORMED ME THAT I WOULD HAVE TO MAKE MY WAY BACK BY LAND.
THE CHANGE IN PRESSURE INVOLVED IN FLYING WOULD CAUSE THE SAMPLES TO EXPLODE.
I HAAAVE...
I HAD TOO MANY SPECIMENS TO GET THEM ALL CHECKED FOR CARRY-ON.
...A DREEEEAM...

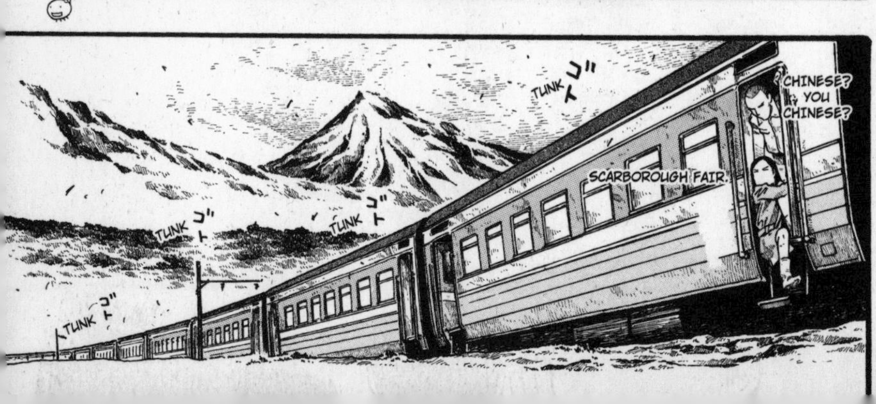
CHINESE? YOU CHINESE?
TUNK
SCARBOROUGH FAIR.
TUNK
TUNK
TUNK

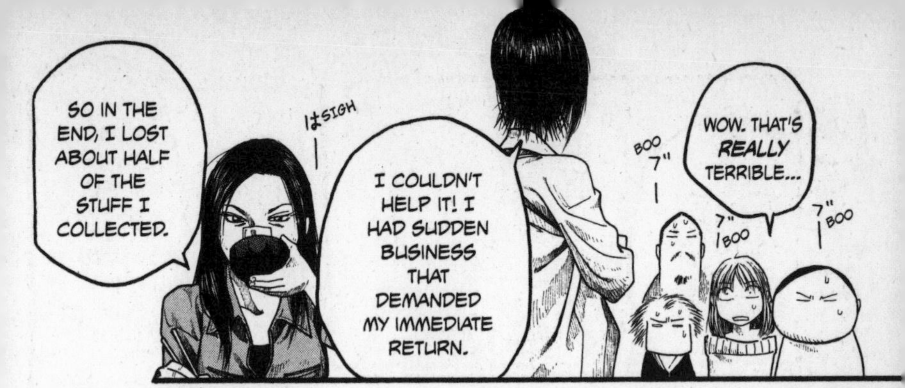
WOW. THAT'S REALLY TERRIBLE...
BOO
BOO
BOO
I COULDN'T HELP IT! I HAD SUDDEN BUSINESS THAT DEMANDED MY IMMEDIATE RETURN.
はSIGH
SO IN THE END, I LOST ABOUT HALF OF THE STUFF I COLLECTED.

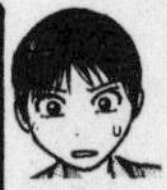

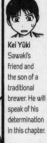

Kei Yūki
Sawaki's friend and the son of a traditional brewer. He will speak of his determination in this chapter.

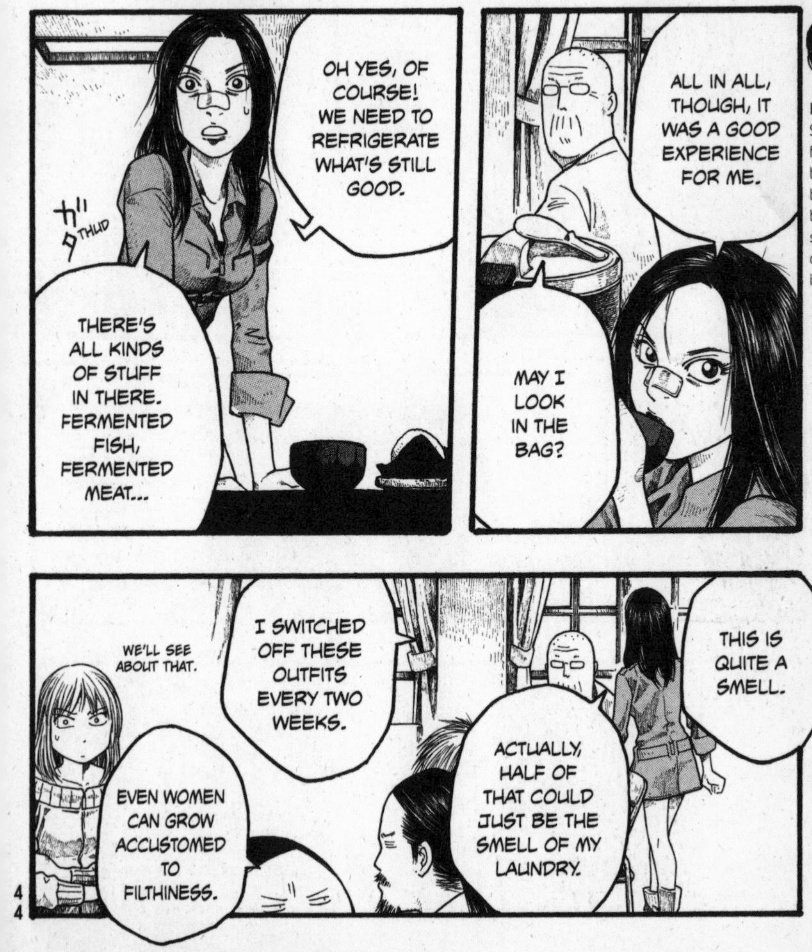
ALL IN ALL, THOUGH, IT WAS A GOOD EXPERIENCE FOR ME.
MAY I LOOK IN THE BAG?
OH YES, OF COURSE! WE NEED TO REFRIGERATE WHAT'S STILL GOOD.
ガタTHUD
THERE'S ALL KINDS OF STUFF IN THERE. FERMENTED FISH, FERMENTED MEAT...
THIS IS QUITE A SMELL.
ACTUALLY, HALF OF THAT COULD JUST BE THE SMELL OF MY LAUNDRY.
I SWITCHED OFF THESE OUTFITS EVERY TWO WEEKS.
WE'LL SEE ABOUT THAT.
EVEN WOMEN CAN GROW ACCUSTOMED TO FILTHINESS.

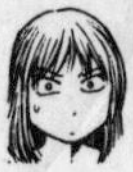

Hazuki Oikawa A freshman like Sawaki and Yûki. Does very little in this chapter.

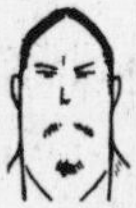

Kaoru Misato Sophomore. Loves *sake* enough to brew his own. He doesn't speak a word in this chapter.

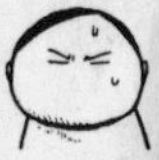

Takuma Kawahama Sophomore. I'm concerned that he's getting more and more overshadowed by everyone else.

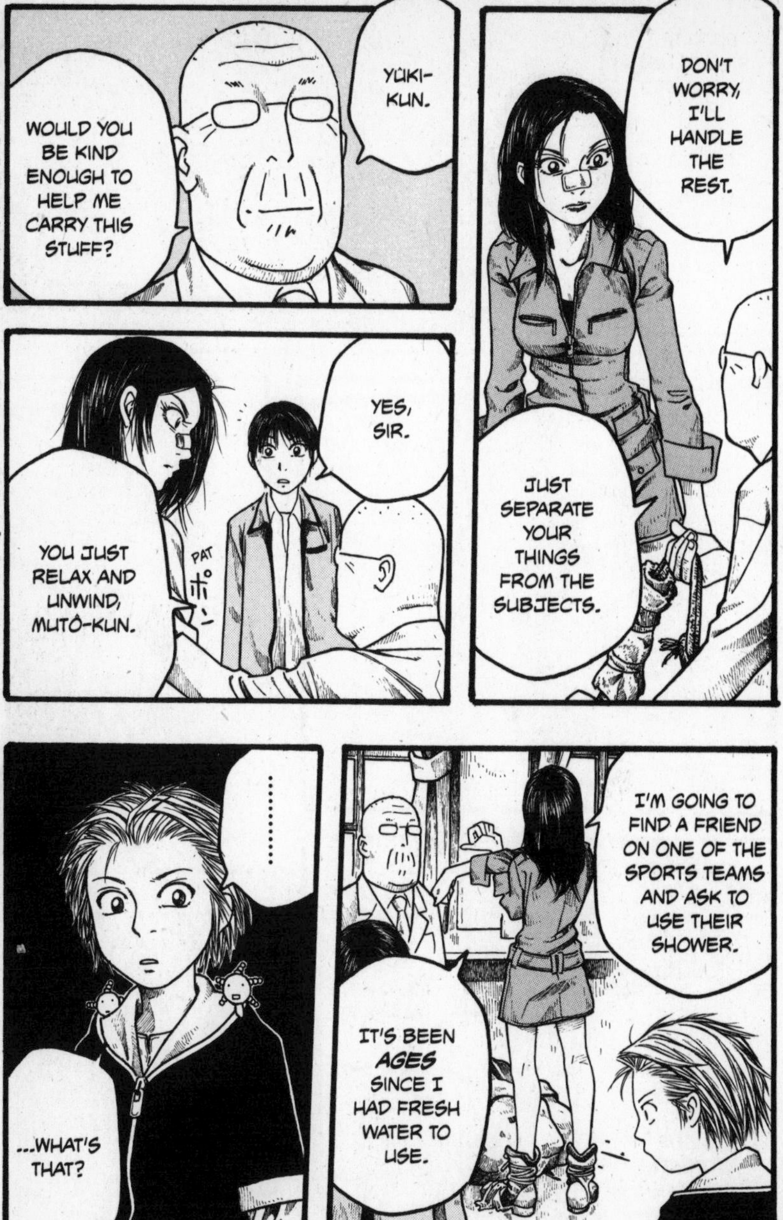

DON'T WORRY, I'LL HANDLE THE REST.
JUST SEPARATE YOUR THINGS FROM THE SUBJECTS.
YŪKI-KUN.
WOULD YOU BE KIND ENOUGH TO HELP ME CARRY THIS STUFF?
YES, SIR.
PAT ポン
YOU JUST RELAX AND UNWIND, MUTÔ-KUN.
I'M GOING TO FIND A FRIEND ON ONE OF THE SPORTS TEAMS AND ASK TO USE THEIR SHOWER.
IT'S BEEN *AGES* SINCE I HAD FRESH WATER TO USE.
....
...WHAT'S THAT?

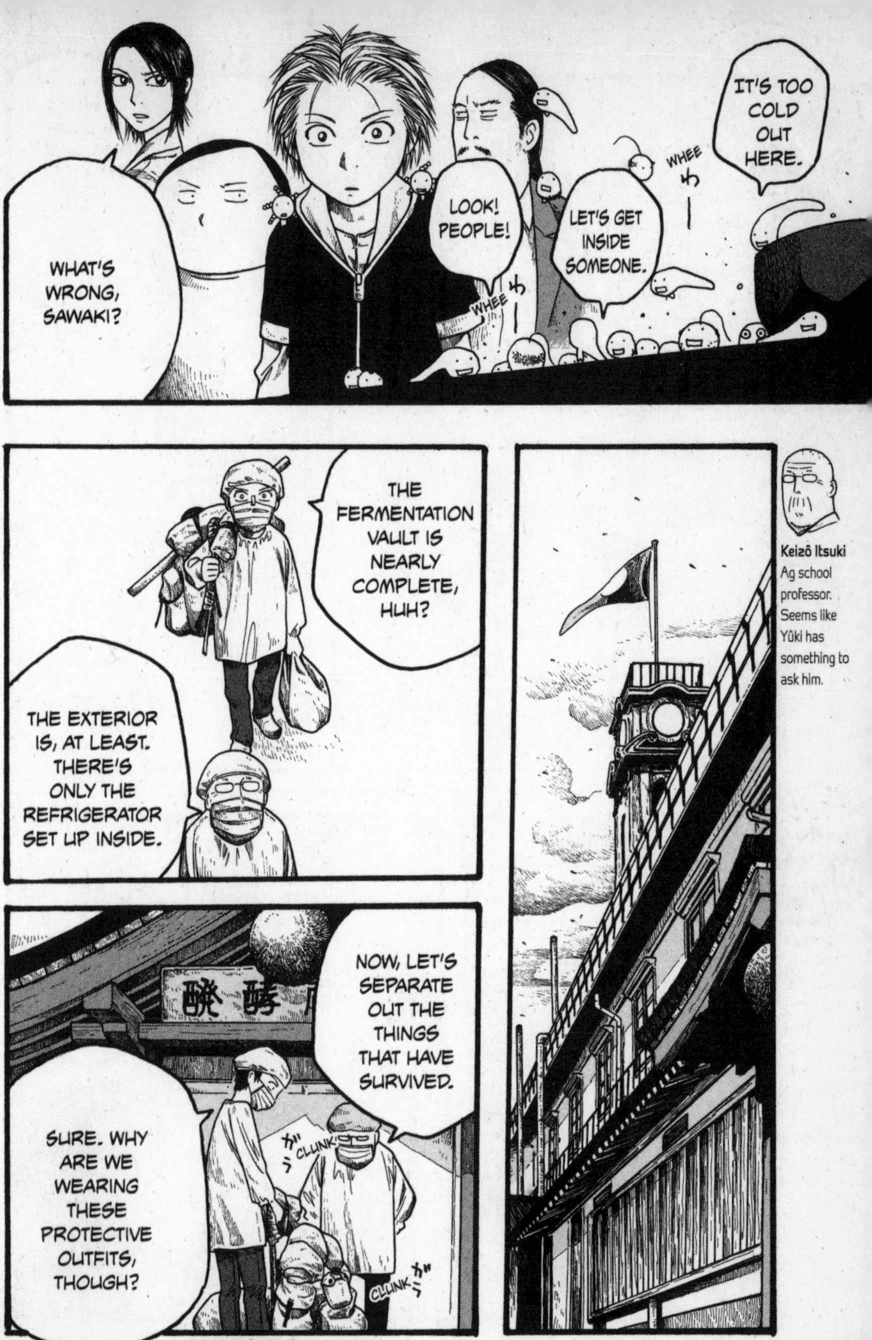
IT'S TOO COLD OUT HERE.
WHEE
LET'S GET INSIDE SOMEONE.
LOOK! PEOPLE!
WHEE
WHAT'S WRONG, SAWAKI?
Keizô Itsuki
Ag school professor. Seems like Yûki has something to ask him.
THE FERMENTATION VAULT IS NEARLY COMPLETE, HUH?
THE EXTERIOR IS, AT LEAST. THERE'S ONLY THE REFRIGERATOR SET UP INSIDE.
醗酵
NOW, LET'S SEPARATE OUT THE THINGS THAT HAVE SURVIVED.
CLUNK
SURE. WHY ARE WE WEARING THESE PROTECTIVE OUTFITS, THOUGH?
CLUNK

Fermentation Vault

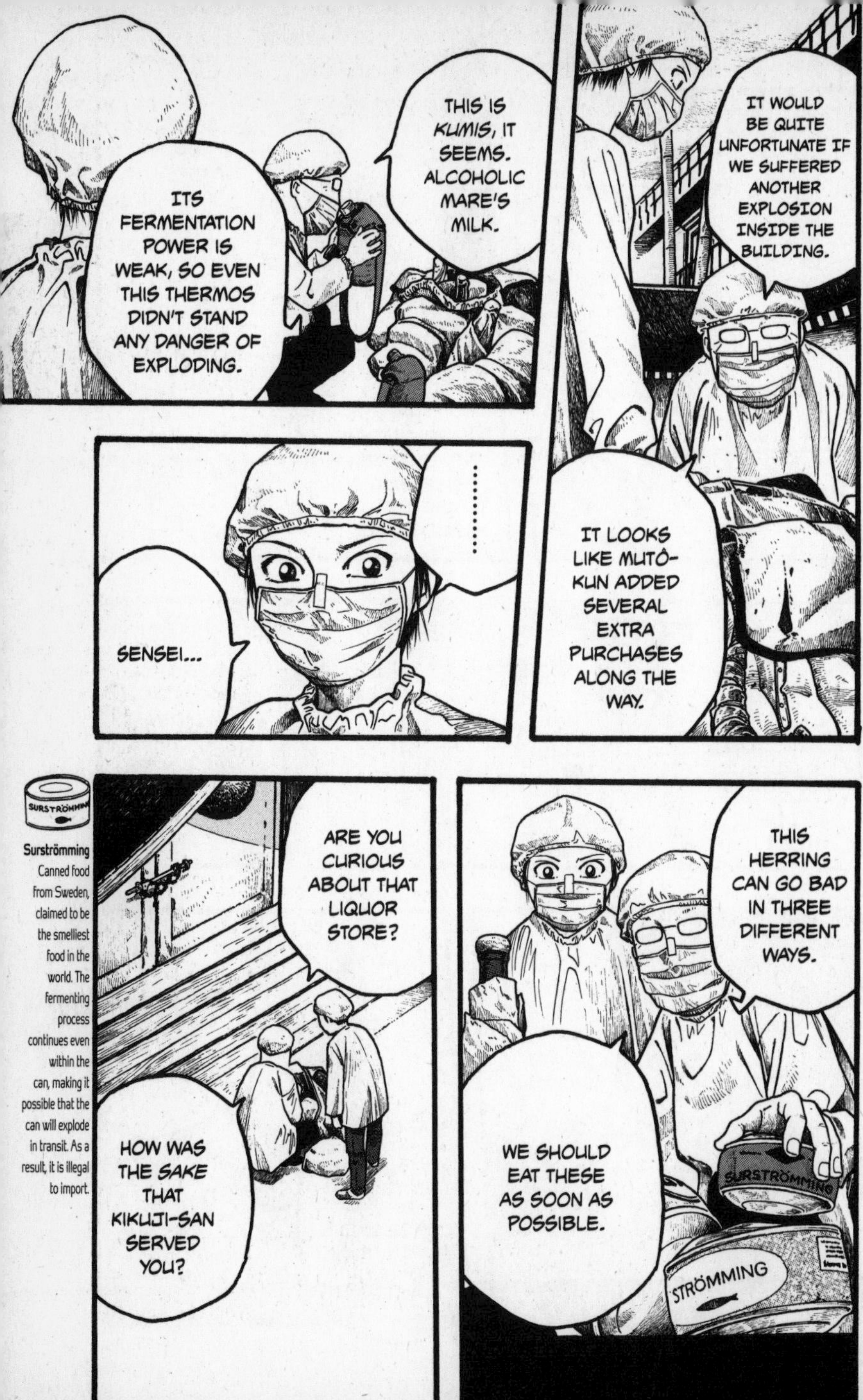
IT WOULD BE QUITE UNFORTUNATE IF WE SUFFERED ANOTHER EXPLOSION INSIDE THE BUILDING.
IT LOOKS LIKE MUTÔ-KUN ADDED SEVERAL EXTRA PURCHASES ALONG THE WAY.
THIS IS *KUMIS*, IT SEEMS. ALCOHOLIC MARE'S MILK.
ITS FERMENTATION POWER IS WEAK, SO EVEN THIS THERMOS DIDN'T STAND ANY DANGER OF EXPLODING.
......
SENSEI...
THIS HERRING CAN GO BAD IN THREE DIFFERENT WAYS.
WE SHOULD EAT THESE AS SOON AS POSSIBLE.
SURSTRÖMMING
STRÖMMING
ARE YOU CURIOUS ABOUT THAT LIQUOR STORE?
HOW WAS THE *SAKE* THAT KIKUJI-SAN SERVED YOU?

SURSTRÖMMING

Surströmming
Canned food from Sweden, claimed to be the smelliest food in the world. The fermenting process continues even within the can, making it possible that the can will explode in transit. As a result, it is illegal to import.

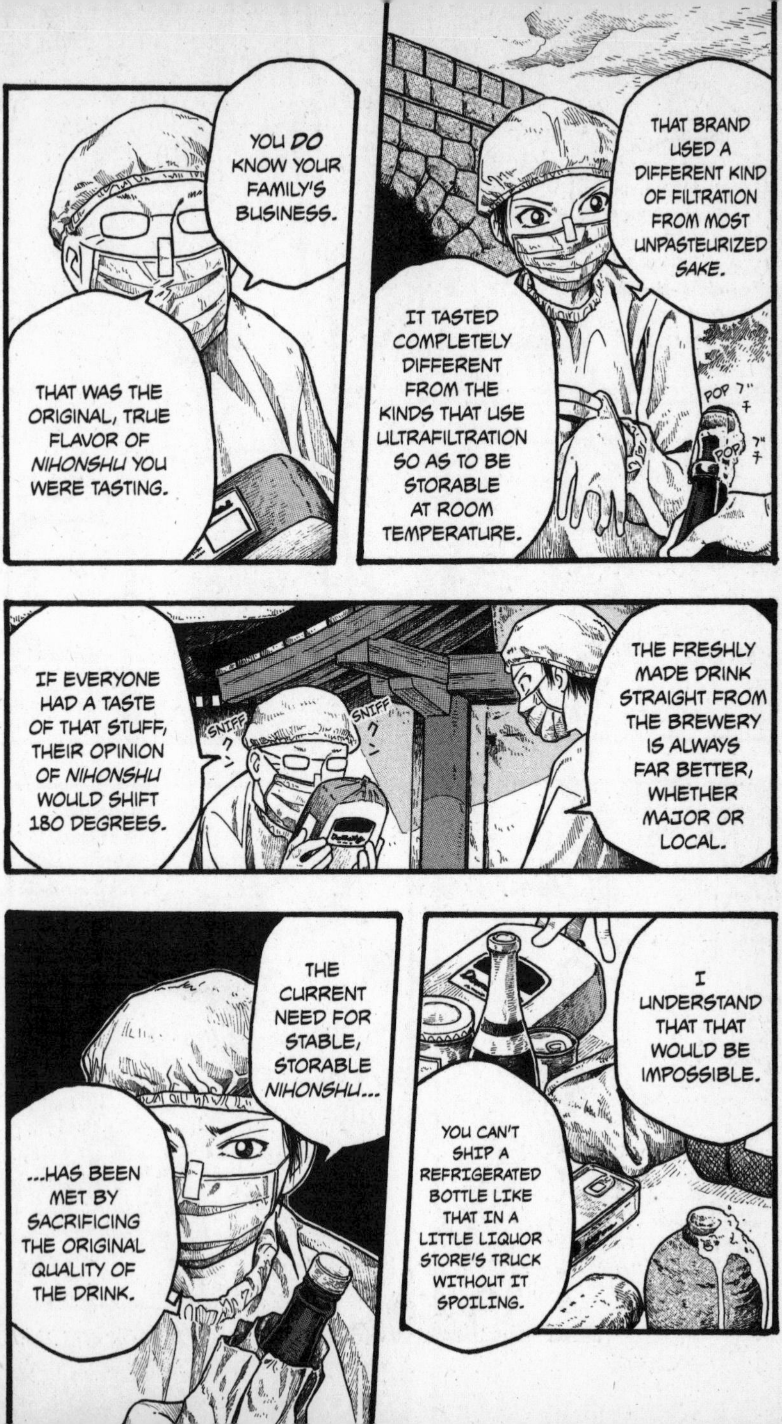
THAT BRAND USED A DIFFERENT KIND OF FILTRATION FROM MOST UNPASTEURIZED *SAKE*.
IT TASTED COMPLETELY DIFFERENT FROM THE KINDS THAT USE ULTRAFILTRATION SO AS TO BE STORABLE AT ROOM TEMPERATURE.
POP
POP
YOU *DO* KNOW YOUR FAMILY'S BUSINESS.
THAT WAS THE ORIGINAL, TRUE FLAVOR OF *NIHONSHU* YOU WERE TASTING.
THE FRESHLY MADE DRINK STRAIGHT FROM THE BREWERY IS ALWAYS FAR BETTER, WHETHER MAJOR OR LOCAL.
SNIFF
SNIFF
IF EVERYONE HAD A TASTE OF THAT STUFF, THEIR OPINION OF *NIHONSHU* WOULD SHIFT 180 DEGREES.
I UNDERSTAND THAT THAT WOULD BE IMPOSSIBLE.
YOU CAN'T SHIP A REFRIGERATED BOTTLE LIKE THAT IN A LITTLE LIQUOR STORE'S TRUCK WITHOUT IT SPOILING.
THE CURRENT NEED FOR STABLE, STORABLE *NIHONSHU*...
...HAS BEEN MET BY SACRIFICING THE ORIGINAL QUALITY OF THE DRINK.

Ultrafiltration
Currently, the chief method of filtration for producing unpasteurized *sake*. The equipment is extremely expensive.

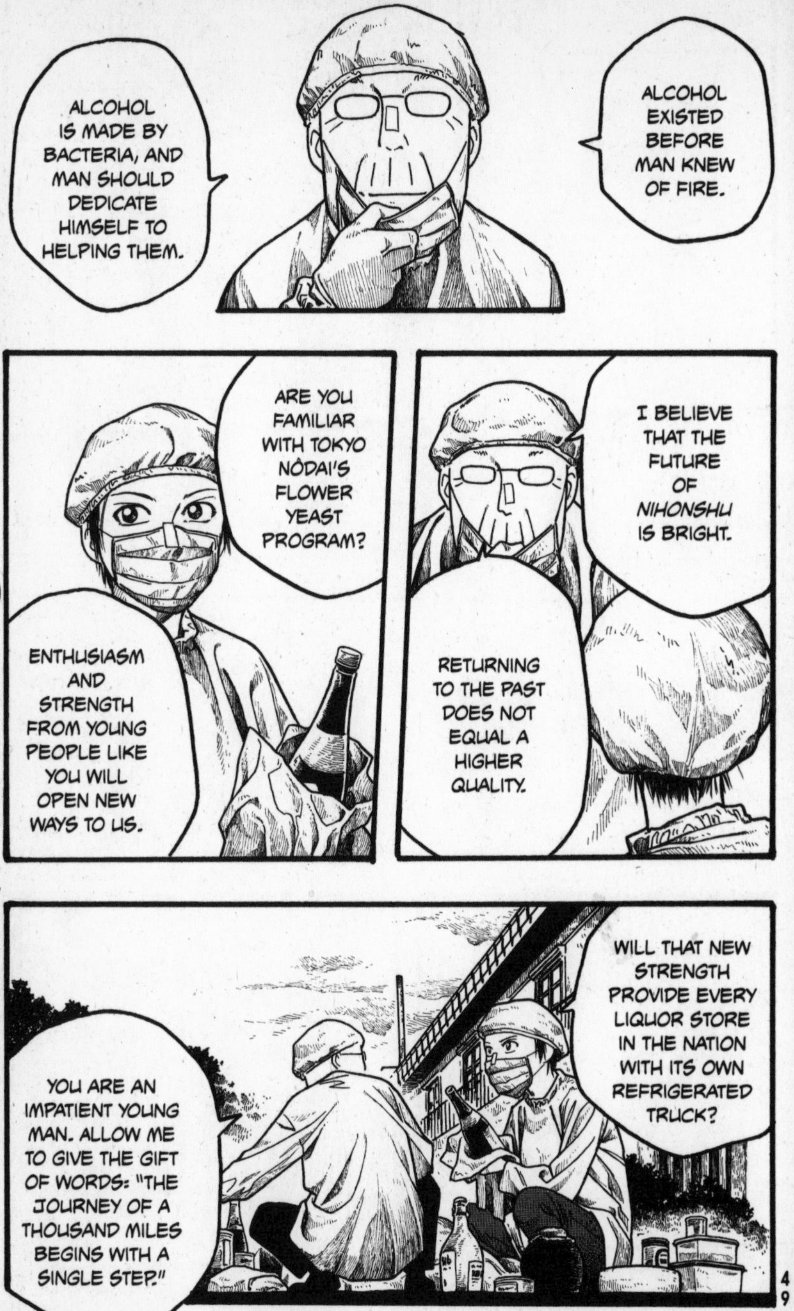
ALCOHOL EXISTED BEFORE MAN KNEW OF FIRE.
ALCOHOL IS MADE BY BACTERIA, AND MAN SHOULD DEDICATE HIMSELF TO HELPING THEM.
I BELIEVE THAT THE FUTURE OF *NIHONSHU* IS BRIGHT.
RETURNING TO THE PAST DOES NOT EQUAL A HIGHER QUALITY.
ARE YOU FAMILIAR WITH TOKYO NÔDAI'S FLOWER YEAST PROGRAM?
ENTHUSIASM AND STRENGTH FROM YOUNG PEOPLE LIKE YOU WILL OPEN NEW WAYS TO US.
WILL THAT NEW STRENGTH PROVIDE EVERY LIQUOR STORE IN THE NATION WITH ITS OWN REFRIGERATED TRUCK?
YOU ARE AN IMPATIENT YOUNG MAN. ALLOW ME TO GIVE THE GIFT OF WORDS: "THE JOURNEY OF A THOUSAND MILES BEGINS WITH A SINGLE STEP."

AB (Abelia) An alum of Tokyo Nôdai runs a brewery which is the center of a research project to expand the use of flower yeast in brewing.

ND (Nadeshiko) In the language of flowers, means "love me always." Just because it's brewed by flower yeast doesn't mean that a *sake* will taste like flowers.

NI (Nichinichi-sô) There's also begonia, cattleya and carnation.

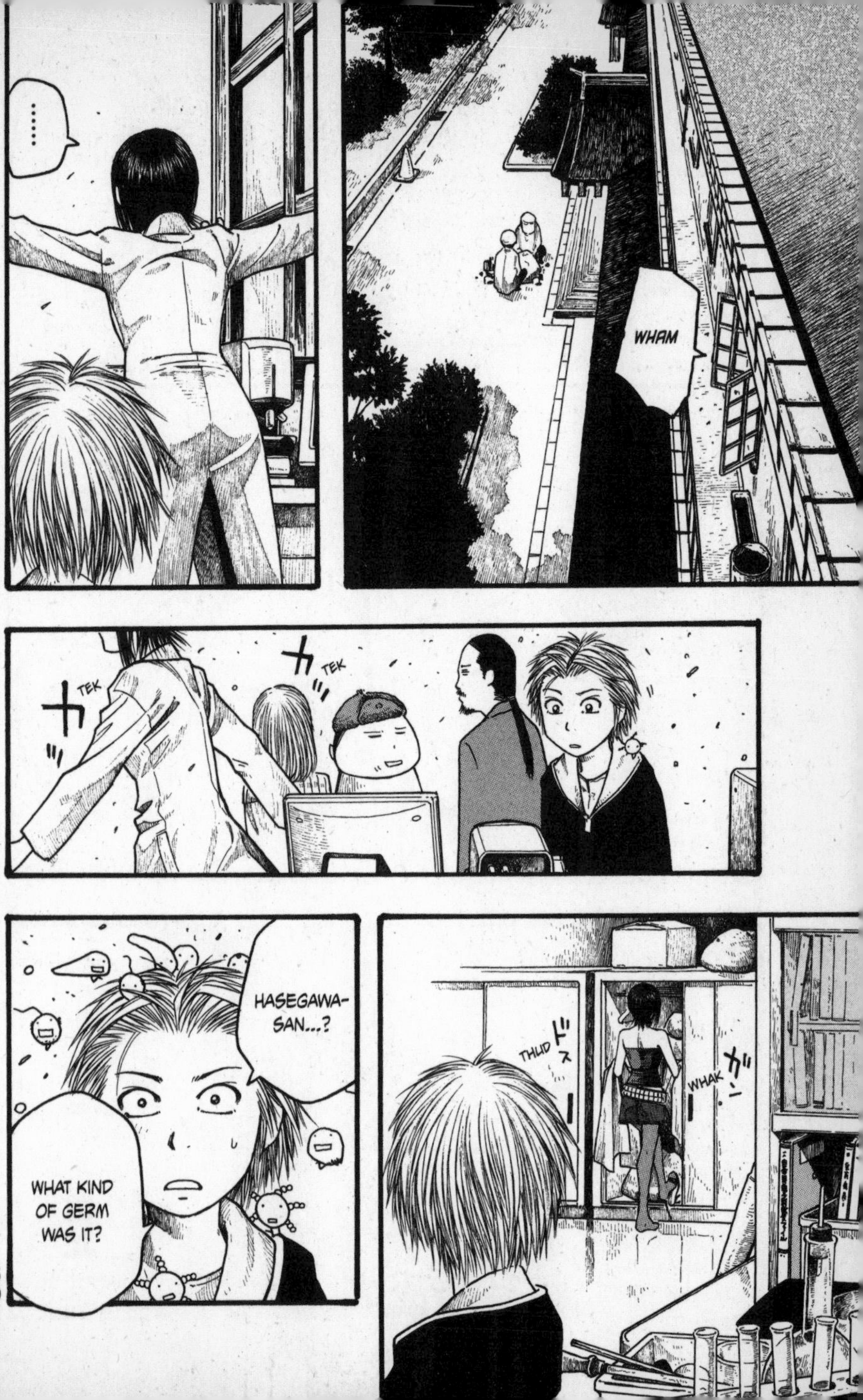
WHAM
……
TEK
TEK
THUD
WHAK
HASEGAWA-SAN...?
WHAT KIND OF GERM WAS IT?

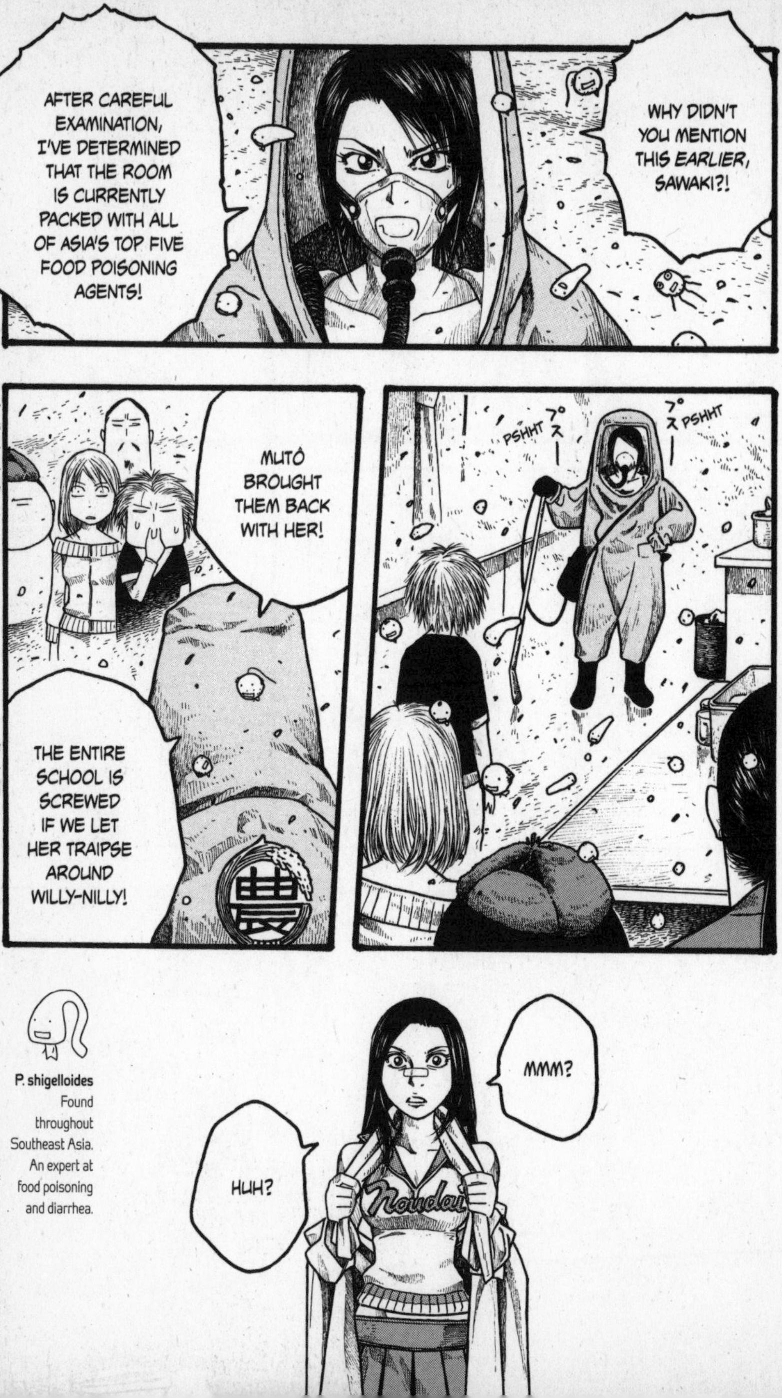
AFTER CAREFUL EXAMINATION, I'VE DETERMINED THAT THE ROOM IS CURRENTLY PACKED WITH ALL OF ASIA'S TOP FIVE FOOD POISONING AGENTS!
WHY DIDN'T YOU MENTION THIS EARLIER, SAWAKI?!
プスー PSHHT
プスー PSHHT
MUTÔ BROUGHT THEM BACK WITH HER!
THE ENTIRE SCHOOL IS SCREWED IF WE LET HER TRAIPSE AROUND WILLY-NILLY!
Noudai
MMM?
HUH?

V. parahaemolyticus
Has one flagellum and a covering of many small hairs.

V. cholerae
Cholera-causing bacteria.

P. shigelloides
Found throughout Southeast Asia. An expert at food poisoning and diarrhea.

S. dysenteriae
The cause of dysentery. Easy to confuse with **P. shigelloides**, so look through the microscope carefully.

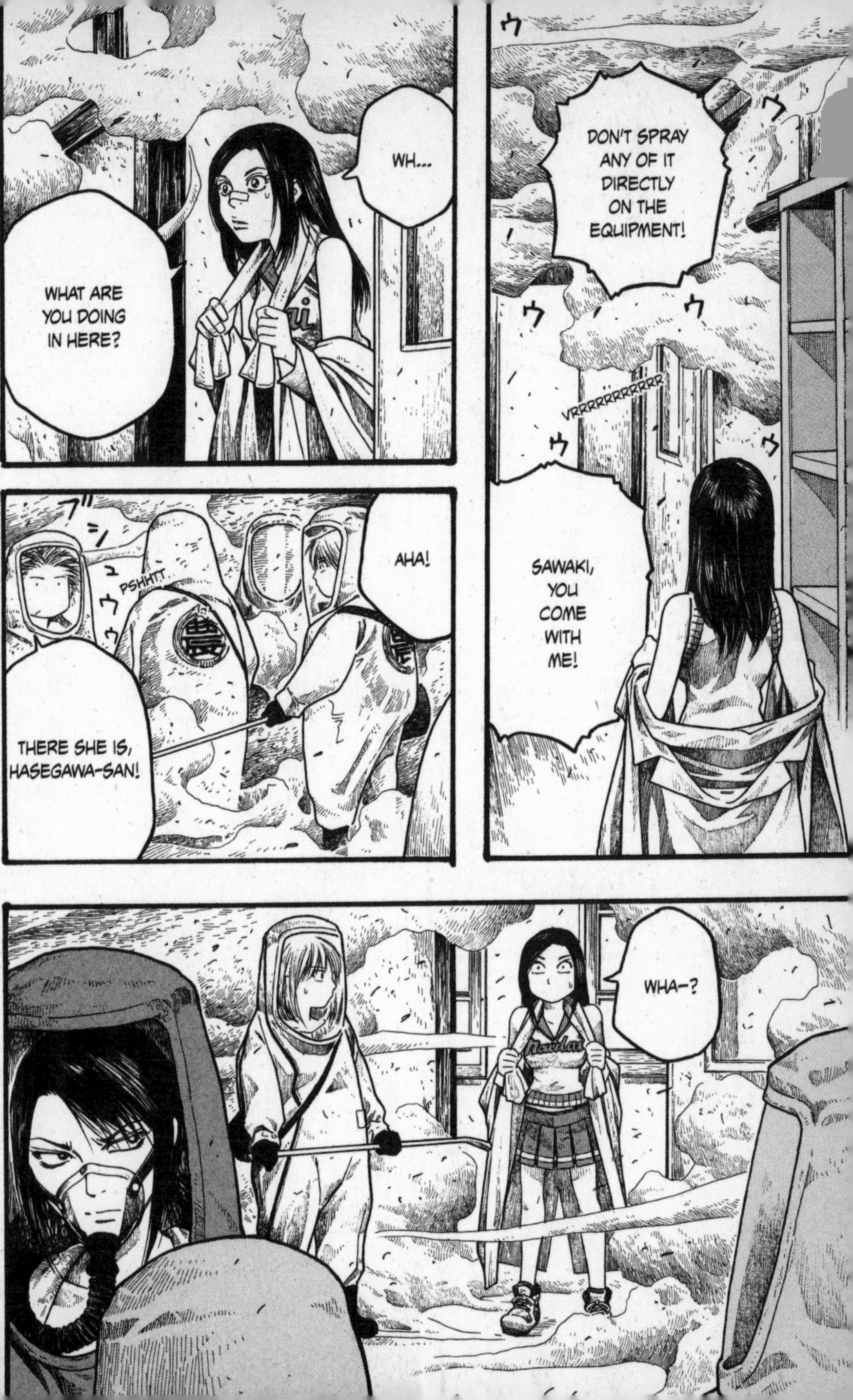
DON'T SPRAY ANY OF IT DIRECTLY ON THE EQUIPMENT!
VRRRRRRRRRRR
SAWAKI, YOU COME WITH ME!
WH...
WHAT ARE YOU DOING IN HERE?
AHA!
PSHHTT
THERE SHE IS, HASEGAWA-SAN!
WHA-?

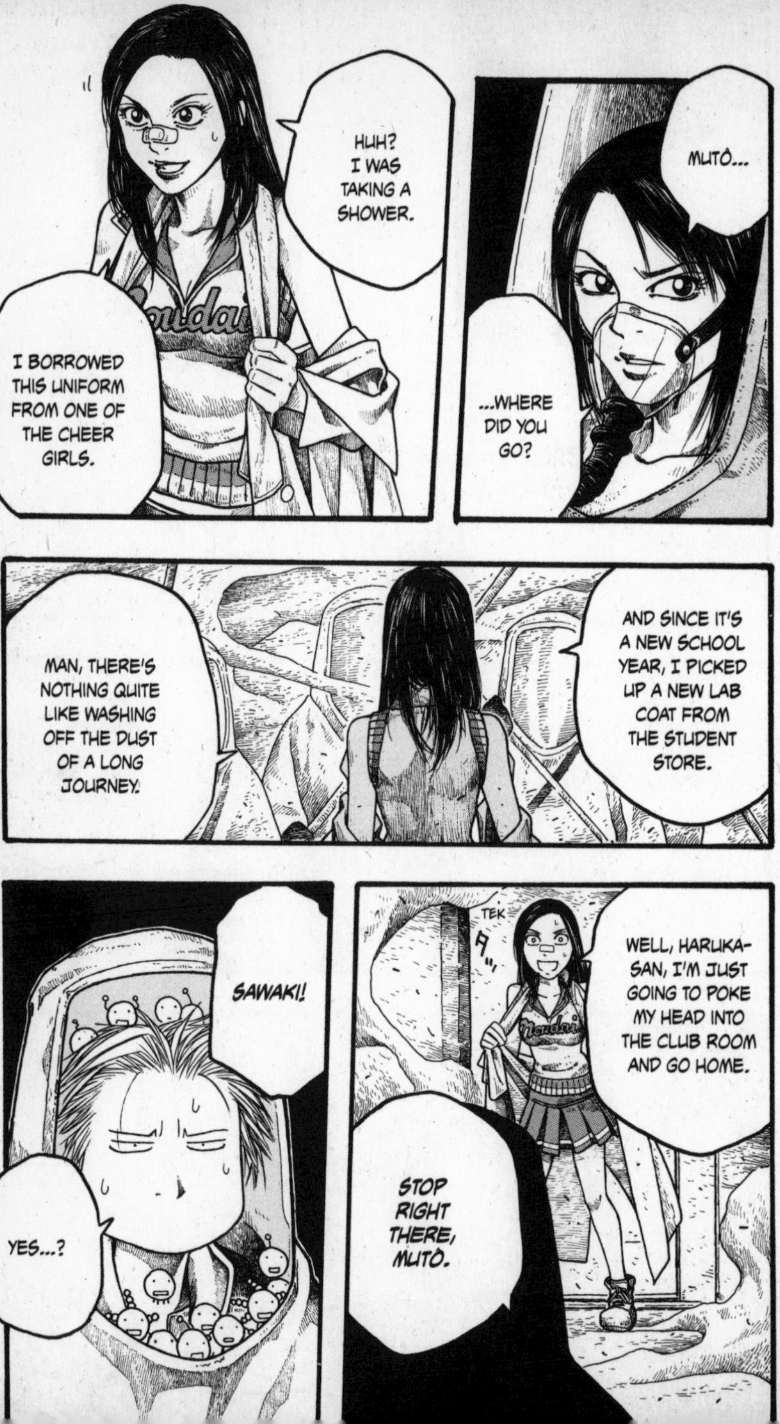
MUTÔ...
...WHERE DID YOU GO?
HUH? I WAS TAKING A SHOWER.
I BORROWED THIS UNIFORM FROM ONE OF THE CHEER GIRLS.
AND SINCE IT'S A NEW SCHOOL YEAR, I PICKED UP A NEW LAB COAT FROM THE STUDENT STORE.
MAN, THERE'S NOTHING QUITE LIKE WASHING OFF THE DUST OF A LONG JOURNEY.
TEK
WELL, HARUKA-SAN, I'M JUST GOING TO POKE MY HEAD INTO THE CLUB ROOM AND GO HOME.
STOP RIGHT THERE, MUTÔ.
SAWAKI!
YES...?

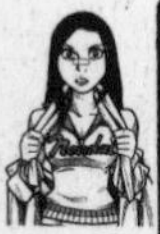

Aoi Mutô (2)
Ed.: "Why a cheerleader outfit?"
M.I.: "It looks hot."

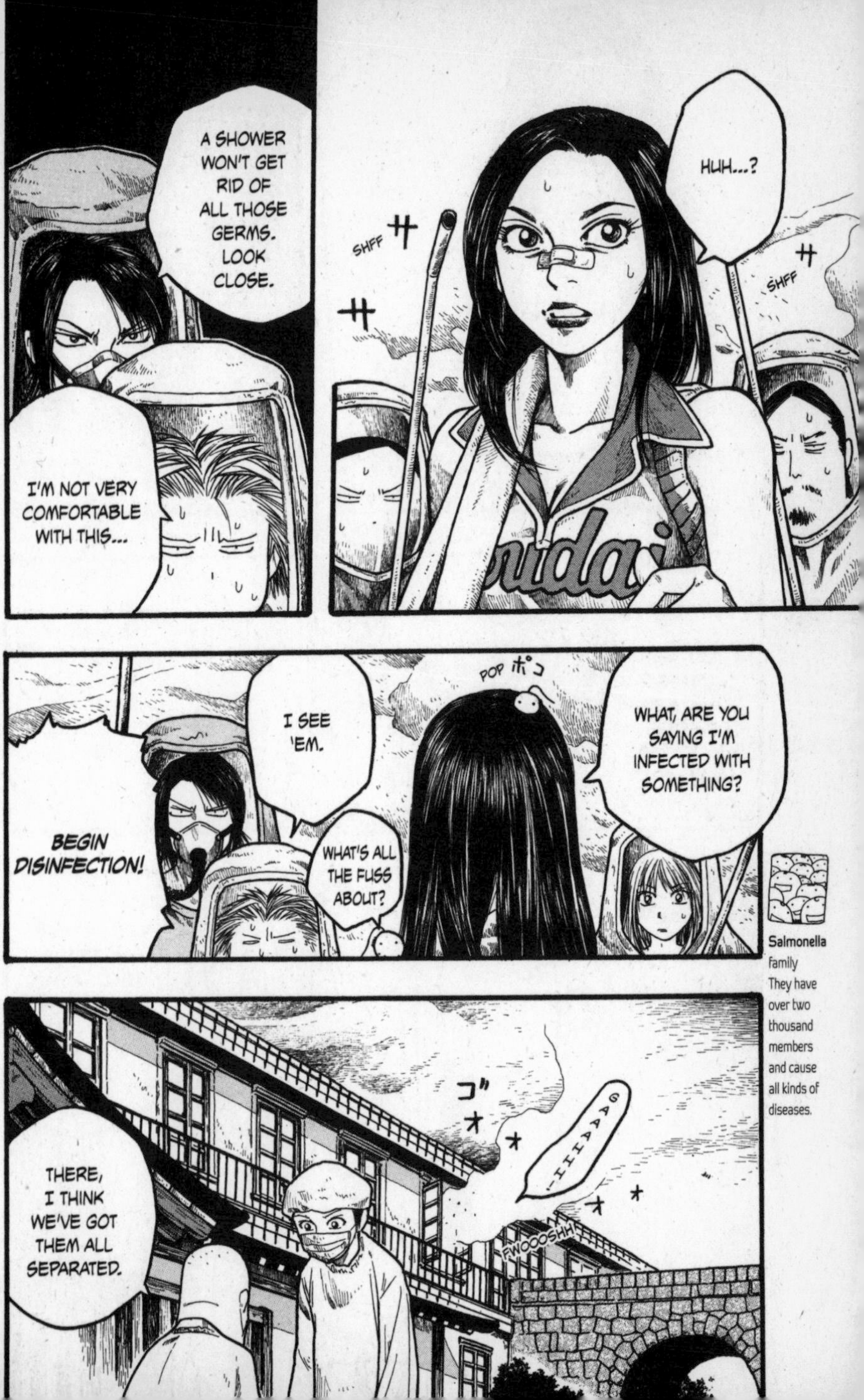
HUH...?
SHFF
SHFF
A SHOWER WON'T GET RID OF ALL THOSE GERMS. LOOK CLOSE.
I'M NOT VERY COMFORTABLE WITH THIS...
WHAT, ARE YOU SAYING I'M INFECTED WITH SOMETHING?
POP ポコ
I SEE 'EM.
WHAT'S ALL THE FUSS ABOUT?
BEGIN DISINFECTION!
ゴォ
GAAAIII!
FWOOOSHH
THERE, I THINK WE'VE GOT THEM ALL SEPARATED.

Salmonella family
They have over two thousand members and cause all kinds of diseases.

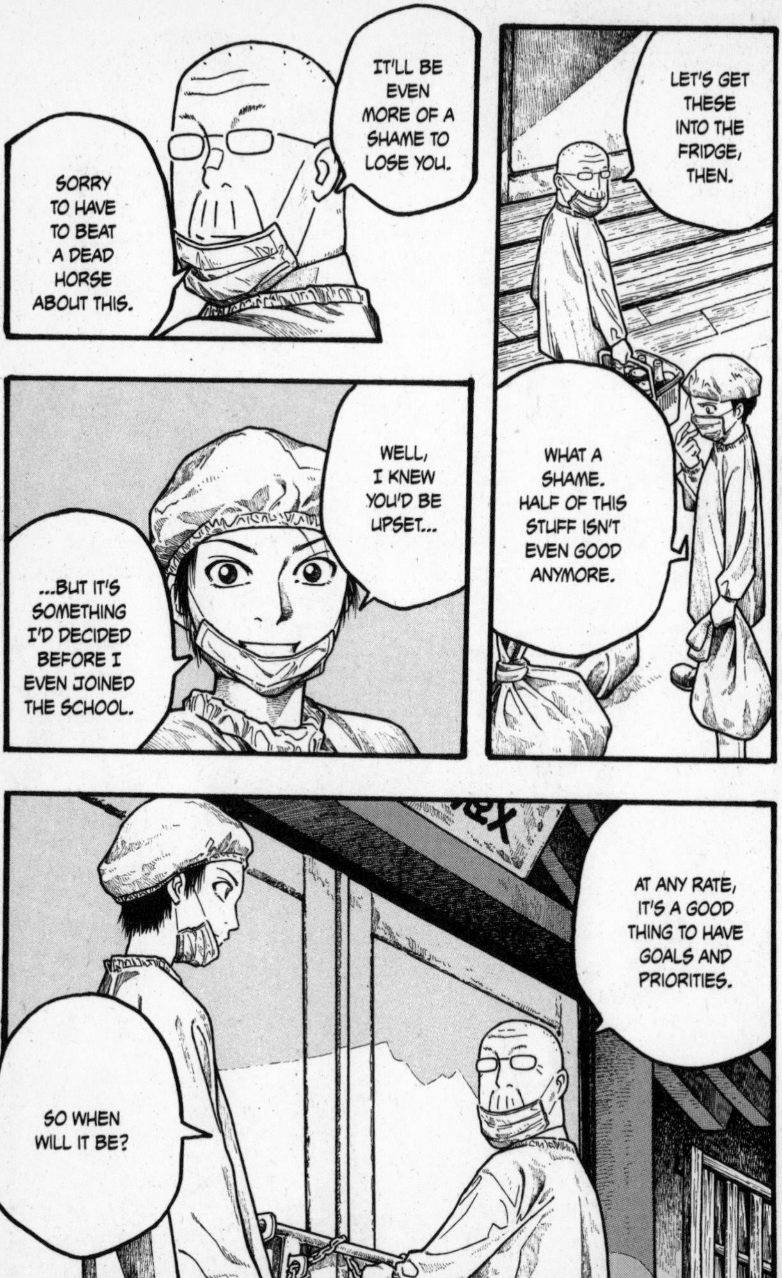
LET'S GET THESE INTO THE FRIDGE, THEN.
WHAT A SHAME. HALF OF THIS STUFF ISN'T EVEN GOOD ANYMORE.
IT'LL BE EVEN MORE OF A SHAME TO LOSE YOU.
SORRY TO HAVE TO BEAT A DEAD HORSE ABOUT THIS.
WELL, I KNEW YOU'D BE UPSET...
...BUT IT'S SOMETHING I'D DECIDED BEFORE I EVEN JOINED THE SCHOOL.
AT ANY RATE, IT'S A GOOD THING TO HAVE GOALS AND PRIORITIES.
SO WHEN WILL IT BE?

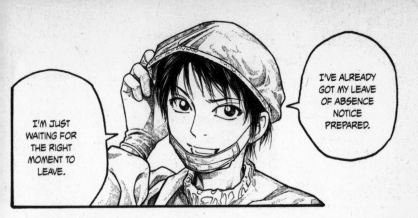

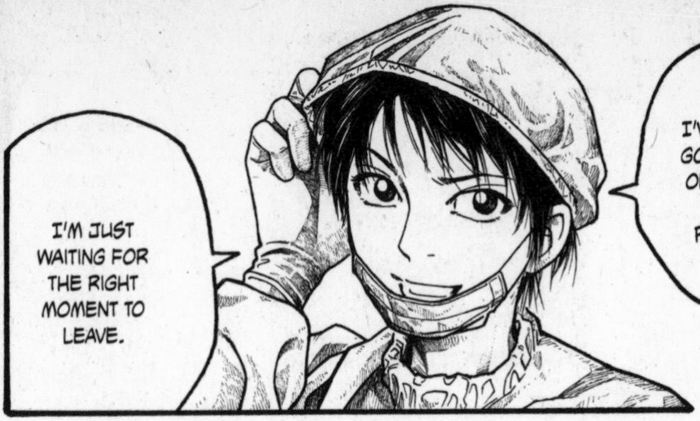
I'VE ALREADY GOT MY LEAVE OF ABSENCE NOTICE PREPARED.
I'M JUST WAITING FOR THE RIGHT MOMENT TO LEAVE.

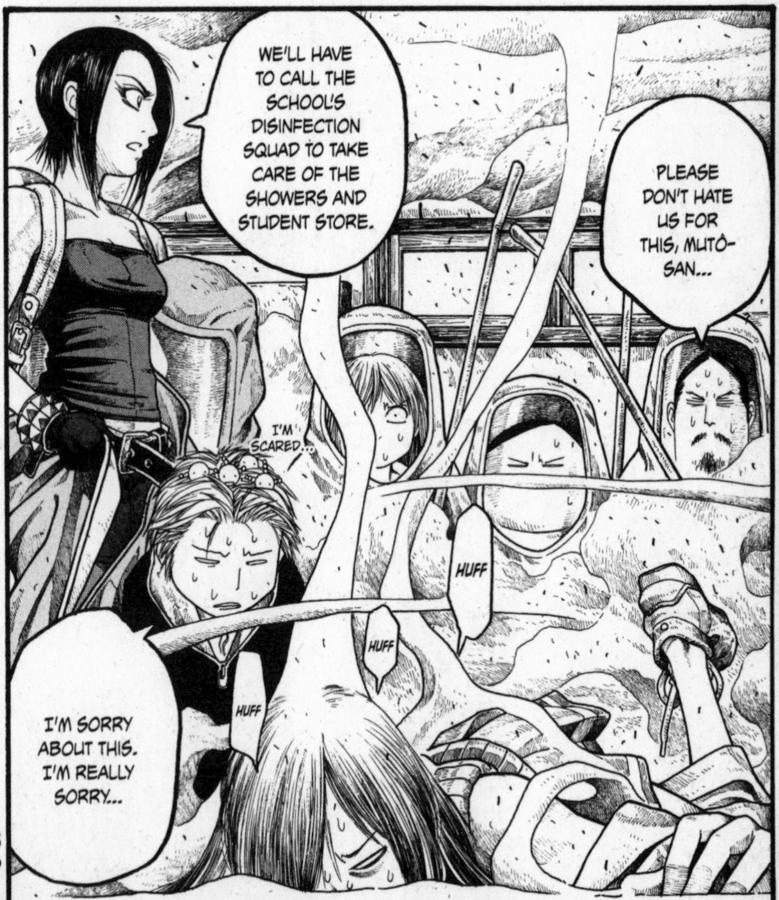
PLEASE DON'T HATE US FOR THIS, MUTÔ-SAN...
WE'LL HAVE TO CALL THE SCHOOL'S DISINFECTION SQUAD TO TAKE CARE OF THE SHOWERS AND STUDENT STORE.
I'M SCARED...
HUFF
HUFF
HUFF
I'M SORRY ABOUT THIS. I'M REALLY SORRY...

Ed.: I've heard that manga artist Yûki Yabuchi is a Tokyo Nôdai graduate.

14 END

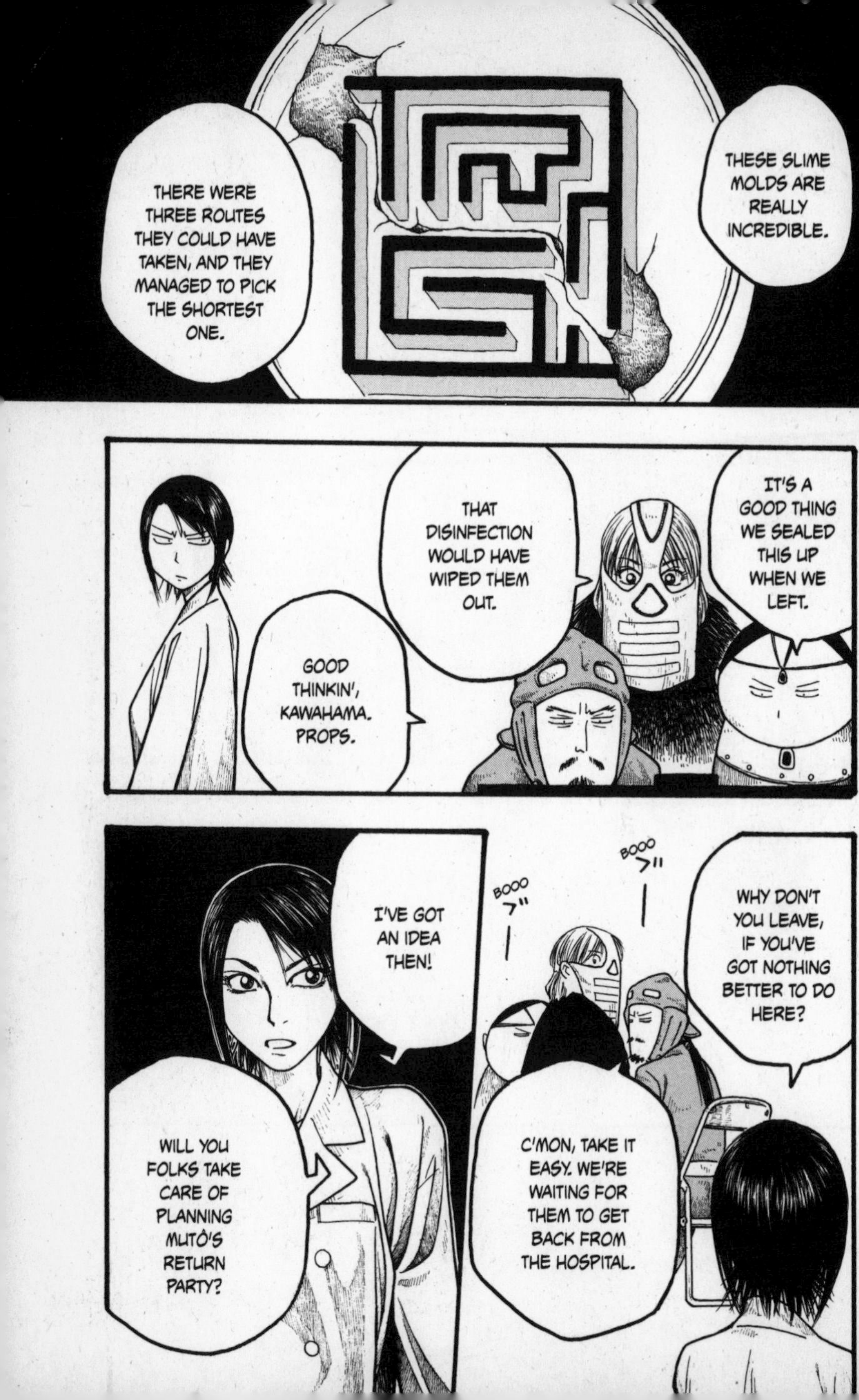
THESE SLIME MOLDS ARE REALLY INCREDIBLE.
THERE WERE THREE ROUTES THEY COULD HAVE TAKEN, AND THEY MANAGED TO PICK THE SHORTEST ONE.
IT'S A GOOD THING WE SEALED THIS UP WHEN WE LEFT.
THAT DISINFECTION WOULD HAVE WIPED THEM OUT.
GOOD THINKIN', KAWAHAMA. PROPS.
BOOO
BOOO
WHY DON'T YOU LEAVE, IF YOU'VE GOT NOTHING BETTER TO DO HERE?
C'MON, TAKE IT EASY. WE'RE WAITING FOR THEM TO GET BACK FROM THE HOSPITAL.
I'VE GOT AN IDEA THEN!
WILL YOU FOLKS TAKE CARE OF PLANNING MUTÔ'S RETURN PARTY?

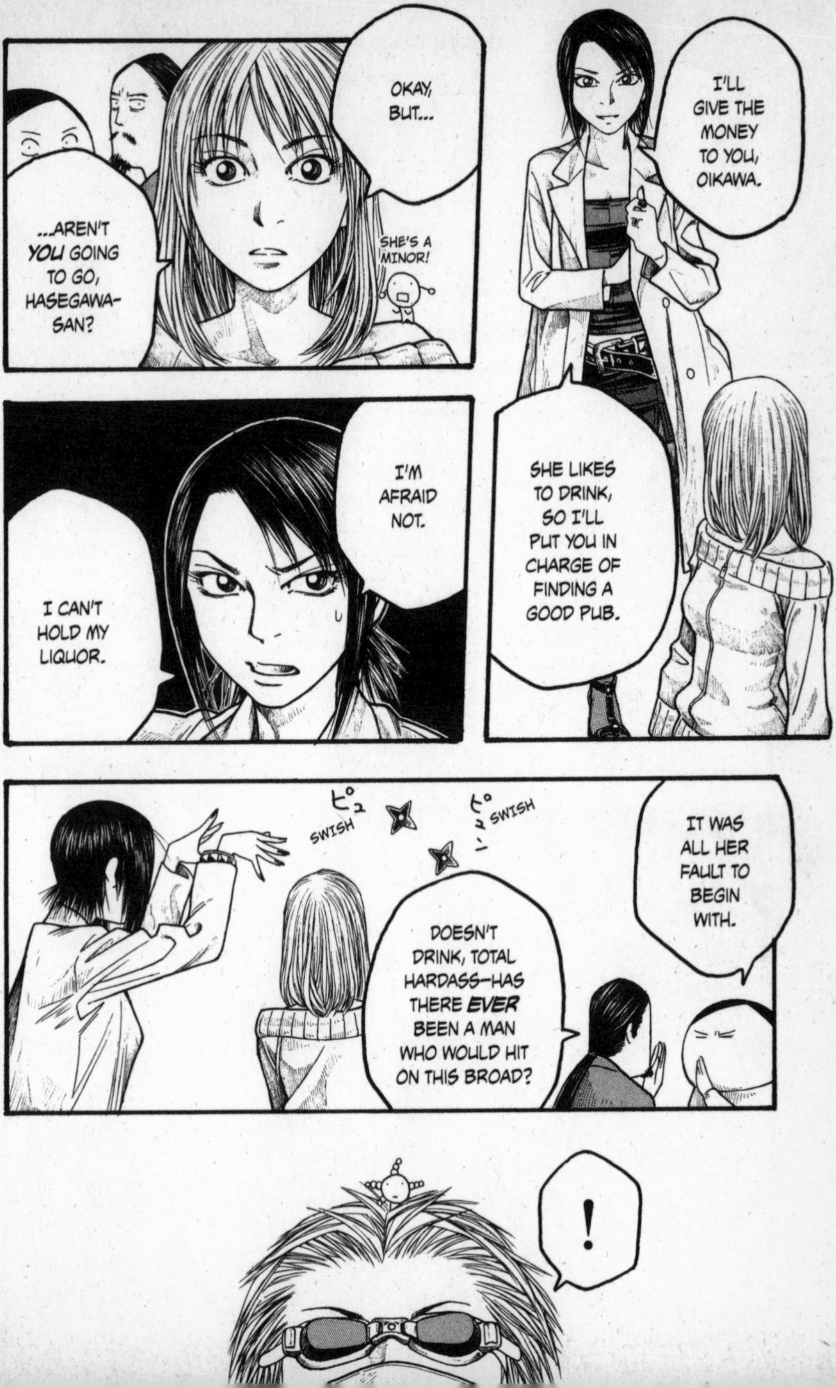
I'LL GIVE THE MONEY TO YOU, OIKAWA.
SHE LIKES TO DRINK, SO I'LL PUT YOU IN CHARGE OF FINDING A GOOD PUB.
OKAY, BUT...
SHE'S A MINOR!
...AREN'T *YOU* GOING TO GO, HASEGAWA-SAN?
I'M AFRAID NOT.
I CAN'T HOLD MY LIQUOR.
IT WAS ALL HER FAULT TO BEGIN WITH.
ピュ SWISH
ピュ SWISH
DOESN'T DRINK, TOTAL HARDASS—HAS THERE *EVER* BEEN A MAN WHO WOULD HIT ON THIS BROAD?
!

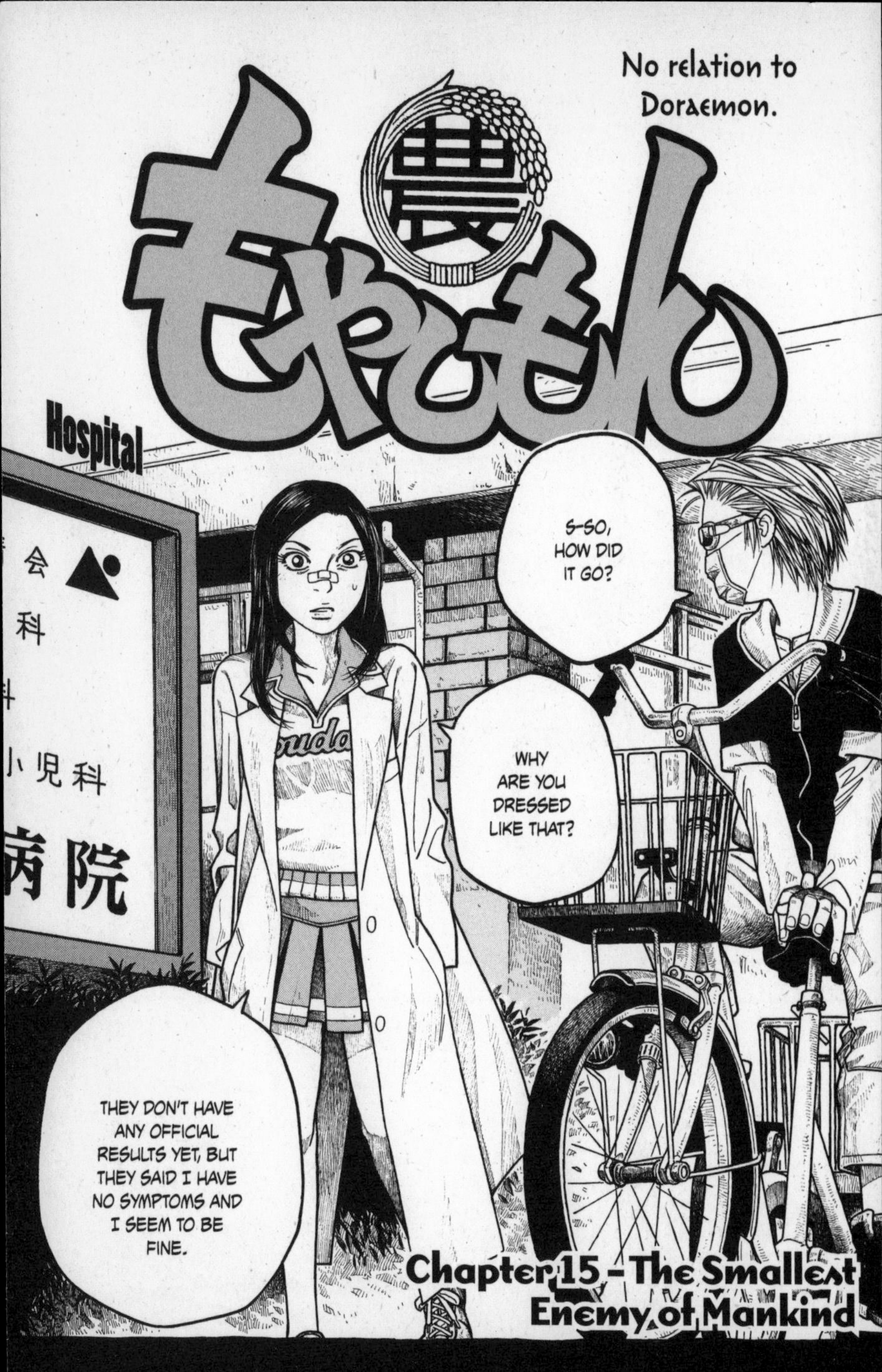
No relation to Doraemon.
もやしもん
Hospital
小児科
病院
S-SO, HOW DID IT GO?
WHY ARE YOU DRESSED LIKE THAT?
THEY DON'T HAVE ANY OFFICIAL RESULTS YET, BUT THEY SAID I HAVE NO SYMPTOMS AND I SEEM TO BE FINE.
Chapter 15 - The Smallest Enemy of Mankind

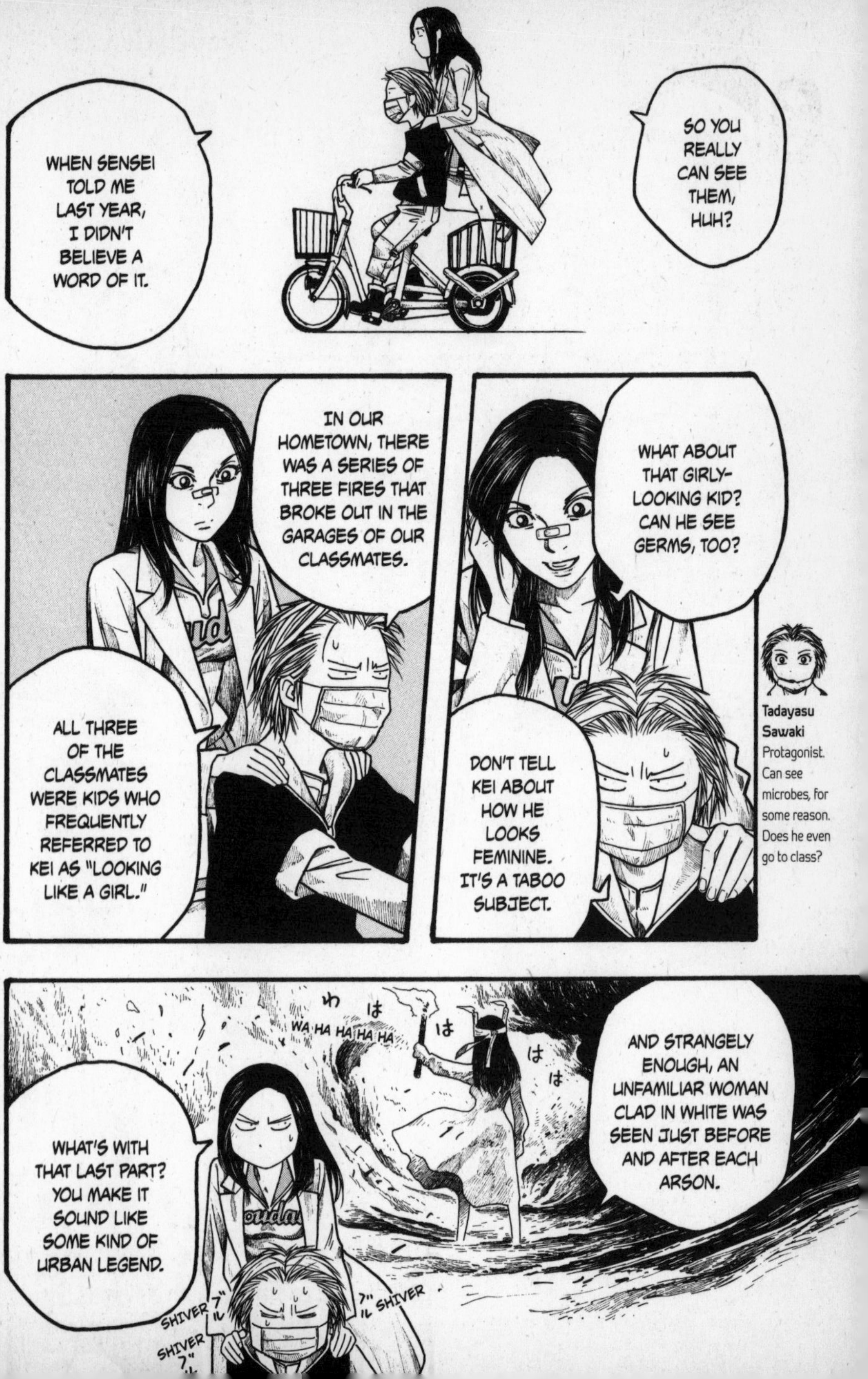
SO YOU REALLY CAN SEE THEM, HUH?
WHEN SENSEI TOLD ME LAST YEAR, I DIDN'T BELIEVE A WORD OF IT.
WHAT ABOUT THAT GIRLY-LOOKING KID? CAN HE SEE GERMS, TOO?
DON'T TELL KEI ABOUT HOW HE LOOKS FEMININE. IT'S A TABOO SUBJECT.
IN OUR HOMETOWN, THERE WAS A SERIES OF THREE FIRES THAT BROKE OUT IN THE GARAGES OF OUR CLASSMATES.
ALL THREE OF THE CLASSMATES WERE KIDS WHO FREQUENTLY REFERRED TO KEI AS "LOOKING LIKE A GIRL."
Tadayasu Sawaki
Protagonist. Can see microbes, for some reason. Does he even go to class?
AND STRANGELY ENOUGH, AN UNFAMILIAR WOMAN CLAD IN WHITE WAS SEEN JUST BEFORE AND AFTER EACH ARSON.
わははははは
WA HA HA HA HA
WHAT'S WITH THAT LAST PART? YOU MAKE IT SOUND LIKE SOME KIND OF URBAN LEGEND.
ブル SHIVER
ブル SHIVER
SHIVER ブル

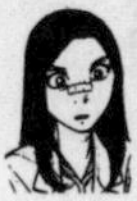

Aoi Mutô
The only seminar student of Itsuki's lab. She takes a lickin' and keeps on tickin'. Masochist?

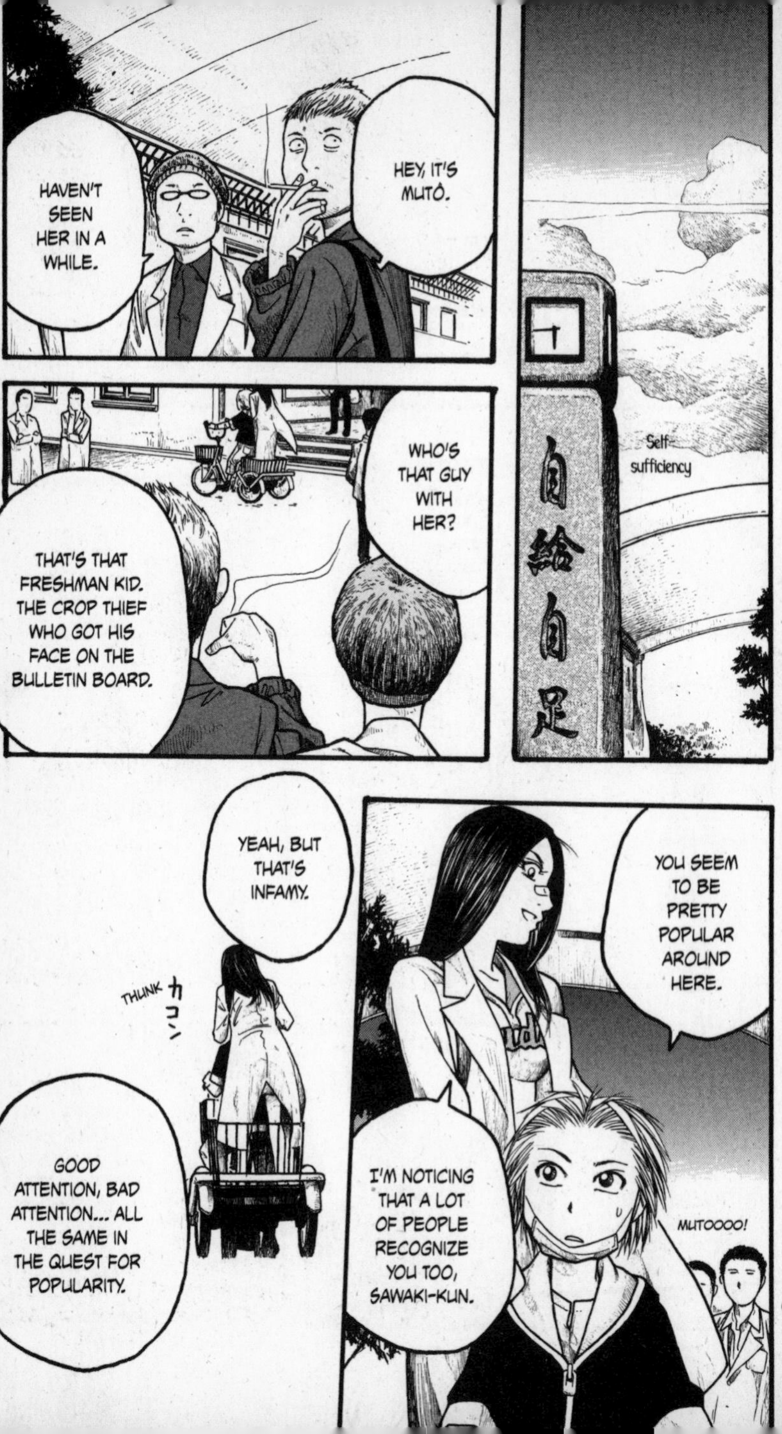

Self-sufficiency
自給自足
HEY, IT'S MUTÔ.
HAVEN'T SEEN HER IN A WHILE.
WHO'S THAT GUY WITH HER?
THAT'S THAT FRESHMAN KID. THE CROP THIEF WHO GOT HIS FACE ON THE BULLETIN BOARD.
YOU SEEM TO BE PRETTY POPULAR AROUND HERE.
I'M NOTICING THAT A LOT OF PEOPLE RECOGNIZE YOU TOO, SAWAKI-KUN.
MUTOOOO!
YEAH, BUT THAT'S INFAMY.
THUNK カコン
GOOD ATTENTION, BAD ATTENTION... ALL THE SAME IN THE QUEST FOR POPULARITY.

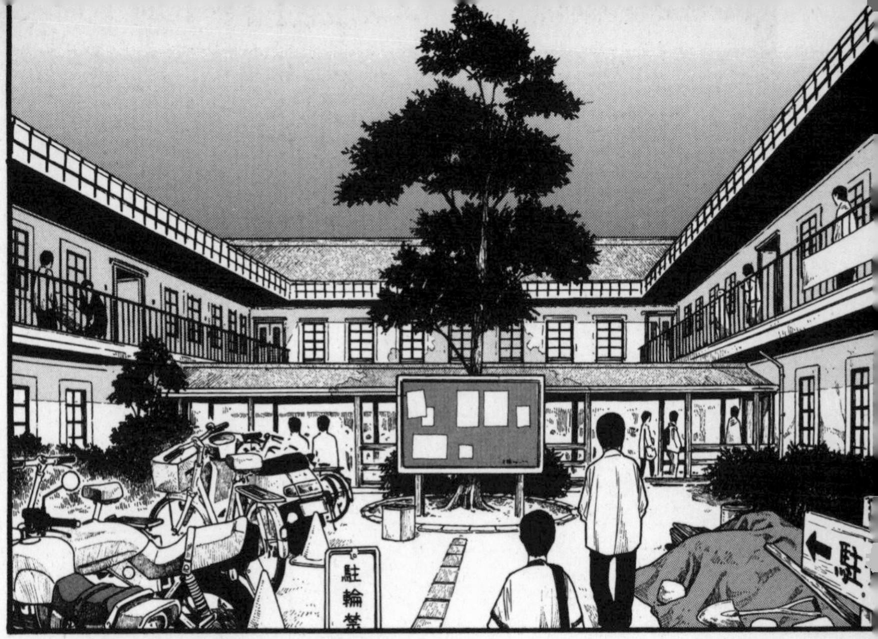
駐輪禁
駐

No Bike Parking

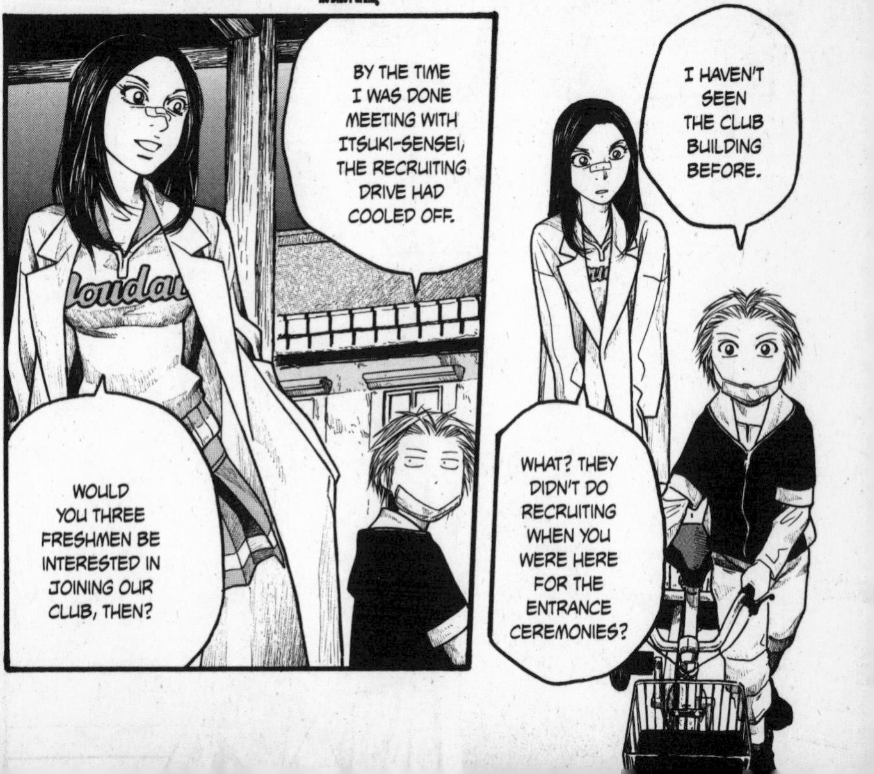
I HAVEN'T SEEN THE CLUB BUILDING BEFORE.
WHAT? THEY DIDN'T DO RECRUITING WHEN YOU WERE HERE FOR THE ENTRANCE CEREMONIES?
BY THE TIME I WAS DONE MEETING WITH ITSUKI-SENSEI, THE RECRUITING DRIVE HAD COOLED OFF.
WOULD YOU THREE FRESHMEN BE INTERESTED IN JOINING OUR CLUB, THEN?

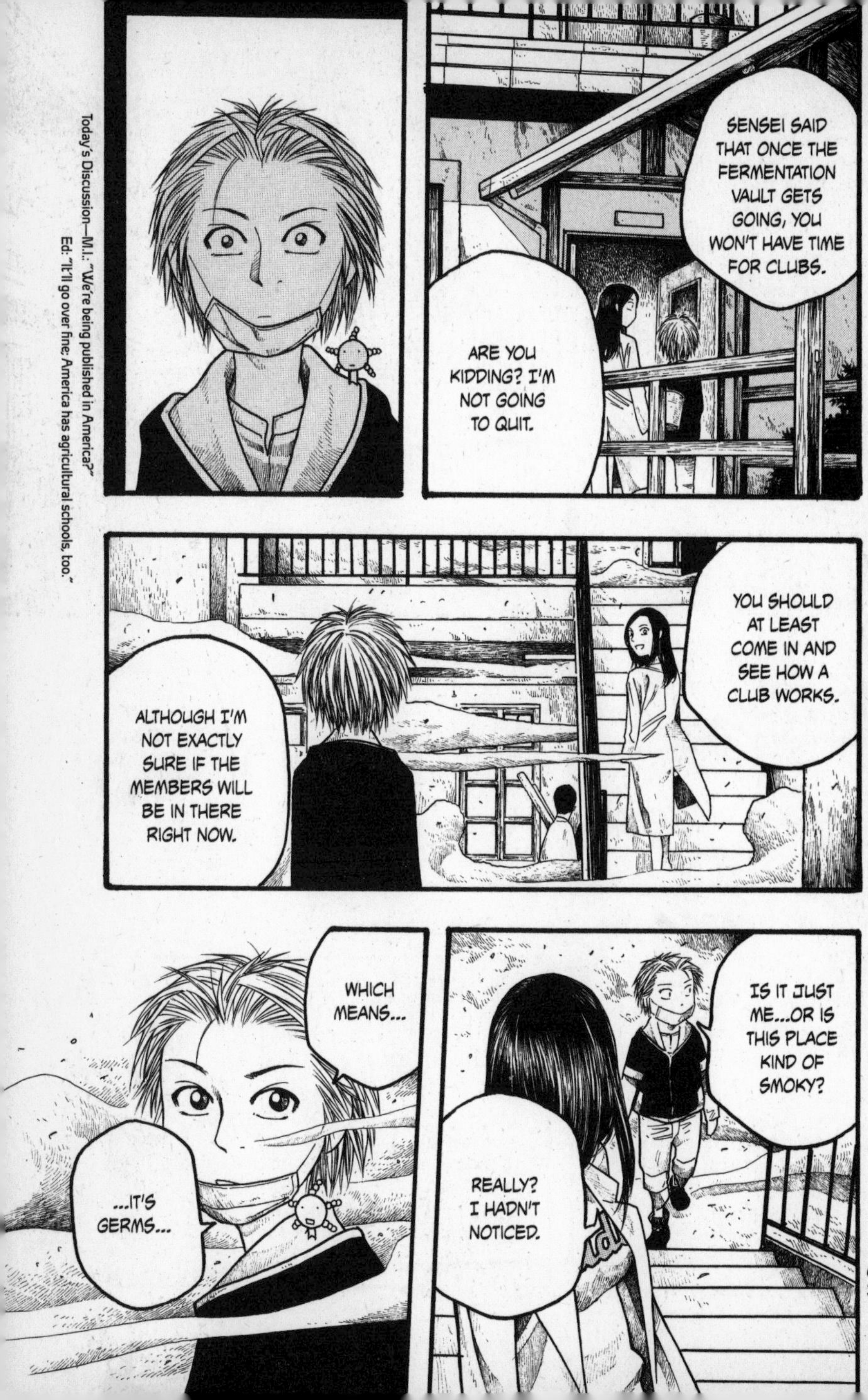
SENSEI SAID THAT ONCE THE FERMENTATION VAULT GETS GOING, YOU WON'T HAVE TIME FOR CLUBS.
ARE YOU KIDDING? I'M NOT GOING TO QUIT.
YOU SHOULD AT LEAST COME IN AND SEE HOW A CLUB WORKS.
ALTHOUGH I'M NOT EXACTLY SURE IF THE MEMBERS WILL BE IN THERE RIGHT NOW.
IS IT JUST ME...OR IS THIS PLACE KIND OF SMOKY?
REALLY? I HADN'T NOTICED.
WHICH MEANS...
...IT'S GERMS...

Today's Discussion—M.I.: "We're being published in America?"
Ed: "It'll go over fine: America has agricultural schools, too."

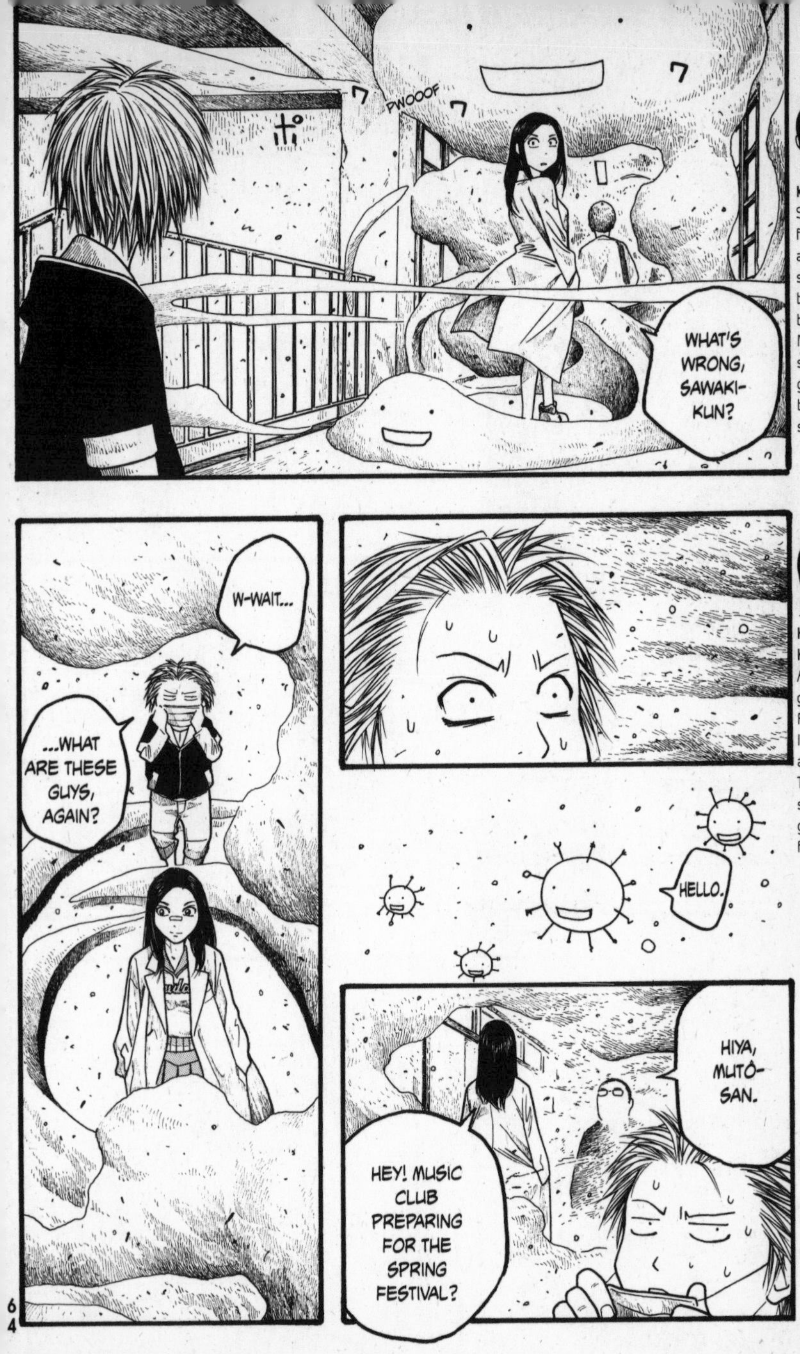
PWOOOF
WHAT'S WRONG, SAWAKI-KUN?
HELLO.
HIYA, MUTÔ-SAN.
HEY! MUSIC CLUB PREPARING FOR THE SPRING FESTIVAL?
W-WAIT...
...WHAT ARE THESE GUYS, AGAIN?

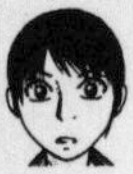

Kei Yûki
Sawaki's friend and the son of a traditional brewer. Now he says he's going to leave school.

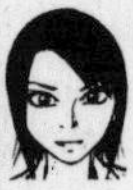

Haruka Hasegawa
Ag school grad student. Professor Itsuki's chief assistant. Totally sadistic. A good match for Mutô?

This Is the Story... ...of Tadayasu Sawaki, an agricultural university student who can see microbes with the naked eye, for some reason. This ability gets him involved in all sorts of trouble. Volume 1 was packed with germs from cover to cover, so you should really check that one out, too.

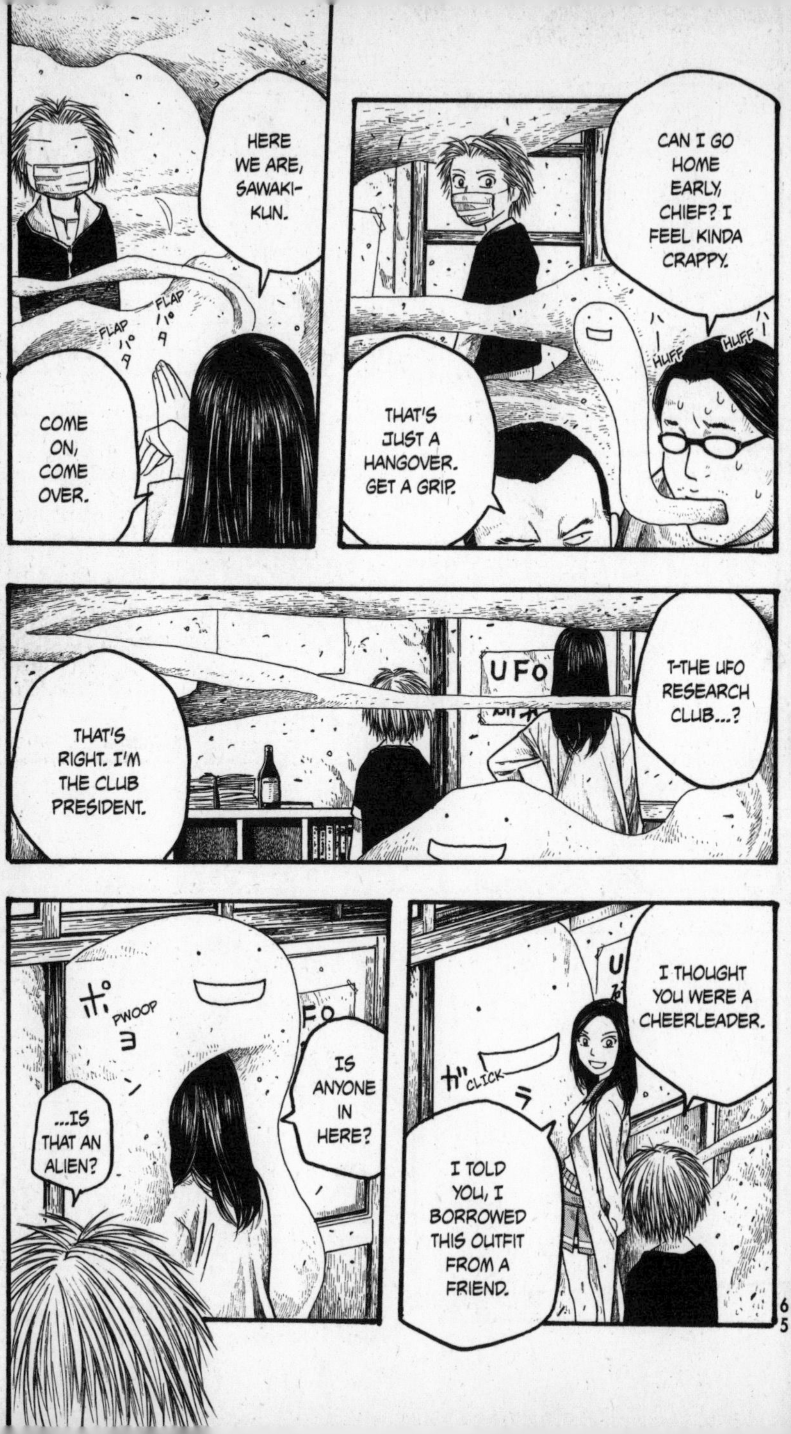
CAN I GO HOME EARLY, CHIEF? I FEEL KINDA CRAPPY.
HUFF
HUFF
THAT'S JUST A HANGOVER. GET A GRIP.
HERE WE ARE, SAWAKI-KUN.
FLAP
FLAP
COME ON, COME OVER.
T-THE UFO RESEARCH CLUB...?
UFO
THAT'S RIGHT. I'M THE CLUB PRESIDENT.
I THOUGHT YOU WERE A CHEERLEADER.
CLICK
I TOLD YOU, I BORROWED THIS OUTFIT FROM A FRIEND.
PWOOP
IS ANYONE IN HERE?
...IS THAT AN ALIEN?

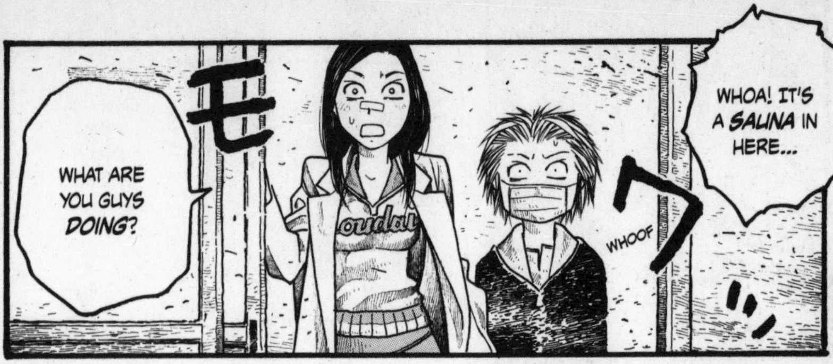
WHOA! IT'S A *SAUNA* IN HERE...
WHOOF
WHAT ARE YOU GUYS *DOING*?

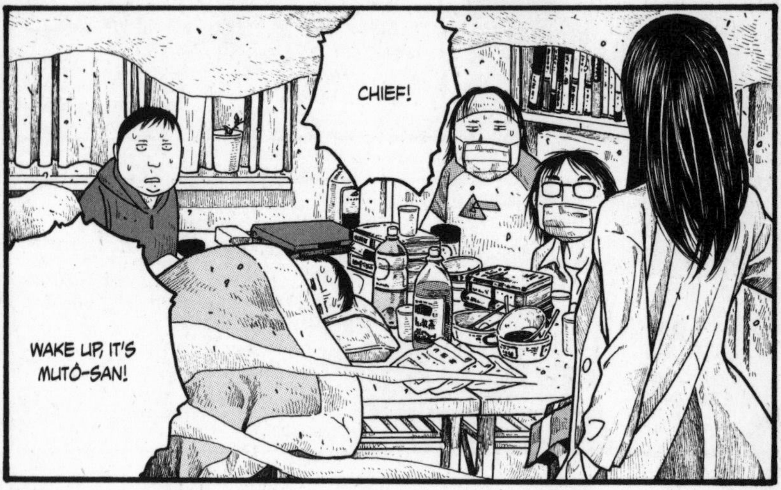
CHIEF!
WAKE UP, IT'S MUTÔ-SAN!

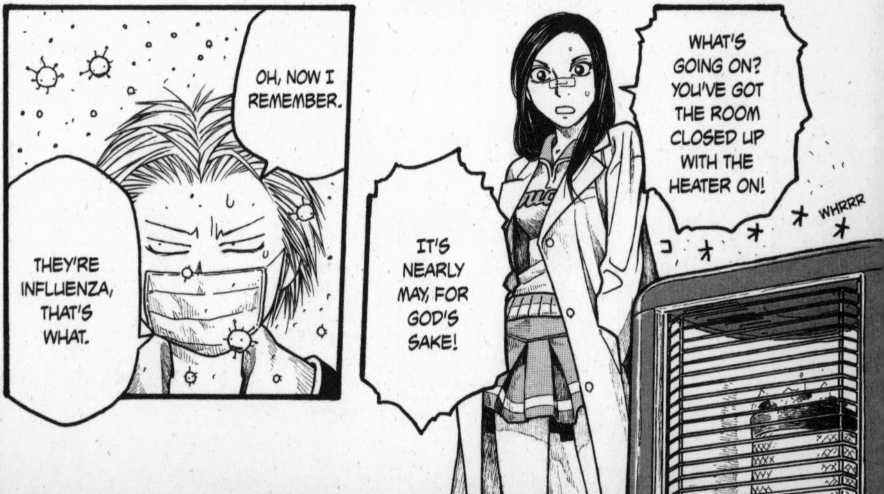
WHAT'S GOING ON? YOU'VE GOT THE ROOM CLOSED UP WITH THE HEATER ON!
WHRRR
IT'S NEARLY MAY, FOR GOD'S SAKE!
OH, NOW I REMEMBER.
THEY'RE INFLUENZA, THAT'S WHAT.

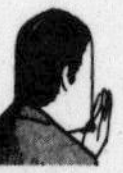

Kaoru Misato
Sophomore. Loves *sake* enough to brew his own. I got a fan letter that said he is identical to some comedian, but my editor didn't know which one. Who is it?

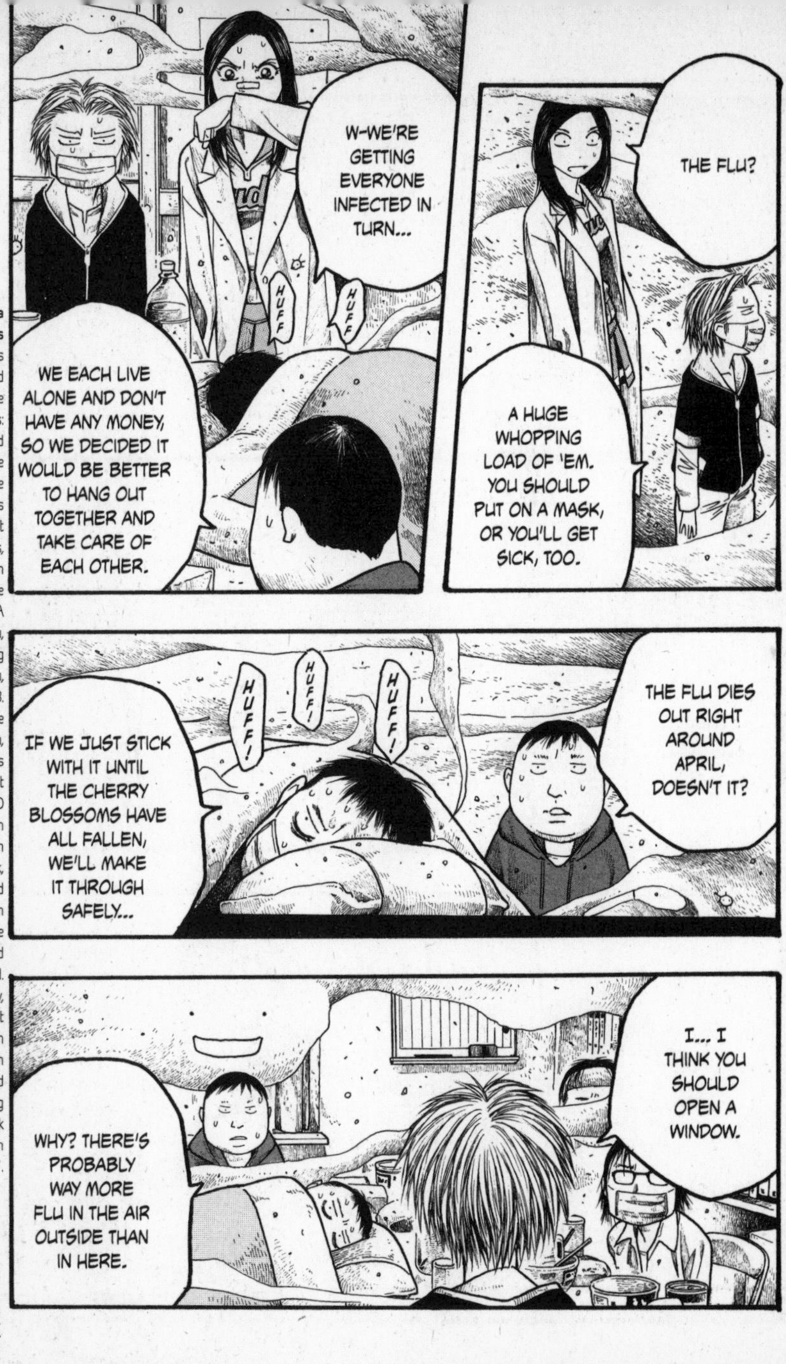
THE FLU?
A HUGE WHOPPING LOAD OF 'EM. YOU SHOULD PUT ON A MASK, OR YOU'LL GET SICK, TOO.
W-WE'RE GETTING EVERYONE INFECTED IN TURN...
HUFF
HUFF
WE EACH LIVE ALONE AND DON'T HAVE ANY MONEY, SO WE DECIDED IT WOULD BE BETTER TO HANG OUT TOGETHER AND TAKE CARE OF EACH OTHER.
THE FLU DIES OUT RIGHT AROUND APRIL, DOESN'T IT?
HUFF!
HUFF!
HUFF!
IF WE JUST STICK WITH IT UNTIL THE CHERRY BLOSSOMS HAVE ALL FALLEN, WE'LL MAKE IT THROUGH SAFELY...
I... I THINK YOU SHOULD OPEN A WINDOW.
WHY? THERE'S PROBABLY WAY MORE FLU IN THE AIR OUTSIDE THAN IN HERE.

Influenza Virus
This virus is classified into three main types: A, B and C. There are three chief flus that affect humans, known in Japanese as Type A Soviet flu, Type A Hong Kong flu, and Type B. For some reason, pandemics occur about every 40 years. When the Spanish flu struck, it killed 20 million people around the world. Funny, the Soviet Union collapsed in 1991, and Hong Kong went back to China in 1997.

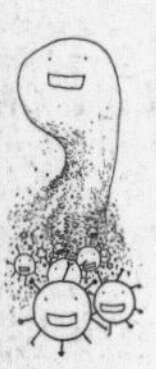

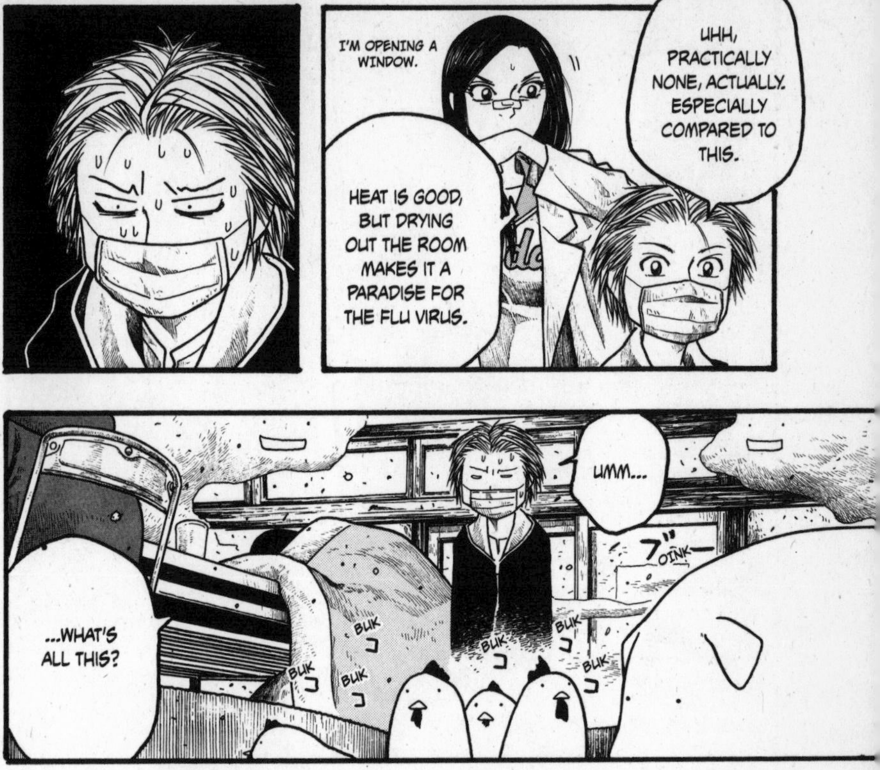
UHH, PRACTICALLY NONE, ACTUALLY. ESPECIALLY COMPARED TO THIS.
I'M OPENING A WINDOW.
HEAT IS GOOD, BUT DRYING OUT THE ROOM MAKES IT A PARADISE FOR THE FLU VIRUS.
UMM...
OINK—
BUK
BUK
BUK
BUK
BUK
...WHAT'S ALL THIS?

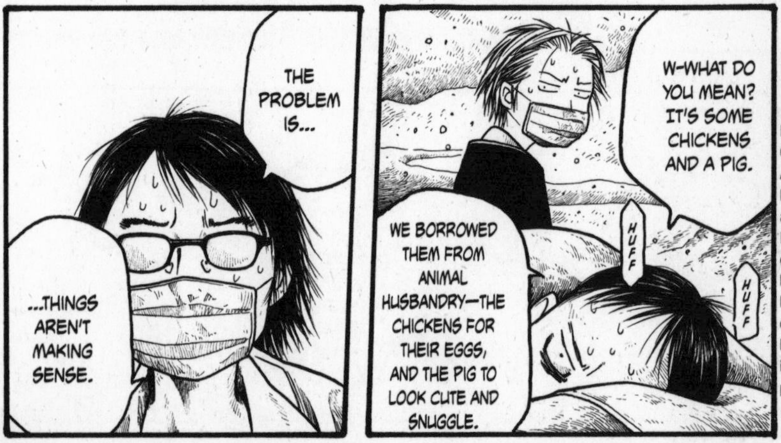
W-WHAT DO YOU MEAN? IT'S SOME CHICKENS AND A PIG.
HUFF
HUFF
WE BORROWED THEM FROM ANIMAL HUSBANDRY—THE CHICKENS FOR THEIR EGGS, AND THE PIG TO LOOK CUTE AND SNUGGLE.
THE PROBLEM IS...
...THINGS AREN'T MAKING SENSE.

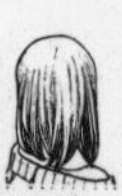

Hazuki Oikawa
A freshman like Sawaki and Yûki. No, she does not have really long bangs covering her face in this picture.

Takuma Kawahama
Sophomore. Only has two lines this chapter.

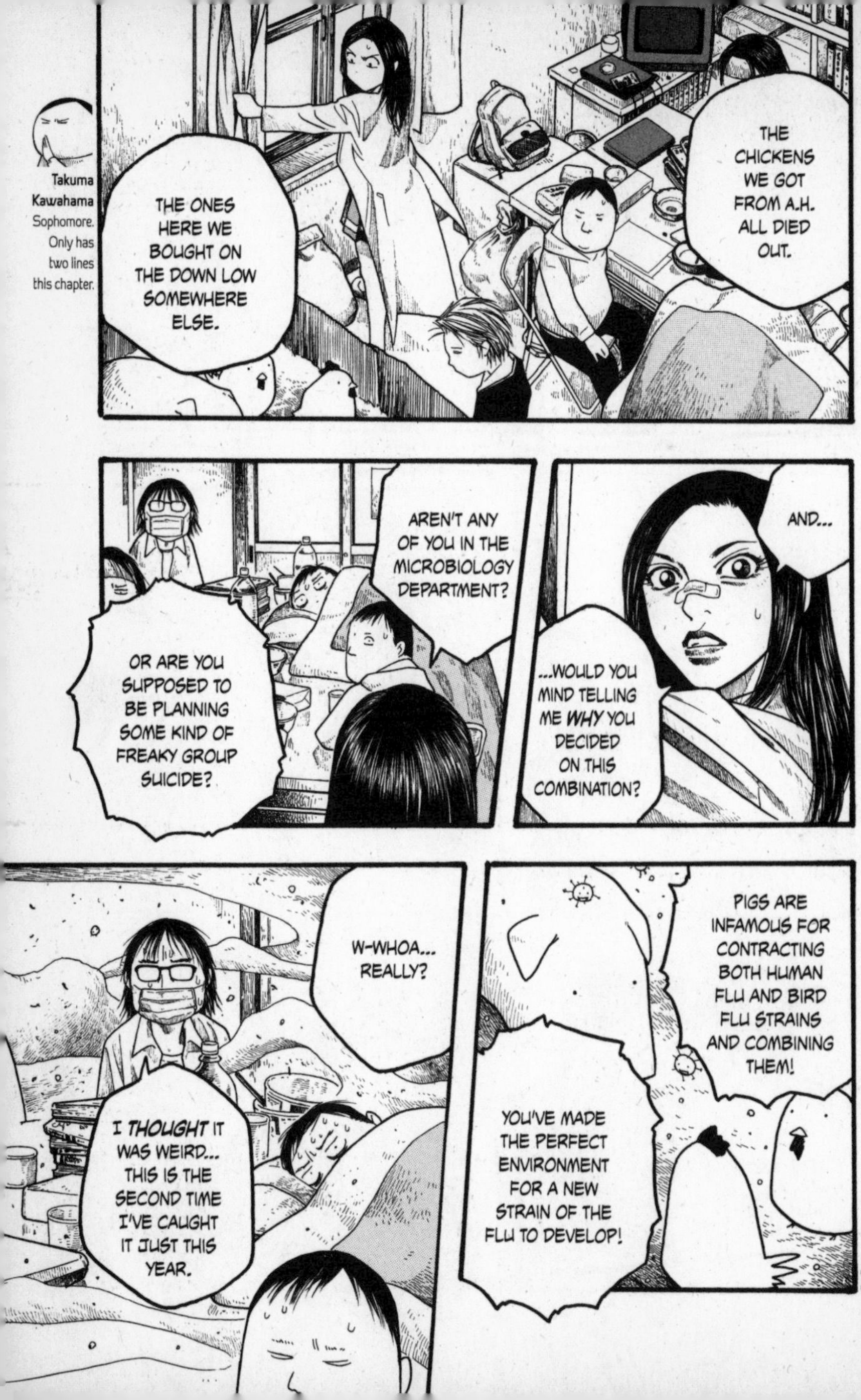
THE CHICKENS WE GOT FROM A.H. ALL DIED OUT.
THE ONES HERE WE BOUGHT ON THE DOWN LOW SOMEWHERE ELSE.
AND...
...WOULD YOU MIND TELLING ME *WHY* YOU DECIDED ON THIS COMBINATION?
AREN'T ANY OF YOU IN THE MICROBIOLOGY DEPARTMENT?
OR ARE YOU SUPPOSED TO BE PLANNING SOME KIND OF FREAKY GROUP SUICIDE?
PIGS ARE INFAMOUS FOR CONTRACTING BOTH HUMAN FLU AND BIRD FLU STRAINS AND COMBINING THEM!
YOU'VE MADE THE PERFECT ENVIRONMENT FOR A NEW STRAIN OF THE FLU TO DEVELOP!
W-WHOA... REALLY?
I *THOUGHT* IT WAS WEIRD... THIS IS THE SECOND TIME I'VE CAUGHT IT JUST THIS YEAR.

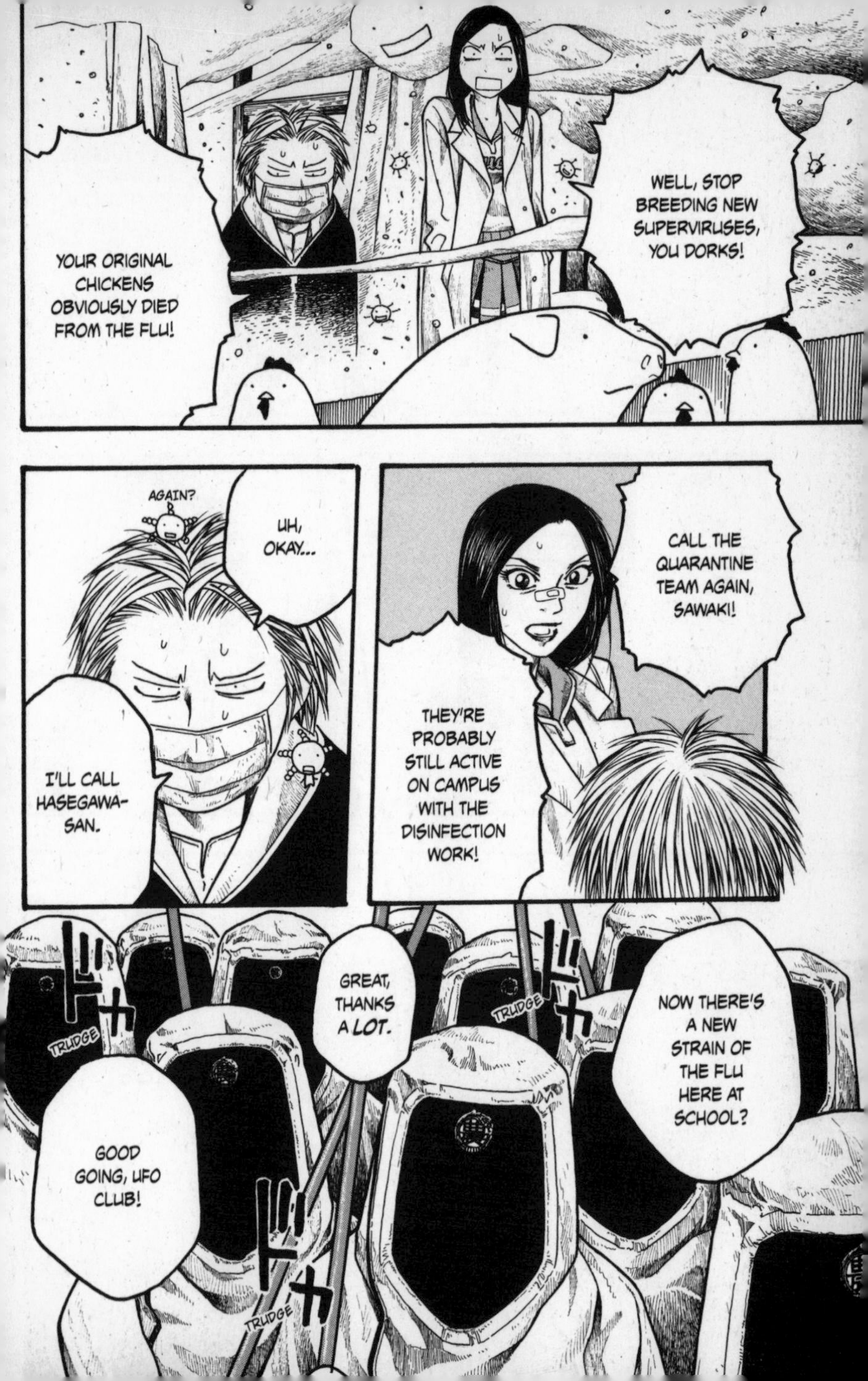
WELL, STOP BREEDING NEW SUPERVIRUSES, YOU DORKS!
YOUR ORIGINAL CHICKENS OBVIOUSLY DIED FROM THE FLU!
CALL THE QUARANTINE TEAM AGAIN, SAWAKI!
THEY'RE PROBABLY STILL ACTIVE ON CAMPUS WITH THE DISINFECTION WORK!
UH, OKAY...
AGAIN?
I'LL CALL HASEGAWA-SAN.
NOW THERE'S A NEW STRAIN OF THE FLU HERE AT SCHOOL?
TRUDGE
GREAT, THANKS A LOT.
TRUDGE
GOOD GOING, UFO CLUB!
TRUDGE

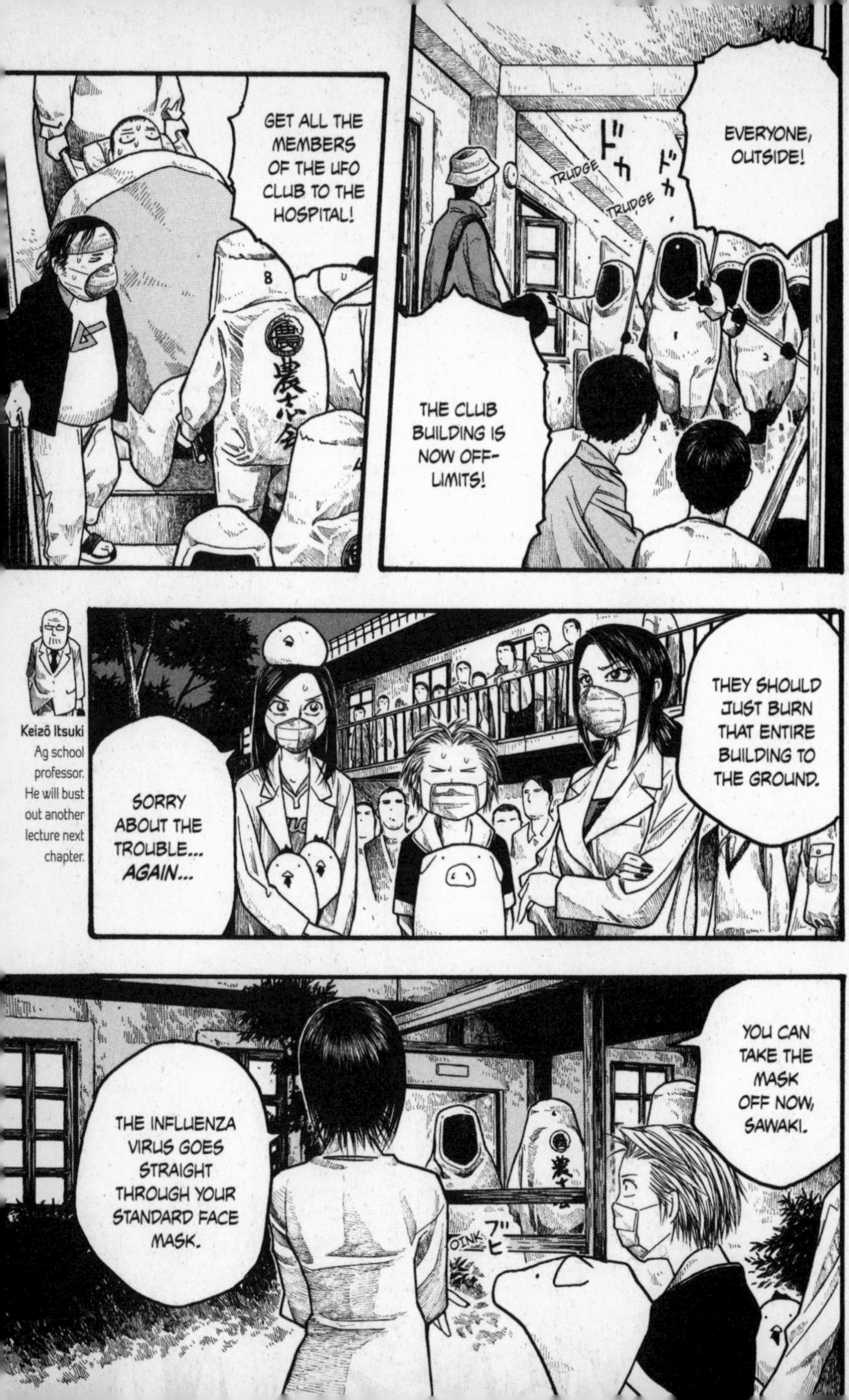
EVERYONE, OUTSIDE!
ドカ
TRUDGE
ドカ
TRUDGE
THE CLUB BUILDING IS NOW OFF-LIMITS!
GET ALL THE MEMBERS OF THE UFO CLUB TO THE HOSPITAL!
THEY SHOULD JUST BURN THAT ENTIRE BUILDING TO THE GROUND.
SORRY ABOUT THE TROUBLE... *AGAIN*...
Keizō Itsuki Ag school professor. He will bust out another lecture next chapter.
YOU CAN TAKE THE MASK OFF NOW, SAWAKI.
ブヒ
OINK
THE INFLUENZA VIRUS GOES STRAIGHT THROUGH YOUR STANDARD FACE MASK.

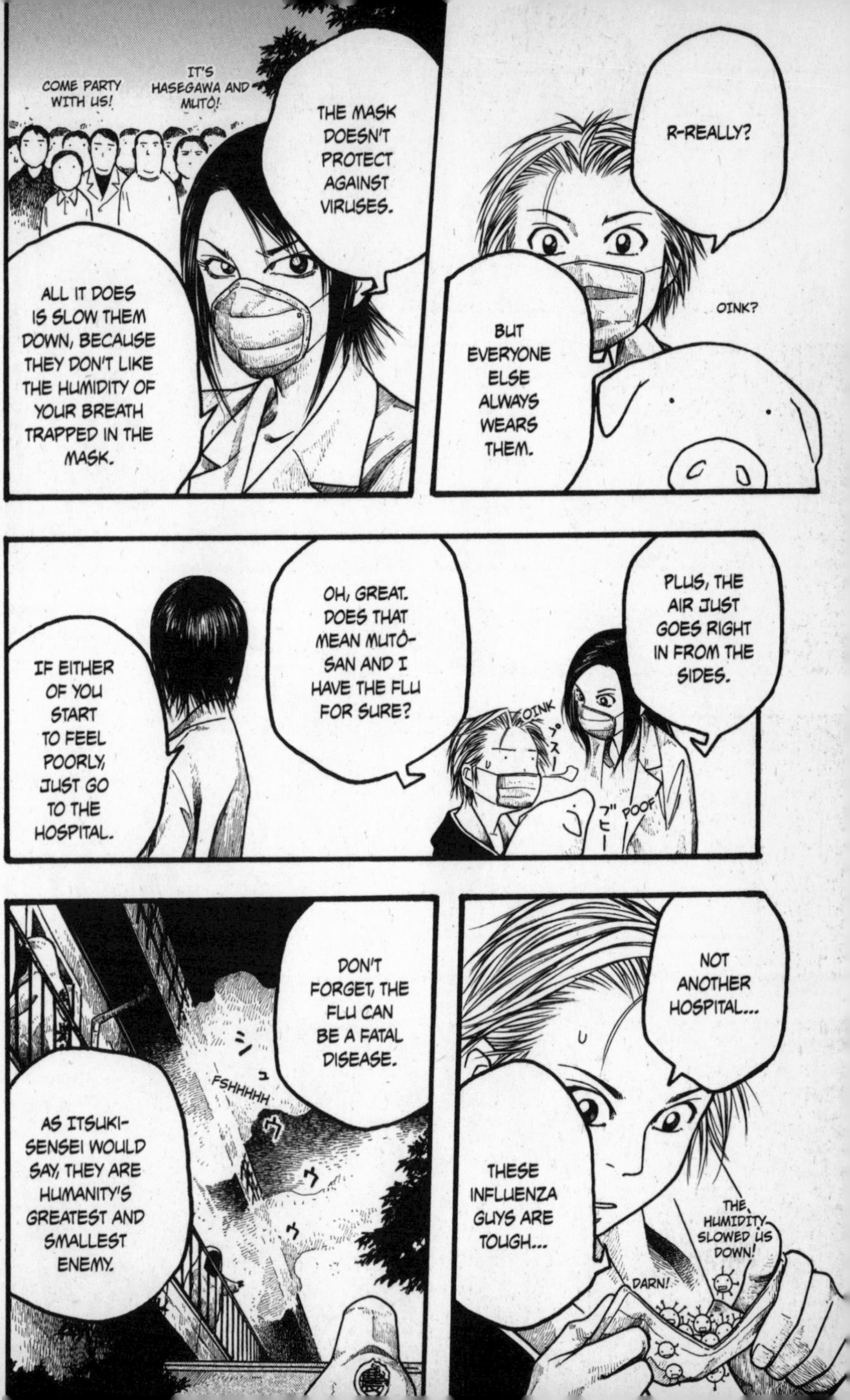
R-REALLY?
OINK?
BUT EVERYONE ELSE ALWAYS WEARS THEM.
THE MASK DOESN'T PROTECT AGAINST VIRUSES.
IT'S HASEGAWA AND MUTÔ!
COME PARTY WITH US!
ALL IT DOES IS SLOW THEM DOWN, BECAUSE THEY DON'T LIKE THE HUMIDITY OF YOUR BREATH TRAPPED IN THE MASK.
PLUS, THE AIR JUST GOES RIGHT IN FROM THE SIDES.
OINK
POOF
OH, GREAT. DOES THAT MEAN MUTÔ-SAN AND I HAVE THE FLU FOR SURE?
IF EITHER OF YOU START TO FEEL POORLY, JUST GO TO THE HOSPITAL.
NOT ANOTHER HOSPITAL...
THE HUMIDITY SLOWED US DOWN!
DARN!
THESE INFLUENZA GUYS ARE TOUGH...
DON'T FORGET, THE FLU CAN BE A FATAL DISEASE.
FSHHHHH
AS ITSUKI-SENSEI WOULD SAY, THEY ARE HUMANITY'S GREATEST AND SMALLEST ENEMY.

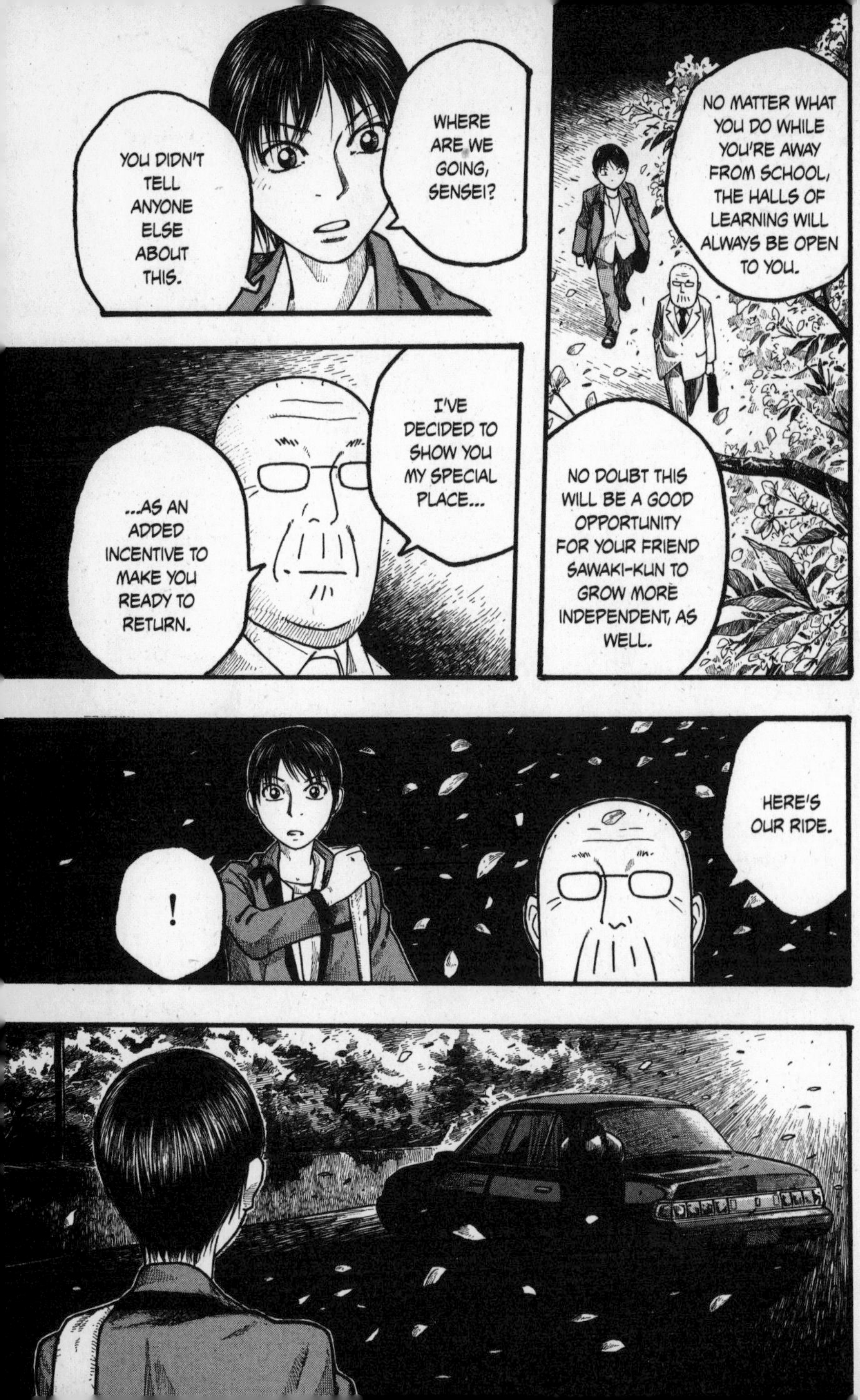
NO MATTER WHAT YOU DO WHILE YOU'RE AWAY FROM SCHOOL, THE HALLS OF LEARNING WILL ALWAYS BE OPEN TO YOU.
NO DOUBT THIS WILL BE A GOOD OPPORTUNITY FOR YOUR FRIEND SAWAKI-KUN TO GROW MORE INDEPENDENT, AS WELL.
WHERE ARE WE GOING, SENSEI?
YOU DIDN'T TELL ANYONE ELSE ABOUT THIS.
I'VE DECIDED TO SHOW YOU MY SPECIAL PLACE...
...AS AN ADDED INCENTIVE TO MAKE YOU READY TO RETURN.
HERE'S OUR RIDE.
!

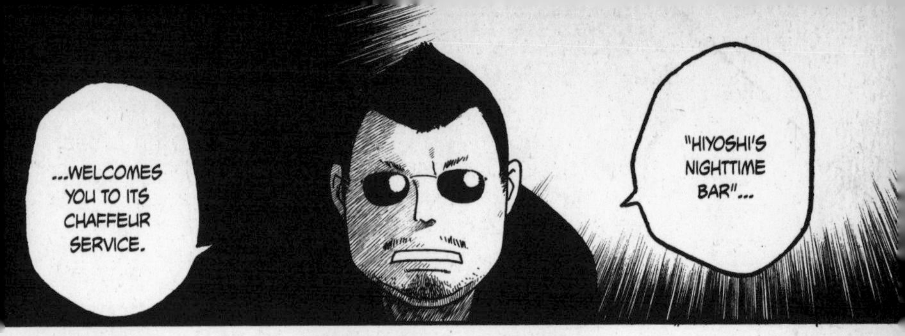
"HIYOSHI'S NIGHTTIME BAR"...
...WELCOMES YOU TO ITS CHAFFEUR SERVICE.

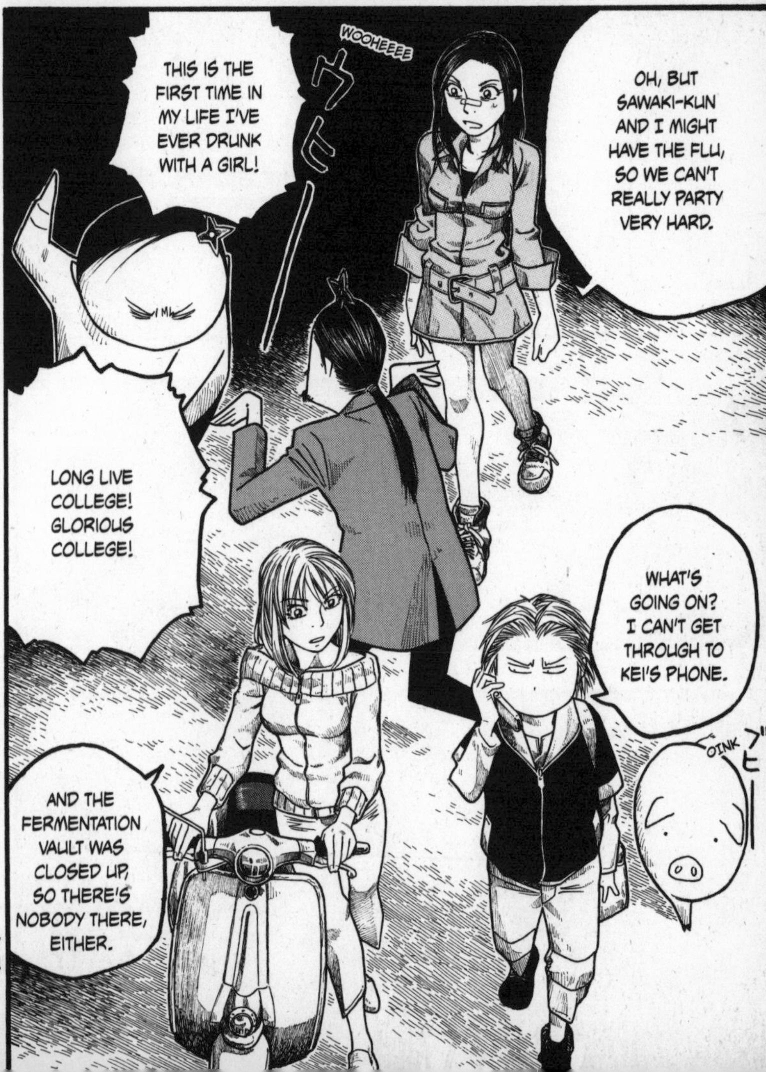
OH, BUT SAWAKI-KUN AND I MIGHT HAVE THE FLU, SO WE CAN'T REALLY PARTY VERY HARD.
WOOHEEEE
ウヒー
THIS IS THE FIRST TIME IN MY LIFE I'VE EVER DRUNK WITH A GIRL!
LONG LIVE COLLEGE! GLORIOUS COLLEGE!
WHAT'S GOING ON? I CAN'T GET THROUGH TO KEI'S PHONE.
OINK
ブヒー
AND THE FERMENTATION VAULT WAS CLOSED UP, SO THERE'S NOBODY THERE, EITHER.

Today's Apology:
In the previous chapter, the name of Mr. Yuki Yabuuchi was incorrectly spelled "Yabuchi."
The author regrets this error. I'm sorry.

15 END

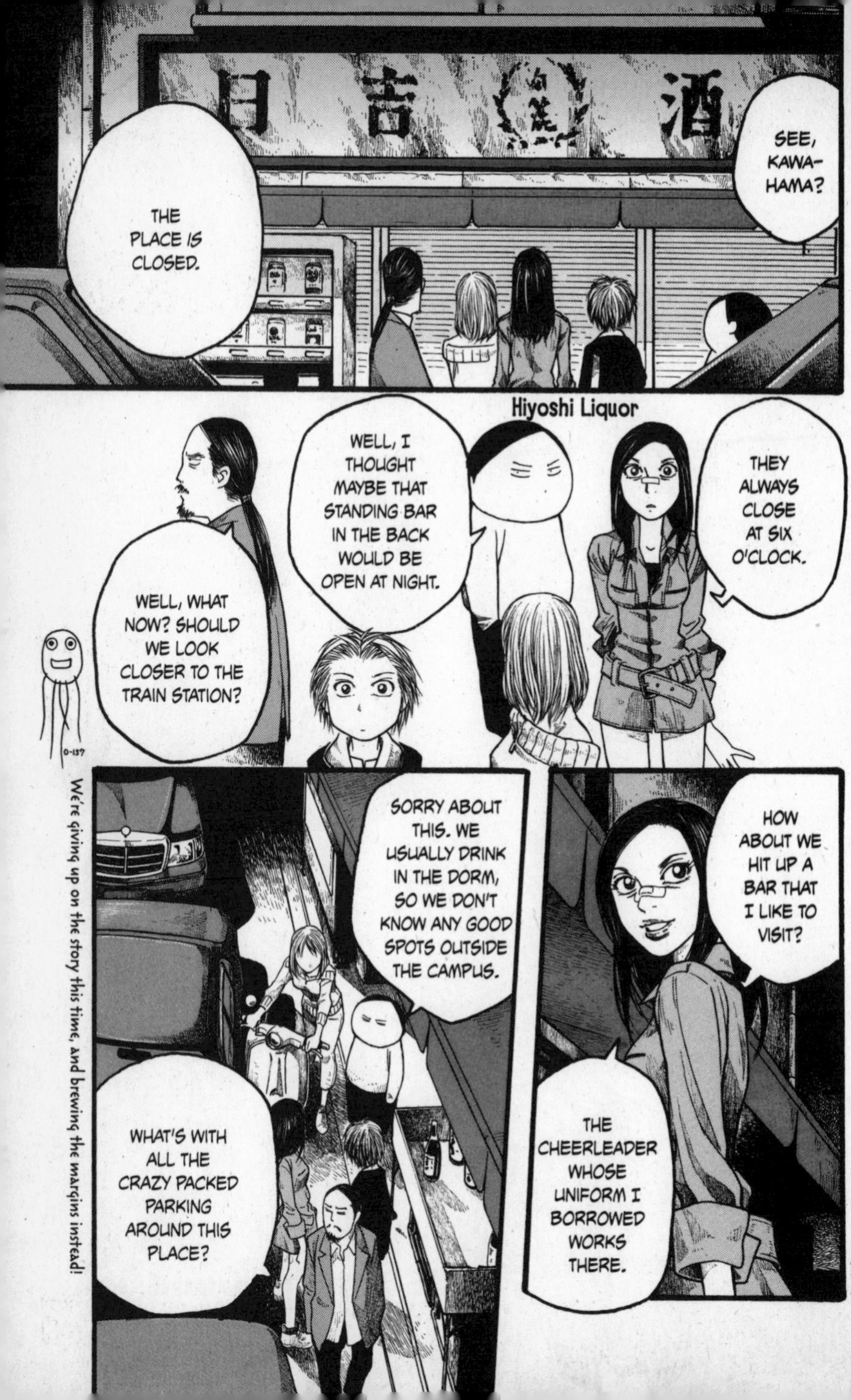
SEE, KAWAHAMA?
THE PLACE IS CLOSED.
Hiyoshi Liquor
THEY ALWAYS CLOSE AT SIX O'CLOCK.
WELL, I THOUGHT MAYBE THAT STANDING BAR IN THE BACK WOULD BE OPEN AT NIGHT.
WELL, WHAT NOW? SHOULD WE LOOK CLOSER TO THE TRAIN STATION?
HOW ABOUT WE HIT UP A BAR THAT I LIKE TO VISIT?
THE CHEERLEADER WHOSE UNIFORM I BORROWED WORKS THERE.
SORRY ABOUT THIS. WE USUALLY DRINK IN THE DORM, SO WE DON'T KNOW ANY GOOD SPOTS OUTSIDE THE CAMPUS.
WHAT'S WITH ALL THE CRAZY PACKED PARKING AROUND THIS PLACE?

0-137

We're giving up on the story this time, and brewing the margins instead!

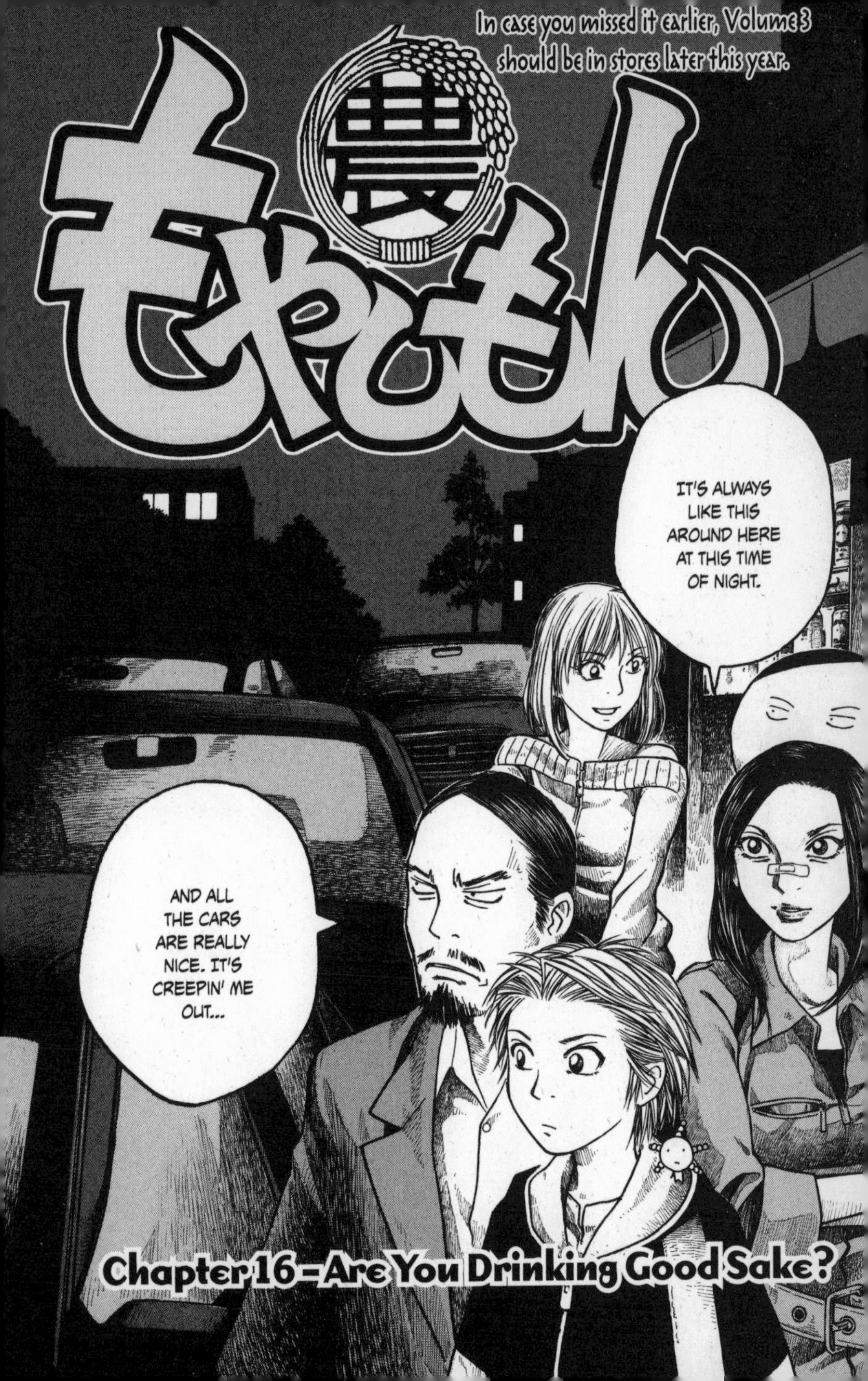
In case you missed it earlier, Volume 3 should be in stores later this year.
もやしもん
IT'S ALWAYS LIKE THIS AROUND HERE AT THIS TIME OF NIGHT.
AND ALL THE CARS ARE REALLY NICE. IT'S CREEPIN' ME OUT...
Chapter 16 - Are You Drinking Good Sake?

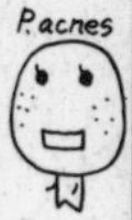
P.acnes

This is a story of a college, germs, viruses, and a few people.

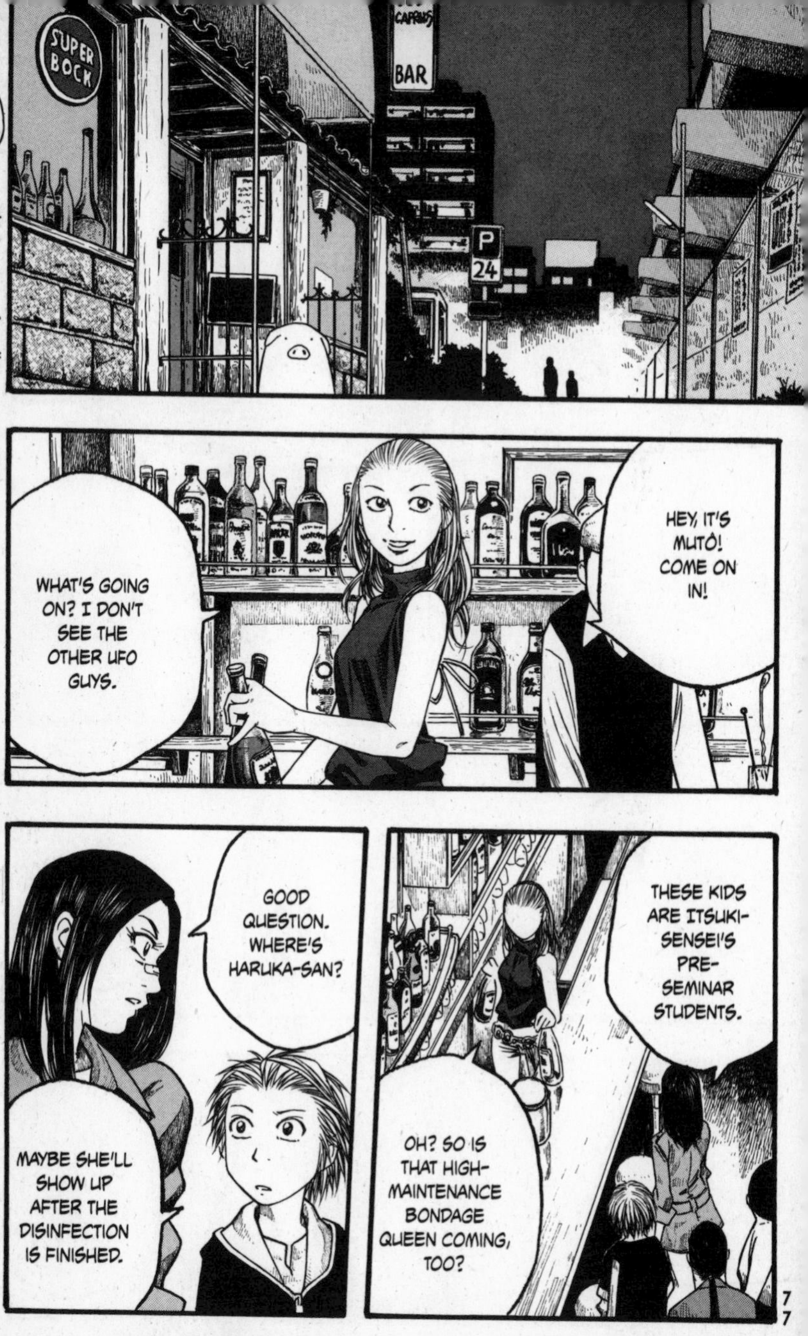
SUPER BOCK
BAR
P 24
HEY, IT'S MUTÔ! COME ON IN!
WHAT'S GOING ON? I DON'T SEE THE OTHER UFO GUYS.
THESE KIDS ARE ITSUKI-SENSEI'S PRE-SEMINAR STUDENTS.
OH? SO IS THAT HIGH-MAINTENANCE BONDAGE QUEEN COMING, TOO?
GOOD QUESTION. WHERE'S HARUKA-SAN?
MAYBE SHE'LL SHOW UP AFTER THE DISINFECTION IS FINISHED.

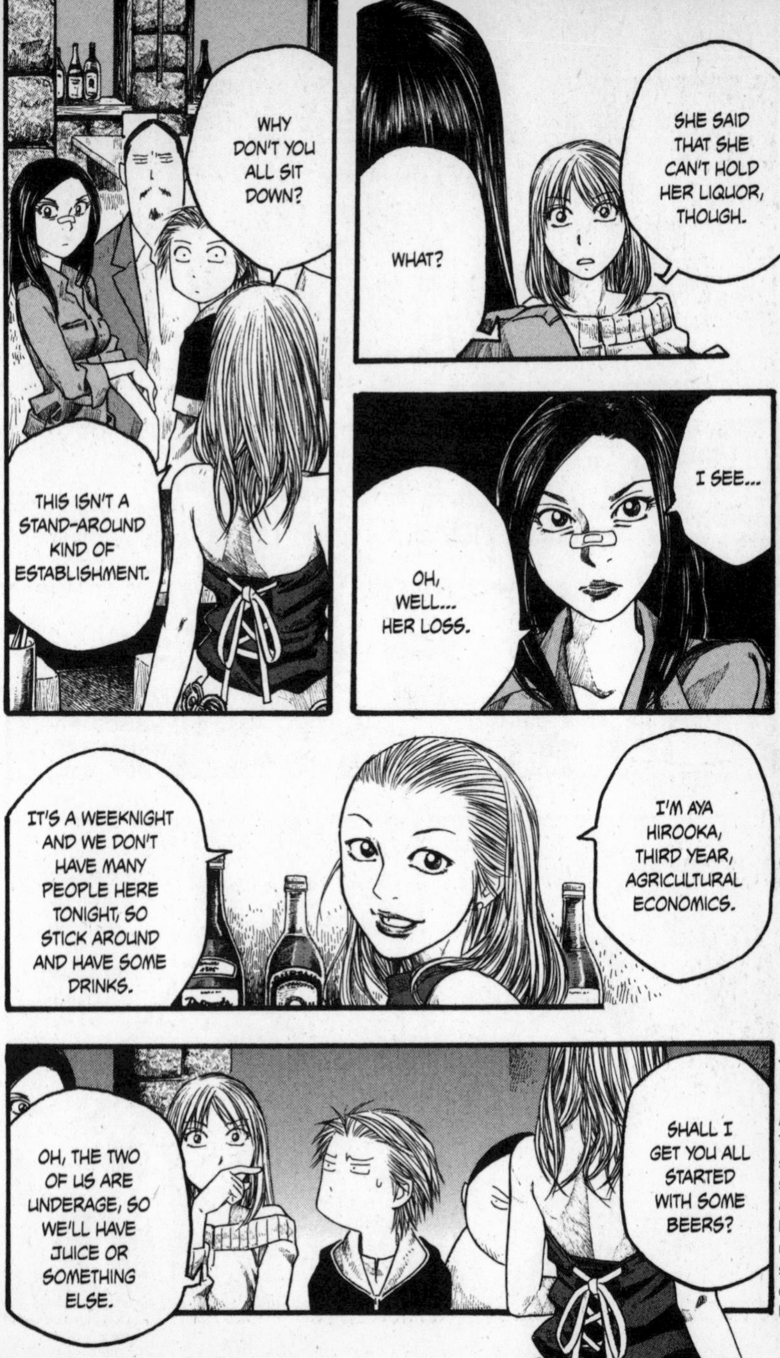
SHE SAID THAT SHE CAN'T HOLD HER LIQUOR, THOUGH.
WHAT?
I SEE...
OH, WELL... HER LOSS.
WHY DON'T YOU ALL SIT DOWN?
THIS ISN'T A STAND-AROUND KIND OF ESTABLISHMENT.
I'M AYA HIROOKA, THIRD YEAR, AGRICULTURAL ECONOMICS.
IT'S A WEEKNIGHT AND WE DON'T HAVE MANY PEOPLE HERE TONIGHT, SO STICK AROUND AND HAVE SOME DRINKS.
SHALL I GET YOU ALL STARTED WITH SOME BEERS?
OH, THE TWO OF US ARE UNDERAGE, SO WE'LL HAVE JUICE OR SOMETHING ELSE.

A.oryzae

Tadayasu Sawaki
Protagonist. Neurotic about his height.

A.niger

Hazuki Oikawa
Started coming to the lab after Professor Itsuki hit on her.

A.aceti

Aoi Mutô
The only seminar student at Itsuki's lab. Her nose got sunburned on her long trip.

P. aeruginosa

Kaoru Misato
Dorm student. Practitioner of *kuchikami sake*.

S. cerevisiae

Takuma Kawahama
Dorm student. Actually fluent in three languages.

P. vulgaris

Aya Hirooka
Mutō's friend and bar employee. Very bad at keeping secrets.

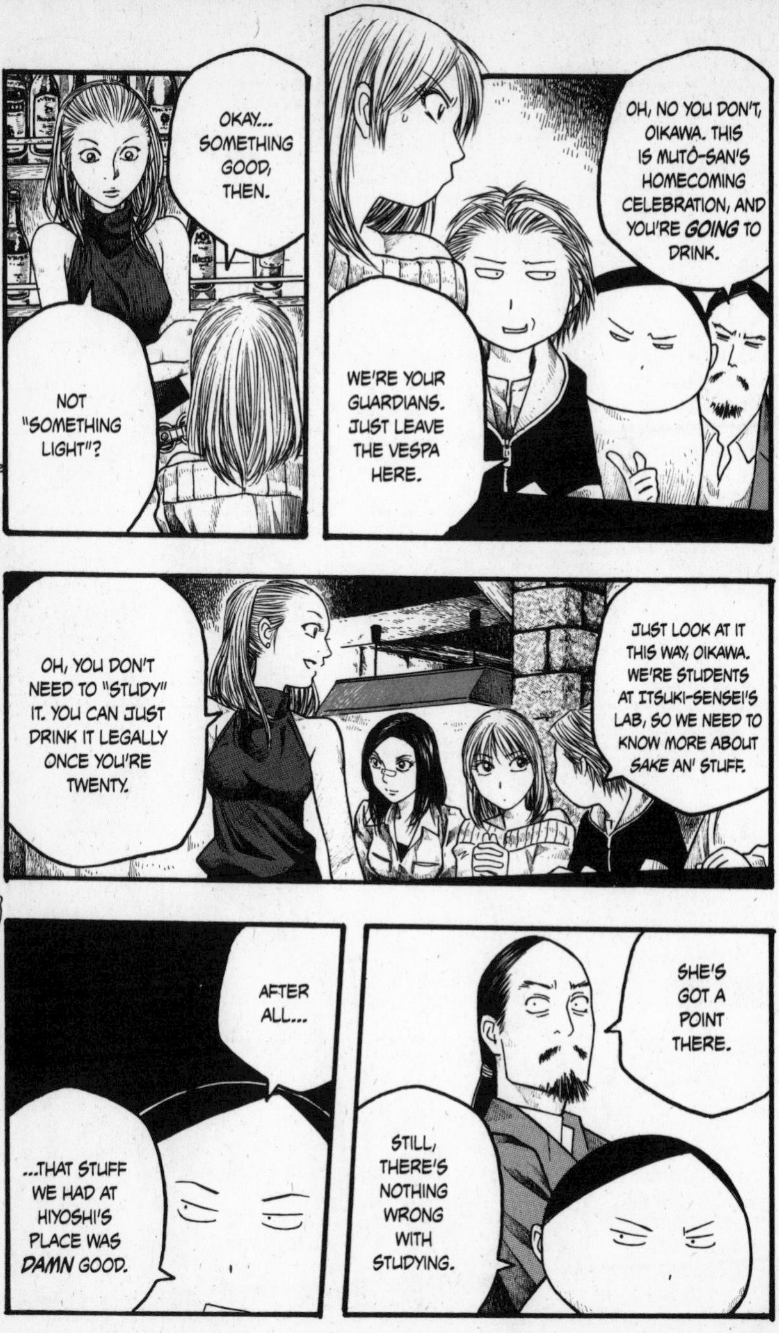

OH, NO YOU DON'T, OIKAWA. THIS IS MUTÔ-SAN'S HOMECOMING CELEBRATION, AND YOU'RE *GOING* TO DRINK.
WE'RE YOUR GUARDIANS. JUST LEAVE THE VESPA HERE.
OKAY... SOMETHING GOOD, THEN.
NOT "SOMETHING LIGHT"?
JUST LOOK AT IT THIS WAY, OIKAWA. WE'RE STUDENTS AT ITSUKI-SENSEI'S LAB, SO WE NEED TO KNOW MORE ABOUT *SAKE* AN' STUFF.
OH, YOU DON'T NEED TO "STUDY" IT. YOU CAN JUST DRINK IT LEGALLY ONCE YOU'RE TWENTY.
SHE'S GOT A POINT THERE.
STILL, THERE'S NOTHING WRONG WITH STUDYING.
AFTER ALL...
...THAT STUFF WE HAD AT HIYOSHI'S PLACE WAS *DAMN* GOOD.

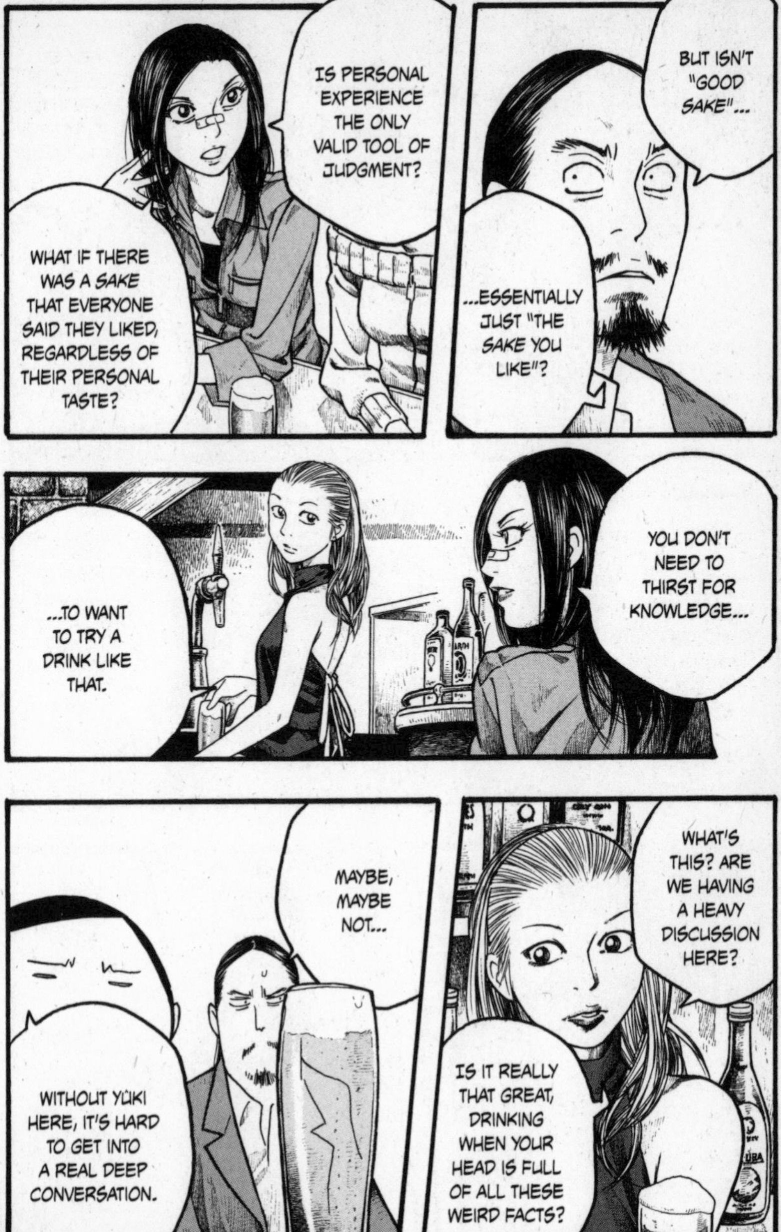
BUT ISN'T "GOOD SAKE"...
...ESSENTIALLY JUST "THE SAKE YOU LIKE"?
IS PERSONAL EXPERIENCE THE ONLY VALID TOOL OF JUDGMENT?
WHAT IF THERE WAS A SAKE THAT EVERYONE SAID THEY LIKED, REGARDLESS OF THEIR PERSONAL TASTE?
YOU DON'T NEED TO THIRST FOR KNOWLEDGE...
...TO WANT TO TRY A DRINK LIKE THAT.
WHAT'S THIS? ARE WE HAVING A HEAVY DISCUSSION HERE?
IS IT REALLY THAT GREAT, DRINKING WHEN YOUR HEAD IS FULL OF ALL THESE WEIRD FACTS?
MAYBE, MAYBE NOT...
WITHOUT YŪKI HERE, IT'S HARD TO GET INTO A REAL DEEP CONVERSATION.

Notice
M. furfur

Today's margins are under germ control!

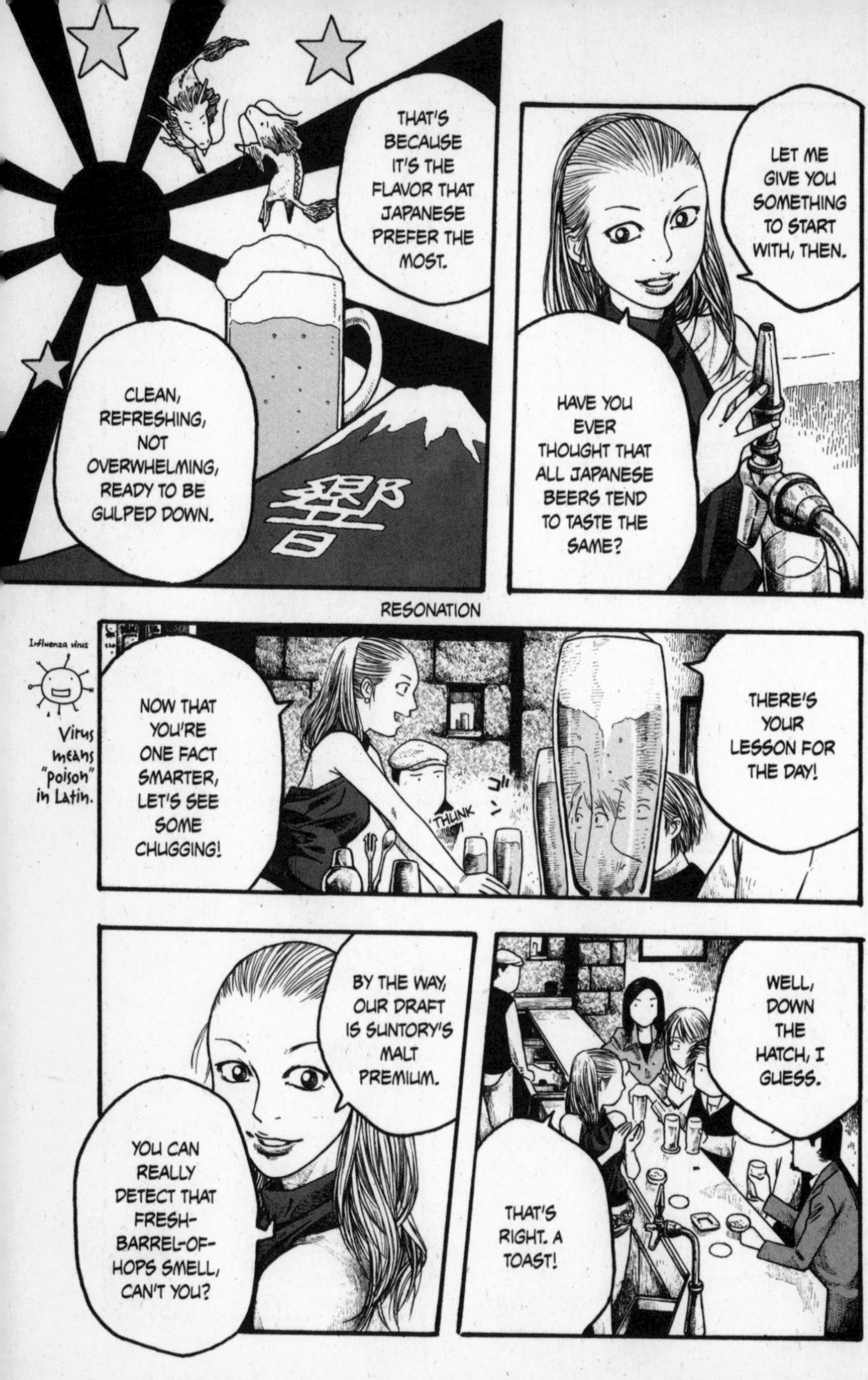
LET ME GIVE YOU SOMETHING TO START WITH, THEN.
HAVE YOU EVER THOUGHT THAT ALL JAPANESE BEERS TEND TO TASTE THE SAME?
THAT'S BECAUSE IT'S THE FLAVOR THAT JAPANESE PREFER THE MOST.
CLEAN, REFRESHING, NOT OVERWHELMING, READY TO BE GULPED DOWN.
RESONATION
THERE'S YOUR LESSON FOR THE DAY!
NOW THAT YOU'RE ONE FACT SMARTER, LET'S SEE SOME CHUGGING!
THUNK
Influenza virus
Virus means "poison" in Latin.
WELL, DOWN THE HATCH, I GUESS.
THAT'S RIGHT. A TOAST!
BY THE WAY, OUR DRAFT IS SUNTORY'S MALT PREMIUM.
YOU CAN REALLY DETECT THAT FRESH-BARREL-OF-HOPS SMELL, CAN'T YOU?

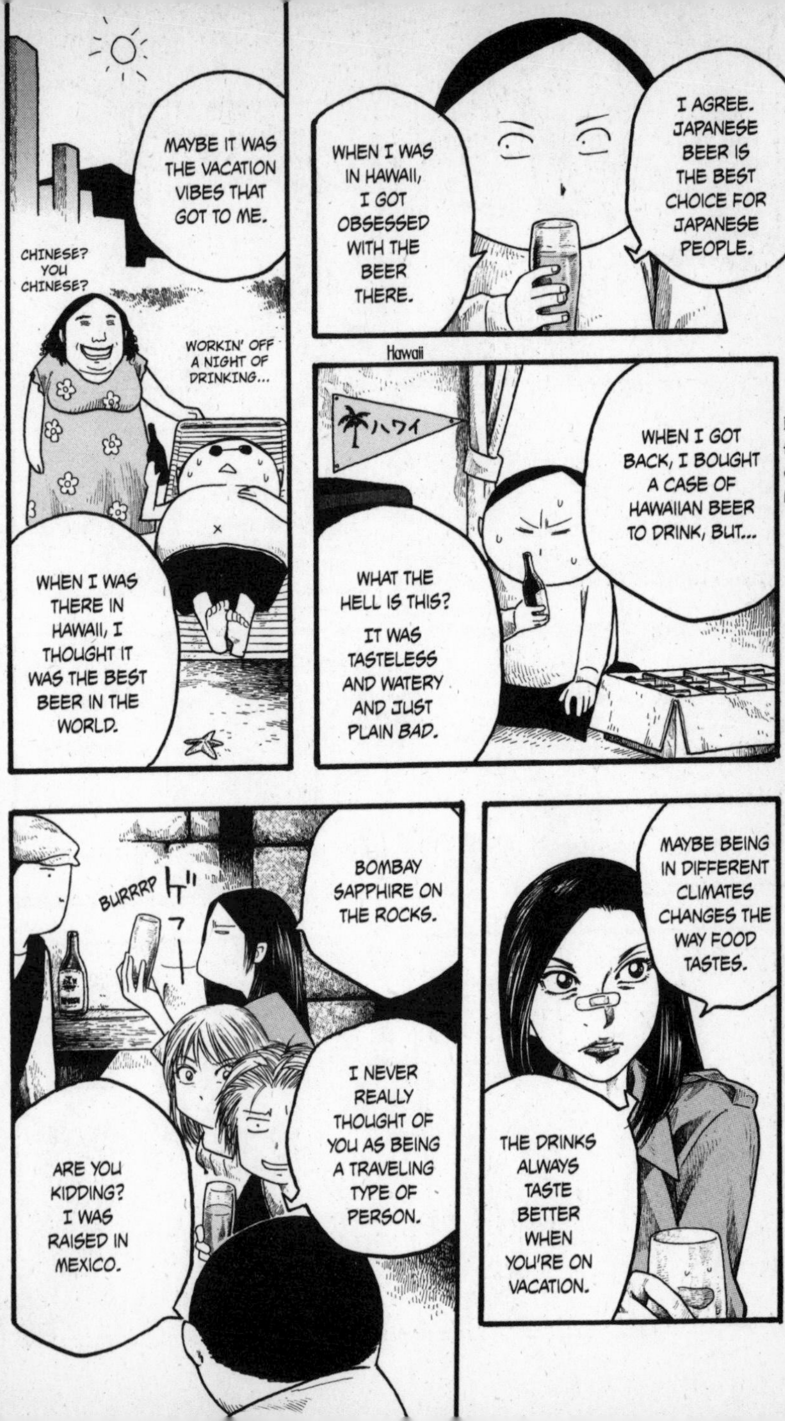
I AGREE. JAPANESE BEER IS THE BEST CHOICE FOR JAPANESE PEOPLE.
WHEN I WAS IN HAWAII, I GOT OBSESSED WITH THE BEER THERE.
ハワイ
Hawaii
WHEN I GOT BACK, I BOUGHT A CASE OF HAWAIIAN BEER TO DRINK, BUT...
WHAT THE HELL IS THIS?
IT WAS TASTELESS AND WATERY AND JUST PLAIN *BAD*.
MAYBE IT WAS THE VACATION VIBES THAT GOT TO ME.
CHINESE? YOU CHINESE?
WORKIN' OFF A NIGHT OF DRINKING...
WHEN I WAS THERE IN HAWAII, I THOUGHT IT WAS THE BEST BEER IN THE WORLD.
MAYBE BEING IN DIFFERENT CLIMATES CHANGES THE WAY FOOD TASTES.
THE DRINKS ALWAYS TASTE BETTER WHEN YOU'RE ON VACATION.
BOMBAY SAPPHIRE ON THE ROCKS.
BURRRP
I NEVER REALLY THOUGHT OF YOU AS BEING A TRAVELING TYPE OF PERSON.
ARE YOU KIDDING? I WAS RAISED IN MEXICO.

S. lactis

Did you know that **nata de coco** is fermented?

A. xylinum
Acetic acid bacteria. When it is added to coconut, the film that results is **nata de coco**.

6 mm

Kowloon Roach

In the past, it was briefly popular to drop two or three of these bugs, alive, into a glass of whisky. Touted as a virility booster, the lack of scientific basis and rumors of the danger of contracting tapeworms quickly scuttled this fad. The bugs are pests.

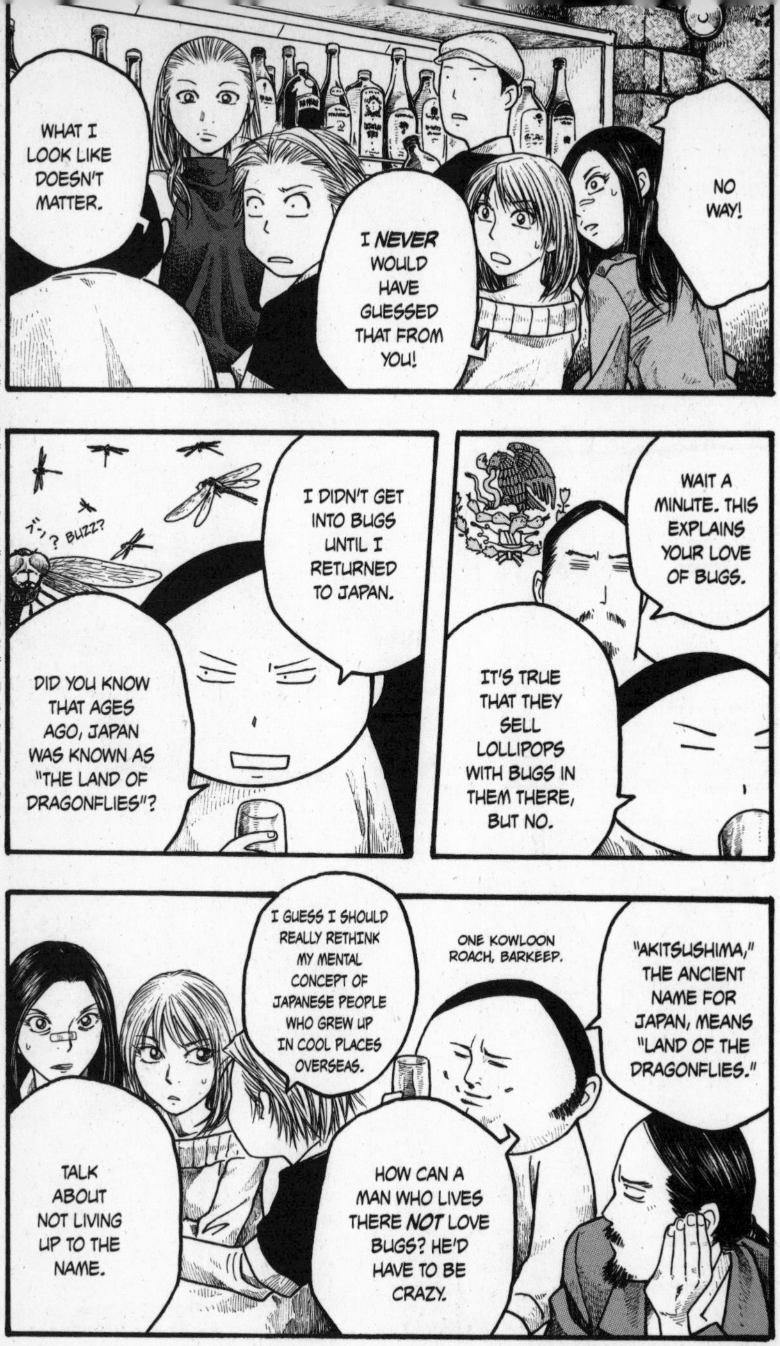

NO WAY!
I NEVER WOULD HAVE GUESSED THAT FROM YOU!
WHAT I LOOK LIKE DOESN'T MATTER.
WAIT A MINUTE. THIS EXPLAINS YOUR LOVE OF BUGS.
IT'S TRUE THAT THEY SELL LOLLIPOPS WITH BUGS IN THEM THERE, BUT NO.
I DIDN'T GET INTO BUGS UNTIL I RETURNED TO JAPAN.
? BUZZ?
DID YOU KNOW THAT AGES AGO, JAPAN WAS KNOWN AS "THE LAND OF DRAGONFLIES"?
"AKITSUSHIMA," THE ANCIENT NAME FOR JAPAN, MEANS "LAND OF THE DRAGONFLIES."
ONE KOWLOON ROACH, BARKEEP.
I GUESS I SHOULD REALLY RETHINK MY MENTAL CONCEPT OF JAPANESE PEOPLE WHO GREW UP IN COOL PLACES OVERSEAS.
HOW CAN A MAN WHO LIVES THERE NOT LOVE BUGS? HE'D HAVE TO BE CRAZY.
TALK ABOUT NOT LIVING UP TO THE NAME.

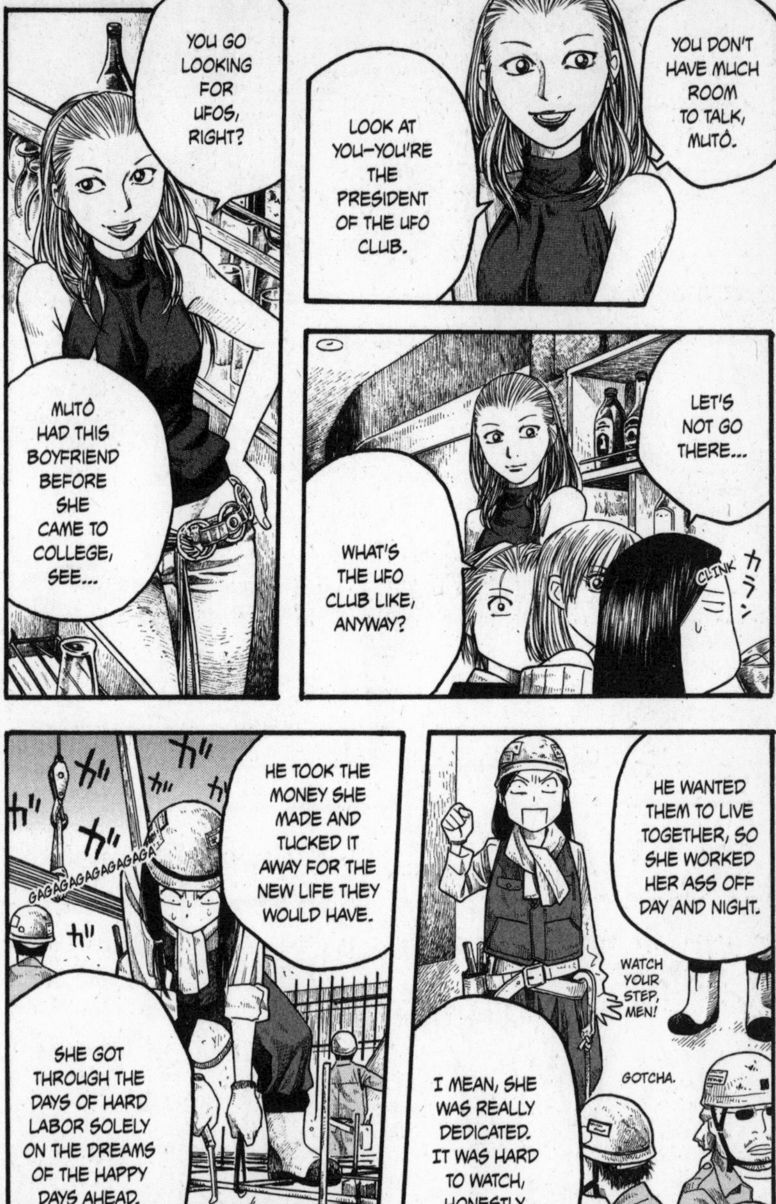
YOU DON'T HAVE MUCH ROOM TO TALK, MUTÔ.
LOOK AT YOU—YOU'RE THE PRESIDENT OF THE UFO CLUB.
LET'S NOT GO THERE...
CLINK
WHAT'S THE UFO CLUB LIKE, ANYWAY?
YOU GO LOOKING FOR UFOS, RIGHT?
MUTÔ HAD THIS BOYFRIEND BEFORE SHE CAME TO COLLEGE, SEE...
HE WANTED THEM TO LIVE TOGETHER, SO SHE WORKED HER ASS OFF DAY AND NIGHT.
WATCH YOUR STEP, MEN!
GOTCHA.
I MEAN, SHE WAS REALLY DEDICATED. IT WAS HARD TO WATCH, HONESTLY.
HE TOOK THE MONEY SHE MADE AND TUCKED IT AWAY FOR THE NEW LIFE THEY WOULD HAVE.
GAGAGAGAGAGAGAGA
SHE GOT THROUGH THE DAYS OF HARD LABOR SOLELY ON THE DREAMS OF THE HAPPY DAYS AHEAD.

Question! Is it just me, or are the margins turning into a place for quotes from the editor?

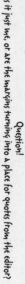

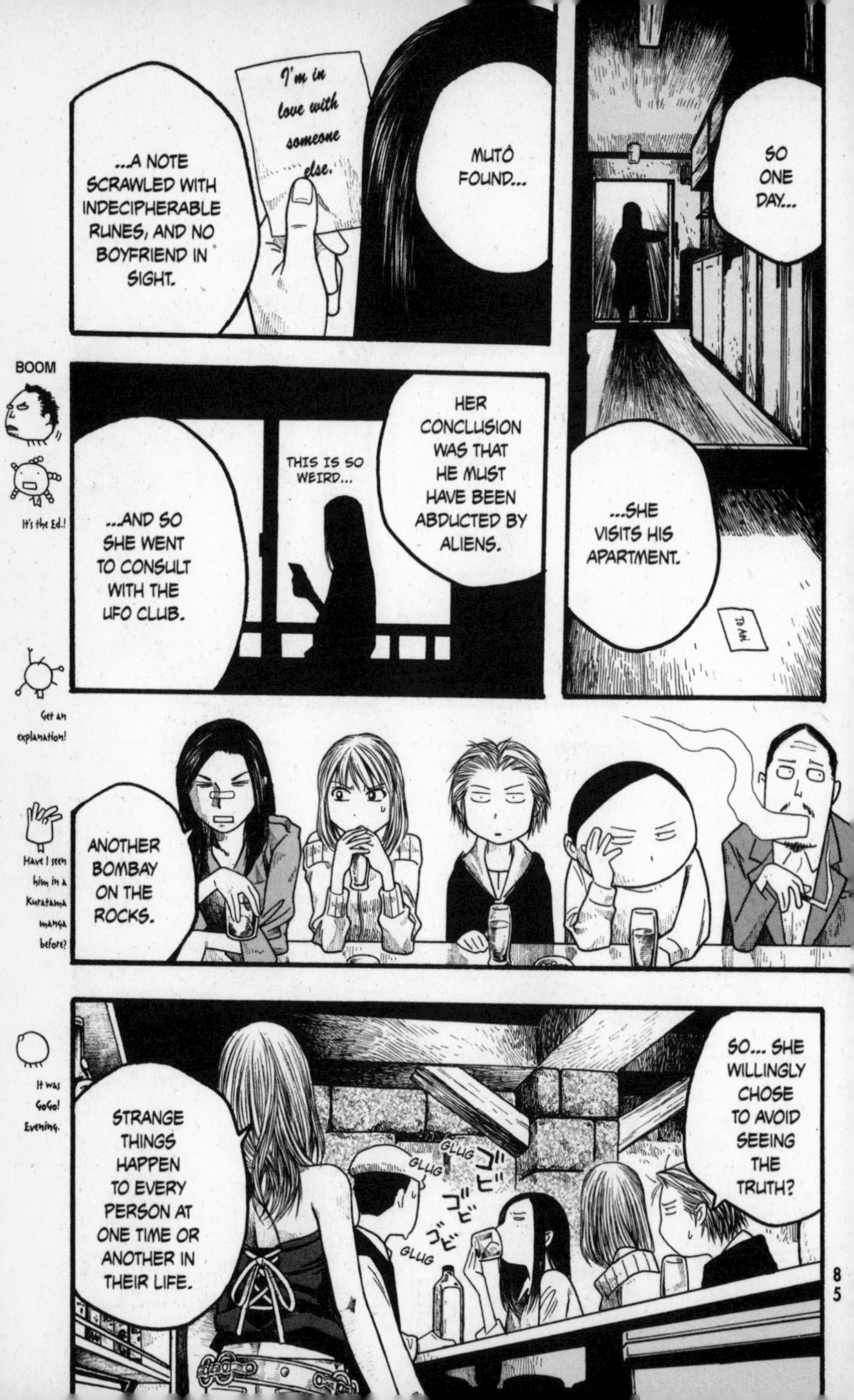
SO ONE DAY...
...SHE VISITS HIS APARTMENT.
To Aoi
MUTO FOUND...
I'm in love with someone else.
...A NOTE SCRAWLED WITH INDECIPHERABLE RUNES, AND NO BOYFRIEND IN SIGHT.
HER CONCLUSION WAS THAT HE MUST HAVE BEEN ABDUCTED BY ALIENS.
THIS IS SO WEIRD...
...AND SO SHE WENT TO CONSULT WITH THE UFO CLUB.
ANOTHER BOMBAY ON THE ROCKS.
SO... SHE WILLINGLY CHOSE TO AVOID SEEING THE TRUTH?
GLUG
GLUG
GLUG
STRANGE THINGS HAPPEN TO EVERY PERSON AT ONE TIME OR ANOTHER IN THEIR LIFE.
BOOM
It's the Ed.!
Get an explanation!
Have I seen him in a Kuratama manga before?
It was GoGo! Evening.

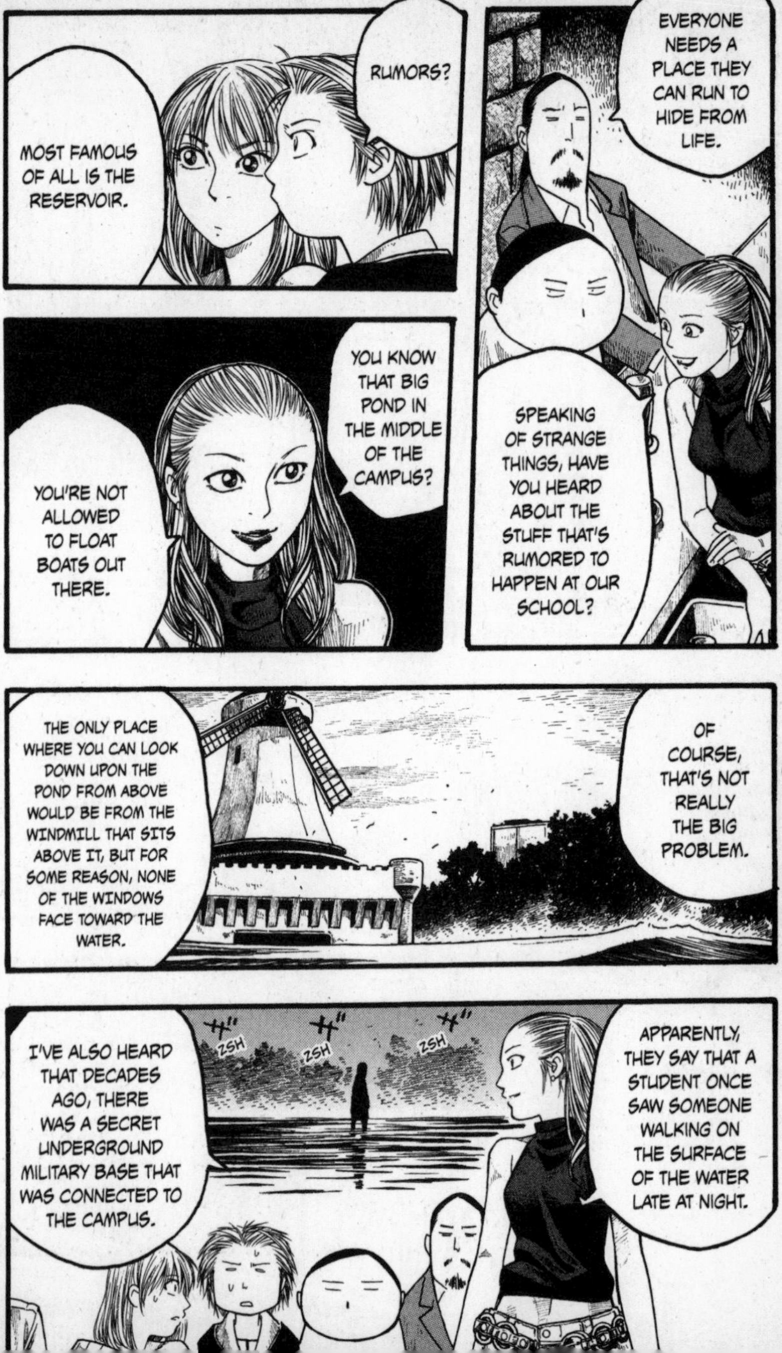
EVERYONE NEEDS A PLACE THEY CAN RUN TO HIDE FROM LIFE.
SPEAKING OF STRANGE THINGS, HAVE YOU HEARD ABOUT THE STUFF THAT'S RUMORED TO HAPPEN AT OUR SCHOOL?
RUMORS?
MOST FAMOUS OF ALL IS THE RESERVOIR.
YOU KNOW THAT BIG POND IN THE MIDDLE OF THE CAMPUS?
YOU'RE NOT ALLOWED TO FLOAT BOATS OUT THERE.
OF COURSE, THAT'S NOT REALLY THE BIG PROBLEM.
THE ONLY PLACE WHERE YOU CAN LOOK DOWN UPON THE POND FROM ABOVE WOULD BE FROM THE WINDMILL THAT SITS ABOVE IT, BUT FOR SOME REASON, NONE OF THE WINDOWS FACE TOWARD THE WATER.
ZSH
ZSH
ZSH
APPARENTLY, THEY SAY THAT A STUDENT ONCE SAW SOMEONE WALKING ON THE SURFACE OF THE WATER LATE AT NIGHT.
I'VE ALSO HEARD THAT DECADES AGO, THERE WAS A SECRET UNDERGROUND MILITARY BASE THAT WAS CONNECTED TO THE CAMPUS.

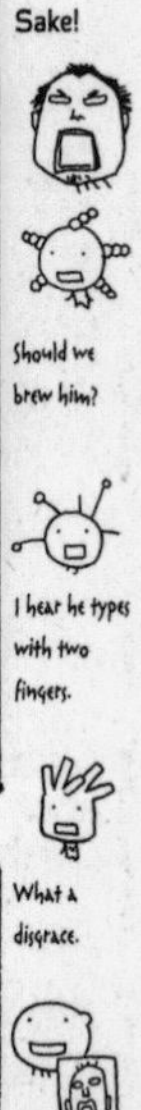
Sake!
Should we brew him?
I hear he types with two fingers.
What a disgrace.
He looked like this in the other manga.

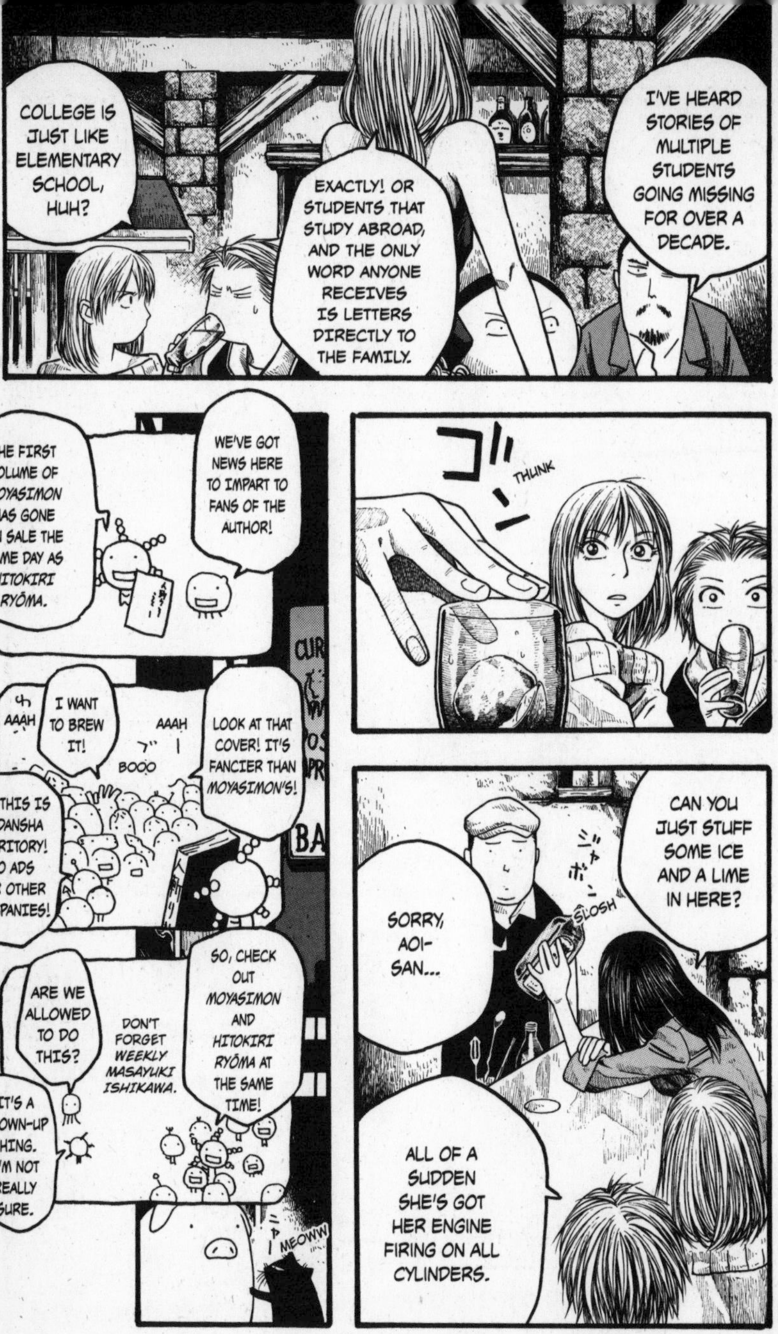
I'VE HEARD STORIES OF MULTIPLE STUDENTS GOING MISSING FOR OVER A DECADE.
EXACTLY! OR STUDENTS THAT STUDY ABROAD, AND THE ONLY WORD ANYONE RECEIVES IS LETTERS DIRECTLY TO THE FAMILY.
COLLEGE IS JUST LIKE ELEMENTARY SCHOOL, HUH?
THUNK
CAN YOU JUST STUFF SOME ICE AND A LIME IN HERE?
SLOSH
SORRY, AOI-SAN...
ALL OF A SUDDEN SHE'S GOT HER ENGINE FIRING ON ALL CYLINDERS.
WE'VE GOT NEWS HERE TO IMPART TO FANS OF THE AUTHOR!
THE FIRST VOLUME OF *MOYASIMON* HAS GONE ON SALE THE SAME DAY AS *HITOKIRI RYŌMA*.
LOOK AT THAT COVER! IT'S FANCIER THAN *MOYASIMON'S*!
AAAH
BOOO
I WANT TO BREW IT!
AAAH
BUT THIS IS KODANSHA TERRITORY! NO ADS FOR OTHER COMPANIES!
SO, CHECK OUT *MOYASIMON* AND *HITOKIRI RYŌMA* AT THE SAME TIME!
DON'T FORGET *WEEKLY MASAYUKI ISHIKAWA*.
ARE WE ALLOWED TO DO THIS?
IT'S A GROWN-UP THING. I'M NOT REALLY SURE.
MEOWW

(Only applies to Japan. Maybe if Moyasimon sells a million copies, they'll come out here, too.)

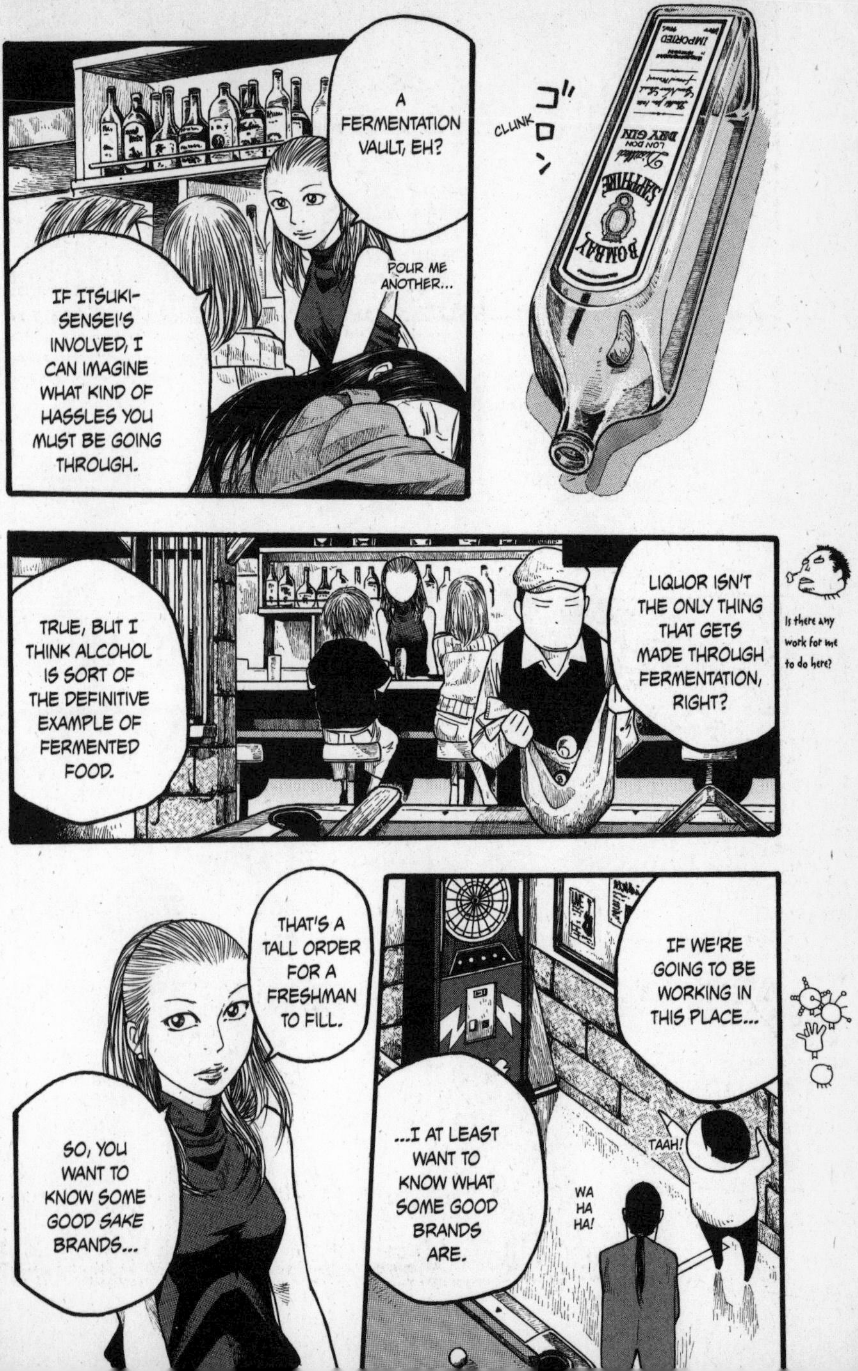
ゴロン
CLUNK
BOMBAY
SAPPHIRE
LON DON
DRY GIN
IMPORTED
A FERMENTATION VAULT, EH?
POUR ME ANOTHER...
IF ITSUKI-SENSEI'S INVOLVED, I CAN IMAGINE WHAT KIND OF HASSLES YOU MUST BE GOING THROUGH.
Is there any work for me to do here?
LIQUOR ISN'T THE ONLY THING THAT GETS MADE THROUGH FERMENTATION, RIGHT?
TRUE, BUT I THINK ALCOHOL IS SORT OF THE DEFINITIVE EXAMPLE OF FERMENTED FOOD.
IF WE'RE GOING TO BE WORKING IN THIS PLACE...
...I AT LEAST WANT TO KNOW WHAT SOME GOOD BRANDS ARE.
TAAH!
WA HA HA!
THAT'S A TALL ORDER FOR A FRESHMAN TO FILL.
SO, YOU WANT TO KNOW SOME GOOD SAKE BRANDS...

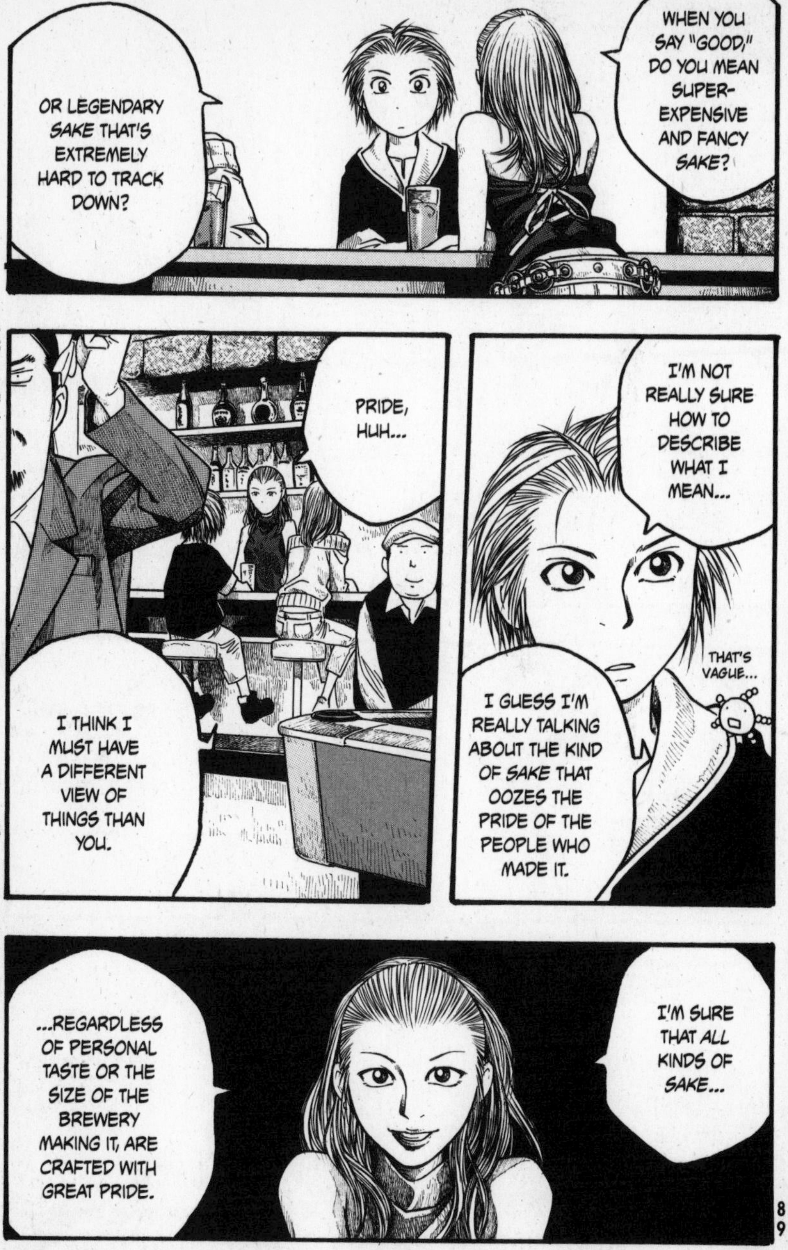
WHEN YOU SAY "GOOD," DO YOU MEAN SUPER-EXPENSIVE AND FANCY SAKE?
OR LEGENDARY SAKE THAT'S EXTREMELY HARD TO TRACK DOWN?
I'M NOT REALLY SURE HOW TO DESCRIBE WHAT I MEAN...
THAT'S VAGUE...
I GUESS I'M REALLY TALKING ABOUT THE KIND OF SAKE THAT OOZES THE PRIDE OF THE PEOPLE WHO MADE IT.
PRIDE, HUH...
I THINK I MUST HAVE A DIFFERENT VIEW OF THINGS THAN YOU.
I'M SURE THAT ALL KINDS OF SAKE...
...REGARDLESS OF PERSONAL TASTE OR THE SIZE OF THE BREWERY MAKING IT, ARE CRAFTED WITH GREAT PRIDE.

Just take it easy for today.

Aww.

R. editorus Converts large amounts of alcohol to ammonia, but loses its potency after turning thirty-five. Never found in the office.

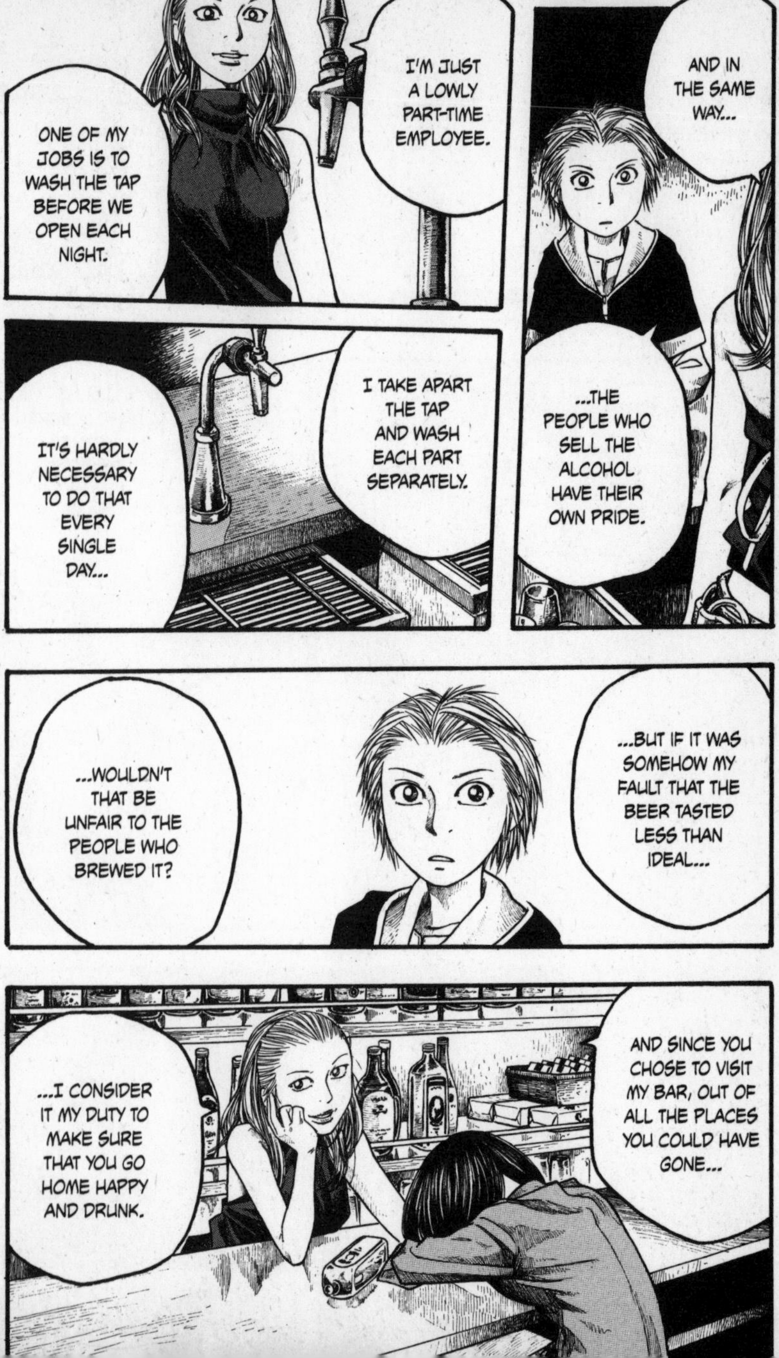
AND IN THE SAME WAY...
...THE PEOPLE WHO SELL THE ALCOHOL HAVE THEIR OWN PRIDE.
I'M JUST A LOWLY PART-TIME EMPLOYEE.
ONE OF MY JOBS IS TO WASH THE TAP BEFORE WE OPEN EACH NIGHT.
I TAKE APART THE TAP AND WASH EACH PART SEPARATELY.
IT'S HARDLY NECESSARY TO DO THAT EVERY SINGLE DAY...
...BUT IF IT WAS SOMEHOW MY FAULT THAT THE BEER TASTED LESS THAN IDEAL...
...WOULDN'T THAT BE UNFAIR TO THE PEOPLE WHO BREWED IT?
AND SINCE YOU CHOSE TO VISIT MY BAR, OUT OF ALL THE PLACES YOU COULD HAVE GONE...
...I CONSIDER IT MY DUTY TO MAKE SURE THAT YOU GO HOME HAPPY AND DRUNK.

C. botulinum

An Apology:
Last chapter, we wrote that "Itsuki will speak" this time. That was a lie.

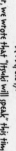

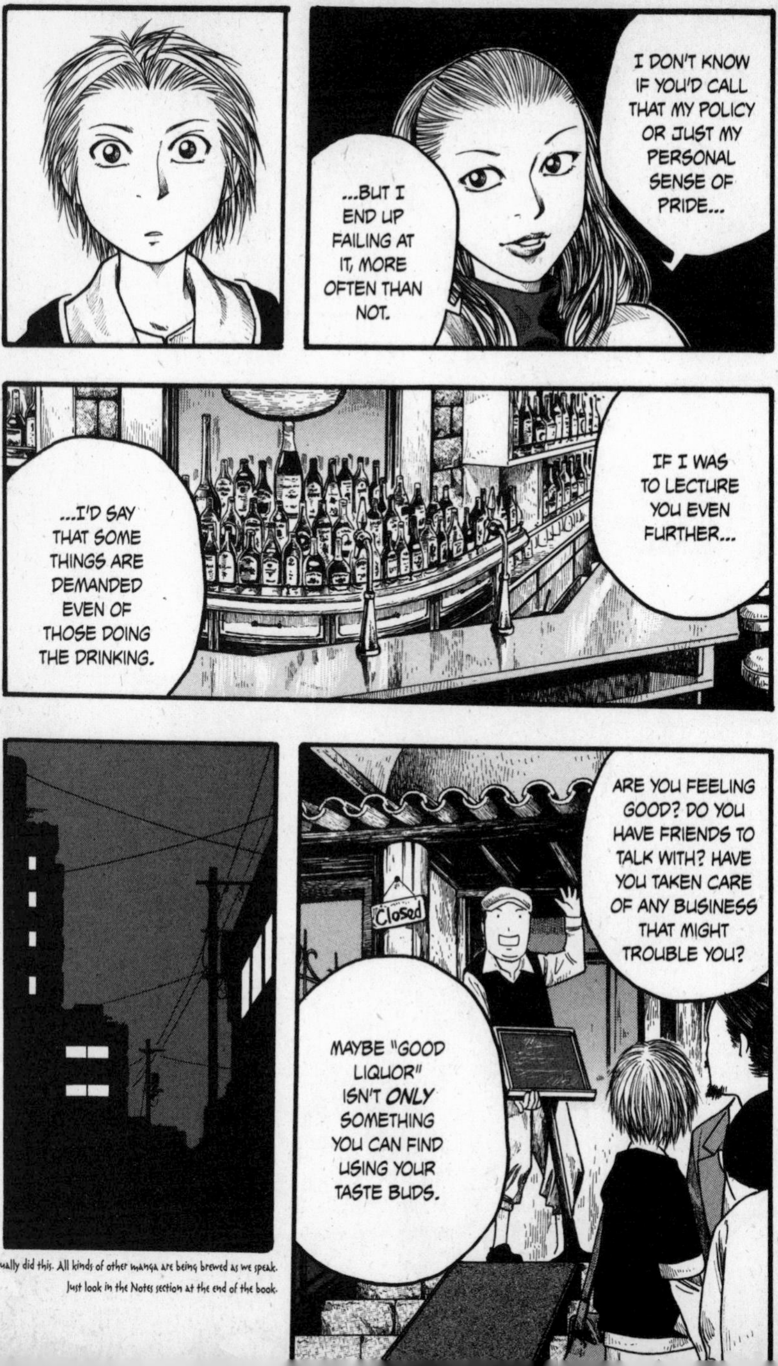
I DON'T KNOW IF YOU'D CALL THAT MY POLICY OR JUST MY PERSONAL SENSE OF PRIDE...
...BUT I END UP FAILING AT IT, MORE OFTEN THAN NOT.
IF I WAS TO LECTURE YOU EVEN FURTHER...
...I'D SAY THAT SOME THINGS ARE DEMANDED EVEN OF THOSE DOING THE DRINKING.
ARE YOU FEELING GOOD? DO YOU HAVE FRIENDS TO TALK WITH? HAVE YOU TAKEN CARE OF ANY BUSINESS THAT MIGHT TROUBLE YOU?
Closed
MAYBE "GOOD LIQUOR" ISN'T *ONLY* SOMETHING YOU CAN FIND USING YOUR TASTE BUDS.

Well, how was that experiment?

I'm feeling unsatisfied.

I want to brew other stuff, too.

Maybe we should brew Metro Police Keisuke--

No! They'll yell at us!

Anyways, we're gonna do stuff outside of Moyasimon soon.

We actually did this. All kinds of other manga are being brewed as we speak. Just look in the Notes section at the end of the book.

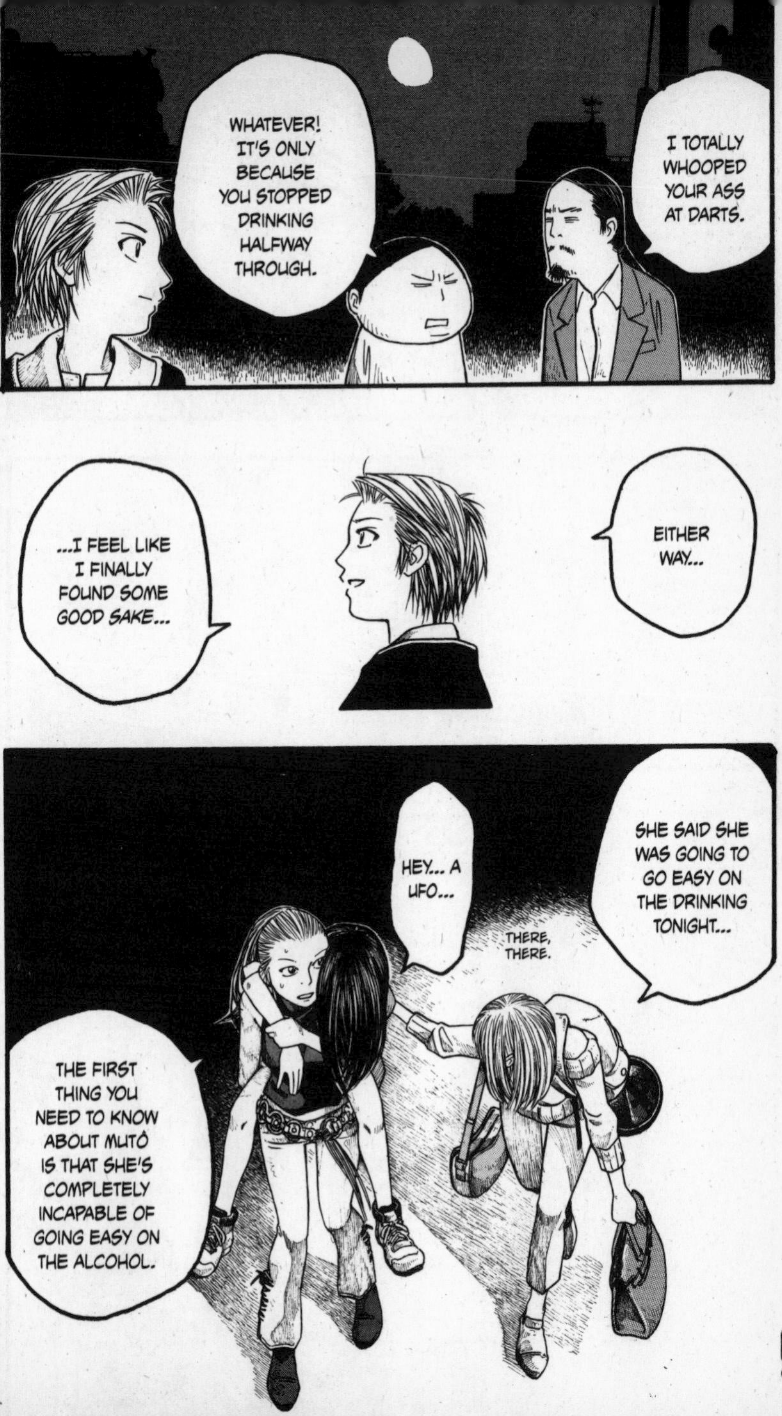
I TOTALLY WHOOPED YOUR ASS AT DARTS.
WHATEVER! IT'S ONLY BECAUSE YOU STOPPED DRINKING HALFWAY THROUGH.
EITHER WAY...
...I FEEL LIKE I FINALLY FOUND SOME GOOD SAKE...
SHE SAID SHE WAS GOING TO GO EASY ON THE DRINKING TONIGHT...
HEY... A UFO...
THERE, THERE.
THE FIRST THING YOU NEED TO KNOW ABOUT MUTÔ IS THAT SHE'S COMPLETELY INCAPABLE OF GOING EASY ON THE ALCOHOL.

In Chapter 17, we're finally going to take over the main story.

16 END

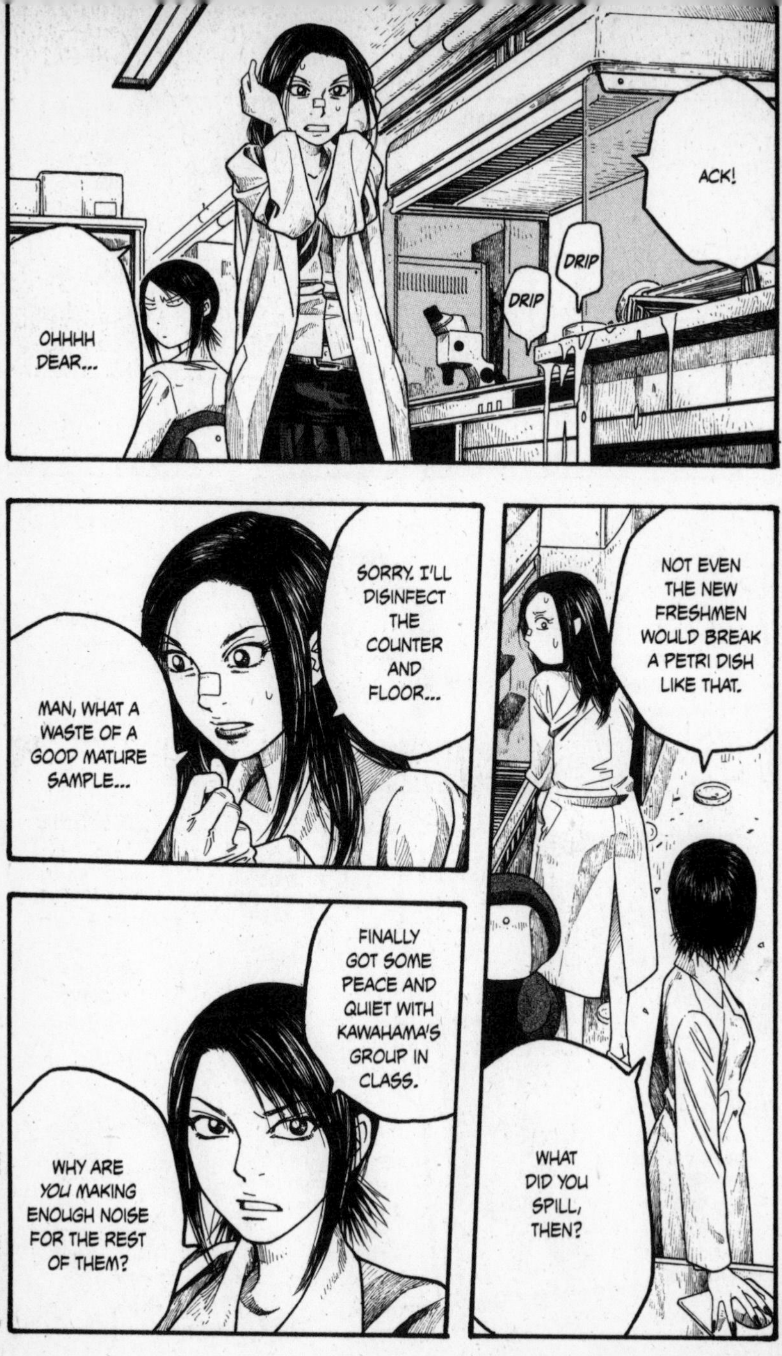
ACK!
DRIP
DRIP
OHHHH DEAR...
NOT EVEN THE NEW FRESHMEN WOULD BREAK A PETRI DISH LIKE THAT.
WHAT DID YOU SPILL, THEN?
SORRY. I'LL DISINFECT THE COUNTER AND FLOOR...
MAN, WHAT A WASTE OF A GOOD MATURE SAMPLE...
FINALLY GOT SOME PEACE AND QUIET WITH KAWAHAMA'S GROUP IN CLASS.
WHY ARE YOU MAKING ENOUGH NOISE FOR THE REST OF THEM?

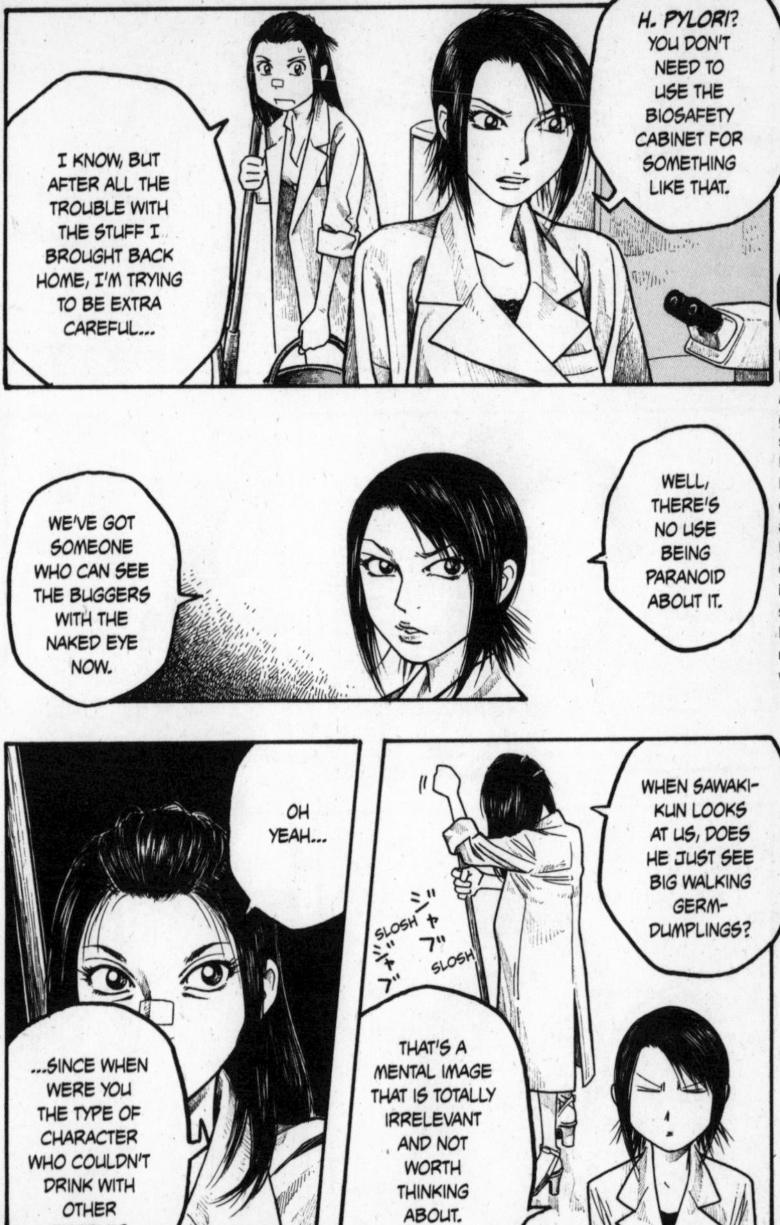
H. PYLORI? YOU DON'T NEED TO USE THE BIOSAFETY CABINET FOR SOMETHING LIKE THAT.
I KNOW, BUT AFTER ALL THE TROUBLE WITH THE STUFF I BROUGHT BACK HOME, I'M TRYING TO BE EXTRA CAREFUL...
WELL, THERE'S NO USE BEING PARANOID ABOUT IT.
WE'VE GOT SOMEONE WHO CAN SEE THE BUGGERS WITH THE NAKED EYE NOW.
WHEN SAWAKI-KUN LOOKS AT US, DOES HE JUST SEE BIG WALKING GERM-DUMPLINGS?
ジャブ
SLOSH
ジャブ
SLOSH
THAT'S A MENTAL IMAGE THAT IS TOTALLY IRRELEVANT AND NOT WORTH THINKING ABOUT.
OH YEAH...
...SINCE WHEN WERE YOU THE TYPE OF CHARACTER WHO COULDN'T DRINK WITH OTHER PEOPLE?

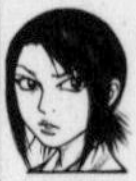

Haruka Hasegawa
Ag school grad student. Professor Itsuki's chief assistant. Recently changed in a very subtle way. Have you noticed what it is?

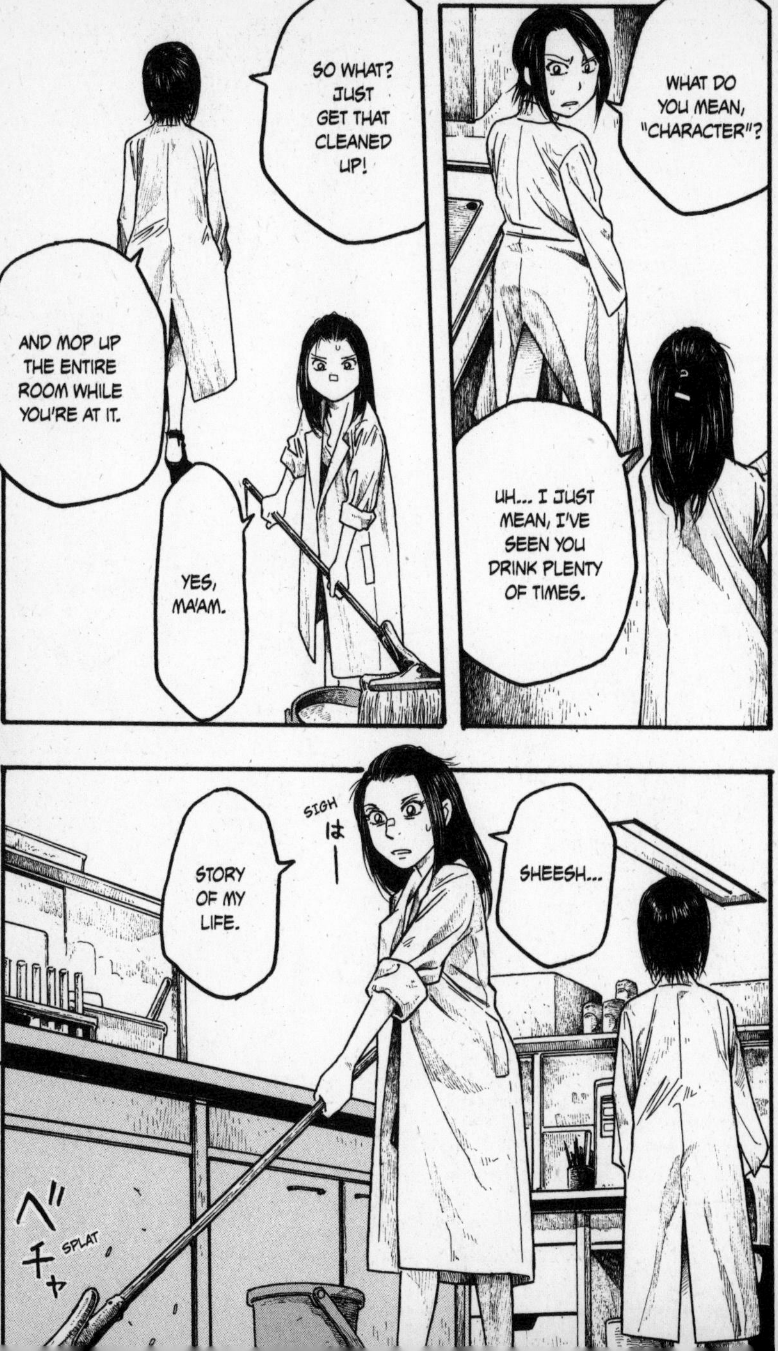
WHAT DO YOU MEAN, "CHARACTER"?
UH... I JUST MEAN, I'VE SEEN YOU DRINK PLENTY OF TIMES.
SO WHAT? JUST GET THAT CLEANED UP!
AND MOP UP THE ENTIRE ROOM WHILE YOU'RE AT IT.
YES, MA'AM.
SHEESH...
SIGH
はー
STORY OF MY LIFE.
ベチャ
SPLAT

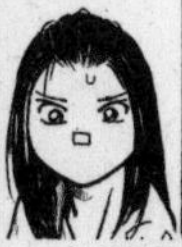

Aoi Mutô
The only seminar student of Itsuki's lab. Known as the "nose tape girl."

Chapter 17 - See Things from Their Perspective

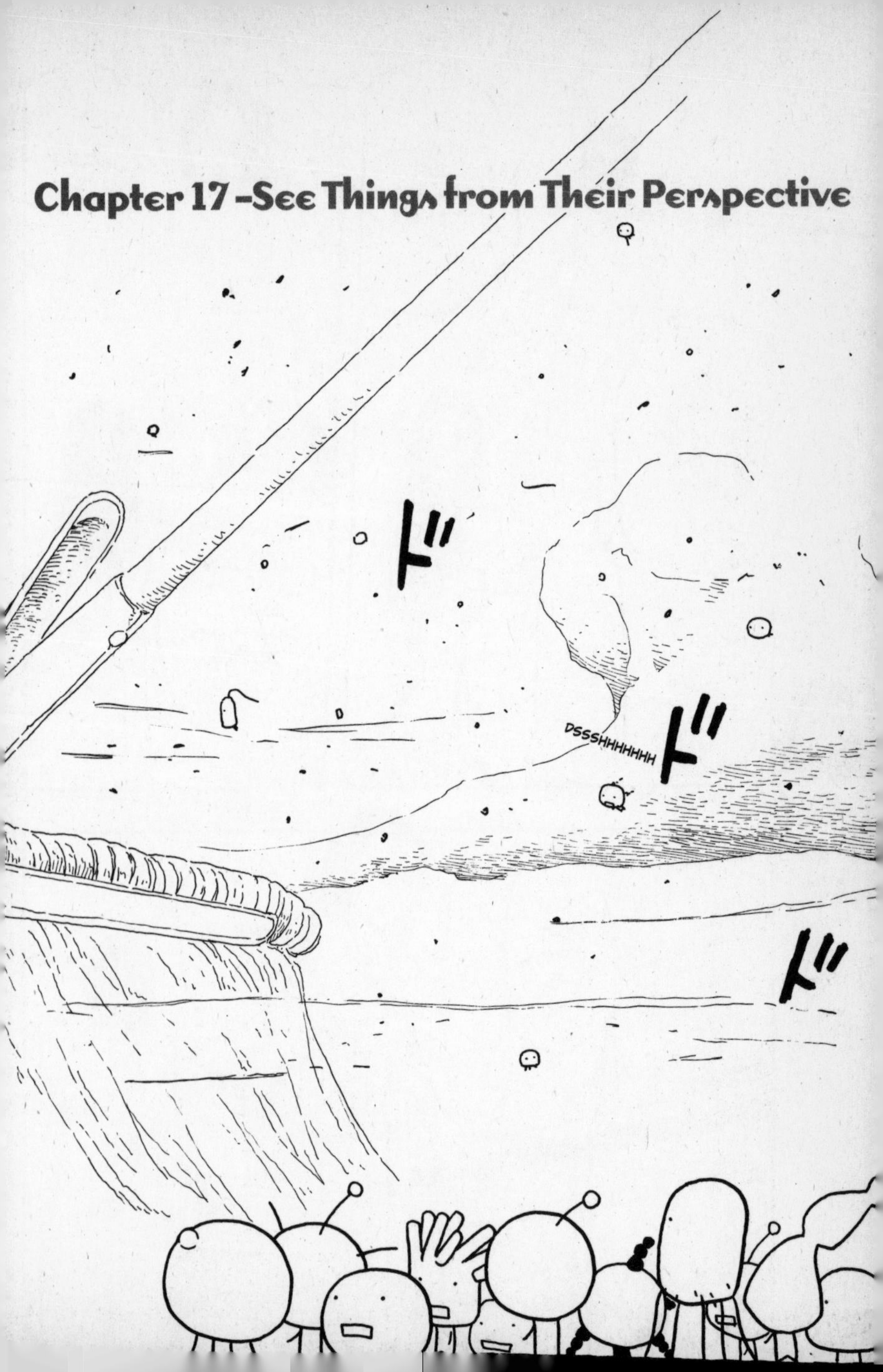
ド
DSSSHHHHHHH
ド
ド

I saw Volume 1 on the microbiology shelf at the education section in the bookstore, even though this book is Manga.

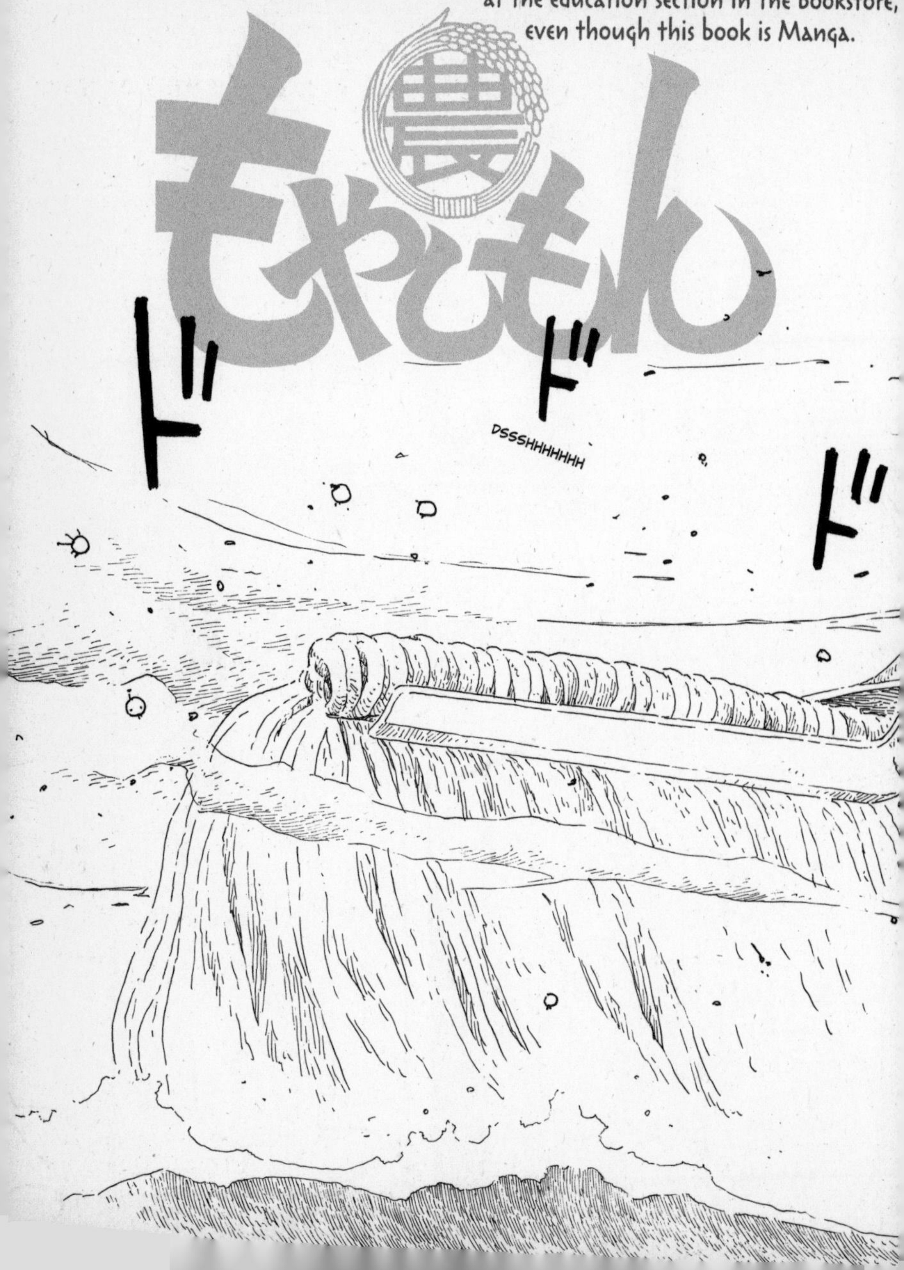
もやしもん
ド
ド
ド
DSSSHHHHHHH

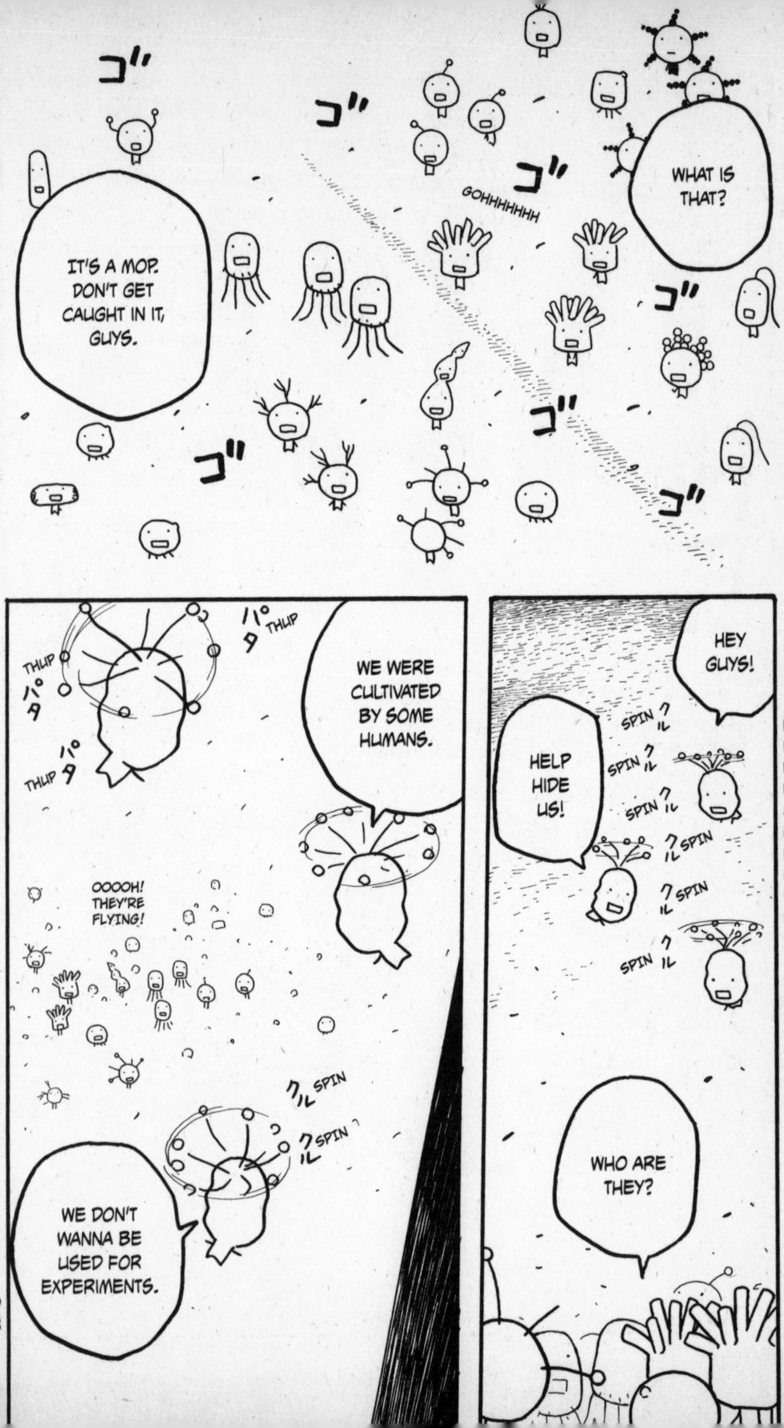
WHAT IS THAT?
ゴ"
GOHHHHHHH
IT'S A MOP. DON'T GET CAUGHT IN IT, GUYS.
HEY GUYS!
SPIN クル
HELP HIDE US!
WHO ARE THEY?
パタ THUP
WE WERE CULTIVATED BY SOME HUMANS.
OOOOH! THEY'RE FLYING!
クル SPIN
WE DON'T WANNA BE USED FOR EXPERIMENTS.

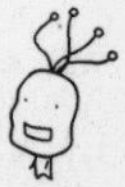

H. pylori
It twists three times to the right and uses its long flagella to move throughout the stomach. It's perfectly fine in stomach acid and can lead to ulcers.

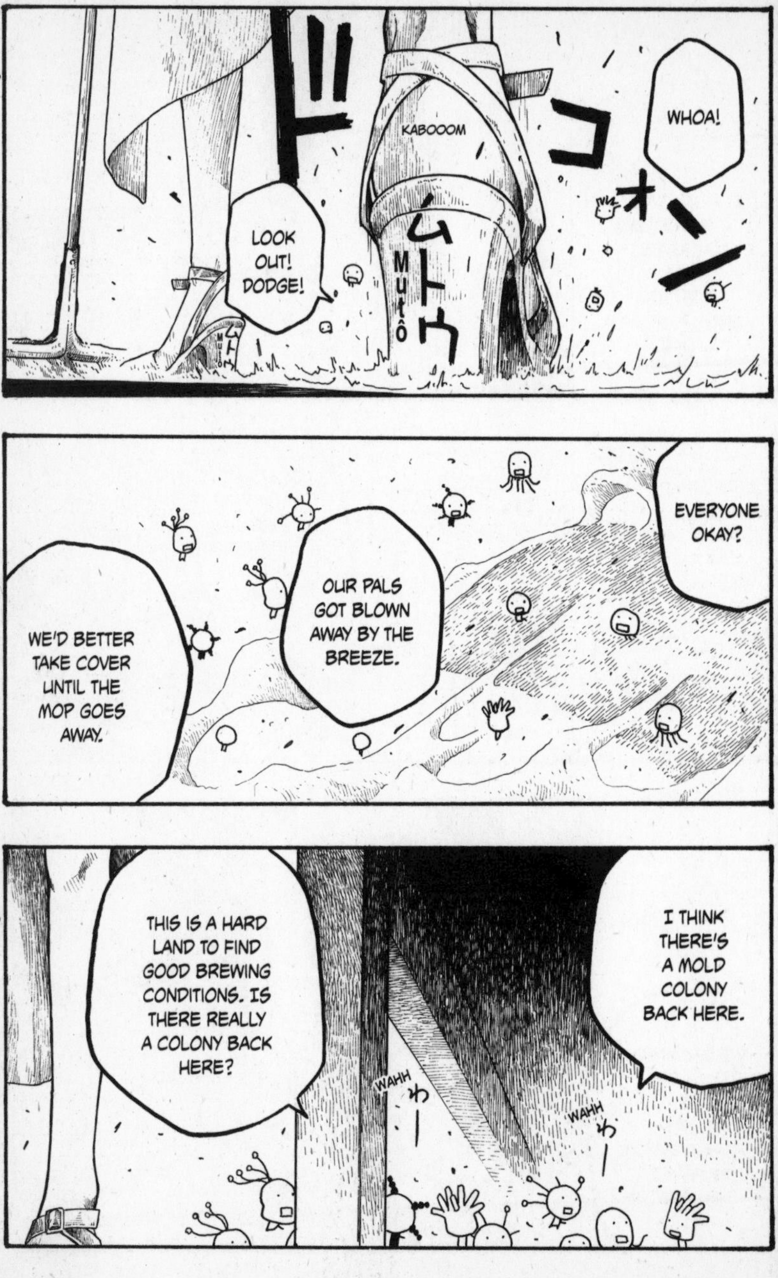
WHOA!
ドコォン
KABOOOM
ムトウ
Mutô
LOOK OUT! DODGE!
Mutô
EVERYONE OKAY?
OUR PALS GOT BLOWN AWAY BY THE BREEZE.
WE'D BETTER TAKE COVER UNTIL THE MOP GOES AWAY.
I THINK THERE'S A MOLD COLONY BACK HERE.
わー
WAHH
わー
WAHH
THIS IS A HARD LAND TO FIND GOOD BREWING CONDITIONS. IS THERE REALLY A COLONY BACK HERE?

A. niger
Widely used in industrial work for its ability to create enzymes and acids, but can also be considered a pest for its robust reproduction.

S. cerevisiae
Eats sugar and makes alcohol. Is used in cosmetic products lately.

A. fumigatus
Infiltrates the lungs of people with weak defenses. Can be a cause of allergies. A good guy at heart.

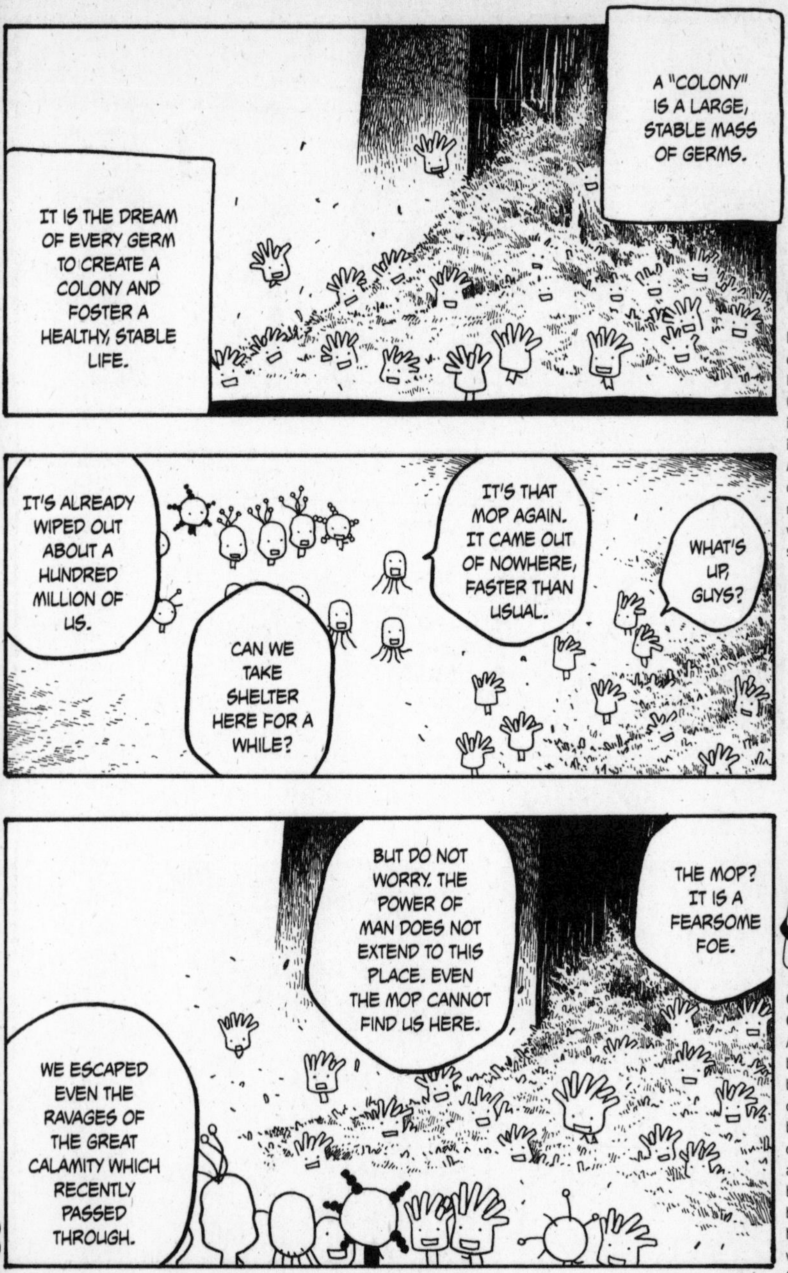
A "COLONY" IS A LARGE, STABLE MASS OF GERMS.
IT IS THE DREAM OF EVERY GERM TO CREATE A COLONY AND FOSTER A HEALTHY, STABLE LIFE.
WHAT'S UP, GUYS?
IT'S THAT MOP AGAIN. IT CAME OUT OF NOWHERE, FASTER THAN USUAL.
IT'S ALREADY WIPED OUT ABOUT A HUNDRED MILLION OF US.
CAN WE TAKE SHELTER HERE FOR A WHILE?
THE MOP? IT IS A FEARSOME FOE.
BUT DO NOT WORRY. THE POWER OF MAN DOES NOT EXTEND TO THIS PLACE. EVEN THE MOP CANNOT FIND US HERE.
WE ESCAPED EVEN THE RAVAGES OF THE GREAT CALAMITY WHICH RECENTLY PASSED THROUGH.

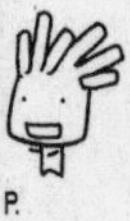

P. **chrysogenum**
Blue mold. One of the ingredients in antibiotics. Appears during the rainy season, where it is shunned.

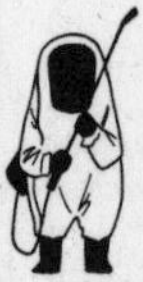

Great Calamity
Apparently this refers to the disinfection that occurred after Mutô brought back all those viruses in Chapter 14.

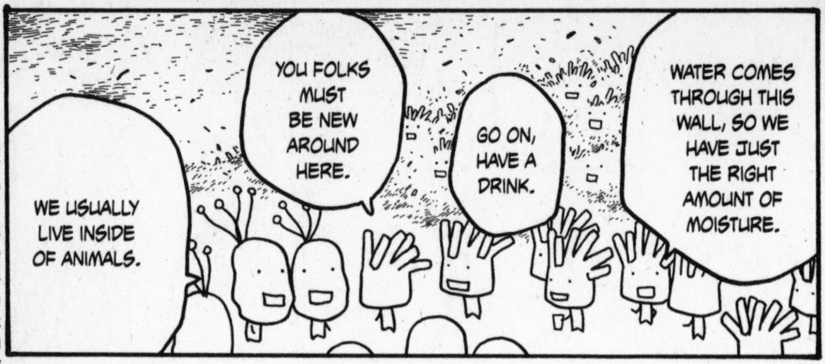
WATER COMES THROUGH THIS WALL, SO WE HAVE JUST THE RIGHT AMOUNT OF MOISTURE.
GO ON, HAVE A DRINK.
YOU FOLKS MUST BE NEW AROUND HERE.
WE USUALLY LIVE INSIDE OF ANIMALS.

R. javanicus Extremely quick to reproduce. Its genus name **Rhizopus** comes from the Greek for "root and foot."

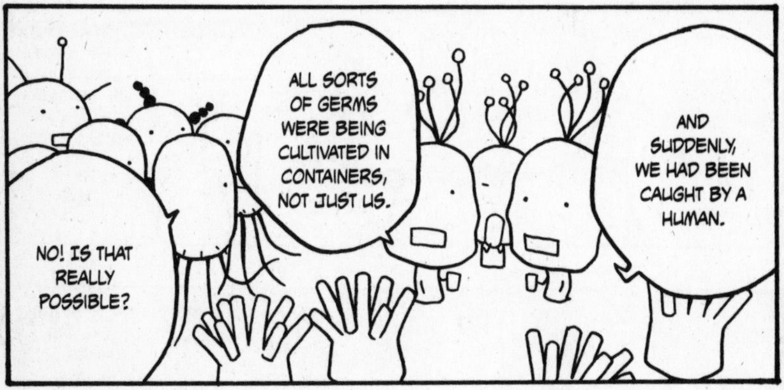
AND SUDDENLY, WE HAD BEEN CAUGHT BY A HUMAN.
ALL SORTS OF GERMS WERE BEING CULTIVATED IN CONTAINERS, NOT JUST US.
NO! IS THAT REALLY POSSIBLE?

E. coli Lives in sinks and other watery places.

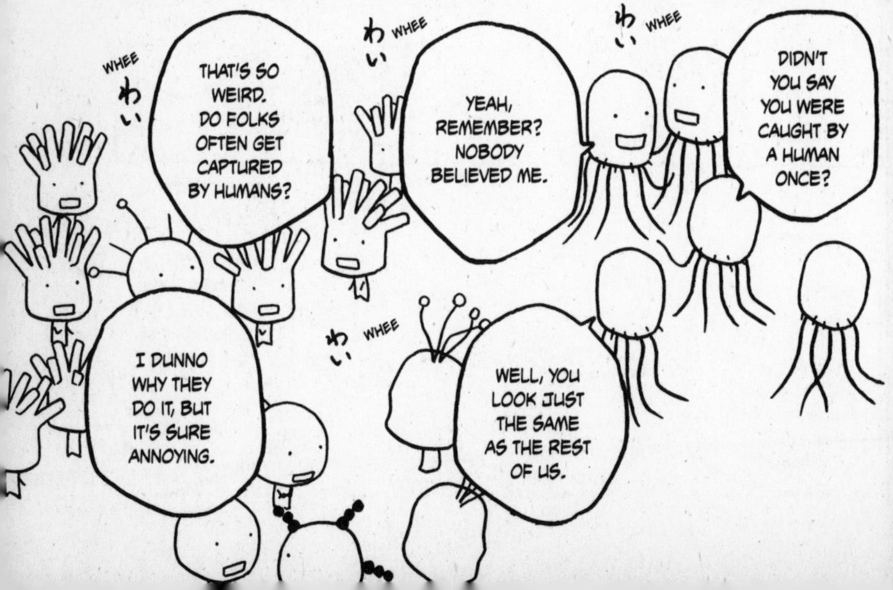
DIDN'T YOU SAY YOU WERE CAUGHT BY A HUMAN ONCE?
わい WHEE
YEAH, REMEMBER? NOBODY BELIEVED ME.
わい WHEE
THAT'S SO WEIRD. DO FOLKS OFTEN GET CAPTURED BY HUMANS?
わい WHEE
WELL, YOU LOOK JUST THE SAME AS THE REST OF US.
わい WHEE
I DUNNO WHY THEY DO IT, BUT IT'S SURE ANNOYING.

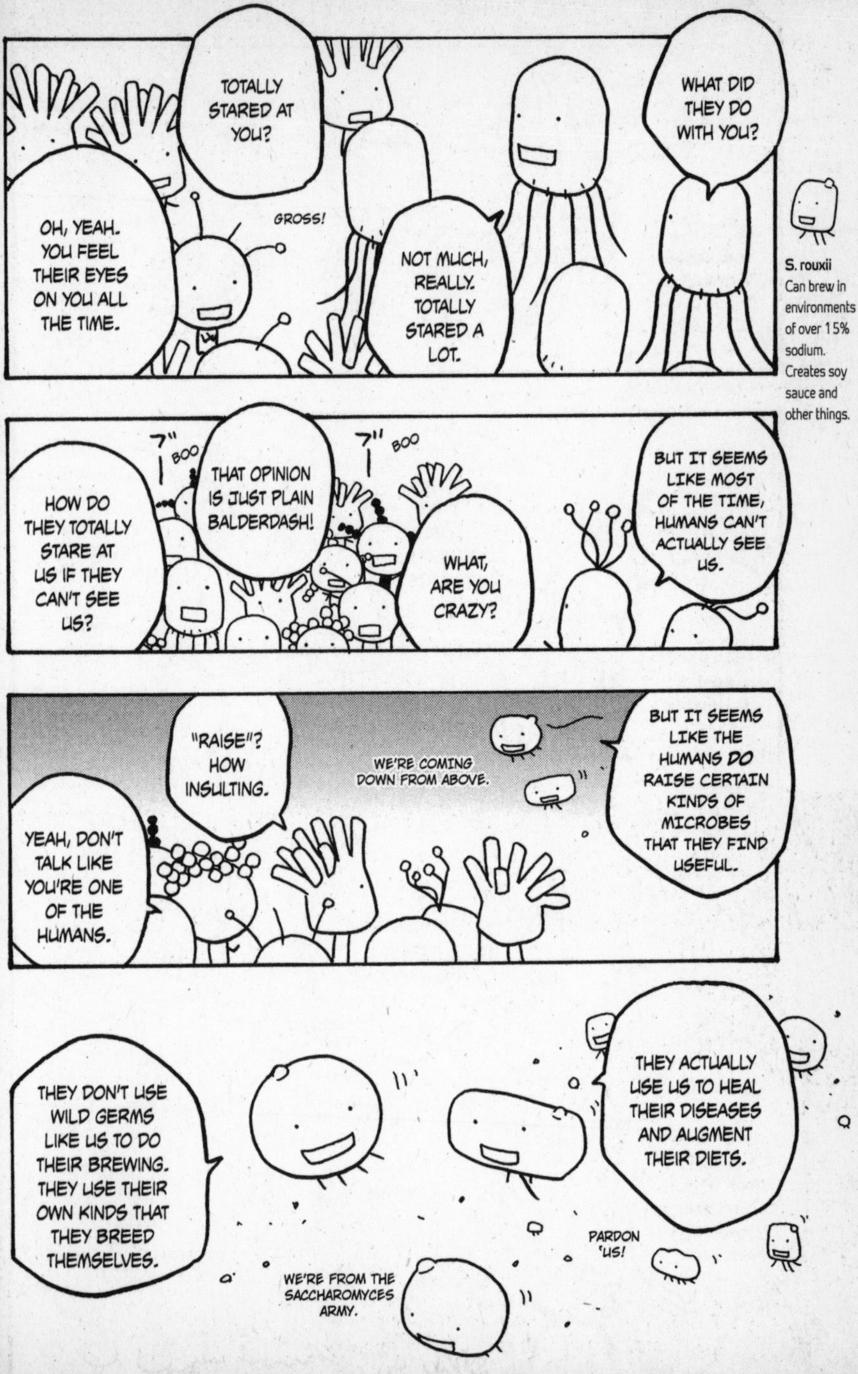
WHAT DID THEY DO WITH YOU?
NOT MUCH, REALLY. TOTALLY STARED A LOT.
TOTALLY STARED AT YOU?
GROSS!
OH, YEAH. YOU FEEL THEIR EYES ON YOU ALL THE TIME.
BUT IT SEEMS LIKE MOST OF THE TIME, HUMANS CAN'T ACTUALLY SEE US.
BOO
WHAT, ARE YOU CRAZY?
THAT OPINION IS JUST PLAIN BALDERDASH!
BOO
HOW DO THEY TOTALLY STARE AT US IF THEY CAN'T SEE US?
BUT IT SEEMS LIKE THE HUMANS *DO* RAISE CERTAIN KINDS OF MICROBES THAT THEY FIND USEFUL.
WE'RE COMING DOWN FROM ABOVE.
"RAISE"? HOW INSULTING.
YEAH, DON'T TALK LIKE YOU'RE ONE OF THE HUMANS.
THEY ACTUALLY USE US TO HEAL THEIR DISEASES AND AUGMENT THEIR DIETS.
PARDON 'US!
WE'RE FROM THE SACCHAROMYCES ARMY.
THEY DON'T USE WILD GERMS LIKE US TO DO THEIR BREWING. THEY USE THEIR OWN KINDS THAT THEY BREED THEMSELVES.

S. rouxii
Can brew in environments of over 15% sodium. Creates soy sauce and other things.

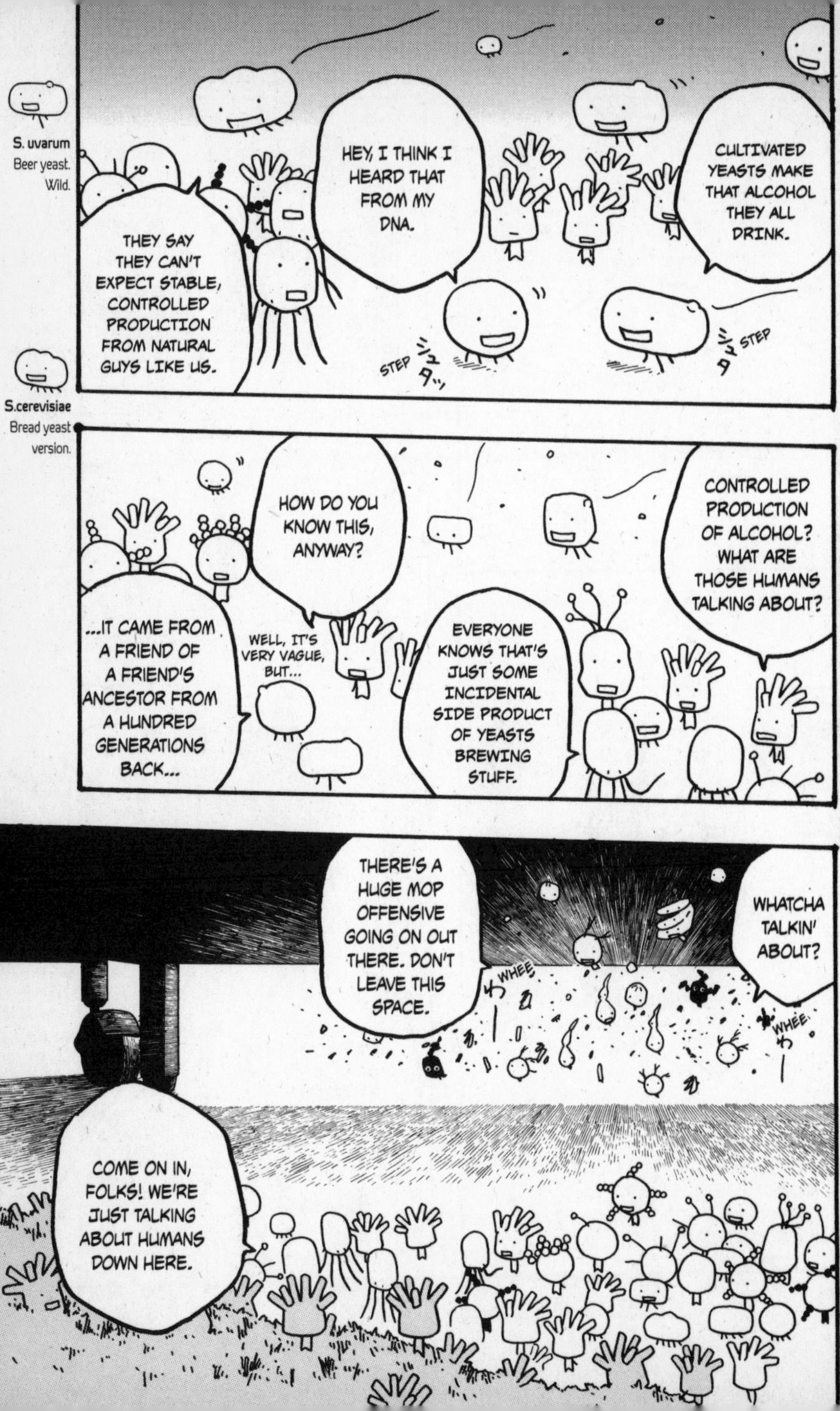
CULTIVATED YEASTS MAKE THAT ALCOHOL THEY ALL DRINK.
HEY, I THINK I HEARD THAT FROM MY DNA.
THEY SAY THEY CAN'T EXPECT STABLE, CONTROLLED PRODUCTION FROM NATURAL GUYS LIKE US.
STEP
STEP
S. uvarum
Beer yeast. Wild.
S.cerevisiae
Bread yeast version.
CONTROLLED PRODUCTION OF ALCOHOL? WHAT ARE THOSE HUMANS TALKING ABOUT?
EVERYONE KNOWS THAT'S JUST SOME INCIDENTAL SIDE PRODUCT OF YEASTS BREWING STUFF.
HOW DO YOU KNOW THIS, ANYWAY?
WELL, IT'S VERY VAGUE, BUT...
...IT CAME FROM A FRIEND OF A FRIEND'S ANCESTOR FROM A HUNDRED GENERATIONS BACK...
WHATCHA TALKIN' ABOUT?
THERE'S A HUGE MOP OFFENSIVE GOING ON OUT THERE. DON'T LEAVE THIS SPACE.
WHEE
WHEE
COME ON IN, FOLKS! WE'RE JUST TALKING ABOUT HUMANS DOWN HERE.

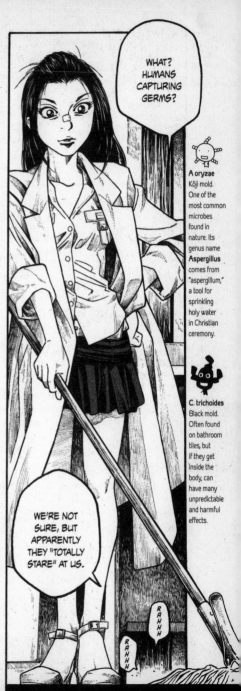

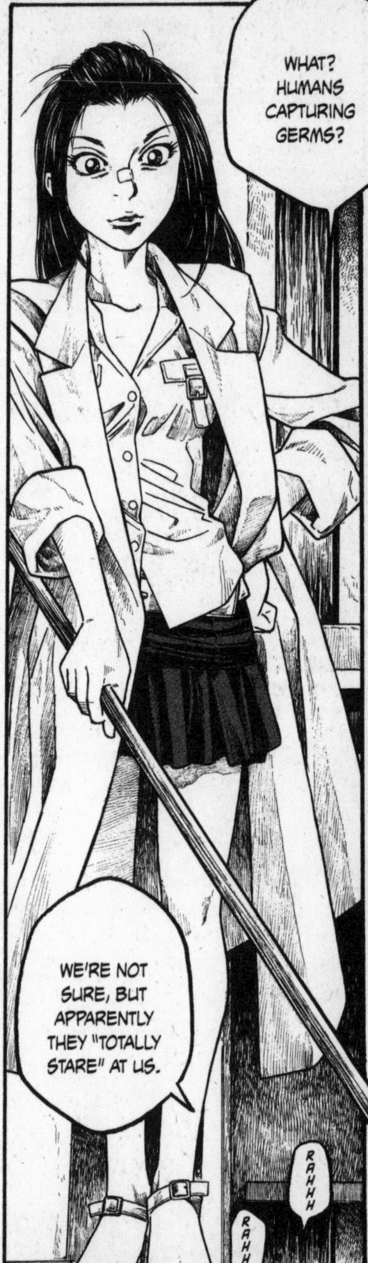
WHAT? HUMANS CAPTURING GERMS?
WE'RE NOT SURE, BUT APPARENTLY THEY "TOTALLY STARE" AT US.
RAHHH
RAHHH

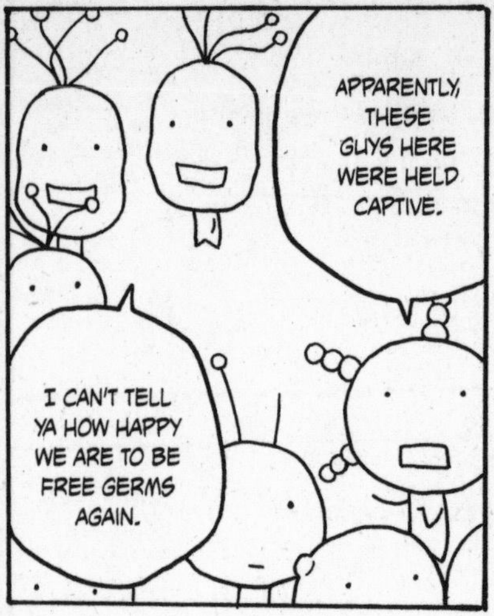
APPARENTLY, THESE GUYS HERE WERE HELD CAPTIVE.
I CAN'T TELL YA HOW HAPPY WE ARE TO BE FREE GERMS AGAIN.

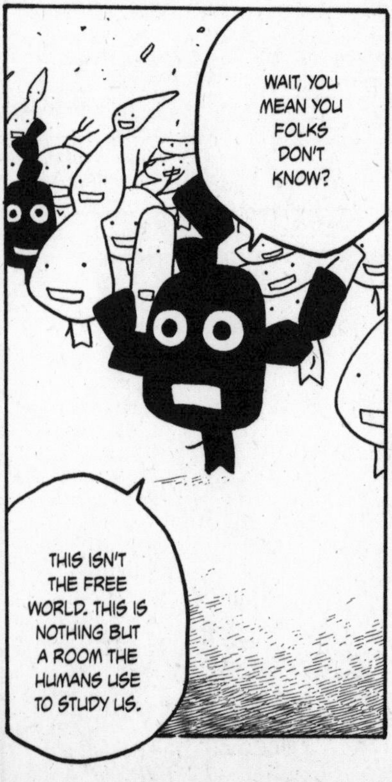
WAIT, YOU MEAN YOU FOLKS DON'T KNOW?
THIS ISN'T THE FREE WORLD. THIS IS NOTHING BUT A ROOM THE HUMANS USE TO STUDY US.

A oryzae
Kôji mold. One of the most common microbes found in nature. Its genus name **Aspergillus** comes from "aspergillum," a tool for sprinkling holy water in Christian ceremony.

C. trichoides
Black mold. Often found on bathroom tiles, but if they get inside the body, can have many unpredictable and harmful effects.

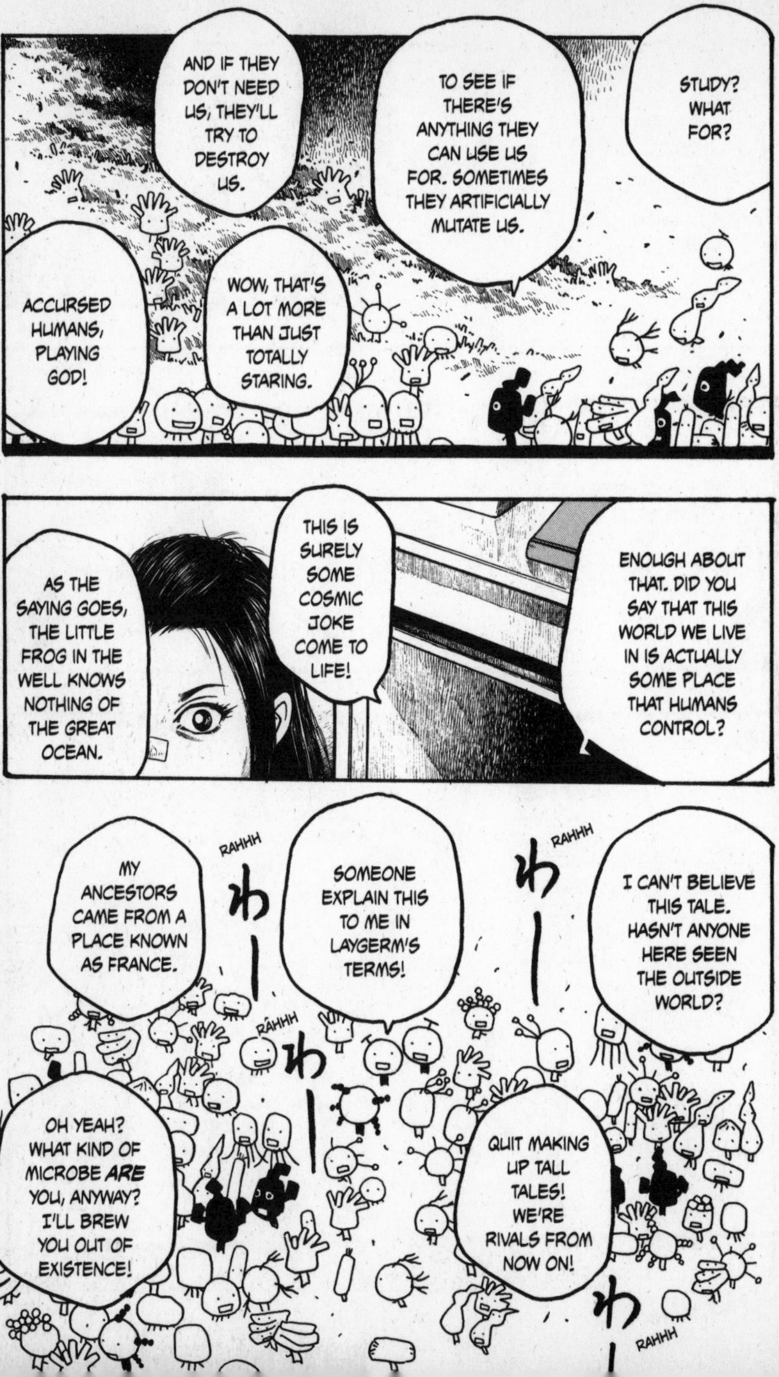
STUDY? WHAT FOR?
TO SEE IF THERE'S ANYTHING THEY CAN USE US FOR. SOMETIMES THEY ARTIFICIALLY MUTATE US.
AND IF THEY DON'T NEED US, THEY'LL TRY TO DESTROY US.
WOW, THAT'S A LOT MORE THAN JUST TOTALLY STARING.
ACCURSED HUMANS, PLAYING GOD!
ENOUGH ABOUT THAT. DID YOU SAY THAT THIS WORLD WE LIVE IN IS ACTUALLY SOME PLACE THAT HUMANS CONTROL?
THIS IS SURELY SOME COSMIC JOKE COME TO LIFE!
AS THE SAYING GOES, THE LITTLE FROG IN THE WELL KNOWS NOTHING OF THE GREAT OCEAN.
I CAN'T BELIEVE THIS TALE. HASN'T ANYONE HERE SEEN THE OUTSIDE WORLD?
わー RAHHH
SOMEONE EXPLAIN THIS TO ME IN LAYGERM'S TERMS!
わー RAHHH
MY ANCESTORS CAME FROM A PLACE KNOWN AS FRANCE.
わー RAHHH
QUIT MAKING UP TALL TALES! WE'RE RIVALS FROM NOW ON!
わー RAHHH
OH YEAH? WHAT KIND OF MICROBE *ARE* YOU, ANYWAY? I'LL BREW YOU OUT OF EXISTENCE!

T. koningii Breaks down wood and paper, and helps cause asthma. Sometimes the dusty stuff you see on rugs and in air-conditioning filters are them.

B. cinerea They've fallen on hard times in this scene, but these proud fellows normally cause "noble rot" in grapes, which makes fancy **pourriture noble** wine. Mutô brought them from France.

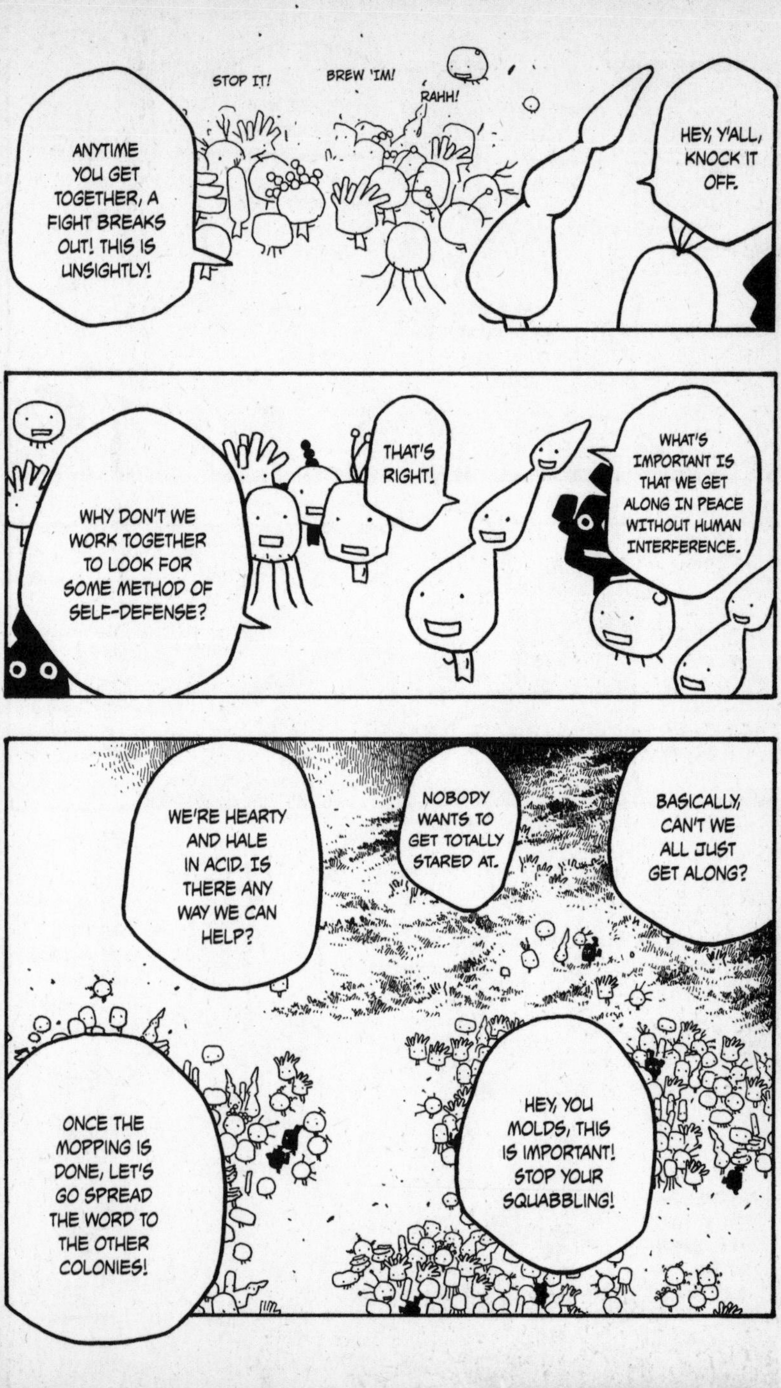
HEY, Y'ALL, KNOCK IT OFF.
RAHH!
BREW 'IM!
STOP IT!
ANYTIME YOU GET TOGETHER, A FIGHT BREAKS OUT! THIS IS UNSIGHTLY!
WHAT'S IMPORTANT IS THAT WE GET ALONG IN PEACE WITHOUT HUMAN INTERFERENCE.
THAT'S RIGHT!
WHY DON'T WE WORK TOGETHER TO LOOK FOR SOME METHOD OF SELF-DEFENSE?
BASICALLY, CAN'T WE ALL JUST GET ALONG?
NOBODY WANTS TO GET TOTALLY STARED AT.
WE'RE HEARTY AND HALE IN ACID. IS THERE ANY WAY WE CAN HELP?
HEY, YOU MOLDS, THIS IS IMPORTANT! STOP YOUR SQUABBLING!
ONCE THE MOPPING IS DONE, LET'S GO SPREAD THE WORD TO THE OTHER COLONIES!

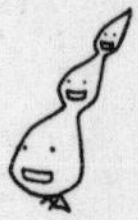

A. alternata
Found everywhere. If you don't take proper care of your contact lens case, they'll brew your lenses and fog them up. It pays to be clean!

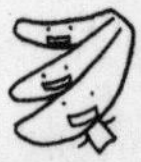

F. roseum
Found everywhere. Looks like a banana. So commonplace that even cleaning products that can't stop them are allowed to be labeled "anti-mold" by law.

T. mentagrophytes Commonly known as "ringworm." Found in watery places.

T. rubrum Athlete's foot. Along with **mentagrophytes,** it creates its own kingdom in the human body. Hasegawa is currently treating for this.

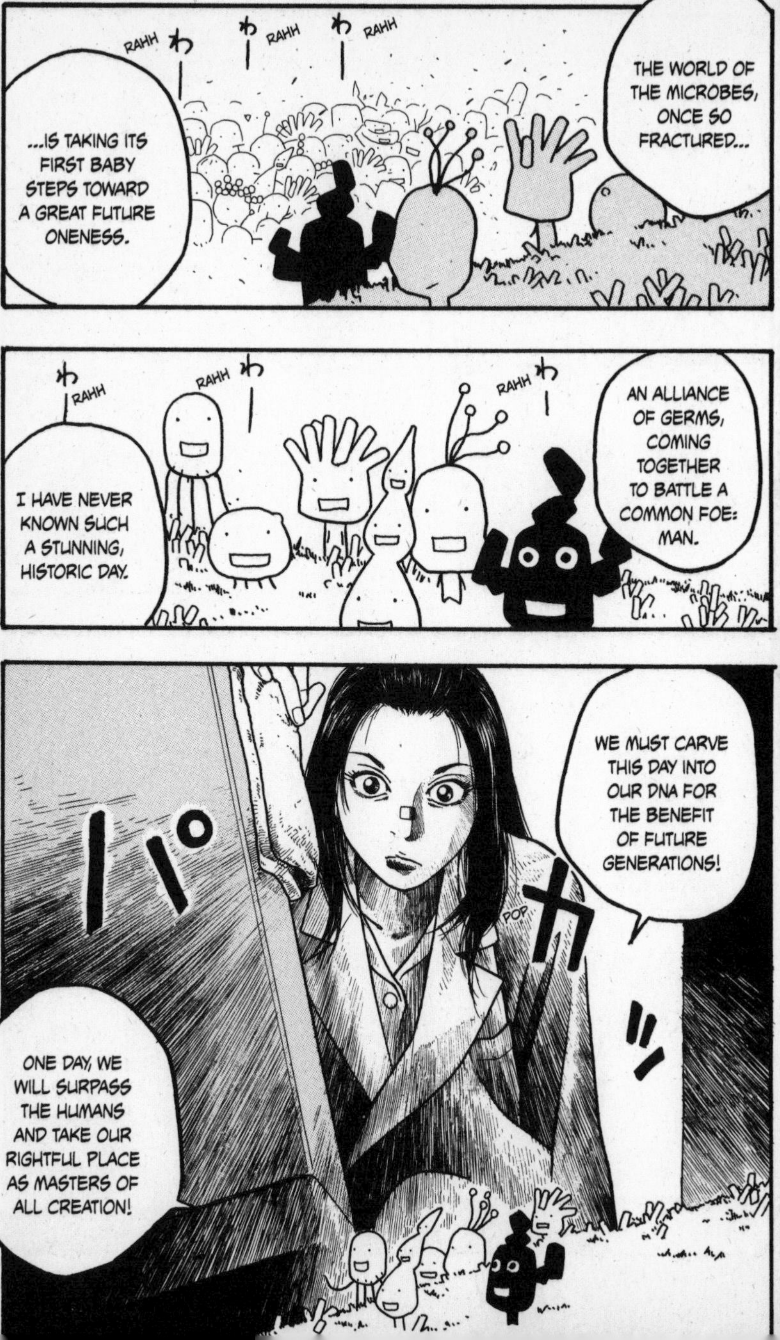
THE WORLD OF THE MICROBES, ONCE SO FRACTURED...
RAHH
RAHH
RAHH
...IS TAKING ITS FIRST BABY STEPS TOWARD A GREAT FUTURE ONENESS.
AN ALLIANCE OF GERMS, COMING TOGETHER TO BATTLE A COMMON FOE: MAN.
RAHH
RAHH
RAHH
I HAVE NEVER KNOWN SUCH A STUNNING, HISTORIC DAY.
WE MUST CARVE THIS DAY INTO OUR DNA FOR THE BENEFIT OF FUTURE GENERATIONS!
POP
ONE DAY, WE WILL SURPASS THE HUMANS AND TAKE OUR RIGHTFUL PLACE AS MASTERS OF ALL CREATION!

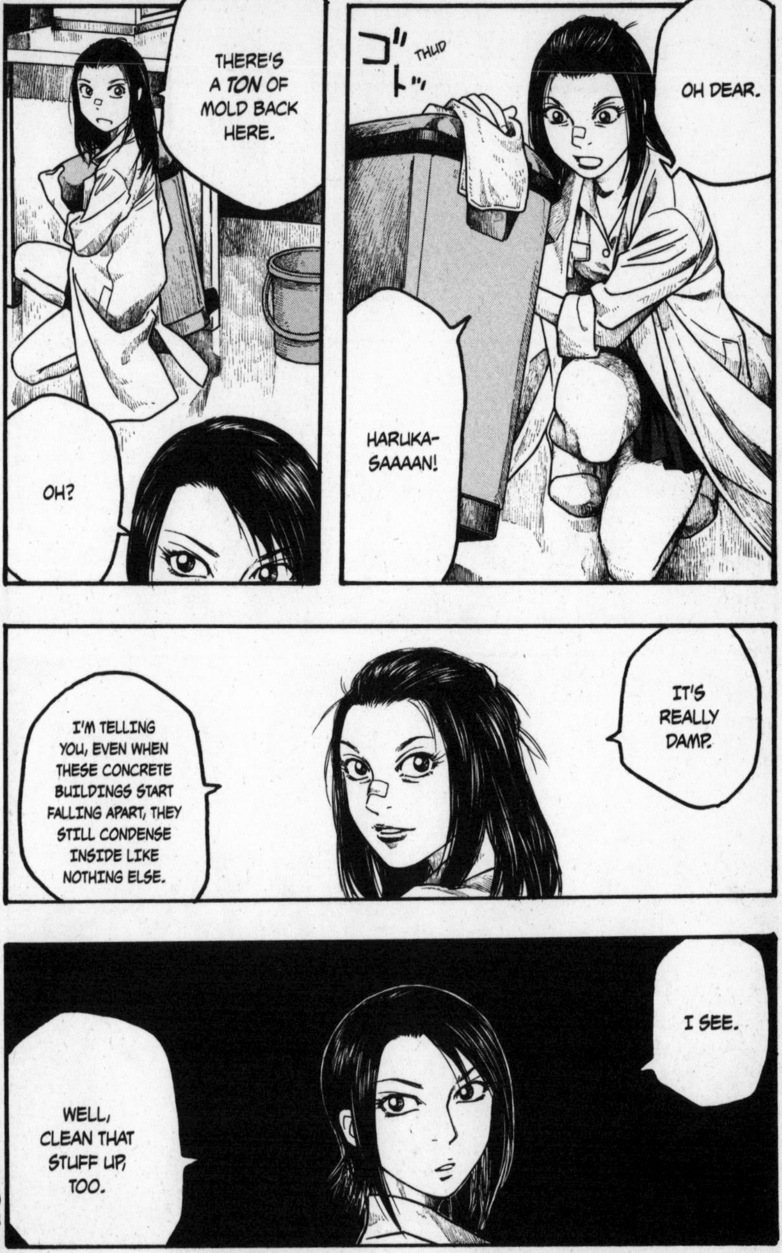
OH DEAR.
ゴトッ
THUD
HARUKA-SAAAAN!
THERE'S A TON OF MOLD BACK HERE.
OH?
IT'S REALLY DAMP.
I'M TELLING YOU, EVEN WHEN THESE CONCRETE BUILDINGS START FALLING APART, THEY STILL CONDENSE INSIDE LIKE NOTHING ELSE.
I SEE.
WELL, CLEAN THAT STUFF UP, TOO.

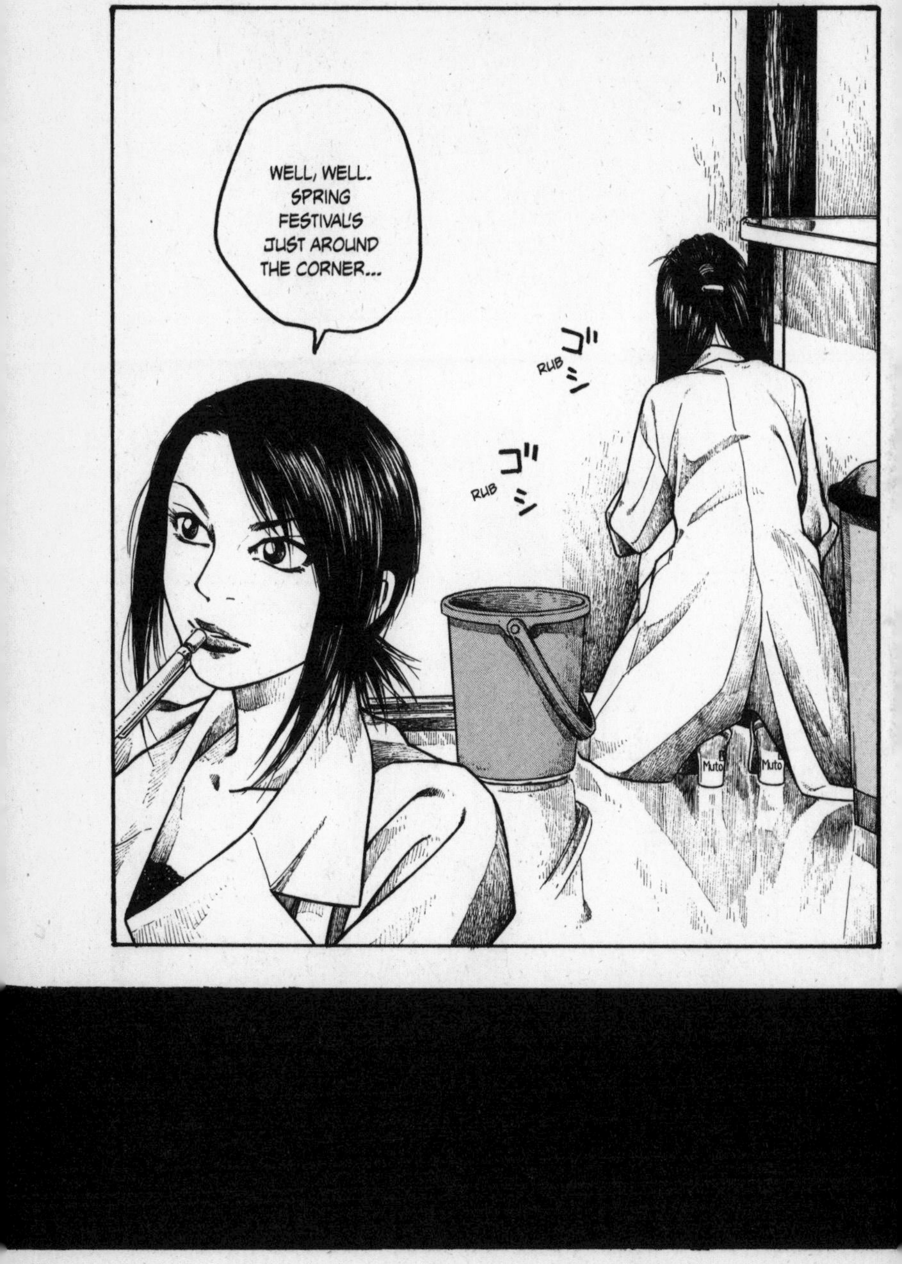
WELL, WELL. SPRING FESTIVAL'S JUST AROUND THE CORNER...
ゴシ
RUB
ゴシ
RUB

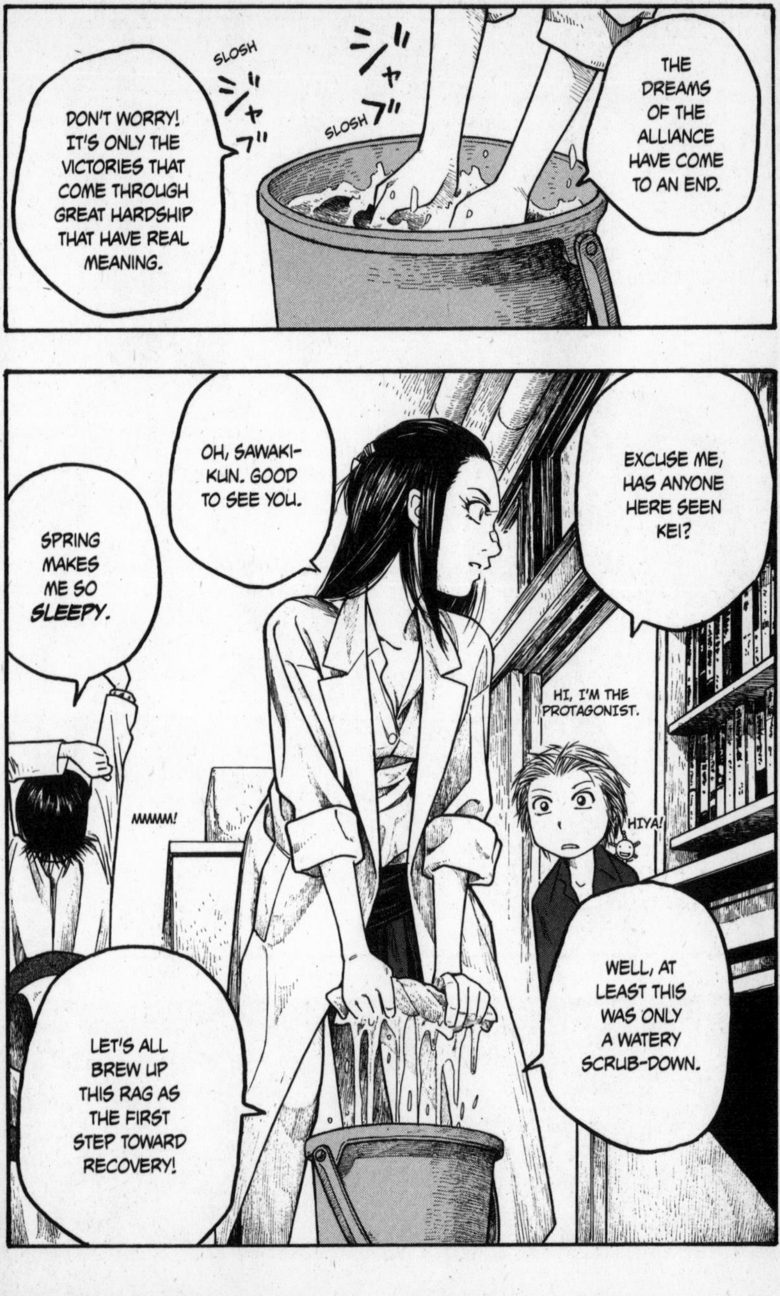
THE DREAMS OF THE ALLIANCE HAVE COME TO AN END.
ジャブ
SLOSH
ジャブ
SLOSH
DON'T WORRY! IT'S ONLY THE VICTORIES THAT COME THROUGH GREAT HARDSHIP THAT HAVE REAL MEANING.
EXCUSE ME, HAS ANYONE HERE SEEN KEI?
OH, SAWAKI-KUN. GOOD TO SEE YOU.
SPRING MAKES ME SO SLEEPY.
HI, I'M THE PROTAGONIST.
HIYA!
MMMM!
WELL, AT LEAST THIS WAS ONLY A WATERY SCRUB-DOWN.
LET'S ALL BREW UP THIS RAG AS THE FIRST STEP TOWARD RECOVERY!

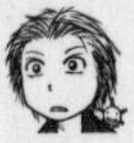

Tadayasu Sawaki
Protagonist. Umm, that's all.

This chapter was a true festival of microbes to celebrate the publication of the first book.

17 END

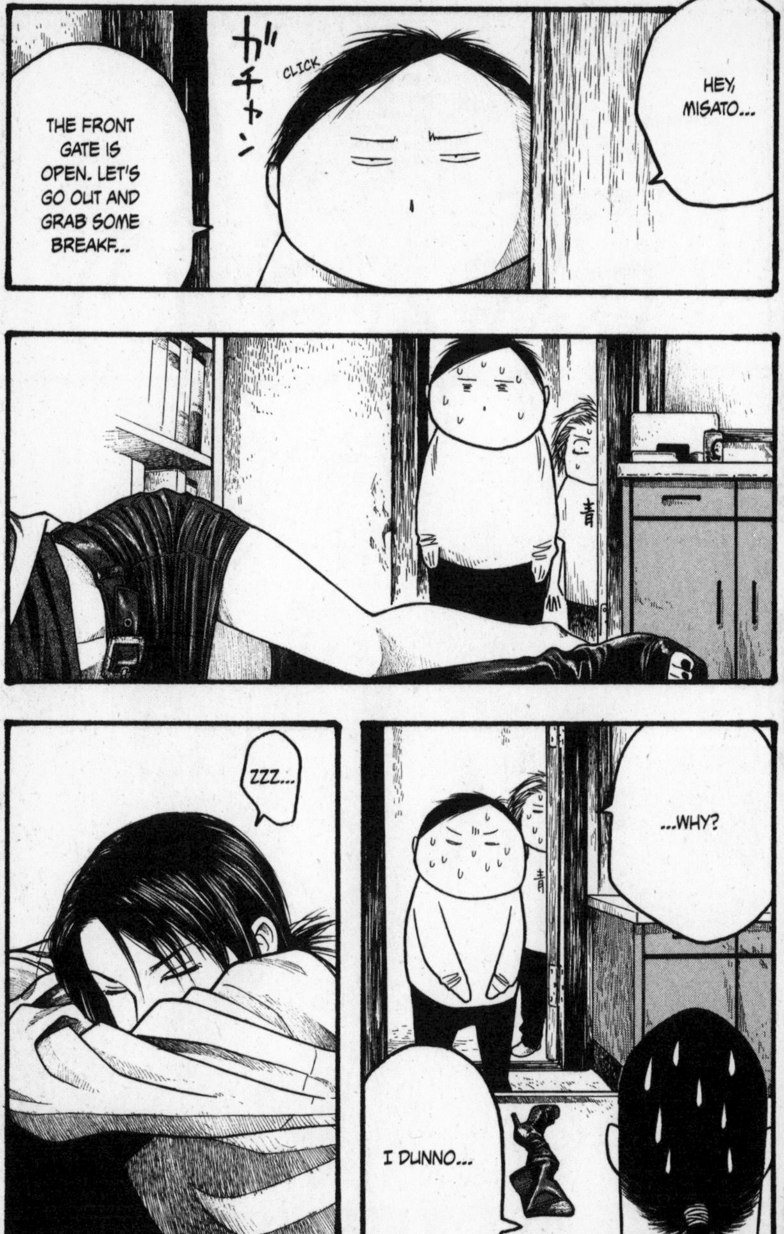
HEY, MISATO...
ガチャン
CLICK
THE FRONT GATE IS OPEN. LET'S GO OUT AND GRAB SOME BREAKF...
...WHY?
I DUNNO...
ZZZ...
青

There's lots of SP in this chapter.

Aww.

SP Short for "sales promotions."

I wish I could get some original cell-phone straps made in America, too.

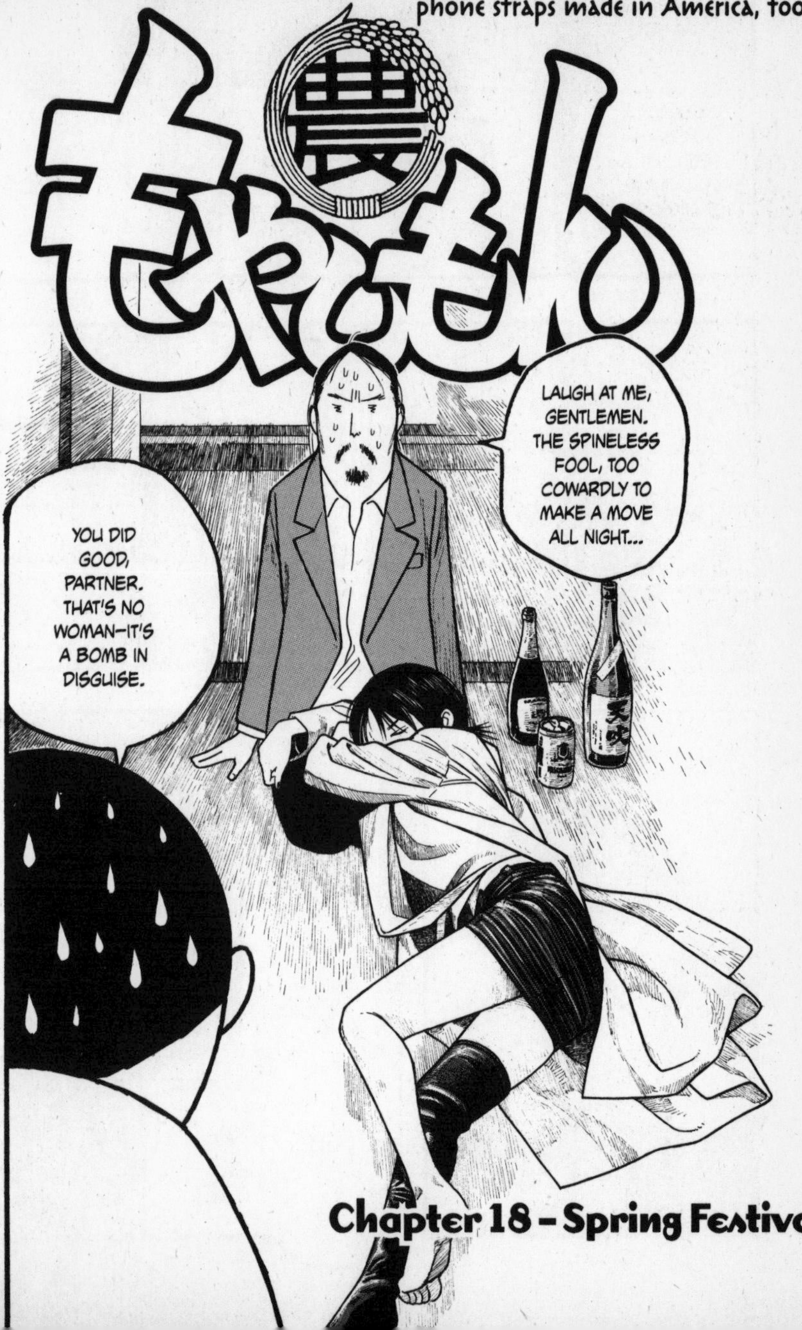

Chapter 18 – Spring Festival

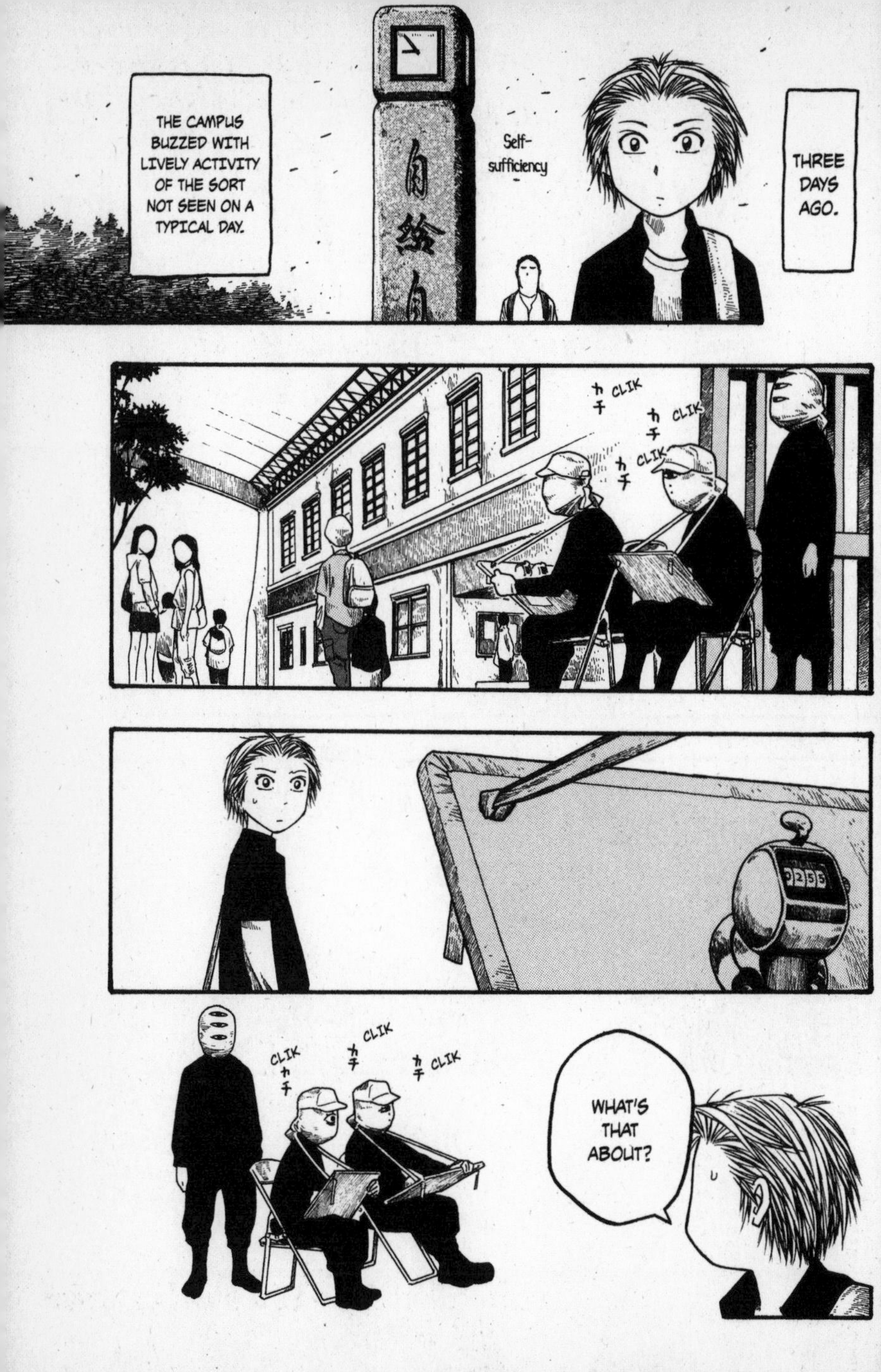
THREE DAYS AGO.
Self-sufficiency
THE CAMPUS BUZZED WITH LIVELY ACTIVITY OF THE SORT NOT SEEN ON A TYPICAL DAY.
カチ CLIK
カチ CLIK
カチ CLIK
WHAT'S THAT ABOUT?
カチ CLIK
カチ CLIK
カチ CLIK

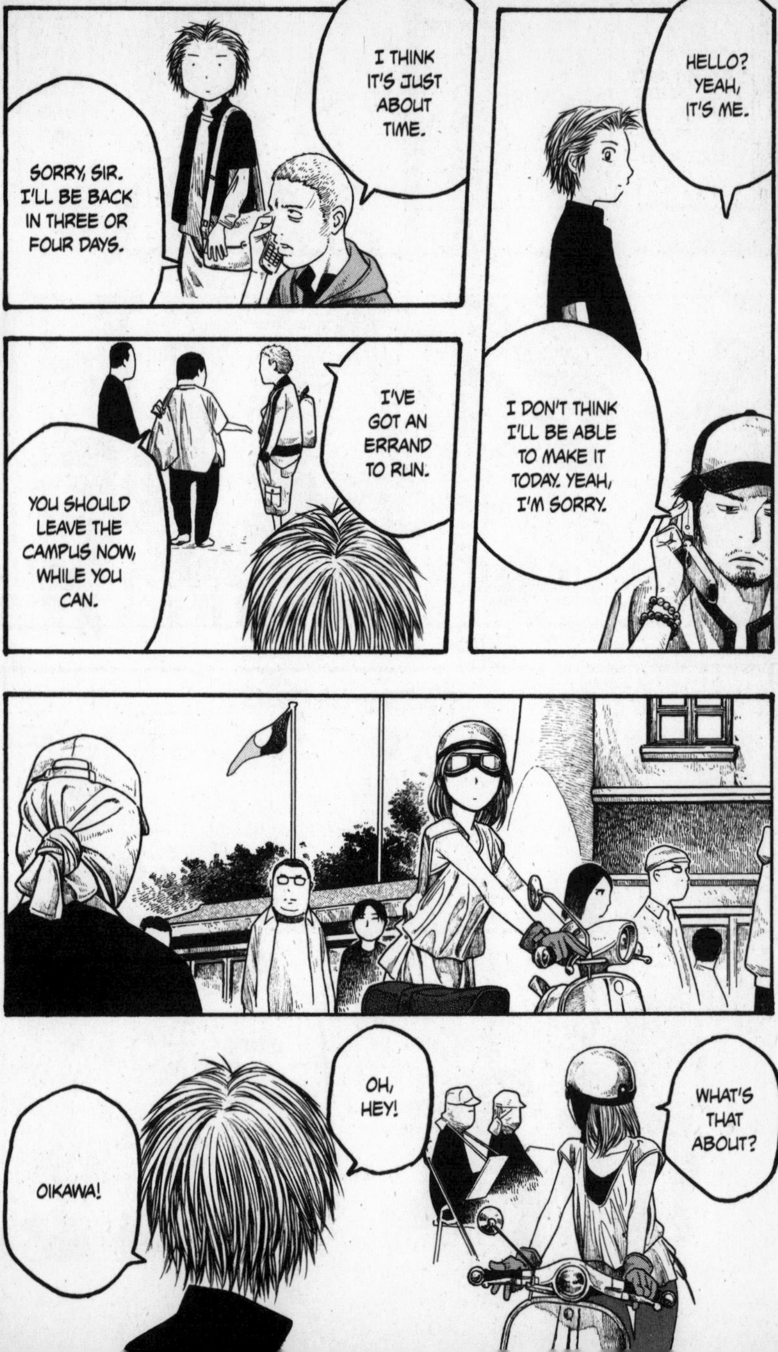
HELLO? YEAH, IT'S ME.
I DON'T THINK I'LL BE ABLE TO MAKE IT TODAY. YEAH, I'M SORRY.
I THINK IT'S JUST ABOUT TIME.
SORRY, SIR. I'LL BE BACK IN THREE OR FOUR DAYS.
I'VE GOT AN ERRAND TO RUN.
YOU SHOULD LEAVE THE CAMPUS NOW, WHILE YOU CAN.
WHAT'S THAT ABOUT?
OH, HEY!
OIKAWA!

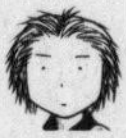

Tadayasu Sawaki
Protagonist. Can see germs with the naked eye. Easily swayed by other people.

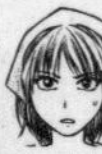

Hazuki Oikawa
Sawaki's classmate. The other day, the publishing office received a fan letter addressed to *her*. Thank you, S-san from Miyagi.

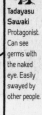

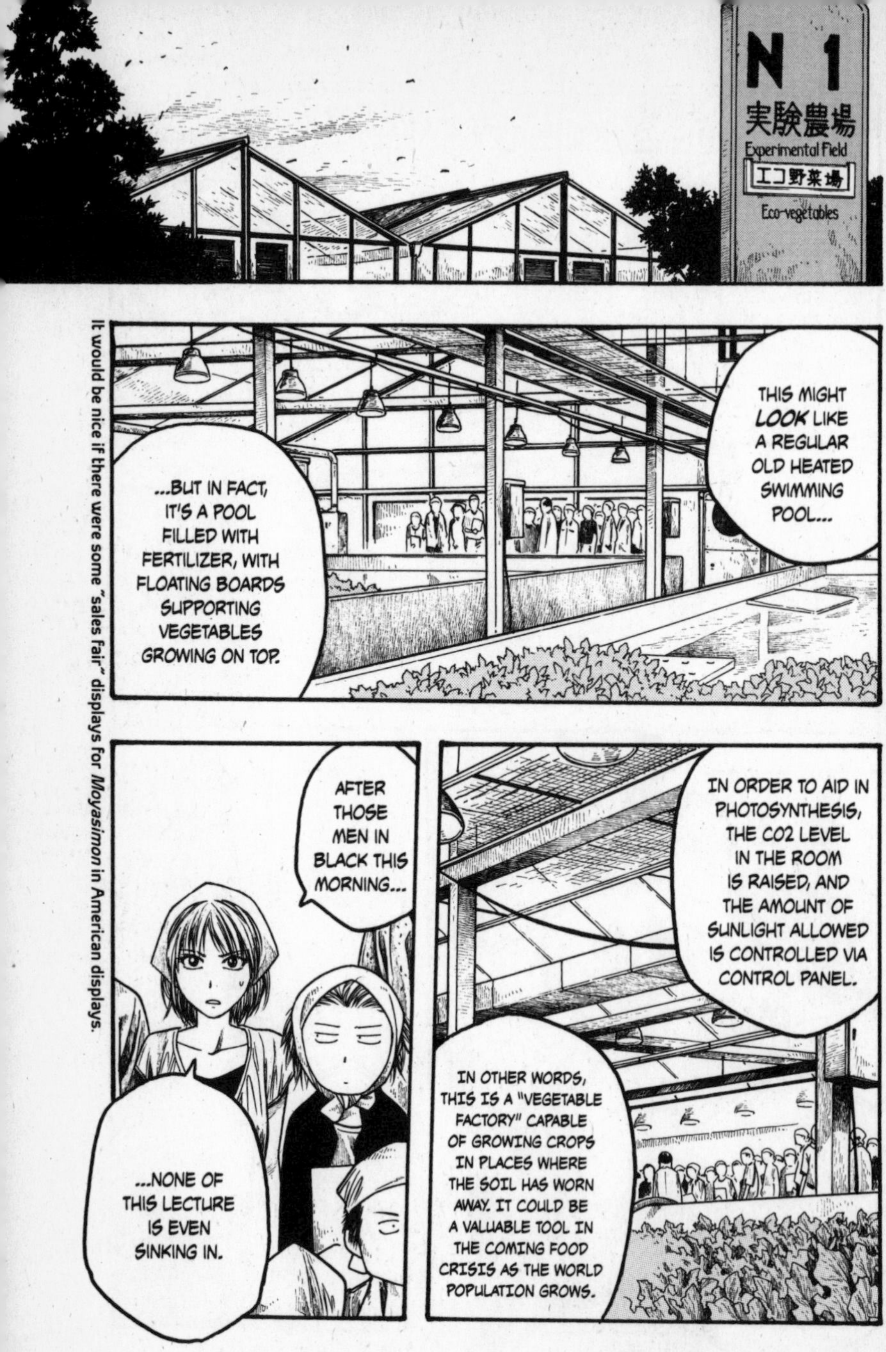
N 1
実験農場
Experimental Field
エコ野菜場
Eco-vegetables
THIS MIGHT LOOK LIKE A REGULAR OLD HEATED SWIMMING POOL...
...BUT IN FACT, IT'S A POOL FILLED WITH FERTILIZER, WITH FLOATING BOARDS SUPPORTING VEGETABLES GROWING ON TOP.
IN ORDER TO AID IN PHOTOSYNTHESIS, THE CO2 LEVEL IN THE ROOM IS RAISED, AND THE AMOUNT OF SUNLIGHT ALLOWED IS CONTROLLED VIA CONTROL PANEL.
IN OTHER WORDS, THIS IS A "VEGETABLE FACTORY" CAPABLE OF GROWING CROPS IN PLACES WHERE THE SOIL HAS WORN AWAY. IT COULD BE A VALUABLE TOOL IN THE COMING FOOD CRISIS AS THE WORLD POPULATION GROWS.
AFTER THOSE MEN IN BLACK THIS MORNING...
...NONE OF THIS LECTURE IS EVEN SINKING IN.

It would be nice if there were some "sales fair" displays for *Moyasimon* in American displays.

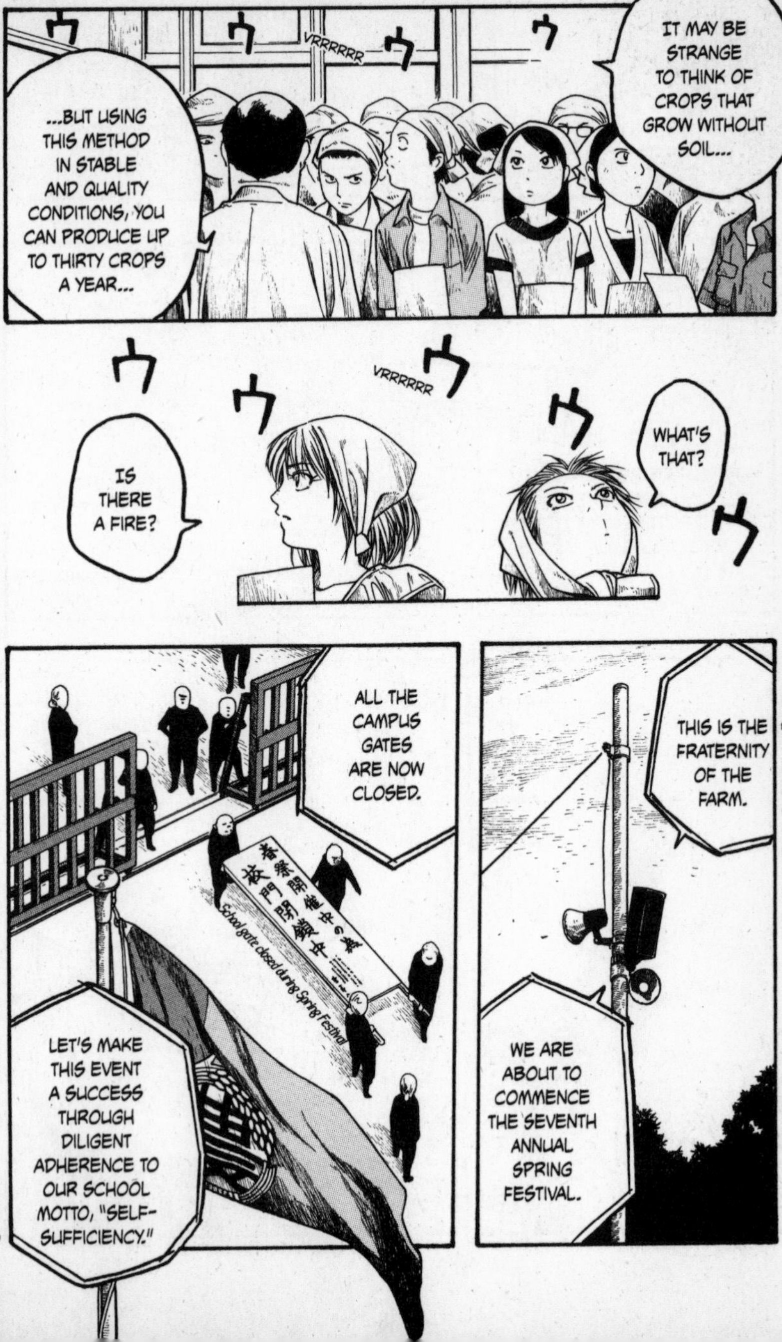
ウ ウ ウ ウ
VRRRRRR
IT MAY BE STRANGE TO THINK OF CROPS THAT GROW WITHOUT SOIL...
...BUT USING THIS METHOD IN STABLE AND QUALITY CONDITIONS, YOU CAN PRODUCE UP TO THIRTY CROPS A YEAR...
ウ ウ ウ ウ ウ
VRRRRRR
WHAT'S THAT?
IS THERE A FIRE?
THIS IS THE FRATERNITY OF THE FARM.
WE ARE ABOUT TO COMMENCE THE SEVENTH ANNUAL SPRING FESTIVAL.
ALL THE CAMPUS GATES ARE NOW CLOSED.
春祭開催中の為
校門閉鎖
School gate closed during Spring Festival
LET'S MAKE THIS EVENT A SUCCESS THROUGH DILIGENT ADHERENCE TO OUR SCHOOL MOTTO, "SELF-SUFFICIENCY."

Fraternity of the Farm
An on-campus student organization. I don't *think* they're clones.

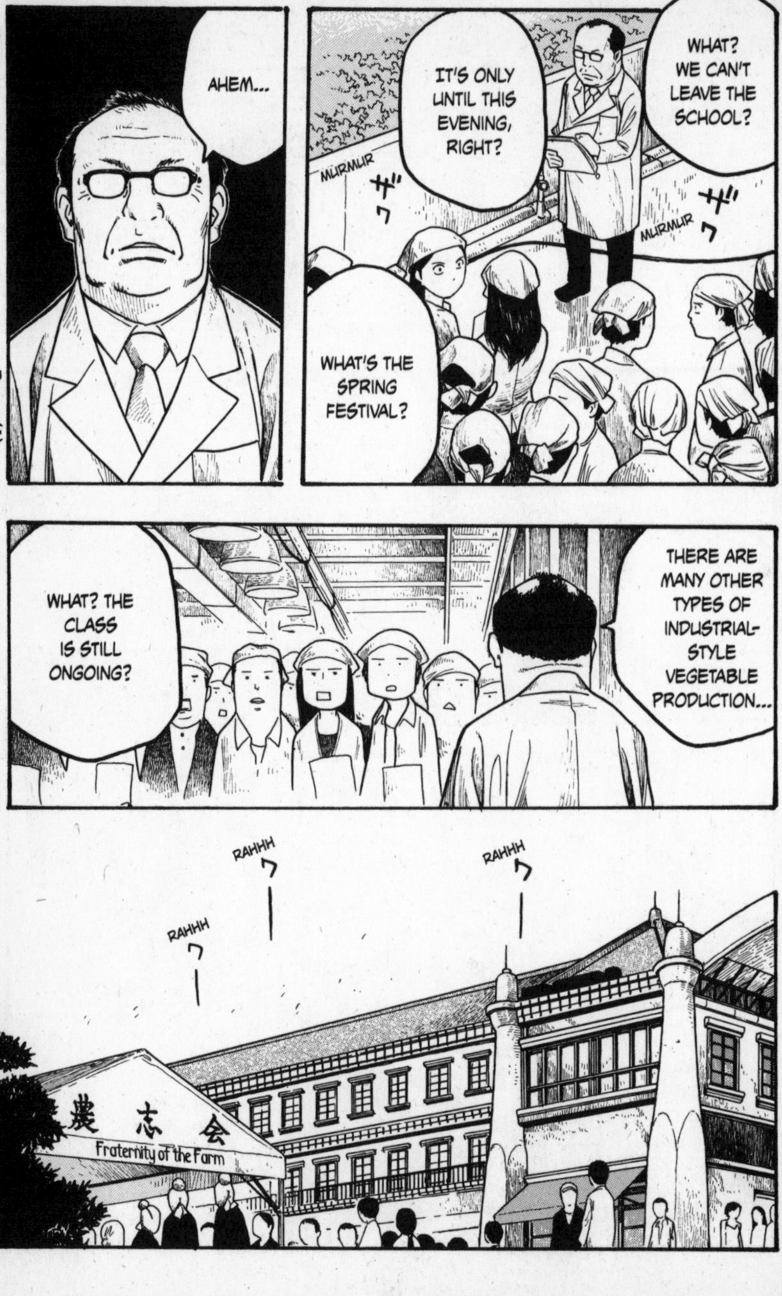
WHAT? WE CAN'T LEAVE THE SCHOOL?
IT'S ONLY UNTIL THIS EVENING, RIGHT?
MURMUR
ザワ
MURMUR
ザワ
WHAT'S THE SPRING FESTIVAL?
AHEM...
THERE ARE MANY OTHER TYPES OF INDUSTRIAL-STYLE VEGETABLE PRODUCTION...
WHAT? THE CLASS IS STILL ONGOING?
RAHHH
ワー
RAHHH
ワー
RAHHH
ワー
農志会
Fraternity of the Farm

Bonus (1):
We'd (hopefully) send posters, figurines, plushies, and other goodies for the displays.

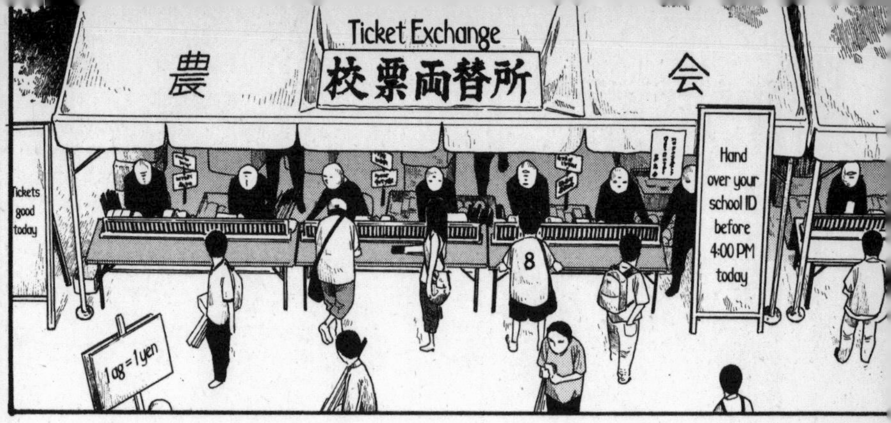
Ticket Exchange
校票両替所
農
会
Hand over your school ID before 4:00 PM today
Tickets good today
1 ag = 1 yen

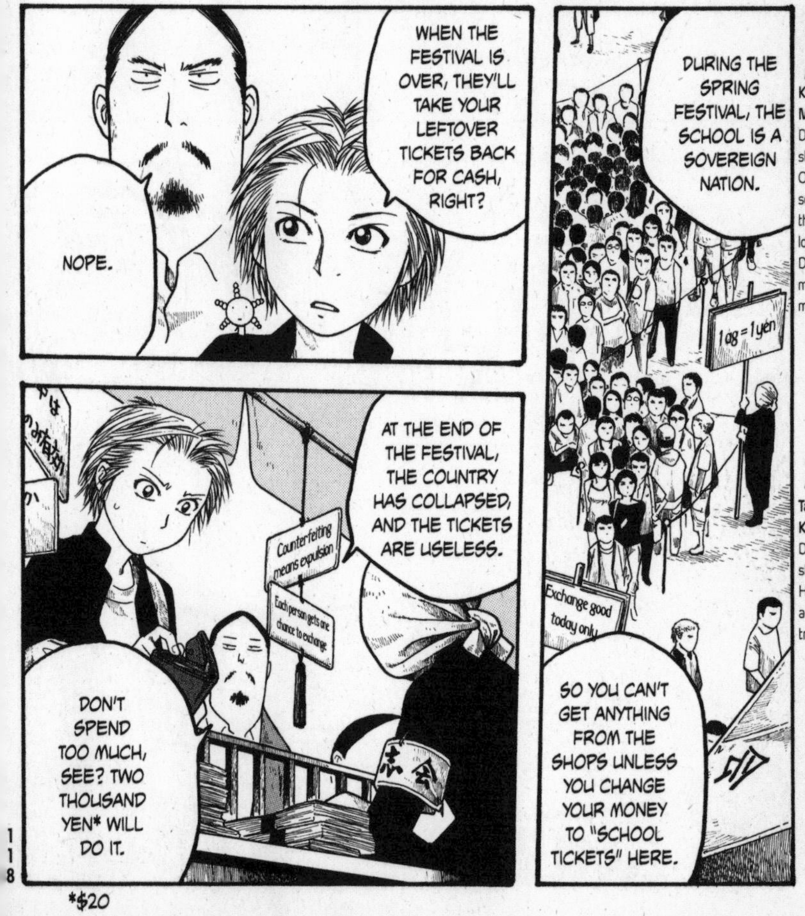
DURING THE SPRING FESTIVAL, THE SCHOOL IS A SOVEREIGN NATION.
1 ag = 1 yen
Exchange good today only
SO YOU CAN'T GET ANYTHING FROM THE SHOPS UNLESS YOU CHANGE YOUR MONEY TO "SCHOOL TICKETS" HERE.
WHEN THE FESTIVAL IS OVER, THEY'LL TAKE YOUR LEFTOVER TICKETS BACK FOR CASH, RIGHT?
NOPE.
AT THE END OF THE FESTIVAL, THE COUNTRY HAS COLLAPSED, AND THE TICKETS ARE USELESS.
Counterfeiting means expulsion
Each person gets one chance to exchange
DON'T SPEND TOO MUCH, SEE? TWO THOUSAND YEN* WILL DO IT.

Kaoru Misato
Dorm student. Only a sophomore, though he looks older. Does that mean he's a minor?

Takuma Kawahama
Dorm student. He's actually trilingual.

*$20

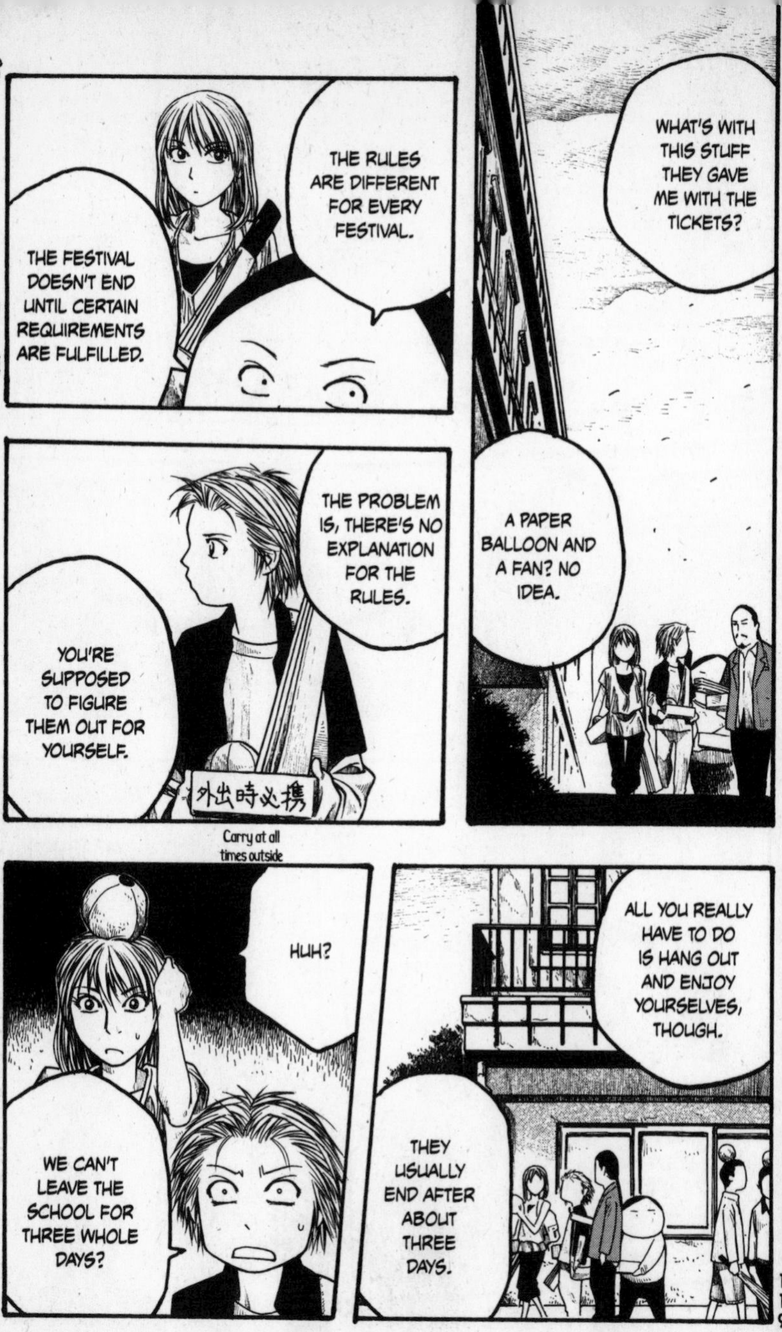
WHAT'S WITH THIS STUFF THEY GAVE ME WITH THE TICKETS?
A PAPER BALLOON AND A FAN? NO IDEA.
THE RULES ARE DIFFERENT FOR EVERY FESTIVAL.
THE FESTIVAL DOESN'T END UNTIL CERTAIN REQUIREMENTS ARE FULFILLED.
THE PROBLEM IS, THERE'S NO EXPLANATION FOR THE RULES.
YOU'RE SUPPOSED TO FIGURE THEM OUT FOR YOURSELF.
外出時必携
Carry at all times outside
ALL YOU REALLY HAVE TO DO IS HANG OUT AND ENJOY YOURSELVES, THOUGH.
THEY USUALLY END AFTER ABOUT THREE DAYS.
HUH?
WE CAN'T LEAVE THE SCHOOL FOR THREE WHOLE DAYS?

Bonus (2):
We'd send autographs from the author, too.

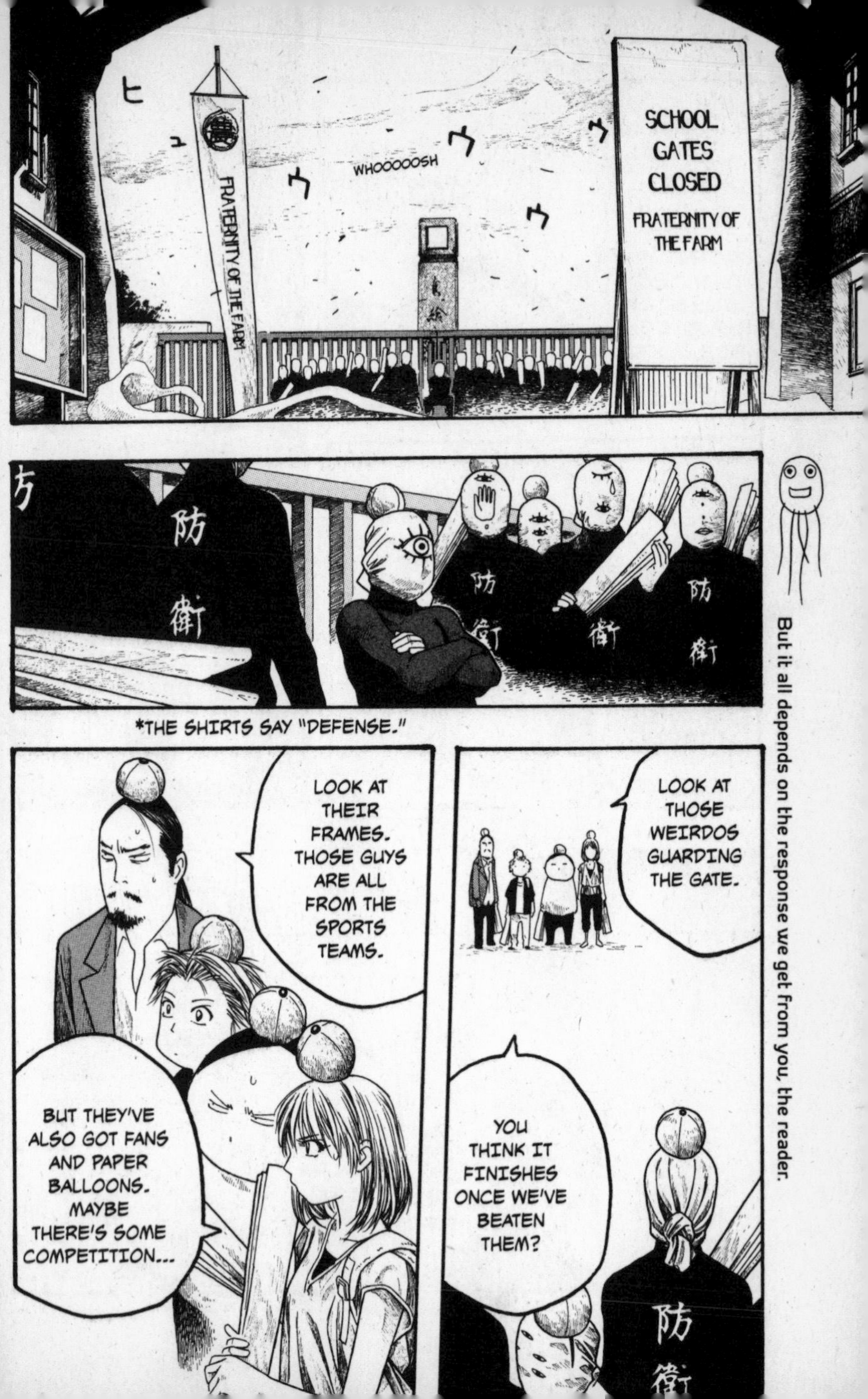
SCHOOL GATES CLOSED
FRATERNITY OF THE FARM
WHOOOOOSH
FRATERNITY OF THE FARM
防衛
*THE SHIRTS SAY "DEFENSE."
LOOK AT THOSE WEIRDOS GUARDING THE GATE.
YOU THINK IT FINISHES ONCE WE'VE BEATEN THEM?
LOOK AT THEIR FRAMES. THOSE GUYS ARE ALL FROM THE SPORTS TEAMS.
BUT THEY'VE ALSO GOT FANS AND PAPER BALLOONS. MAYBE THERE'S SOME COMPETITION...
But it all depends on the response we get from you, the reader.

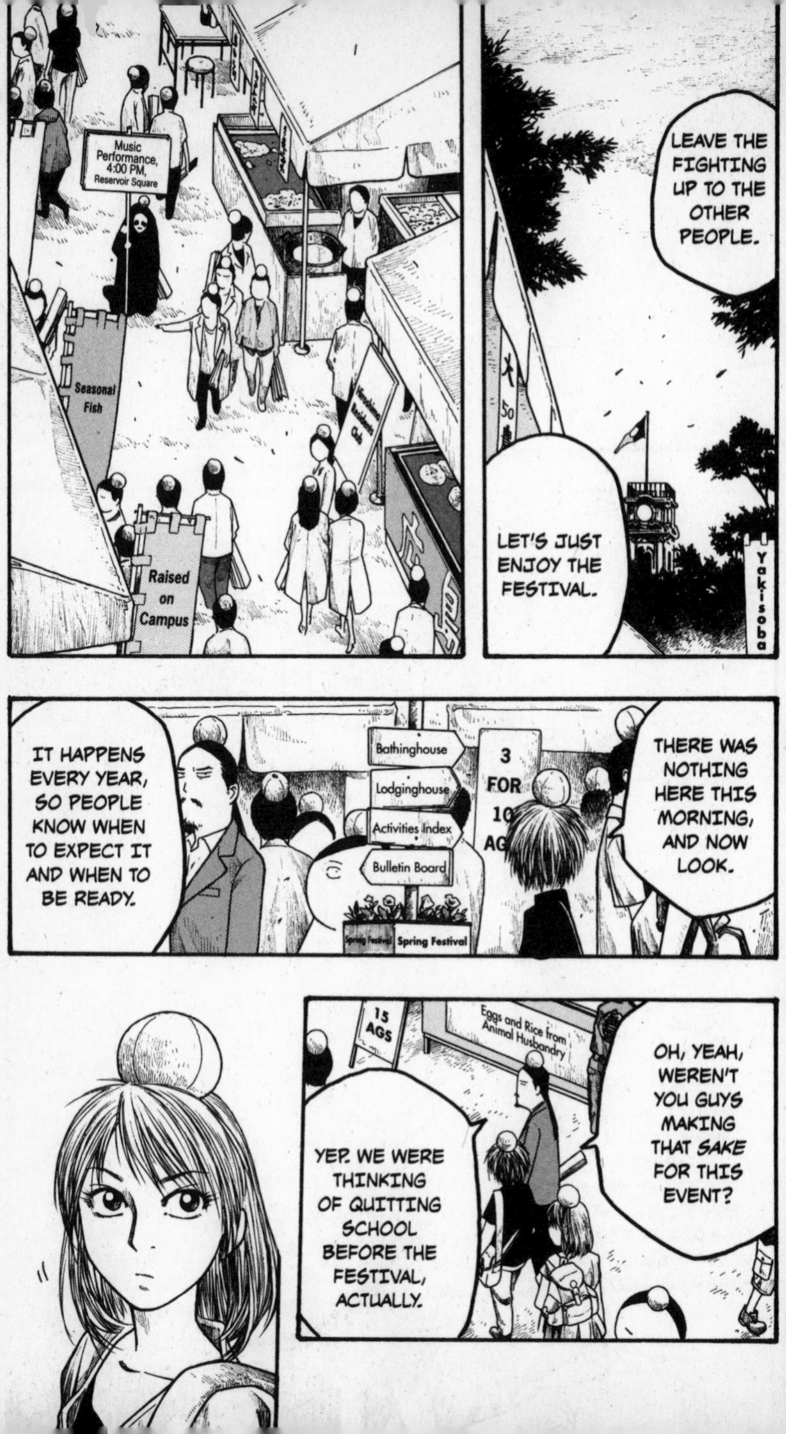
LEAVE THE FIGHTING UP TO THE OTHER PEOPLE.
LET'S JUST ENJOY THE FESTIVAL.
Yakisoba
Music Performance, 4:00 PM, Reservoir Square
Seasonal Fish
Raised on Campus
THERE WAS NOTHING HERE THIS MORNING, AND NOW LOOK.
IT HAPPENS EVERY YEAR, SO PEOPLE KNOW WHEN TO EXPECT IT AND WHEN TO BE READY.
Bathinghouse
Lodginghouse
Activities Index
Bulletin Board
Spring Festival
Spring Festival
OH, YEAH, WEREN'T YOU GUYS MAKING THAT *SAKE* FOR THIS EVENT?
Eggs and Rice from Animal Husbandry
15 AGS
YEP. WE WERE THINKING OF QUITTING SCHOOL BEFORE THE FESTIVAL, ACTUALLY.

This is not a joke.

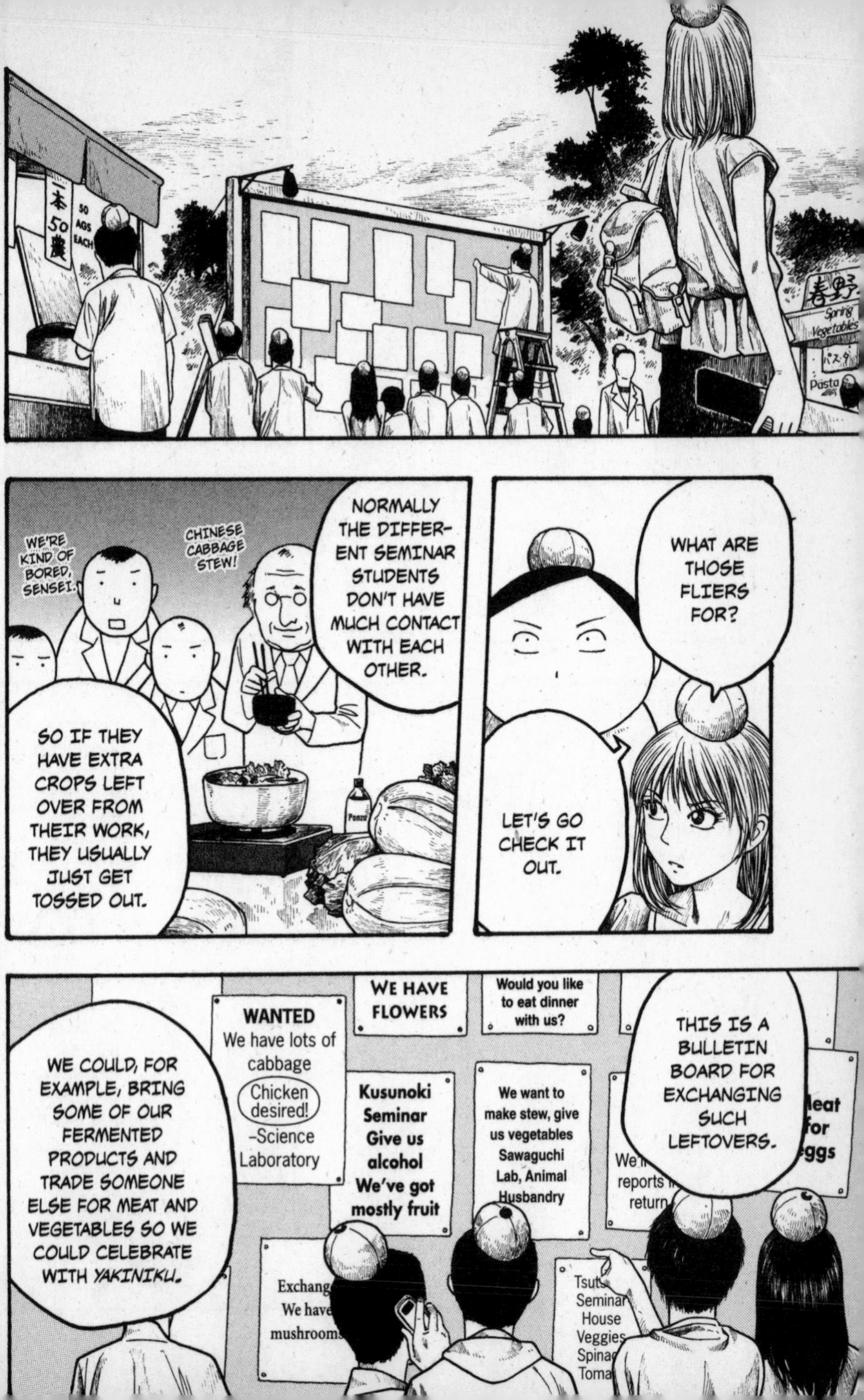
一本50農
50 AGS EACH
春野
Spring Vegetables
パスタ
Pasta
WHAT ARE THOSE FLIERS FOR?
LET'S GO CHECK IT OUT.
NORMALLY THE DIFFER-ENT SEMINAR STUDENTS DON'T HAVE MUCH CONTACT WITH EACH OTHER.
CHINESE CABBAGE STEW!
WE'RE KIND OF BORED, SENSEI.
SO IF THEY HAVE EXTRA CROPS LEFT OVER FROM THEIR WORK, THEY USUALLY JUST GET TOSSED OUT.
Ponzu
THIS IS A BULLETIN BOARD FOR EXCHANGING SUCH LEFTOVERS.
Would you like to eat dinner with us?
WE HAVE FLOWERS
WANTED We have lots of cabbage Chicken desired! –Science Laboratory
We want to make stew, give us vegetables Sawaguchi Lab, Animal Husbandry
Kusunoki Seminar Give us alcohol We've got mostly fruit
Seminar House Veggies
WE COULD, FOR EXAMPLE, BRING SOME OF OUR FERMENTED PRODUCTS AND TRADE SOMEONE ELSE FOR MEAT AND VEGETABLES SO WE COULD CELEBRATE WITH *YAKINIKU*.

It is actually our deepest desire.

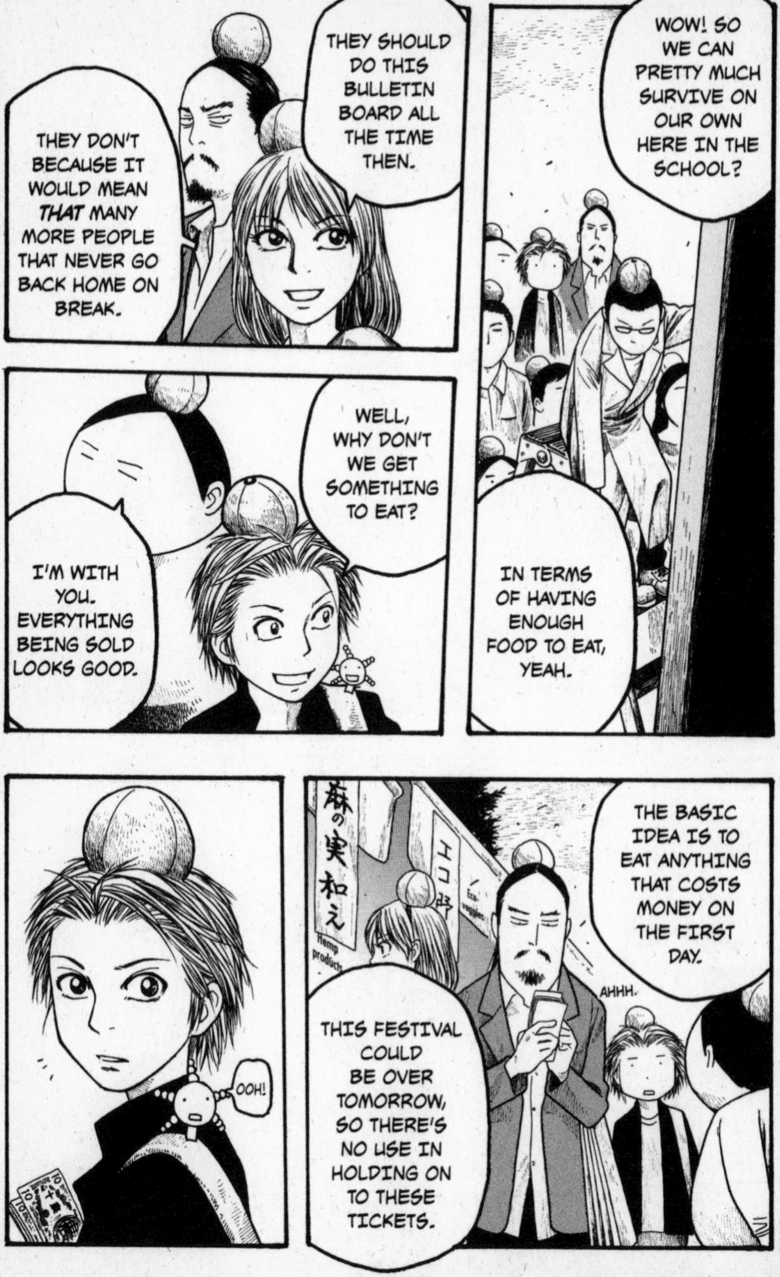

WOW! SO WE CAN PRETTY MUCH SURVIVE ON OUR OWN HERE IN THE SCHOOL?
IN TERMS OF HAVING ENOUGH FOOD TO EAT, YEAH.
THEY SHOULD DO THIS BULLETIN BOARD ALL THE TIME THEN.
THEY DON'T BECAUSE IT WOULD MEAN THAT MANY MORE PEOPLE THAT NEVER GO BACK HOME ON BREAK.
WELL, WHY DON'T WE GET SOMETHING TO EAT?
I'M WITH YOU. EVERYTHING BEING SOLD LOOKS GOOD.
麻の実和え
Hemp products
エコ野
Eco-veggies
THE BASIC IDEA IS TO EAT ANYTHING THAT COSTS MONEY ON THE FIRST DAY.
AHHH.
THIS FESTIVAL COULD BE OVER TOMORROW, SO THERE'S NO USE IN HOLDING ON TO THESE TICKETS.
OOH!

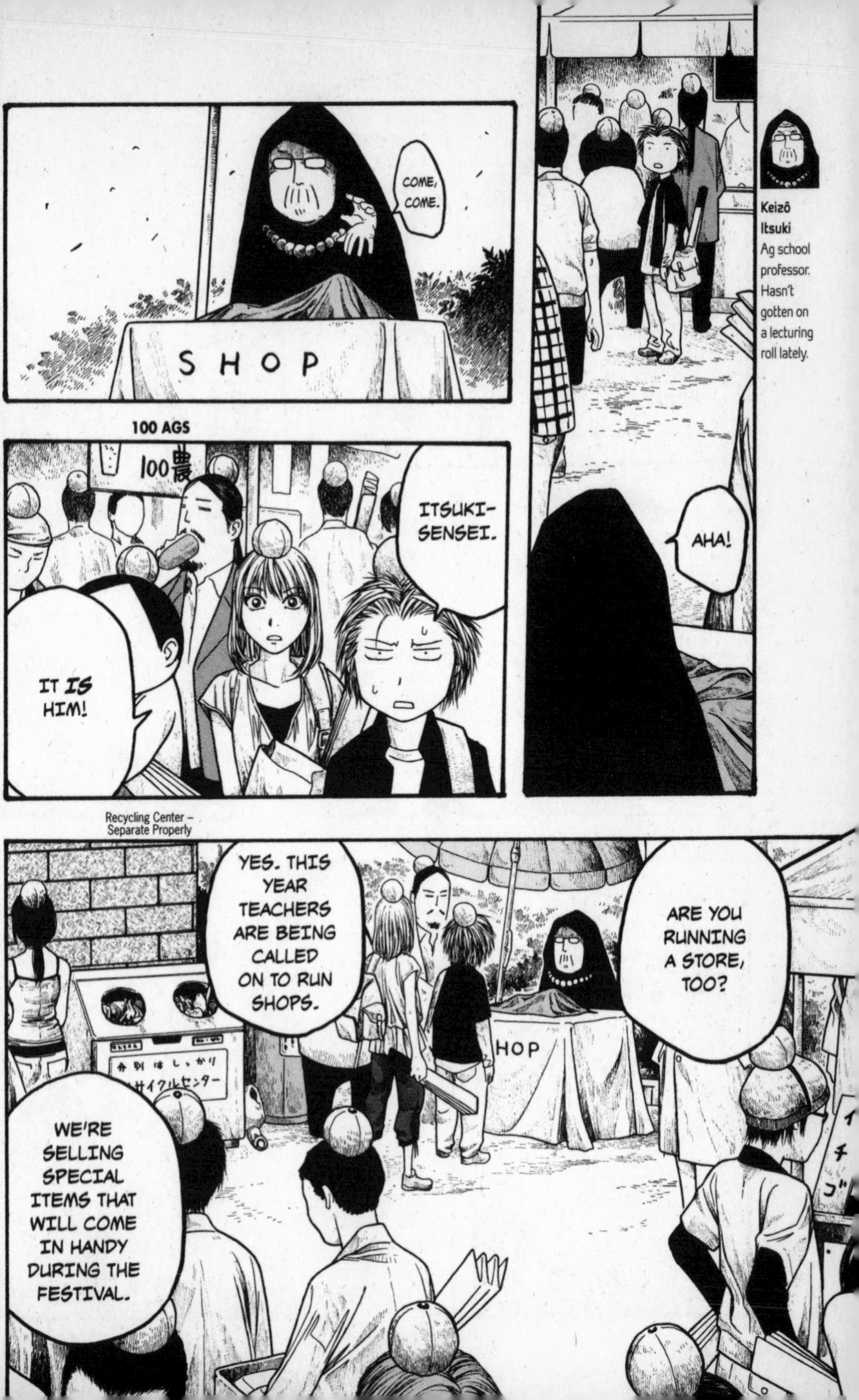
Keizô Itsuki
Ag school professor. Hasn't gotten on a lecturing roll lately.
AHA!
COME, COME.
SHOP
100 AGS
100農
ITSUKI-SENSEI.
IT IS HIM!
Recycling Center – Separate Properly
ARE YOU RUNNING A STORE, TOO?
YES. THIS YEAR TEACHERS ARE BEING CALLED ON TO RUN SHOPS.
HOP
分別はしっかり
WE'RE SELLING SPECIAL ITEMS THAT WILL COME IN HANDY DURING THE FESTIVAL.

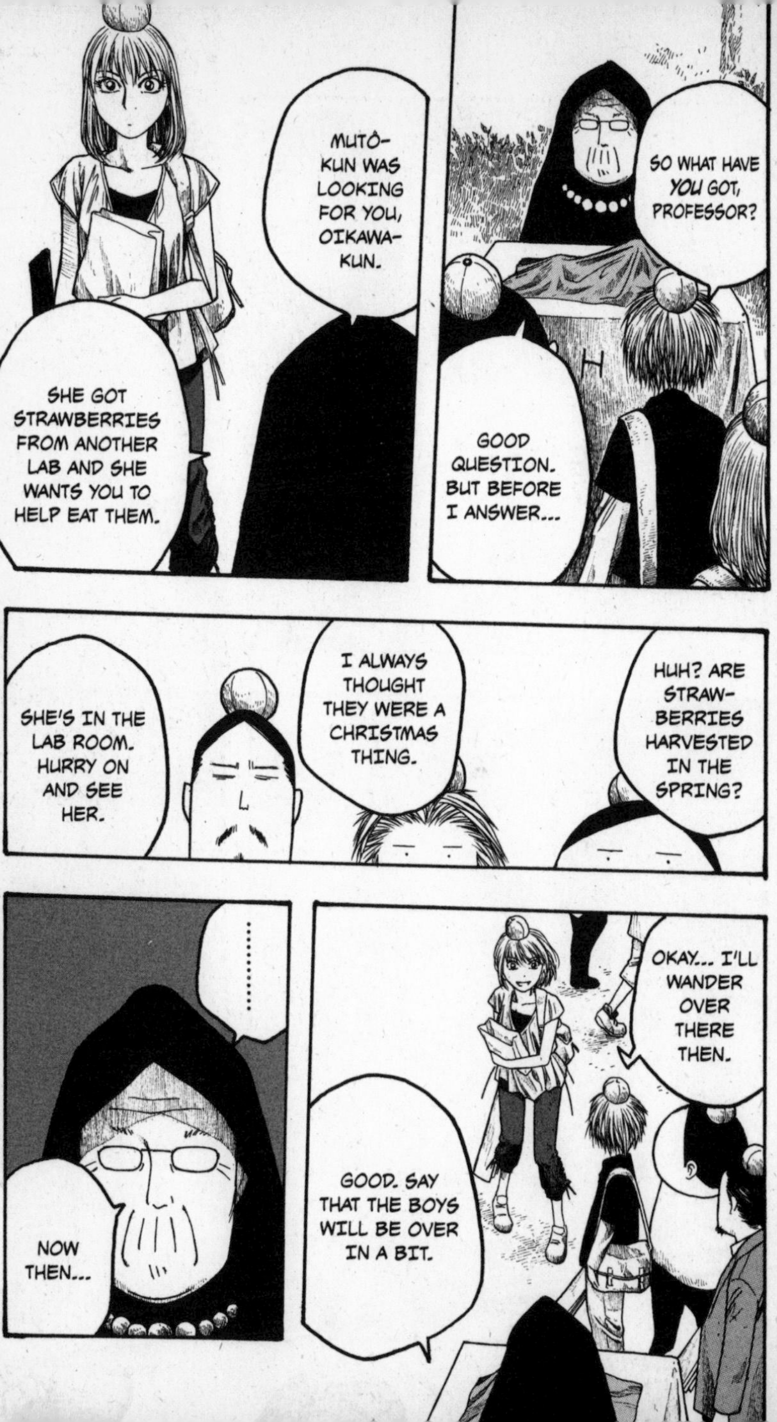
SO WHAT HAVE YOU GOT, PROFESSOR?
GOOD QUESTION. BUT BEFORE I ANSWER...
MUTÔ-KUN WAS LOOKING FOR YOU, OIKAWA-KUN.
SHE GOT STRAWBERRIES FROM ANOTHER LAB AND SHE WANTS YOU TO HELP EAT THEM.
HUH? ARE STRAW-BERRIES HARVESTED IN THE SPRING?
I ALWAYS THOUGHT THEY WERE A CHRISTMAS THING.
SHE'S IN THE LAB ROOM. HURRY ON AND SEE HER.
OKAY... I'LL WANDER OVER THERE THEN.
GOOD. SAY THAT THE BOYS WILL BE OVER IN A BIT.
....
NOW THEN...

By the way, we have a request for our American readers.

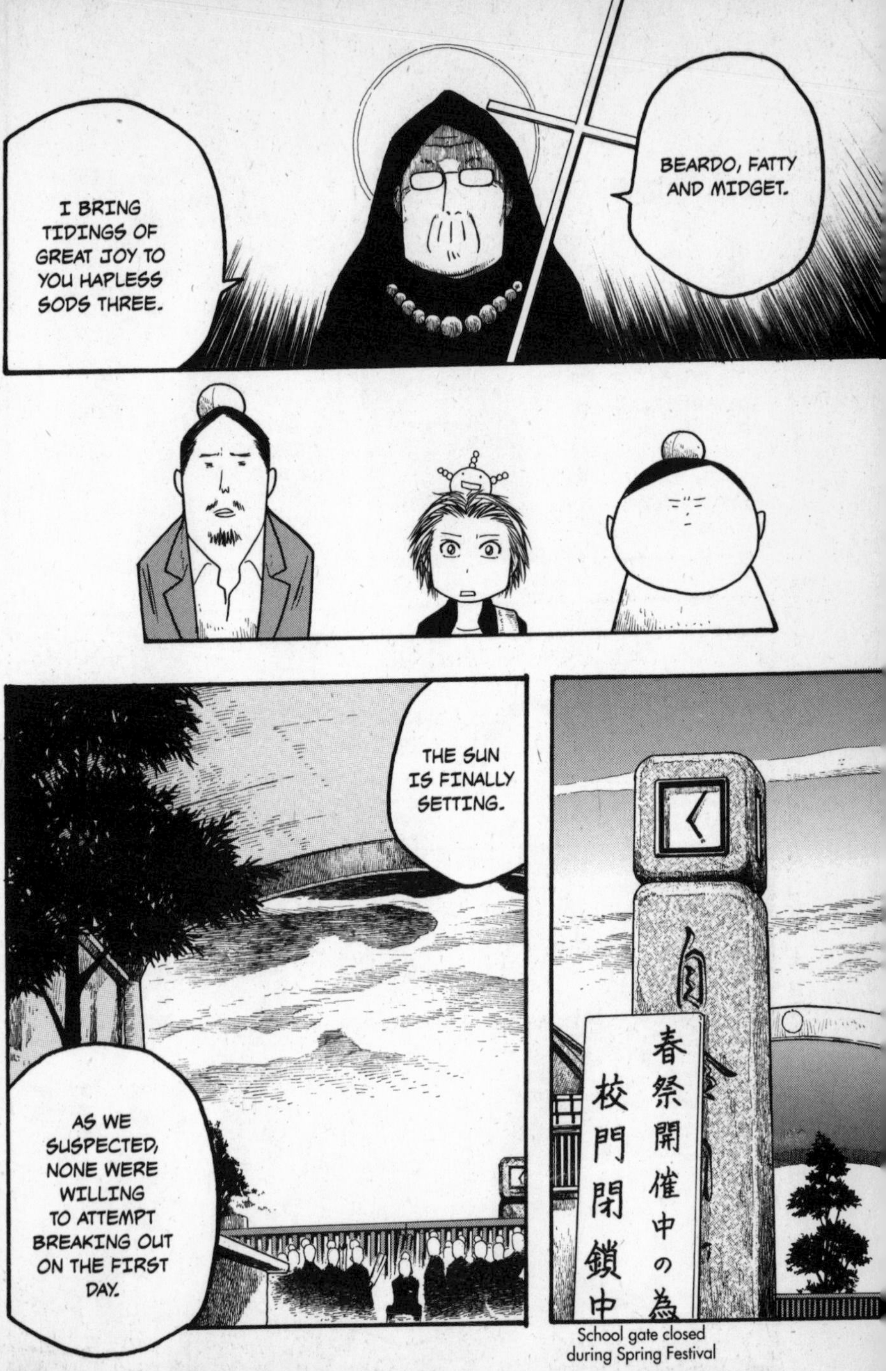
I BRING TIDINGS OF GREAT JOY TO YOU HAPLESS SODS THREE.
BEARDO, FATTY AND MIDGET.
THE SUN IS FINALLY SETTING.
AS WE SUSPECTED, NONE WERE WILLING TO ATTEMPT BREAKING OUT ON THE FIRST DAY.
春祭開催中の為
校門閉鎖中
School gate closed during Spring Festival

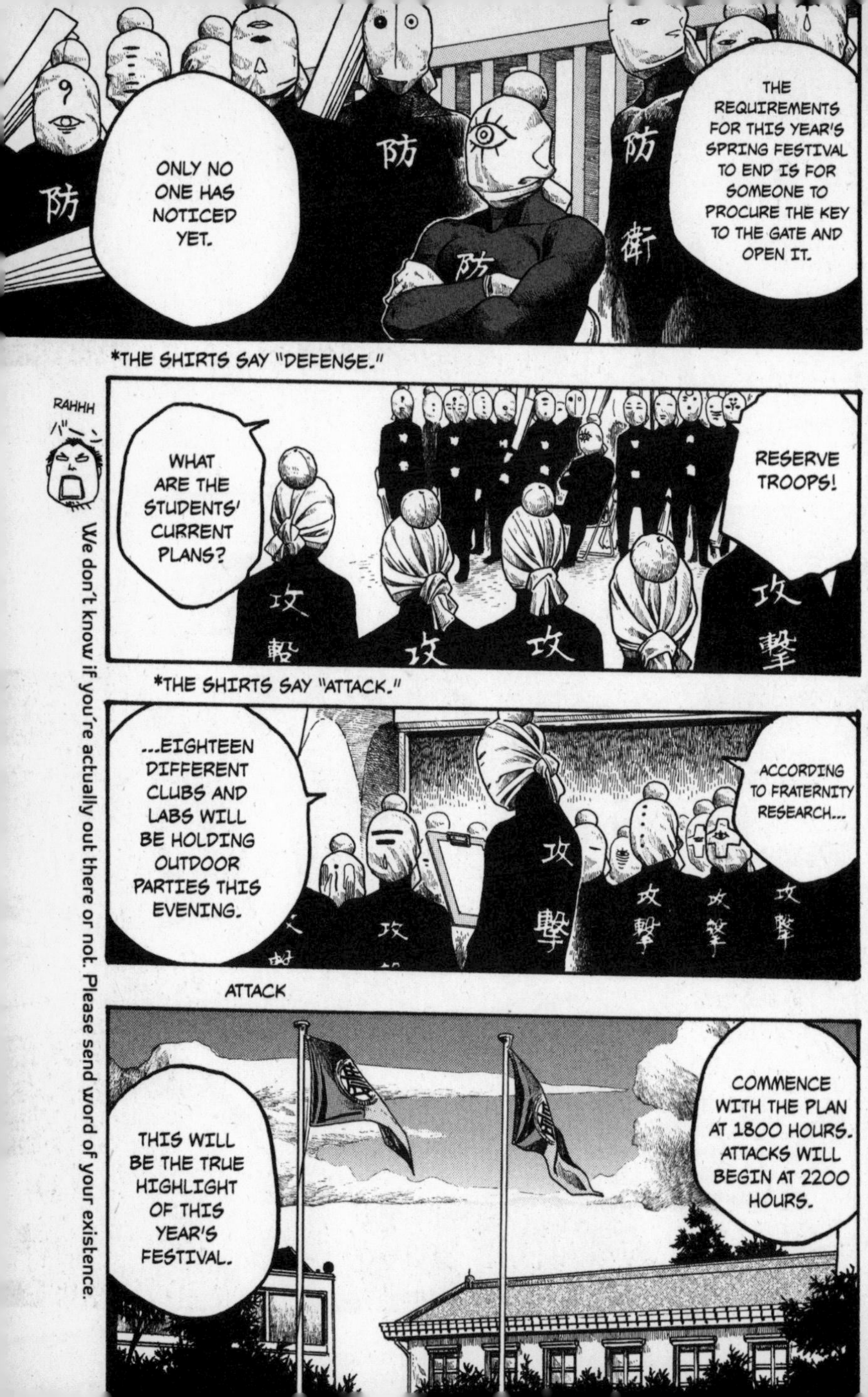
THE REQUIREMENTS FOR THIS YEAR'S SPRING FESTIVAL TO END IS FOR SOMEONE TO PROCURE THE KEY TO THE GATE AND OPEN IT.
ONLY NO ONE HAS NOTICED YET.
防
防衛
*THE SHIRTS SAY "DEFENSE."
RESERVE TROOPS!
WHAT ARE THE STUDENTS' CURRENT PLANS?
RAHHH
バーン
攻撃
攻
*THE SHIRTS SAY "ATTACK."
ACCORDING TO FRATERNITY RESEARCH...
...EIGHTEEN DIFFERENT CLUBS AND LABS WILL BE HOLDING OUTDOOR PARTIES THIS EVENING.
攻撃
ATTACK
COMMENCE WITH THE PLAN AT 1800 HOURS. ATTACKS WILL BEGIN AT 2200 HOURS.
THIS WILL BE THE TRUE HIGHLIGHT OF THIS YEAR'S FESTIVAL.

We don't know if you're actually out there or not. Please send word of your existence.

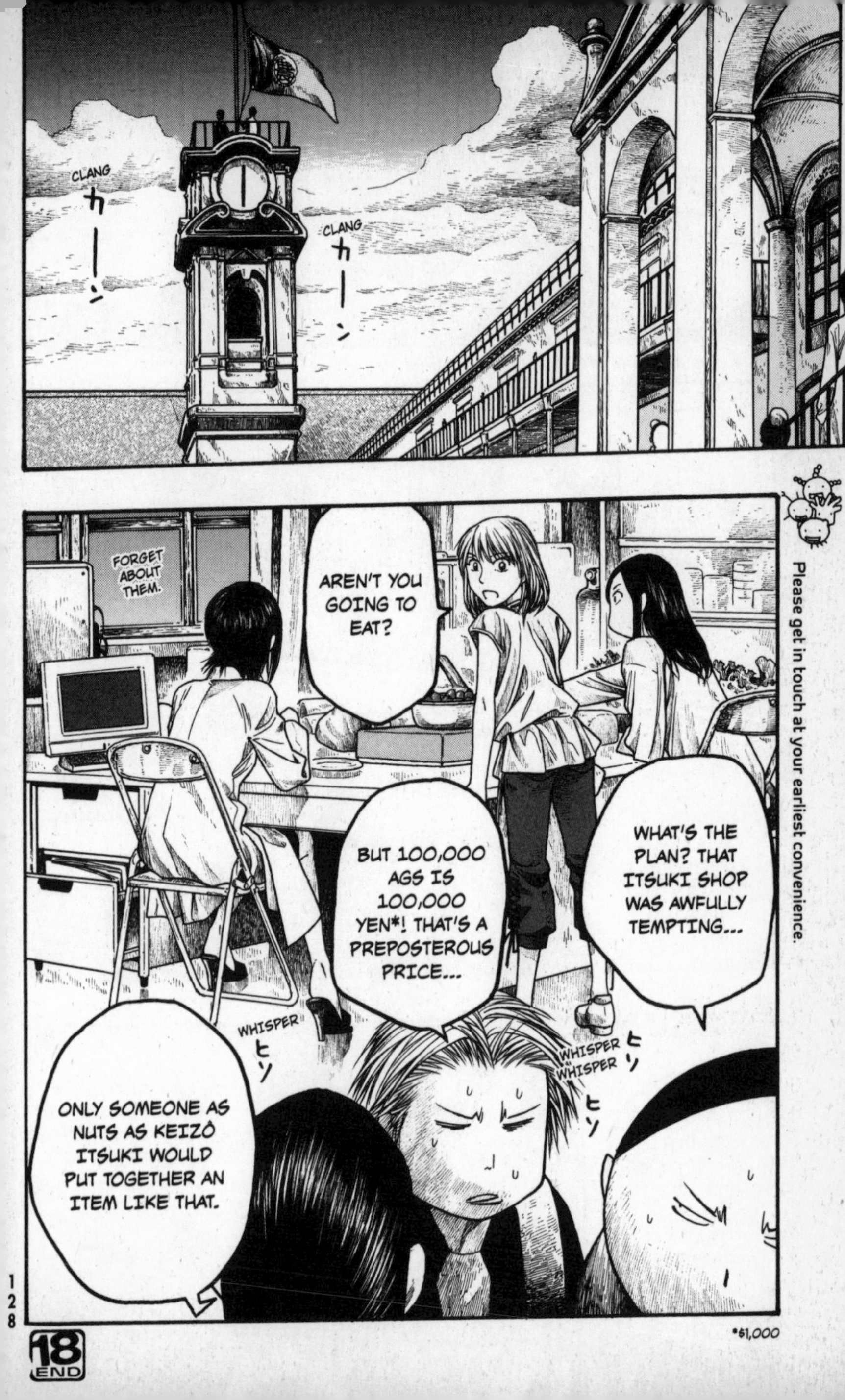
CLANG
カーン
CLANG
カーン
AREN'T YOU GOING TO EAT?
FORGET ABOUT THEM.
WHAT'S THE PLAN? THAT ITSUKI SHOP WAS AWFULLY TEMPTING...
BUT 100,000 AGS IS 100,000 YEN*! THAT'S A PREPOSTEROUS PRICE...
WHISPER
ヒソ
WHISPER
ヒソ
WHISPER
ヒソ
ONLY SOMEONE AS NUTS AS KEIZÔ ITSUKI WOULD PUT TOGETHER AN ITEM LIKE THAT.

Please get in touch at your earliest convenience.

*$1,000

18 END

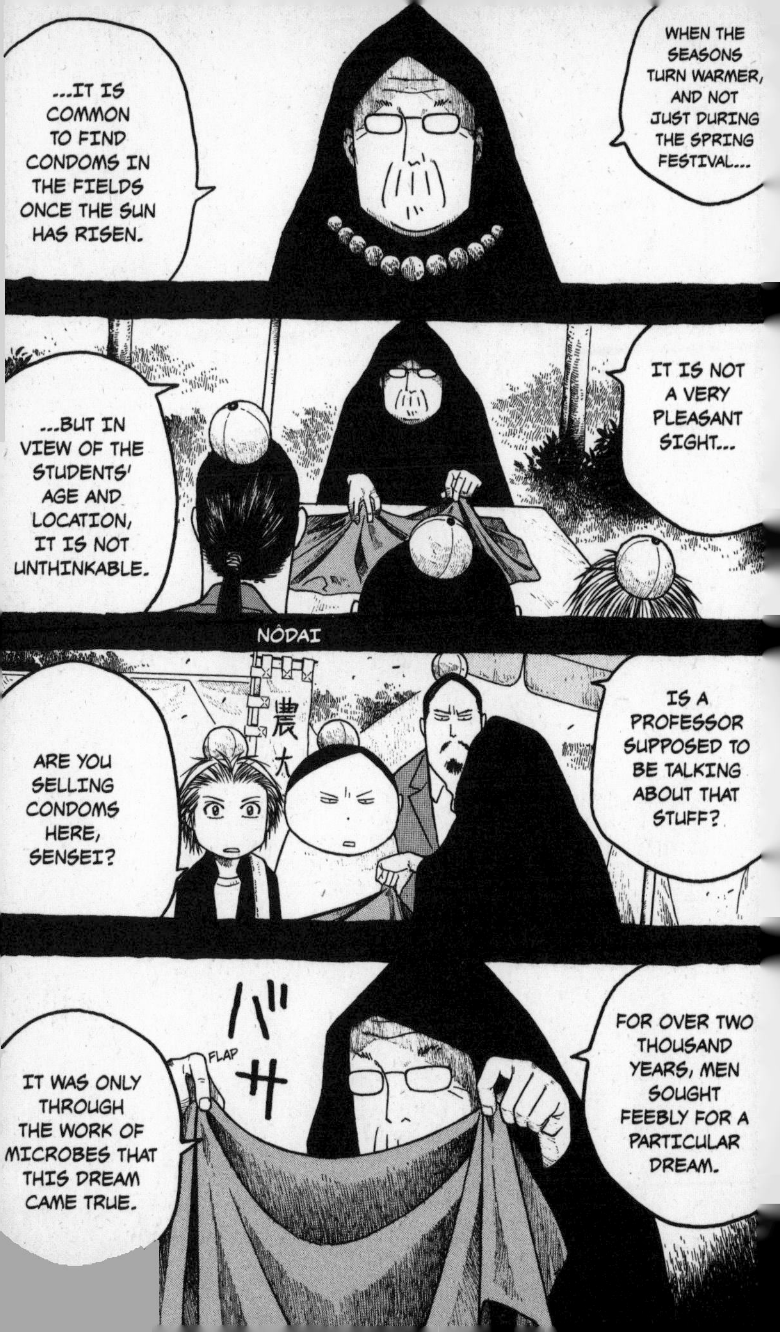
WHEN THE SEASONS TURN WARMER, AND NOT JUST DURING THE SPRING FESTIVAL...
...IT IS COMMON TO FIND CONDOMS IN THE FIELDS ONCE THE SUN HAS RISEN.
IT IS NOT A VERY PLEASANT SIGHT...
...BUT IN VIEW OF THE STUDENTS' AGE AND LOCATION, IT IS NOT UNTHINKABLE.
NÔDAI
農大
IS A PROFESSOR SUPPOSED TO BE TALKING ABOUT THAT STUFF?
ARE YOU SELLING CONDOMS HERE, SENSEI?
FOR OVER TWO THOUSAND YEARS, MEN SOUGHT FEEBLY FOR A PARTICULAR DREAM.
バサ
FLAP
IT WAS ONLY THROUGH THE WORK OF MICROBES THAT THIS DREAM CAME TRUE.

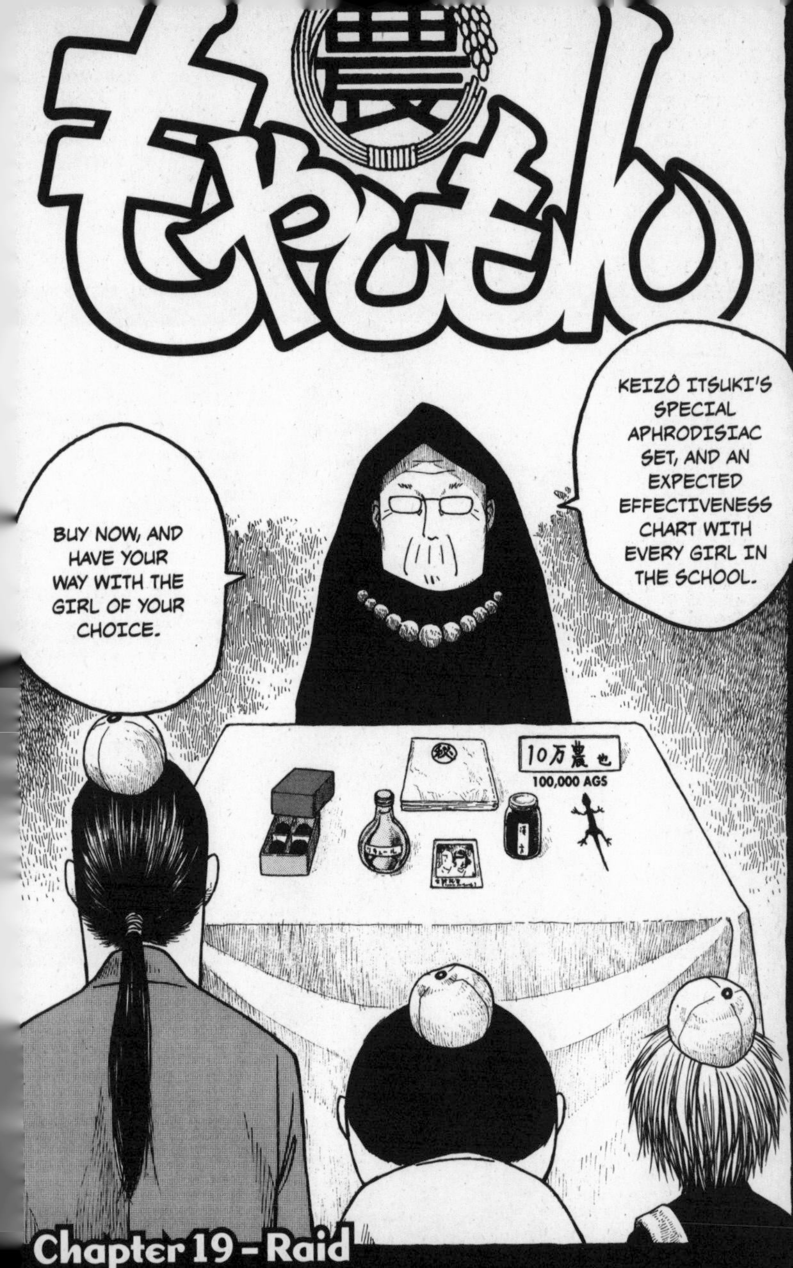
KEIZÔ ITSUKI'S SPECIAL APHRODISIAC SET, AND AN EXPECTED EFFECTIVENESS CHART WITH EVERY GIRL IN THE SCHOOL.
BUY NOW, AND HAVE YOUR WAY WITH THE GIRL OF YOUR CHOICE.
10万農也
100,000 AGS

Chapter 19 - Raid

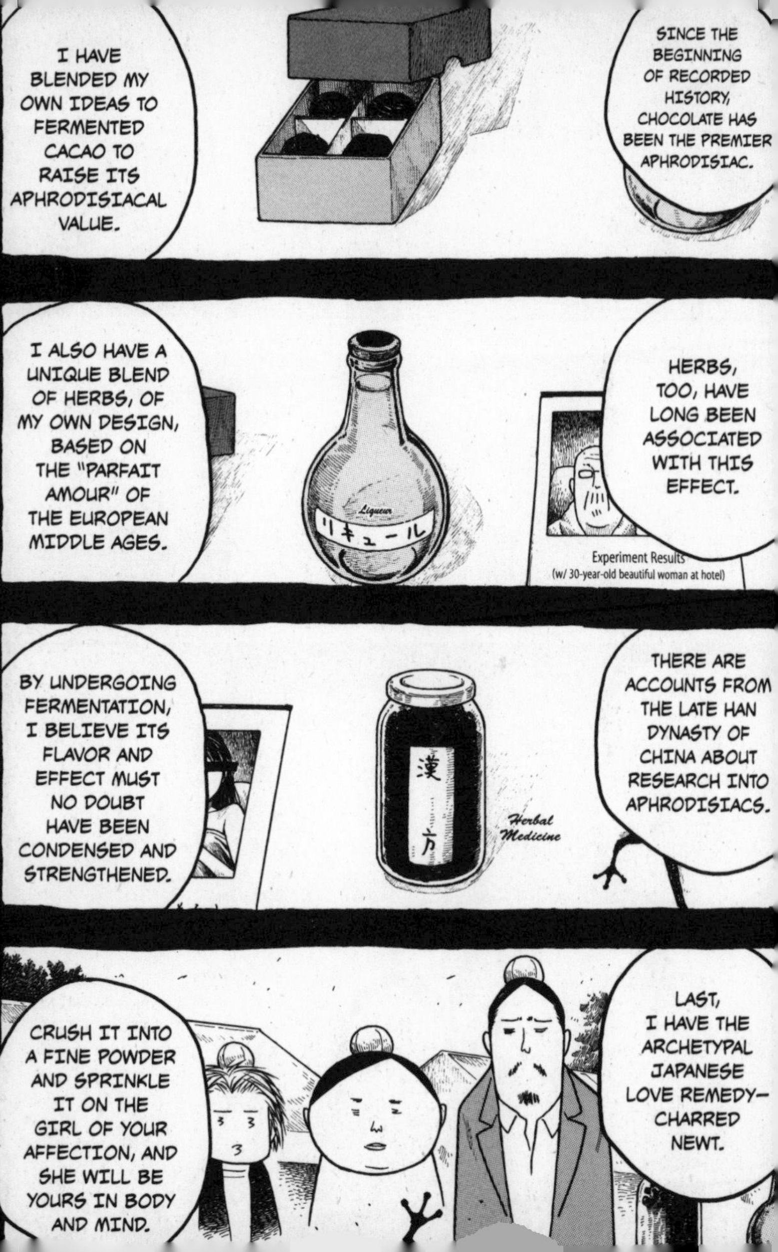
SINCE THE BEGINNING OF RECORDED HISTORY, CHOCOLATE HAS BEEN THE PREMIER APHRODISIAC.
I HAVE BLENDED MY OWN IDEAS TO FERMENTED CACAO TO RAISE ITS APHRODISIACAL VALUE.
HERBS, TOO, HAVE LONG BEEN ASSOCIATED WITH THIS EFFECT.
Experiment Results
(w/ 30-year-old beautiful woman at hotel)
Liqueur
リキュール
I ALSO HAVE A UNIQUE BLEND OF HERBS, OF MY OWN DESIGN, BASED ON THE "PARFAIT AMOUR" OF THE EUROPEAN MIDDLE AGES.
THERE ARE ACCOUNTS FROM THE LATE HAN DYNASTY OF CHINA ABOUT RESEARCH INTO APHRODISIACS.
Herbal Medicine
漢方
BY UNDERGOING FERMENTATION, I BELIEVE ITS FLAVOR AND EFFECT MUST NO DOUBT HAVE BEEN CONDENSED AND STRENGTHENED.
LAST, I HAVE THE ARCHETYPAL JAPANESE LOVE REMEDY—CHARRED NEWT.
CRUSH IT INTO A FINE POWDER AND SPRINKLE IT ON THE GIRL OF YOUR AFFECTION, AND SHE WILL BE YOURS IN BODY AND MIND.

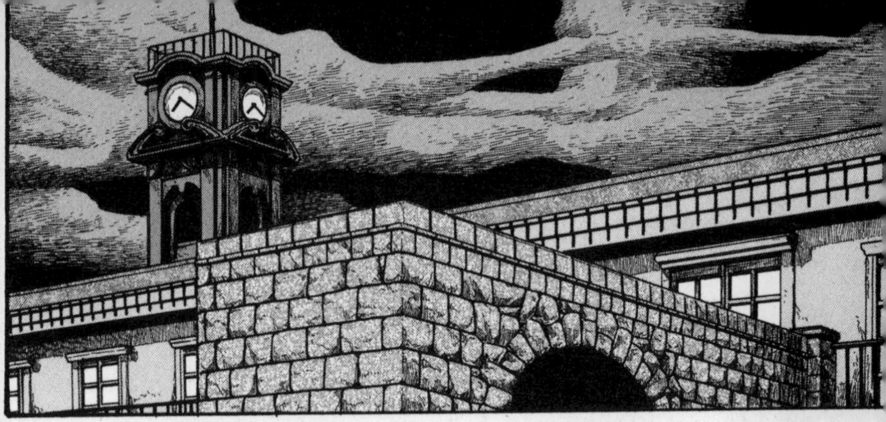

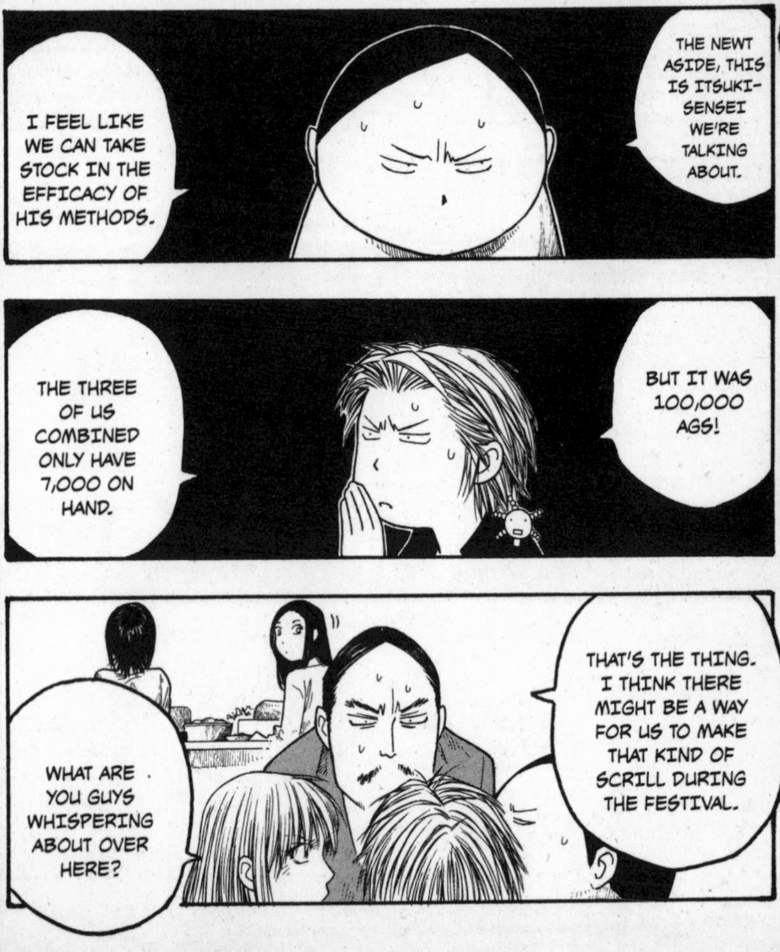
THE NEWT ASIDE, THIS IS ITSUKI-SENSEI WE'RE TALKING ABOUT.
I FEEL LIKE WE CAN TAKE STOCK IN THE EFFICACY OF HIS METHODS.
BUT IT WAS 100,000 AGS!
THE THREE OF US COMBINED ONLY HAVE 7,000 ON HAND.
THAT'S THE THING. I THINK THERE MIGHT BE A WAY FOR US TO MAKE THAT KIND OF SCRILL DURING THE FESTIVAL.
WHAT ARE YOU GUYS WHISPERING ABOUT OVER HERE?

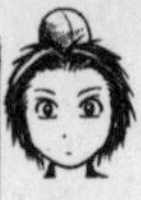

Tadayasu Sawaki
Protagonist. Can see germs. That's a paper balloon on his head.

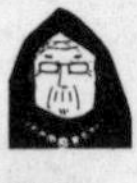

Keizō Itsuki
Ag school professor. Only has one seminar student.

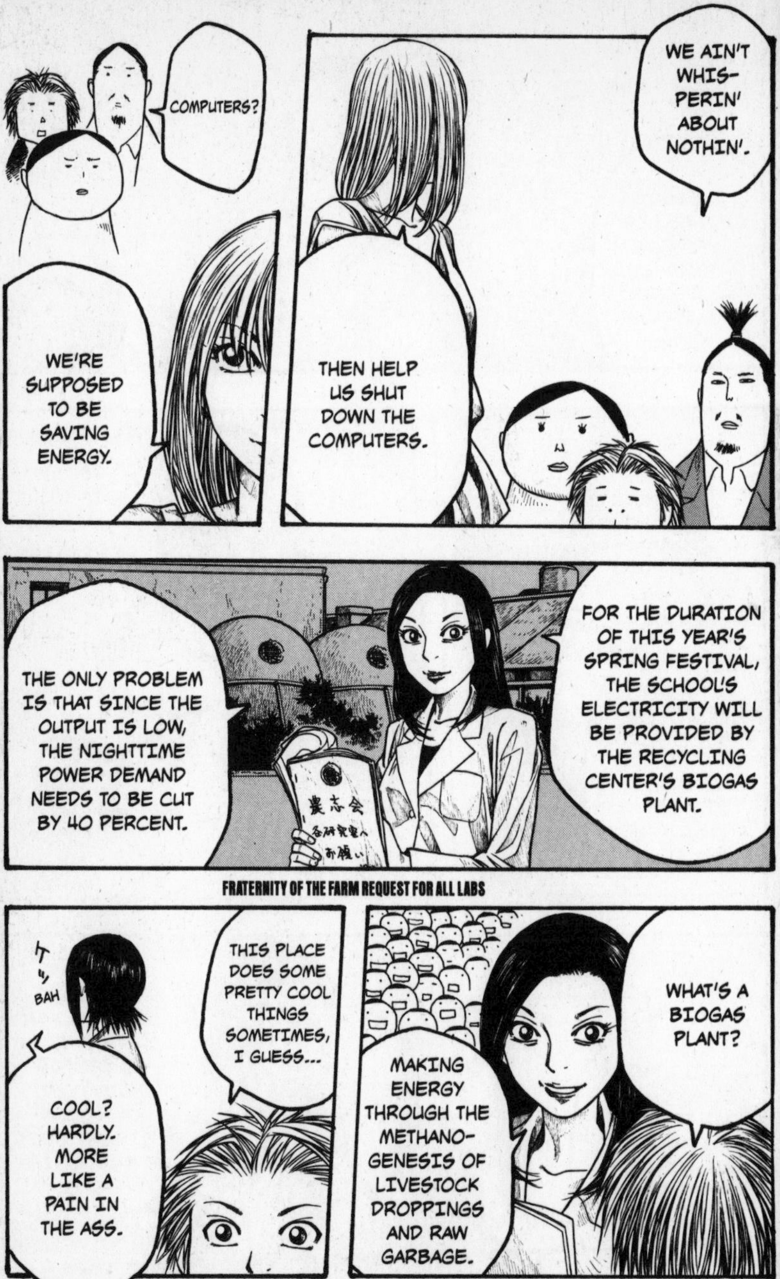
WE AIN'T WHISPERIN' ABOUT NOTHIN'.
THEN HELP US SHUT DOWN THE COMPUTERS.
COMPUTERS?
WE'RE SUPPOSED TO BE SAVING ENERGY.
FOR THE DURATION OF THIS YEAR'S SPRING FESTIVAL, THE SCHOOL'S ELECTRICITY WILL BE PROVIDED BY THE RECYCLING CENTER'S BIOGAS PLANT.
農志会
各研究室へ
お願い
THE ONLY PROBLEM IS THAT SINCE THE OUTPUT IS LOW, THE NIGHTTIME POWER DEMAND NEEDS TO BE CUT BY 40 PERCENT.
FRATERNITY OF THE FARM REQUEST FOR ALL LABS
WHAT'S A BIOGAS PLANT?
MAKING ENERGY THROUGH THE METHANOGENESIS OF LIVESTOCK DROPPINGS AND RAW GARBAGE.
THIS PLACE DOES SOME PRETTY COOL THINGS SOMETIMES, I GUESS...
ケッ
BAH
COOL? HARDLY. MORE LIKE A PAIN IN THE ASS.

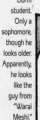

Kaoru Misato
Dorm student. Only a sophomore, though he looks older. Apparently, he looks like the guy from "Warai Meshi."

Takuma Kawahama
Dorm student. Former expatriate, current bug-eater. He'll do more bug-eating in the future.

Methanogens
Classified as archaea, these anaerobic extremophiles create methane gas from organic matter in all kinds of environments. Some of the powers they harbor are still unknown.

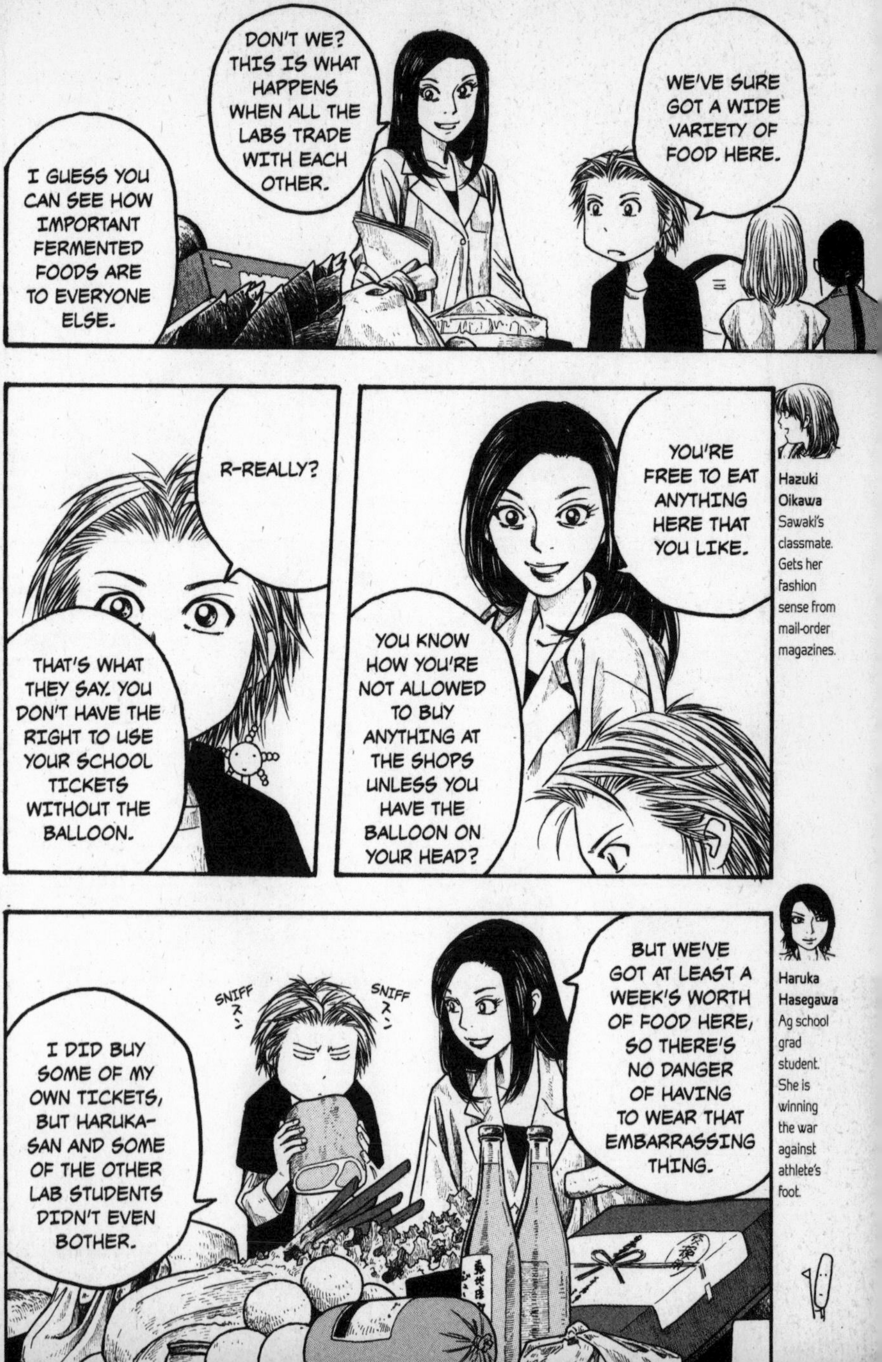
WE'VE SURE GOT A WIDE VARIETY OF FOOD HERE.
DON'T WE? THIS IS WHAT HAPPENS WHEN ALL THE LABS TRADE WITH EACH OTHER.
I GUESS YOU CAN SEE HOW IMPORTANT FERMENTED FOODS ARE TO EVERYONE ELSE.
Hazuki Oikawa
Sawaki's classmate. Gets her fashion sense from mail-order magazines.
YOU'RE FREE TO EAT ANYTHING HERE THAT YOU LIKE.
YOU KNOW HOW YOU'RE NOT ALLOWED TO BUY ANYTHING AT THE SHOPS UNLESS YOU HAVE THE BALLOON ON YOUR HEAD?
R-REALLY?
THAT'S WHAT THEY SAY. YOU DON'T HAVE THE RIGHT TO USE YOUR SCHOOL TICKETS WITHOUT THE BALLOON.
Haruka Hasegawa
Ag school grad student. She is winning the war against athlete's foot.
BUT WE'VE GOT AT LEAST A WEEK'S WORTH OF FOOD HERE, SO THERE'S NO DANGER OF HAVING TO WEAR THAT EMBARRASSING THING.
SNIFF スン
SNIFF スン
I DID BUY SOME OF MY OWN TICKETS, BUT HARUKA-SAN AND SOME OF THE OTHER LAB STUDENTS DIDN'T EVEN BOTHER.

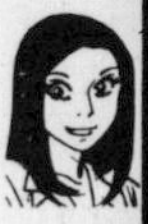

Aoi Mutô
The only seminar student of Itsuki's lab. She took off the bandage.

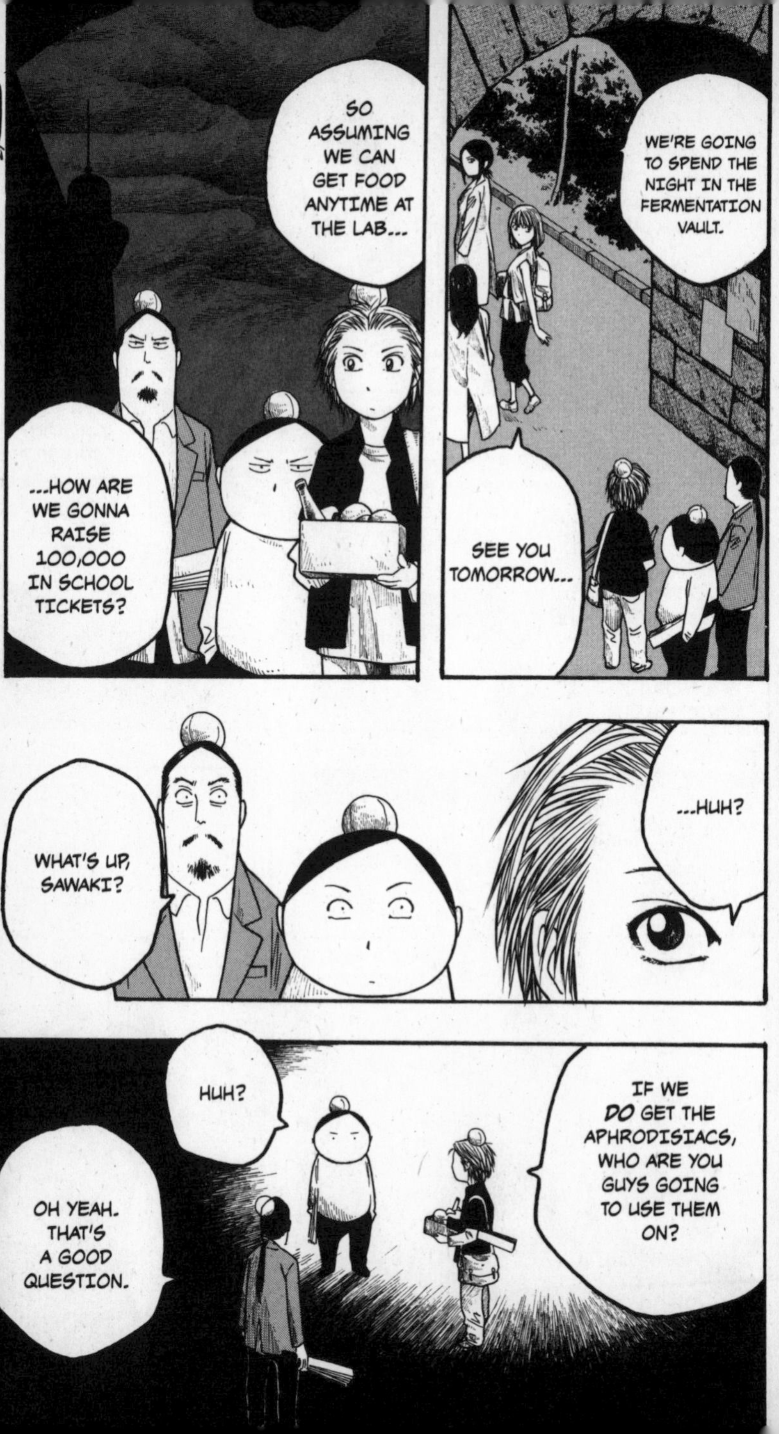
WE'RE GOING TO SPEND THE NIGHT IN THE FERMENTATION VAULT.
SEE YOU TOMORROW...
SO ASSUMING WE CAN GET FOOD ANYTIME AT THE LAB...
...HOW ARE WE GONNA RAISE 100,000 IN SCHOOL TICKETS?
...HUH?
WHAT'S UP, SAWAKI?
IF WE *DO* GET THE APHRODISIACS, WHO ARE YOU GUYS GOING TO USE THEM ON?
HUH?
OH YEAH. THAT'S A GOOD QUESTION.

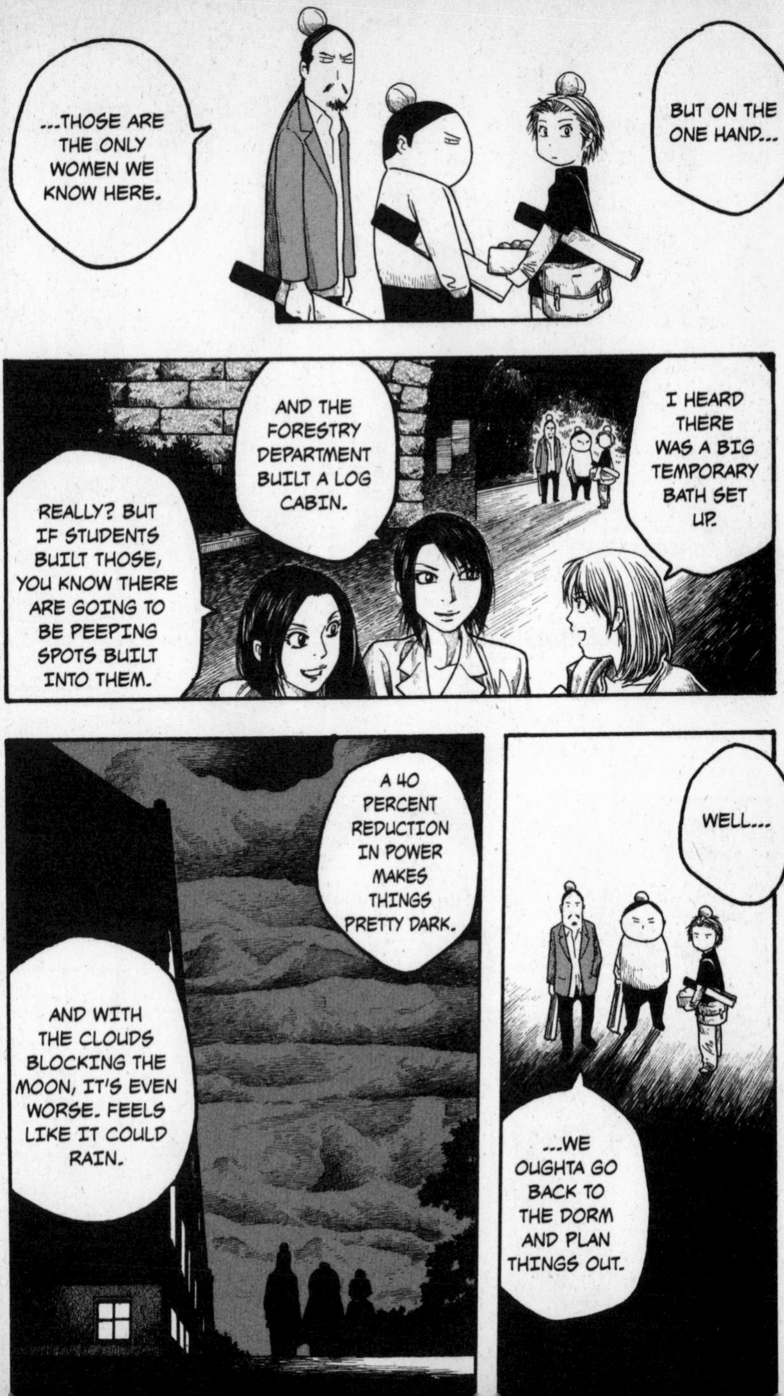
BUT ON THE ONE HAND...
...THOSE ARE THE ONLY WOMEN WE KNOW HERE.
I HEARD THERE WAS A BIG TEMPORARY BATH SET UP.
AND THE FORESTRY DEPARTMENT BUILT A LOG CABIN.
REALLY? BUT IF STUDENTS BUILT THOSE, YOU KNOW THERE ARE GOING TO BE PEEPING SPOTS BUILT INTO THEM.
WELL...
...WE OUGHTA GO BACK TO THE DORM AND PLAN THINGS OUT.
A 40 PERCENT REDUCTION IN POWER MAKES THINGS PRETTY DARK.
AND WITH THE CLOUDS BLOCKING THE MOON, IT'S EVEN WORSE. FEELS LIKE IT COULD RAIN.

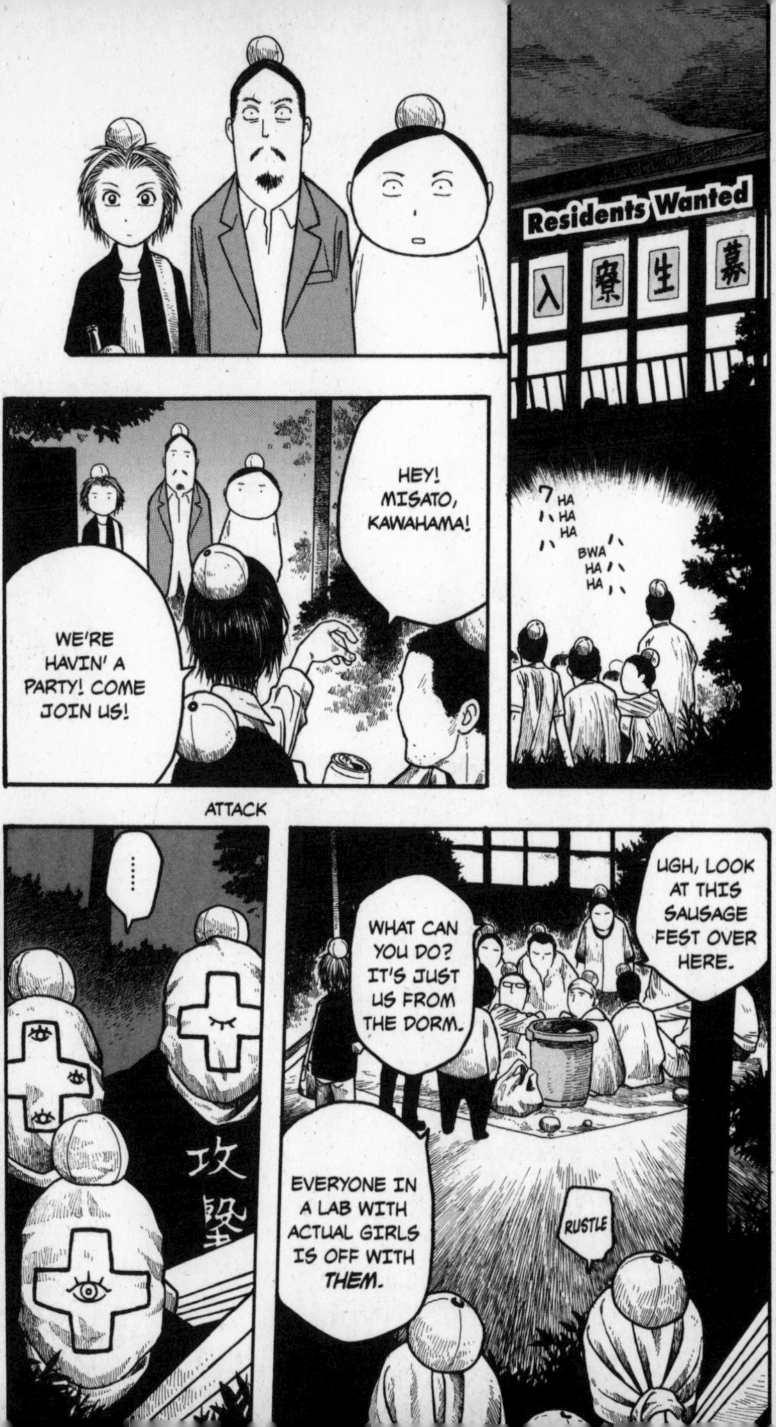
Residents Wanted
入寮生募
HA HA HA
BWA HA HA
HEY! MISATO, KAWAHAMA!
WE'RE HAVIN' A PARTY! COME JOIN US!
UGH, LOOK AT THIS SAUSAGE FEST OVER HERE.
WHAT CAN YOU DO? IT'S JUST US FROM THE DORM.
EVERYONE IN A LAB WITH ACTUAL GIRLS IS OFF WITH *THEM*.
RUSTLE
......
攻撃
ATTACK

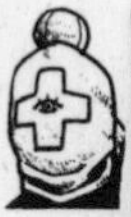

Fraternity of the Farm (Roving Squad) Scouts for the on-campus student organization. Incidentally, in regard to the original **Mobile Suit Gundam**, the author is a fan of the Federation, while the editor prefers Zeon.

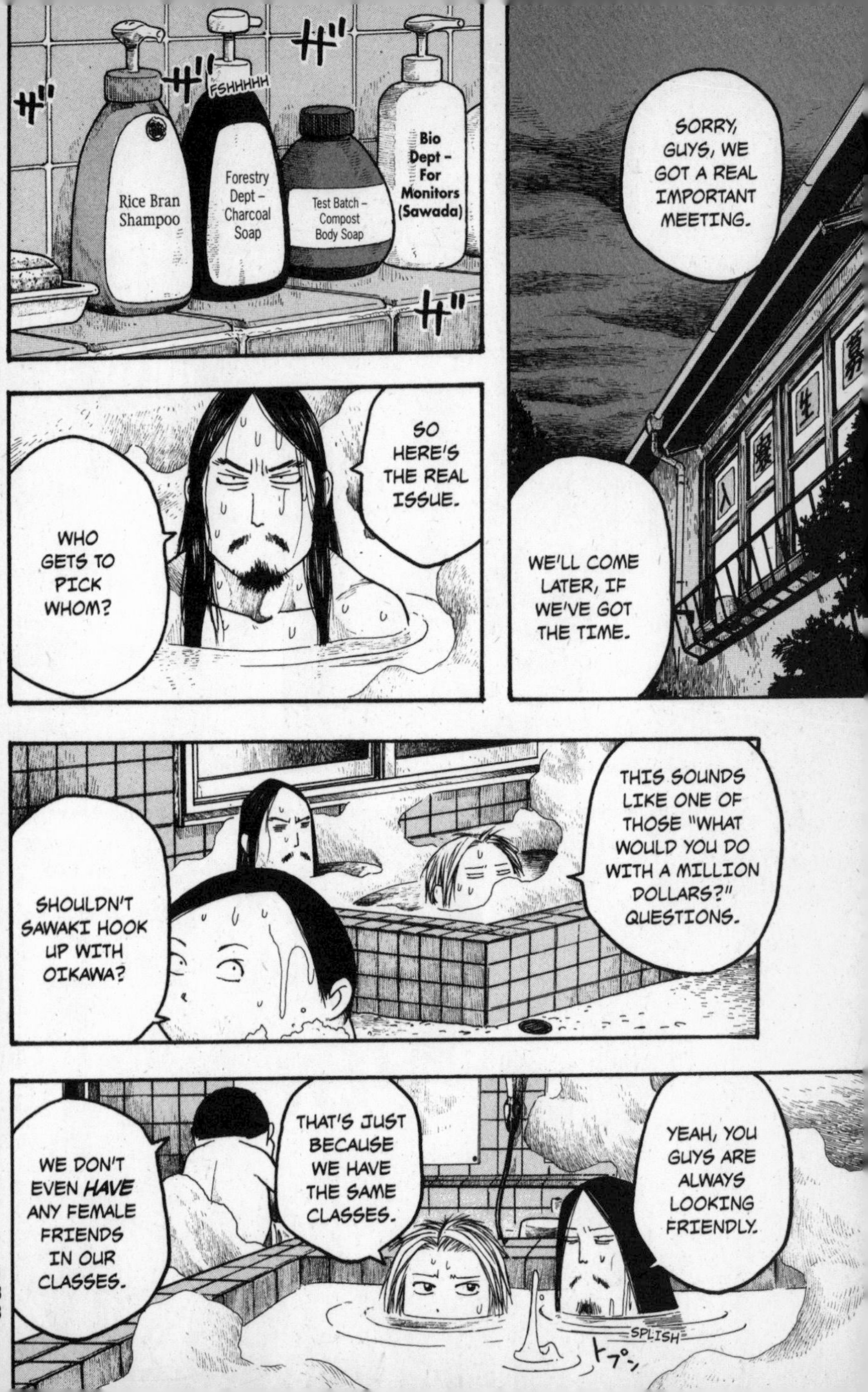
SORRY, GUYS, WE GOT A REAL IMPORTANT MEETING.
WE'LL COME LATER, IF WE'VE GOT THE TIME.
FSHHHHH
Bio Dept – For Monitors (Sawada)
Test Batch – Compost Body Soap
Forestry Dept – Charcoal Soap
Rice Bran Shampoo
SO HERE'S THE REAL ISSUE.
WHO GETS TO PICK WHOM?
THIS SOUNDS LIKE ONE OF THOSE "WHAT WOULD YOU DO WITH A MILLION DOLLARS?" QUESTIONS.
SHOULDN'T SAWAKI HOOK UP WITH OIKAWA?
YEAH, YOU GUYS ARE ALWAYS LOOKING FRIENDLY.
THAT'S JUST BECAUSE WE HAVE THE SAME CLASSES.
WE DON'T EVEN *HAVE* ANY FEMALE FRIENDS IN OUR CLASSES.
SPLISH

C. trichoides
Black mold. In the past, they would breed in the ink for fountain pens, raising a considerable fuss around the world. If you read the first three pages of this chapter very intently, your fingers might turn black, but this has nothing to do with microbes.

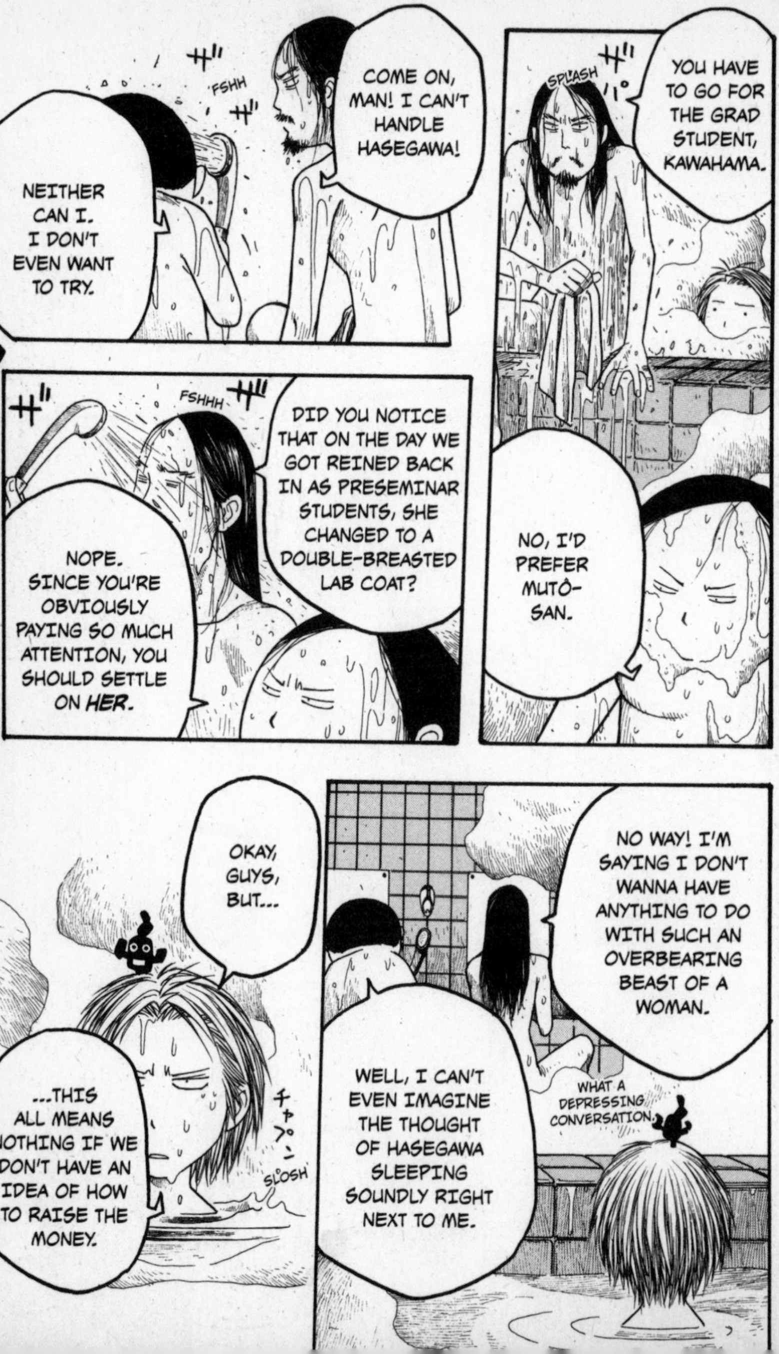
SPLASH
YOU HAVE TO GO FOR THE GRAD STUDENT, KAWAHAMA.
NO, I'D PREFER MUTÔ-SAN.
FSHH
COME ON, MAN! I CAN'T HANDLE HASEGAWA!
NEITHER CAN I. I DON'T EVEN WANT TO TRY.
FSHHH
DID YOU NOTICE THAT ON THE DAY WE GOT REINED BACK IN AS PRESEMINAR STUDENTS, SHE CHANGED TO A DOUBLE-BREASTED LAB COAT?
NOPE. SINCE YOU'RE OBVIOUSLY PAYING SO MUCH ATTENTION, YOU SHOULD SETTLE ON HER.
NO WAY! I'M SAYING I DON'T WANNA HAVE ANYTHING TO DO WITH SUCH AN OVERBEARING BEAST OF A WOMAN.
WELL, I CAN'T EVEN IMAGINE THE THOUGHT OF HASEGAWA SLEEPING SOUNDLY RIGHT NEXT TO ME.
WHAT A DEPRESSING CONVERSATION.
OKAY, GUYS, BUT...
チャプン
SLOSH
...THIS ALL MEANS NOTHING IF WE DON'T HAVE AN IDEA OF HOW TO RAISE THE MONEY.

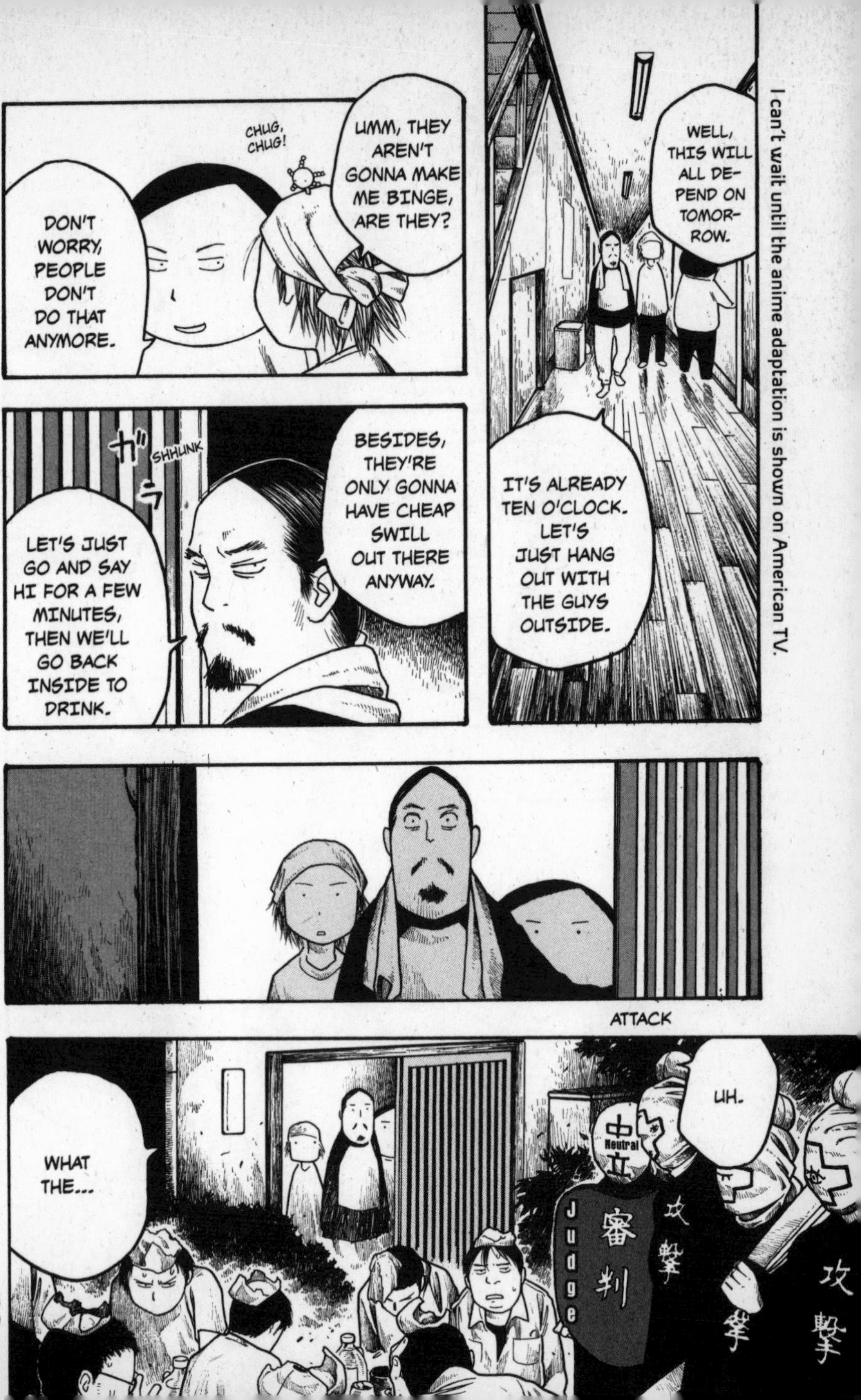
WELL, THIS WILL ALL DE-PEND ON TOMOR-ROW.
IT'S ALREADY TEN O'CLOCK. LET'S JUST HANG OUT WITH THE GUYS OUTSIDE.
UMM, THEY AREN'T GONNA MAKE ME BINGE, ARE THEY?
CHUG, CHUG!
DON'T WORRY, PEOPLE DON'T DO THAT ANYMORE.
BESIDES, THEY'RE ONLY GONNA HAVE CHEAP SWILL OUT THERE ANYWAY.
ガラ
SHHUNK
LET'S JUST GO AND SAY HI FOR A FEW MINUTES, THEN WE'LL GO BACK INSIDE TO DRINK.
ATTACK
攻撃
攻撃
UH.
中立
Neutral
審判
Judge
攻撃
WHAT THE...

I can't wait until the anime adaptation is shown on American TV.

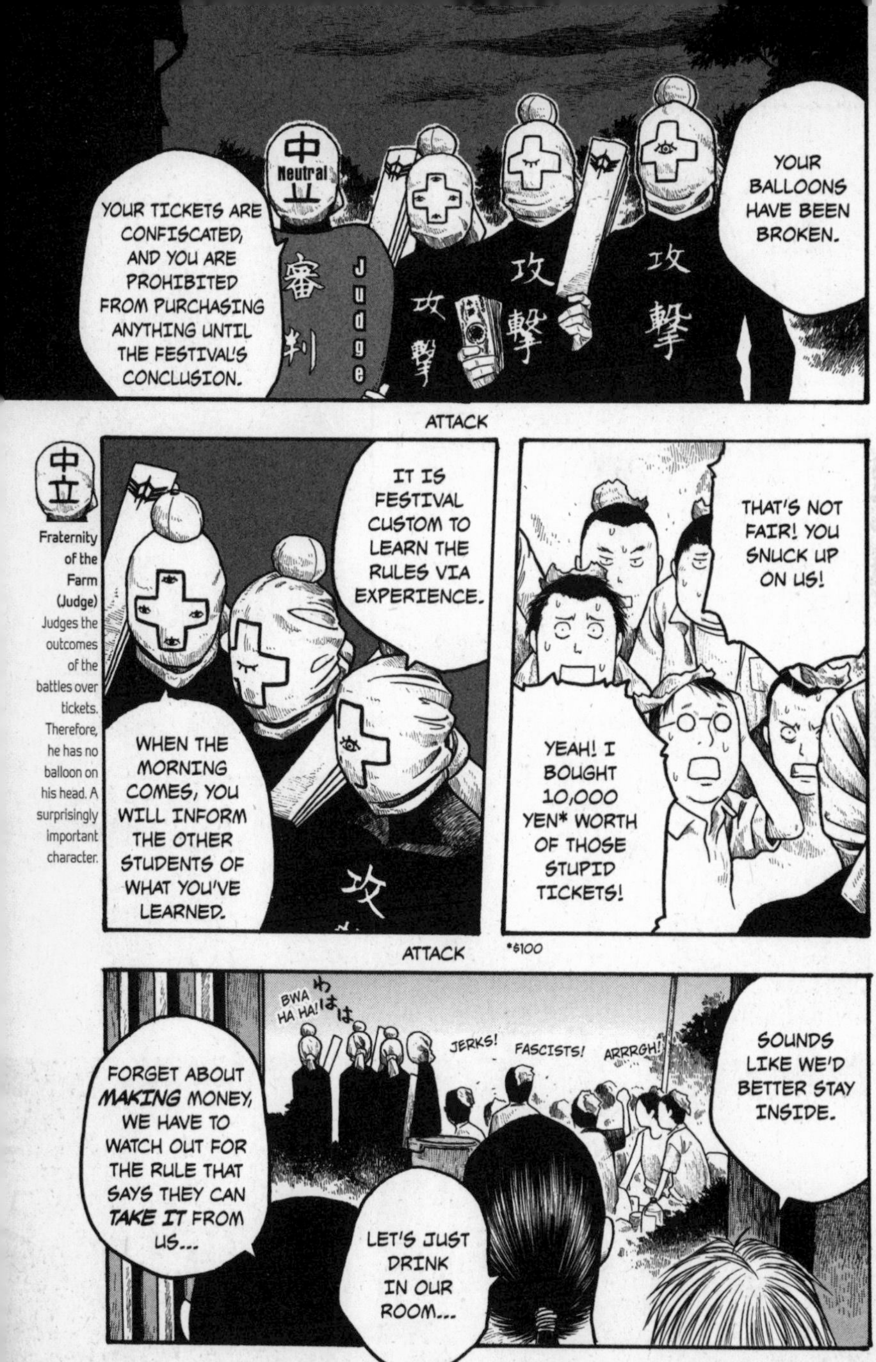
YOUR BALLOONS HAVE BEEN BROKEN.
YOUR TICKETS ARE CONFISCATED, AND YOU ARE PROHIBITED FROM PURCHASING ANYTHING UNTIL THE FESTIVAL'S CONCLUSION.
中立 Neutral
審判 Judge
攻撃
攻撃
攻撃
ATTACK
THAT'S NOT FAIR! YOU SNUCK UP ON US!
YEAH! I BOUGHT 10,000 YEN* WORTH OF THOSE STUPID TICKETS!
IT IS FESTIVAL CUSTOM TO LEARN THE RULES VIA EXPERIENCE.
WHEN THE MORNING COMES, YOU WILL INFORM THE OTHER STUDENTS OF WHAT YOU'VE LEARNED.
中立
Fraternity of the Farm (Judge) Judges the outcomes of the battles over tickets. Therefore, he has no balloon on his head. A surprisingly important character.
ATTACK
*$100
SOUNDS LIKE WE'D BETTER STAY INSIDE.
ARRRGH!
FASCISTS!
JERKS!
わはは BWA HA HA!
FORGET ABOUT *MAKING* MONEY, WE HAVE TO WATCH OUT FOR THE RULE THAT SAYS THEY CAN *TAKE IT* FROM US...
LET'S JUST DRINK IN OUR ROOM...

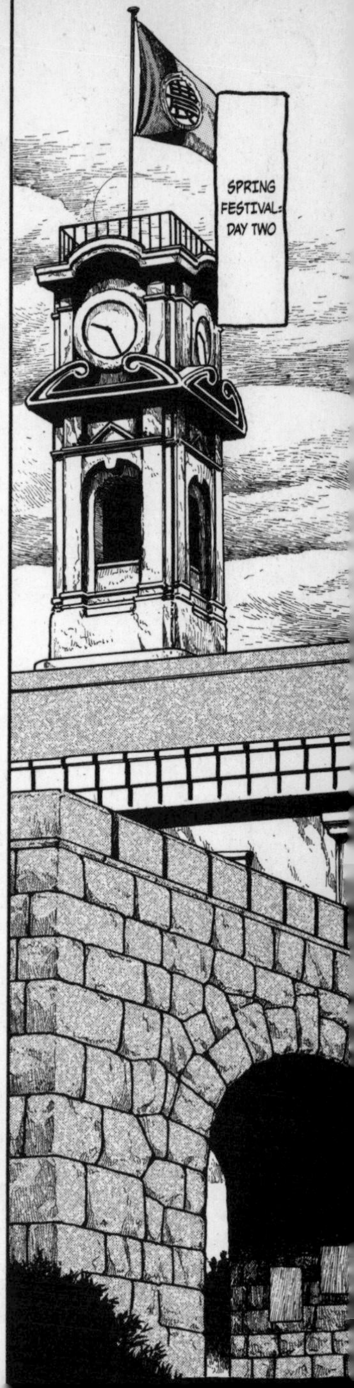
SPRING FESTIVAL: DAY TWO

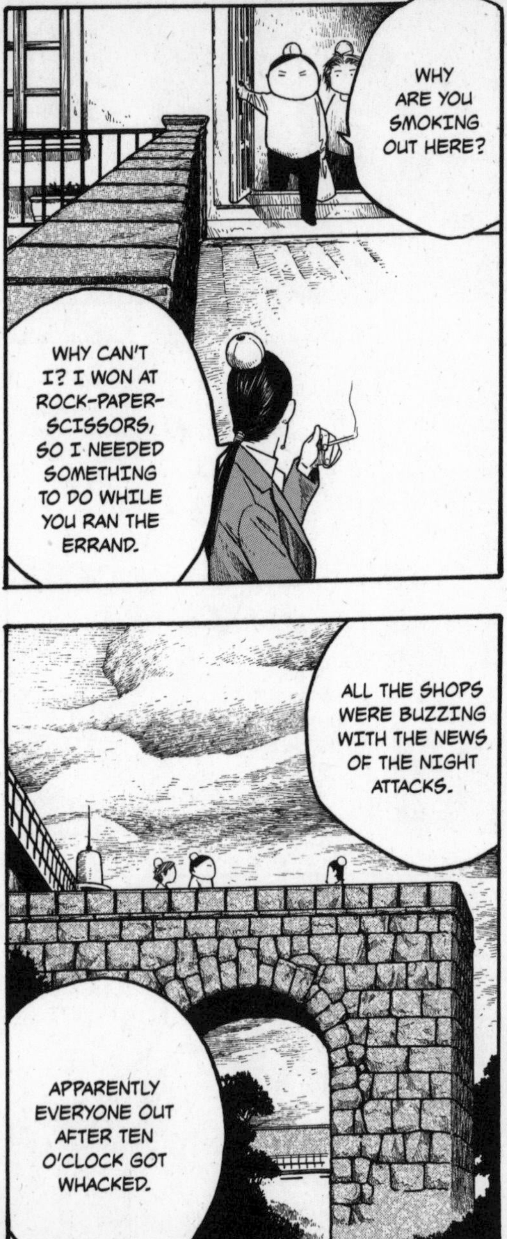
WHY ARE YOU SMOKING OUT HERE?
WHY CAN'T I? I WON AT ROCK-PAPER-SCISSORS, SO I NEEDED SOMETHING TO DO WHILE YOU RAN THE ERRAND.
ALL THE SHOPS WERE BUZZING WITH THE NEWS OF THE NIGHT ATTACKS.
APPARENTLY EVERYONE OUT AFTER TEN O'CLOCK GOT WHACKED.

Hopefully we'll get a chance to show off all the neat *Moyasimon* merchandise.

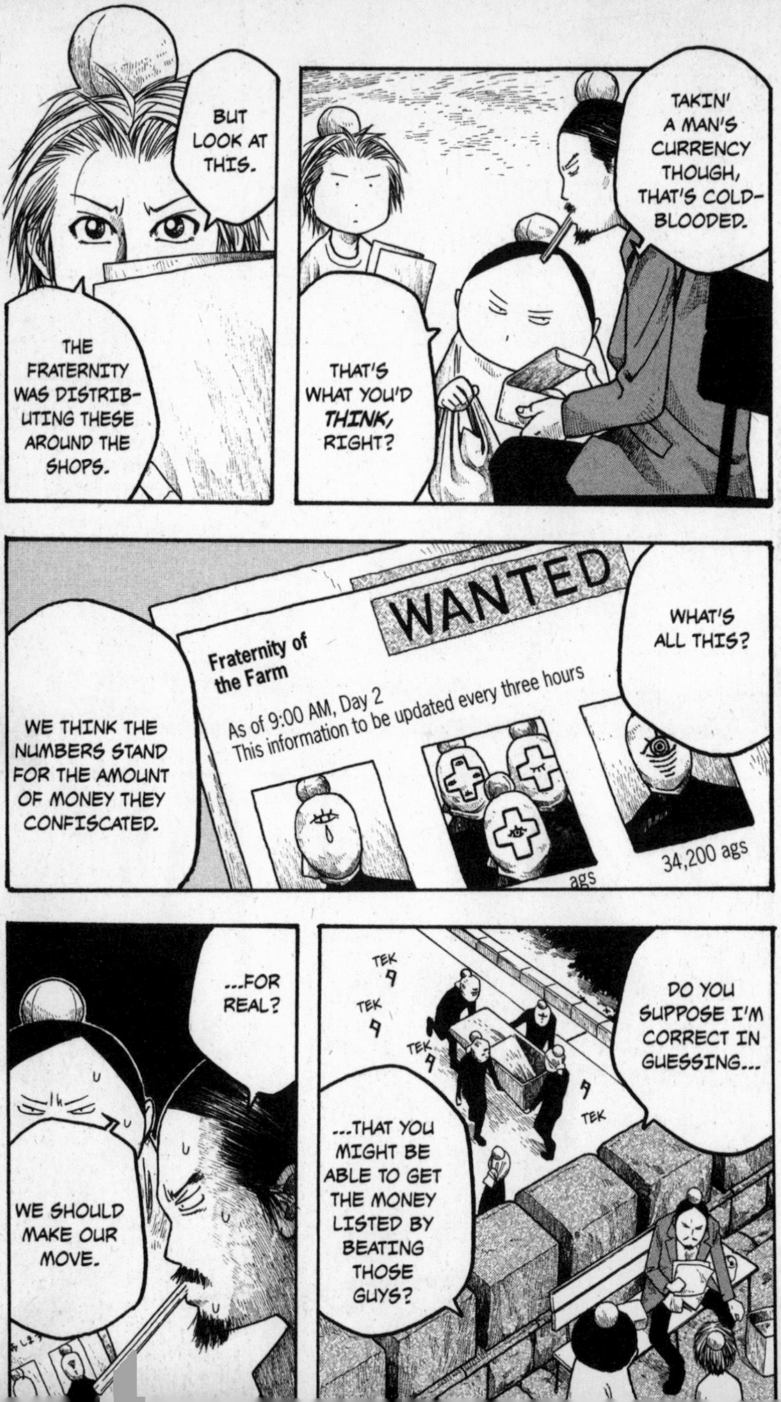

TAKIN' A MAN'S CURRENCY THOUGH, THAT'S COLD-BLOODED.
THAT'S WHAT YOU'D *THINK*, RIGHT?
BUT LOOK AT THIS.
THE FRATERNITY WAS DISTRIBUTING THESE AROUND THE SHOPS.
WHAT'S ALL THIS?
WANTED
Fraternity of the Farm
As of 9:00 AM, Day 2
This information to be updated every three hours
34,200 ags
ags
WE THINK THE NUMBERS STAND FOR THE AMOUNT OF MONEY THEY CONFISCATED.
TEK
TEK
TEK
TEK
DO YOU SUPPOSE I'M CORRECT IN GUESSING...
...THAT YOU MIGHT BE ABLE TO GET THE MONEY LISTED BY BEATING THOSE GUYS?
...FOR REAL?
WE SHOULD MAKE OUR MOVE.

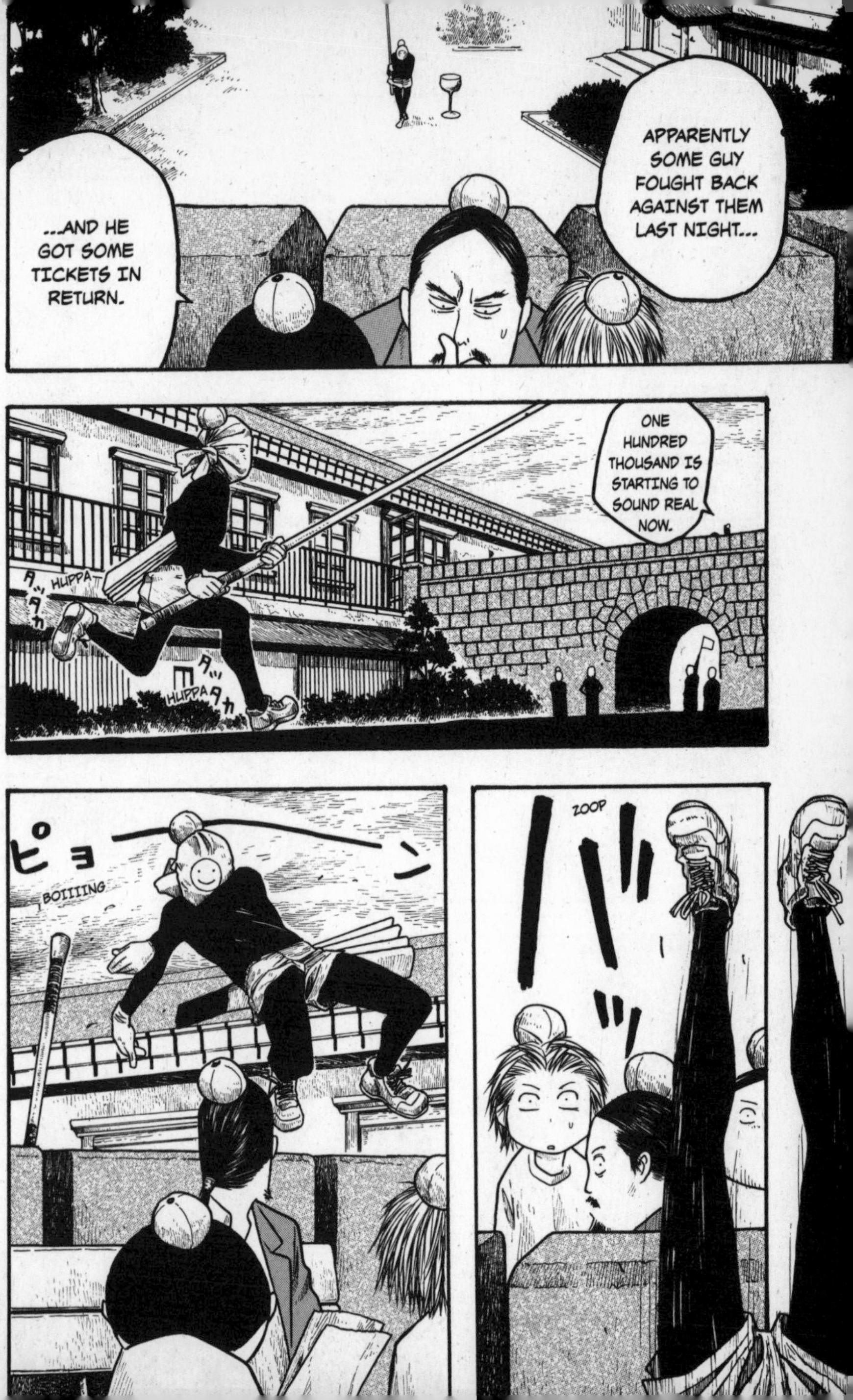
APPARENTLY SOME GUY FOUGHT BACK AGAINST THEM LAST NIGHT...
...AND HE GOT SOME TICKETS IN RETURN.
ONE HUNDRED THOUSAND IS STARTING TO SOUND REAL NOW.
タッタカ
HUPPA
タッタカ
HUPPA
バッ
ZOOP
ピョーン
BOIIIING

WHAT'S GOING ON?!

THEY'LL ATTACK US IN THE DAYTIME, TOO?!

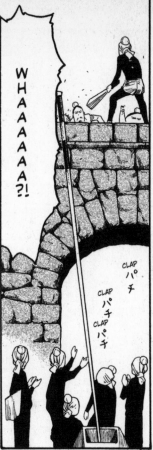

WHAAAAAA?!

CLAP パチ

CLAP パチ

CLAP パチ

SETTLE DOWN! THERE ARE THREE OF US!

WE CAN TAKE HIM!

WHOA!

AAAAHHH!!

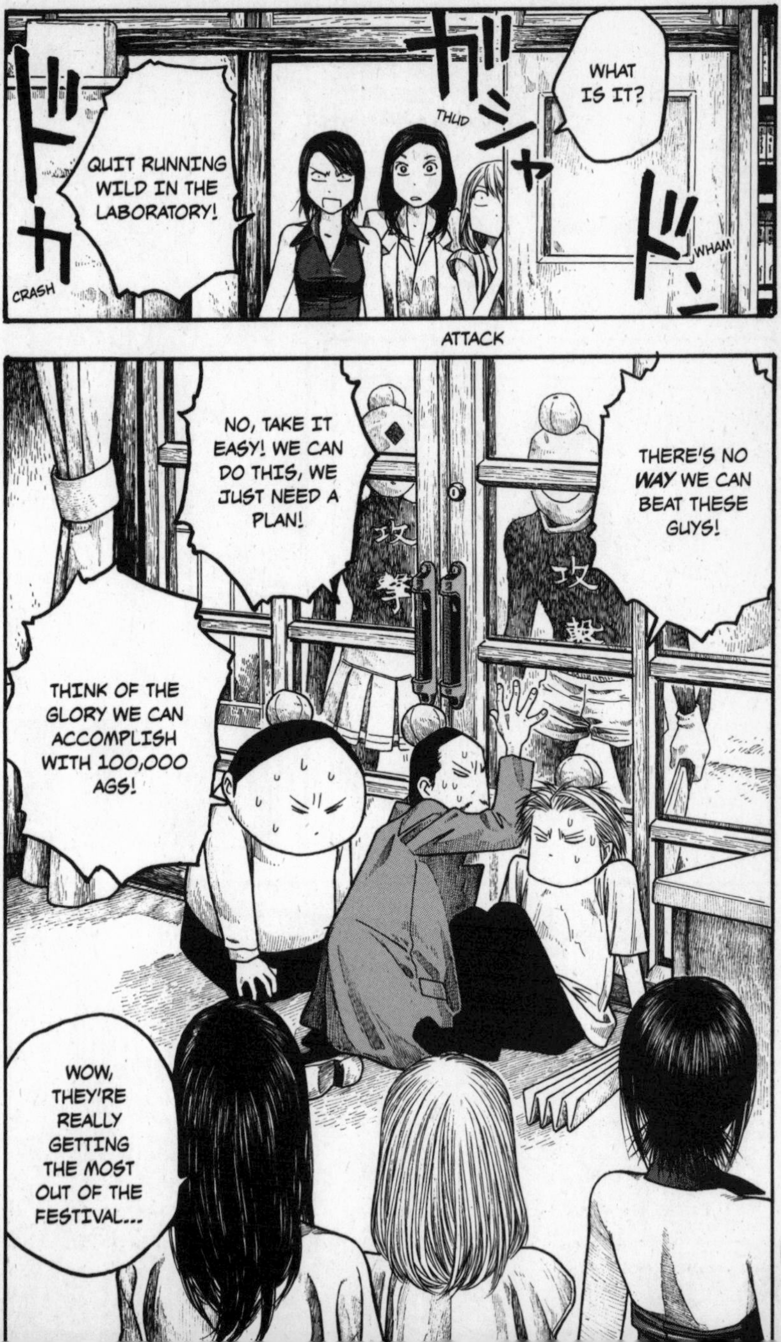
WHAT IS IT?
ドン
WHAM
ガシャ
THUD
QUIT RUNNING WILD IN THE LABORATORY!
ドカ
CRASH
ATTACK
THERE'S NO *WAY* WE CAN BEAT THESE GUYS!
NO, TAKE IT EASY! WE CAN DO THIS, WE JUST NEED A PLAN!
THINK OF THE GLORY WE CAN ACCOMPLISH WITH 100,000 AGS!
WOW, THEY'RE REALLY GETTING THE MOST OUT OF THE FESTIVAL...

I wonder what campus festivals are like in America.

19 END

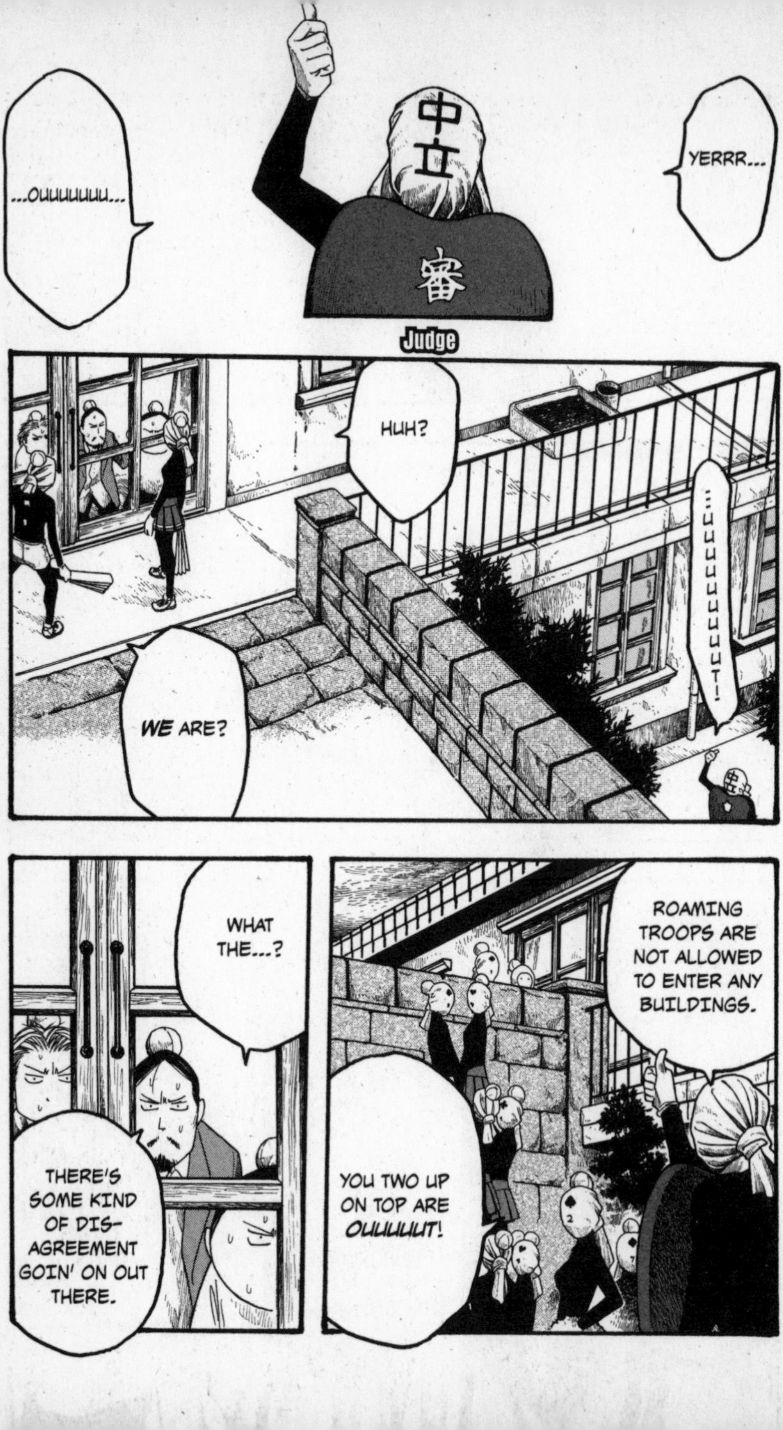
YERRR...
...OUUUUUUU...
Judge
...UUUUUUUUUT!
HUH?
WE ARE?
ROAMING TROOPS ARE NOT ALLOWED TO ENTER ANY BUILDINGS.
YOU TWO UP ON TOP ARE OUUUUUT!
WHAT THE...?
THERE'S SOME KIND OF DIS-AGREEMENT GOIN' ON OUT THERE.

America is the home of baseball, right?

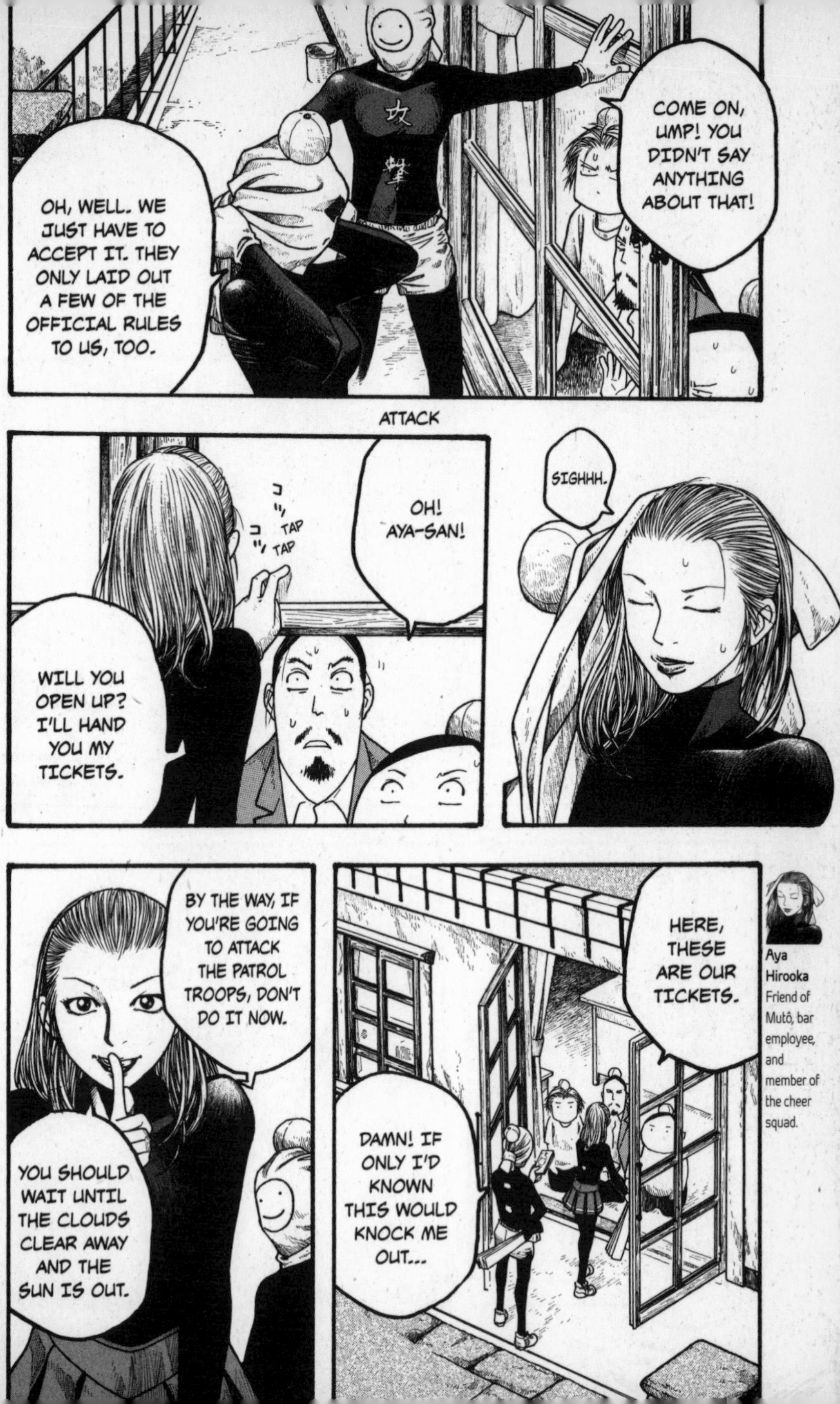
COME ON, UMP! YOU DIDN'T SAY ANYTHING ABOUT THAT!
OH, WELL. WE JUST HAVE TO ACCEPT IT. THEY ONLY LAID OUT A FEW OF THE OFFICIAL RULES TO US, TOO.
ATTACK
SIGHHH.
OH! AYA-SAN!
TAP TAP
WILL YOU OPEN UP? I'LL HAND YOU MY TICKETS.
HERE, THESE ARE OUR TICKETS.
DAMN! IF ONLY I'D KNOWN THIS WOULD KNOCK ME OUT...
BY THE WAY, IF YOU'RE GOING TO ATTACK THE PATROL TROOPS, DON'T DO IT NOW.
YOU SHOULD WAIT UNTIL THE CLOUDS CLEAR AWAY AND THE SUN IS OUT.
Aya Hirooka
Friend of Mutô, bar employee, and member of the cheer squad.

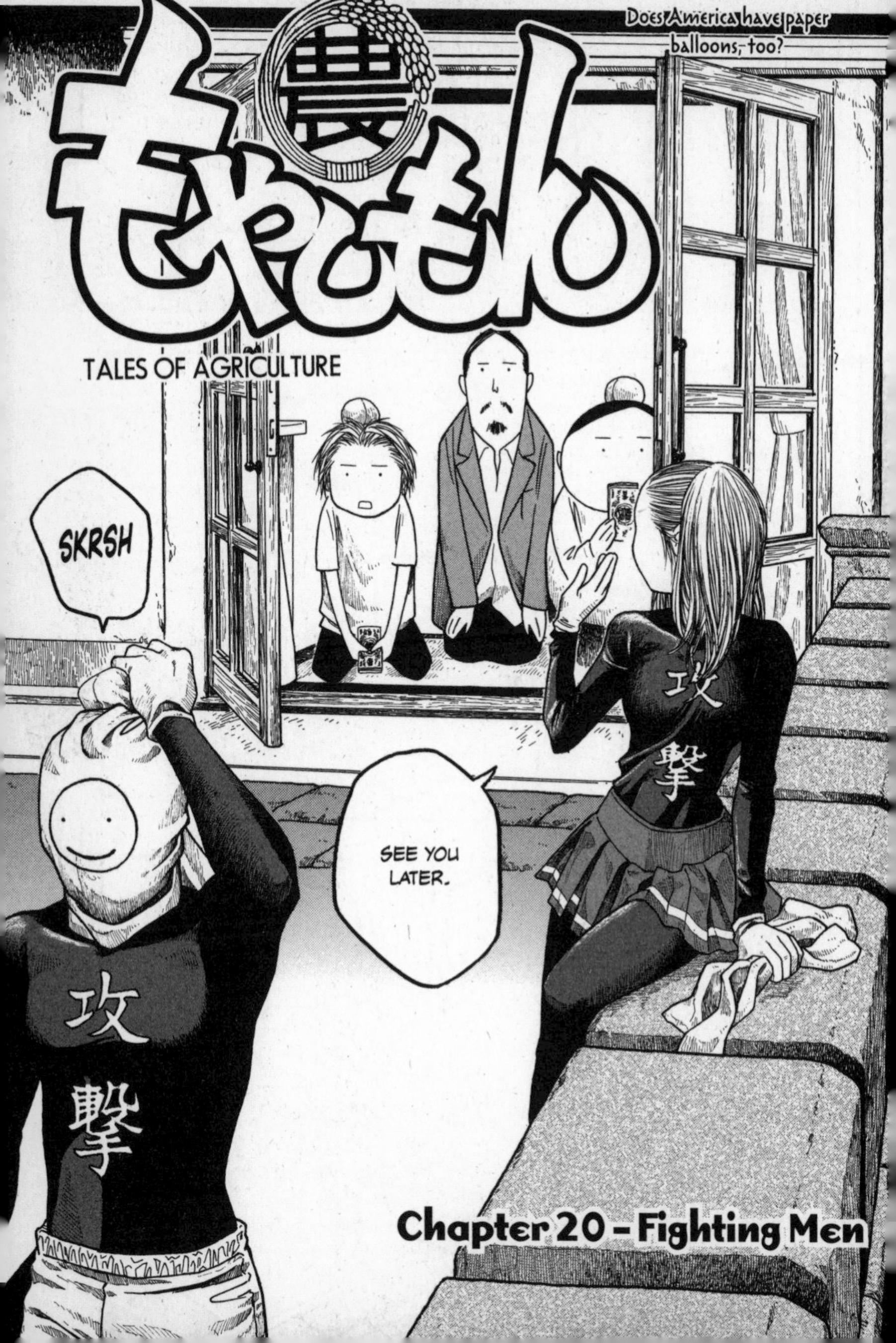
もやしもん
TALES OF AGRICULTURE
Does America have paper balloons, too?
SKRSH
SEE YOU LATER.
攻撃
攻撃
Chapter 20 - Fighting Men

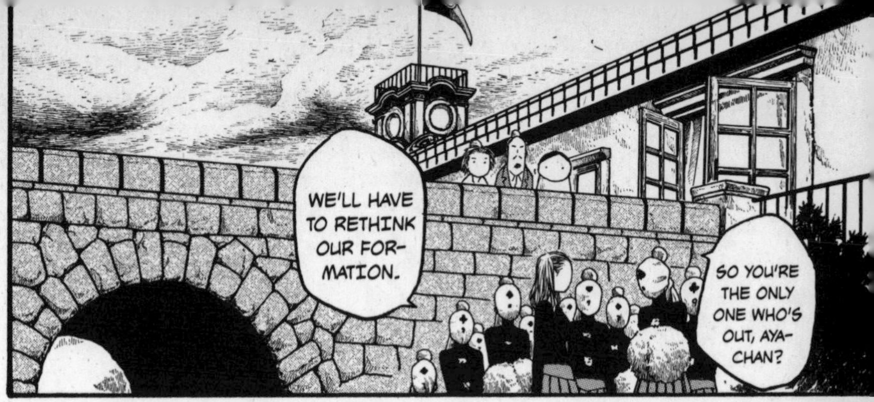
SO YOU'RE THE ONLY ONE WHO'S OUT, AYA-CHAN?
WE'LL HAVE TO RETHINK OUR FOR-MATION.

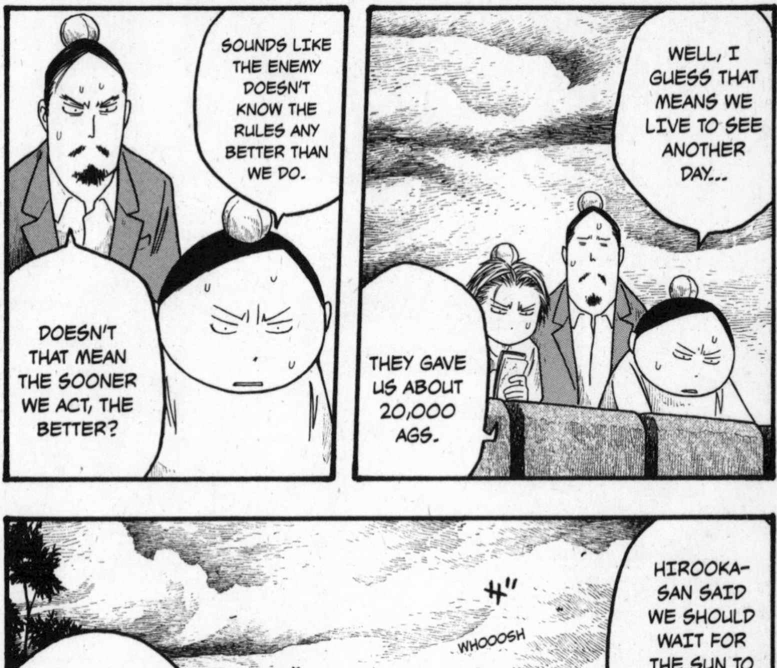
WELL, I GUESS THAT MEANS WE LIVE TO SEE ANOTHER DAY...
THEY GAVE US ABOUT 20,000 AGS.
SOUNDS LIKE THE ENEMY DOESN'T KNOW THE RULES ANY BETTER THAN WE DO.
DOESN'T THAT MEAN THE SOONER WE ACT, THE BETTER?
HIROOKA-SAN SAID WE SHOULD WAIT FOR THE SUN TO COME OUT.
ザ"
WHOOOSH
ザ"
ザ"
出店エリア
YEAH, BUT A STUDENT ISN'T GOING TO MAKE 100,000 WITHOUT TAKING A FEW RISKS HERE AND THERE.

Store Area

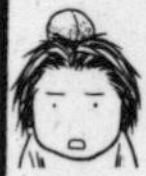

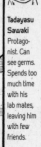

Tadayasu Sawaki
Protagonist. Can see germs. Spends too much time with his lab mates, leaving him with few friends.

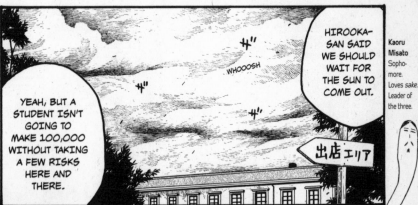

Kaoru Misato
Sophomore. Loves *sake*. Leader of the three.

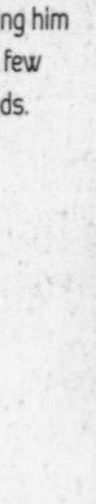

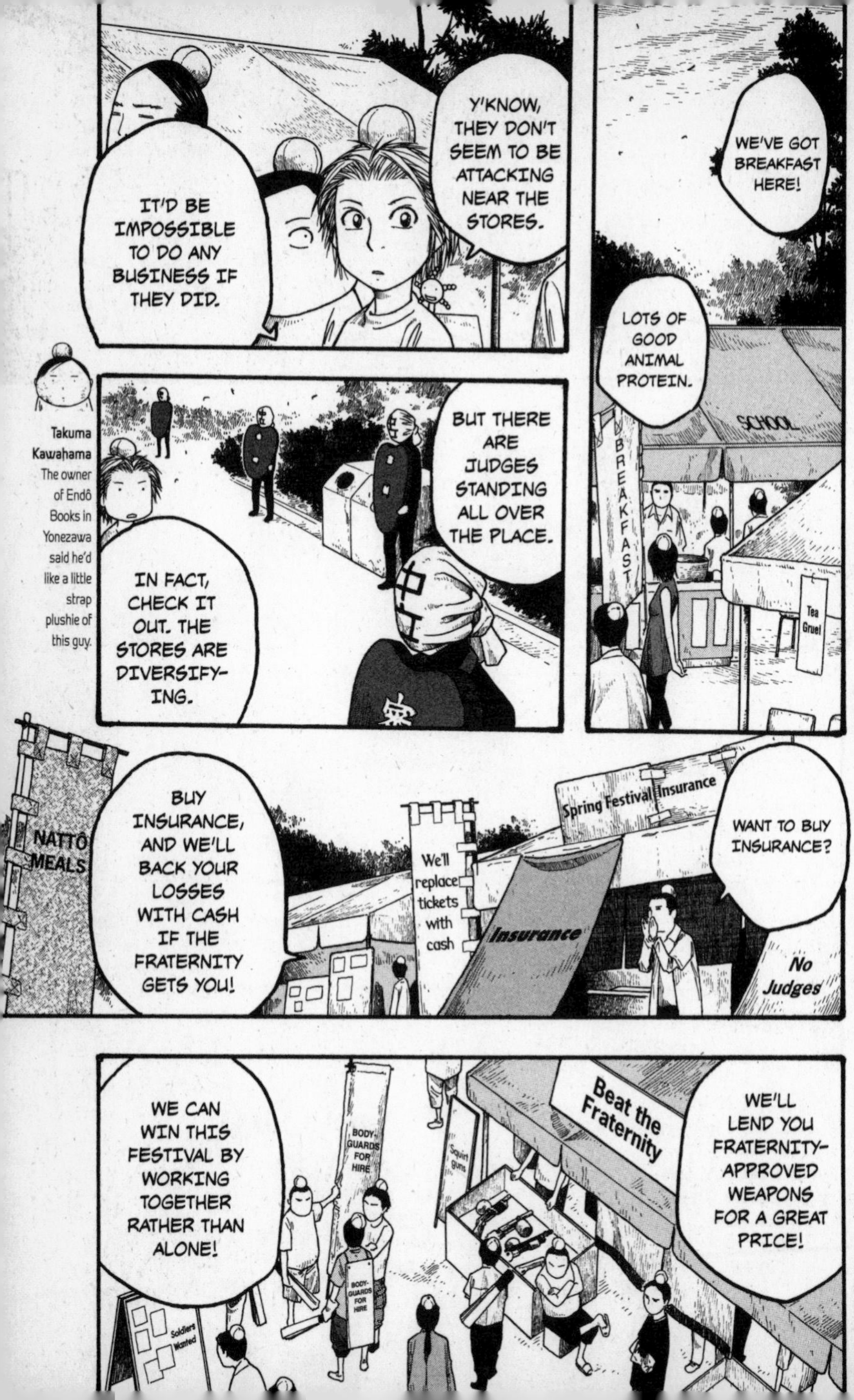
WE'VE GOT BREAKFAST HERE!
LOTS OF GOOD ANIMAL PROTEIN.
SCHOOL
BREAKFAST
Tea Gruel
Y'KNOW, THEY DON'T SEEM TO BE ATTACKING NEAR THE STORES.
IT'D BE IMPOSSIBLE TO DO ANY BUSINESS IF THEY DID.
BUT THERE ARE JUDGES STANDING ALL OVER THE PLACE.
IN FACT, CHECK IT OUT. THE STORES ARE DIVERSIFY-ING.
Takuma Kawahama The owner of Endô Books in Yonezawa said he'd like a little strap plushie of this guy.
Spring Festival Insurance
WANT TO BUY INSURANCE?
No Judges
Insurance
We'll replace tickets with cash
BUY INSURANCE, AND WE'LL BACK YOUR LOSSES WITH CASH IF THE FRATERNITY GETS YOU!
NATTÔ MEALS
Beat the Fraternity
WE'LL LEND YOU FRATERNITY-APPROVED WEAPONS FOR A GREAT PRICE!
Squirt guns
BODY-GUARDS FOR HIRE
WE CAN WIN THIS FESTIVAL BY WORKING TOGETHER RATHER THAN ALONE!
BODY-GUARDS FOR HIRE
Soldiers Wanted

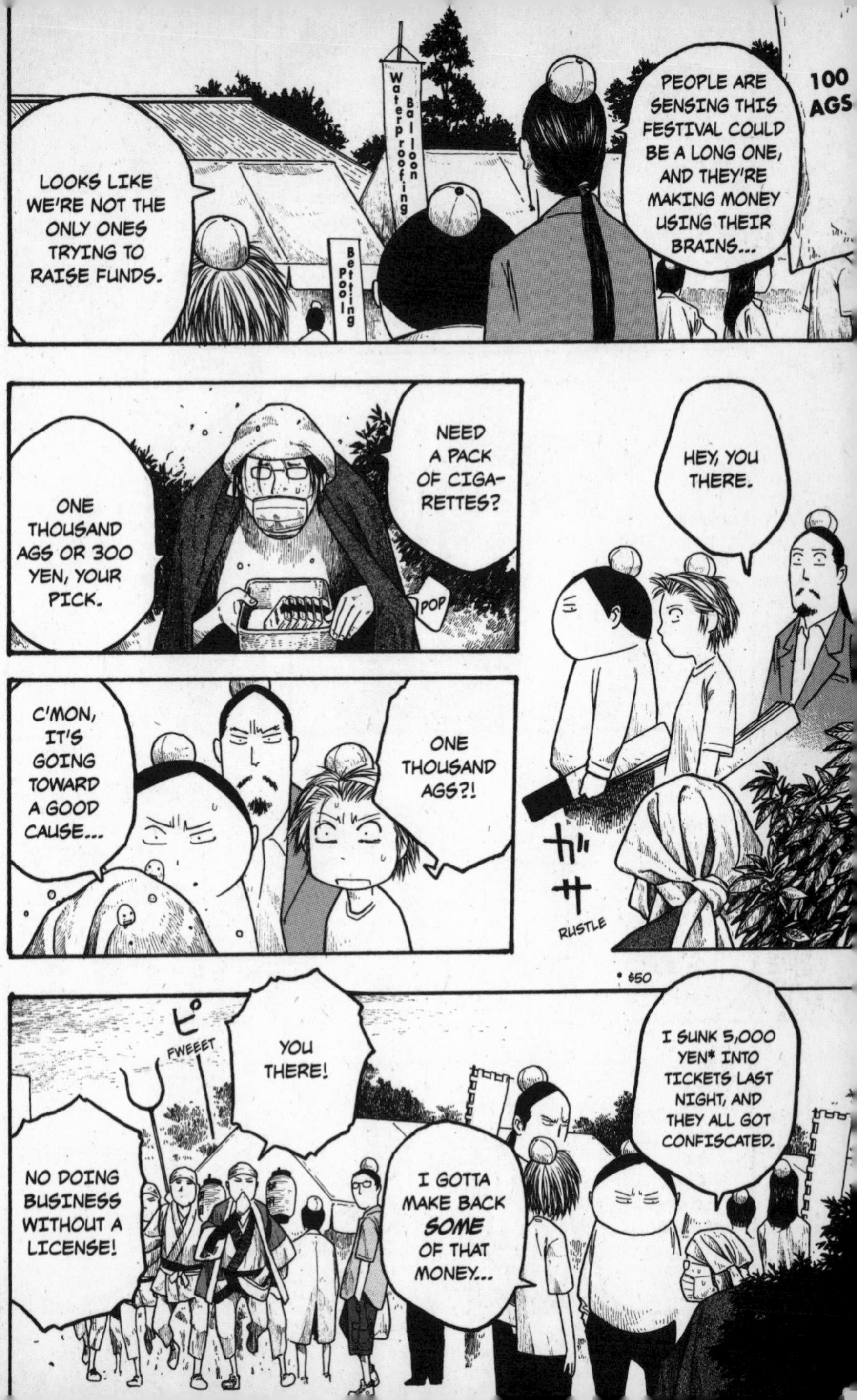
100 AGS
PEOPLE ARE SENSING THIS FESTIVAL COULD BE A LONG ONE, AND THEY'RE MAKING MONEY USING THEIR BRAINS...
Balloon Waterproofing
Betting Pool
LOOKS LIKE WE'RE NOT THE ONLY ONES TRYING TO RAISE FUNDS.
HEY, YOU THERE.
ガサ
RUSTLE
NEED A PACK OF CIGARETTES?
POP
ONE THOUSAND AGS OR 300 YEN, YOUR PICK.
ONE THOUSAND AGS?!
C'MON, IT'S GOING TOWARD A GOOD CAUSE...
* $50
I SUNK 5,000 YEN* INTO TICKETS LAST NIGHT, AND THEY ALL GOT CONFISCATED.
I GOTTA MAKE BACK *SOME* OF THAT MONEY...
YOU THERE!
ピ
FWEEET
NO DOING BUSINESS WITHOUT A LICENSE!

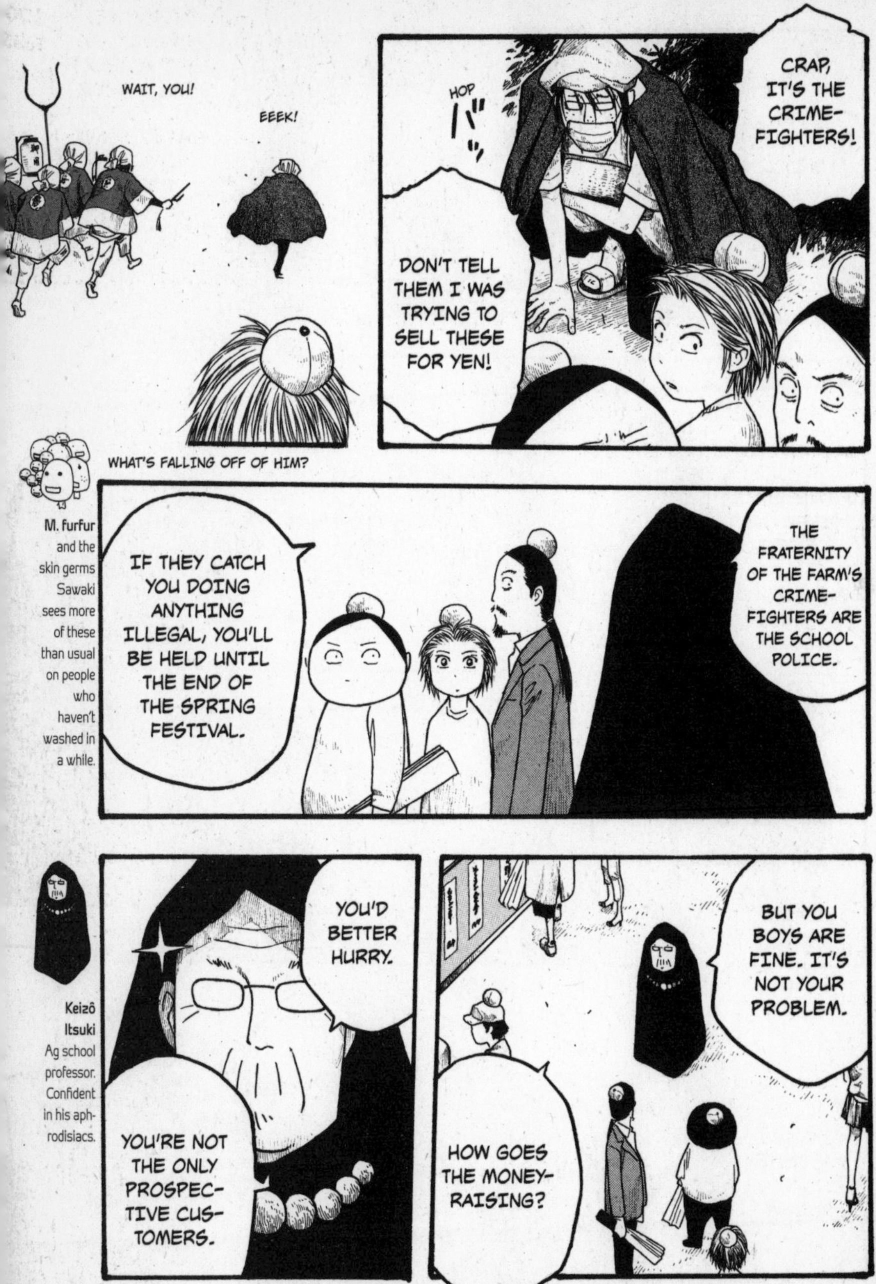
CRAP, IT'S THE CRIME-FIGHTERS!
HOP
バッ
DON'T TELL THEM I WAS TRYING TO SELL THESE FOR YEN!
WAIT, YOU!
EEEK!
WHAT'S FALLING OFF OF HIM?
M. furfur and the skin germs Sawaki sees more of these than usual on people who haven't washed in a while.
THE FRATERNITY OF THE FARM'S CRIME-FIGHTERS ARE THE SCHOOL POLICE.
IF THEY CATCH YOU DOING ANYTHING ILLEGAL, YOU'LL BE HELD UNTIL THE END OF THE SPRING FESTIVAL.
BUT YOU BOYS ARE FINE. IT'S NOT YOUR PROBLEM.
HOW GOES THE MONEY-RAISING?
YOU'D BETTER HURRY.
YOU'RE NOT THE ONLY PROSPEC-TIVE CUS-TOMERS.
Keizô Itsuki Ag school professor. Confident in his aph-rodisiacs.

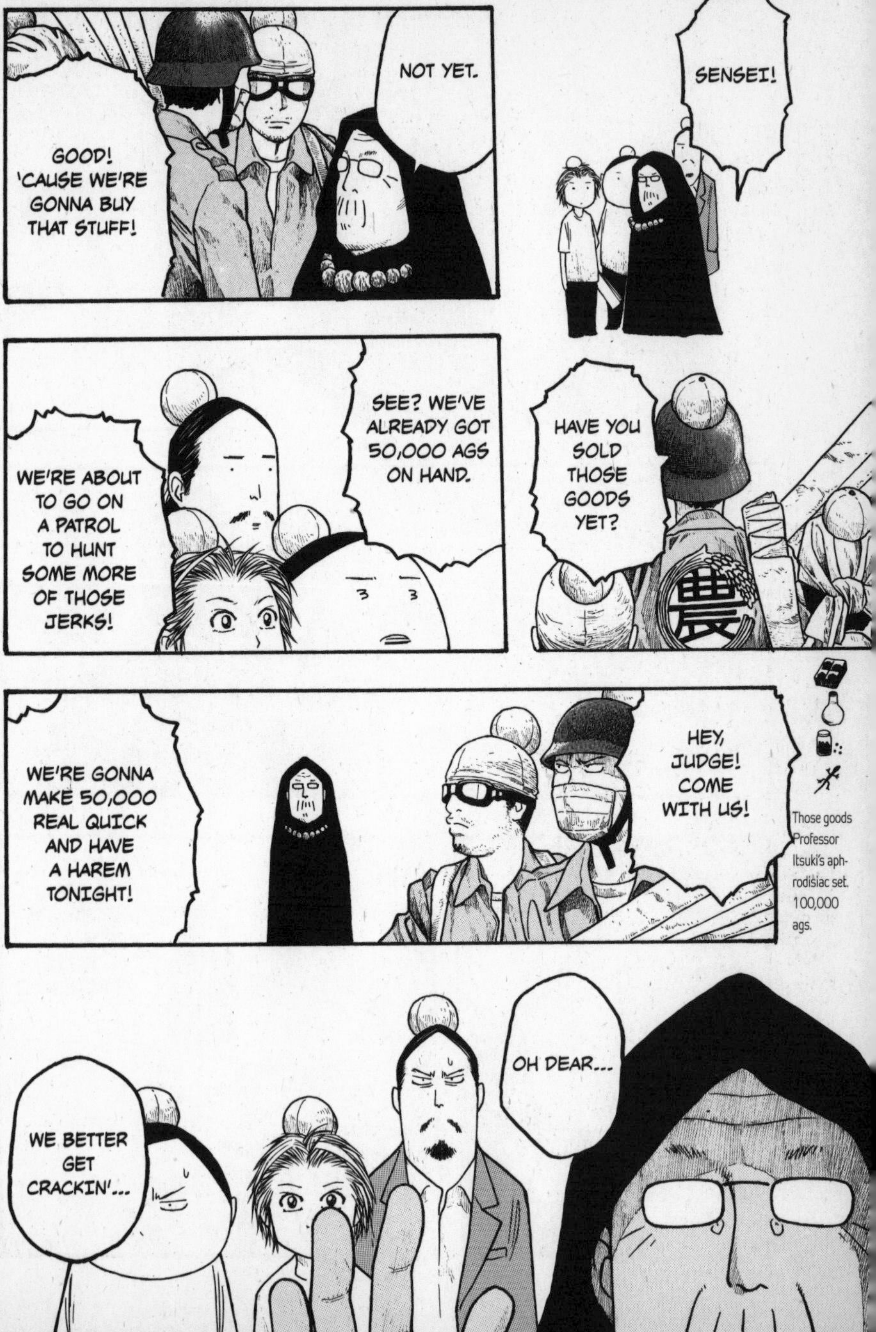
SENSEI!
NOT YET.
GOOD! 'CAUSE WE'RE GONNA BUY THAT STUFF!
HAVE YOU SOLD THOSE GOODS YET?
SEE? WE'VE ALREADY GOT 50,000 AGS ON HAND.
WE'RE ABOUT TO GO ON A PATROL TO HUNT SOME MORE OF THOSE JERKS!
HEY, JUDGE! COME WITH US!
WE'RE GONNA MAKE 50,000 REAL QUICK AND HAVE A HAREM TONIGHT!
Those goods Professor Itsuki's aphrodisiac set. 100,000 ags.
OH DEAR...
WE BETTER GET CRACKIN'...

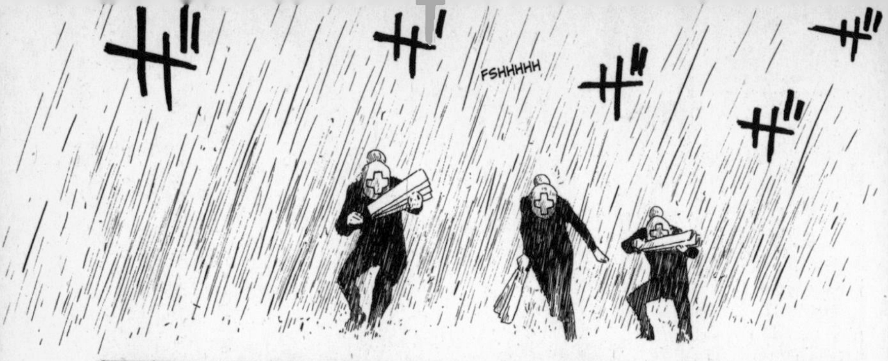
FSHHHHH

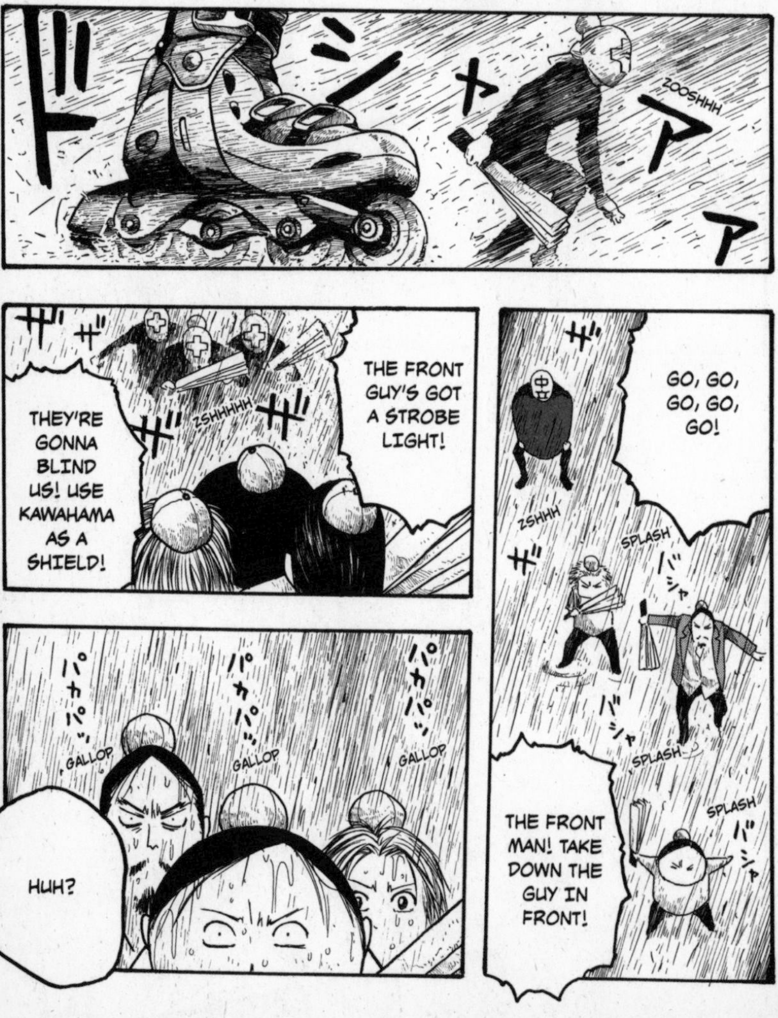
ZOOSHHH
ZSHHH
GO, GO, GO, GO, GO!
SPLASH
SPLASH
SPLASH
THE FRONT MAN! TAKE DOWN THE GUY IN FRONT!
THE FRONT GUY'S GOT A STROBE LIGHT!
ZSHHHHH
THEY'RE GONNA BLIND US! USE KAWAHAMA AS A SHIELD!
GALLOP
GALLOP
GALLOP
HUH?

Fraternity of the Farm Reserves (Black Tri-Stars) Members of the ice hockey team. People don't call these "roller skates" anymore, do they? FYI, if you do not know what Black Tri-Star is, please watch *Gundam*.

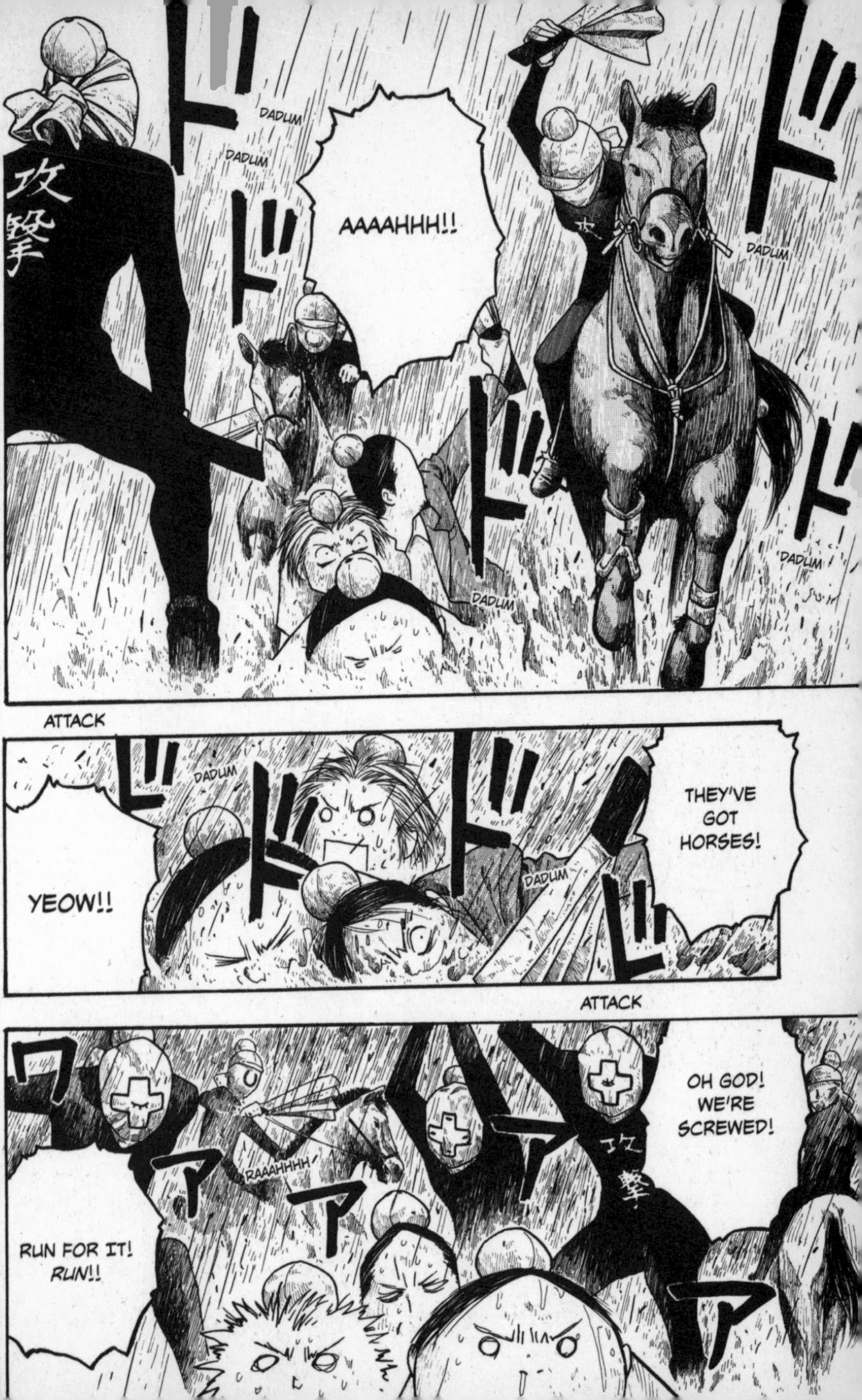
DADUM
AAAAHHH!!
DADUM
DADUM
DADUM
DADUM
攻撃
ATTACK
THEY'VE GOT HORSES!
DADUM
DADUM
YEOW!!
ATTACK
OH GOD! WE'RE SCREWED!
攻撃
RAAAHHHH
RUN FOR IT! RUN!!

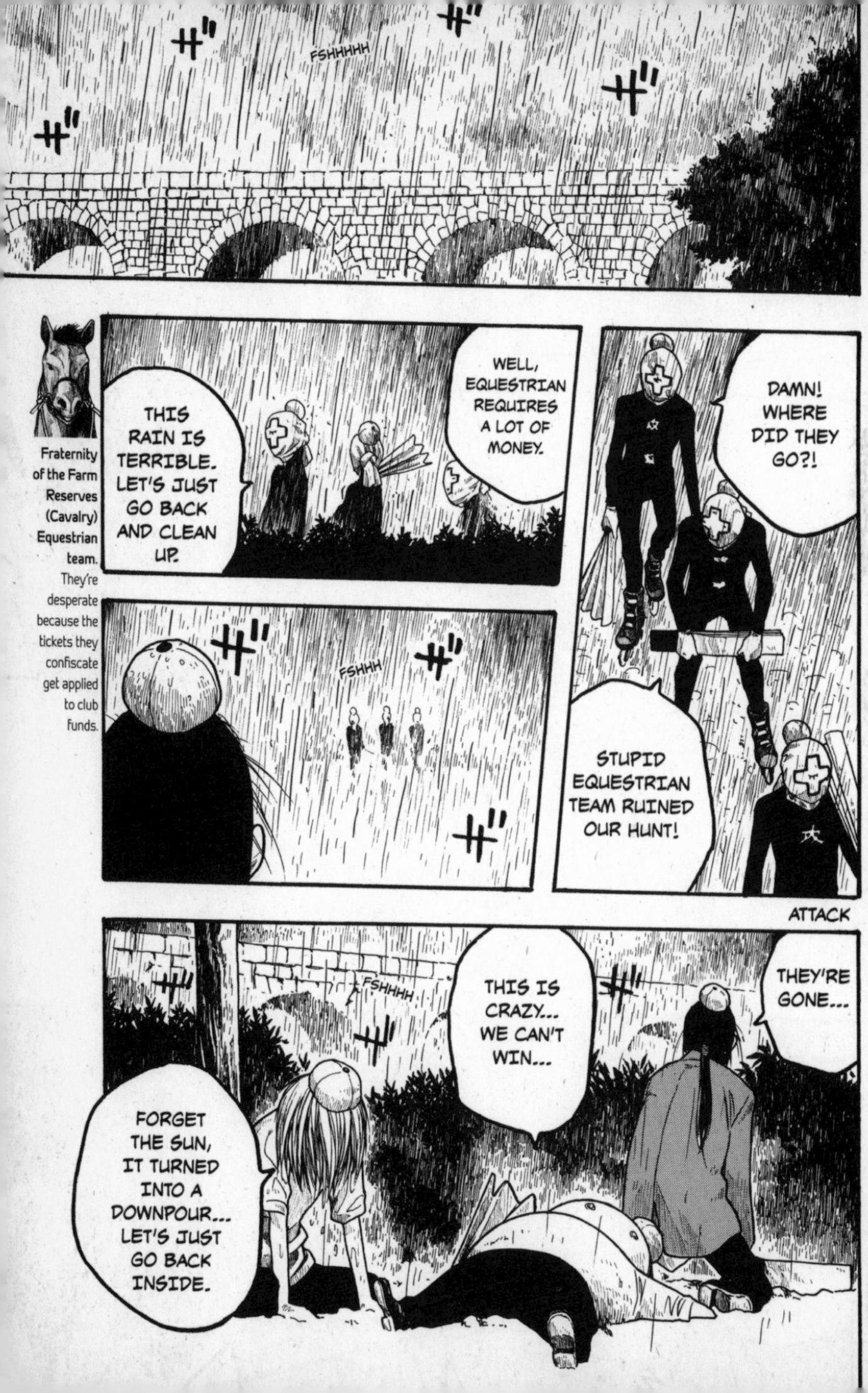
FSHHHHH
DAMN! WHERE DID THEY GO?!
STUPID EQUESTRIAN TEAM RUINED OUR HUNT!
WELL, EQUESTRIAN REQUIRES A LOT OF MONEY.
THIS RAIN IS TERRIBLE. LET'S JUST GO BACK AND CLEAN UP.
Fraternity of the Farm Reserves (Cavalry) Equestrian team. They're desperate because the tickets they confiscate get applied to club funds.
FSHHH
ATTACK
THEY'RE GONE...
THIS IS CRAZY... WE CAN'T WIN...
FSHHHH
FORGET THE SUN, IT TURNED INTO A DOWNPOUR... LET'S JUST GO BACK INSIDE.

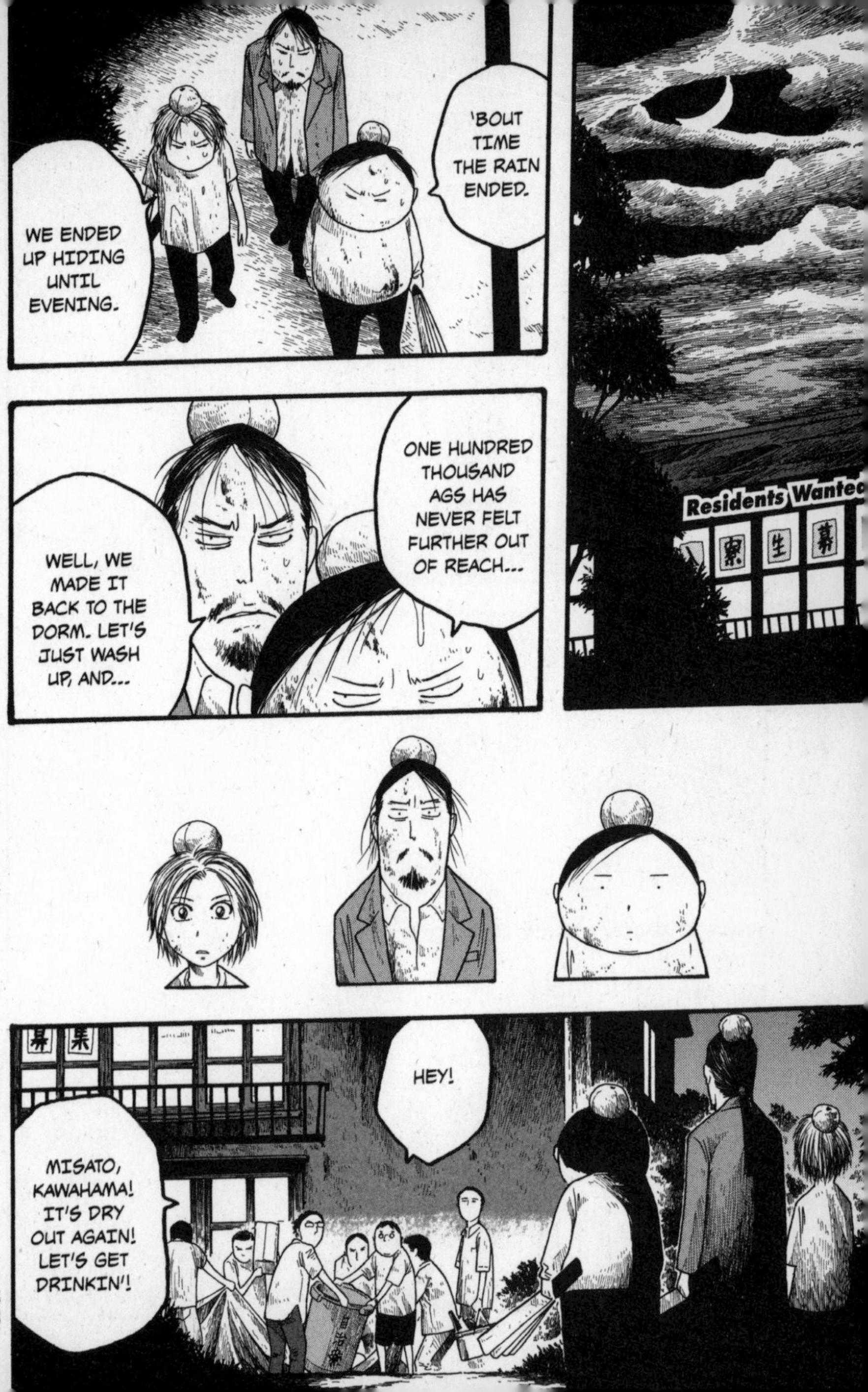
Residents Wanted
'BOUT TIME THE RAIN ENDED.
WE ENDED UP HIDING UNTIL EVENING.
ONE HUNDRED THOUSAND AGS HAS NEVER FELT FURTHER OUT OF REACH...
WELL, WE MADE IT BACK TO THE DORM. LET'S JUST WASH UP, AND...
HEY!
MISATO, KAWAHAMA! IT'S DRY OUT AGAIN! LET'S GET DRINKIN'!

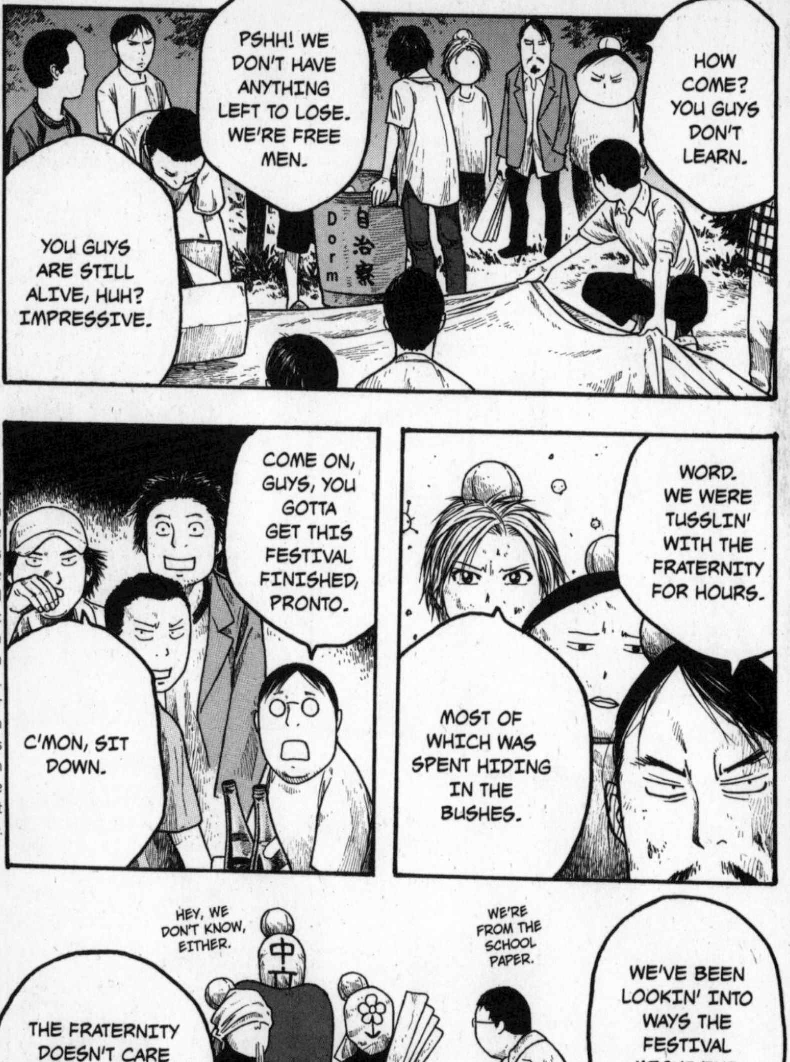
HOW COME? YOU GUYS DON'T LEARN.
PSHH! WE DON'T HAVE ANYTHING LEFT TO LOSE. WE'RE FREE MEN.
YOU GUYS ARE STILL ALIVE, HUH? IMPRESSIVE.
Dorm
WORD. WE WERE TUSSLIN' WITH THE FRATERNITY FOR HOURS.
MOST OF WHICH WAS SPENT HIDING IN THE BUSHES.
COME ON, GUYS, YOU GOTTA GET THIS FESTIVAL FINISHED, PRONTO.
C'MON, SIT DOWN.
WE'VE BEEN LOOKIN' INTO WAYS THE FESTIVAL MIGHT END.
WE'RE FROM THE SCHOOL PAPER.
NOT REALLY.
HEY, WE DON'T KNOW, EITHER.
THE FRATERNITY DOESN'T CARE ABOUT GUYS WHOSE BALLOONS HAVE ALREADY BEEN POPPED, SO IT WAS EASY TO GATHER INFORMATION.

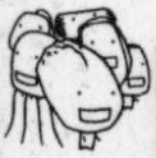

C. botulinum and the soil germs They're covered with dirt germs from hiding on the ground. Remember to wash your hands and mouth every time you get home.

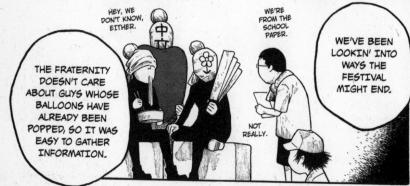

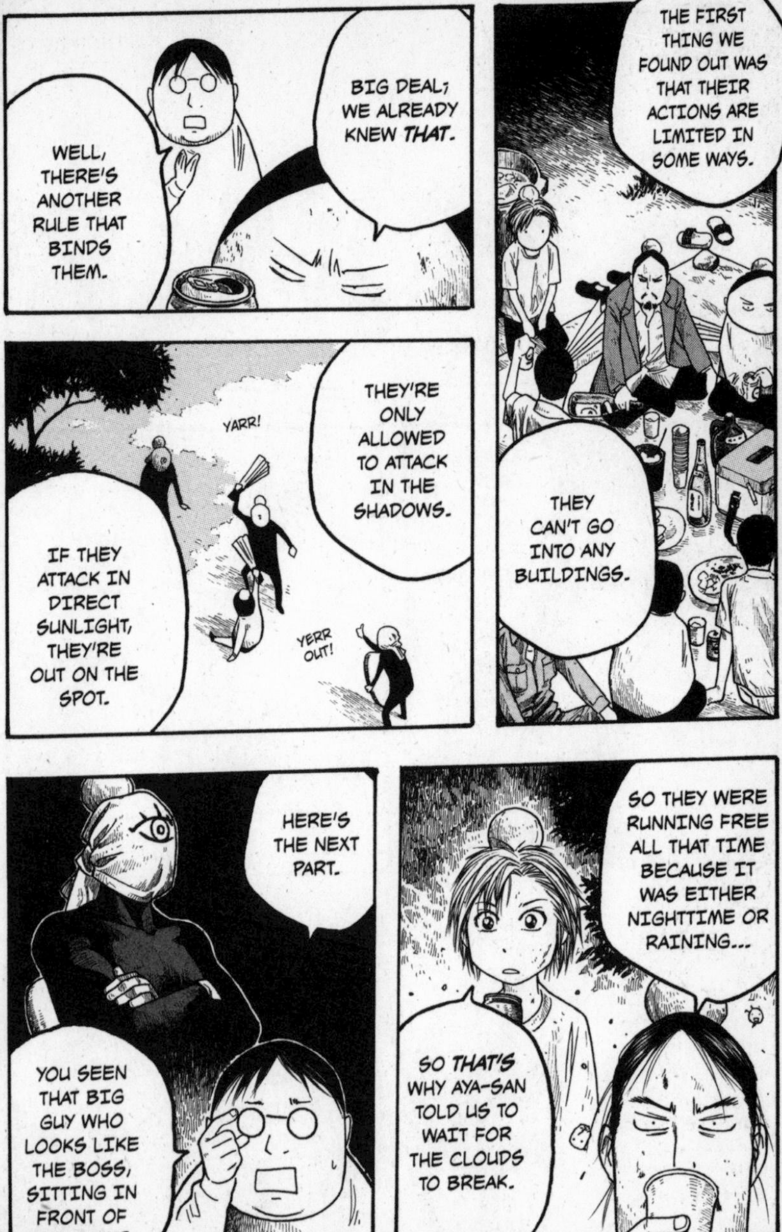
THE FIRST THING WE FOUND OUT WAS THAT THEIR ACTIONS ARE LIMITED IN SOME WAYS.
THEY CAN'T GO INTO ANY BUILDINGS.
BIG DEAL; WE ALREADY KNEW *THAT*.
WELL, THERE'S ANOTHER RULE THAT BINDS THEM.
THEY'RE ONLY ALLOWED TO ATTACK IN THE SHADOWS.
YARR!
YERR OUT!
IF THEY ATTACK IN DIRECT SUNLIGHT, THEY'RE OUT ON THE SPOT.
SO THEY WERE RUNNING FREE ALL THAT TIME BECAUSE IT WAS EITHER NIGHTTIME OR RAINING...
SO *THAT'S* WHY AYA-SAN TOLD US TO WAIT FOR THE CLOUDS TO BREAK.
HERE'S THE NEXT PART.
YOU SEEN THAT BIG GUY WHO LOOKS LIKE THE BOSS, SITTING IN FRONT OF THE GATE?

Do American kids play "Shadow Tag"?

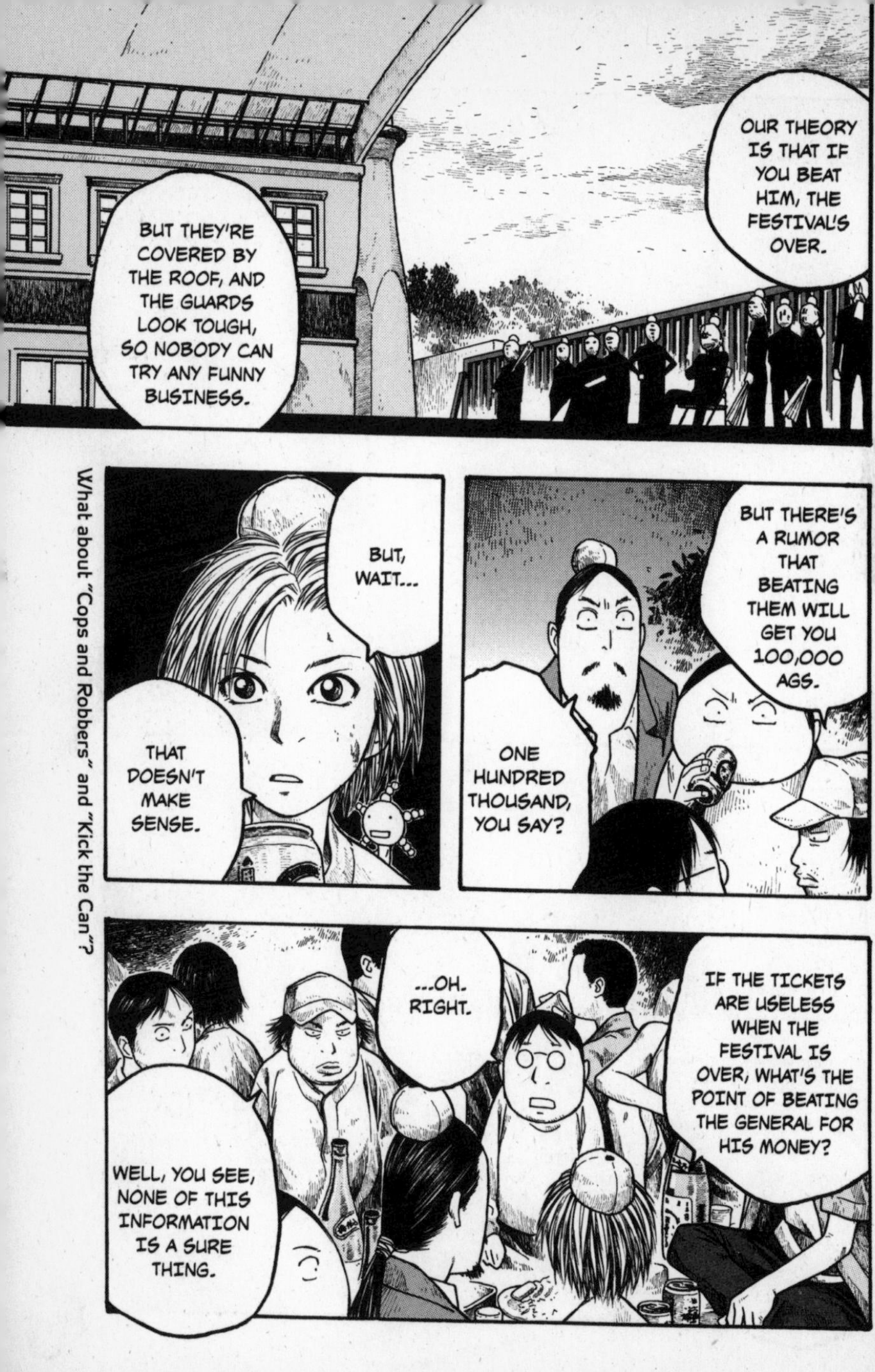
OUR THEORY IS THAT IF YOU BEAT HIM, THE FESTIVAL'S OVER.
BUT THEY'RE COVERED BY THE ROOF, AND THE GUARDS LOOK TOUGH, SO NOBODY CAN TRY ANY FUNNY BUSINESS.
BUT THERE'S A RUMOR THAT BEATING THEM WILL GET YOU 100,000 AGS.
ONE HUNDRED THOUSAND, YOU SAY?
BUT, WAIT...
THAT DOESN'T MAKE SENSE.
IF THE TICKETS ARE USELESS WHEN THE FESTIVAL IS OVER, WHAT'S THE POINT OF BEATING THE GENERAL FOR HIS MONEY?
...OH. RIGHT.
WELL, YOU SEE, NONE OF THIS INFORMATION IS A SURE THING.

What about "Cops and Robbers" and "Kick the Can"?

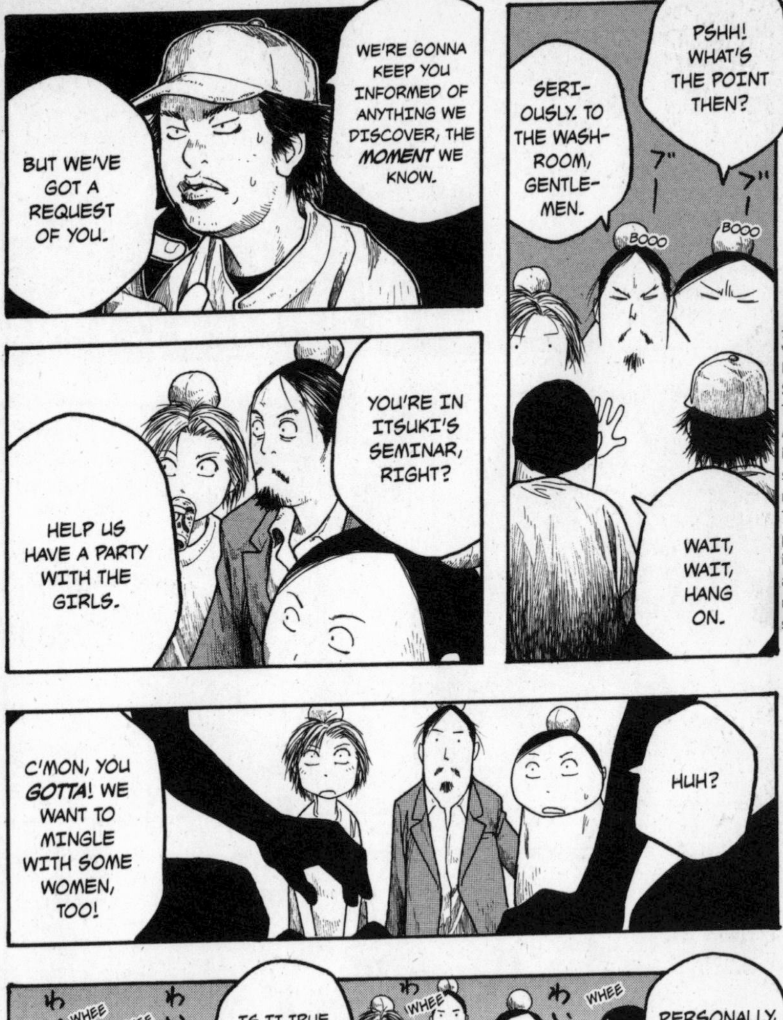
PSHH! WHAT'S THE POINT THEN?
SERI-OUSLY. TO THE WASH-ROOM, GENTLE-MEN.
BOOO
BOOO
WAIT, WAIT, HANG ON.
WE'RE GONNA KEEP YOU INFORMED OF ANYTHING WE DISCOVER, THE *MOMENT* WE KNOW.
BUT WE'VE GOT A REQUEST OF YOU.
YOU'RE IN ITSUKI'S SEMINAR, RIGHT?
HELP US HAVE A PARTY WITH THE GIRLS.
HUH?
C'MON, YOU *GOTTA*! WE WANT TO MINGLE WITH SOME WOMEN, TOO!
WHEE
PERSONALLY, I'M *REALLY* INTO HASEGAWA-SAN.
WHAT'S SHE LIKE IN PERSON?
WHEE
IS IT TRUE THAT SHE COMES FROM A SUPER-RICH FAMILY?
WHEE
WHEE
DOES SHE DRESS LIKE A BONDAGE CHICK IN THE LAB, TOO?

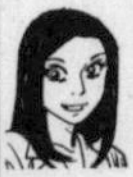

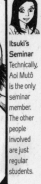

Itsuki's Seminar
Technically, Aoi Mutô is the only seminar member. The other people involved are just regular students.

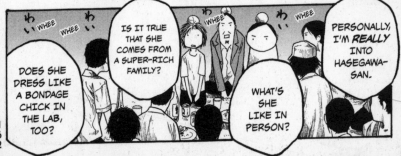

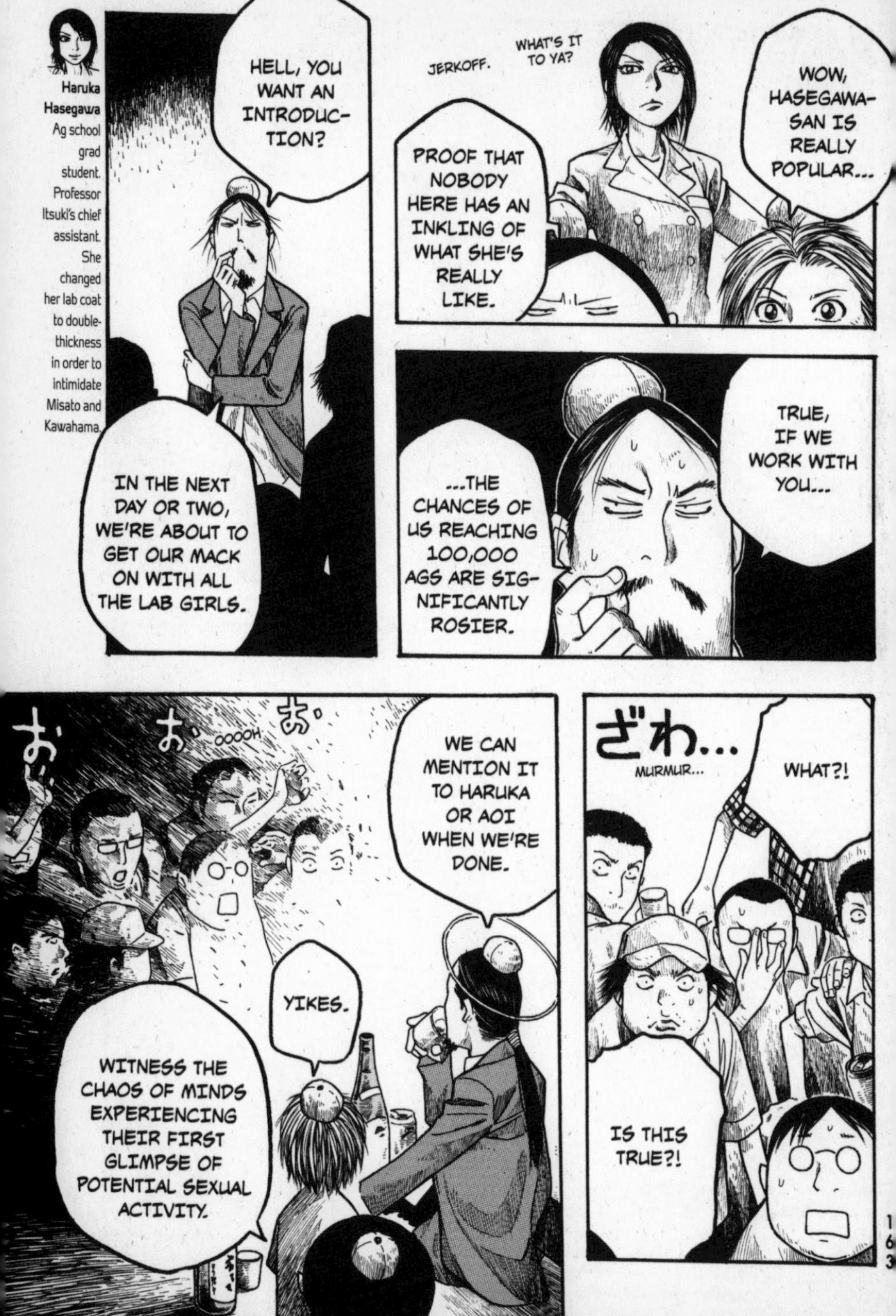
WOW, HASEGAWA-SAN IS REALLY POPULAR...
PROOF THAT NOBODY HERE HAS AN INKLING OF WHAT SHE'S REALLY LIKE.
WHAT'S IT TO YA?
JERKOFF.
TRUE, IF WE WORK WITH YOU...
...THE CHANCES OF US REACHING 100,000 AGS ARE SIGNIFICANTLY ROSIER.
HELL, YOU WANT AN INTRODUCTION?
IN THE NEXT DAY OR TWO, WE'RE ABOUT TO GET OUR MACK ON WITH ALL THE LAB GIRLS.
WHAT?!
ざわ...
MURMUR...
IS THIS TRUE?!
WE CAN MENTION IT TO HARUKA OR AOI WHEN WE'RE DONE.
お
お
OOOOH
お
YIKES.
WITNESS THE CHAOS OF MINDS EXPERIENCING THEIR FIRST GLIMPSE OF POTENTIAL SEXUAL ACTIVITY.

Haruka Hasegawa
Ag school grad student. Professor Itsuki's chief assistant. She changed her lab coat to double-thickness in order to intimidate Misato and Kawahama.

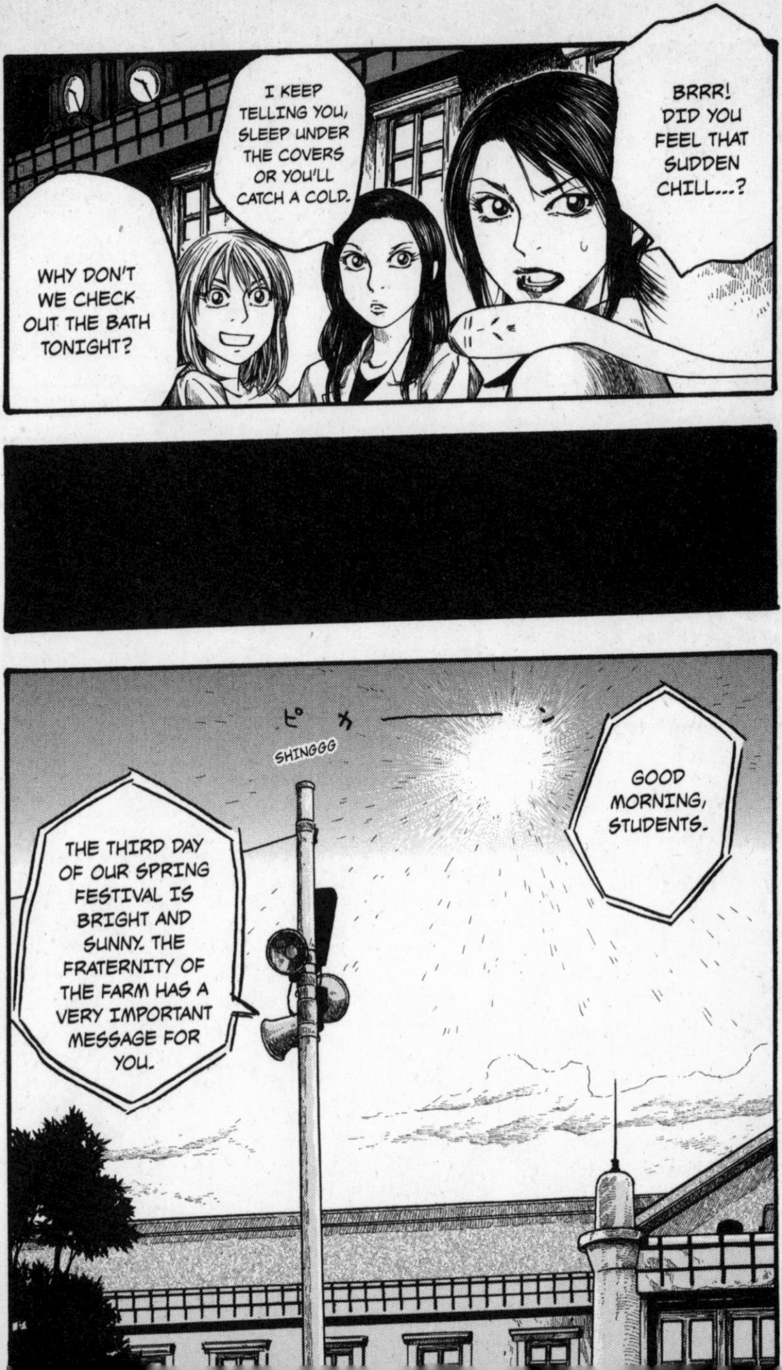
BRRR! DID YOU FEEL THAT SUDDEN CHILL...?
I KEEP TELLING YOU, SLEEP UNDER THE COVERS OR YOU'LL CATCH A COLD.
WHY DON'T WE CHECK OUT THE BATH TONIGHT?
ピカー
SHINGGG
GOOD MORNING, STUDENTS.
THE THIRD DAY OF OUR SPRING FESTIVAL IS BRIGHT AND SUNNY. THE FRATERNITY OF THE FARM HAS A VERY IMPORTANT MESSAGE FOR YOU.

I wonder how people in America pronounce the title of this manga.

20 END

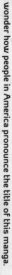

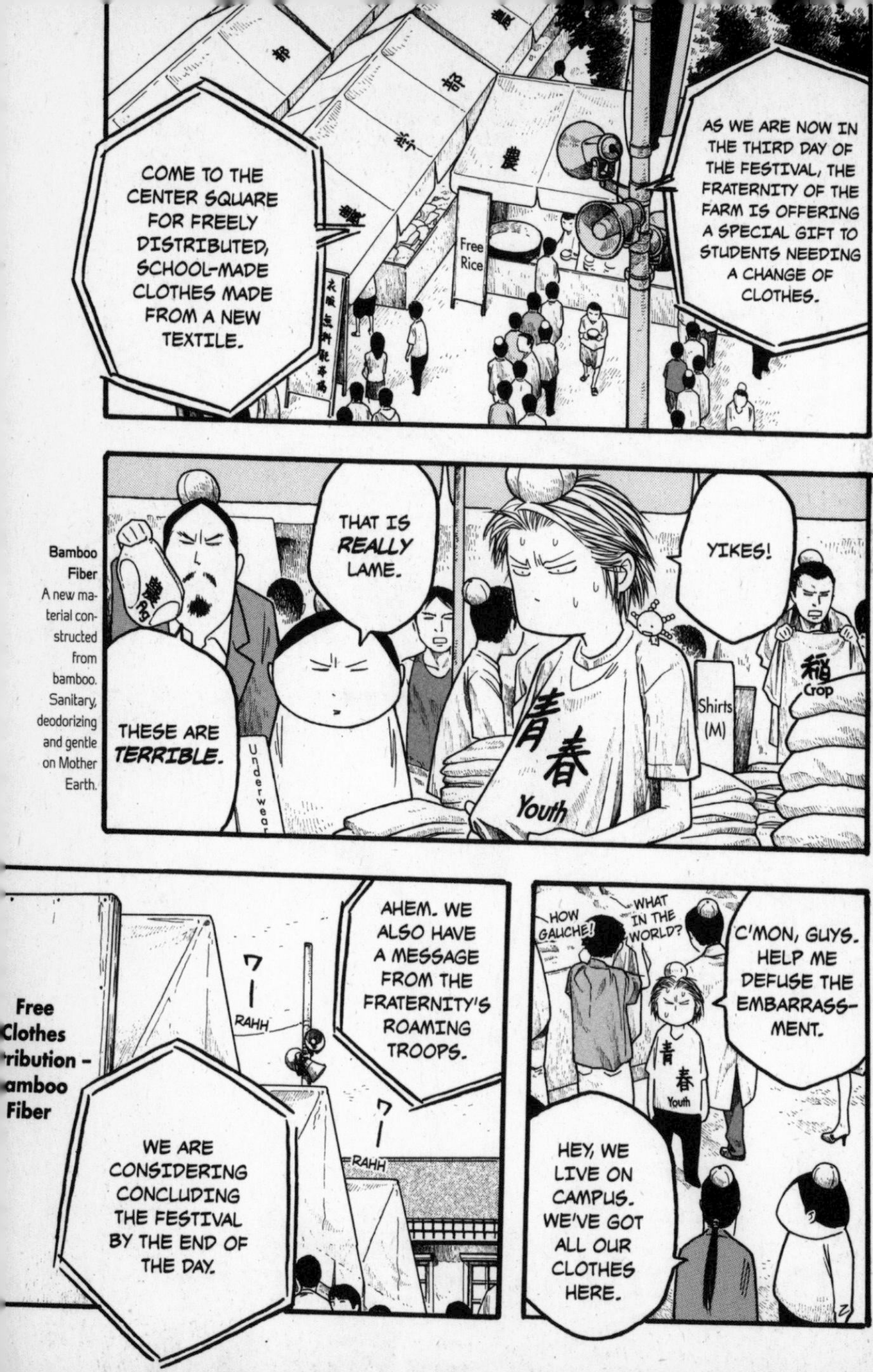
AS WE ARE NOW IN THE THIRD DAY OF THE FESTIVAL, THE FRATERNITY OF THE FARM IS OFFERING A SPECIAL GIFT TO STUDENTS NEEDING A CHANGE OF CLOTHES.
COME TO THE CENTER SQUARE FOR FREELY DISTRIBUTED, SCHOOL-MADE CLOTHES MADE FROM A NEW TEXTILE.
Free Rice
YIKES!
Shirts (M)
稲
Crop
青春
Youth
THAT IS REALLY LAME.
THESE ARE TERRIBLE.
Underwear
C'MON, GUYS. HELP ME DEFUSE THE EMBARRASSMENT.
WHAT IN THE WORLD?
HOW GAUCHE!
青春
Youth
HEY, WE LIVE ON CAMPUS. WE'VE GOT ALL OUR CLOTHES HERE.
AHEM. WE ALSO HAVE A MESSAGE FROM THE FRATERNITY'S ROAMING TROOPS.
ワー
RAHH
ワー
RAHH
WE ARE CONSIDERING CONCLUDING THE FESTIVAL BY THE END OF THE DAY.

Bamboo Fiber A new material constructed from bamboo. Sanitary, deodorizing and gentle on Mother Earth.

Free Clothes Distribution – Bamboo Fiber

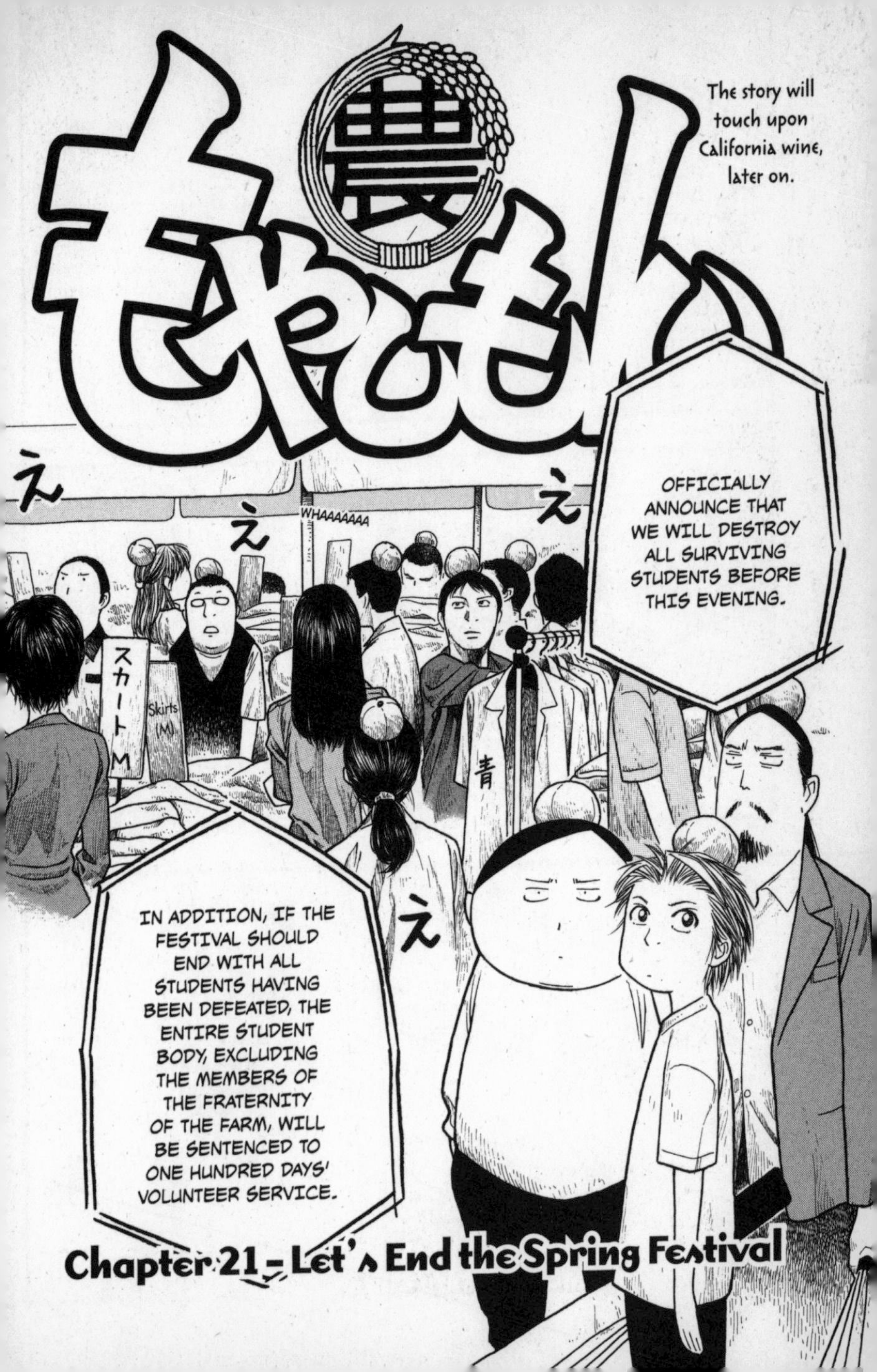
The story will touch upon California wine, later on.
もやしもん
え
え
え
WHAAAAAAA
OFFICIALLY ANNOUNCE THAT WE WILL DESTROY ALL SURVIVING STUDENTS BEFORE THIS EVENING.
スカートM
Skirts (M)
青
え
IN ADDITION, IF THE FESTIVAL SHOULD END WITH ALL STUDENTS HAVING BEEN DEFEATED, THE ENTIRE STUDENT BODY, EXCLUDING THE MEMBERS OF THE FRATERNITY OF THE FARM, WILL BE SENTENCED TO ONE HUNDRED DAYS' VOLUNTEER SERVICE.
Chapter 21 - Let's End the Spring Festival

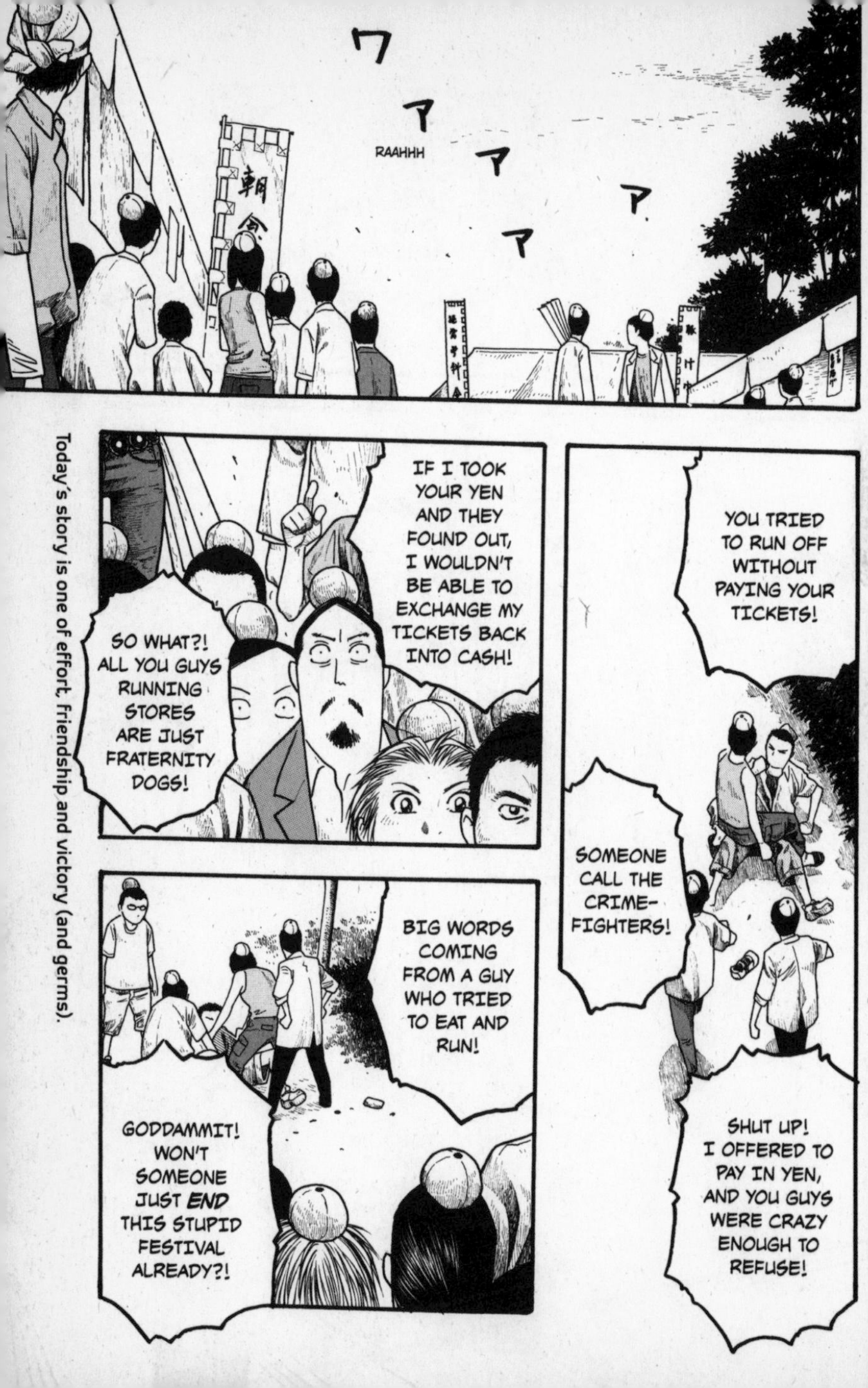
ワァアアア
RAAHHH
YOU TRIED TO RUN OFF WITHOUT PAYING YOUR TICKETS!
SOMEONE CALL THE CRIME-FIGHTERS!
SHUT UP! I OFFERED TO PAY IN YEN, AND YOU GUYS WERE CRAZY ENOUGH TO REFUSE!
IF I TOOK YOUR YEN AND THEY FOUND OUT, I WOULDN'T BE ABLE TO EXCHANGE MY TICKETS BACK INTO CASH!
SO WHAT?! ALL YOU GUYS RUNNING STORES ARE JUST FRATERNITY DOGS!
BIG WORDS COMING FROM A GUY WHO TRIED TO EAT AND RUN!
GODDAMMIT! WON'T SOMEONE JUST *END* THIS STUPID FESTIVAL ALREADY?!

Today's story is one of effort, friendship and victory (and germs).

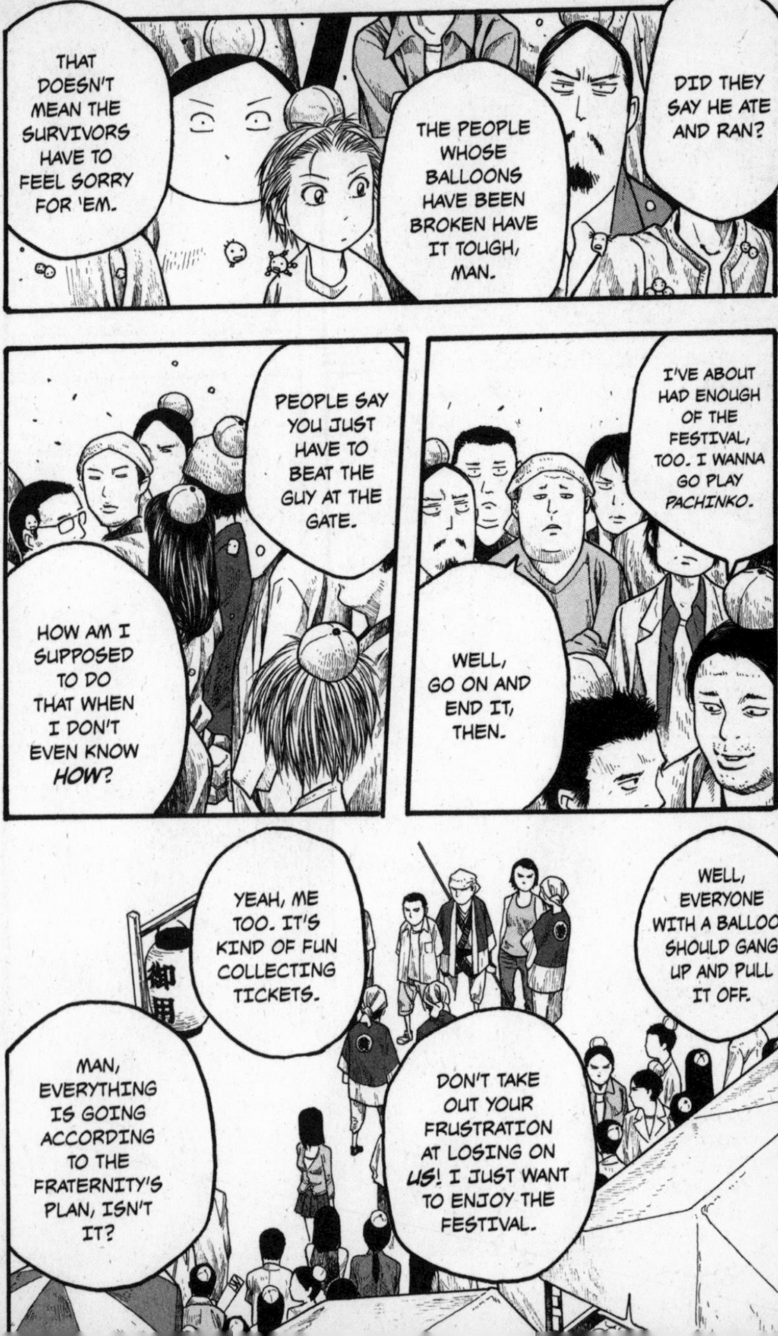
DID THEY SAY HE ATE AND RAN?
THE PEOPLE WHOSE BALLOONS HAVE BEEN BROKEN HAVE IT TOUGH, MAN.
THAT DOESN'T MEAN THE SURVIVORS HAVE TO FEEL SORRY FOR 'EM.
I'VE ABOUT HAD ENOUGH OF THE FESTIVAL, TOO. I WANNA GO PLAY PACHINKO.
WELL, GO ON AND END IT, THEN.
PEOPLE SAY YOU JUST HAVE TO BEAT THE GUY AT THE GATE.
HOW AM I SUPPOSED TO DO THAT WHEN I DON'T EVEN KNOW HOW?
WELL, EVERYONE WITH A BALLOON SHOULD GANG UP AND PULL IT OFF.
YEAH, ME TOO. IT'S KIND OF FUN COLLECTING TICKETS.
DON'T TAKE OUT YOUR FRUSTRATION AT LOSING ON US! I JUST WANT TO ENJOY THE FESTIVAL.
MAN, EVERYTHING IS GOING ACCORDING TO THE FRATERNITY'S PLAN, ISN'T IT?

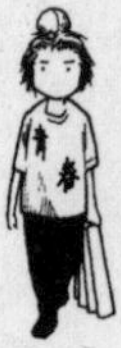

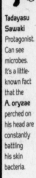

Tadayasu Sawaki Protagonist. Can see microbes. It's a little-known fact that the **A. oryzae** perched on his head are constantly battling his skin bacteria.

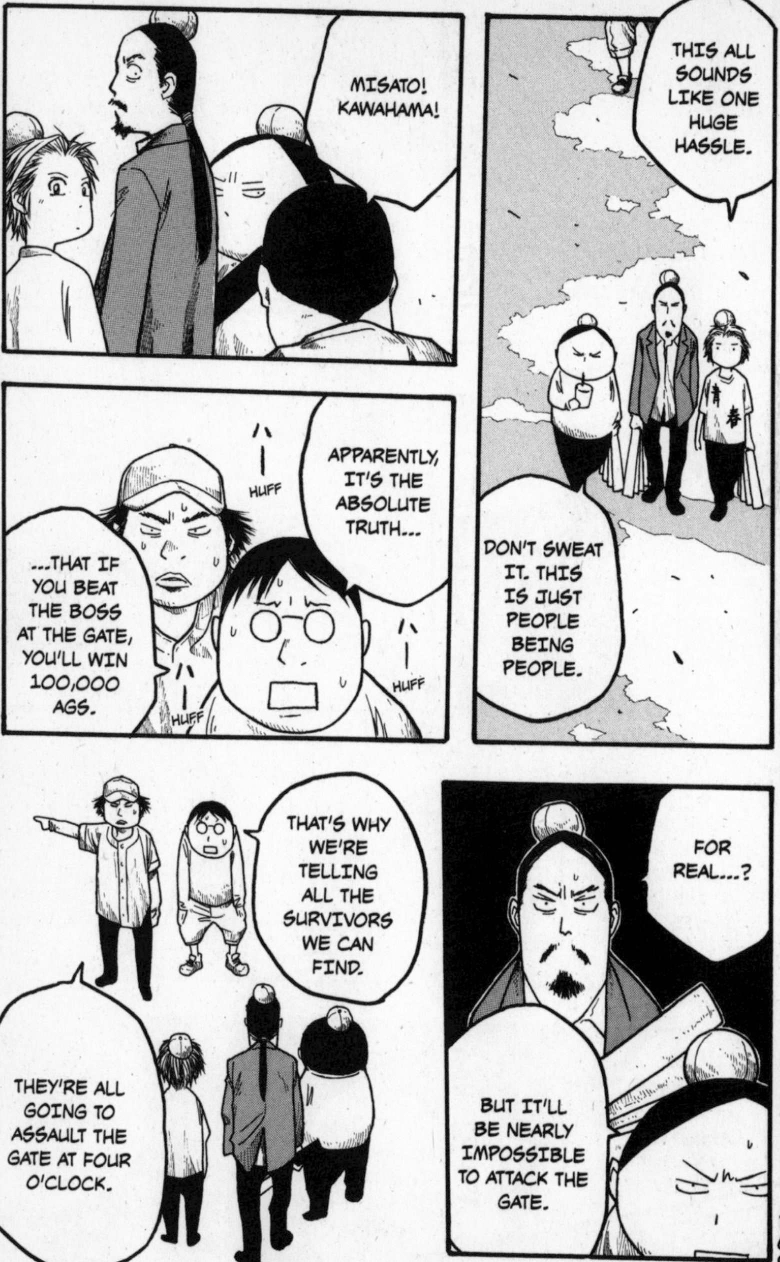
THIS ALL SOUNDS LIKE ONE HUGE HASSLE.
DON'T SWEAT IT. THIS IS JUST PEOPLE BEING PEOPLE.
MISATO! KAWAHAMA!
HUFF
APPARENTLY, IT'S THE ABSOLUTE TRUTH...
HUFF
...THAT IF YOU BEAT THE BOSS AT THE GATE, YOU'LL WIN 100,000 AGS.
HUFF
FOR REAL...?
BUT IT'LL BE NEARLY IMPOSSIBLE TO ATTACK THE GATE.
THAT'S WHY WE'RE TELLING ALL THE SURVIVORS WE CAN FIND.
THEY'RE ALL GOING TO ASSAULT THE GATE AT FOUR O'CLOCK.

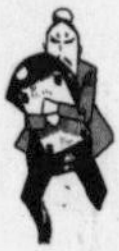

Kaoru Misato Sophomore. In his native Kansai dialect, they don't say "second year student," but "second-timer."

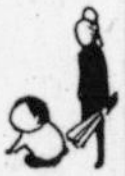

Takuma Kawahama (Left) Sophomore. Dorm student, like Misato. His frame is recognizable from a hundred meters away.

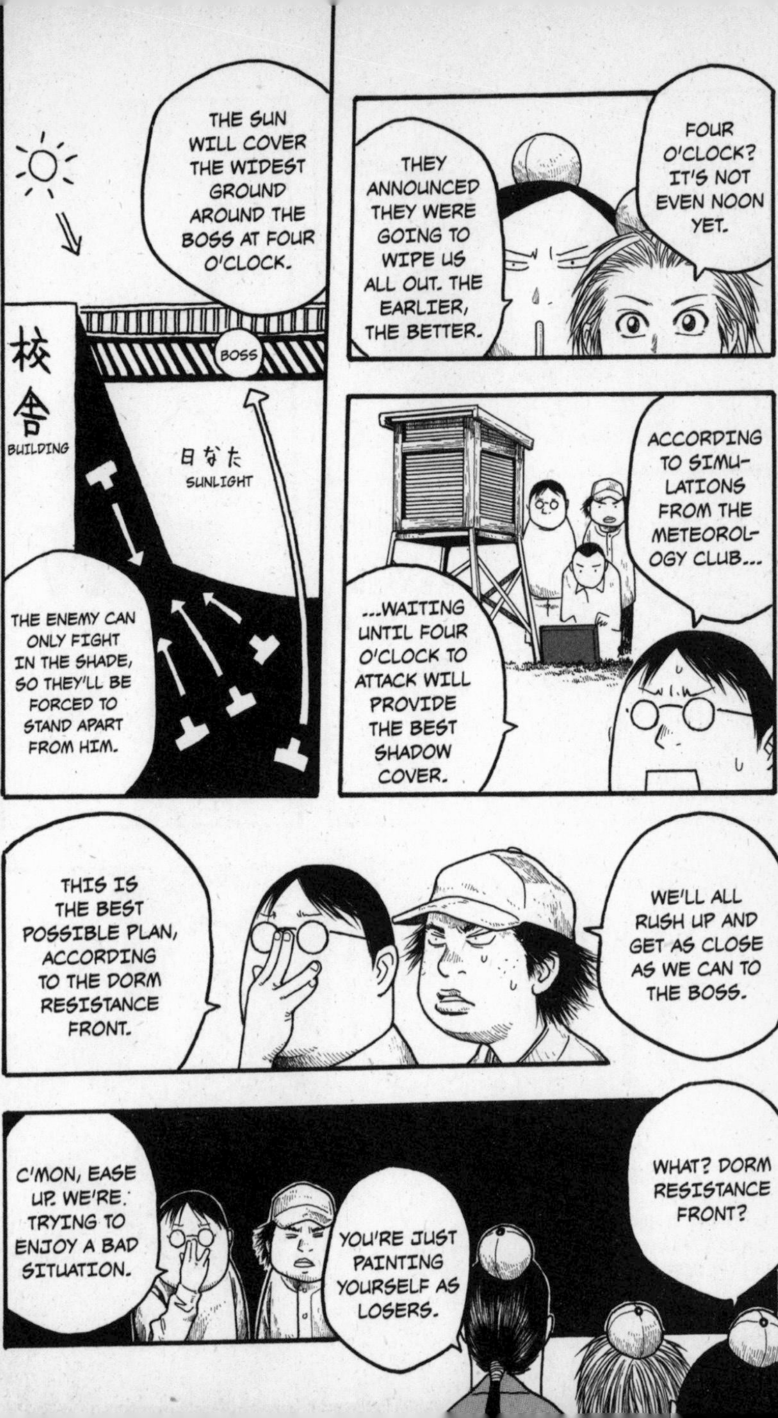
FOUR O'CLOCK? IT'S NOT EVEN NOON YET.
THEY ANNOUNCED THEY WERE GOING TO WIPE US ALL OUT. THE EARLIER, THE BETTER.
ACCORDING TO SIMULATIONS FROM THE METEOROLOGY CLUB...
...WAITING UNTIL FOUR O'CLOCK TO ATTACK WILL PROVIDE THE BEST SHADOW COVER.
THE SUN WILL COVER THE WIDEST GROUND AROUND THE BOSS AT FOUR O'CLOCK.
校舎
BUILDING
BOSS
日なた
SUNLIGHT
THE ENEMY CAN ONLY FIGHT IN THE SHADE, SO THEY'LL BE FORCED TO STAND APART FROM HIM.
WE'LL ALL RUSH UP AND GET AS CLOSE AS WE CAN TO THE BOSS.
THIS IS THE BEST POSSIBLE PLAN, ACCORDING TO THE DORM RESISTANCE FRONT.
WHAT? DORM RESISTANCE FRONT?
YOU'RE JUST PAINTING YOURSELF AS LOSERS.
C'MON, EASE UP. WE'RE TRYING TO ENJOY A BAD SITUATION.

The author is a big fan of wine. He visited Bourgogne in France and Napa Valley in the United States (and drank, of course).

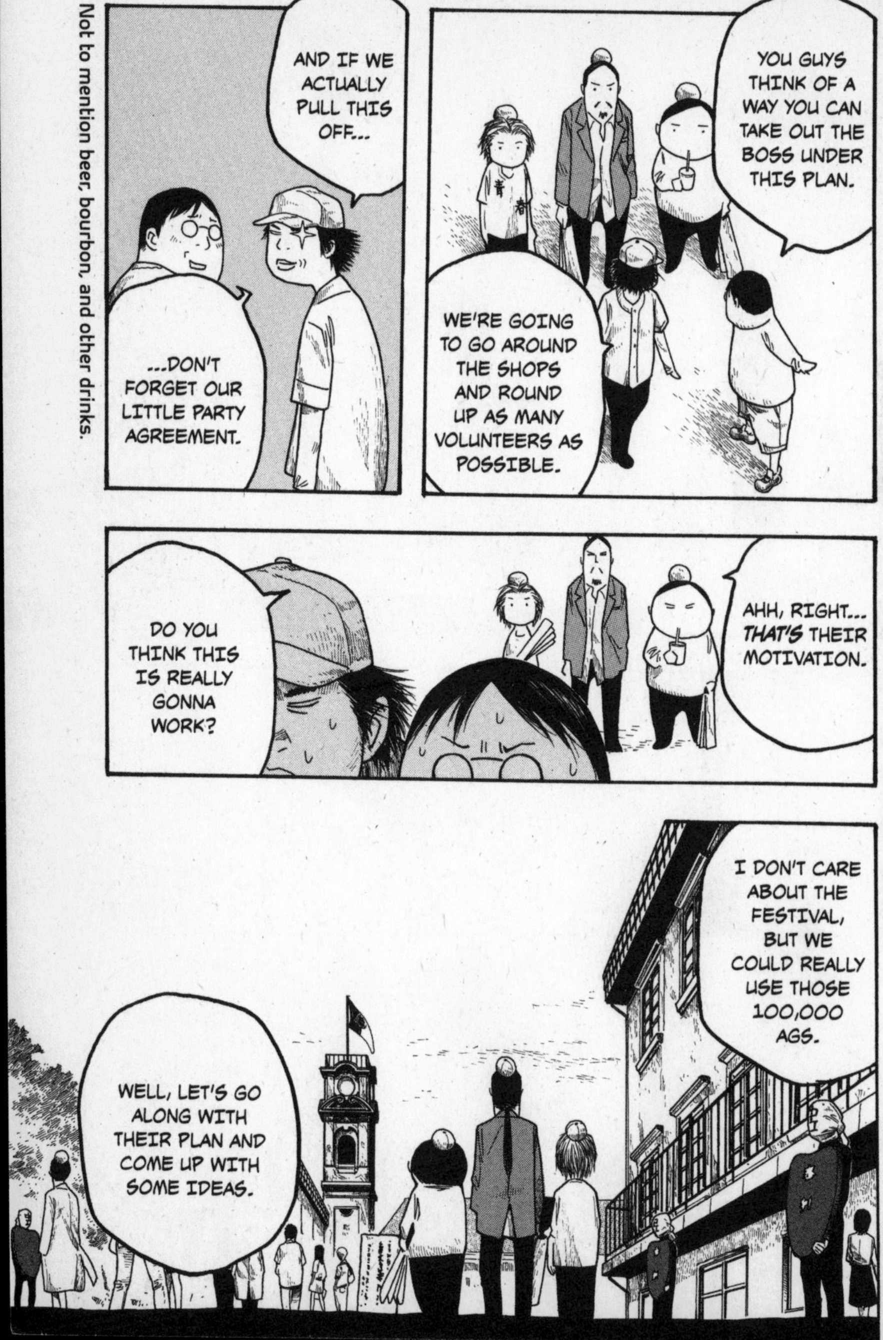

YOU GUYS THINK OF A WAY YOU CAN TAKE OUT THE BOSS UNDER THIS PLAN.
WE'RE GOING TO GO AROUND THE SHOPS AND ROUND UP AS MANY VOLUNTEERS AS POSSIBLE.
AND IF WE ACTUALLY PULL THIS OFF...
...DON'T FORGET OUR LITTLE PARTY AGREEMENT.
AHH, RIGHT... *THAT'S* THEIR MOTIVATION.
DO YOU THINK THIS IS REALLY GONNA WORK?
I DON'T CARE ABOUT THE FESTIVAL, BUT WE COULD REALLY USE THOSE 100,000 AGS.
WELL, LET'S GO ALONG WITH THEIR PLAN AND COME UP WITH SOME IDEAS.

Not to mention beer, bourbon, and other drinks.

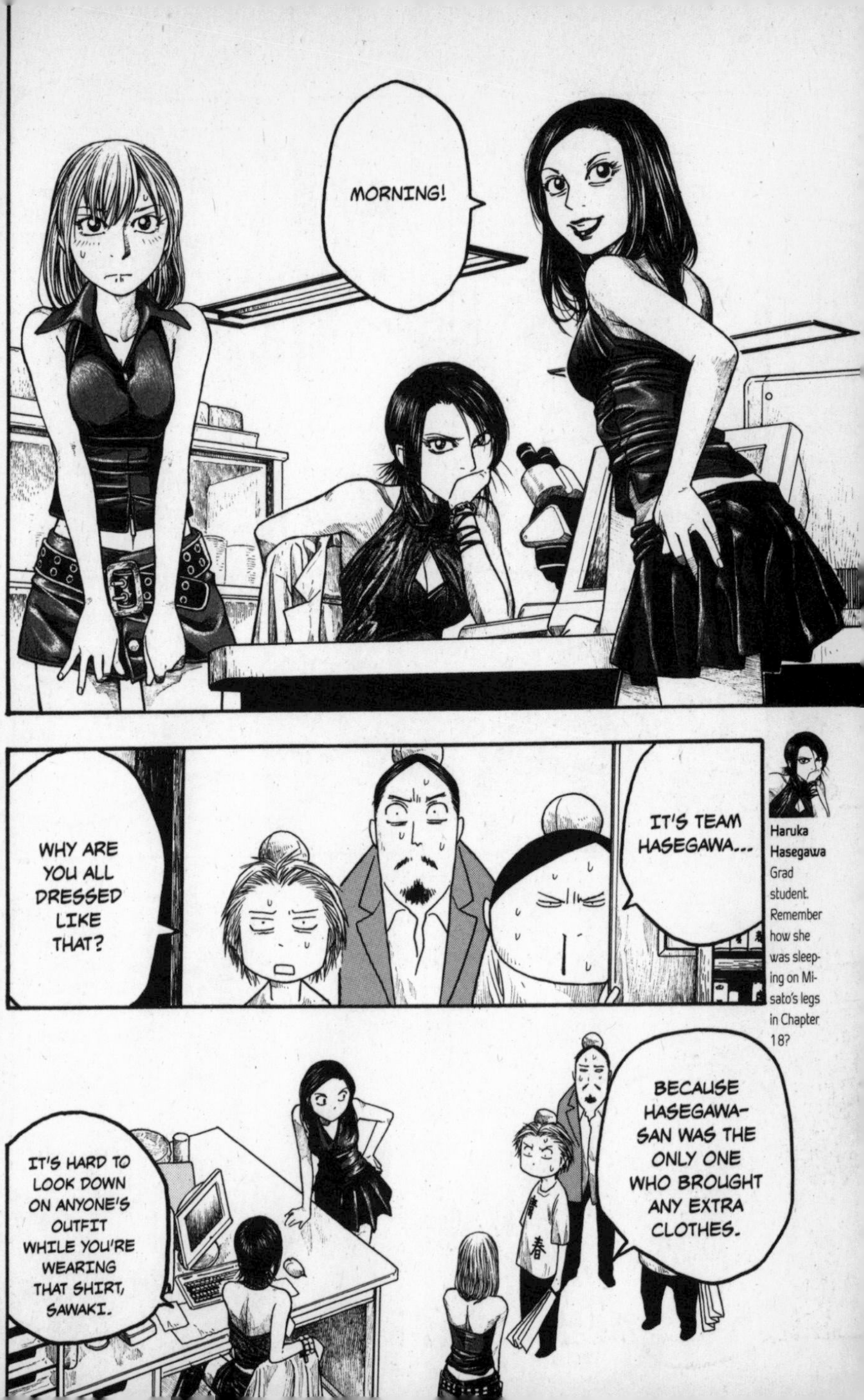
MORNING!
IT'S TEAM HASEGAWA...
WHY ARE YOU ALL DRESSED LIKE THAT?
BECAUSE HASEGAWA-SAN WAS THE ONLY ONE WHO BROUGHT ANY EXTRA CLOTHES.
IT'S HARD TO LOOK DOWN ON ANYONE'S OUTFIT WHILE YOU'RE WEARING THAT SHIRT, SAWAKI.

Haruka Hasegawa
Grad student. Remember how she was sleeping on Misato's legs in Chapter 18?

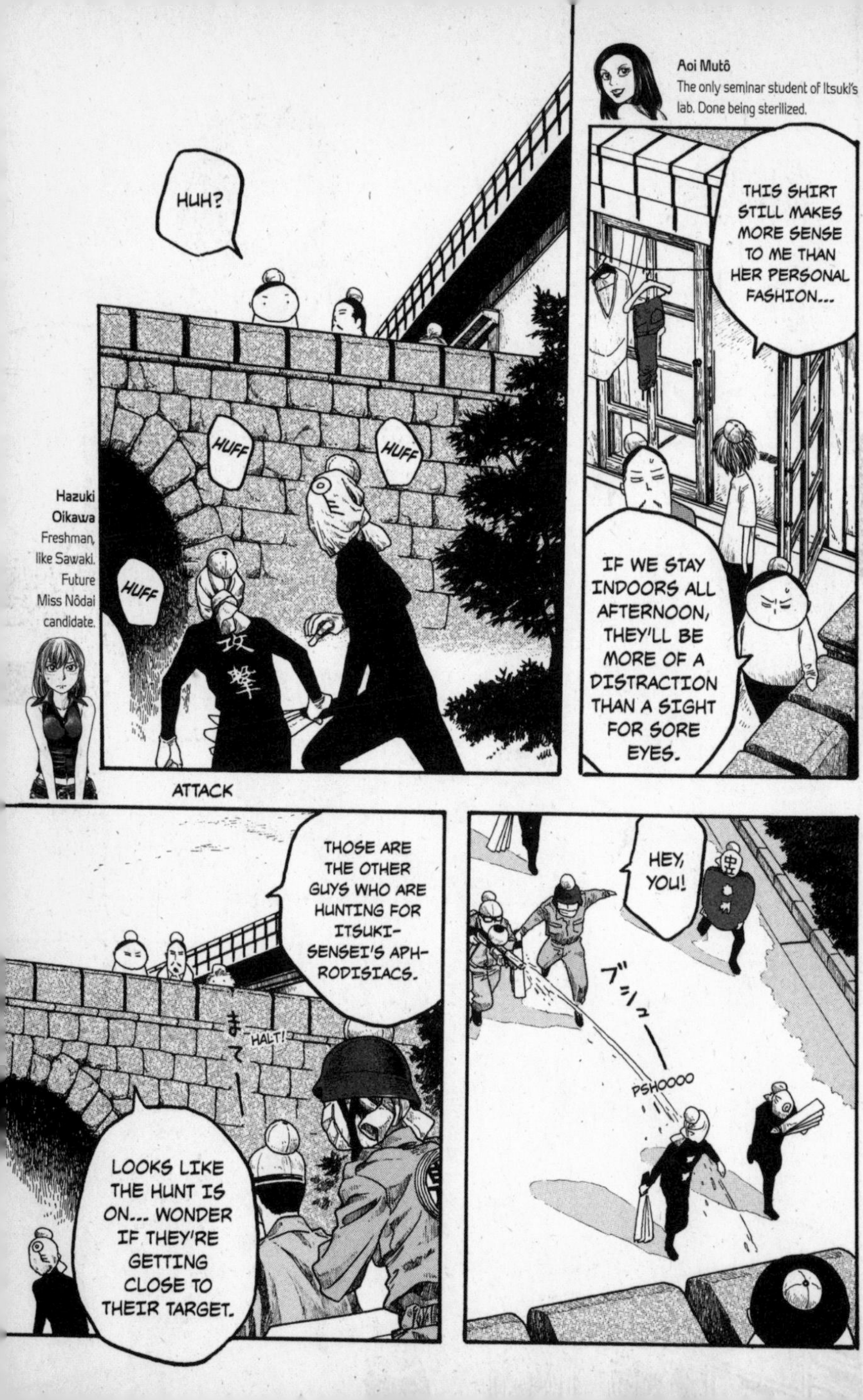
Aoi Mutô
The only seminar student of Itsuki's lab. Done being sterilized.
THIS SHIRT STILL MAKES MORE SENSE TO ME THAN HER PERSONAL FASHION...
IF WE STAY INDOORS ALL AFTERNOON, THEY'LL BE MORE OF A DISTRACTION THAN A SIGHT FOR SORE EYES.
HUH?
HUFF
HUFF
HUFF
攻撃
ATTACK
Hazuki Oikawa
Freshman, like Sawaki. Future Miss Nôdai candidate.
HEY, YOU!
ブシュー
PSHOOOO
THOSE ARE THE OTHER GUYS WHO ARE HUNTING FOR ITSUKI-SENSEI'S APHRODISIACS.
まてー
HALT!
LOOKS LIKE THE HUNT IS ON... WONDER IF THEY'RE GETTING CLOSE TO THEIR TARGET.

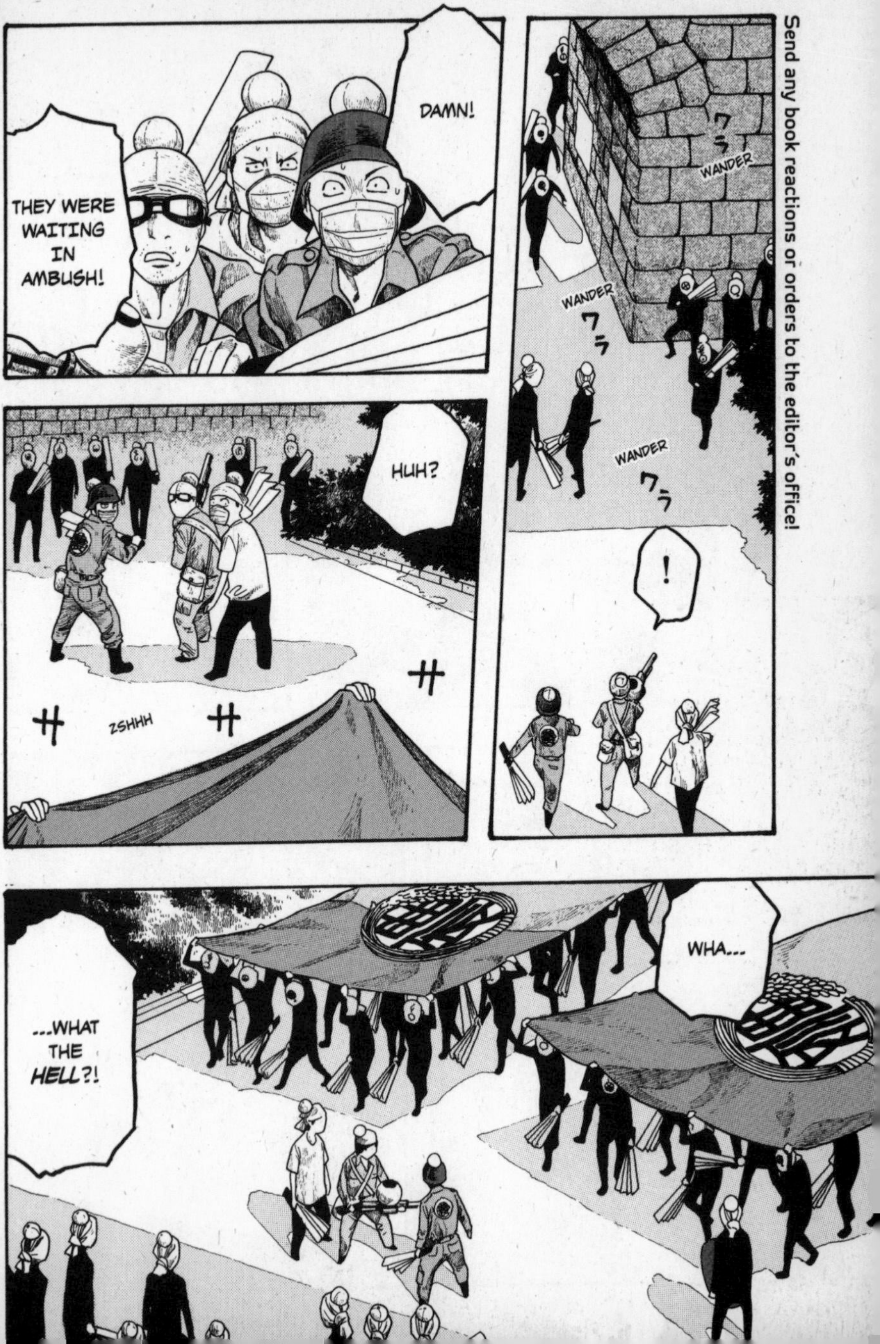
WANDER
ワラ
WANDER
ワラ
WANDER
ワラ
!
DAMN!
THEY WERE WAITING IN AMBUSH!
HUH?
ザ
ZSHHH
ザ
ザ
WHA...
...WHAT THE *HELL*?!

Send any book reactions or orders to the editor's office!

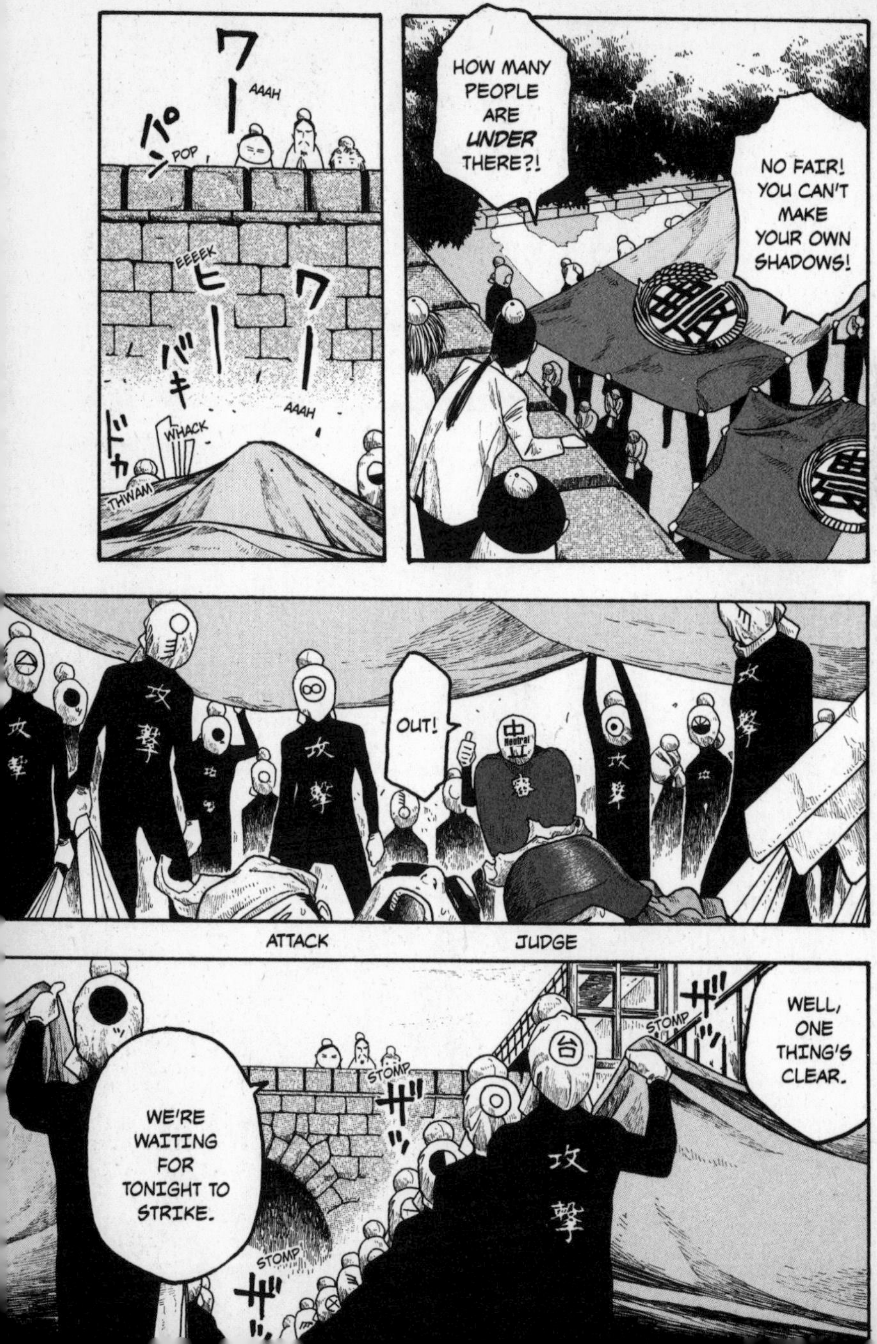
HOW MANY PEOPLE ARE UNDER THERE?!
NO FAIR! YOU CAN'T MAKE YOUR OWN SHADOWS!
ワー
AAAH
パン
POP
ワー
AAAH
ヒー
EEEEK
バキ
WHACK
ドカ
THWAM
OUT!
ATTACK
JUDGE
WELL, ONE THING'S CLEAR.
ザッ
STOMP
WE'RE WAITING FOR TONIGHT TO STRIKE.
ザッ
STOMP
ザッ
STOMP

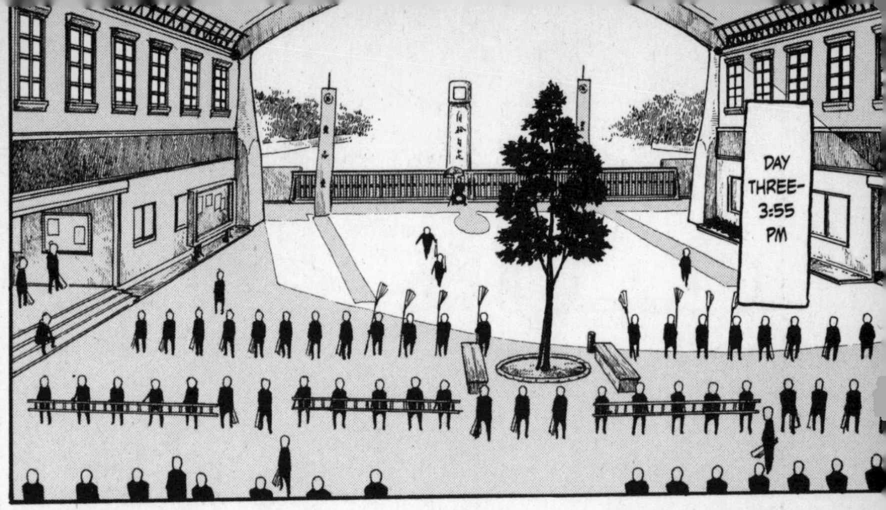
DAY THREE- 3:55 PM

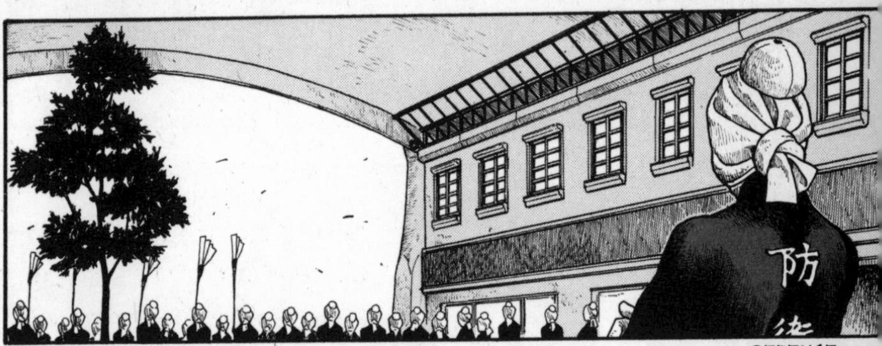

DEFENSE

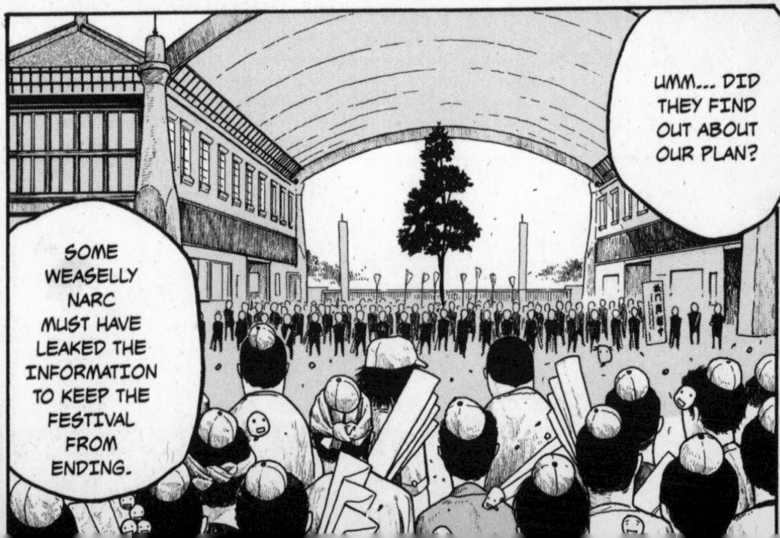
UMM... DID THEY FIND OUT ABOUT OUR PLAN?
SOME WEASELLY NARC MUST HAVE LEAKED THE INFORMATION TO KEEP THE FESTIVAL FROM ENDING.

S. epidermis Beneficial skin bacteria. If they are healthy, you won't smell so bad.

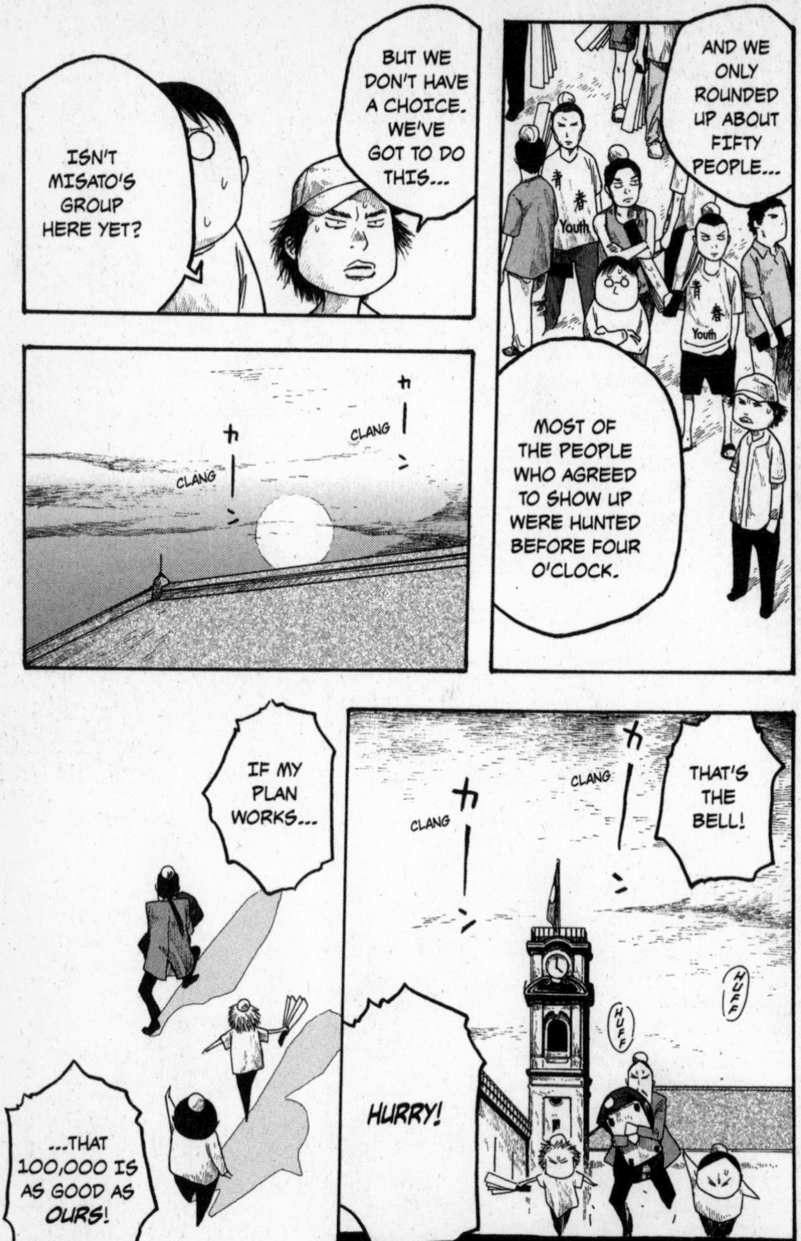
AND WE ONLY ROUNDED UP ABOUT FIFTY PEOPLE...
Youth
Youth
MOST OF THE PEOPLE WHO AGREED TO SHOW UP WERE HUNTED BEFORE FOUR O'CLOCK.
BUT WE DON'T HAVE A CHOICE. WE'VE GOT TO DO THIS...
ISN'T MISATO'S GROUP HERE YET?
カーン
CLANG
カーン
CLANG
THAT'S THE BELL!
カーン
CLANG
カーン
CLANG
HUFF
HUFF
HURRY!
IF MY PLAN WORKS...
...THAT 100,000 IS AS GOOD AS OURS!

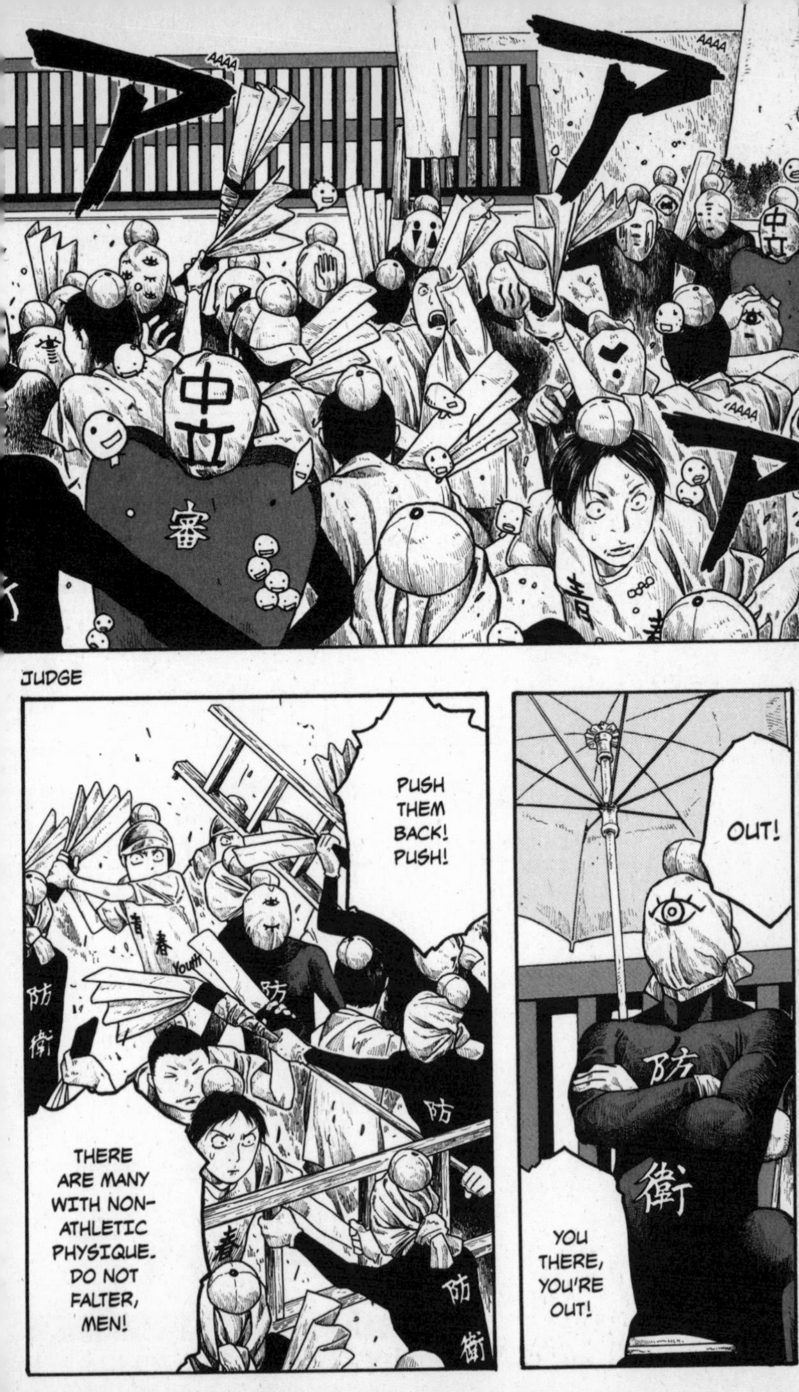
AAAA
AAAA
AAAA
JUDGE
OUT!
YOU THERE, YOU'RE OUT!
PUSH THEM BACK! PUSH!
Youth
THERE ARE MANY WITH NON-ATHLETIC PHYSIQUE. DO NOT FALTER, MEN!

T. tonsurans Friend of ringworm. This little bugger will make your scalp peel.

M. furfur A cause of dandruff. There's no use fretting over them. They're there.

A. calcoaceticus Out of all the skin bacteria, these are the most likely to show up where the skin temperature is hottest.

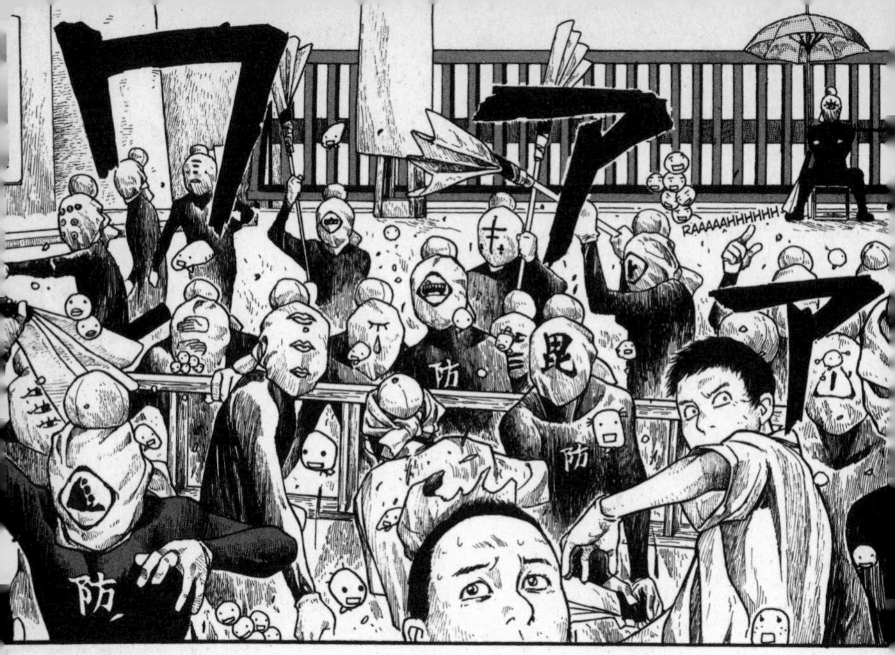
ワ
ア
ア
RAAAAAHHHHHH

DEFENSE

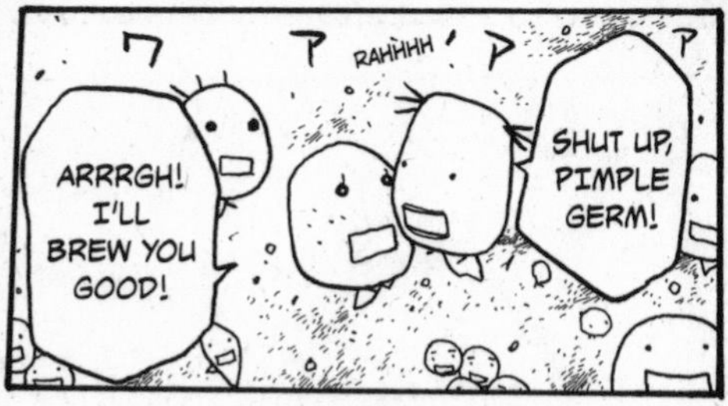
ワ
ア
RAHHHH
ア
ア
SHUT UP, PIMPLE GERM!
ARRRGH! I'LL BREW YOU GOOD!

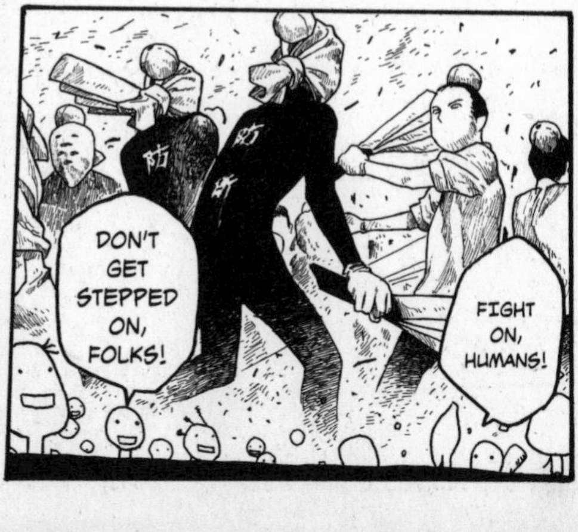
FIGHT ON, HUMANS!
DON'T GET STEPPED ON, FOLKS!

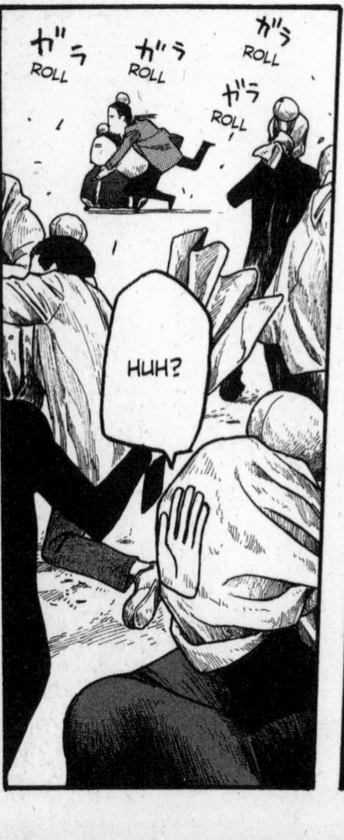
ガラ
ROLL
ガラ
ROLL
ガラ
ROLL
ガラ
ROLL
HUH?

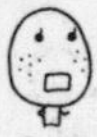

P. acnes
The cause of pimples.

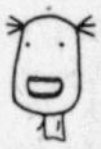

C. diphtheroid
If you clean your body too rigorously, the **S. epidermis** will disappear, and you might end up with these guys, instead.

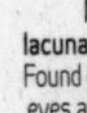

M. lacunata
Found on eyes and membranes. They're fence-straddlers.

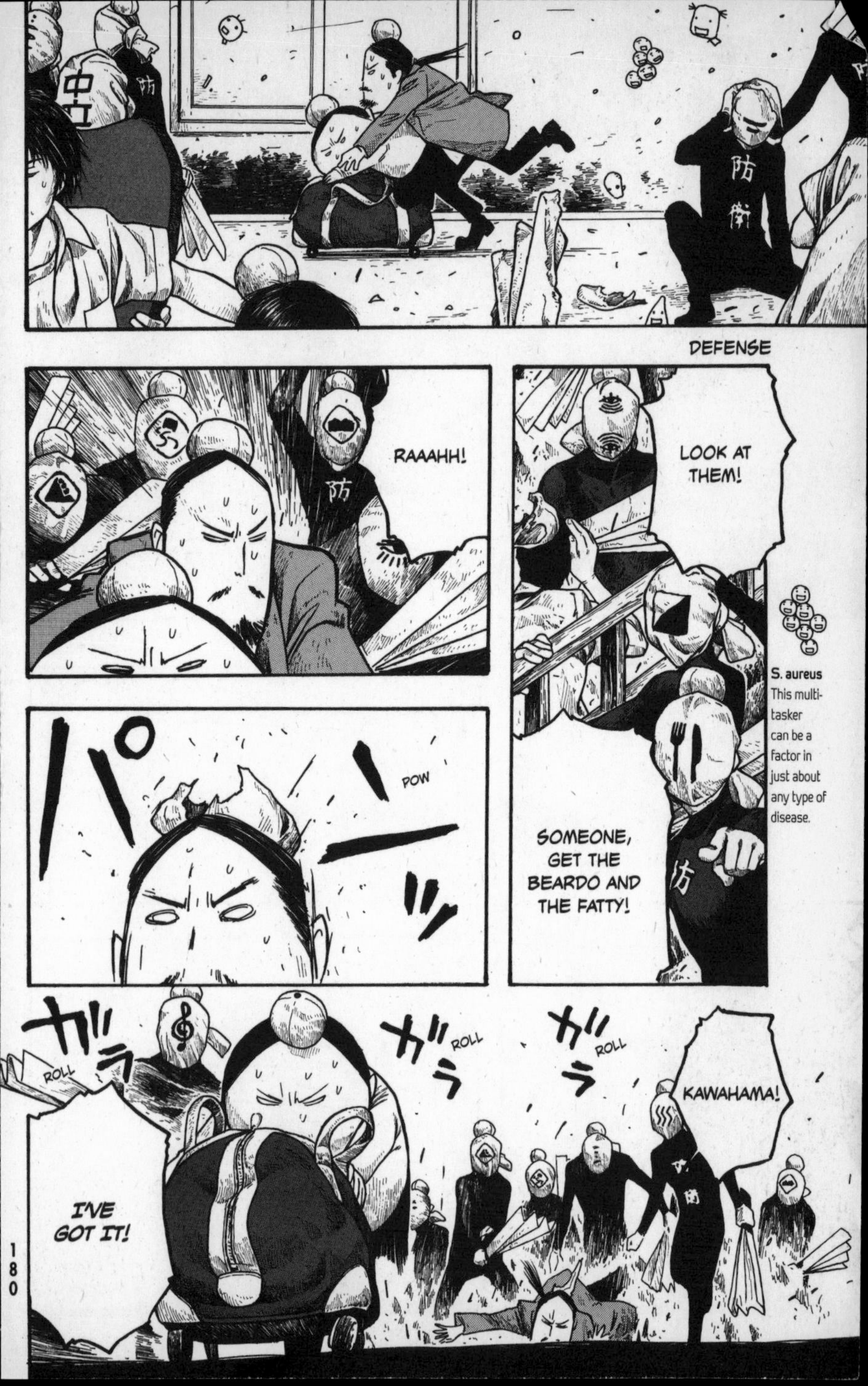
DEFENSE
LOOK AT THEM!
SOMEONE, GET THE BEARDO AND THE FATTY!
RAAAHH!
POW
ROLL
ROLL
KAWAHAMA!
ROLL
I'VE GOT IT!

S. aureus
This multi-tasker can be a factor in just about any type of disease.

M. canis You can get him from your pets. Just as big a trouble-maker as **tonsurans.**

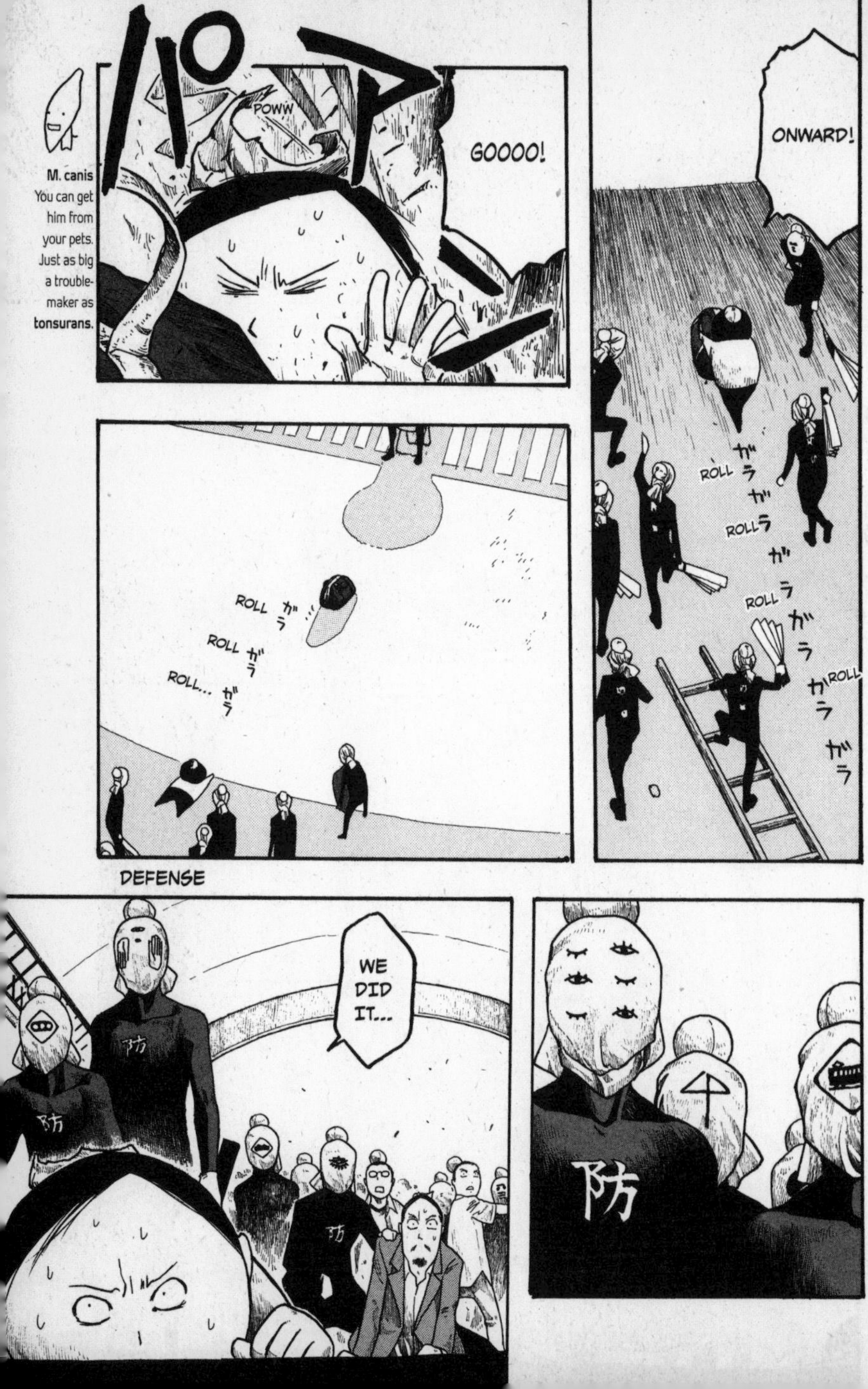

ONWARD!
ROLL ガラ
ROLL ガラ
ROLL ガラ
ROLL ガラ
ガラ
パ
POWW
GOOOO!
ROLL ガラ
ROLL ガラ
ROLL... ガラ
DEFENSE
WE DID IT...

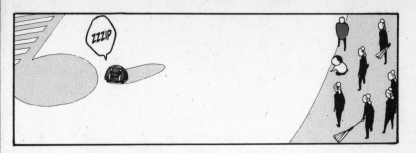

ZZZIP

ポ POP

ン

!

DEFENSE

防

21
END

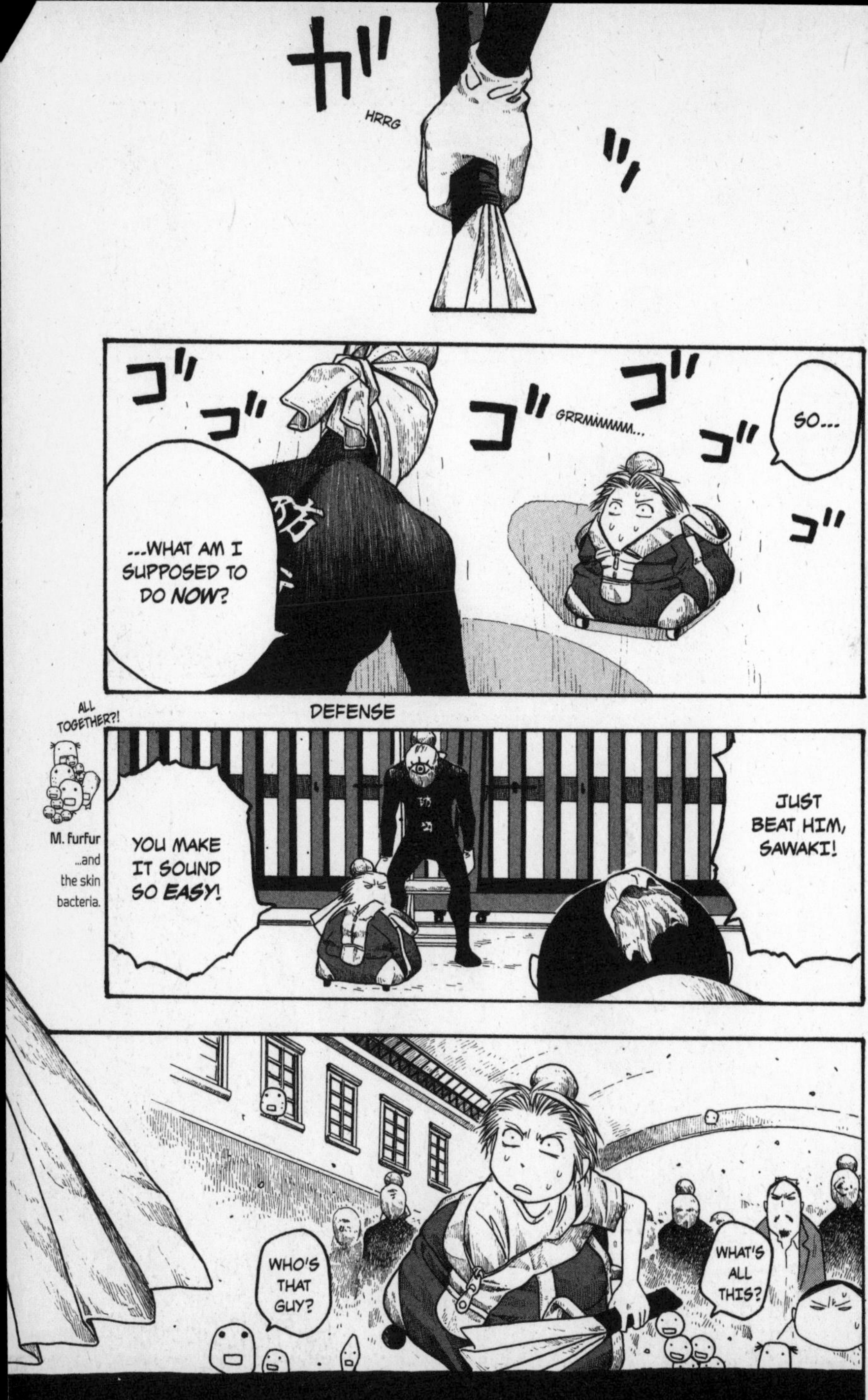
ガッ
HRRG
SO...
ゴゴゴゴゴゴ
GRRMMMMM...
...WHAT AM I SUPPOSED TO DO NOW?
JUST BEAT HIM, SAWAKI!
DEFENSE
YOU MAKE IT SOUND SO EASY!
WHAT'S ALL THIS?
WHO'S THAT GUY?
ALL TOGETHER?!
M. furfur ...and the skin bacteria.

Now I hear the Mycological Society of Japan is interested.

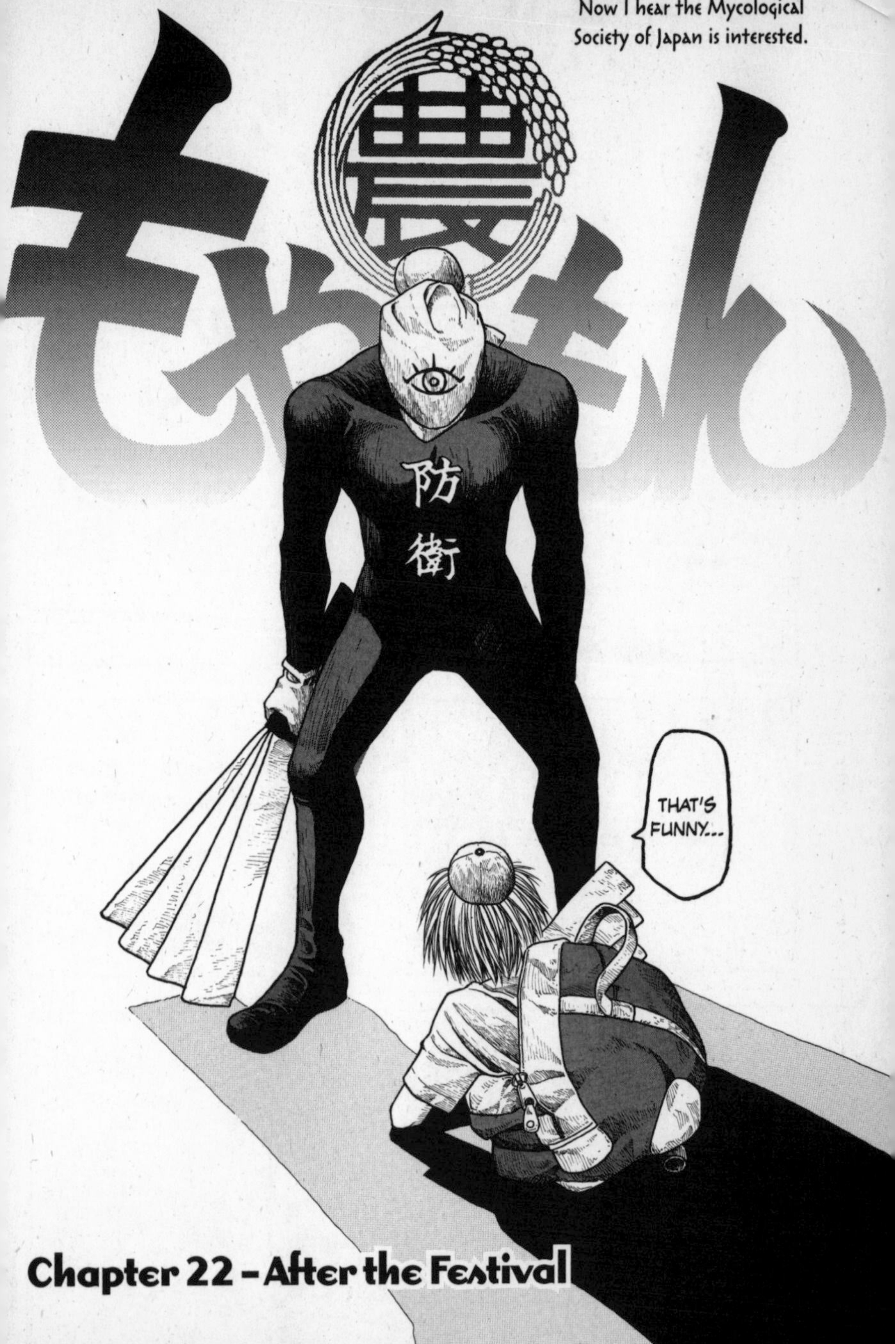
防衛
THAT'S FUNNY...

Chapter 22 – After the Festival

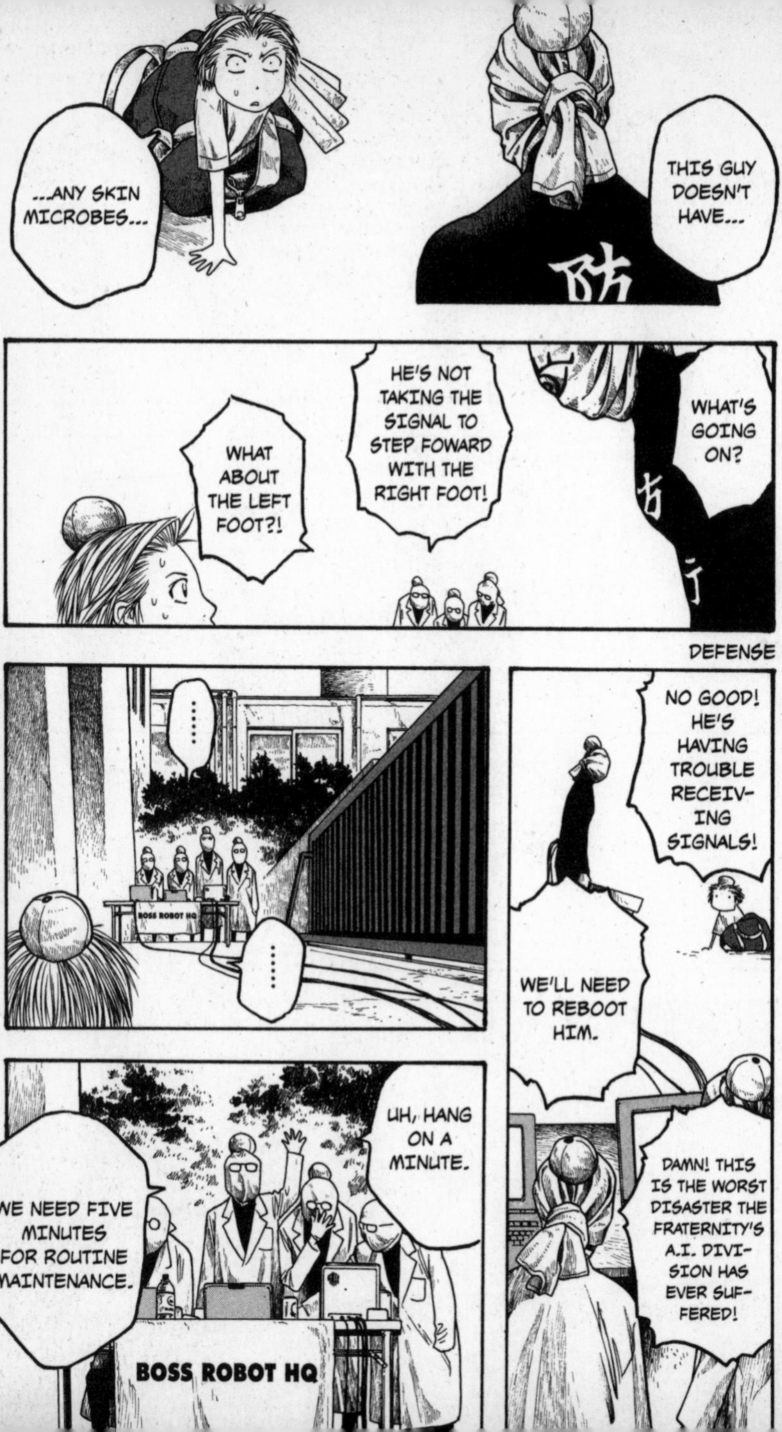
THIS GUY DOESN'T HAVE...
...ANY SKIN MICROBES...
WHAT'S GOING ON?
HE'S NOT TAKING THE SIGNAL TO STEP FOWARD WITH THE RIGHT FOOT!
WHAT ABOUT THE LEFT FOOT?!
DEFENSE
NO GOOD! HE'S HAVING TROUBLE RECEIV-ING SIGNALS!
WE'LL NEED TO REBOOT HIM.
DAMN! THIS IS THE WORST DISASTER THE FRATERNITY'S A.I. DIVI-SION HAS EVER SUF-FERED!
......
BOSS ROBOT HQ
......
UH, HANG ON A MINUTE.
WE NEED FIVE MINUTES FOR ROUTINE MAINTENANCE.
BOSS ROBOT HQ

This is the story.....that has led readers to inform me via fan letter that they want to go to college at an agricultural university. That doesn't change the fact that this story is pure fiction.

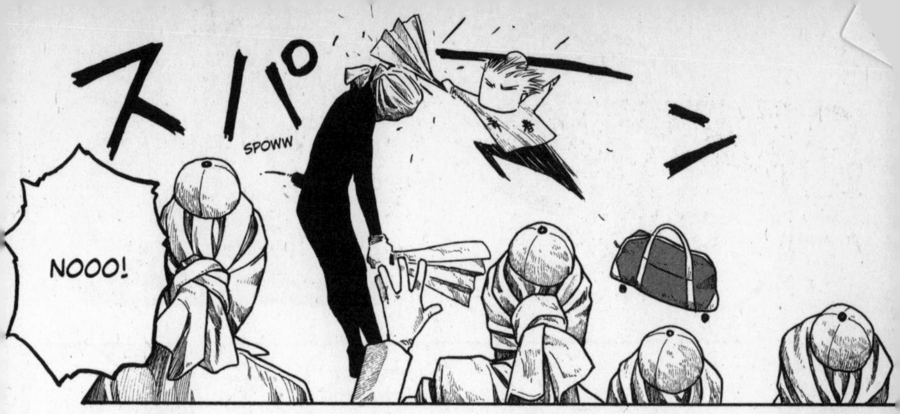
スパーン
SPOWW
NOOO!

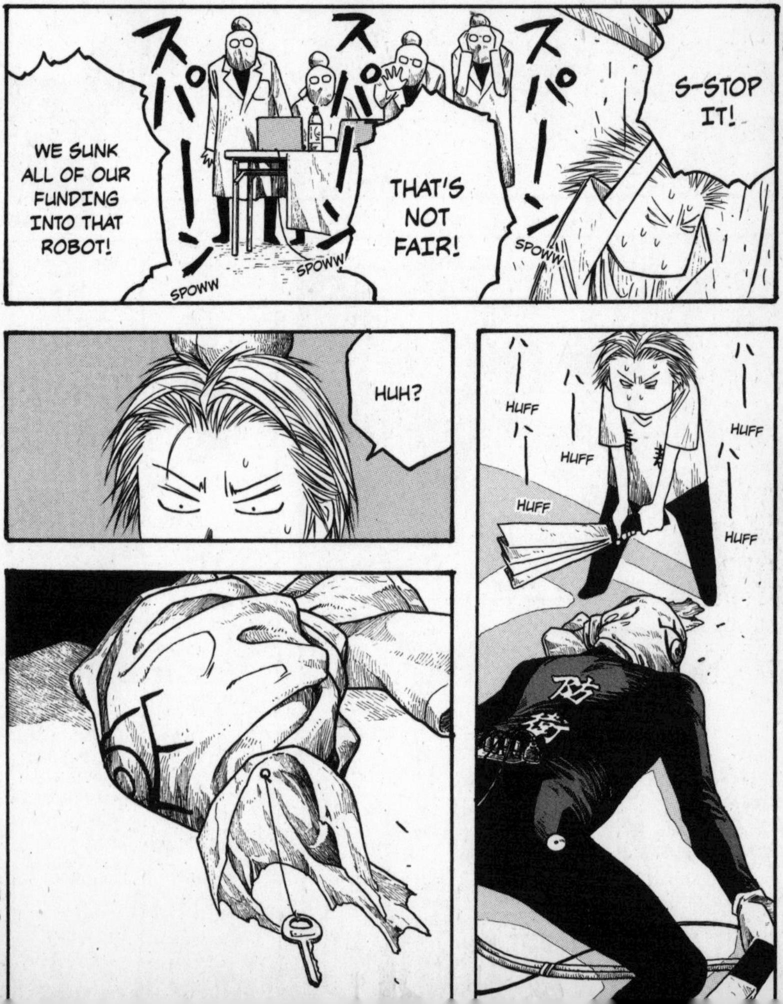
S-STOP IT!
スパーン
SPOWW
THAT'S NOT FAIR!
スパーン
SPOWW
WE SUNK ALL OF OUR FUNDING INTO THAT ROBOT!
スパーン
SPOWW
ハー
HUFF
ハー
HUFF
ハー
HUFF
ハー
HUFF
HUH?

Tadayasu Sawaki
Protagonist. Can see germs. His hair has grown out a bit.

Kaoru Misato
Sophomore. Despite all his faults, he still wants to be a hit with the ladies.

Takuma Kawahama
Sophomore. Lives in a student-run dorm with Misato. Scheduled to achieve great things in the near future.

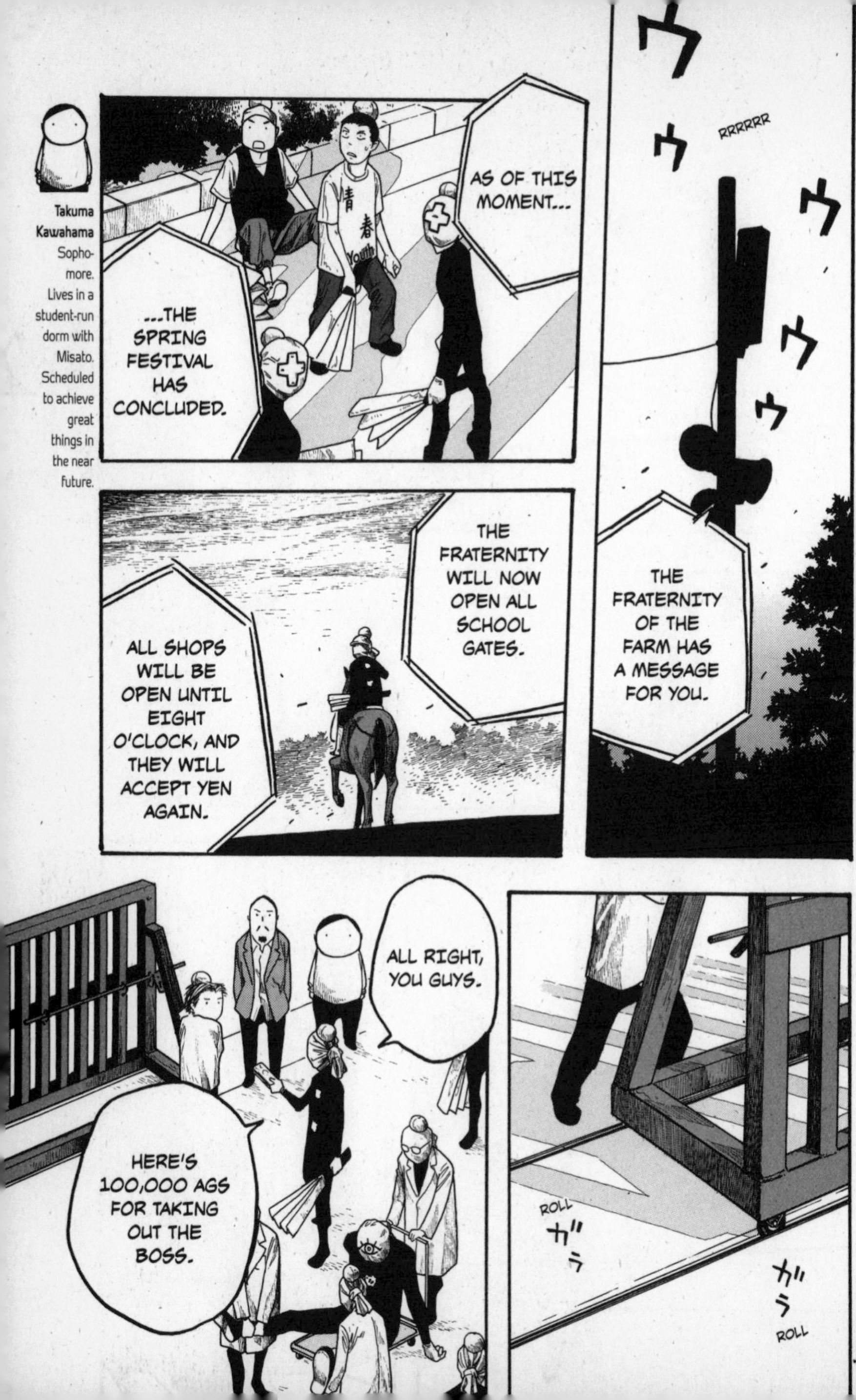
ウウ
RRRRRR
ウウウ
THE FRATERNITY OF THE FARM HAS A MESSAGE FOR YOU.
AS OF THIS MOMENT...
...THE SPRING FESTIVAL HAS CONCLUDED.
THE FRATERNITY WILL NOW OPEN ALL SCHOOL GATES.
ALL SHOPS WILL BE OPEN UNTIL EIGHT O'CLOCK, AND THEY WILL ACCEPT YEN AGAIN.
ガラ
ROLL
ROLL
ガラ
ALL RIGHT, YOU GUYS.
HERE'S 100,000 AGS FOR TAKING OUT THE BOSS.

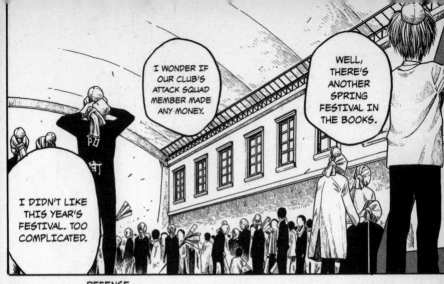

WELL, THERE'S ANOTHER SPRING FESTIVAL IN THE BOOKS.
I WONDER IF OUR CLUB'S ATTACK SQUAD MEMBER MADE ANY MONEY.
I DIDN'T LIKE THIS YEAR'S FESTIVAL. TOO COMPLICATED.
DEFENSE
FINALLY, I CAN WALK AROUND AND CHECK OUT THE SHOPS WITHOUT THIS MASK ON.
LET'S GO GET SOME DRINKS BEFORE THE CLOCK HITS EIGHT.
SAWAKI...
I DID IT... WE GOT OUR 100,000.
HELLO THERE.
YOUTH

Keizô Itsuki
Ag school professor. Say, I never gave the school an official name, did I?

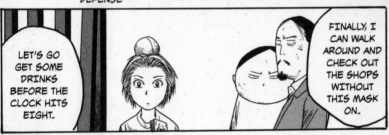

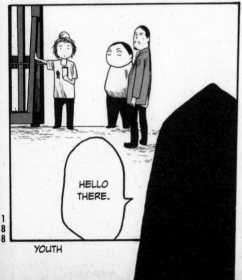

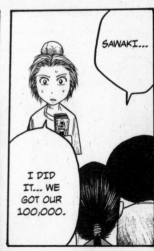

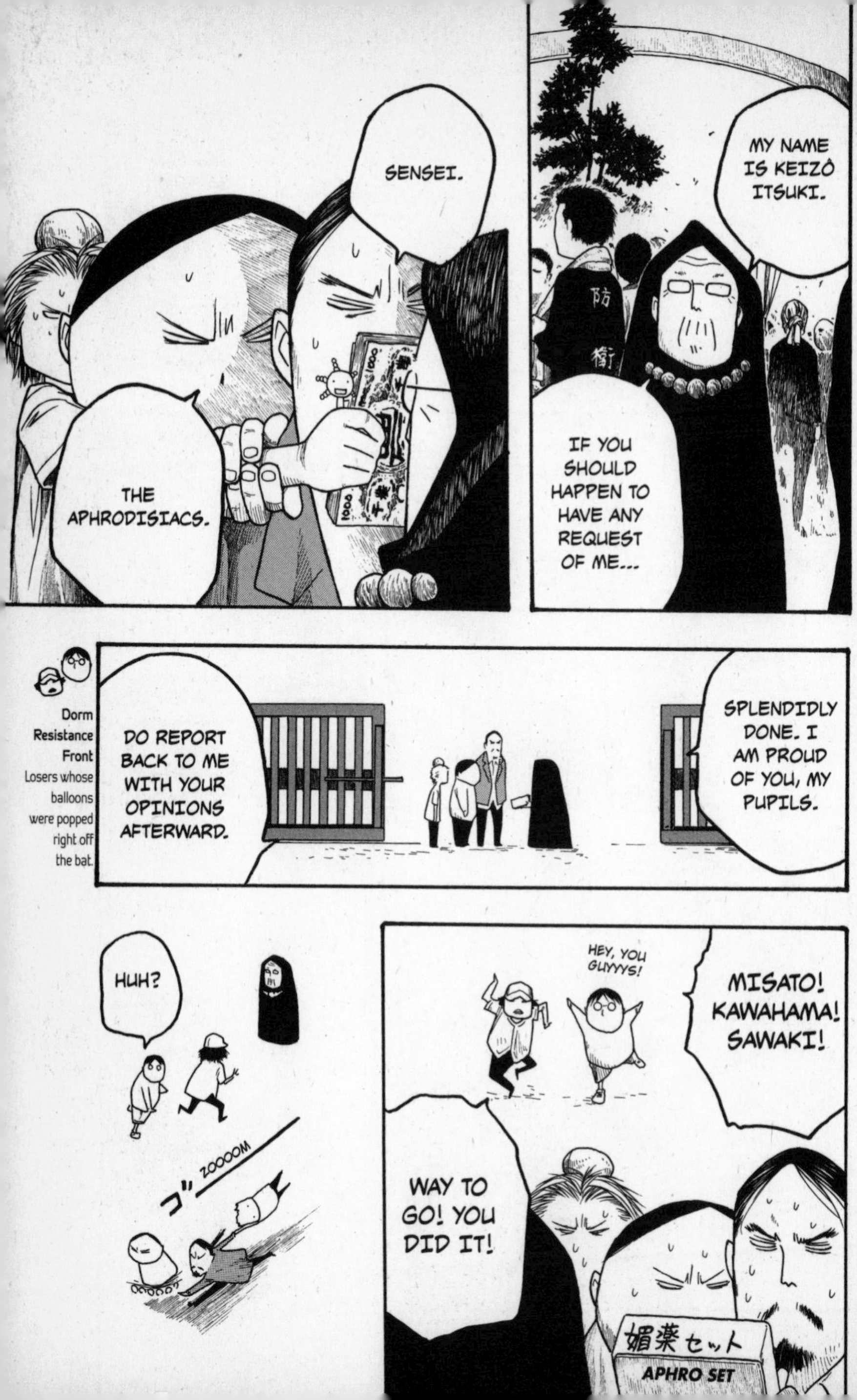
MY NAME IS KEIZÔ ITSUKI.
IF YOU SHOULD HAPPEN TO HAVE ANY REQUEST OF ME...
SENSEI.
THE APHRODISIACS.
SPLENDIDLY DONE. I AM PROUD OF YOU, MY PUPILS.
DO REPORT BACK TO ME WITH YOUR OPINIONS AFTERWARD.
Dorm Resistance Front
Losers whose balloons were popped right off the bat.
MISATO! KAWAHAMA! SAWAKI!
HEY, YOU GUYYYS!
WAY TO GO! YOU DID IT!
媚薬セット
APHRO SET
HUH?
ゴ
ZOOOOM

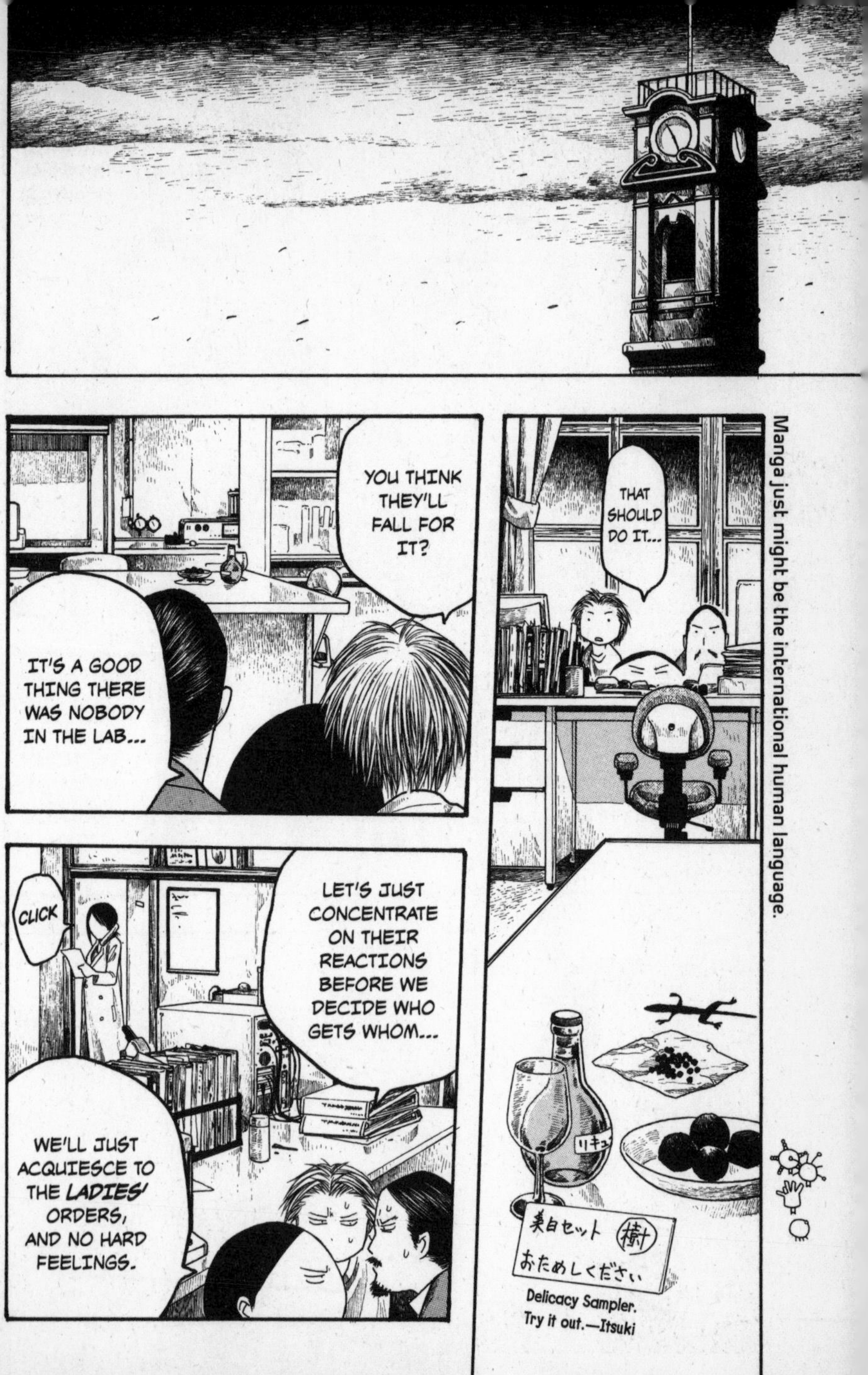
THAT SHOULD DO IT...
YOU THINK THEY'LL FALL FOR IT?
IT'S A GOOD THING THERE WAS NOBODY IN THE LAB...
リキュ
美白セット 樹
おためしください
Delicacy Sampler. Try it out.—Itsuki
LET'S JUST CONCENTRATE ON THEIR REACTIONS BEFORE WE DECIDE WHO GETS WHOM...
CLICK
WE'LL JUST ACQUIESCE TO THE *LADIES'* ORDERS, AND NO HARD FEELINGS.

Manga just might be the international human language.

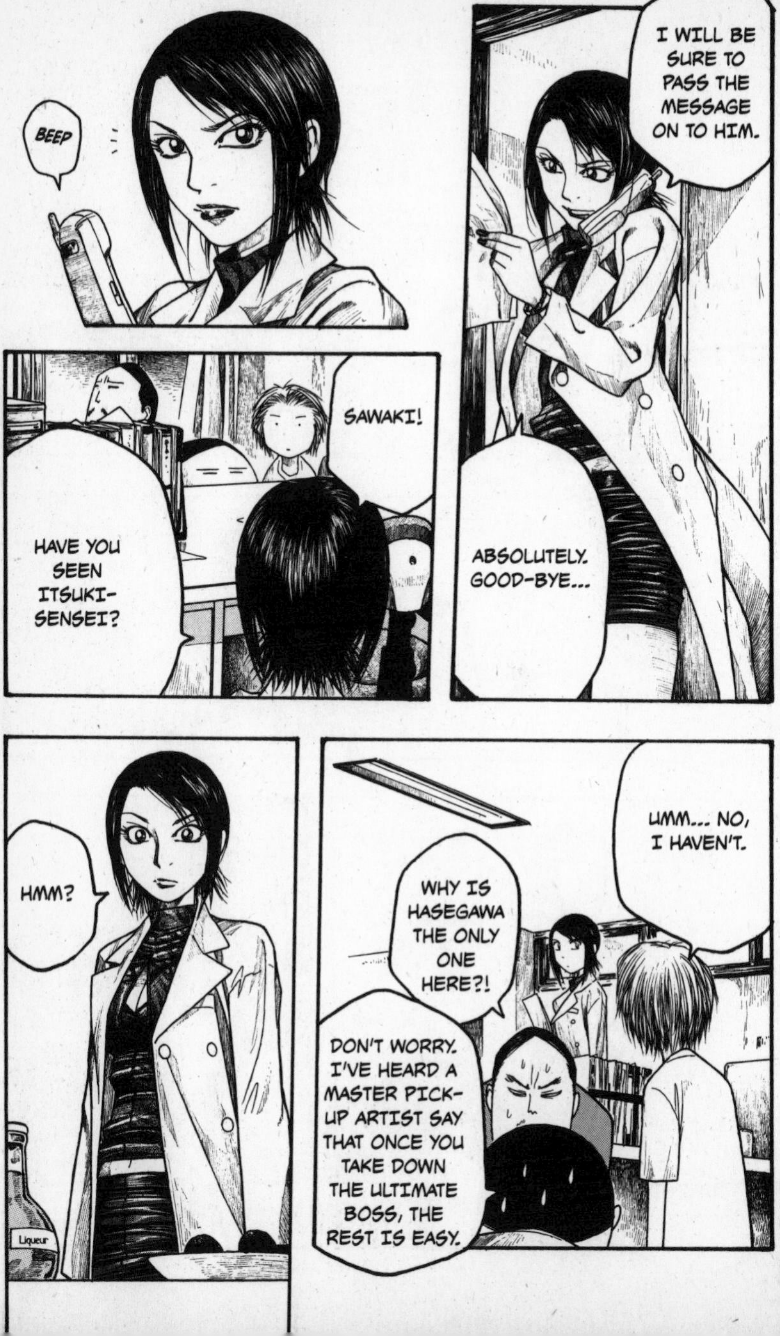
I WILL BE SURE TO PASS THE MESSAGE ON TO HIM.
ABSOLUTELY. GOOD-BYE...
BEEP
SAWAKI!
HAVE YOU SEEN ITSUKI-SENSEI?
UMM... NO, I HAVEN'T.
WHY IS HASEGAWA THE ONLY ONE HERE?!
DON'T WORRY. I'VE HEARD A MASTER PICK-UP ARTIST SAY THAT ONCE YOU TAKE DOWN THE ULTIMATE BOSS, THE REST IS EASY.
HMM?
Liqueur

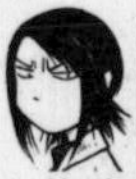

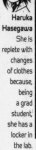

Haruka Hasegawa
She is replete with changes of clothes because, being a grad student, she has a locker in the lab.

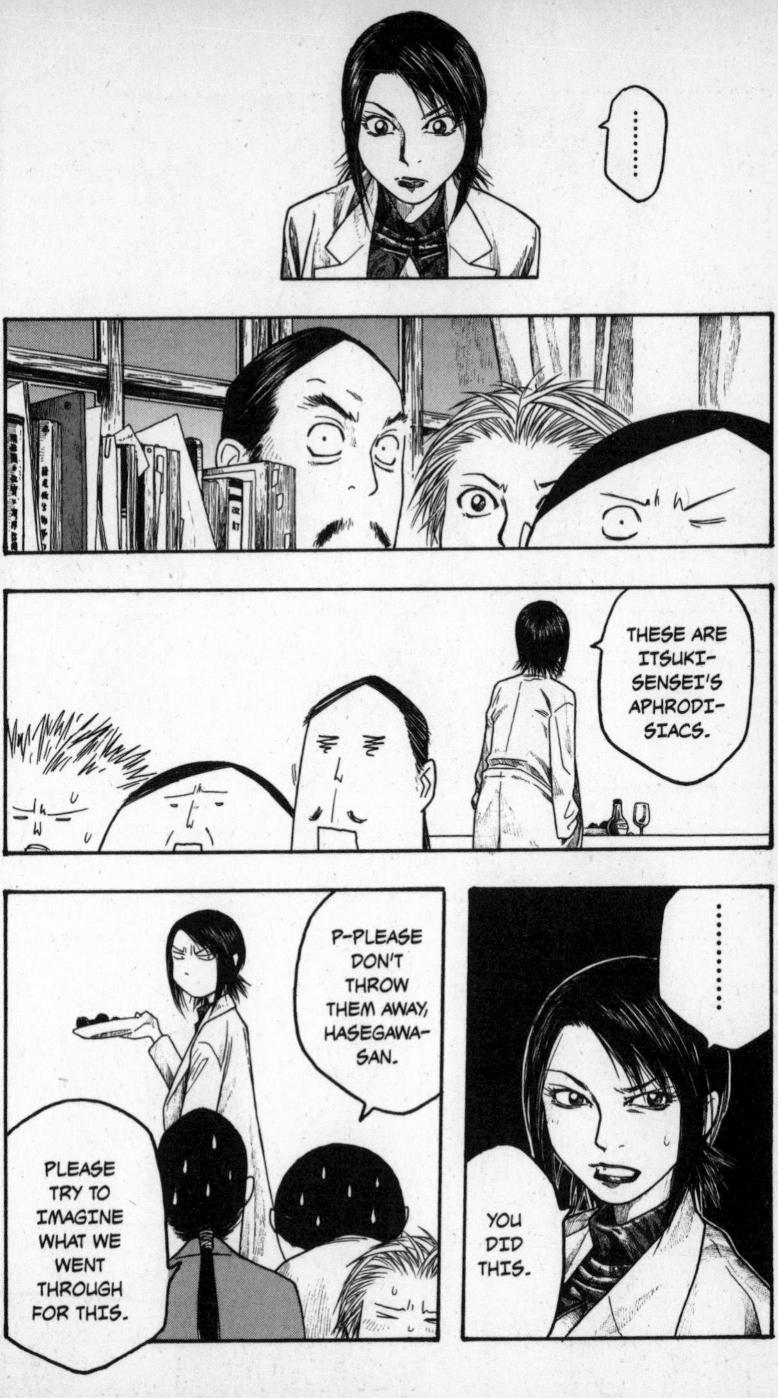
……
THESE ARE ITSUKI-SENSEI'S APHRODISIACS.
………
YOU DID THIS.
P-PLEASE DON'T THROW THEM AWAY, HASEGAWA-SAN.
PLEASE TRY TO IMAGINE WHAT WE WENT THROUGH FOR THIS.

It is capable of producing the same feelings in people separated by great distances.

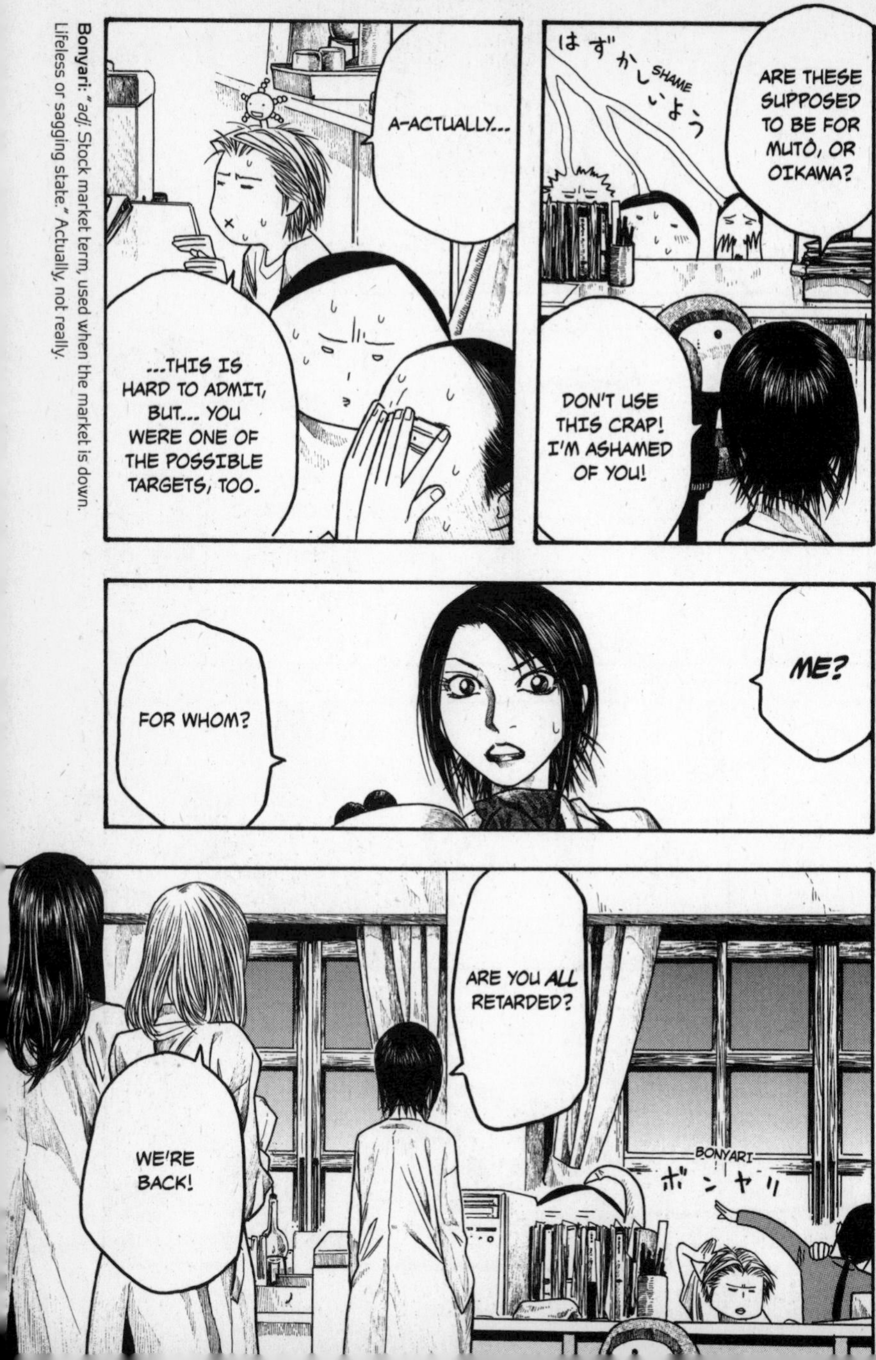
ARE THESE SUPPOSED TO BE FOR MUTÔ, OR OIKAWA?
はずかしいよう
SHAME
DON'T USE THIS CRAP! I'M ASHAMED OF YOU!
A-ACTUALLY...
...THIS IS HARD TO ADMIT, BUT... YOU WERE ONE OF THE POSSIBLE TARGETS, TOO.
ME?
FOR WHOM?
ARE YOU ALL RETARDED?
BONYARI
ボンヤリ
WE'RE BACK!

Bonyari: "*adj.* Stock market term, used when the market is down. Lifeless or sagging state." Actually, not really.

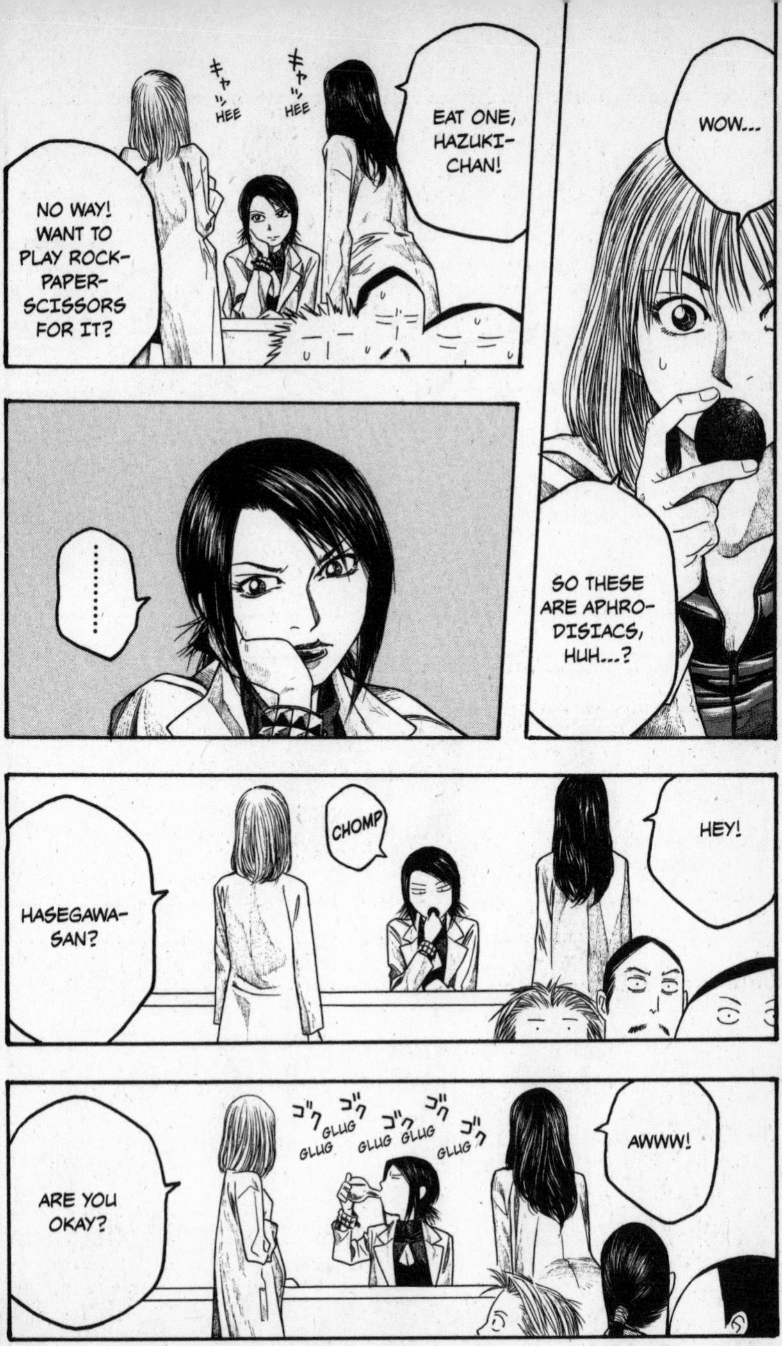
WOW...
SO THESE ARE APHRODISIACS, HUH...?
EAT ONE, HAZUKI-CHAN!
キャッ HEE
キャッ HEE
NO WAY! WANT TO PLAY ROCK-PAPER-SCISSORS FOR IT?
....
HEY!
CHOMP
HASEGAWA-SAN?
AWWW!
ゴク ゴク GLUG GLUG
ゴク ゴク GLUG GLUG
ゴク GLUG
ARE YOU OKAY?

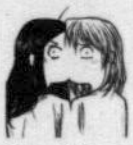

Hazuki Oikawa (R) and **Aoi Mutô** (L)
Oikawa is a freshman, like Sawaki. Mutô is Itsuki's only seminar student. They both look surprisingly good in bondage gear, but they're only just getting started.

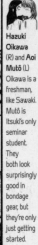

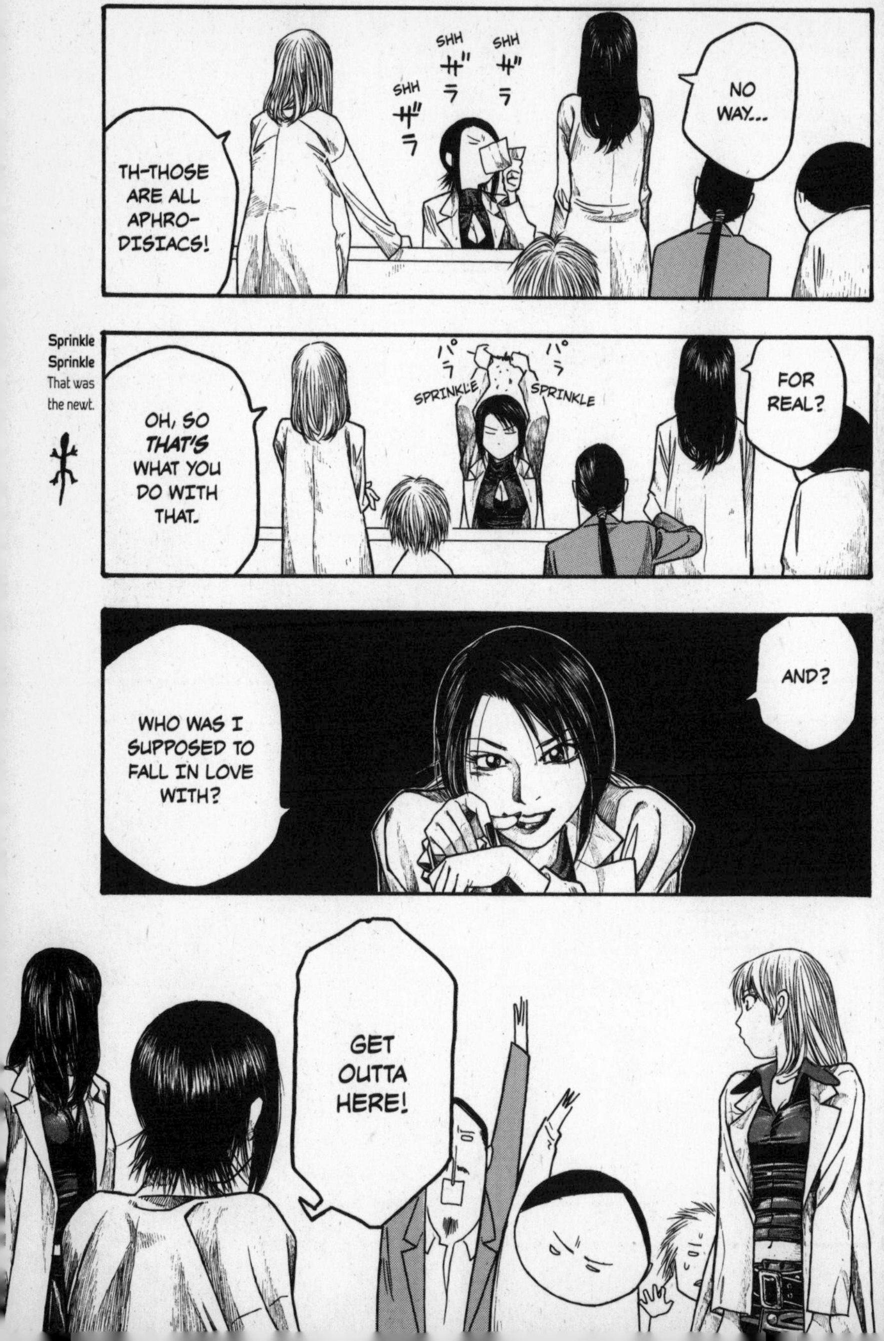
NO WAY...
SHH SHH SHH
TH-THOSE ARE ALL APHRODISIACS!
FOR REAL?
SPRINKLE SPRINKLE
OH, SO THAT'S WHAT YOU DO WITH THAT.
Sprinkle Sprinkle That was the newt.
AND?
WHO WAS I SUPPOSED TO FALL IN LOVE WITH?
GET OUTTA HERE!

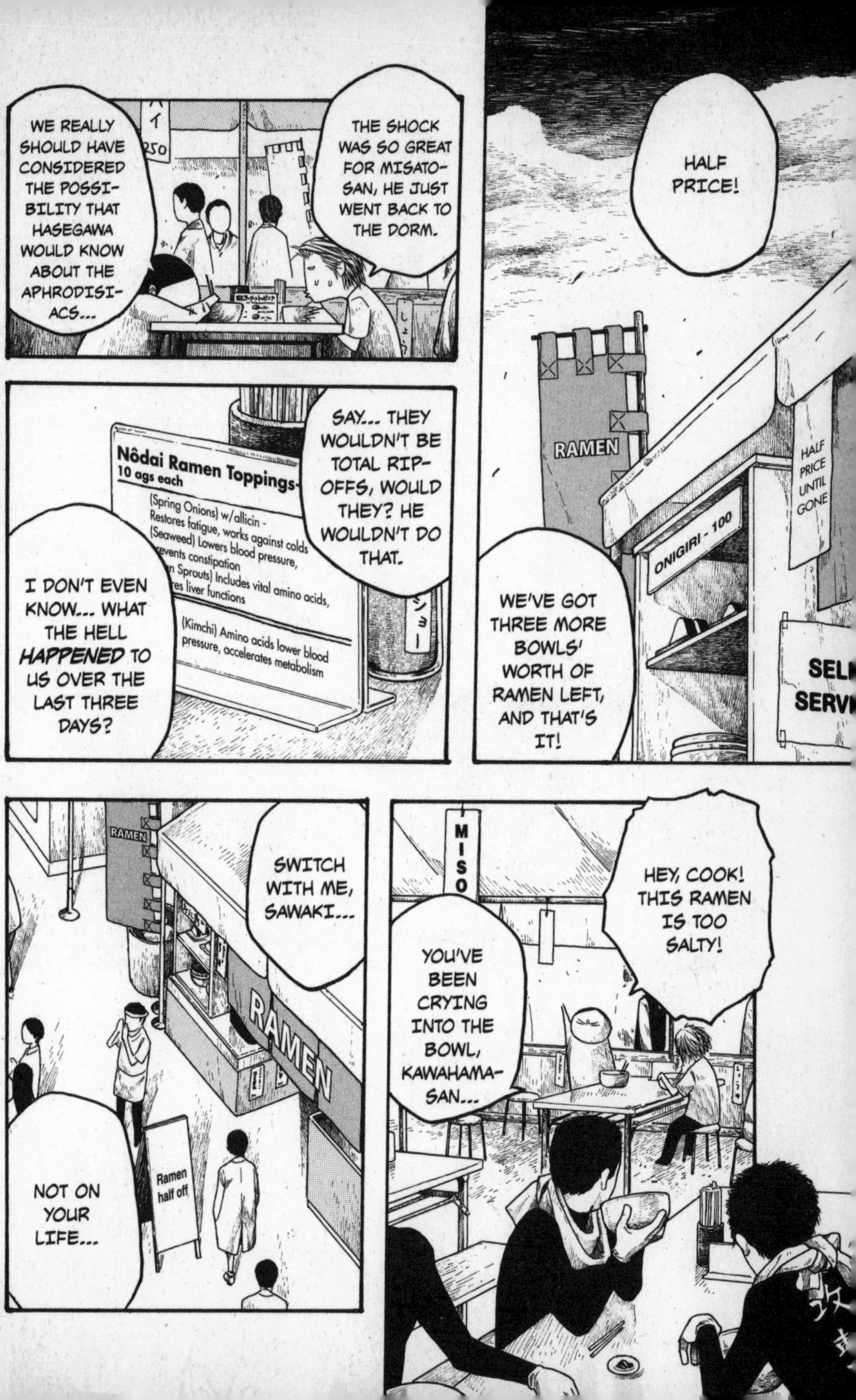
HALF PRICE!
RAMEN
HALF PRICE UNTIL GONE
ONIGIRI - 100
WE'VE GOT THREE MORE BOWLS' WORTH OF RAMEN LEFT, AND THAT'S IT!
SELF SERV
THE SHOCK WAS SO GREAT FOR MISATO-SAN, HE JUST WENT BACK TO THE DORM.
WE REALLY SHOULD HAVE CONSIDERED THE POSSIBILITY THAT HASEGAWA WOULD KNOW ABOUT THE APHRODISIACS...
SAY... THEY WOULDN'T BE TOTAL RIP-OFFS, WOULD THEY? HE WOULDN'T DO THAT.
Nôdai Ramen Toppings
10 ags each
(Spring Onions) w/allicin - Restores fatigue, works against colds
(Seaweed) Lowers blood pressure,
revents constipation
n Sprouts) Includes vital amino acids,
res liver functions
(Kimchi) Amino acids lower blood pressure, accelerates metabolism
I DON'T EVEN KNOW... WHAT THE HELL *HAPPENED* TO US OVER THE LAST THREE DAYS?
HEY, COOK! THIS RAMEN IS TOO SALTY!
MISO
YOU'VE BEEN CRYING INTO THE BOWL, KAWAHAMA-SAN...
RAMEN
SWITCH WITH ME, SAWAKI...
RAMEN
NOT ON YOUR LIFE...
Ramen half off

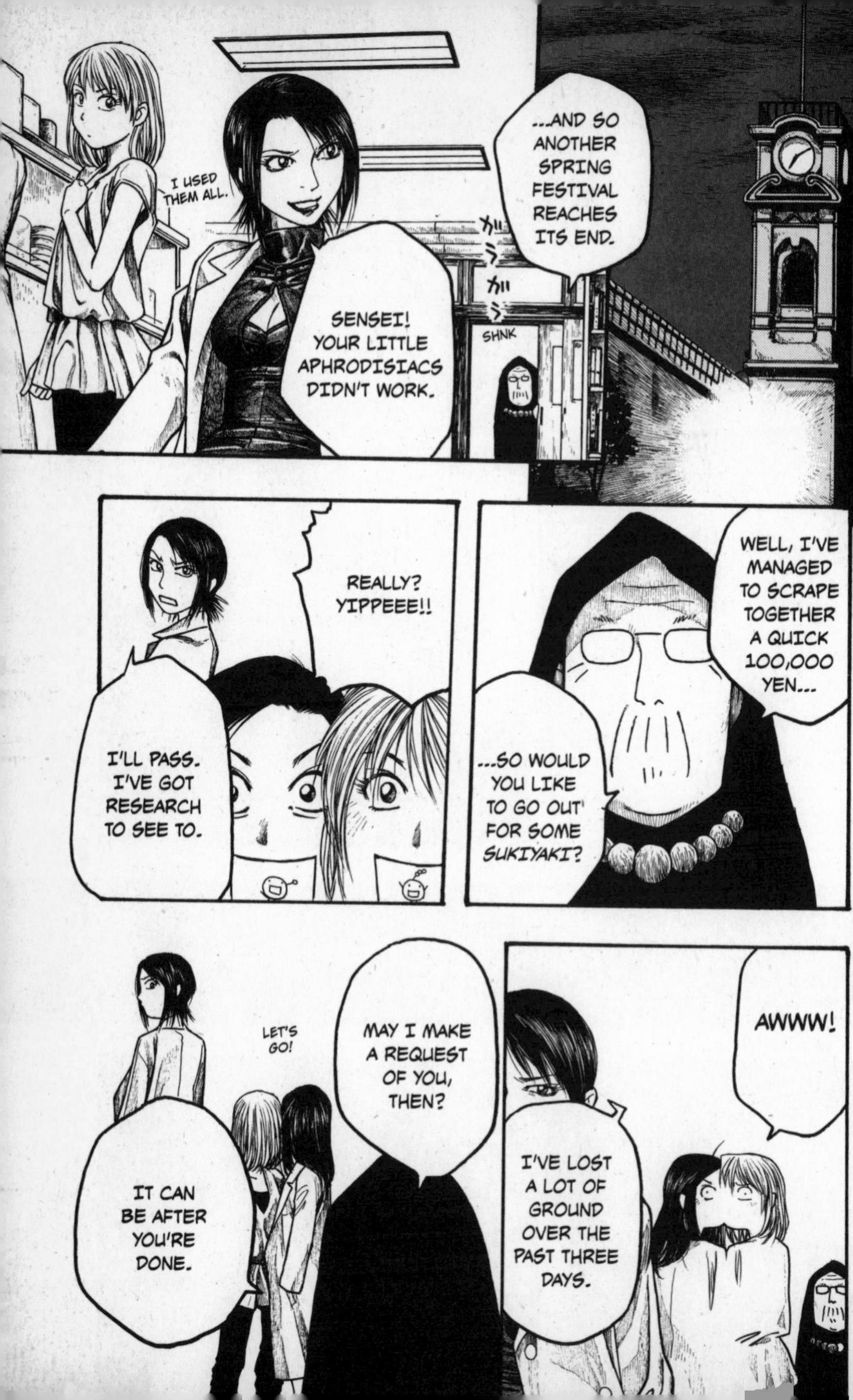
...AND SO ANOTHER SPRING FESTIVAL REACHES ITS END.
ガラガラ
SHNK
SENSEI! YOUR LITTLE APHRODISIACS DIDN'T WORK.
I USED THEM ALL.
WELL, I'VE MANAGED TO SCRAPE TOGETHER A QUICK 100,000 YEN...
...SO WOULD YOU LIKE TO GO OUT FOR SOME SUKIYAKI?
REALLY? YIPPEEE!!
I'LL PASS. I'VE GOT RESEARCH TO SEE TO.
AWWW!
I'VE LOST A LOT OF GROUND OVER THE PAST THREE DAYS.
MAY I MAKE A REQUEST OF YOU, THEN?
LET'S GO!
IT CAN BE AFTER YOU'RE DONE.

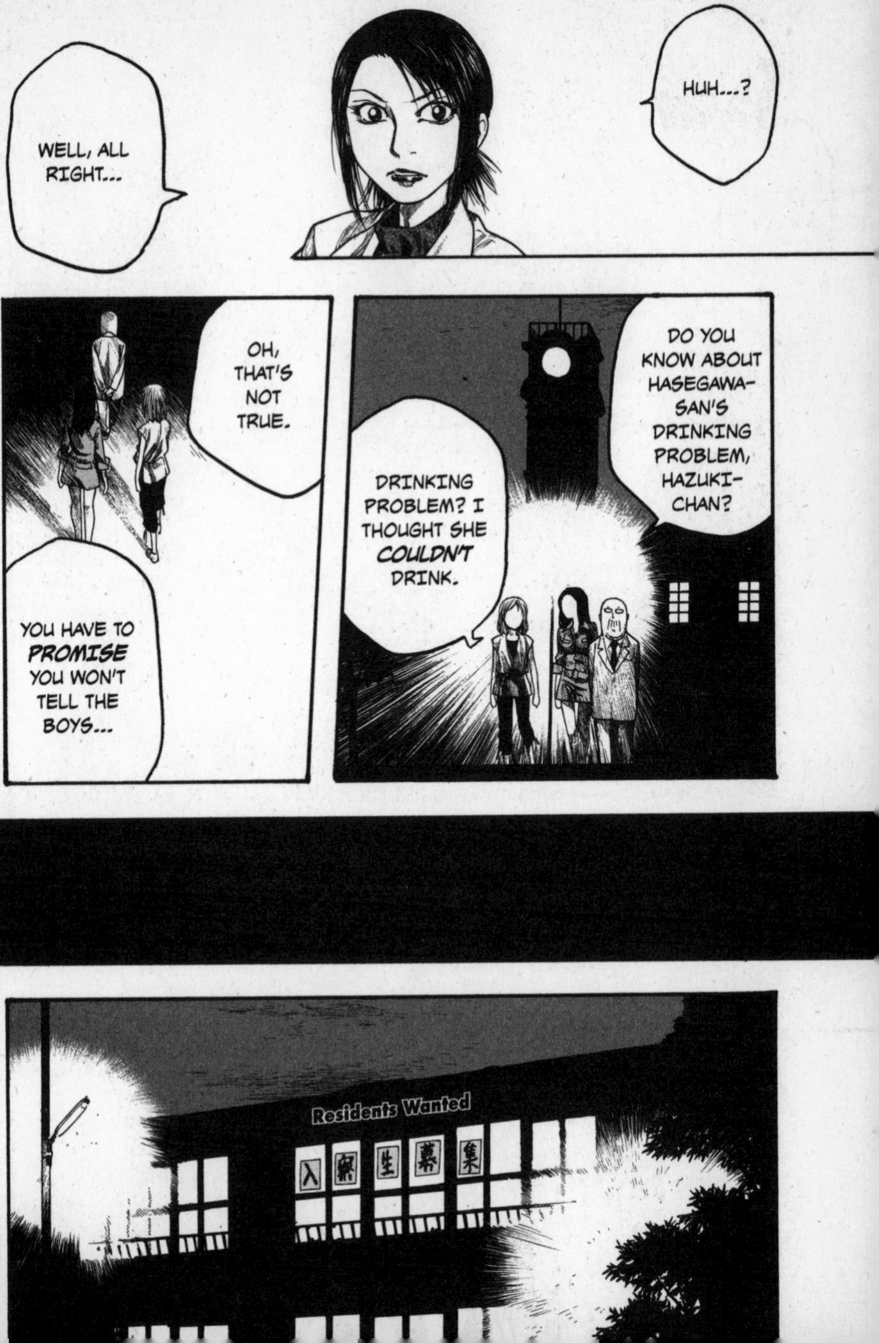
HUH...?
WELL, ALL RIGHT...
DO YOU KNOW ABOUT HASEGAWA-SAN'S DRINKING PROBLEM, HAZUKI-CHAN?
DRINKING PROBLEM? I THOUGHT SHE *COULDN'T* DRINK.
OH, THAT'S NOT TRUE.
YOU HAVE TO *PROMISE* YOU WON'T TELL THE BOYS...
Residents Wanted
入寮生募集

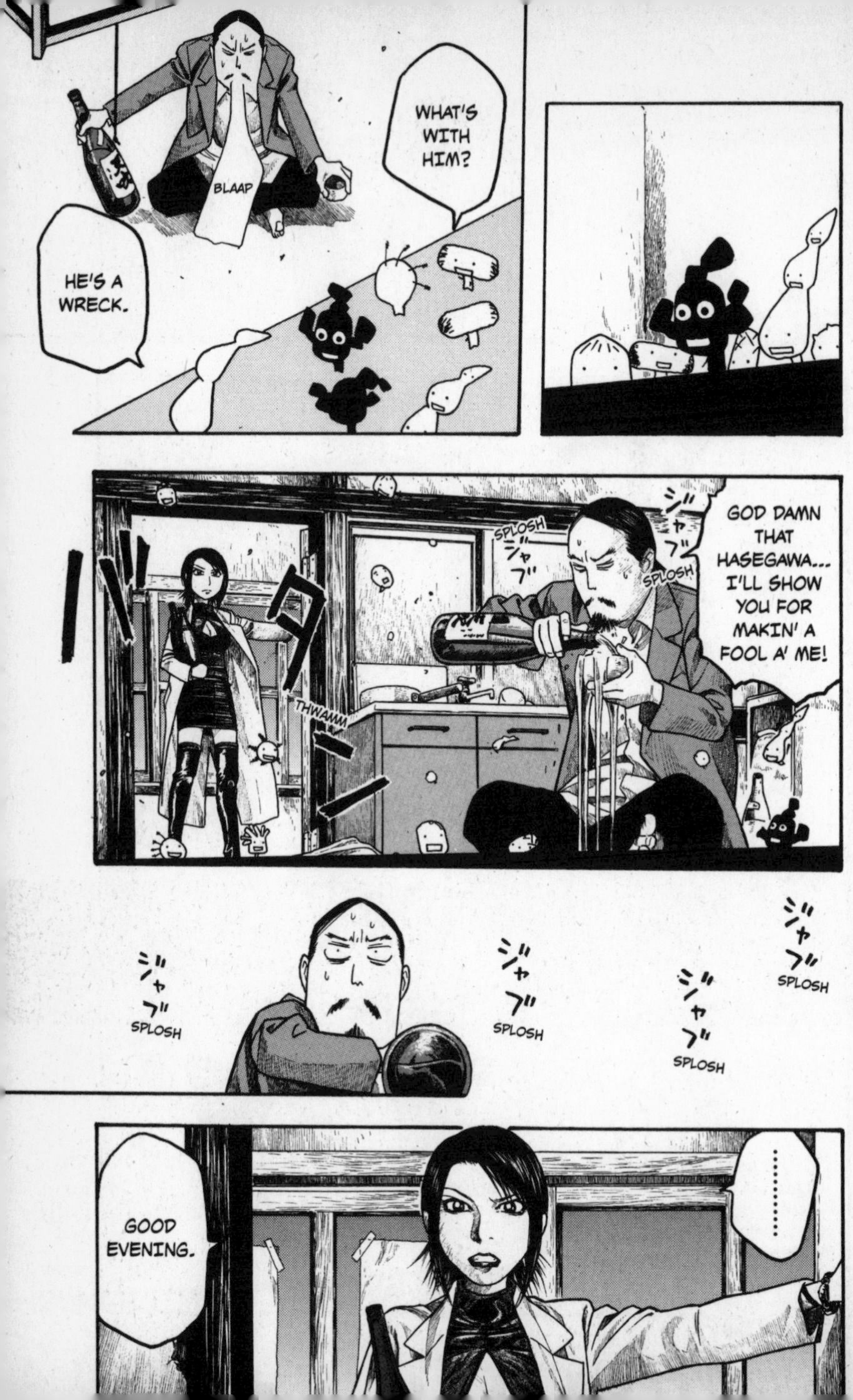

WHAT'S WITH HIM?
BLAAP
HE'S A WRECK.
GOD DAMN THAT HASEGAWA... I'LL SHOW YOU FOR MAKIN' A FOOL A' ME!
ジャブ
SPLOSH
ジャブ
SPLOSH
THWAMM
ジャブ
SPLOSH
ジャブ
SPLOSH
ジャブ
SPLOSH
ジャブ
SPLOSH
....
GOOD EVENING.

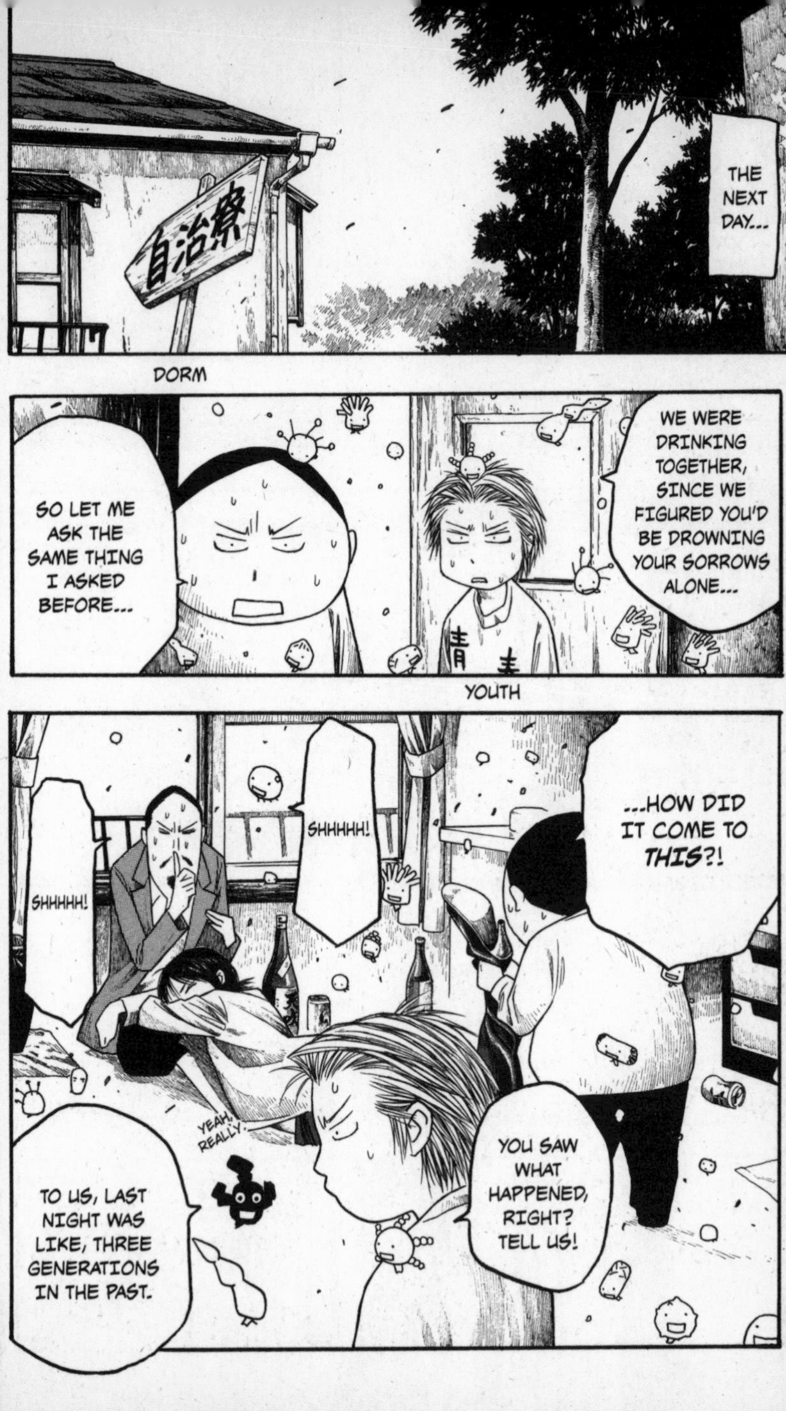
THE NEXT DAY...
DORM
WE WERE DRINKING TOGETHER, SINCE WE FIGURED YOU'D BE DROWNING YOUR SORROWS ALONE...
SO LET ME ASK THE SAME THING I ASKED BEFORE...
YOUTH
...HOW DID IT COME TO *THIS*?!
SHHHHH!
SHHHHH!
YOU SAW WHAT HAPPENED, RIGHT? TELL US!
YEAH, REALLY.
TO US, LAST NIGHT WAS LIKE, THREE GENERATIONS IN THE PAST.

The Germs of Misato's Room
Just a random assortment of "germs," in the most common sense of the word.

HOW RUDE!

22
END

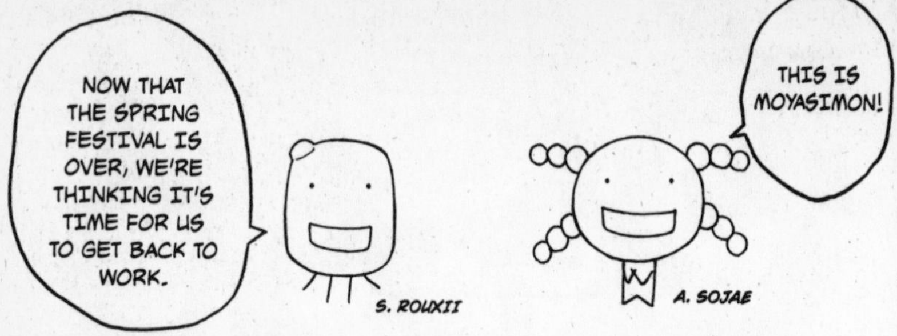
THIS IS MOYASIMON!
A. SOJAE
NOW THAT THE SPRING FESTIVAL IS OVER, WE'RE THINKING IT'S TIME FOR US TO GET BACK TO WORK.
S. ROUXII

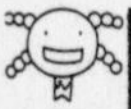

A. sojae
Can even brew in high-sodium environments, making them a valuable tool in the creation of soy sauce and *miso*.

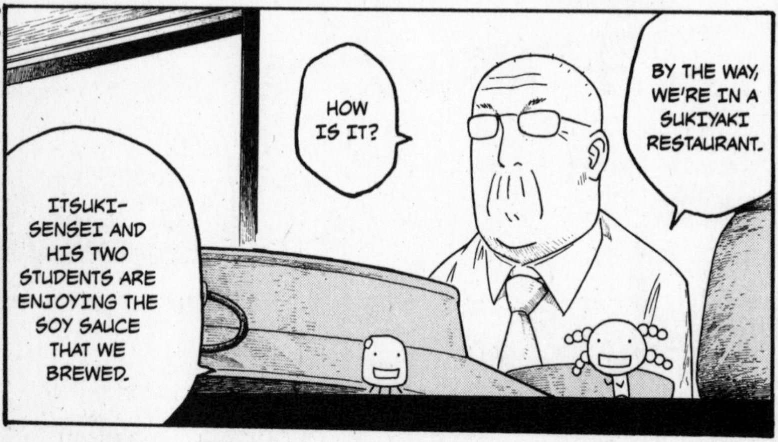
BY THE WAY, WE'RE IN A SUKIYAKI RESTAURANT.
HOW IS IT?
ITSUKI-SENSEI AND HIS TWO STUDENTS ARE ENJOYING THE SOY SAUCE THAT WE BREWED.

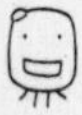

S. rouxii
Soy sauce actually involves the work of many different microbes. If you took a peek, you'd see a parade of germs. That's just how soy sauce is.

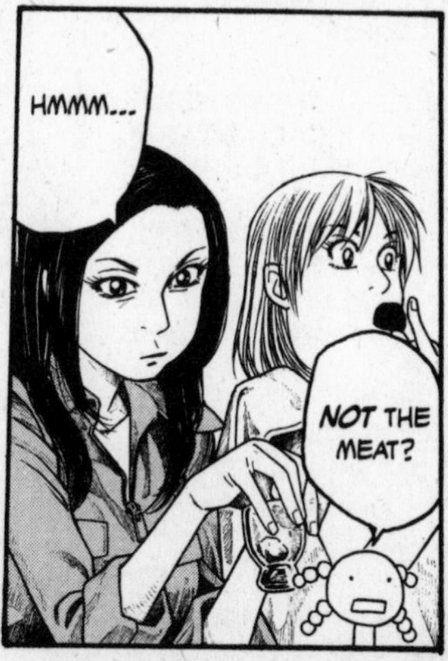
HMMM...
NOT THE MEAT?

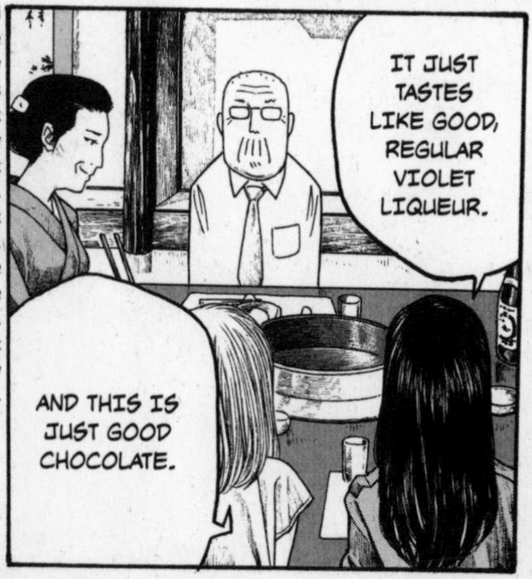
IT JUST TASTES LIKE GOOD, REGULAR VIOLET LIQUEUR.
AND THIS IS JUST GOOD CHOCOLATE.

もやしもん

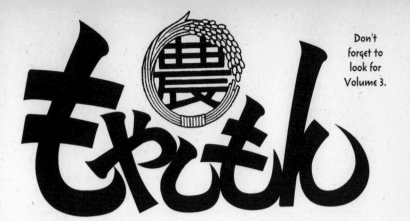

Don't forget to look for Volume 3.

Chapter 23 – Mornings

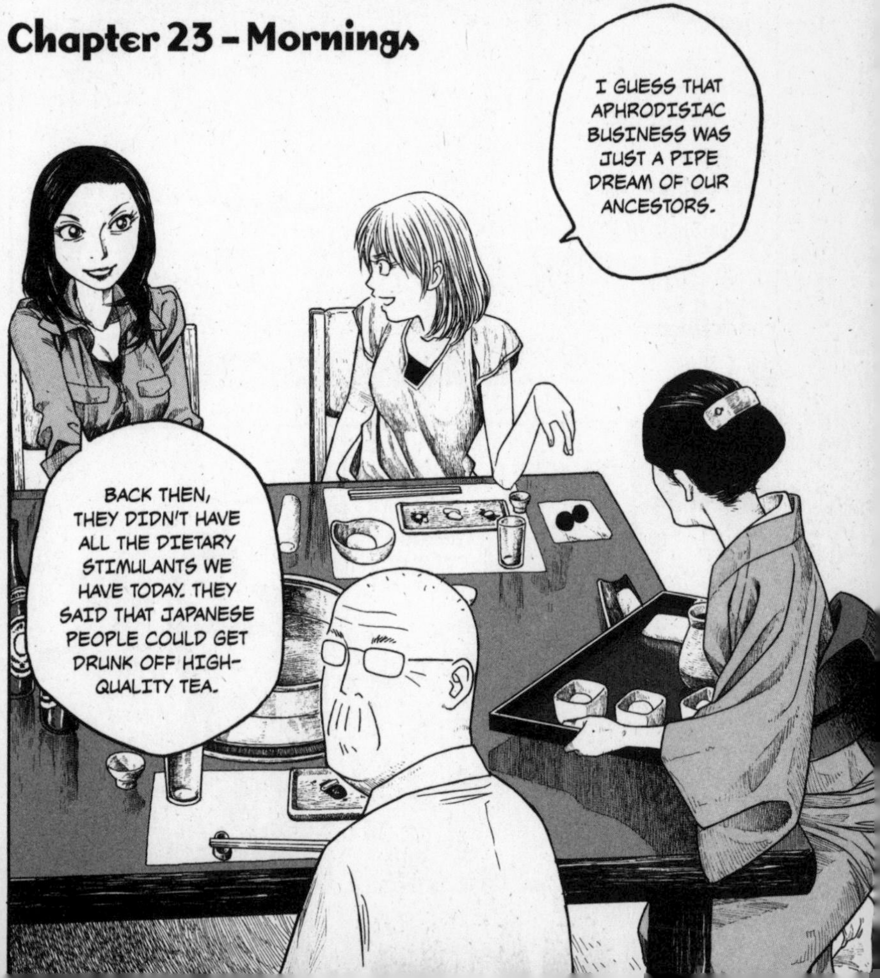

I GUESS THAT APHRODISIAC BUSINESS WAS JUST A PIPE DREAM OF OUR ANCESTORS.
BACK THEN, THEY DIDN'T HAVE ALL THE DIETARY STIMULANTS WE HAVE TODAY. THEY SAID THAT JAPANESE PEOPLE COULD GET DRUNK OFF HIGH-QUALITY TEA.

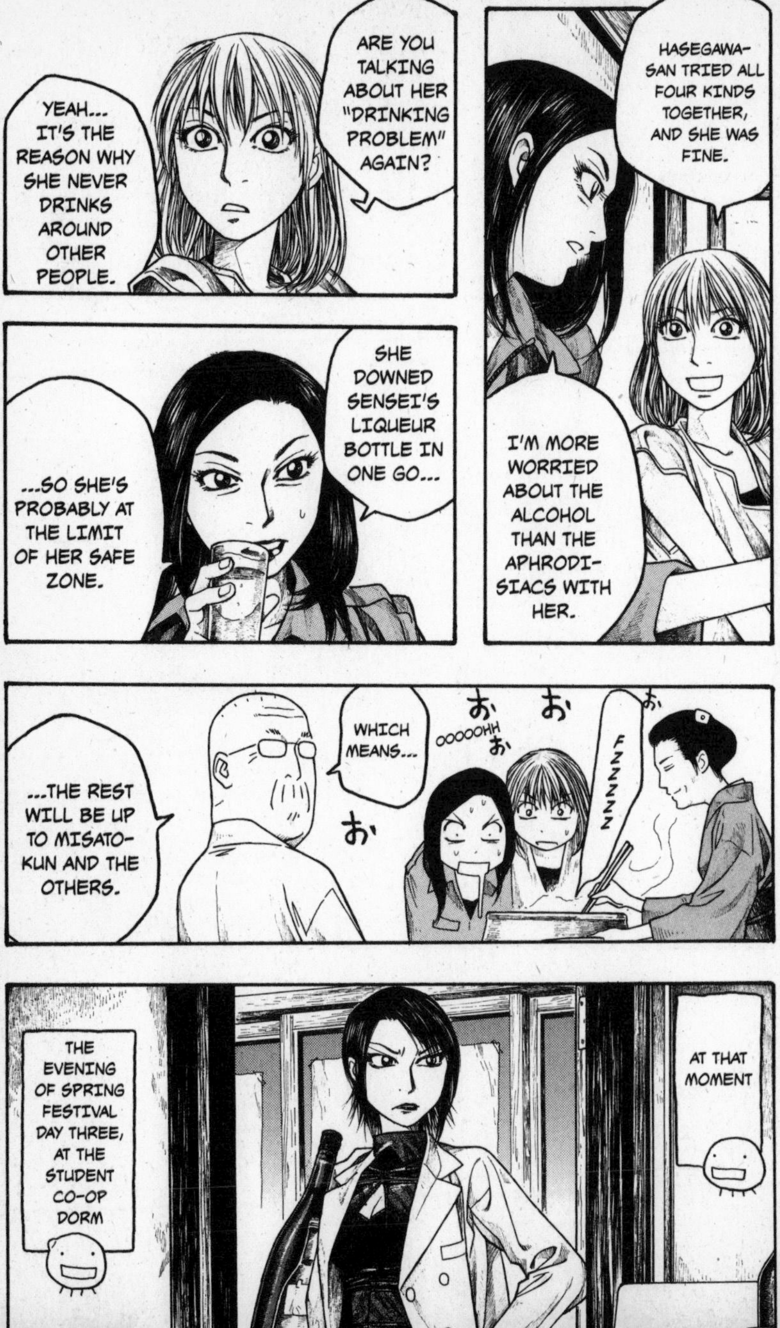
HASEGAWA-SAN TRIED ALL FOUR KINDS TOGETHER, AND SHE WAS FINE.
I'M MORE WORRIED ABOUT THE ALCOHOL THAN THE APHRODISIACS WITH HER.
ARE YOU TALKING ABOUT HER "DRINKING PROBLEM" AGAIN?
YEAH... IT'S THE REASON WHY SHE NEVER DRINKS AROUND OTHER PEOPLE.
SHE DOWNED SENSEI'S LIQUEUR BOTTLE IN ONE GO...
...SO SHE'S PROBABLY AT THE LIMIT OF HER SAFE ZONE.
お
FZZZZZ
お
お
OOOOOHH
お
WHICH MEANS...
お
...THE REST WILL BE UP TO MISATO-KUN AND THE OTHERS.
AT THAT MOMENT
THE EVENING OF SPRING FESTIVAL DAY THREE, AT THE STUDENT CO-OP DORM

This is the story.....that some have called the "First Germ Manga in Japan," but *Nausicaä of the Valley of the Wind* was a story about germs saving the world, and in Part 5 of *Jojo's Bizarre Adventurae*, there was that mold-based Stand called "Green Day." What am I trying to say? That this manga is fiction.

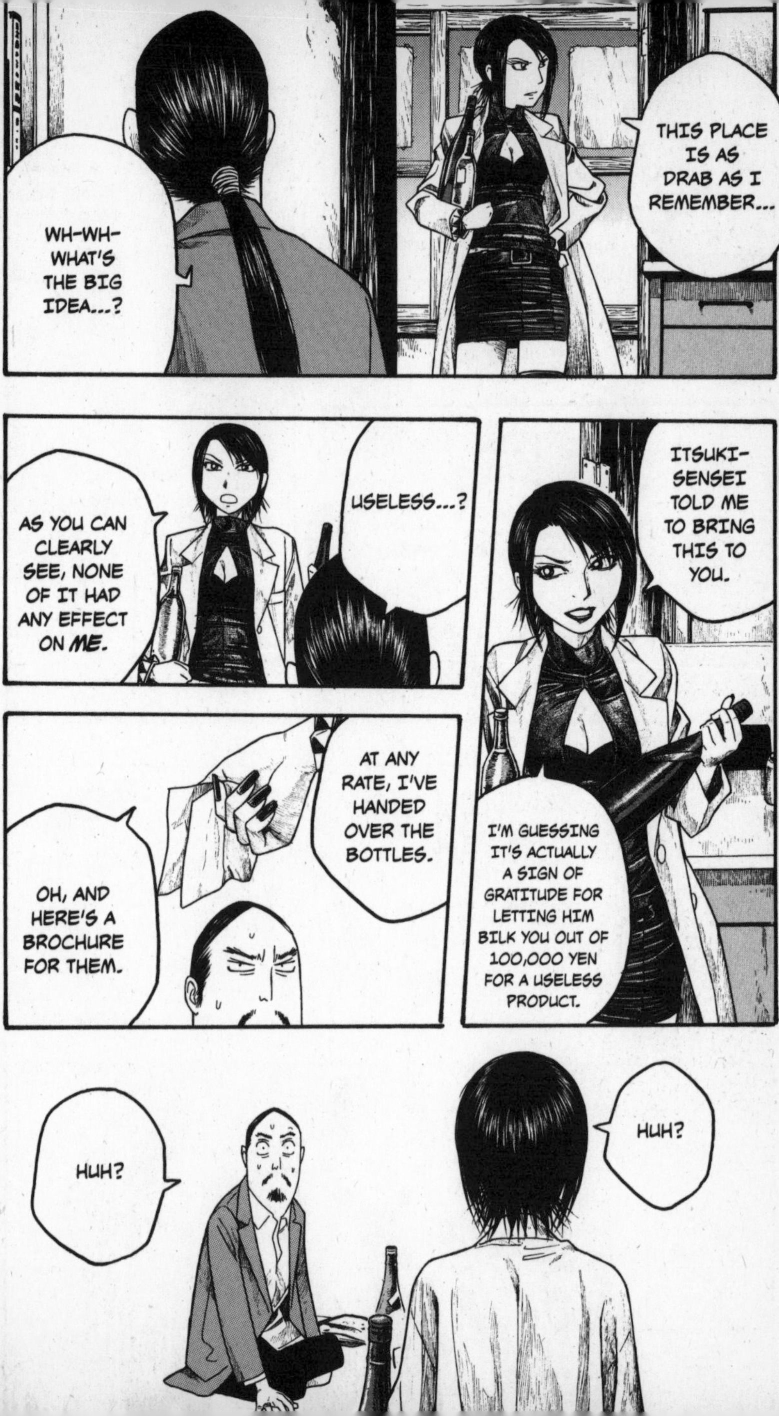
THIS PLACE IS AS DRAB AS I REMEMBER...
WH-WH-WHAT'S THE BIG IDEA...?
ITSUKI-SENSEI TOLD ME TO BRING THIS TO YOU.
I'M GUESSING IT'S ACTUALLY A SIGN OF GRATITUDE FOR LETTING HIM BILK YOU OUT OF 100,000 YEN FOR A USELESS PRODUCT.
USELESS...?
AS YOU CAN CLEARLY SEE, NONE OF IT HAD ANY EFFECT ON *ME*.
AT ANY RATE, I'VE HANDED OVER THE BOTTLES.
OH, AND HERE'S A BROCHURE FOR THEM.
HUH?
HUH?

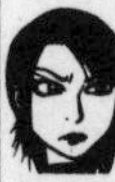

Haruka Hasegawa
Ag school grad student. For the last year, we have only seen her stern and disapproving look, but today will bring something new to the table.

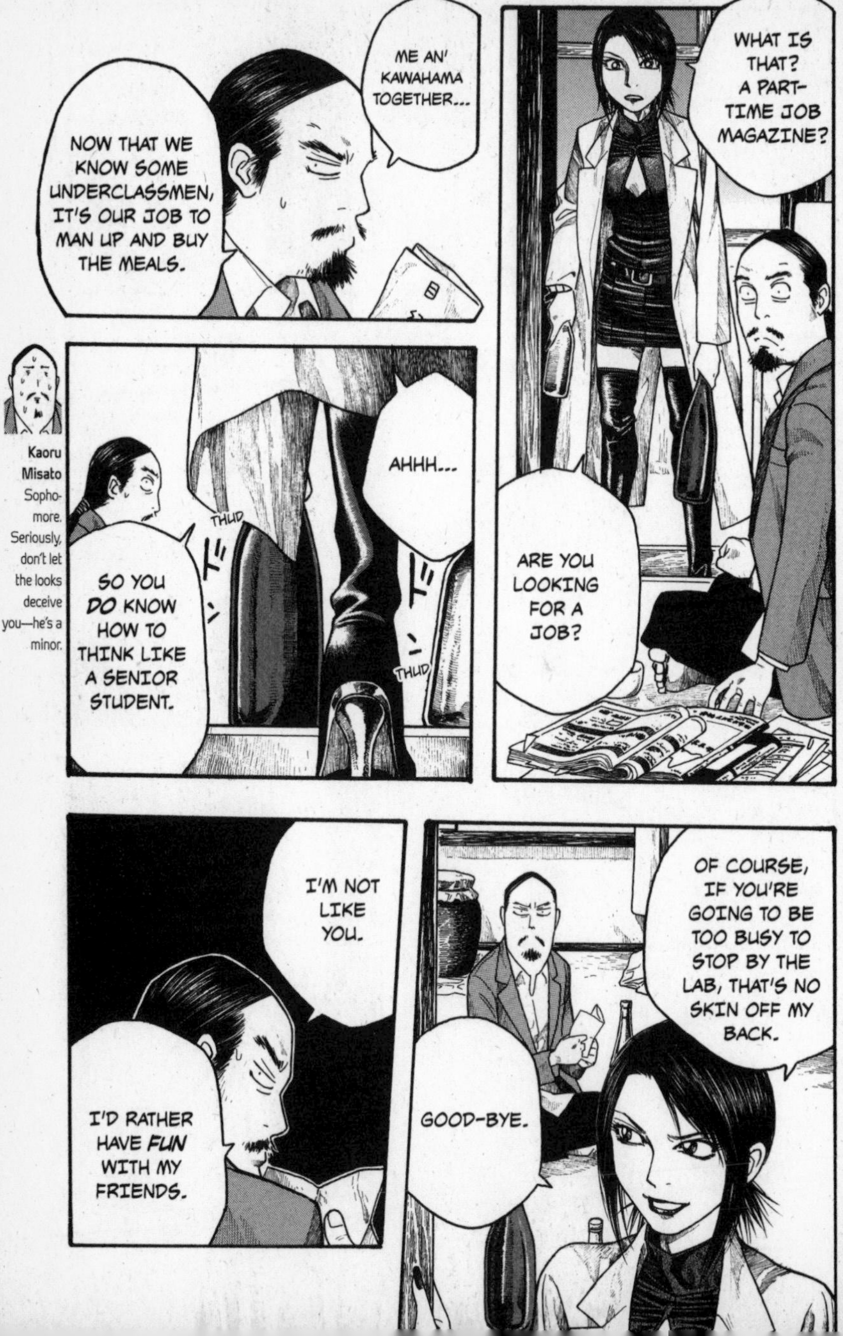
WHAT IS THAT? A PART-TIME JOB MAGAZINE?
ARE YOU LOOKING FOR A JOB?
ME AN' KAWAHAMA TOGETHER...
NOW THAT WE KNOW SOME UNDERCLASSMEN, IT'S OUR JOB TO MAN UP AND BUY THE MEALS.
AHHH...
THUD
THUD
SO YOU *DO* KNOW HOW TO THINK LIKE A SENIOR STUDENT.
Kaoru Misato
Sophomore. Seriously, don't let the looks deceive you—he's a minor.
OF COURSE, IF YOU'RE GOING TO BE TOO BUSY TO STOP BY THE LAB, THAT'S NO SKIN OFF MY BACK.
GOOD-BYE.
I'M NOT LIKE YOU.
I'D RATHER HAVE *FUN* WITH MY FRIENDS.

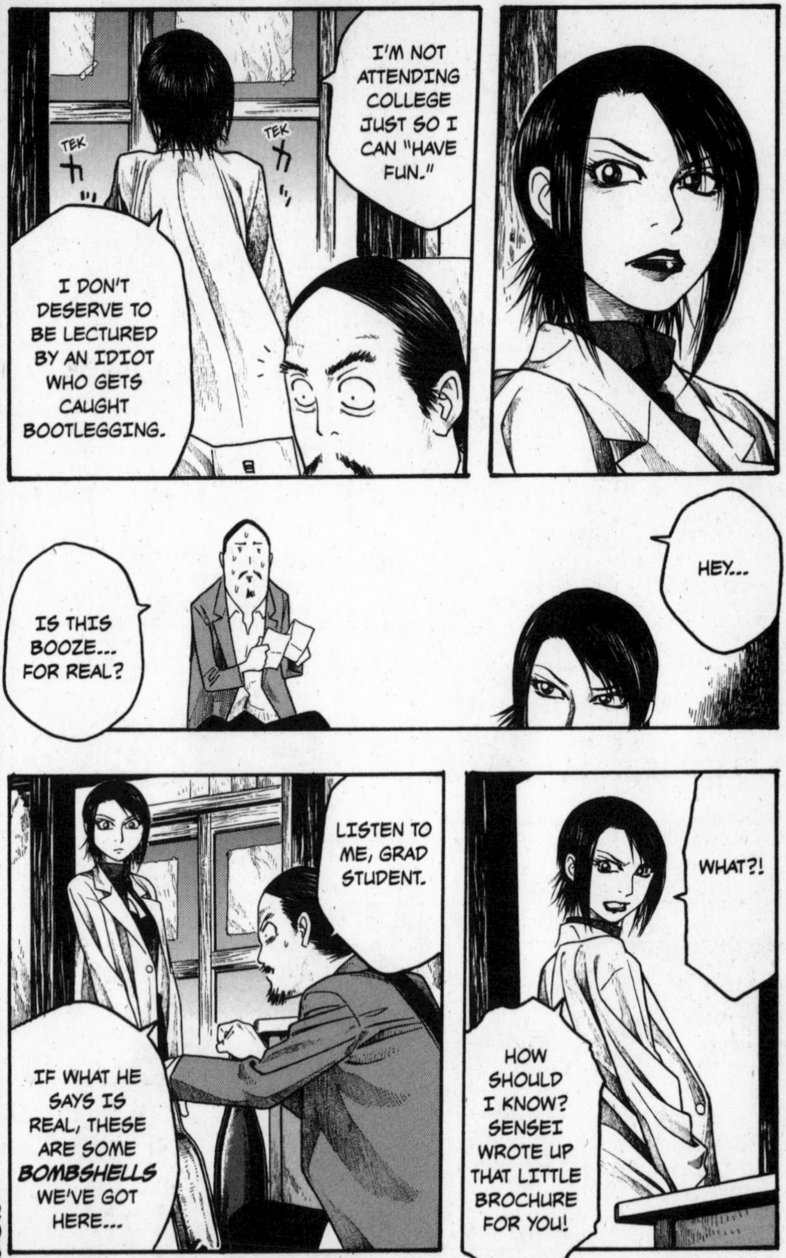
I'M NOT ATTENDING COLLEGE JUST SO I CAN "HAVE FUN."
TEK
TEK
I DON'T DESERVE TO BE LECTURED BY AN IDIOT WHO GETS CAUGHT BOOTLEGGING.
HEY...
IS THIS BOOZE... FOR REAL?
WHAT?!
HOW SHOULD I KNOW? SENSEI WROTE UP THAT LITTLE BROCHURE FOR YOU!
LISTEN TO ME, GRAD STUDENT.
IF WHAT HE SAYS IS REAL, THESE ARE SOME *BOMBSHELLS* WE'VE GOT HERE...

Hope you will check out Volume 3 as well.

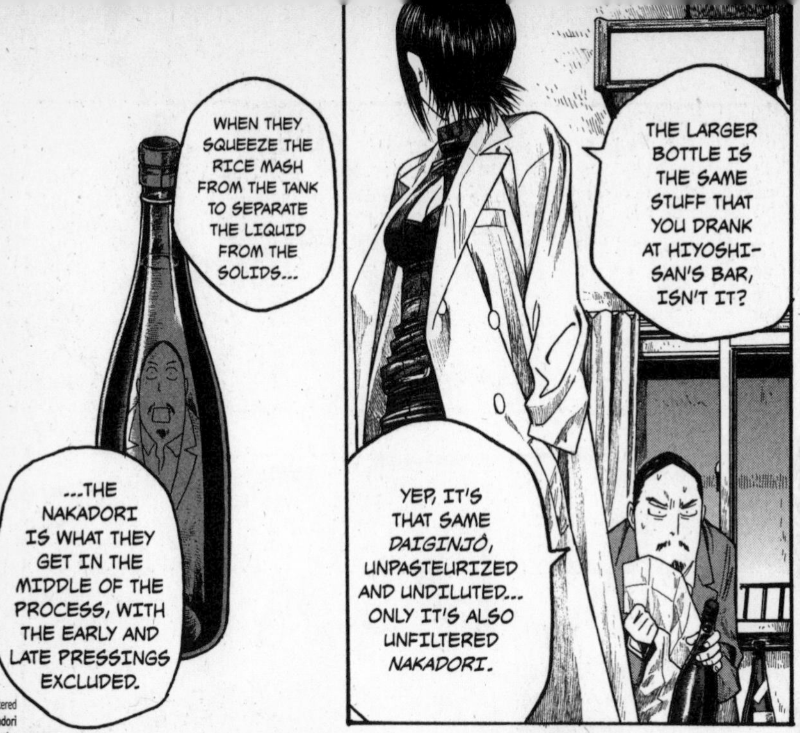
THE LARGER BOTTLE IS THE SAME STUFF THAT YOU DRANK AT HIYOSHI-SAN'S BAR, ISN'T IT?
YEP, IT'S THAT SAME *DAIGINJÔ*, UNPASTEURIZED AND UNDILUTED... ONLY IT'S ALSO UNFILTERED *NAKADORI*.
WHEN THEY SQUEEZE THE RICE MASH FROM THE TANK TO SEPARATE THE LIQUID FROM THE SOLIDS...
...THE NAKADORI IS WHAT THEY GET IN THE MIDDLE OF THE PROCESS, WITH THE EARLY AND LATE PRESSINGS EXCLUDED.

Unfiltered **nakadori**
When **nihonshu** is first pressed, the "eyes" of the filter are the widest, allowing some solid pieces to pass through and causing the flavor to be harsh, but after time, the filter will grow finer, leading to a clear and pure liquid and flavor. When this purer product is set aside, it is called **nakadori** ("taking the middle"). At the end, extra pressure must be applied to get the last bits of liquid out, which naturally causes more flavor fluctuation. Basically, the **nakadori** is the stuff for **sake** gourmets.

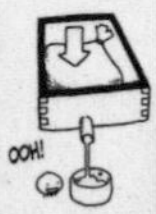
OOH!

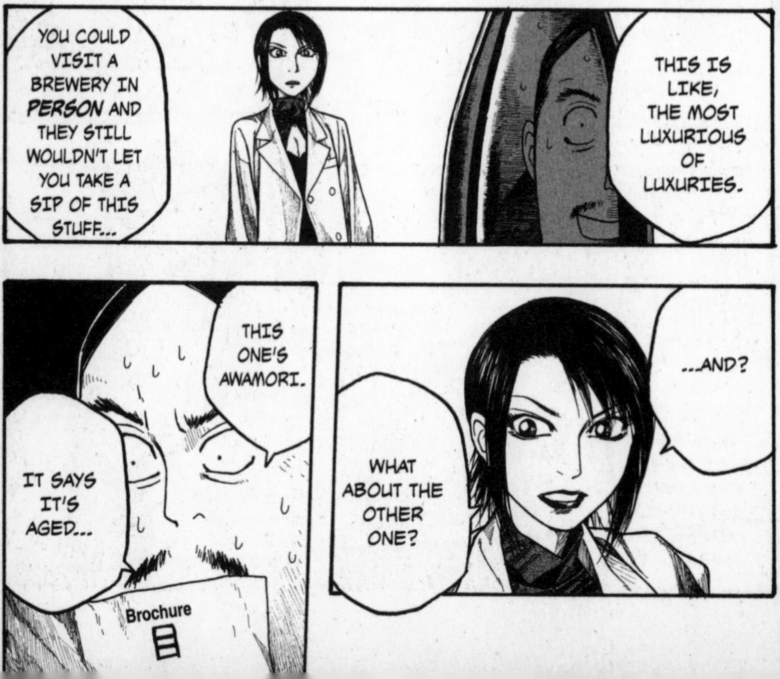
THIS IS LIKE, THE MOST LUXURIOUS OF LUXURIES.
YOU COULD VISIT A BREWERY IN ***PERSON*** AND THEY STILL WOULDN'T LET YOU TAKE A SIP OF THIS STUFF...
...AND?
WHAT ABOUT THE OTHER ONE?
THIS ONE'S AWAMORI.
IT SAYS IT'S AGED...
Brochure

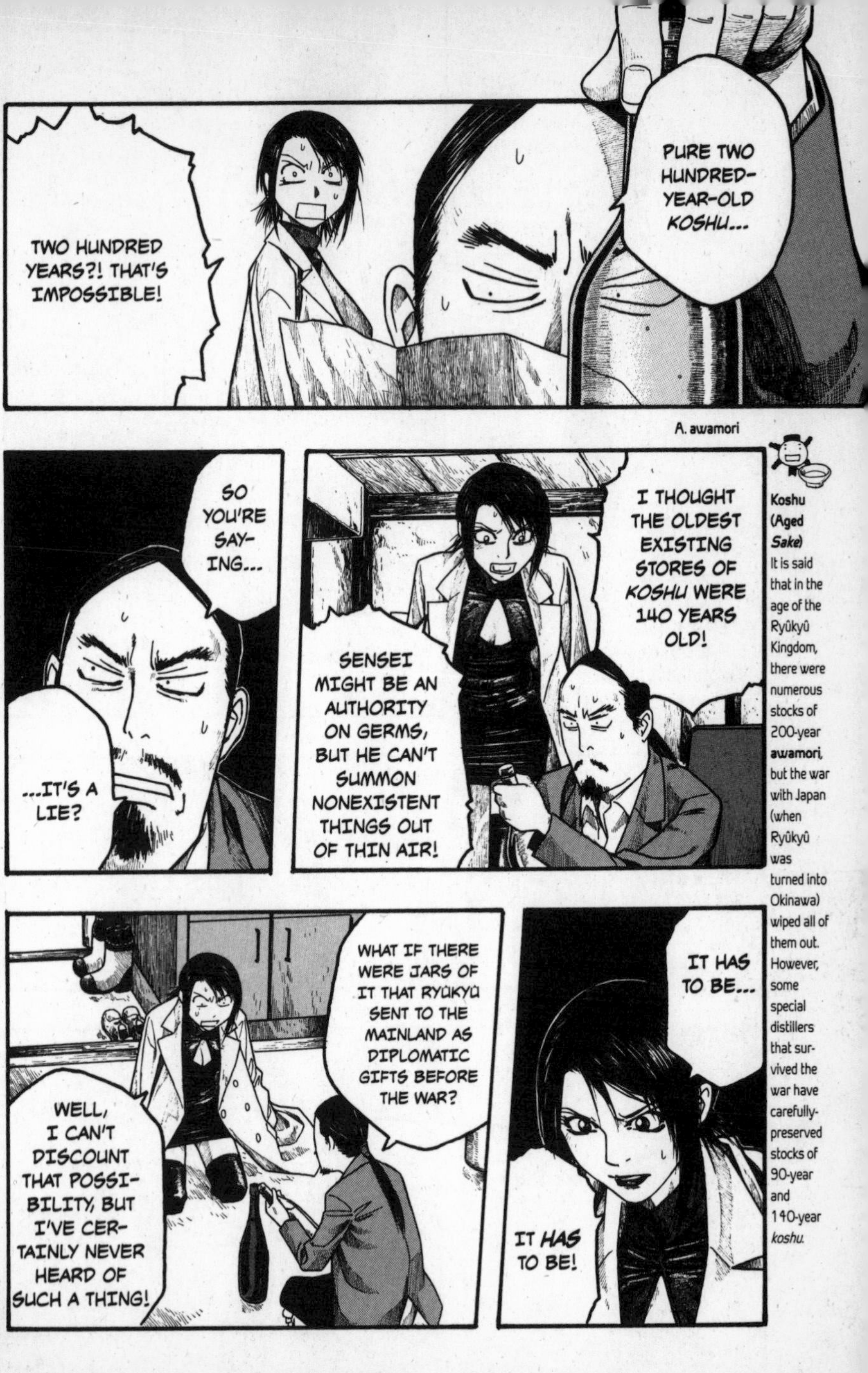
PURE TWO HUNDRED-YEAR-OLD KOSHU...
TWO HUNDRED YEARS?! THAT'S IMPOSSIBLE!
I THOUGHT THE OLDEST EXISTING STORES OF KOSHU WERE 140 YEARS OLD!
SENSEI MIGHT BE AN AUTHORITY ON GERMS, BUT HE CAN'T SUMMON NONEXISTENT THINGS OUT OF THIN AIR!
SO YOU'RE SAY-ING...
...IT'S A LIE?
IT HAS TO BE...
IT HAS TO BE!
WHAT IF THERE WERE JARS OF IT THAT RYŪKYŪ SENT TO THE MAINLAND AS DIPLOMATIC GIFTS BEFORE THE WAR?
WELL, I CAN'T DISCOUNT THAT POSSI-BILITY, BUT I'VE CER-TAINLY NEVER HEARD OF SUCH A THING!

A. awamori

Koshu (Aged *Sake*)
It is said that in the age of the Ryûkyû Kingdom, there were numerous stocks of 200-year **awamori**, but the war with Japan (when Ryûkyû was turned into Okinawa) wiped all of them out. However, some special distillers that survived the war have carefully-preserved stocks of 90-year and 140-year *koshu*.

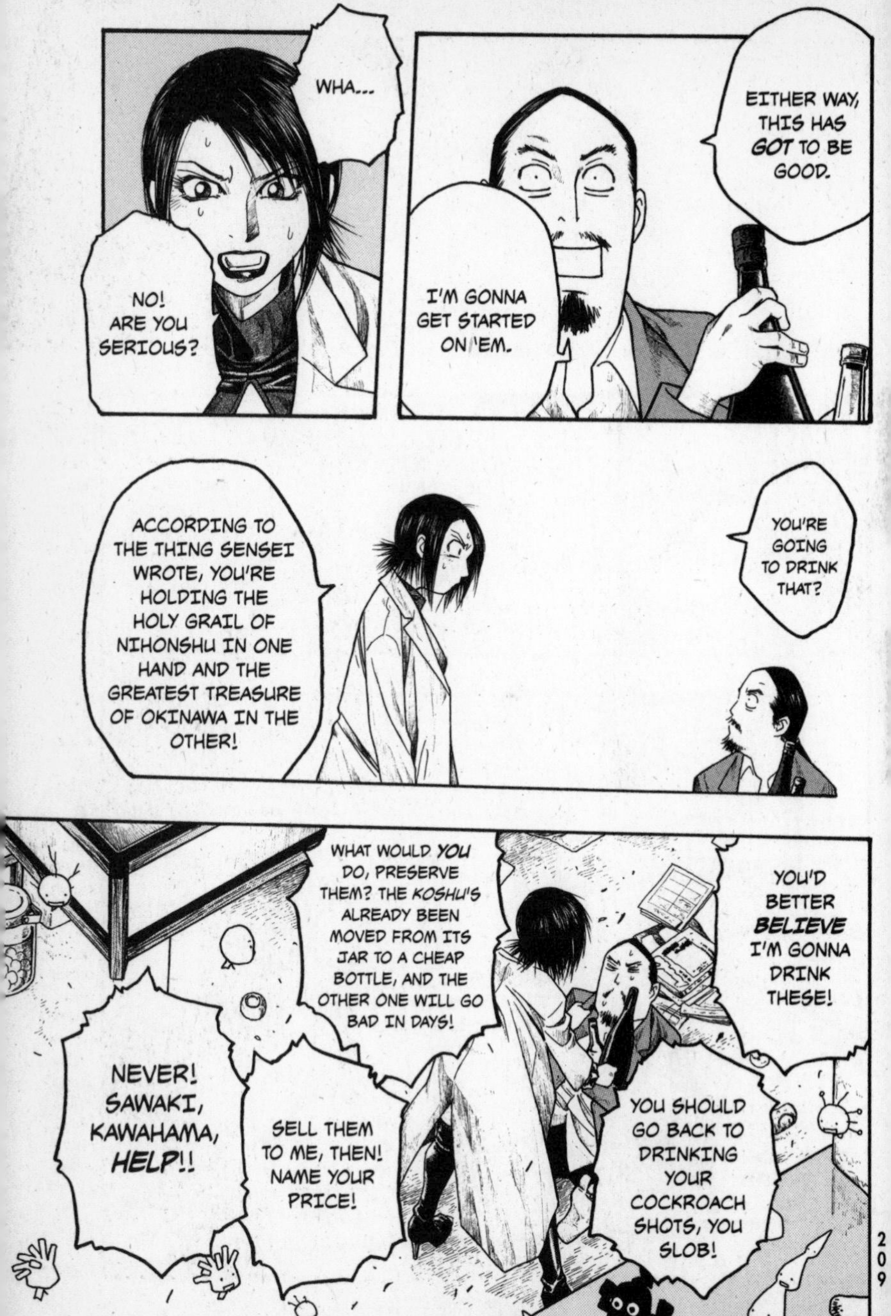
EITHER WAY, THIS HAS *GOT* TO BE GOOD.
I'M GONNA GET STARTED ON 'EM.
WHA...
NO! ARE YOU SERIOUS?
YOU'RE GOING TO DRINK THAT?
ACCORDING TO THE THING SENSEI WROTE, YOU'RE HOLDING THE HOLY GRAIL OF NIHONSHU IN ONE HAND AND THE GREATEST TREASURE OF OKINAWA IN THE OTHER!
YOU'D BETTER ***BELIEVE*** I'M GONNA DRINK THESE!
WHAT WOULD *YOU* DO, PRESERVE THEM? THE *KOSHU'S* ALREADY BEEN MOVED FROM ITS JAR TO A CHEAP BOTTLE, AND THE OTHER ONE WILL GO BAD IN DAYS!
YOU SHOULD GO BACK TO DRINKING YOUR COCKROACH SHOTS, YOU SLOB!
SELL THEM TO ME, THEN! NAME YOUR PRICE!
NEVER! SAWAKI, KAWAHAMA, ***HELP***!!

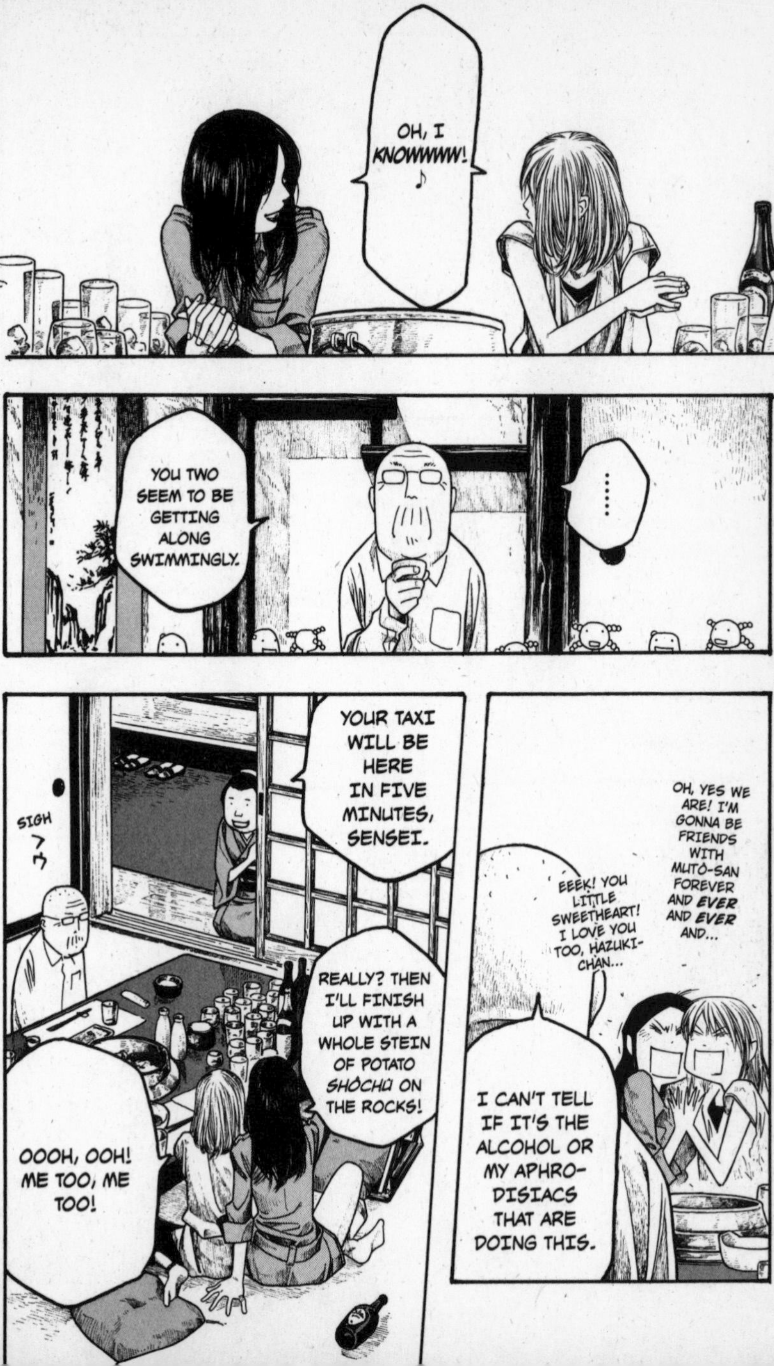
OH, I KNOWWWW! ♪
......
YOU TWO SEEM TO BE GETTING ALONG SWIMMINGLY.
OH, YES WE ARE! I'M GONNA BE FRIENDS WITH MUTÔ-SAN FOREVER AND EVER AND EVER AND...
EEEK! YOU LITTLE SWEETHEART! I LOVE YOU TOO, HAZUKI-CHAN...
I CAN'T TELL IF IT'S THE ALCOHOL OR MY APHRO-DISIACS THAT ARE DOING THIS.
YOUR TAXI WILL BE HERE IN FIVE MINUTES, SENSEI.
SIGH
REALLY? THEN I'LL FINISH UP WITH A WHOLE STEIN OF POTATO *SHÔCHÛ* ON THE ROCKS!
OOOH, OOH! ME TOO, ME TOO!

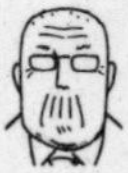

Keizô Itsuki
Ag school professor. I received a letter reminding me that he still hasn't done any lecturing recently.

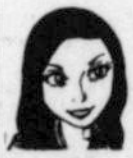

Aoi Mutô
The only seminar student of Itsuki's lab. Last year's "Miss Nôdai."

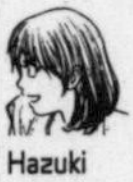

Hazuki Oikawa
A freshman, like Sawaki. Did she come from an all-girls' high school?

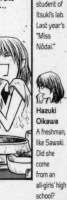

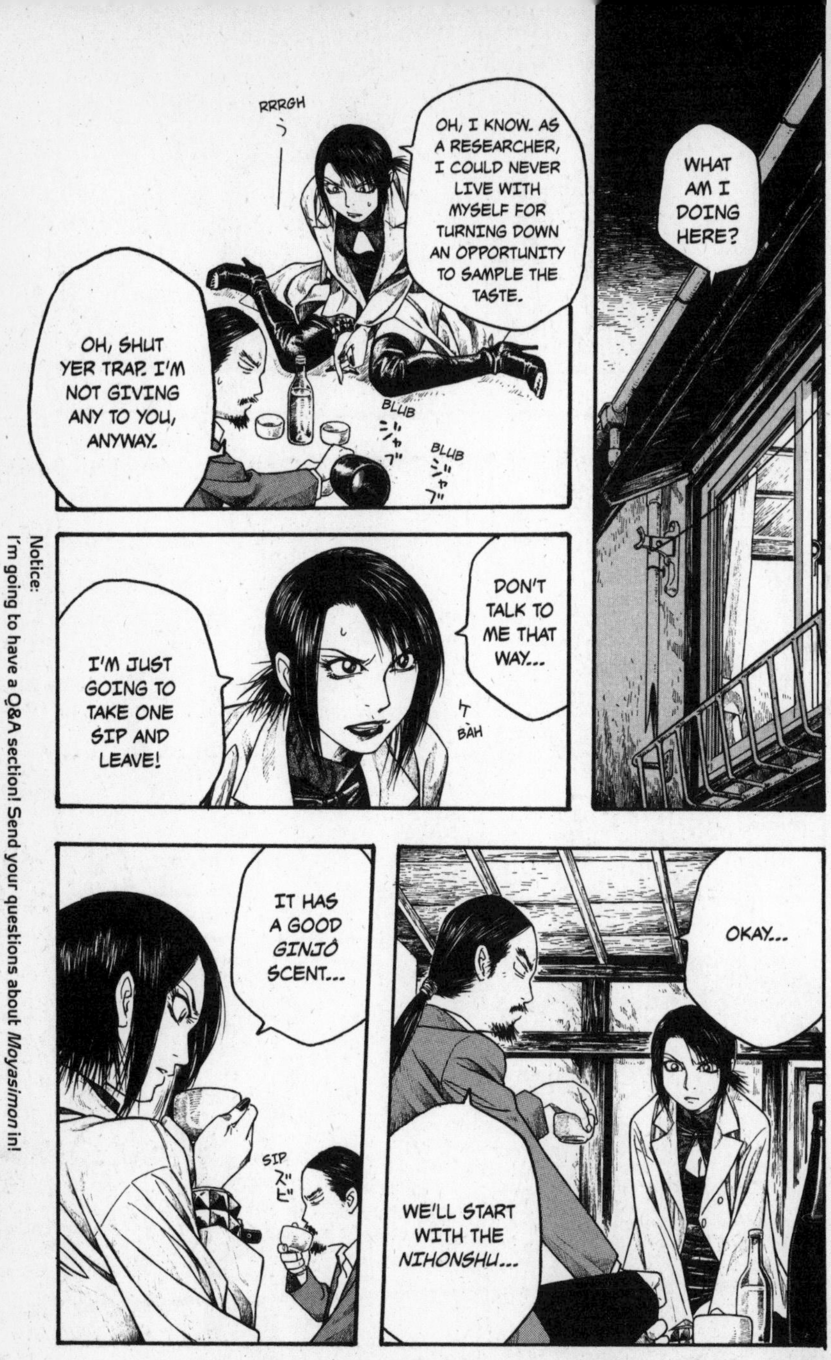
WHAT AM I DOING HERE?
OH, I KNOW. AS A RESEARCHER, I COULD NEVER LIVE WITH MYSELF FOR TURNING DOWN AN OPPORTUNITY TO SAMPLE THE TASTE.
RRRGH
OH, SHUT YER TRAP. I'M NOT GIVING ANY TO YOU, ANYWAY.
BLUB ジャブ
BLUB ジャブ
DON'T TALK TO ME THAT WAY...
BAH
I'M JUST GOING TO TAKE ONE SIP AND LEAVE!
OKAY...
WE'LL START WITH THE *NIHONSHU*...
IT HAS A GOOD GINJŌ SCENT...
SIP ズビ

Notice:
I'm going to have a Q&A section! Send your questions about *Moyasimon* in!

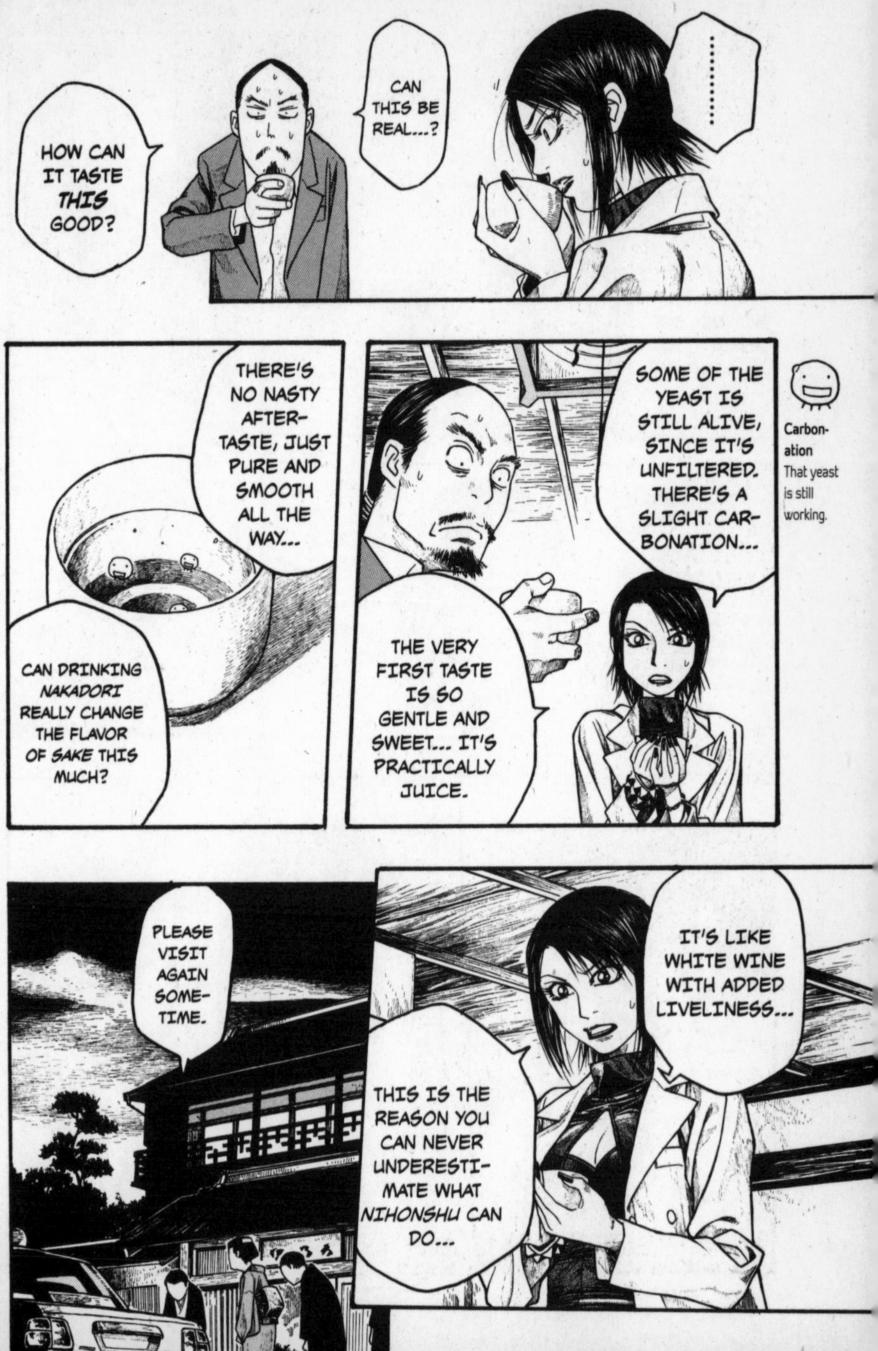
......
CAN THIS BE REAL...?
HOW CAN IT TASTE THIS GOOD?
SOME OF THE YEAST IS STILL ALIVE, SINCE IT'S UNFILTERED. THERE'S A SLIGHT CARBONATION...
THE VERY FIRST TASTE IS SO GENTLE AND SWEET... IT'S PRACTICALLY JUICE.
THERE'S NO NASTY AFTERTASTE, JUST PURE AND SMOOTH ALL THE WAY...
CAN DRINKING NAKADORI REALLY CHANGE THE FLAVOR OF SAKE THIS MUCH?
IT'S LIKE WHITE WINE WITH ADDED LIVELINESS...
THIS IS THE REASON YOU CAN NEVER UNDERESTIMATE WHAT NIHONSHU CAN DO...
PLEASE VISIT AGAIN SOMETIME.

Carbonation That yeast is still working.

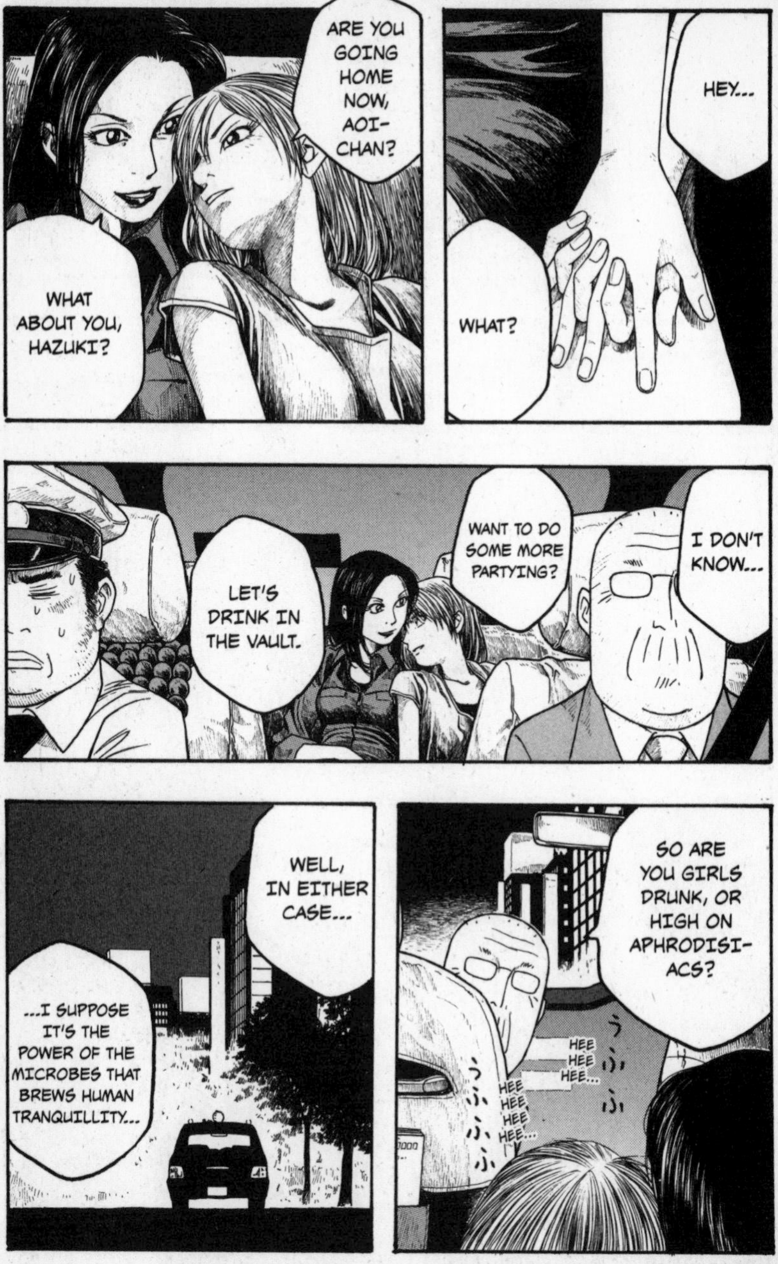
HEY...
WHAT?
ARE YOU GOING HOME NOW, AOI-CHAN?
WHAT ABOUT YOU, HAZUKI?
I DON'T KNOW...
WANT TO DO SOME MORE PARTYING?
LET'S DRINK IN THE VAULT.
SO ARE YOU GIRLS DRUNK, OR HIGH ON APHRODISI-ACS?
うふふ
HEE HEE HEE...
うふふふ
HEE HEE HEE HEE...
WELL, IN EITHER CASE...
...I SUPPOSE IT'S THE POWER OF THE MICROBES THAT BREWS HUMAN TRANQUILLITY...

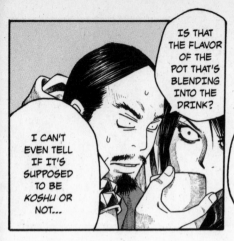

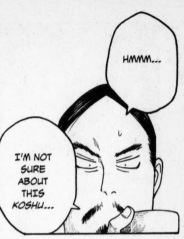

HMMM...
I'M NOT SURE ABOUT THIS KOSHU...
IS THAT THE FLAVOR OF THE POT THAT'S BLENDING INTO THE DRINK?
I CAN'T EVEN TELL IF IT'S SUPPOSED TO BE KOSHU OR NOT...
......
...YES, MA'AM?
DO YOU LIKE RAW MEAT?
HUH?
RAW MEAT.
UHH... I LIKE... YUKHOE...
CAN I BITE OFF YOUR EAR?
UMM... NO...

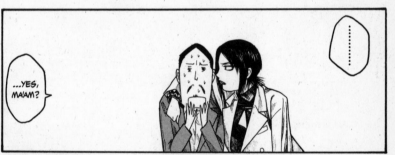

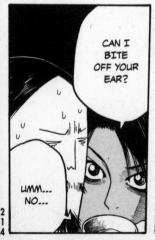

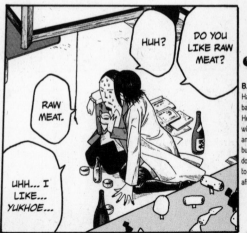

B. subtilis
Hay bacillus. He's friends with anthrax, but you don't need to be afraid.

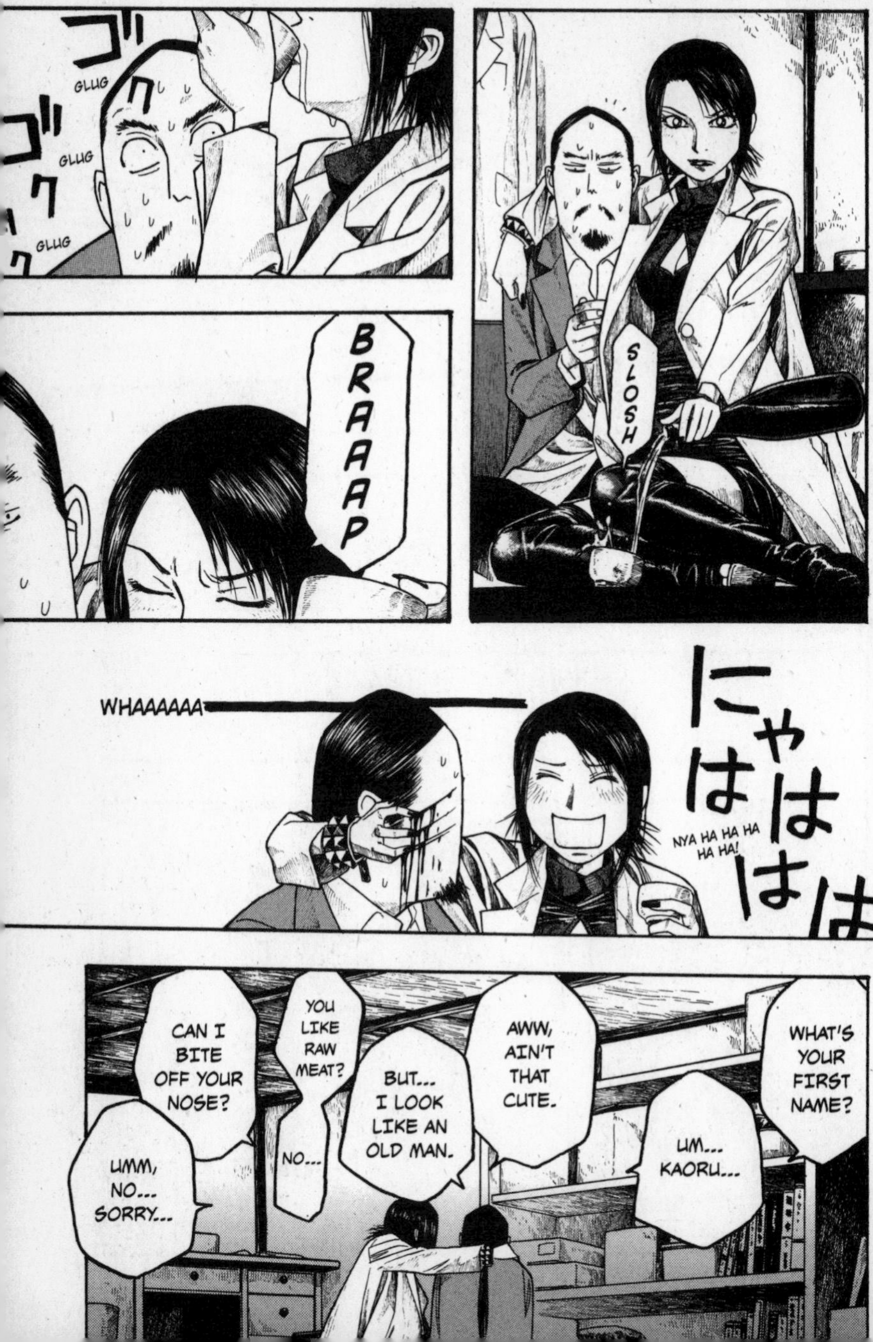
SLOSH
ゴク
GLUG
ゴク
GLUG
GLUG
BRAAAAAP
にゃははは
NYA HA HA HA HA HA!
WHAAAAAAA
WHAT'S YOUR FIRST NAME?
UM... KAORU...
AWW, AIN'T THAT CUTE.
BUT... I LOOK LIKE AN OLD MAN.
YOU LIKE RAW MEAT?
NO...
CAN I BITE OFF YOUR NOSE?
UMM, NO... SORRY...

POP

カ

UGH....

自治寮
DORM

WHA...

!

バカ
MORON

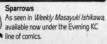

Sparrows
As seen in *Weekly Masayuki Ishikawa*, available now under the Evening KC line of comics.

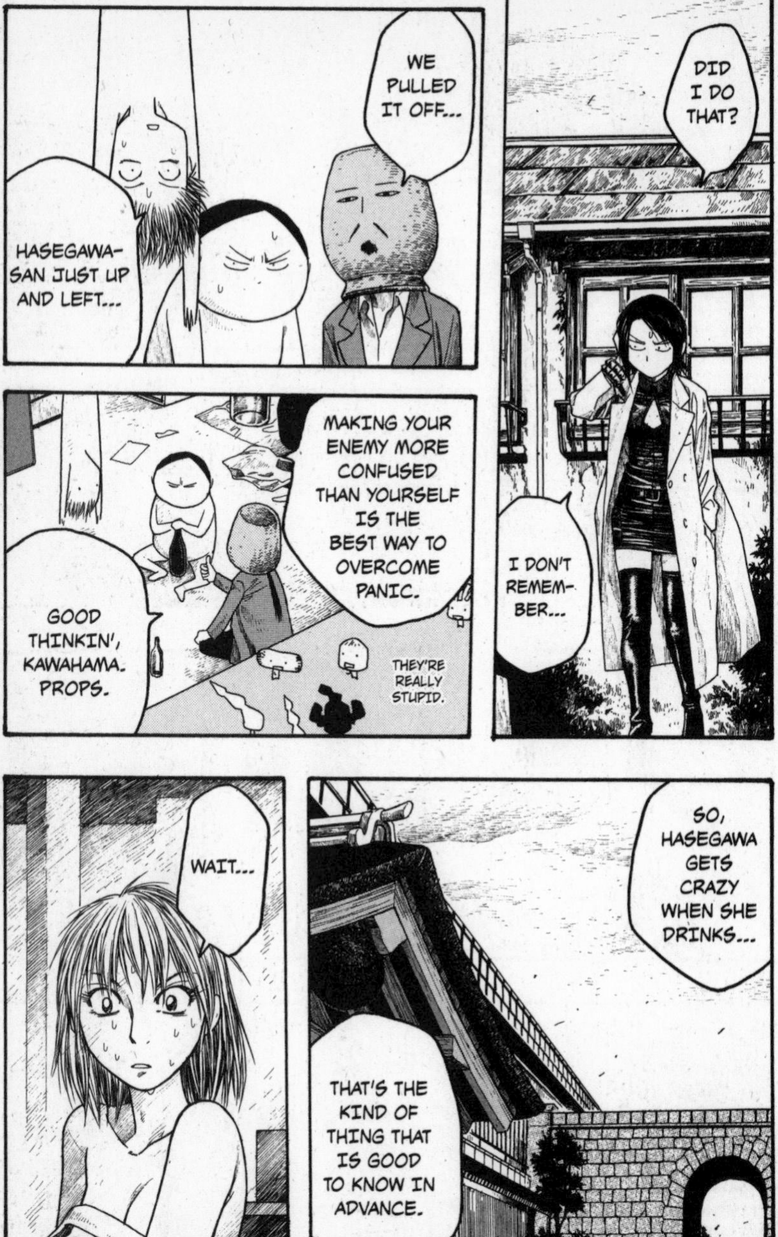
DID I DO THAT?
I DON'T REMEMBER...
WE PULLED IT OFF...
HASEGAWA-SAN JUST UP AND LEFT...
MAKING YOUR ENEMY MORE CONFUSED THAN YOURSELF IS THE BEST WAY TO OVERCOME PANIC.
GOOD THINKIN', KAWAHAMA. PROPS.
THEY'RE REALLY STUPID.
SO, HASEGAWA GETS CRAZY WHEN SHE DRINKS...
THAT'S THE KIND OF THING THAT IS GOOD TO KNOW IN ADVANCE.
WAIT...

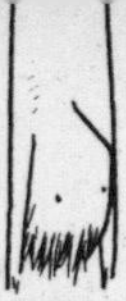

Tadayasu Sawaki
Protagonist. Can see germs. This is all he does this chapter.

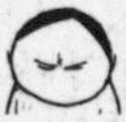

Takuma Kawahama
Sophomore. Dorm student, like Misato. The brains of the three.

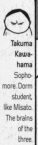

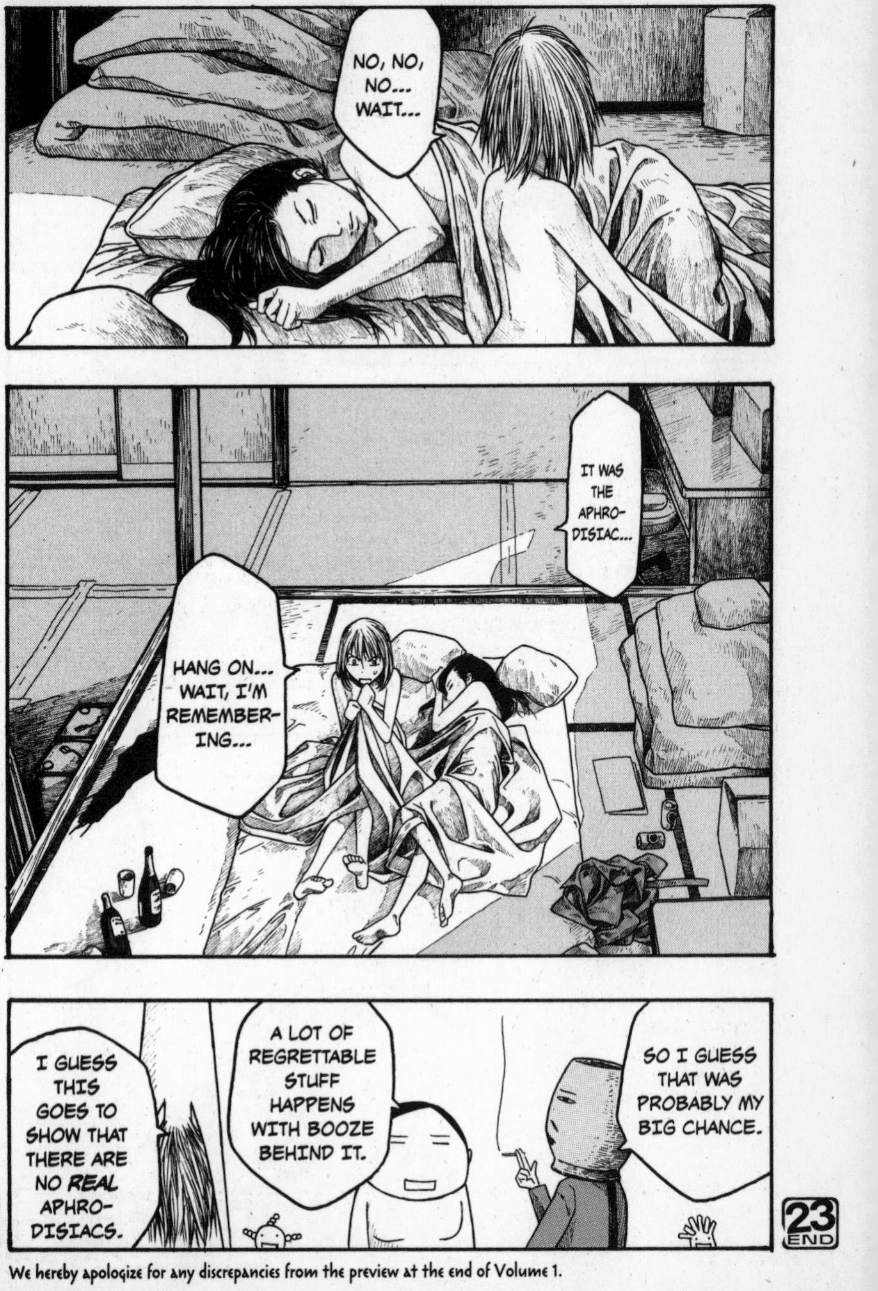
NO, NO, NO... WAIT...
IT WAS THE APHRO-DISIAC...
HANG ON... WAIT, I'M REMEMBER-ING...
SO I GUESS THAT WAS PROBABLY MY BIG CHANCE.
A LOT OF REGRETTABLE STUFF HAPPENS WITH BOOZE BEHIND IT.
I GUESS THIS GOES TO SHOW THAT THERE ARE NO *REAL* APHRO-DISIACS.

23 END

We hereby apologize for any discrepancies from the preview at the end of Volume 1.

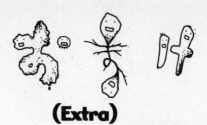

(Extra)

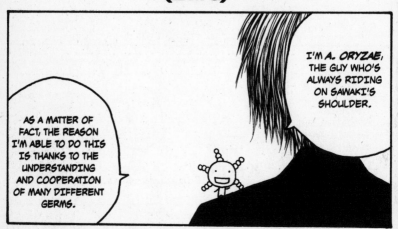

I'M A. ORYZAE, THE GUY WHO'S ALWAYS RIDING ON SAWAKI'S SHOULDER.
AS A MATTER OF FACT, THE REASON I'M ABLE TO DO THIS IS THANKS TO THE UNDERSTANDING AND COOPERATION OF MANY DIFFERENT GERMS.
IN EVERY LOCATION OF YOUR BODY, THERE IS AN ARMY DEFENDING YOU FROM HOSTILE INVADERS.
表皮常在菌
Skin Bacteria
TODAY, WE'RE GOING TO TALK ABOUT THE BACTERIA THAT LIVE ON YOUR SKIN.

THIS LECTURE ONLY DEALS WITH HEALTHY, NORMAL CIRCUMSTANCES, AS THINGS WILL BE DIFFERENT IN A HOSPITAL, FOR EXAMPLE.

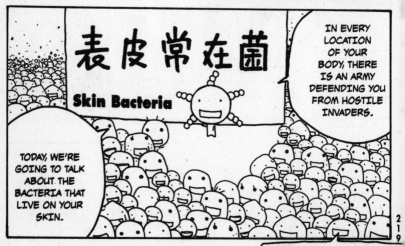

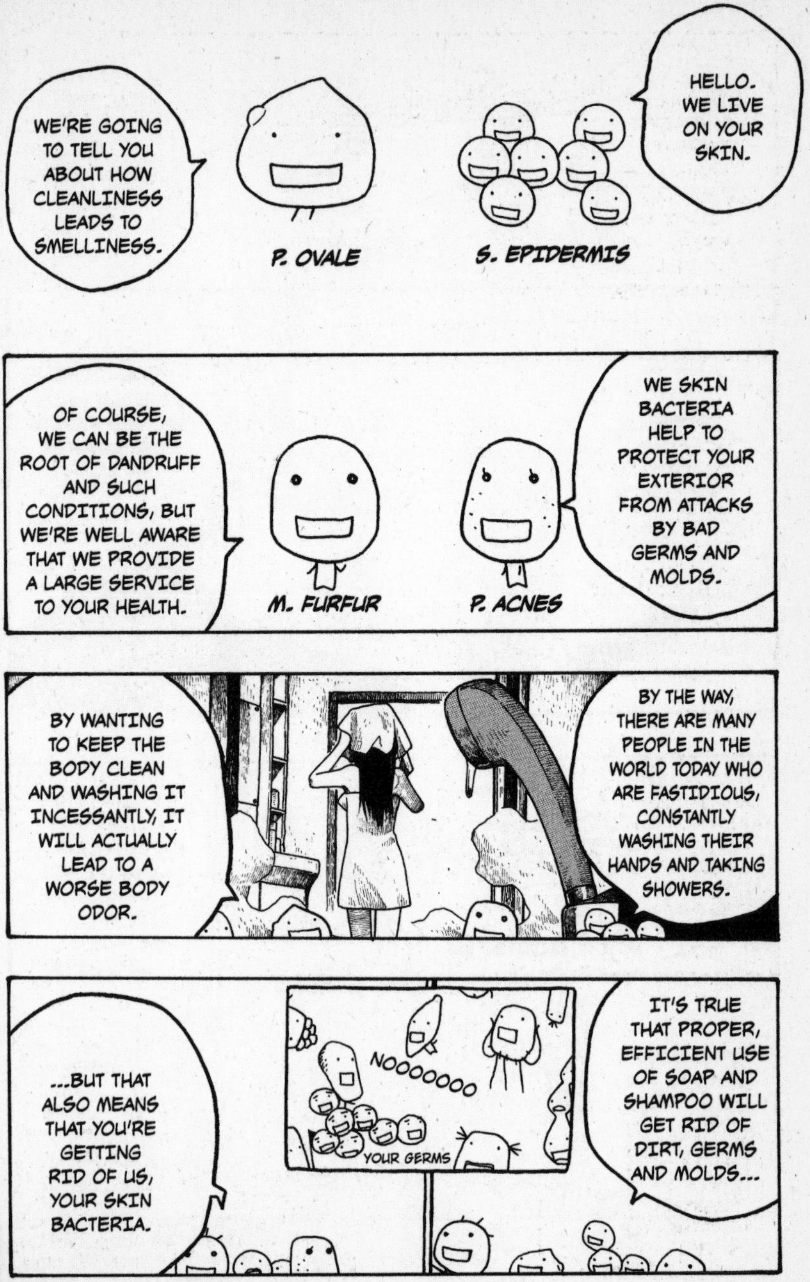
HELLO. WE LIVE ON YOUR SKIN.
S. EPIDERMIS
P. OVALE
WE'RE GOING TO TELL YOU ABOUT HOW CLEANLINESS LEADS TO SMELLINESS.
WE SKIN BACTERIA HELP TO PROTECT YOUR EXTERIOR FROM ATTACKS BY BAD GERMS AND MOLDS.
P. ACNES
M. FURFUR
OF COURSE, WE CAN BE THE ROOT OF DANDRUFF AND SUCH CONDITIONS, BUT WE'RE WELL AWARE THAT WE PROVIDE A LARGE SERVICE TO YOUR HEALTH.
BY THE WAY, THERE ARE MANY PEOPLE IN THE WORLD TODAY WHO ARE FASTIDIOUS, CONSTANTLY WASHING THEIR HANDS AND TAKING SHOWERS.
BY WANTING TO KEEP THE BODY CLEAN AND WASHING IT INCESSANTLY, IT WILL ACTUALLY LEAD TO A WORSE BODY ODOR.
IT'S TRUE THAT PROPER, EFFICIENT USE OF SOAP AND SHAMPOO WILL GET RID OF DIRT, GERMS AND MOLDS...
NOOOOOOO
YOUR GERMS
...BUT THAT ALSO MEANS THAT YOU'RE GETTING RID OF US, YOUR SKIN BACTERIA.

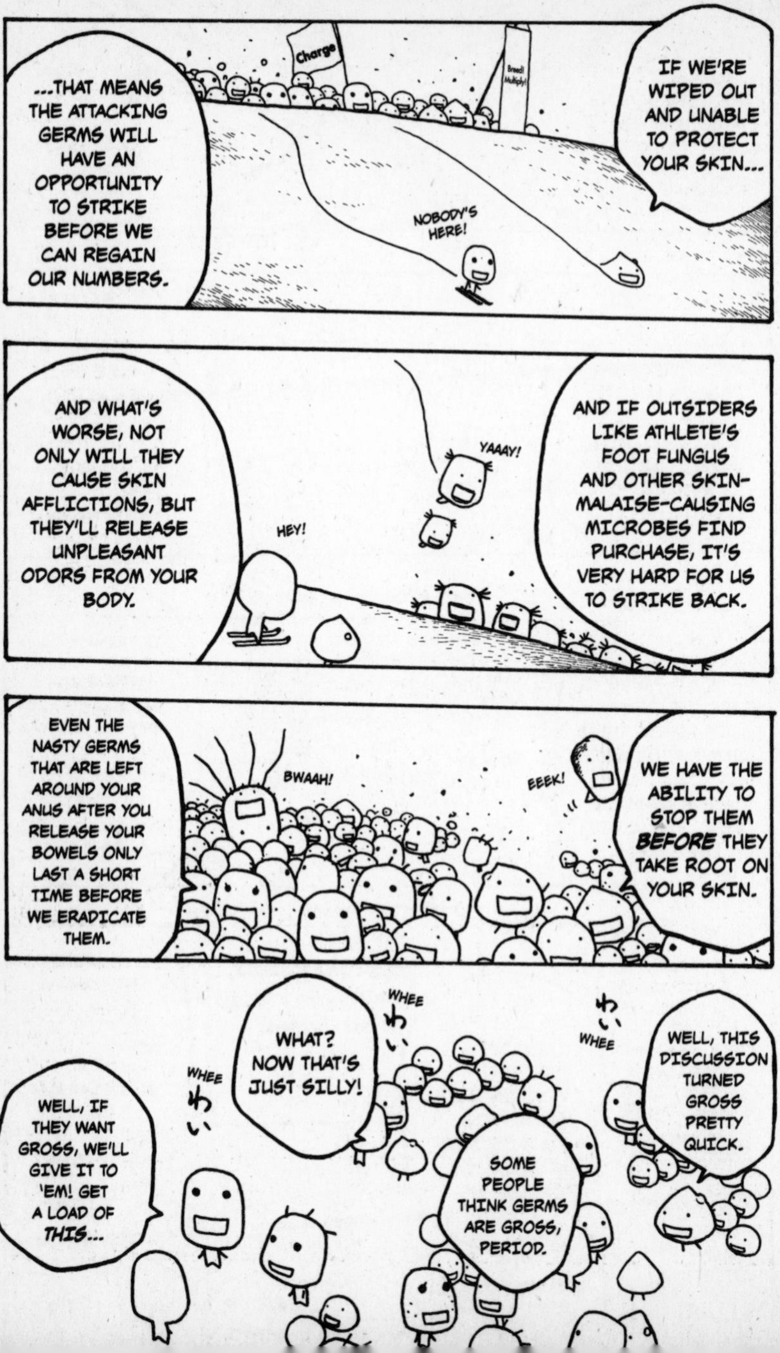
IF WE'RE WIPED OUT AND UNABLE TO PROTECT YOUR SKIN...
Breed! Multiply!
Charge
NOBODY'S HERE!
...THAT MEANS THE ATTACKING GERMS WILL HAVE AN OPPORTUNITY TO STRIKE BEFORE WE CAN REGAIN OUR NUMBERS.
AND IF OUTSIDERS LIKE ATHLETE'S FOOT FUNGUS AND OTHER SKIN-MALAISE-CAUSING MICROBES FIND PURCHASE, IT'S VERY HARD FOR US TO STRIKE BACK.
YAAAY!
HEY!
AND WHAT'S WORSE, NOT ONLY WILL THEY CAUSE SKIN AFFLICTIONS, BUT THEY'LL RELEASE UNPLEASANT ODORS FROM YOUR BODY.
WE HAVE THE ABILITY TO STOP THEM *BEFORE* THEY TAKE ROOT ON YOUR SKIN.
EEEK!
BWAAH!
EVEN THE NASTY GERMS THAT ARE LEFT AROUND YOUR ANUS AFTER YOU RELEASE YOUR BOWELS ONLY LAST A SHORT TIME BEFORE WE ERADICATE THEM.
WELL, THIS DISCUSSION TURNED GROSS PRETTY QUICK.
わい
WHEE
SOME PEOPLE THINK GERMS ARE GROSS, PERIOD.
WHEE
わい
WHAT? NOW THAT'S JUST SILLY!
WHEE
わい
WELL, IF THEY WANT GROSS, WE'LL GIVE IT TO 'EM! GET A LOAD OF *THIS*...

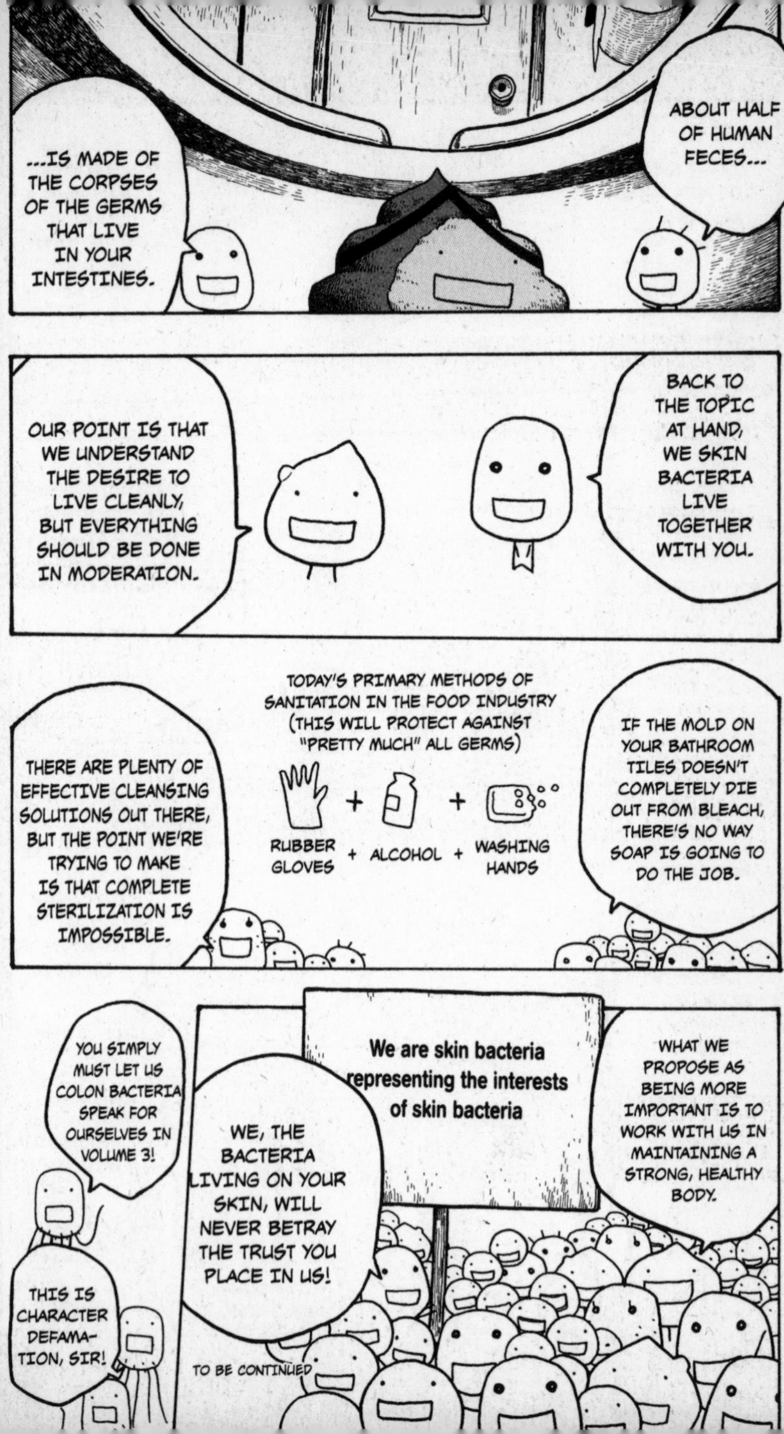
ABOUT HALF OF HUMAN FECES...
...IS MADE OF THE CORPSES OF THE GERMS THAT LIVE IN YOUR INTESTINES.
BACK TO THE TOPIC AT HAND, WE SKIN BACTERIA LIVE TOGETHER WITH YOU.
OUR POINT IS THAT WE UNDERSTAND THE DESIRE TO LIVE CLEANLY, BUT EVERYTHING SHOULD BE DONE IN MODERATION.
IF THE MOLD ON YOUR BATHROOM TILES DOESN'T COMPLETELY DIE OUT FROM BLEACH, THERE'S NO WAY SOAP IS GOING TO DO THE JOB.
TODAY'S PRIMARY METHODS OF SANITATION IN THE FOOD INDUSTRY (THIS WILL PROTECT AGAINST "PRETTY MUCH" ALL GERMS)
RUBBER GLOVES + ALCOHOL + WASHING HANDS
THERE ARE PLENTY OF EFFECTIVE CLEANSING SOLUTIONS OUT THERE, BUT THE POINT WE'RE TRYING TO MAKE IS THAT COMPLETE STERILIZATION IS IMPOSSIBLE.
WHAT WE PROPOSE AS BEING MORE IMPORTANT IS TO WORK WITH US IN MAINTAINING A STRONG, HEALTHY BODY.
We are skin bacteria representing the interests of skin bacteria
WE, THE BACTERIA LIVING ON YOUR SKIN, WILL NEVER BETRAY THE TRUST YOU PLACE IN US!
YOU SIMPLY MUST LET US COLON BACTERIA SPEAK FOR OURSELVES IN VOLUME 3!
THIS IS CHARACTER DEFAMATION, SIR!
TO BE CONTINUED

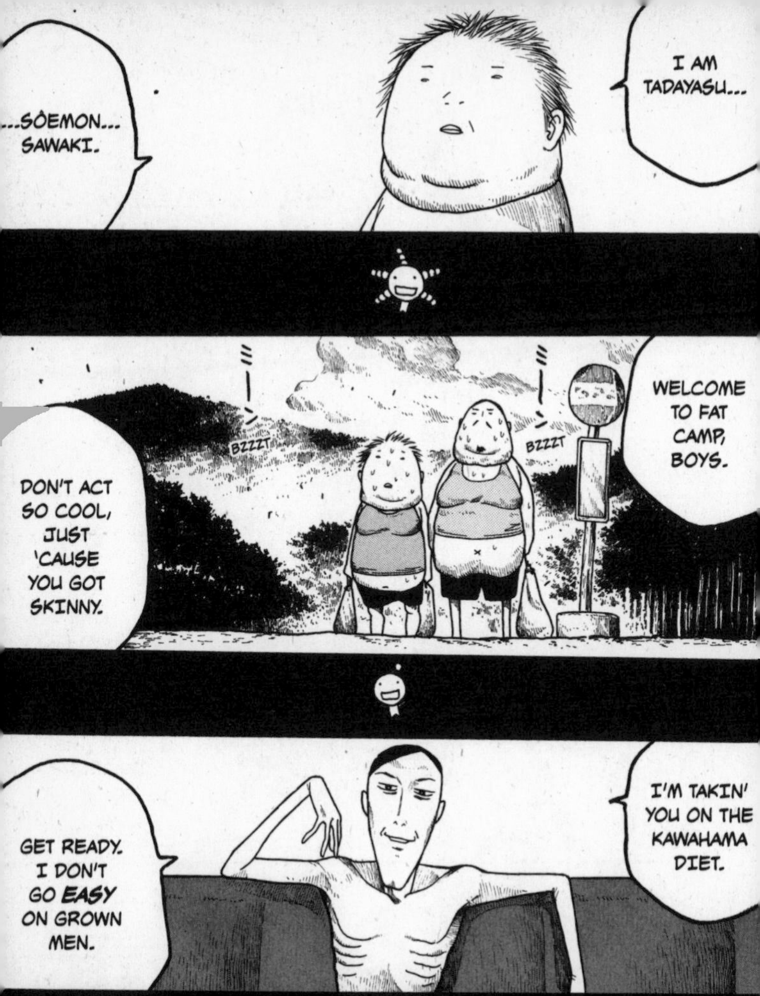
I AM TADAYASU...
...SÔEMON... SAWAKI.
WELCOME TO FAT CAMP, BOYS.
BZZZT
BZZZT
DON'T ACT SO COOL, JUST 'CAUSE YOU GOT SKINNY.
I'M TAKIN' YOU ON THE KAWAHAMA DIET.
GET READY. I DON'T GO *EASY* ON GROWN MEN.

MOYASIMON 3

CONTENTS SUBJECT TO CHANGE

FROM ISSUE 18, 2005 OF *EVENING*

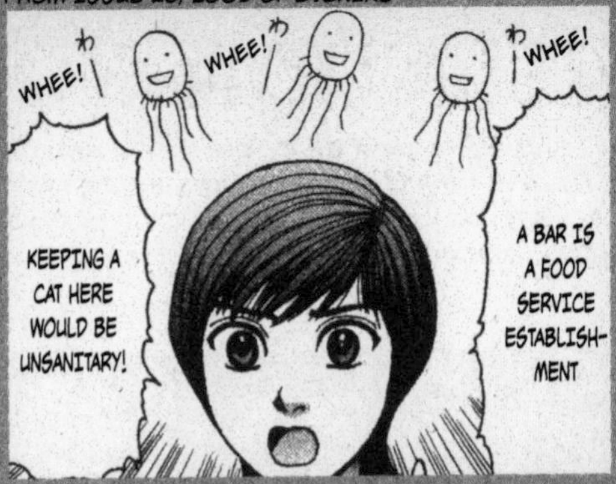
わ
WHEE!
わ
WHEE!
わ
WHEE!
A BAR IS A FOOD SERVICE ESTABLISHMENT
KEEPING A CAT HERE WOULD BE UNSANITARY!

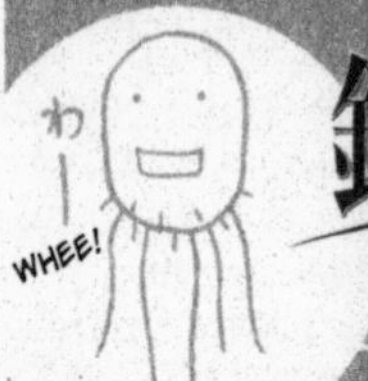
わ
WHEE!

銀座の番ねこ
The watch cats of ginza

MIDORI TAKANASHI

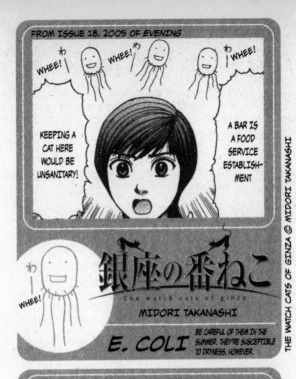

E. COLI BE CAREFUL OF THEM IN THE SUMMER. THEY'RE SUSCEPTIBLE TO DRYNESS, HOWEVER.

FROM ISSUE 16, 2005 OF *EVENING*

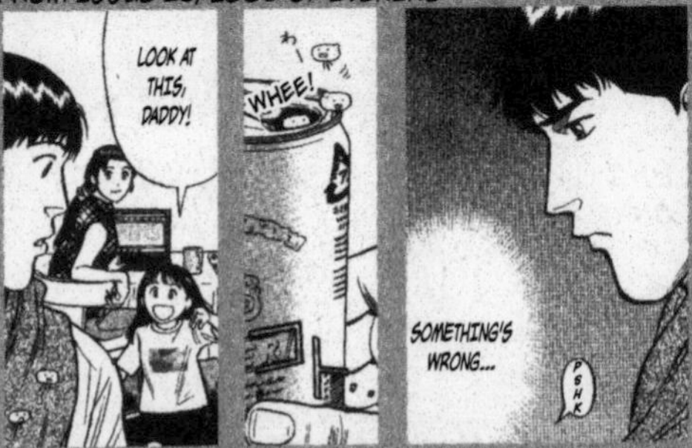
SOMETHING'S WRONG...
PSHK
わ
WHEE!
LOOK AT THIS, DADDY!

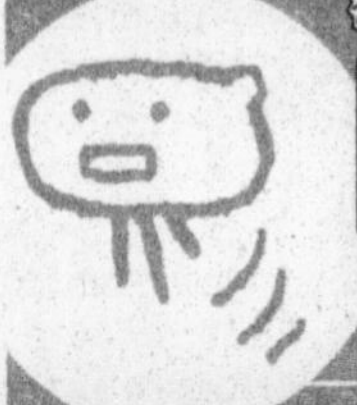

KEISHISEI
SHIINA KEISUKE

椎名啓介

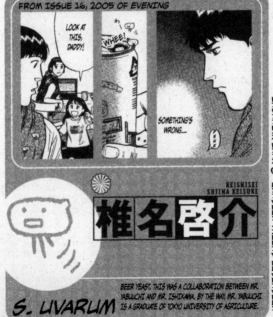

S. UVARUM BEER YEAST. THIS WAS A COLLABORATION BETWEEN MR. YABUUCHI AND MR. ISHIKAWA. BY THE WAY, MR. YABUUCHI IS A GRADUATE OF TOKYO UNIVERSITY OF AGRICULTURE.

TRANSLATION NOTES

Japanese is a tricky language for most Westerners, and translation is often more art than science. For your edification and reading pleasure, here are notes on some of the places where we could have gone in a different direction with our translation of the work, or where a Japanese cultural reference is used.

Character profiles and comments

When manga are originally published in magazines (*Moyasimon* appears in Kodansha's *Evening* magazine twice a month), the margins and title/final pages will usually be stuffed with information—messages from the author, advertisements or announcements of new releases, character profiles, teaser statements about upcoming chapters, etc. When virtually every manga is collected into book form, these tidbits are removed to streamline the reading process, but author Masayuki Ishikawa, perhaps pleased with his extra info and jokes, decided to keep them. So enjoy these extra treats from Ishikawa-sensei's brain!

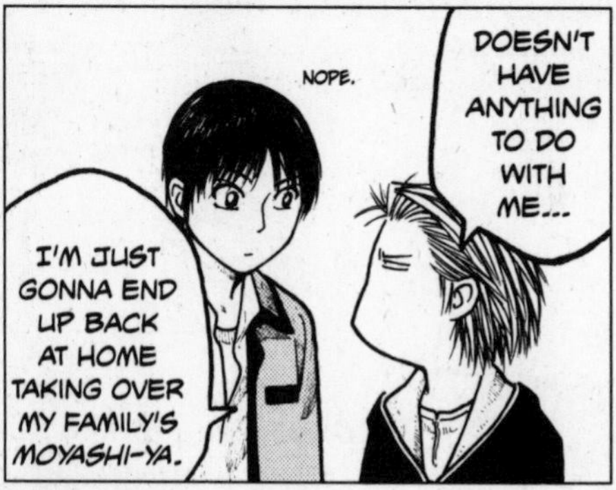
DOESN'T HAVE ANYTHING TO DO WITH ME...
NOPE.
I'M JUST GONNA END UP BACK AT HOME TAKING OVER MY FAMILY'S MOYASHI-YA.

Moyashi/Tane-kôji, page 8

Kôji is the Japanese term for a special kind of mold (*Aspergillus oryzae*) that is applied to cooked grains or beans. *Kôji* is the first step in the process of creating many fermented food products, such as *sake*, *miso* and soy sauce, and different combinations of base material and mold strains will be suited for different products. A *tane-kôji* is the "starter *kôji*" that food producers will use to create batches of their product, and they will purchase those from a *tane-kôji-ya*: a cultivator of *kôji*. *Moyashi* is another word for *kôji* mold, which makes the title of this story, "*Moyasimon*," something like "*moyashi* man." (The spelling in the title is slightly altered at the author's request.)

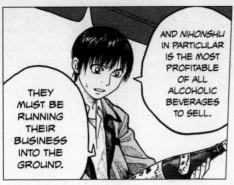

***Nihonshu*, page 16**

While outside of Japan, most people are familiar with "sake" or "rice wine," within Japan this alcoholic staple is called *nihonshu*, or "Japanese liquor." The linguistic confusion probably arose because in Japanese, "*sake*" can refer to any alcoholic beverage.

AND NIHONSHU IN PARTICULAR IS THE MOST PROFITABLE OF ALL ALCOHOLIC BEVERAGES TO SELL.
THEY MUST BE RUNNING THEIR BUSINESS INTO THE GROUND.

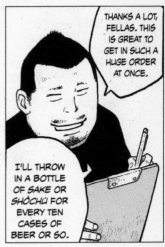

THANKS A LOT, FELLAS. THIS IS GREAT TO GET IN SUCH A HUGE ORDER AT ONCE.
I'LL THROW IN A BOTTLE OF SAKE OR SHÔCHŪ FOR EVERY TEN CASES OF BEER OR SO.

***Shôchû*, page 17**

The traditional spirit of the Japanese island of Kyûshû, this drink is distilled from barley, sweet potato or rice, and has grown so popular in recent years that it has even eclipsed *nihonshu* production.

***Ginjô*, page 25**

A type of *sake* made with rice grains that have been milled to remove the outer edges, which contain proteins, fats and amino acids. This leaves only the starch at the center and creates a purer, high-quality taste, making it the *sake* equivalent of "single malt scotch." In technical terms, *ginjô* uses rice that has been at least 40 percent milled away, leaving 60 percent of the grain. An even higher quality, *daiginjô*, is at least 50 percent milled.

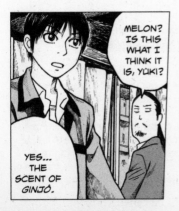

MELON? IS THIS WHAT I THINK IT IS, YŪKI?
YES... THE SCENT OF GINJÔ.

***Tôji*, page 33**
The master brewer of a *sake* brewery.

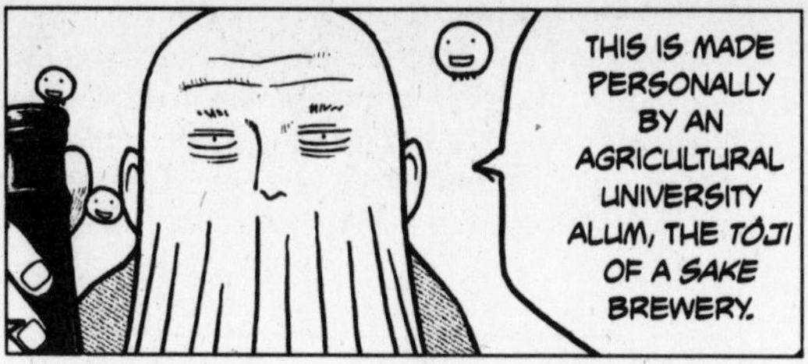
THIS IS MADE PERSONALLY BY AN AGRICULTURAL UNIVERSITY ALUM, THE *TÔJI* OF A *SAKE* BREWERY.

Nôdai, page 42

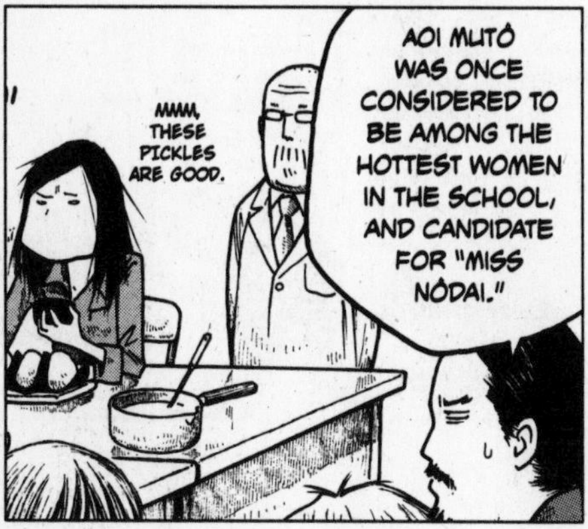
AOI MUTÔ WAS ONCE CONSIDERED TO BE AMONG THE HOTTEST WOMEN IN THE SCHOOL, AND CANDIDATE FOR "MISS NÔDAI."
MMM, THESE PICKLES ARE GOOD.

An abbreviation of *nôgyô daigaku* (agricultural university). When used as a proper noun, this is commonly understood to refer to Tokyo University of Agriculture, which is widely recognized as a model for the school in *Moyasimon*. However, as a fictional manga, *Moyasimon* does not draw any direct connections to the existing college. In fact, at no point is an official name for the school provided, only the generic "Nôdai." Therefore, when this term appears, keep in mind that it refers to an indefinite (*a* Nôdai) rather than a definite (*the* Nôdai) institution.

***Nata de coco*, page 82**
A jelly-like food created by fermenting coconut water, and commonly sweetened to be a dessert. *Nata de coco* originates from the Philippines.

Kuratama, page 85

The nickname of manga artist Mayumi Kurata. Known for her mostly autobiographical manga style and her simple artwork, most of her stories revolve around relationships with worthless men. *GoGo! Evening* is the title of one of her stories, and based on what is said here, it seems possible that Masayuki Ishikawa's editor was also the editor for *GoGo! Evening*.

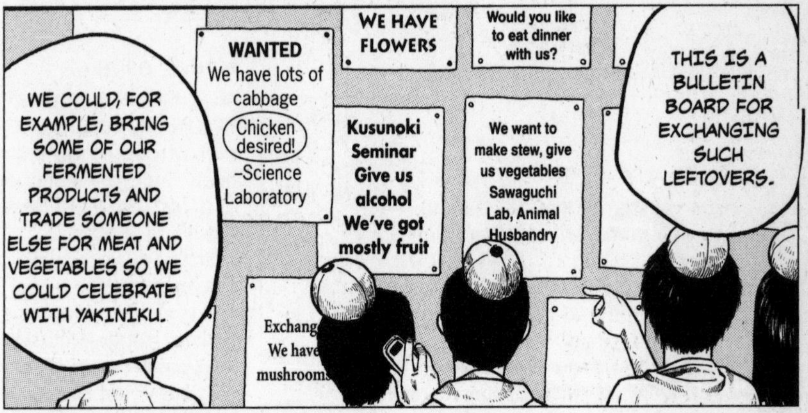
THIS IS A BULLETIN BOARD FOR EXCHANGING SUCH LEFTOVERS.
Would you like to eat dinner with us?
WE HAVE FLOWERS
WANTED We have lots of cabbage Chicken desired! –Science Laboratory
We want to make stew, give us vegetables Sawaguchi Lab, Animal Husbandry
Kusunoki Seminar Give us alcohol We've got mostly fruit
WE COULD, FOR EXAMPLE, BRING SOME OF OUR FERMENTED PRODUCTS AND TRADE SOMEONE ELSE FOR MEAT AND VEGETABLES SO WE COULD CELEBRATE WITH YAKINIKU.

Yakiniku, page 122

A Japanese dish based on Korean barbecue, in which beef and vegetables are grilled over a small electric or gas grill.

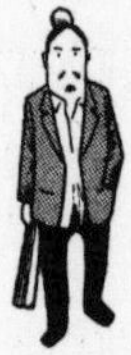

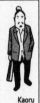

Kaoru Misato
Dorm student. Only a sophomore, though he looks older. Apparently, he looks like the guy from "Waral Meshi."

Warai Meshi, page 133

A Japanese comedy duo. One of the members' signature look is a mustache/goatee combo with long hair pulled back into a ponytail.

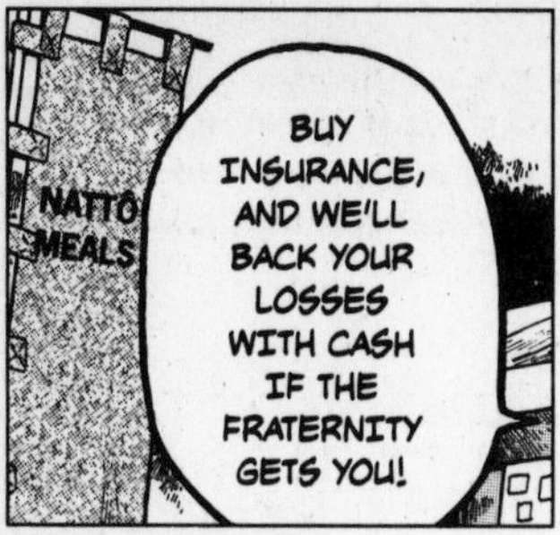
NATTO MEALS
BUY INSURANCE, AND WE'LL BACK YOUR LOSSES WITH CASH IF THE FRATERNITY GETS YOU!

Nattô**,** page 151

A traditional Japanese dish made from fermented soybeans and most often eaten over rice. It takes the form of soybeans in a sticky, stringy paste. It has a very strong smell, texture and flavor, making it considered an acquired taste.

Pachinko**,** page 168

A game resembling vertical pinball. Money is converted to little *pachinko* balls and winning will result in the machine spitting out more balls that can be converted to prizes that are exchanged for cash at a nearby pawnshop. While organized gambling is illegal in Japan, *pachinko* operates in a gray area that is legally accepted.

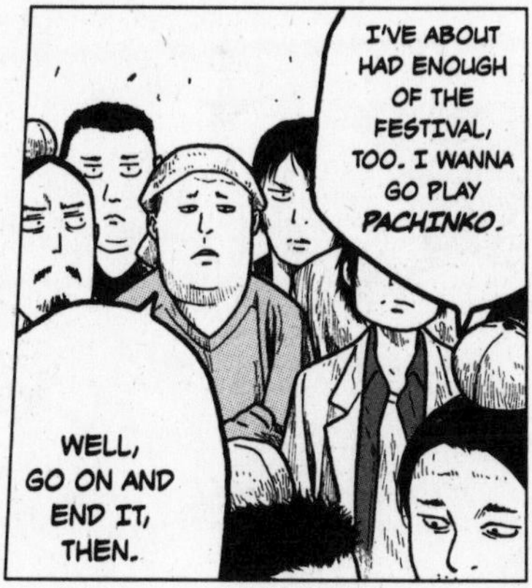
I'VE ABOUT HAD ENOUGH OF THE FESTIVAL, TOO. I WANNA GO PLAY PACHINKO.
WELL, GO ON AND END IT, THEN.

Sukiyaki, page 197

A stew usually eaten during the colder times of the year, made with slices of beef, tôfu, Chinese cabbage, mushrooms, noodles and other ingredients.

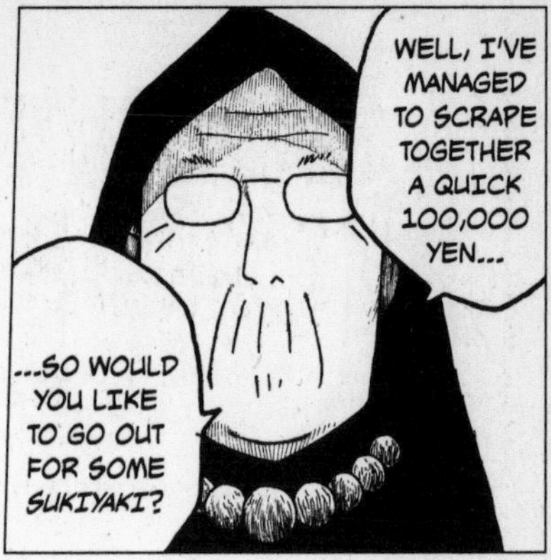
WELL, I'VE MANAGED TO SCRAPE TOGETHER A QUICK 100,000 YEN...
...SO WOULD YOU LIKE TO GO OUT FOR SOME SUKIYAKI?

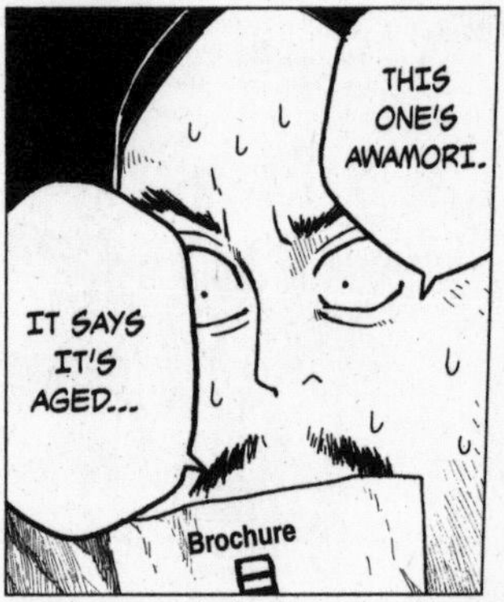
THIS ONE'S AWAMORI.
IT SAYS IT'S AGED...
Brochure

Awamori, page 207

Awamori is the chief alcoholic drink of the Japanese island of Okinawa. Like *nihonshu*, it is made from rice, but is distilled rather than brewed. Though distinct from *shôchû*, they are both made in similar ways and originated from the same drinks from mainland Asia centuries ago.

Yukhoe, page 214

A Korean dish of raw beef, served with soy sauce, sesame oil, garlic, green onion, pepper and a raw egg on top.

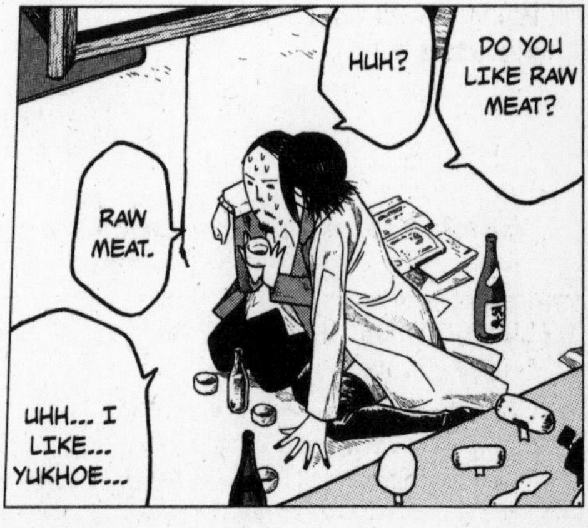
DO YOU LIKE RAW MEAT?
HUH?
RAW MEAT.
UHH... I LIKE... YUKHOE...

SAYONARA, ZETSUBOU-SENSEI

BY KOJI KUMETA

THE POWER OF NEGATIVE THINKING
VOLUME 1

Nozomu Itoshiki is depressed. Very depressed. He's certifiably suicidal, but he's also the beloved schoolteacher of a class of unique students, each charming in her own way. For all of them, it's a special time, when the right teacher can have a lasting positive effect on their lives. But is that teacher Itoshiki, a.k.a. Zetsubou-sensei, who just wants to find the perfect place to die?

SAYONARA, ZETSUBOU-SENSEI
THE POWER OF NEGATIVE THINKING
VOLUME 1
KOJI KUMETA

Available anywhere books or comics are sold!

VISIT WWW.DELREYMANGA.COM TO:
- Read sample pages
- View release date calendars for upcoming volumes
- Sign up for Del Rey's free manga e-newsletter
- Find out the latest about new Del Rey Manga series

RATING OT AGES 16+

DEL REY MANGA デルレイ
www.delreymanga.com

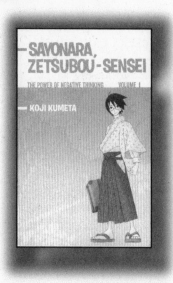

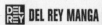

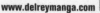

NINJA LOVE!

The horn growing on Raizo's forehead is proof that he is the lost illegitimate son of the once-mighty Katana family.

Now a band of loyal and lovely female ninjas devise a scheme to elevate their newfound master to greatness. But does the shy outcast have what it takes to become the ruler of a kingdom?

Special extras in each volume! Read them all!

WITHDRAWN
TOMARE
[STOP!]

You're going the wrong way!

Manga is a completely different
type of reading experience.

To start at the *beginning,*
go to the *end*!

That's right! Authentic manga is read the traditional Japanese way—
from right to left, exactly the *opposite* of how American books are read.
It's easy to follow: Just go to the other end of the book, and read
each page—and each panel—from right side to left side, starting at
the top right. Now you're experiencing manga as it was meant to be.